ECONOMIC REPORT

OF THE

PRESIDENT

TRANSMITTED TO THE CONGRESS

MARCH 2014

TOGETHER WITH

THE ANNUAL REPORT

OF THE

COUNCIL OF ECONOMIC ADVISERS

UNITED STATES GOVERNMENT PRINTING OFFICE

WASHINGTON : 2014

C O N T E N T S

---

*For a detailed table of contents of the Council's Report, see page 11.

ECONOMIC REPORT
OF THE
PRESIDENT

ECONOMIC REPORT OF THE PRESIDENT

To the Congress of the United States:

This year's *Economic Report of the President* describes how after 5 years of grit and determined effort, the United States is better-positioned for the 21st century than any other nation on Earth. We've now experienced 4 straight years of economic growth with more than 8 million new private-sector jobs. Our unemployment rate is the lowest it's been in more than 5 years. Our deficits have been cut by more than half. For the first time in nearly 20 years, we produce more oil at home than we buy from the rest of the world. The housing market is rebounding, manufacturers are adding jobs for the first time since the 1990s, and we sell more of what we make to the rest of the world than ever before.

But in many ways, the trends that have threatened the middle class for decades have grown even starker. While those at the top are doing better than ever, average wages have barely budged. Inequality has deepened. Too many Americans are working harder and harder just to get by, and too many still aren't working at all. Our job is to reverse those trends. It is time to restore opportunity for all—the idea that no matter who you are or how you started out, with hard work and responsibility, you can get ahead.

That's why this must be a year of action. I'm eager to work with the Congress to speed up economic growth, strengthen the middle class, and build new ladders of opportunity into the middle class. But America does not stand still, and neither will I. Wherever and whenever I can take steps without legislation to expand opportunity for more American families, I will. Because opportunity is who we are. And the defining project of our generation is to restore that promise.

Simply put, this opportunity agenda has four parts. Number one is more new jobs. Number two is training more Americans with the skills to fill those jobs. Number three is guaranteeing every child access to a world-class education. And number four is making sure hard work pays off for every American.

With the economy picking up speed, companies say they intend to hire more people this year. We should make that decision even easier for them by closing wasteful tax loopholes and lowering tax rates for businesses that create jobs here at home, and use the money we save in the process to create jobs rebuilding our roads, upgrading our ports, and unclogging our commutes. We should help America win the race for the next wave of high-tech manufacturing jobs by connecting businesses and universities in hubs for innovation. We should do more to boost exports and fund basic research. We should maintain our commitment to an all-of-the-above-energy strategy that is creating jobs and leading to a safer planet. Finally, we should heed the call of business leaders, labor leaders, faith leaders, and law enforcement, and fix our broken immigration system. Independent economists say this will grow our economy and shrink our deficits by almost $1 trillion in the next two decades. We should get it done this year.

Creating jobs is step one, but in this rapidly-changing economy, we also must make sure every American has the skills to fill those jobs. I've asked Vice President Biden to lead an across-the-board reform of America's training programs to make sure they have one mission: training Americans with the skills employers need, and matching them to good jobs that need to be filled right now. That means more on-the-job training, and more apprenticeships that set a young worker on an upward trajectory for life. It means connecting companies to community colleges that can help design training to fill their specific needs.

I'm also convinced we can help Americans return to the workforce faster by reforming unemployment insurance so that it's more effective in today's economy. But first, the Congress needs to restore the unemployment insurance it let expire at the end of last year, affecting around 2 million workers.

Of course, it's not enough to train today's workforce. We also have to prepare tomorrow's workforce, by guaranteeing every child access to a world-class education. Our high school graduation rate is higher than it's been in 30 years, and more young people are earning college degrees than ever before. The problem is we're still not reaching enough kids, and we're not reaching them in time.

That has to change. I am repeating a request I made last year asking you to help States make high-quality preschool available to every four year-old. In the meantime, I'm going to pull together a coalition of elected officials, business leaders, and philanthropists willing to help more kids access the high-quality early education they need. I'll also work to redesign high schools and partner them with colleges and employers that offer the real-world education and hands-on training that can lead directly to a job and career, and follow through on my pledge to connect 99 percent of our students to high-speed broadband over the next 4 years. With the support of the FCC, we've announced a down payment to start connecting more than 15,000 schools and 20 million students over the next 2 years, without adding a dime to the deficit, and with the help of some of America's top companies, we're going to make the most of these new connections.

My Administration is also shaking up our system of higher education, so that no middle-class family is priced out of a college education. We're offering millions the opportunity to cap their monthly student loan payments to ten percent of their income, and I will continue to look for other ways to see how we can help even more Americans who feel trapped by student loan debt.

But we know our opportunity agenda won't be complete—and too many young people entering the workforce today will see the American Dream as an empty promise—unless we do more to make sure hard work pays off for every single American. This year, we should do more to secure a women's right to equal pay for equal work. We should expand the Earned Income Tax Credit to help more workers without children make ends meet, and help more Americans save for retirement through the new "MyRA" plans my Administration is creating. We should protect taxpayers from ever footing the bill for a housing crisis ever again. And we will continue the work of making sure every American has access to affordable, quality health insurance that's there for them when they need it.

And we should raise a minimum wage that in real terms is worth less than it was when Ronald Reagan took office. In the year since I first asked the Congress to raise the minimum wage, six States raised theirs, and more companies like Costco see paying fair wages as one of the best ways to reduce turnover, increase productivity, and boost profits. As America's chief executive, I agree, which is why I signed an Executive Order requiring Federal contractors to pay their federally funded employees a fair wage of at least $10.10 an hour for new contracts. There is a bill in front of both the House and the Senate that would raise the minimum wage to $10.10 for all Americans. The Congress should pass that bill and give America a raise.

I believe this can be a breakthrough year for America. But it falls to all of us to grow the economy and create new jobs, to strengthen the middle class, and to build new ladders of opportunity for folks to work their way into the middle class. So in the coming months, let's see where we can make progress together. Let's continue to make this a year of action. Together, we can restore an economy that works for everybody, and our founding vision of opportunity for all.

THE WHITE HOUSE
MARCH 2014

THE ANNUAL REPORT
OF THE
COUNCIL OF ECONOMIC ADVISERS

LETTER OF TRANSMITTAL

COUNCIL OF ECONOMIC ADVISERS
Washington, D.C., March 10, 2014

MR. PRESIDENT:

The Council of Economic Advisers herewith submits its 2014 Annual Report in accordance of the Employment Act of 1946 as amended by the Full Employment and Balanced Growth Act of 1978.

Sincerely yours,

Jason Furman
Chairman

Betsey Stevenson
Member

James H. Stock
Member

CONTENTS

FIGURES

TABLES

BOXES

C H A P T E R 1

PROMOTING OPPORTUNITY AND SHARED, SUSTAINABLE GROWTH

As the 2014 *Economic Report of the President* goes to press, the U.S. economy stands five years removed from one of the most tumultuous and challenging periods in its history. The state of acute crisis that emerged in the months just before President Obama took office was, in some respects, worse than the initial shock that touched off the Great Depression. The plunge in stock prices in late 2008 proved similar to what occurred in late 1929, but was compounded by sharper home price declines, ultimately leading to a drop in overall household wealth that was substantially greater than the loss in wealth at the outset of the Great Depression (Romer 2009; see also Greenspan 2013, Almunia et al. 2010). As the recession unfolded, the economy's total output contracted more sharply than at any other time since World War II, and the fallout ultimately cost the country a staggering 8.8 million private-sector jobs.

As of early 2014, however, the economic landscape looks vastly different: total output has grown for 11 consecutive quarters, businesses have added 8.5 million jobs since February 2010, and a range of analysts are optimistic that the economy will further strengthen in the years ahead. Yet despite this progress, many American families are still struggling to join the middle class or to stay there, as they face the lingering after-effects of the crisis on top of a long-standing trend of widening inequality that has caused the rungs on the economic ladder to grow further apart. This fundamental issue—making sure the economy provides opportunity for every American—is the President's central economic focus.

To move toward the President's goal of a broader, more solid foundation for future growth, three key imperatives must be addressed. The first and most immediate imperative is to continue to restore the economy to its full potential. Although the recovery from the Great Recession is well underway, it remains incomplete. The second imperative is to expand the economy's potential. In the decades after World War II, rapid productivity

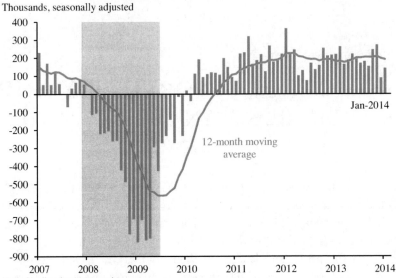

Figure 1-1
Monthly Change in Private Nonfarm Payrolls, 2007–2014

Thousands, seasonally adjusted

Jan-2014

12-month moving average

Note: Shading denotes recession.
Source: Bureau of Labor Statistics, Current Employment Statistics.

growth propelled the American economy forward and grew the middle class. The historic surge of women into the labor force further transformed America's society and economic capacity. But in the last several decades, productivity growth has declined relative to the early postwar years, and looking ahead, America's workforce is now expected to grow more slowly as members of the baby-boom generation move into retirement. As a result, efforts to enhance overall productivity and the skills of American workers, and to expand the labor force, will be as critical as ever. The third imperative is to ensure that the economy provides all Americans with greater opportunity to realize their full individual potential and to experience the prosperity they work to create. A typical family's inflation-adjusted income barely budged in the years leading up to the crisis, which placed undue strain on millions of hardworking households, contributed to instability in the overall economy, and raised questions about how the American ideals of opportunity and mobility would manifest themselves in the 21st century.

These challenges are substantial, but so is America's potential. As discussed in the remainder of this chapter and throughout this report, the President has set out an ambitious agenda to make progress on all three imperatives, both by working with Congress and by taking action on his own where possible. To return the economy to its full potential more quickly, the President has called for a range of measures including an

Opportunity, Growth, and Security initiative, along with steps to pair business tax reform with a major effort to upgrade our Nation's infrastructure. To expand the economy's potential, the President continues to urge the House of Representatives to follow the Senate's lead and pass commonsense immigration reform, which would help attract a new wave of inventors and entrepreneurs to American soil. The President also wants to build on the great strides that have already been made in the technology and energy sectors, which are laying the groundwork for a more productive economy in the years ahead. And to make sure that the economy provides opportunity for every American, the President's agenda includes improved job training programs and an increase in the minimum wage, because no one working full time should have to raise their family in poverty. In addition, the President has set a goal of preschool for all, since one of the best ways to ensure that all Americans have a chance to succeed is to invest in their early childhood development. Implementation of the Affordable Care Act is another critical step in this direction, because it is helping to provide financial security for more American families and to slow the growth in health care costs that cut into workers' take-home pay.

The President is calling for significant legislative measures in these areas, but will continue to pursue progress through executive authority by, for example, streamlining the infrastructure-permitting process, creating new products to improve retirement security, and raising wages for Federal contractors. The President is also using his influence to work with businesses, universities, and nonprofits to, for instance, help low-income students succeed in college and ensure that the long-term unemployed have a fair shot at a new job. These are just a few of the President's key efforts in what he has described as "a year of action," and the President remains ready to work with anyone offering constructive ideas to move forward.

THE ECONOMY FIVE YEARS AFTER THE CRISIS

The recovery from the Great Recession took another major step forward in 2013, as detailed in Chapter 2. Businesses added 2.4 million jobs over the course of the year, or 197,000 a month, marking the third consecutive year that private employment increased by more than 2 million. From its trough in February 2010 through January 2014, private employment has risen in 47 consecutive months for a total of 8.5 million jobs added (Figure 1-1). The unemployment rate remains unacceptably high, primarily due to the continued elevation of long-term unemployment, but it has continued to recover, reaching a five-year low of 6.6 percent in January. The housing and automotive sectors—two areas that were especially hard-hit by the

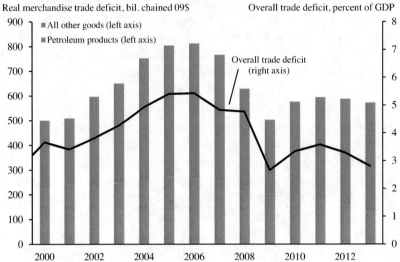

Figure 1-2
U.S. Merchandise and Overall Trade Deficits, 2000–2013

Real merchandise trade deficit, bil. chained 09$ Overall trade deficit, percent of GDP

Note: "All other goods" includes a residual due to chained-dollar price adjustment.
Source: Census Bureau, U.S. International Trade in Goods and Services; Bureau of Economic Analysis, National Income and Product Accounts; CEA calculations.

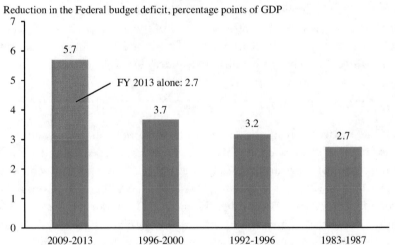

Figure 1-3
**Major Deficit Reduction Episodes Over a Four-Year Period
Since the Demobilization from WWII**

Reduction in the Federal budget deficit, percentage points of GDP

Source: Office of Management and Budget; Bureau of Economic Analysis, National Income and Product Accounts; CEA calculations.

crisis—continue to rebound and contribute to growth, as real (inflation-adjusted) residential investment rose more than 6 percent over the four quarters of the year, while motor vehicle production rose 9 percent. And in October 2013, the amount of crude oil produced domestically exceeded the amount imported for the first time since 1995, providing further evidence of a domestic energy boom that is supporting jobs and helping to sustain a markedly narrower trade deficit relative to the years leading up to the crisis (Figure 1-2).

The progress seen in 2013 is notable in part because the steep decline in the Federal budget deficit during the year was a major headwind on macroeconomic performance. Figure 1-3 shows the largest four-year reductions in the Federal budget deficit since the demobilization from World War II. Since the end of fiscal year 2009, the deficit has fallen by 5.7 percentage points of GDP, with nearly half of that reduction—2.7 percentage points of GDP—coming in FY 2013 alone. Some of the deficit reduction in 2013 was a natural consequence of the gradual improvement in the economy, and a large portion of it was due to policy decisions, like the spending caps agreed to in the Budget Control Act of 2011, the increase in tax rates for top earners at the beginning of 2013, as well as the end of the temporary payroll tax holiday. The fiscal contraction would, of course, have been much worse were it not for the permanent extension of tax cuts for middle-income households. While these factors reflected a balanced approach to making progress toward fiscal sustainability, they were unnecessarily compounded with the onset of budget sequestration in March, which the Congressional Budget Office (CBO 2013a) estimated slowed real GDP growth over the four quarters of the year by 0.6 percentage point and reduced employment by the equivalent of roughly 750,000 full-time jobs.

On top of the fiscal headwinds, the economy was also forced to contend with a disruptive government shutdown for 16 days in October, as well as dangerous brinksmanship over raising the Federal debt limit. The shutdown cost the government more than $2 billion in lost productivity alone as Federal workers were furloughed for a combined 6.6 million days. In addition, families were unable to travel to national parks, oil and gas drilling permits were delayed, Small Business Administration loans were put on hold, and licenses to export high-tech products could not be granted, to name just a few effects. Consumer sentiment, as measured by the Reuters/University of Michigan Index, fell to its lowest point of the year in October, and fourth-quarter GDP growth was constrained by a large negative contribution from the Federal sector. Moreover, because Congress was slow to act to raise the debt ceiling, several large investment management firms announced that they had divested from Treasury securities maturing around the time of the potential debt-ceiling breach. Ultimately, the episode provided yet another reminder of the need for policymakers to avoid self-inflicted wounds to the economy and to stay focused on constructive steps that support growth and job creation.

How We Got Here: The Administration's Response to the Crisis

In considering the recovery over the last five years and the sources of optimism for the years ahead, it is important not to lose sight of the critical policy decisions that averted a second Great Depression and made it possible for the economy to arrive at this point. Recoveries from financial crises tend to be slower than from recessions caused by other types of shocks because heavy household debt burdens and tight credit conditions can linger for an extended period of time. However, the U.S. economy has fared better than most other developed countries in recent years. As shown in Figure 1-4, among the 12 countries that experienced a systemic financial crisis in 2007 and 2008, the United States is one of just two in which output per working-age population has returned to pre-crisis levels. The fact that the United States has been one of the best performing economies in the wake of the crisis supports the view that the full set of policy interventions in the United States made a major difference in averting a substantially worse outcome.

Chapter 3 looks back at the American Recovery and Reinvestment Act of 2009 (the Recovery Act), along with more than a dozen subsequent jobs measures that the President signed into law, including the payroll tax cut, extensions of unemployment insurance, and tax cuts for business investment and hiring. At the macroeconomic level, CEA estimates that the Recovery Act, by itself, cumulatively saved or created about 6 million job-years, where a job-year is defined as one full-time job for one year (equivalent to an average of 1.6 million jobs a year for four years). Adding in the subsequent jobs measures, the cumulative gain in employment through the end of 2012 grows to 9 million job-years (Figure 1-5). This analysis is broadly similar to others provided by a variety of sources, including the Congressional Budget Office, and is generally consistent with a growing academic literature that is discussed in Chapter 3. In addition to the macroeconomic impact, Chapter 3 also reviews the Recovery Act's key investments in areas like education, clean energy, physical infrastructure, and technological infrastructure that will continue to pay dividends long after the Recovery Act has phased out.

Fiscal measures were only part of the overall policy response. The President acted decisively to save the American auto industry and the suppliers and economic ecosystem that depend on it. The Administration also

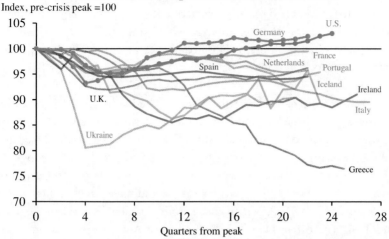

Figure 1-4
**Real GDP Per Working-Age Population
in 2007–2008 Banking Crisis Countries, 2007–2013**

Index, pre-crisis peak =100

Quarters from peak

Note: U.S. as of 2013:Q4, all others as of 2013:Q3 except Iceland (Q2). Working-age population is 16-64
for U.S. and 15-64 for all others. Population for Ukraine is interpolated from annual estimates. Selection
of countries based on Reinhart and Rogoff (forthcoming).
Source: Statistical Office of the European Communities; national sources; CEA calculations.

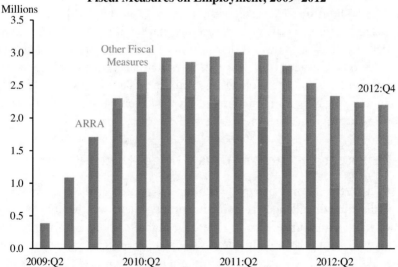

Figure 1-5
**Quarterly Effect of the Recovery Act and Subsequent
Fiscal Measures on Employment, 2009–2012**

Millions

Source: Bureau of Economic Analysis, National Income and Product Accounts; Congressional Budget
Office; CEA calculations.

instituted a range of measures that helped families stay in their homes, facilitated refinancing into lower interest rates, and took steps toward alleviating the housing blight that can threaten neighborhoods and restrain home values. Furthermore, the Treasury Department promoted financial stability and instituted a range of programs to help restore the flow of credit for both large and small businesses. The Federal Reserve undertook important independent actions as well, which are more fully described in Bernanke (2012, 2014).

Another positive but less widely appreciated story from the recession and recovery is the performance of America's social safety net. Though employment and incomes declined sharply as the recession unfolded, millions of Americans were kept out of poverty by tax credits and programs like Social Security, nutrition assistance, and unemployment insurance. Excluding these measures, the poverty rate would have risen 4.5 percentage points from 2007 to 2010, but in fact it only rose half a percentage point (Figure 1-6). The direct effect of the Recovery Act on incomes, not even counting its impact on jobs and the broader economy, reduced the poverty rate in 2010 by 1.7 percentage points, equal to 5.3 million people kept out of poverty. As discussed in Chapter 6, these developments represent the continuation of a longer-running trend in which essentially all of the progress made in reducing poverty has come as a direct consequence of government programs. The poverty rate excluding tax credits and public programs actually rose from 1967 to 2012, but when tax credits and programs are included, the poverty rate was cut by 38 percent (Wimer et al. 2013). Nevertheless, with 49.7 million Americans still living in poverty as of 2012, far more work remains to be done. As the Nation recently marked the 50th anniversary of President Lyndon B. Johnson's declaration of a war on poverty, Chapter 6 details lessons that have been learned, ways that antipoverty programs can be strengthened, and other policies that can help take the next step forward by achieving meaningful reductions in poverty even before tax credits and government programs kick in.

SOURCES OF OPPORTUNITY IN 2014 AND BEYOND

The U.S. economy has made substantial gains over the last five years, and while many challenges remain, including recent weather-related disruptions and some turbulence in emerging markets, there are a number of reasons to be optimistic about the economy's prospects. Cyclical developments like diminished fiscal headwinds and an improvement in household finances are likely to contribute to a strengthening of the recovery in the near-term. At the same time, emerging structural trends like the decline in

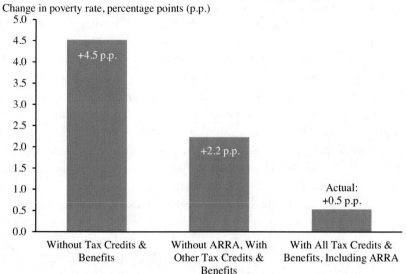

Figure 1-6
**Change in Poverty Rate From 2007–2010,
With and Without Tax Credits and Benefits**

Change in poverty rate, percentage points (p.p.)

Without Tax Credits & Benefits	+4.5 p.p.
Without ARRA, With Other Tax Credits & Benefits	+2.2 p.p.
With All Tax Credits & Benefits, Including ARRA	Actual: +0.5 p.p.

Source: Wimer et al. (2013); CEA calculations.

the rate of health care cost growth, the surge in domestic energy production, and continued technological progress will support growth on a sustained basis into the future. As these developments unfold, it will be critical to take additional steps to ensure that the middle class and those striving to join it have opportunities to succeed. But these emerging trends will help create the framework for the sustainable, broad-based growth that the President is seeking to promote.

Cyclical Factors

Diminished fiscal headwinds. The most predictable reason for optimism about the U.S. economy in 2014 is the waning drag from fiscal policy and reduced fiscal uncertainty. In December, a bipartisan budget agreement averted a second round of discretionary sequester cuts that were scheduled to go into effect in January and also relieved a portion of the cuts that had already taken place during the preceding year. While Congress could do substantially more to support job growth and economic opportunity, the economy is unlikely to face anything like the fiscal consolidation seen at the Federal level in 2013, with deficit reduction continuing at a much more gradual pace going forward. As part of the budget deal, Congress also agreed on discretionary funding levels for the remainder of FY 2014 and all of FY 2015, offering a way to avoid another counterproductive shutdown. Earlier this year, Congress passed appropriations bills for FY 2014 consistent with these spending levels and also extended the debt limit into 2015.

As fiscal headwinds ease at the Federal level, State and local governments are also showing encouraging signs. After shedding more than 700,000 jobs from 2009 to 2012, State and local governments added 32,000 jobs in 2013.

Improved household finances. American households saw trillions of dollars in wealth wiped out as a result of the recession, but recent data indicate that a large degree of progress has been made in the recovery. As of the third quarter of 2013, real per-capita household wealth had recouped over 80 percent of the large decline from its peak, reflecting gains in housing and stock prices, as well as the progress households have made in deleveraging. Moreover, the household debt service ratio—the estimated required payments on mortgage and consumer debt as a share of disposable income—was 9.9 percent in the third quarter of 2013, the lowest since the data began in 1980, and down from 13 percent in 2007. Further improvements in household finances and expanded access to credit will contribute to strengthening in consumer spending. Looking over the course of the recovery, real personal consumption expenditures have grown just 2.2 percent at an annual rate, compared with the 2.9 percent pace during the 2000s expansion period, a fact that partly reflects the lingering after-effects of the financial crisis. A noticeable pickup in consumer spending—which comprises more than two-thirds of the U.S. economy—would represent an important step toward turning the page on the crisis era.

While the aggregate statistics on household wealth paint a picture of improvement, too many families have not shared in the gains. For instance, middle-income households have on average a larger fraction of wealth in their homes relative to equities, and house prices—despite recent improvements—have not recovered as sharply as equities, which represent a larger fraction of the wealth held by upper-income households. The challenges of ensuring that more Americans share in the gains from economic growth are discussed in additional detail later in the chapter.

Structural Trends

Along with these positive near-term developments, this report also highlights three longer-term, structural trends that have emerged recently and will support growth on a sustained basis into the future.

Domestic energy boom and changes in energy use. The first major trend is the dramatic increase in domestic energy production combined with a shift in the use of energy that represents an important opportunity not just for the economy, but also for America's security and climate. Current

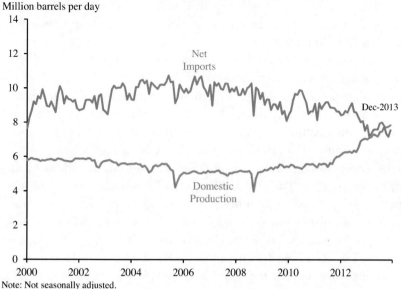

Figure 1-7
Domestic Crude Oil Production and Net Imports, 2000–2013
Million barrels per day

Note: Not seasonally adjusted.
Source: Energy Information Administration, Petroleum Supply Monthly.

projections indicate that the United States became the world's largest producer of oil and gas in 2013, exceeding both Russia and Saudi Arabia. As noted earlier, domestic production of crude oil rose above imports in October for the first time since 1995 (Figure 1-7), and further increases in domestic production and reduced oil imports are expected in the coming years. Moreover, natural gas production continued to rise in 2013 from the 2012 record high and is up more than 20 percent over the past five years. The power sector has undertaken a shift from coal to natural gas, which was responsible for 27 percent of our overall energy consumption in 2012, up from 24 percent in 2008. But the progress is not limited to oil and gas—consistent with the President's "all of the above" energy strategy, great strides have also been made in renewables and energy efficiency. Wind and solar power generation have each more than doubled since the President took office, while oil consumption has fallen over this time, as stronger fuel economy standards and investments in cutting-edge technologies have led to the most fuel-efficient light vehicle fleet ever. This broad-based energy boom supports jobs directly in production and distribution, and also indirectly, by making the United States more attractive as a location for multi-national firms in energy-intensive industries like manufacturing.

The President recently announced new steps to further capitalize on these exciting developments in the energy sector and reduce our dependence on foreign energy sources while creating new jobs. In the 2014 State of the Union address, the President announced his intention to forge ahead with new executive actions that will improve the fuel efficiency of the nation's trucking fleet and help states and localities attract investment in new factories powered by natural gas.

Although many of the recent trends in the energy sector are positive, looking ahead over the coming decades, climate change continues to pose considerable threats to America's environment, economy, and national security. The combined effects of shifting electricity production from coal to cleaner-burning natural gas, large increases in wind and solar power generation, and ongoing progress in energy efficiency have made a large contribution to reducing national energy-related carbon dioxide emissions by more than 10 percent since 2005. In his Climate Action Plan, the President set out the concrete steps that the Administration is taking to address the costs of climate change through new actions to reduce greenhouse gas emissions and prepare for the future climate changes that are an inevitable consequence of past emissions. The President has also recently directed his Administration to continue working with states, utilities, and other stakeholders to set new standards on carbon pollution from power plants.

Health care cost slowdown. The second structural trend is the slowdown in the growth of health care costs. The growth rate of real per-capita health care expenditures from 2010 to 2012 was the lowest since the Center for Medicare and Medicaid Services data began in the 1960s (Figure 1-8), and preliminary data and projections indicate that slow growth continued into 2013. As detailed in Chapter 4, this historic slowdown in health care cost growth does not appear to be merely an after-effect of the recession. The slowdown has persisted even as the economic recovery has unfolded, and it is evident in areas like Medicare as well as in the gap between health care price inflation and overall inflation, neither of which should be sensitive to cyclical fluctuations. Chapter 4 also presents evidence that some already-implemented features of the Affordable Care Act, including reductions in overpayments to Medicare providers and private insurers as well as payment reforms that incentivize better patient outcomes, are contributing to this trend. Primarily as a consequence of slower health care cost growth, the Congressional Budget Office has marked down its forecast of spending on Medicare and Medicaid in the year 2020 by about 13 percent relative to the projection it issued in August 2010. Employers and families are also likely to see significant benefits as health care places less pressure on employers' compensation costs, and the resulting savings are passed on to workers in the form of higher wages.

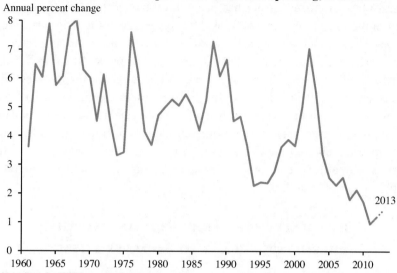

Figure 1-8
Growth in Real Per Capita National Health Spending, 1961–2013

Annual percent change

2013

Note: Data for 2013 is a projection.
Source: Centers for Medicare and Medicaid Services, National Health Expenditure Accounts; Bureau of Economic Analysis, National Income and Product Accounts; CEA calculations.

Expansion of innovation. The third emerging trend that presents a major opportunity for long-term growth is the rapid advance in telecommunications technology, particularly in fast and widely available wired and wireless broadband networks, and in their capacity to allow mobile devices to take advantage of cloud computing. The economic potential of these technologies and the broader context of U.S. productivity growth are discussed in greater detail in Chapter 5. From 2009 to 2012, annual investment in U.S. wireless networks grew more than 40 percent from $21 billion to $30 billion, and the United States now leads the world in the availability of advanced 4G wireless broadband Internet services. This infrastructure is at the center of a vibrant ecosystem that includes smartphone design, mobile app development, and the deployment of these technologies in sectors like business, health care, education, public safety, entertainment, and more. All told, the expansion of advanced telecommunications technology—along with the slowdown in health care cost growth and the rise in domestic energy production—are major reasons to be upbeat about the U.S. economy's growth prospects in the coming years.

Long-Term Fiscal Sustainability

To the extent these structural trends continue to unfold and support stronger-than-projected economic growth in the years ahead, they will help move the Federal government closer to fiscal sustainability over the medium- and long-run. The steep decline in the Federal deficit over the last several years discussed earlier has been accompanied by similar improvement in the long-term fiscal outlook. One key gauge of the long-term fiscal outlook is the fiscal gap, which represents the amount of tax increases or spending cuts as a share of GDP required in the present to stabilize the debt-to-GDP ratio over the next 75 years. While long-run fiscal projections are always subject to a wide margin of error, recent estimates of the fiscal gap are smaller than those issued just a few years ago. These improvements are thanks in large part to the aforementioned slowdown in health care cost growth, including the cost-saving measures in the Affordable Care Act together with other spending restraint and the restoration of higher tax rates on high-income households.

THE CHALLENGES THAT REMAIN AND THE PRESIDENT'S PLANS TO ADDRESS THEM

In the five years since the depths of the Great Recession, the U.S. economy has strengthened considerably. Nevertheless, many of the challenges left in the wake of the recession linger, as do other challenges that built up in the decades before the recession. Presently, the first and most immediate imperative is to support the recovery and continue to restore the economy to its full potential. But going forward, it will also be critical to find ways to expand the economy's potential and to ensure that all Americans have the opportunity to experience the prosperity that they help create.

Continuing to Restore the Economy to its Full Potential

Despite the 8.5 million private-sector jobs added over the last 47 months and the decline in the unemployment rate to a five-year low, the economy has not fully healed from the massive blow of the Great Recession, and helping restore the economy to its full potential is the most immediate challenge policymakers face. This imperative can in large part be understood through the prism of the U.S. labor market, which is currently subject to multiple distinct but closely related challenges. First, given the magnitude of the job losses stemming from the Great Recession and the need to add jobs to support a growing working-age population, the economy continues to exhibit an absolute shortfall in the number of jobs.

Moreover, while the long-term unemployment rate has trended down, it still remains markedly elevated. As shown in Figure 1-9, the prevalence of persons unemployed for 26 weeks or less has returned to its pre-recession average (4.2 percent of the labor force in January 2014, same as the average

Figure 1-9
Unemployment Rate by Duration, 1994–2014

Percent of labor force

Note: Dotted lines represent average during the December 2001 to December 2007 expansion period as defined by the National Bureau of Economic Research. Shading denotes recession.
Source: Bureau of Labor Statistics, Current Population Survey; CEA calculations.

from 2001 to 2007), but the long-term unemployment rate is more than twice what it was during the pre-crisis years (2.3 percent in January 2014 compared with 1.0 percent on average from 2001 to 2007). Reducing long-term unemployment presents a major challenge because these individuals may face stigmatization from employers or experience skill deterioration.

Even as the economy continues to add jobs, it will also be important to see a concurrent recovery in the volume of job-to-job mobility. The flow of workers across firms plays a critical role in the economy because job mobility enables rising productivity and wages as individuals switch to jobs for which they are better suited. However, in recent months there have been fewer than 9 million combined hires and separations a month, compared with more than 10 million a month on average from 2005 to 2007. The rate of voluntary separations—a measure of workers' confidence in labor market conditions—also remains below pre-recession levels.

As the unemployment rate trends down and worker mobility picks up, real wages should grow more quickly; but currently, the sluggish real wage growth seen in recent years represents another serious outstanding challenge in the labor market. Real wage growth remained positive for most of 2013, a key sign of the progress being made (Figure 1-10). However, as discussed in greater depth below, substantially faster real wage increases will

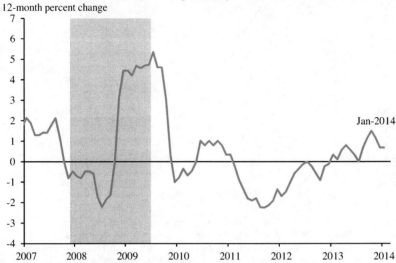

Figure 1-10
**Growth in Real Average Hourly Earnings for
Production and Nonsupervisory Workers, 2007–2014**

12-month percent change

Jan-2014

Note: Shading denotes recession.
Source: Bureau of Labor Statistics, Real Earnings.

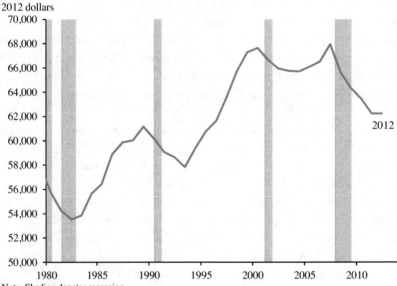

Figure 1-11
Real Median Family Income, 1980–2012

2012 dollars

2012

Note: Shading denotes recession.
Source: Census Bureau, Historical Income Data.

be needed to make up for a decades-long trend of average wages failing to keep pace with productivity gains.

The typical family's inflation-adjusted income has also been slow to recover. The Census Bureau reported in September that the median family earned $62,241 during 2012, little changed in real terms from the preceding year (Figure 1-11). After increasing cumulatively less than half a percent in the seven years leading up to the recession, real median family income fell markedly during the recession and its aftermath and, as of 2012, was still 8 percent below its previous peak. Going forward, this is an important indicator of the way in which the recovery makes progress for the middle class.

To speed the recovery, boost job creation, and tighten labor markets so as to put upward pressure on median wages, the President has repeatedly called for investment in America's infrastructure. This type of investment would not only help address the 11 percent average unemployment rate in the construction sector during 2013, but would also foster stronger long-run growth. In the 2014 State of the Union, the President renewed his call for using the one-time revenue associated with the transition to a reformed business tax system to finance a major modernization of U.S. transportation infrastructure. But in the absence of the necessary Congressional action on this proposal, the President will press ahead in other ways by speeding up the permitting process for new construction projects.

In addition, the President's budget includes an Opportunity, Growth, and Security initiative, which will finance additional discretionary investments in areas such as education, research, infrastructure, and national security. The $56 billion initiative is evenly split between defense and non-defense and is fully paid for with mandatory spending reforms and tax loophole closers—and would both speed the return of the economy to its full potential and also expand that potential.

In addition to the challenges in the areas of jobs and income, the housing sector represents another key area with scope for further improvement. As shown in Figure 1-12, construction activity fell so far in the wake of the recession that, despite notable gains in recent years, the rate of permitting for new residential sites still remains well below the level suggested by demographic trends and home depreciation. To help unlock this potential, steps must be taken to bring certainty to the mortgage finance system, and also to support communities that were particularly hard hit when the housing bubble burst and are still coping with a legacy of foreclosures and blight.

Expanding the Economy's Potential

In addition to taking steps that speed the economy's return to full potential, the Administration continues to push simultaneously for

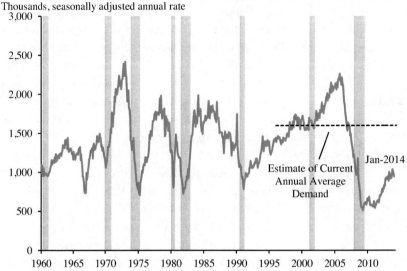

Figure 1-12
Building Permits for New Residential Units, 1960–2014
Thousands, seasonally adjusted annual rate

Note: CEA estimates that approximately 1.6 million new units per year are needed to keep pace with household formation and home depreciation. Shading denotes recession.
Source: Census Bureau, New Residential Construction; CEA calculations.

measures that will expand that potential. To understand the importance of this goal, consider that an American worker in 2012 could produce more than four times as much per hour as his or her counterpart in 1948. About 10 percent of the increase is due to improvements in the composition of labor, mostly because of greater education, and 38 percent is due to increases in the amounts of capital that workers have at their disposal. Fully 52 percent is due to increases in total factor productivity, or what the Bureau of Labor Statistics calls multifactor productivity, which reflects technological change as well as the scale of markets and organization of production processes.

The growth of total factor productivity can vary widely year-to-year, but the longer-term trends can be broadly illustrated by splitting the last 60 years into three periods, as shown in Figure 1-13. First, from the 1950s through the early 1970s, total factor productivity grew at a relatively rapid 1.8 percent annual rate, fueled in part by public investments like the interstate highway system and the commercialization of innovations from World War II like the jet engine and synthetic rubber. Then, from the mid 1970s to the mid 1990s, the rate of total factor productivity growth slowed substantially, to just 0.4 percent a year. The causes of this slowdown have been the subject of extensive academic debate, with some evidence pointing to the disruptive effect of higher and volatile oil prices. Finally, from the mid 1990s through the latest available data for 2012, total factor productivity growth

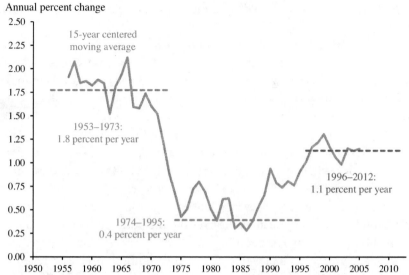

Figure 1-13
Growth in Total Factor Productivity, 1953–2012

Annual percent change

15-year centered
moving average

1953–1973:
1.8 percent per year

1996–2012:
1.1 percent per year

1974–1995:
0.4 percent per year

1950   1955   1960   1965   1970   1975   1980   1985   1990   1995   2000   2005   2010

Note: The dotted lines divide the last 60 years into three periods that broadly reflect three "episodes" in productivity growth. For the nonfarm business sector.
Source: Bureau of Labor Statistics, Multifactor Productivity; CEA calculations.

picked up to a 1.1 percent-a-year rate, in part reflecting vast improvements in computer technology and software during this time. Although differences across these episodes may seem small, over time they compound to enormous differences in output and living standards.

While the growth rate of total factor productivity is always critical to an economy's long-run potential, the projected slowdown in the growth of America's workforce due to the aging of the population places even greater emphasis on productivity going forward. Since an economy's potential output depends fundamentally on the number of workers and the average output per worker, slower productivity growth can in theory be offset by rapid population growth. And during the aforementioned 1974 to 1995 period marked by slower total factor productivity growth, the working-age (16 to 64) population continued to expand at a solid rate of more than 1 percent a year. However, the Census Bureau projects that over the 20 years from 2012 to 2032, the working-age population will grow only 0.3 percent a year, largely a consequence of the aging of the baby boomers into retirement. Thus, looking ahead, productivity-enhancing investments are likely to be as critical as ever.

The President has several key proposals that will expand the U.S. economy's long-run potential. Comprehensive immigration reform would counteract the slower growth of America's workforce by attracting highly skilled inventors and entrepreneurs to create jobs in the United States. The Congressional Budget Office (2013b) has affirmed that the bipartisan bill passed by the Senate would raise the economy's productivity and total output.

In addition, while the Opportunity, Growth and Security initiative, infrastructure investments, and business tax reform proposals discussed earlier will speed the recovery in the near term, these steps will also help make the economy more productive over the long run. Specifically, the President's framework for business tax reform would expand the economy's potential by reducing the distortions in the current system that skew investment decisions. By developing a system that is more neutral, corporate decision makers can act for business reasons, not tax reasons, creating an environment in which capital will flow to the most efficient purposes.

Expanding the economy's potential also means ensuring that the Federal budget is fiscally sustainable over the medium- and long-run. Fiscal sustainability frees up resources for productive investment and reduces borrowing from abroad that would ultimately require commensurate reductions in future national income. For these reasons, the President's budget proposals have repeatedly included additional steps toward long-run fiscal sustainability, including proposals to promote additional efficiencies in the health care system and limit tax benefits and loopholes for the highest earners. The Administration has also placed substantial emphasis on using evidence and evaluation in the budgeting process, as discussed in Chapter 7. These practices will help make the Federal Government more efficient and save taxpayer money for years to come.

Executive actions—including establishing new, innovative manufacturing institutes and expanding the SelectUSA initiative to attract foreign investment—will also help improve productivity and create well-paying jobs in the United States. Further, the Administration continues to negotiate new trade and investment partnerships with Europe and Asia, to help American consumers, the American businesses that sell their products overseas, and the workers they employ. The President is asking Congress for the Trade Promotion Authority he will need to make these agreements a reality.

Promoting Economic Opportunity

The third major challenge the economy faces is the need to ensure that every American has an opportunity to realize their full potential and partake in the prosperity they help create. Since the late 1970s, the United States has seen a major increase in income inequality due to a combination of technological change, globalization, changes in social norms, and institutional shifts like the erosion of the inflation-adjusted minimum wage and

Figure 1-14
Share of National Income Earned by Top 1 Percent, 1915–2012

Note: Excludes capital gains.
Source: September 2013 update to Piketty and Saez (2003).

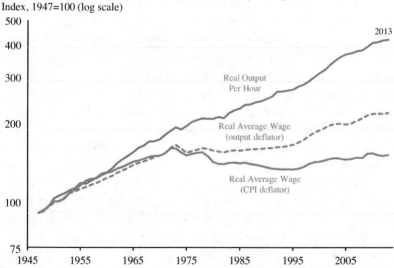

Figure 1-15
Growth in Productivity and Average Wage, 1947–2013

Note: Real output per hour is for all workers in the nonfarm business sector. Average wage is for private production and nonsupervisory workers. Output deflator is the price index for nonfarm business output. CPI deflator is the CPI-W. Data on wages before 1964 reflect SIC-based industry classifications.
Source: Bureau of Labor Statistics, Productivity and Costs, Current Employment Statistics; CEA calculations.

the decline in union membership. As shown earlier, in 2012, the median U.S. family's inflation-adjusted income was less than it was in 1997. In contrast, separate data derived from administrative tax records show that the top 1 percent of tax units—who earned an average of more than $1 million in 2012—received 19.3 percent of total income (excluding income from capital gains, which can be highly volatile year-to-year), the largest share since 1928 (Figure 1-14).

These statistics are symptomatic of a troubling disconnect between the economy's productivity and ordinary workers' wages that has emerged over the last 40 years. As shown in Figure 1-15, real average hourly earnings for production and nonsupervisory employees roughly kept pace with productivity growth in the nonfarm business sector during the early postwar years. But starting around the 1970s, a large gap emerged between overall productivity and an ordinary worker's take-home pay. Several factors may be contributing to this gap, including the relatively rapid increase in non-wage compensation like employer-sponsored health insurance, as well as the likelihood that productivity gains may translate into higher pay differently across occupations. Moreover, the gap is substantial regardless of whether one adjusts for inflation using the Consumer Price Index, which is more indicative of the typical household's purchasing power, or using the price index for total nonfarm business output, which allows for a more direct comparison with the productivity data. Ultimately, the Figure illustrates the growing concern that too many ordinary workers are being left behind, and helps explain why the President has said that the basic bargain in America—that those who work hard will have the chance to get ahead—has frayed.

To address this issue and to restore a greater measure of fairness and opportunity to the economy, the President has proposed a number of important measures. In the near term, the most direct step is to raise the minimum wage, which, after adjusting for inflation, has declined by more than one-third from its peak in the 1960s and is now worth less than it was when President Ronald Reagan first took office in 1981. Along with a minimum wage increase, the President has also called for other measures that would help those striving to join the middle class, including an expansion of the Earned Income Tax Credit for workers without children. In addition to these immediate steps, the President has set out a range of ideas to invest in education and equip workers with the skills they will need to compete in the global economy for years to come. For instance, the ConnectEd program continues to move forward, putting high-speed Internet in classrooms across America, and the Administration has also secured over 150 new commitments from universities, businesses, and nonprofits to improve college opportunity and outcomes for students from low-income families.

Along with steps that create jobs, boost incomes, and invest in educational opportunities, the President is pursuing measures to ensure that families can experience a greater degree of financial security. Three million young adults under age 26 have gained coverage through their parents' plans because of the Affordable Care Act, another 4 million people enrolled in insurance plans through State and Federal marketplaces as of late February, and millions more have been determined eligible for State Medicaid programs. Additionally, in the 2014 State of the Union, the President announced the creation of MyRA, a new safe and easy-to-use savings vehicle that can help millions Americans start saving for retirement.

CONCLUSION

The challenges discussed above are substantial, but the President believes that it is well within our capacity as a Nation to address these issues and to move toward shared and sustainable growth. The President has set out an ambitious agenda to support the recovery in the near term, while building on emerging strengths to expand the economy's potential over the long term. In this context, the President also remains focused on restoring greater measures of fairness and opportunity to our economy, to strengthen the middle class and give a boost to those striving to join it. This agenda includes measures to create new well-paying jobs, continue to reduce dependence on foreign energy sources, equip workers with skills to compete in the global economy, support those hardest hit by economic change, and provide families with a greater sense of financial security. These steps, and the rationale underlying them, are the focus of the pages that follow.

CHAPTER 2

THE YEAR IN REVIEW AND THE YEARS AHEAD

The economy continued to recover and strengthen in 2013, nearly five years after the worst of the financial crisis. Building on the progress of the previous two years, businesses added 2.4 million jobs over the 12 months of 2013: in total, the private sector added 8.5 million jobs during 47 months of consecutive job growth. The unemployment rate fell 1.2 percentage points in 2013, a larger decline than in previous years and more than was forecast by most private-sector economists. Output growth started the year slowly, largely because of headwinds from fiscal drag and slow growth among many of our trading partners that reduced demand for U.S. exports. Output strengthened, however, in the second half of the year. Overall, real gross domestic product (GDP) grew 2.5 percent during the four quarters of the year, up from the 2.0 percent growth during each of the preceding two years. Growth in consumer spending, homebuilding, and exports supported aggregate demand growth. Inventory investment was also a positive factor, partially due to an increase in agricultural production reflecting a plentiful crop in 2013 following a year of drought in 2012. Federal fiscal policy was a drag on the economy because of the tightening due to the expiration of the temporary payroll tax cut and sequester-related spending cuts beginning in March, and because of the uncertainty caused by a partial government shutdown in October and the brinksmanship over the debt limit. Inflation remained low and roughly stable, with the consumer price index (CPI) up 1.5 percent during the 12 months of 2013, and the CPI excluding food and energy up 1.7 percent over this period, slightly below the year-earlier pace.

Looking ahead, a wide variety of indicators suggest that the economy is well situated for a pickup in growth in 2014. Following the largest four-year reduction in the Federal deficit as a share of GDP since the post-WWII demobilization, Federal fiscal policy will be much less of a drag in 2014 and thus will likely constrain overall growth by less than during the preceding years. State and local government spending appears to have turned the corner, with purchases increasing during the second and third quarters of 2013. The mid-February action of Congress to suspend the debt limit until March 2015 relaxes a situation that had been headed towards unwelcome uncertainty.

Although the economy still remains challenging for many, households—on average—are in an improved position to increase spending as they have further reduced their debt burden and seen a substantial increase in housing and stock-market wealth. More household wealth will facilitate an increase in spending on consumer durables such as motor vehicles, which are showing their age and due for replacement. Homebuilding, which grew rapidly last year, is likely to continue growing on a path up to levels consistent with the demographic forces of the next decade, with mortgage interest rates still below their pre-recession levels, despite a mid-2013 rise. Business fixed investment also has potential to accelerate after relatively slow growth in 2013 as aggregate demand picks up and businesses can take advantage of their sizeable cash flows.

Nevertheless, several downside risks to economic growth remain in 2014 as unforeseen events both domestically and internationally may pose a risk to the economy. Recently, for example, severe cold weather and storms in the United States and a global reduction in asset prices have contributed to some economic activity falling below trend rates of growth in the last few months.

The pace of the recovery will depend, in part, on policy choices. Additional measures that increase aggregate demand would add impetus to the economy in 2014. In particular, the Budget also includes the Opportunity, Growth, and Security initiative, which will finance additional discretionary investments in areas such as education, research, infrastructure, and national security. The $56 billion initiative is evenly split between defense and non-defense and is fully paid for with mandatory spending reforms and tax loophole closers. In addition, investments in infrastructure or extending emergency unemployment benefits would expand demand immediately while measures like business tax reform would help the economy by increasing certainty.

KEY EVENTS OF 2013

Aggregate Output Growth During the Year

Growth in aggregate economic activity was fairly steady during 2013, with quarterly growth rates between 1.8 and 3.0 percent at an annual rate for the first three quarters of the year, as measured by the average of the

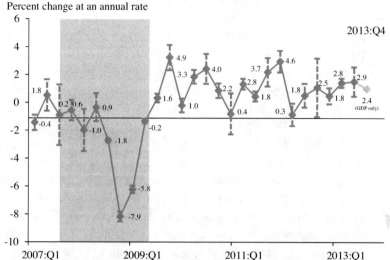

Figure 2-1
Mean GDP Growth, 2007–2013

Percent change at an annual rate

Note: Mean real GDP growth is the average of the growth rates of real GDP and real gross domestic income (GDI). The bullets show mean GDP and the bars show the GDP and GDI growth in each quarter. The estimate for 2013:Q4 is for GDP only. Shading denotes recession.
Source: Bureau of Economic Analysis, National Income and Product Accounts; CEA calculations.

income- and product-side of real GDP (Figure 2-1).[1] During the four quarters of the year, growth was strong in exports (4.9 percent) and in residential investment (6.6 percent), and moderate in business fixed investment (3.0 percent) and consumer spending (2.1 percent). State and local purchases edged up slightly following four years of decline, while Federal spending fell 6.2 percent.

Fiscal Policy

Federal fiscal policy evolved through several near- or after-deadline Congressional actions that made fiscal policy uncertain and created a difficult planning environment for businesses and consumers.

Toward the end of 2012, policy focused on the potential negative effects of the "fiscal cliff," a confluence of expiring tax cuts and scheduled spending declines that were on track to occur simultaneously, which might have resulted in a sharp fiscal-policy tightening on January 1, 2013. The Congressional Budget Office (CBO) estimated that these policies, if allowed to occur, would have lowered real GDP growth by about 2.25 percent during

[1] Research shows that an average of the two growth rates is better correlated with a wide variety of economic indicators than either the product-side measure (which is headlined in the Commerce Department reports) or the income-side measure alone (Nalewaik 2010, Economic Report of the President 1997, pp. 72-74).

the four quarters of 2013, or enough to cause a decline in real GDP. On the tax side, the 2001 tax cuts, previously extended through 2012, were expiring. Also expiring at the end of 2012 was a 2-percentage point cut in the Social Security payroll tax that was first instituted for one year in 2011, and an increase of the threshold for the Alternative Minimum Tax (AMT). On the spending side, defense and nondefense spending were each scheduled for across-the-board cuts (sequestration) of $55 billion. Medicare payments to physicians and emergency unemployment benefits were among other spending programs scheduled to be cut in January 2013.

On January 1, 2013, Congress passed the American Taxpayer Relief Act of 2012 (ATRA). The ATRA addressed the revenue side of the fiscal cliff by making permanent the middle-class tax cuts, indexing the AMT to inflation permanently, and raising revenues over 10 years by allowing high-income tax cuts to expire. The ATRA also allowed the temporary payroll tax cut to lapse. On the spending side, the ATRA extended Emergency Unemployment Compensation and delayed the Medicare physician cuts for an additional year, but the Act delayed sequestration only until March 1, 2013.

When Congress failed to reach a budget agreement by March 1, allowing the sequester to go into effect, cuts to discretionary and non-exempt mandatory programs were distributed over the remaining seven months of the fiscal year (rather than the full fiscal year in the sequester's original design). As a result, many Federal agencies furloughed civil servants, which reduced Federal compensation by $0.6 billion at an annual rate in the second quarter and by $5.5 billion at an annual rate during the third quarter of 2013 (a total of $1.5 billion not at an annual rate). The CBO projected that the sequester would cut 750,000 jobs and reduce growth during the four quarters of 2013 by a 0.6-percentage point.

The debt ceiling had technically been reached on December 31, 2012 when the Treasury Department commenced "extraordinary measures" to enable the continued financing of the government through mid-February. Around the end of February, however, Congress passed and the President signed a bill that suspended the debt limit though May 18. The next day, on May 19, the debt ceiling was reinstated at a level that reflected borrowing during the suspension period, but no more. As a result, the Treasury began applying extraordinary measures once again and, in late September, the Treasury announced that these extraordinary measures would be exhausted by October 17.

Adding to the debt-ceiling stress, more uncertainty arose in early October when the continuing resolution needed to fund the government was not extended into the new fiscal year beginning on October 1. As a result, the U.S. Government went into a partial shutdown. About 850,000 Federal civilian employees were initially put on temporary leave, but many civilian Defense Department employees were recalled during the second week of the shutdown. An agreement for a continuing resolution to end the shutdown and extend the debt ceiling was reached on October 16, and the Federal government returned to normal operations the next day. The Bureau of Economic Analysis (BEA) has estimated that the shutdown was directly responsible for a 0.3 percentage point reduction in the annualized GDP growth rate for the fourth quarter, although this estimate does not incorporate indirect effects that operate through reductions in private activity dependent on government services, reductions in confidence, or increases in uncertainty. Confidence in government policy, as measured by the Thompson Reuters-University of Michigan Survey, fell to a level in October which was in the bottom 5 percent of the monthly series since it began in 1978.

The agreement to end the shutdown (the Continuing Appropriations Act of 2014) funded the government through January 15, 2014, and suspended the debt ceiling until February 7, 2014, after which time it was suspended again until March 2015. In mid-December, Congress passed an agreement to provide partial relief from the automatic sequestration of discretionary spending in FY 2014 and 2015, and offset those increases with increased pension contributions from new Federal civilian employees, as well as a variety of higher fees and spending reductions. The bill provided only an overall discretionary cap and, in January, Congress passed FY 2014 appropriations bills consistent with these spending levels. Notably, the bill would fully restore cuts to Head Start programs, which provide early childhood education to children from low-income families, partially restore cuts to medical research and job training programs, and finance new programs to combat sexual assault in the military.

As a result of this fiscal stringency and continued GDP growth, the Federal deficit-to-GDP ratio fell 2.7 percentage points to 4.1 percent in FY 2013 and ranks among one of the largest year-over-year declines ever (Figure 2-2). The deficit-to-GDP ratio in FY 2009 was elevated by the steep recession as well as the fiscal stimulus to combat that recession (See Chapter 3). Since then, the four-year decline in the deficit-to-GDP ratio of 5.7 percentage points was the largest since the demobilization at the end of World War II. Overall fiscal support substantially raised the level of output and employment since 2009, as discussed in Chapter 3. But the reduction in the deficit, especially in 2013, has acted as a drag on growth rates. One reason for the fiscal drag was the winding down of various countercyclical fiscal policies taken during the recession. Fiscal drag is likely to moderate substantially in

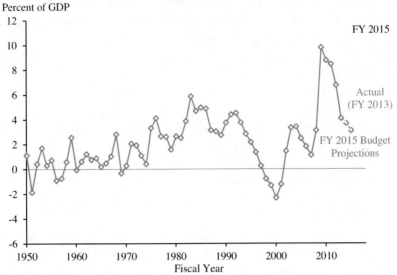

Figure 2-2
Federal Budget Deficit, 1950–2015

Percent of GDP

FY 2015

Actual
(FY 2013)

FY 2015 Budget
Projections

Fiscal Year

Source: Bureau of Economic Analysis, National Income and Product Accounts; Office of
Management and Budget.

FY 2014, with a projected further 0.4 percentage point decline to 3.7 percent
in the deficit to GDP ratio under the President's policies.

Monetary Policy

In 2013, the Federal Open Market Committee (FOMC) continued to
provide substantial policy accommodation. With its usual tool—the federal
funds rate—near its effective lower bound, the Committee employed both
forward guidance for the federal funds rate and additional purchases of
longer-term securities.

The FOMC made clear its intention to keep the target range for
the federal funds rate "exceptionally low" and maintained throughout the
year the forward guidance it issued in December 2012 indicating that the
Committee will maintain the current level of the federal funds rate at least
"as long as the unemployment rate remains above 6.5 percent, inflation
between one and two years ahead is projected to be no more than half a percentage point above the Committee's 2 percent longer-run goal, and longer-
term inflation expectations continue to be well anchored." Moreover, in its
December 2013 statement, the FOMC added to its forward guidance, stating
that "The Committee now anticipates, based on its assessment of these factors (labor market conditions, inflation, and inflation expectations), that

it likely will be appropriate to maintain the current target range [of 0 to ¼ percent] for the federal funds rate well past the time that the unemployment rate declines below 6-1/2 percent (emphasis added), especially if projected inflation continues to run below the Committee's 2 percent longer-run goal." This additional information was intended to provide greater clarity on the Committee's policy intentions once the unemployment threshold is crossed.

With regard to asset purchases during 2013, the Federal Reserve continued expanding its holding of mortgage-backed securities at a rate of $40 billion a month and longer-term Treasury securities at a pace of $45 billion a month in an attempt to "support a stronger economic recovery and to help ensure that inflation, over time, is at the rate most consistent with its dual mandate," to achieve "maximum employment and price stability." In the period leading up to the June FOMC meeting, financial market participants interpreted some Federal Reserve communications as implying an earlier-than-expected reduction in the pace of purchases. This interpretation contributed to an increase in market volatility and a marked rise in longer-term Treasury yields over the summer that were only partly reversed in the fall, as the Federal Reserve continued to purchase assets at an unchanged pace. However, at its December meeting the FOMC decided to begin reducing the pace of its purchases in January, cutting the monthly increase in its holdings by $10 billion to $75 billion. In addition, the Committee indicated that if incoming information broadly supports its expectation of ongoing improvement in labor market conditions and inflation moving back toward its longer-run objective, it will likely reduce the pace of asset purchases in further measured steps at future meetings. This tapering of asset purchases was continued in January 2014 as announced in the FOMC meeting that month.

Financial Markets

Financial developments over the course of the year reflected the evolving economic outlook as well as Federal Reserve communications. In the spring and the summer, speculation about a possible reduction in the pace of Federal Reserve asset purchases contributed to a sizeable increase in longer-term interest rates (Figure 2-3).

Yields on 10-year Treasury notes were 1.7 percent at the start of May before rising to 2.6 percent in July, and yields continued to rise to about 2.9 percent just before the September FOMC meeting. In response to the Committee's decision to leave the pace of purchases unchanged in September, the 10-year yield retraced part of the summer increase, dropping to 2.6 percent for the month of October. In addition, Federal Reserve

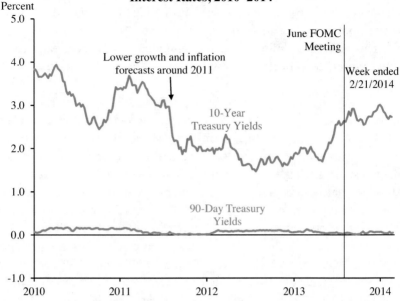

Figure 2-3
Interest Rates, 2010–2014

Percent

Lower growth and inflation
forecasts around 2011

June FOMC
Meeting

Week ended
2/21/2014

10-Year
Treasury Yields

90-Day Treasury
Yields

Source: Federal Reserve Board, H.15.

communications appeared to lead investors to push back their expectations for the timing of the first increase in the federal funds rate during the fall. Toward the end of the year, however, the better-than-expected readings on payroll employment and on other economic indicators, followed by the FOMC's decision to reduce the pace of its asset purchases, boosted longer-term Treasury yields in the final weeks of 2013. The 10-year Treasury yield closed 2013 at roughly 3 percent. Short-term rates (such as the rate on federal funds, and the 91-day Treasury bill rate) were more stable throughout the year—remaining under 0.2 percent—although expectations of future short-term rates fluctuated.

In October, brinksmanship over the debt ceiling—which was expected to be hit soon after October 17—and the two-week government shutdown weighed heavily on financial markets. Through September and early October, several indicators of financial stress reflected market participants' concerns about the debt limit. As shown in Figure 2-4, yields on specific Treasury bills maturing around that time increased in anticipation of potential delayed payments.

Moreover, institutional money market funds saw a sizeable $86 billion of outflows (about 5 percent of assets) in the three-week period that ended October 16. Fidelity Investments—the nation's largest manager of money market mutual funds—declared publicly in early October its decision not

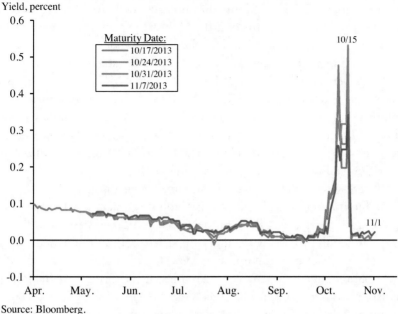

Figure 2-4
Treasury Bills Maturing in Late October–Early November, 2013

Source: Bloomberg.

to hold U.S. government debt set to mature around the date of the potential debt ceiling breach. Finally, interest rates on overnight repurchase agreements, or repos, collateralized by Treasury securities, a common source of funding for financial institutions, spiked in early October. With the resolution of the debt ceiling debate, all such indicators returned to normal levels.

Reflecting the ongoing economic recovery and the improved outlook over the course of the year, U.S. equity markets remained on a general upward path despite the increase in interest rates. The Standard and Poor's 500 rose by 30 percent in 2013, reaching a record high in nominal terms at year-end. When adjusted for GDP price inflation, however, it remained below its March 2000 peak. The Standard and Poor's edged up slightly during the first two months of 2014.

International Developments

The past year also saw the beginnings of a recovery in Europe, with real GDP edging up between 1.0 and 1.6 percent annual rate in the second, third, and fourth quarters of 2013. These were the first three consecutive quarters of positive real GDP growth for the 28-country European Union since 2011. Concerns about the stability of the European monetary union (the 17-country "euro area") that surfaced in 2011 and 2012 have subsided.

In the euro area, the unemployment rate stabilized at a record high of 12.1 percent from April to September before ticking down to 12.0 percent in the fourth quarter. Euro area inflation was subdued, declining to only 0.8 percent during the 12 months of 2013 from 2.2 percent a year earlier. The recent low rate of inflation has fueled concerns about possible deflation. The European Central Bank policy target for price stability is "below, but close to, 2 percent." The Central Bank's Outright Monetary Transactions program, first announced in August 2012, has helped bring a measure of stability to European sovereign debt markets, with Italy and Spain's 10-year yields ending the year right around a manageable 4 percent. During the year, euro area states made substantial progress to centralize and harmonize bank supervision and regulation at the euro level.

There were notable developments in several European countries as well. In the runup to the euro area crisis, countries including Greece, Spain and Portugal saw a large runup in their current account deficits to finance private and public borrowing that supported consumption and investment. In the wake of the euro area crisis, these countries have adjusted, largely eliminating their current account deficits through reductions in unit labor costs and improved price competiveness, as shown in Figure 2-5. Nevertheless, unemployment rates remain particularly high in these countries.

Japan's real GDP grew a solid 2.7 percent during the four quarters of 2013 following a 0.4 percent decline during 2012. Japan's core consumer price index (that is, excluding food and energy) turned positive, 0.7 percent during the 12 months of 2013, up from a 0.6 percent decline during 2012. This follows in the wake of the election of Shinzo Abe in December 2012, the appointment of a new governor of the Bank of Japan in March, and the announcement in April that the Bank intended to double the monetary base by the end of 2014. Under this policy, bond purchases amount to about $80 billion a month (basically, the same pace as the Federal Reserve but in a smaller economy). Expansionary monetary policy was part of a three-prong strategy that initially included fiscal stimulus and structural reforms meant to support positive growth and to keep Japan from slipping back into a period of deflation.

China's real GDP grew 7.7 percent during the four quarters of 2013, slightly below the year-earlier pace, but noticeably slower than 10 percent and 9 percent growth rates during 2010 and 2011, respectively. Xi Jinping assumed the presidency in March and presided over the Third Plenary Session of the Communist Party, which resulted in a raft of economic reform proposals. China's interbank lending rates have spiked on several occasions this year. During these episodes, the People's Bank of China was

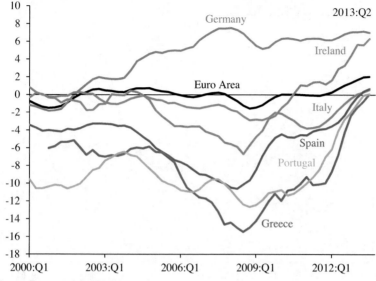

Figure 2-5
Current Account Balance by Country, 2000–2013

Percent of GDP, four-quarter moving average

Source: Eurostat; national sources.

slow to inject liquidity, which many interpreted as a warning to banks that have increased off-balance sheet commitments to bypass administrative and regulatory controls and expand lending.

Among other emerging market economies, the pace of real GDP growth fell in Indonesia, Malaysia, Mexico, South Africa and Thailand. But growth also increased in a few, such as Brazil, India, and Turkey. Low interest rates in the United States since the recession coupled with higher investment return prospects in emerging market economies prompted an increase in capital flows toward emerging markets. As interest rates in the United States began to rise and growth prospects abroad waned, however, investors started adjusting their portfolios, which in some cases had adverse effects on emerging-market currencies and interest rates. Foreign mutual funds withdrew $53 billion from emerging markets between mid-May and August, leading to sharp drops in a number of currencies and emerging market equity indexes and causing central banks in several affected countries (India, Indonesia, Turkey, Brazil, and Pakistan) to raise domestic policy interest rates. Nevertheless, even with the withdrawals, investment holdings remained well above the levels of just a few years ago as shown in Figure 2-6. In some instances, currencies and bond markets have retraced their earlier losses, especially as global investors have increasingly differentiated

Figure 2-6

Cumulative Flows into Mutual and Exchange-Traded Funds Investing in Emerging Markets, 2010–2014

Billions of dollars, cumulative since January 2010

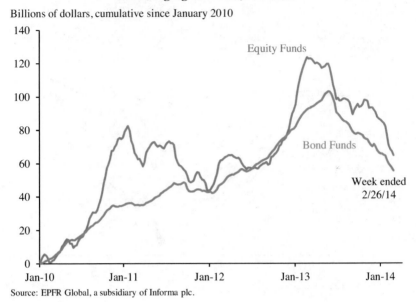

Source: EPFR Global, a subsidiary of Informa plc.

debt by country according to the underlying economic fundamentals of each country's economy.

DEVELOPMENTS IN 2013 AND THE NEAR-TERM OUTLOOK

Consumer Spending

Real consumer spending grew about 2 percent during each of the past three years. With consumer spending constituting 68 percent of GDP, that stability explains much of the stability of the growth of aggregate demand during those three years. Yet the stability of consumption growth during 2013 results from several offsetting developments. The termination of the temporary 2-percentage point cut in payroll taxes reduced disposable income during 2013 by $115 billion relative to 2012. This subtracted about 0.9 percent from disposable income, and held down consumption growth by about half a percent. Higher taxes on high-income households from the American Taxpayer Relief Act likely had little impact on spending due to their smaller aggregate size and the relatively low marginal propensities to consume for high-income households. Also, by reducing the medium- and long-term budget deficit, the higher tax rates on high-income households will contribute to stronger and more-sustainable growth over time.

Strong gains in aggregate household net worth—both an increase in assets and a decline in the debt burden—have supported aggregate consumer spending. Debt service (that is, required minimum payments on household debt) has fallen from 13 percent of disposable income at the end of 2008 to 10 percent by the third quarter of 2013 (the latest data available, Figure 2-7). Some of the decline in debt service is due to declines in interest rates on mortgages and consumer credit, but some of the decline is due to declines in the ratio of household debt to income, a process called deleveraging. Debt has fallen from about 1.3 times annual income in 2008 to 1.1 times annual income by the third quarter of 2013—with most of the decline in this ratio due to rising nominal incomes, although nominal debt has edged down 5 percent. Together, these declines in household debt and debt-service relative to income show that the household sector as a whole has progressed in reducing these burdens. Although these figures are relevant for projecting aggregate output and consumption growth, they do not reflect the change in debt and debt service for moderate-income and median-income households who, in many cases, continued to face challenges in 2013.

Overall wealth also grew in 2013, as shown in Figure 2-8. Although these wealth increases were in all categories of holdings, wealth likely increased substantially more for high-income households (which have a larger share of their wealth in equities) than for the typical household (which has more of their wealth in housing that appreciated more slowly than equities in 2013). As a result, this suggests that wealth inequality continued to grow as middle-class families faced persistent economic challenges. While gains in stock-market wealth have been happening since the trough of the recession in 2009, those increases were particularly sharp during 2013, when the Wilshire 5000 stock market index increased 31 percent. During the four quarters of 2013, stock market wealth is estimated to have increased by an amount equivalent to 39 percent of annual disposable income. Housing wealth (net of mortgage liability) also increased notably during the year. Housing prices, as measured by the CoreLogic National House Price Index, hit bottom around March 2011 and have increased 11 percent during the 12 months of 2013. As a result, net housing wealth is on track to increase by another 13 percent of annual disposable income in 2013.

The increases in stock market and housing assets point to an increase in the ratio of net worth to income amounting to 52 percent of annual disposable income. An increase in wealth raises annual consumer spending by about 3 percent of that increase. As a result, the expansion of wealth alone

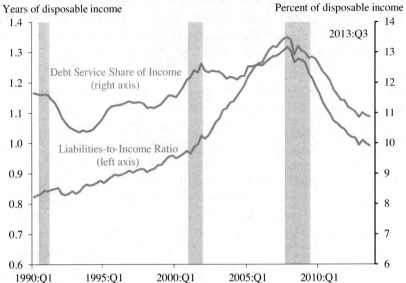

Figure 2-7
Household Deleveraging, 1990–2013

Years of disposable income

Percent of disposable income

2013:Q3

Debt Service Share of Income
(right axis)

Liabilities-to-Income Ratio
(left axis)

Note: Shading denotes recession.
Source: Federal Reserve Board, Financial Accounts of the United States.

Figure 2-8
**Consumption and Wealth Relative to Disposable
Personal Income (DPI), 1952–2013**

Consumption/DPI ratio

Years of disposable income

2013:Q4

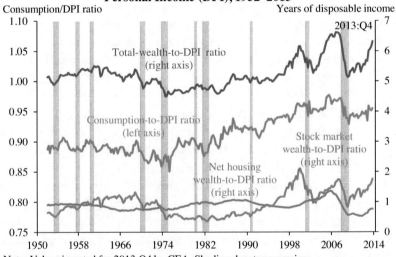

Total-wealth-to-DPI ratio
(right axis)

Consumption-to-DPI ratio
(left axis)

Stock market
wealth-to-DPI ratio
(right axis)

Net housing
wealth-to-DPI ratio
(right axis)

Note: Values imputed for 2013:Q4 by CEA. Shading denotes recession.
Source: Bureau of Economic Analysis, National Income and Product Accounts; Federal
Reserve Board, Financial Accounts of the United States; CEA calculations.

could support a rise in consumption of 1.7 percent of disposable income, or more than enough to offset the rise in taxes in 2013.

Looking ahead, consumer spending in 2014 is likely to grow faster than its 2-percent rate during the past three years. The rise in wealth and the progress in deleveraging have created a more-stable platform on which to base the growth of consumer spending. The rapid growth of consumer durables during 2013 (5.6 percent) is likely to continue or increase further. The average age of light motor vehicles on the road has risen to 11.4 years and it appears likely that some pent-up demand remains for motor vehicles and other durables whose purchases have been delayed during the recession and the slow recovery.

Business Investment

Business Fixed Investment. Real business fixed investment grew moderately, 3.0 percent during the four quarters of 2013, down from a 5.0 percent increase during 2012. The slower pace of business investment during 2013 was concentrated in structures and equipment investment, while investment in intellectual property products grew faster in 2013 than the year earlier. Investment in nonresidential structures declined 0.2 percent following robust growth of 9.2 percent during 2012. Investment in equipment slowed to 3.8 percent, following a 4.5 percent increase in 2012. In contrast, investment in intellectual property products picked up to 4.0 percent during 2013 from 2.9 percent in 2012. (In July 2013, as part of a comprehensive revision to the National Income and Product Accounts, the Bureau of Economic Analysis revised its classifications for business fixed investment to include 1) Research and Development and 2) Entertainment, Literary, and Artistic originals in a new category of Intellectual Property Products, which also includes software investment. See Box 2-1 on the July 2013 benchmark of the National Income and Product Accounts.)

Within equipment investment, major components such as information processing equipment and transportation equipment posted less robust growth in 2013 than in 2012, offsetting stronger growth in industrial equipment investment. Within investment in information processing equipment, declines were posted in investment in computers and photocopy equipment. Within transportation equipment, growth was not as fast as 2012 for investment in autos, aircraft, and ships.

Real investment in nonresidential structures edged down 0.2 percent during the four quarters of 2013, down from growth of 9.3 percent in 2012. Solid growth in petroleum and natural gas drilling was offset by declines in the construction of manufacturing structures and power and communication facilities.

Box 2-1: The 2013 Comprehensive Revision to the National Income and Product Accounts

In July 2013, the Commerce Department released the results of the first comprehensive revision to its National Income and Product Accounts—the raw material underlying the calculation of gross domestic product (GDP)—since 2009. These revisions, which reach back to 1929, include additional source data as well as methodological changes designed to reflect the evolving nature of the U.S. economy. In particular, the Bureau of Economic Analysis has expanded its definition of business investment to include spending on research and development (R&D) and the creation of original works of art like movies, all of which are now recorded as intellectual property products. The Commerce Department also recognized the increase in pension obligations as savings for households and a liability for governments and businesses. In the Federal Reserve's Financial Accounts of the United States, the cumulative values of these liabilities are now recognized as assets of the household sector and liabilities of governments and businesses.

All told, these and other changes effectively increased the size of the economy as measured in the first quarter of 2013 by $551 billion dollars at an annual rate (or 3.4 percent). The changes also held implications for the path of growth of GDP over time, with the statistical updates from the new annual source data affecting mainly more recent years, while

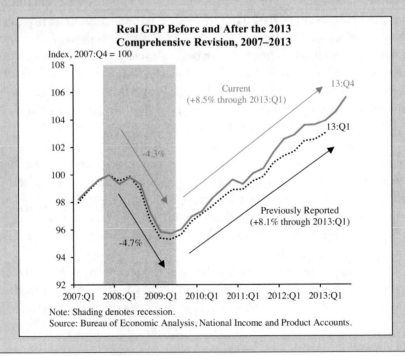

Real GDP Before and After the 2013 Comprehensive Revision, 2007–2013

Index, 2007:Q4 = 100

Current (+8.5% through 2013:Q1)

13:Q4

-4.3%

13:Q1

Previously Reported (+8.1% through 2013:Q1)

-4.7%

2007:Q1   2008:Q1   2009:Q1   2010:Q1   2011:Q1   2012:Q1   2013:Q1

Note: Shading denotes recession.
Source: Bureau of Economic Analysis, National Income and Product Accounts.

the methodological revisions (such as intellectual property) affected the entire historical series. Real GDP growth during the 16 quarters following the end of the recession in the second quarter of 2009 was revised up by an average of 0.1 percentage point to 2.2 percent a year, and the decline in GDP observed during the recession (starting in the fourth quarter of 2007) was revised up 0.3 percentage point to -2.9 percent at an annual rate, making the recession less steep and the recovery stronger than what was previously reported. The cumulative decline in real GDP during the recession is now reported at 4.3 percent rather than 4.7 percent, followed by an increase during the expansion of 8.5 percent through the first quarter of 2013, as opposed to 8.1 percent published previously (see Figure).

Since the beginning of 2009, the average absolute revision (without regard to sign) from the advance quarterly estimate of real GDP growth to the latest data was 1.3 percentage points. The magnitude of these changes highlights the difficulty in measuring economic performance real-time.

The pace of growth of business fixed investment is puzzling because interest rates are low and the internal funds available for investment are high. Interest rates on corporate Baa bonds were low in both nominal and real terms. Nominal Baa rates averaged 5 percent during 2013, and adjusted for expected inflation of about 2 percent, this translates into a real rate of 3 percent, substantially below the 60-year average of about 4.7 percent.

Funds for investment were also easily available from internal sources such as undistributed profits and depreciation. For the nonfinancial business sector, the sum of these sources, known as cash flow in national income accounting, was 10.1 percent of GDP in the first three quarters of 2013, well above the historical average of 8.7 percent. Historically, nonfinancial corporate investment averages 103 percent of cash flow, with the sector as a whole borrowing from banks and the public for the rest. In contrast, during the first three quarters of 2013, investment was only 90 percent of cash flow. The cash flow that was not available for investment appears to have been spent on share repurchases, a way of returning funds to shareholders that is similar to dividends, but more volatile.

With interest rates low and internal funds readily available, the growth rate of investment might be attributable to low expectations of output growth. In a relationship known as "the accelerator," the growth of investment is related to the change in growth (that is, the acceleration) of output, as shown in Figure 2-9. For example, when output accelerated in 2010 (that is, when output growth increased from negative in 2009 to

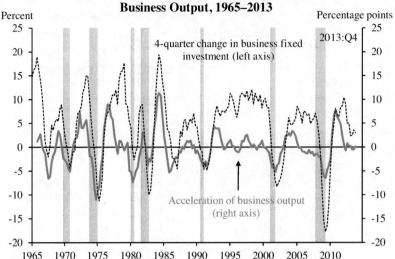

Figure 2-9
**Business Investment and the Acceleration of
Business Output, 1965–2013**

Note: The accelerator is the 6-quarter percent change in business output (AR) less the 6-quarter ago 6-quarter percent change in business output (AR). Shading denotes recession.
Source: Bureau of Economic Analysis, National Income and Product Accounts.

positive in 2010), investment increased very fast so that the capital stock could service the new level of demand. But when business output growth settled down to an annual rate of roughly 3 percent during the three years through 2013, investment did not need to grow so fast, and indeed it has slowed, as shown in Figure 2-9.

Inventory Investment. Inventory investment made a substantial contribution to real GDP growth during the four quarters of 2013 when it accounted for 0.8 percentage point of the 2.5 percent total growth. An increase in agricultural inventory investment accounts for 0.3 percentage point of that overall 0.8 percentage-point contribution and reflects the rebound to a strong harvest following a severe drought in 2012. In the manufacturing and trade sector, the buildup of inventories through the year was no faster than sales, so that by December, inventory stocks were at a 1.30 months' supply, roughly the same level as at year-end 2012.

State and Local Governments

Although State and local governments continued to experience fiscal pressure in 2013, the four-year contraction in the sector—measured in terms of both purchases (consumption and investment) and employment—finally appears to have ended. State and local purchases, which had generally

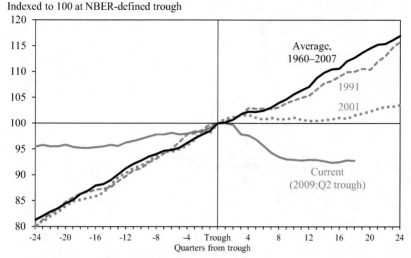

Figure 2-10
Real State and Local Government Purchases During Recoveries

Indexed to 100 at NBER-defined trough

Note: The 1960–2007 average excludes the 1980 recession due to overlap with the
1981–82 recession.
Source: Bureau of Economic Analysis, National Income and Product Accounts; National Bureau of
Economic Research; CEA calculations.

declined for 13 quarters through the first quarter of 2013, ended the year at a higher level than in the first quarter, marking its first increase over three quarters since 2009. The cumulative decline in State and local purchases during this recovery contrasts with the usual experience during recoveries (Figure 2-10). In a typical recovery, growth in State and local government bolsters the economic recovery. In contrast, declines in State and local government have been a headwind to private-sector growth and hiring during the first four years of this recovery.

Similar to the 2013 pickup in spending, State and local employment has begun to show signs of life, adding 32,000 jobs during the 12 months of 2013, after shedding almost 700,000 jobs from the end of the recession through year-end 2012.

Despite these positive signals during 2013, major obstacles to growth remain: in particular, the burden of unfunded pension obligations of State and local governments. In its benchmark revision to the National Income and Product Accounts of the United States in July 2013, the Commerce Department, in cooperation with the Federal Reserve, began to measure State and local defined-benefit plans on an accrual basis rather than a cash basis, thereby tracking funded and unfunded pension liabilities. As can be seen in Figure 2-11, the size of these liabilities relative to State and local receipts ballooned immediately after the recession and remains elevated at a

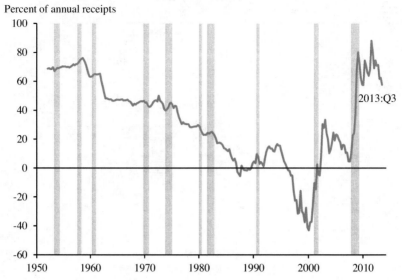

Figure 2-11
State and Local Pension Fund Liabilities, 1952–2013

Percent of annual receipts

Note: Shading denotes recession.
Source: Federal Reserve Board, Financial Accounts of the United States.

level that is currently at about 60 percent of a year's revenue for the sector. Adding in State and local bond liabilities does not change the shape of the plot shown in the figure, although they elevate the level of the liabilities-to-receipts ratio to about two hundred percent of a year's revenue.

International Trade

In 2013, U.S. exports of goods and services to the world averaged nearly $189 billion a month and imports averaged nearly $229 billion a month (Figure 2-12). Exports accounted for 13.5 percent of U.S. production (GDP) in 2013, the same as in 2011 and 2012.

The U.S. trade deficit, the excess of the Nation's imports over its exports, averaged nearly $40 billion a month in 2013. Import demand fell during the recession and, as a result, the trade deficit fell from $66 billion in July 2008 to $25 billion in May 2009. Exports fell too because of recession-related declines in domestic demand abroad (see Figure 2-13), but the recession was not as severe in many parts of the global economy as in the United States. Since May 2009, growth rates of exports and imports have each been averaging about 0.8 percent a month.

Figure 2-13 suggests that slower economic growth among our main trading partners dampens U.S. export growth. In recent years, the top five

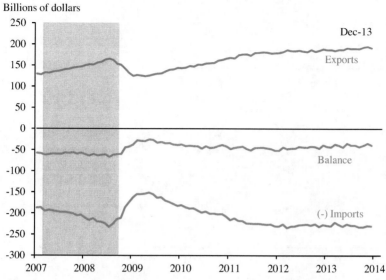

Figure 2-12
Trade in Goods and Services, 2007–2013

Source: U.S. Census Bureau, Foreign Trade Division.

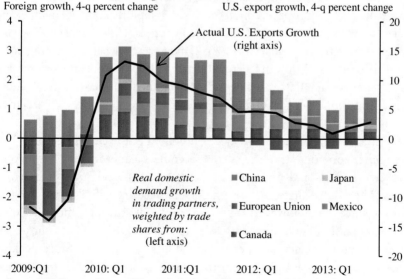

Figure 2-13
U.S. Exports Growth, 2009–2013

Source: IMF; Eurostat; Bureau of Economic Analysis; U.S. Census Bureau, Foreign Tade Divison.

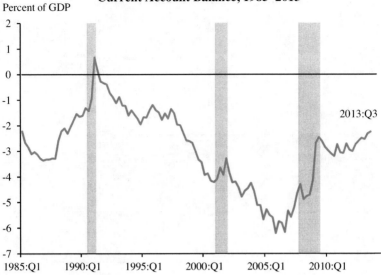

Figure 2-14
Current Account Balance, 1985–2013

Percent of GDP

Note: Shading denotes recession.
Source: Bureau of Economic Analysis, National Income and Product Accounts.

destinations for U.S. exports, in order from highest to lowest typically were: Canada, the European Union, Mexico, China, and Japan. While growth generally slowed in all these trading partners, it actually turned to recession for a time in our No.2 (European Union) and No. 5 (Japan) export recipients, and their recoveries look to be gradual. In the European Union, real GDP fell 0.7 percent during the four quarters of 2012, then grew 1.1 percent during 2013, and is forecasted to grow 1.4 percent during 2014 (European Commission 2013). Japan's real GDP fell 0.4 percent during the four quarters of 2012, but grew 2.7 percent during 2013, but is projected to edge up only 0.6 percent in 2014 (OECD 2013).

The trade balance is the major component of the current account balance. Other components of the current account balance include net income on overseas assets and unilateral transfers such as foreign aid and remittances. The United States has run a current account deficit in all but two quarters since 1985; however, the trend from 1990 through the mid-2000s of ever-increasing deficits appears to have reversed. Figure 2-14 shows the current account balance as a percentage of GDP since 1985. Since peaking at more than 6 percent of GDP in the fourth quarter of 2005, the current account balance has fallen as a share of GDP by more than 3 percentage points. The sharpest decrease occurred during the recession of 2008-09, and although there have been some periods of increase since then, the current account deficit recently reached a 15-year low in the third quarter of 2013 of 2.3 percent. An important driver of the decrease in current account deficit in recent years is the increased domestic production of oil and gas, and the associated reduced demand for imported oil, a shift discussed in more detail later in the chapter. Removing oil, which depends on prices that are set on world markets, the U.S. current account deficit is substantially smaller.

The United States has one of the most open and transparent trade and investment regimes in the world, with a trade weighted applied tariff of 1.3 percent, making it a friendly market for imports and foreign investment. A prime motivation behind U.S. trade policy initiatives is to ensure that our accommodative trade and business environment is reciprocated when U.S. actors have the same opportunities to compete in other markets that foreign exporters and investors have in the United States. U.S. trade policy also seeks to level the playing field, including by seeking to raise standards abroad so they are closer to our own in key areas such as intellectual property, labor, and environment. Box 2-2 discusses Administration trade policy initiatives.

Housing Markets

Housing activity continued its recovery in 2013 despite headwinds from mortgage interest rates that rose approximately 1 percentage point in mid-summer, continued tight credit conditions, and waning investor demand for foreclosed properties. On the production side, new housing starts for both single-family and multi-family structures continued their 2012 growth during 2013, despite relatively higher mortgage rates. For 2013 as a whole, starts were roughly 930,000 units, up from 780,000 in 2012, and up from an all-time low of 554,000 units in 2009 (Figure 2-15).

Demand for housing increased, with new and existing home sales reaching their highest levels in 2013 since the Great Recession. With the lowest level of mortgage delinquencies and foreclosure completions in five years, the composition of sales shifted markedly to non-foreclosure proper-ties as fewer households sold homes under distressed conditions.

Supported by a tight supply of homes for sale, housing prices climbed further in 2013, according to every major measure of house prices (Figure 2-16). As of November 2013, quality-adjusted house prices—as measured by the FHFA index—were 7.7 percent higher than their year-ago level and 15.3 percent higher than at their trough in early 2011. Two considerations provide some context for the brisk growth in house prices in 2013. First, such behavior appears to be typical following recessions. Even though house prices bottomed out well after the end of the Great Recession, the recovery since then has, on net, been at a rate just below the average growth rate in house prices seen during the aftermath of the eight post-war recessions of

Box 2-2. Administration Trade Policy Initiatives

The United States has been pursuing the most ambitious trade agenda in a generation. In the President's first term, this included upgrading, passing and implementing market-opening trade agreements with Korea, Panama, and Colombia. U.S. tariffs on imports from those countries were generally much lower than were the tariffs on U.S. exports to those countries at the start of negotiations, and while the United States did further lower tariff barriers as a result of the agreements, the larger barriers were removed by U.S. trading partners.

In December 2013, the United States played a leadership role, working with the 159 countries of the World Trade Organization (WTO), to conclude a Trade Facilitation Agreement, the first multilateral trade agreement concluded by that body in its 20-year history. This global agreement will expedite the movement of goods and services across borders and improve customs cooperation among WTO Members, making it easier to support jobs through trade. Among other things, the Agreement seeks to reduce documentary requirements, require transparency in customs regulations and procedures, encourage countries to accept electronic payments of customs duties and charges, and ensure the quick release of perishable goods. Streamlined procedures and enhanced transparency reduce the costs to businesses of exporting and particularly assist small business for which logistical complexity can be particularly challenging.[1]

The United States is currently pursuing two comprehensive, high-standard regional trade agreements that are ambitious in the size of the overall markets that they seek to affect and in the scope of provisions to be covered under the agreements. Negotiations are nearing completion on the Trans-Pacific Partnership Agreement (TPP), which includes 12 nations that rim the Asia-Pacific region. Negotiations between the United States and the 28-country European Union (EU) for the Transatlantic Trade and Investment Partnership (T-TIP) are at an earlier stage.

The Figure in this box demonstrates the importance of the regions encompassed by these two proposed agreements to U.S. trade. Together, the partner countries in the TPP and the T-TIP buy around 60 percent of all U.S. exports and provide about 53 percent of U.S imports. The TPP and T-TIP therefore seek to build on already robust trading relationships.

---

[1] USTR. 2013a. "Weekly Trade Spotlight: The Benefits of the WTO Trade Facilitation Agreement to Small Business." (http://www.ustr.gov/about-us/press-office/blog/2013/December/Benefits-of-WTO-Trade-Facilitation-Agreement-to-Small-Business).

According to the Office of the United States Trade Representative (USTR 2013a), the TPP "… is the foundation of the Obama Administration's economic policy in the Asia-Pacific Region" and "promotes regional integration by establishing a common set of trade and investment commitments, and also addresses 21st century issues like state-owned enterprises, intellectual property rights, regulatory convergence, and global supply chains."[2]

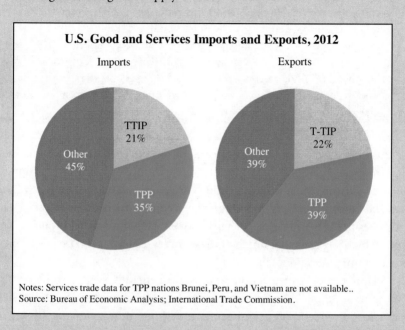

U.S. Good and Services Imports and Exports, 2012

Imports

Exports

TTIP 21%

Other 45%

TPP 35%

T-TIP 22%

Other 39%

TPP 39%

Notes: Services trade data for TPP nations Brunei, Peru, and Vietnam are not available..
Source: Bureau of Economic Analysis; International Trade Commission.

The T-TIP seeks to strengthen trade and investment linkages between the United States and the European Union and to set a template for raising standards across the global trading system. It aims to create new openings for service providers and to make regulations and standards more compatible between the two parties. The T-TIP should also create new channels of cooperation to address shared interests in global trade (USTR 2013b).[3]

---

[2] USTR. 2013b. "Acting Deputy U.S. Trade Representative Wendy Cutler discusses Japan and the TPP at the Peterson Institute for International Economics." ("http://www.ustr.gov/about-us/press-office/blog/2013/November/Cutler-TPP-Japan-PIIE"). The TPP participants are: Australia, Brunei Darussalam, Canada, Chile, Japan, Malaysia, Mexico, New Zealand, Peru, Singapore, Vietnam, and the United States.

[3] USTR. 2013b. "Ambassador Froman discusses the Transatlantic Trade and Investment Partnership at the Munich Security Conference." ("http://www.ustr.gov/about-us/press-office/blog/2013/November/Froman-Munich-Security-Conference").

Upon completion, the TPP and T-TIP agreements, together, will place the United States at the center of an open trade zone representing around two thirds of global economic output. The United States is also in the process of negotiating several other agreements: an International Services Agreement that would liberalize trade in services among countries representing nearly 70 percent of the global services market; another agreement that would further liberalize trade in information technology products among countries representing 90 percent of that market; and an agreement that would liberalize trade in environmental goods among countries representing 86 percent of that market.

The Administration's trade policy initiatives provide production and consumption opportunities otherwise not available to the American economy, and serve the ultimate goals of promoting growth, supporting higher-paying jobs, and thus strengthening the middle class.

the 20th century. Second, house prices at the end of 2013 appear close to their long-run relationship with rents, one measure of housing's fundamental value. During the mid-2000s, house prices increased much more rapidly than did rents before plummeting. The recent growth in house prices has left prices broadly in line or perhaps above their long-run relationship with rents, which suggests that much of these increases have been tied to improving economic fundamentals.

Home sales, construction, and prices generally appear to be on firm footing in spite of higher mortgage rates, which increased about 100 basis points to 4.4 percent, on net, after the May-July interest rate rise (discussed earlier in this chapter) and remained close to that level for the remainder of 2013. Although nominal mortgage rates remain low by historical standards, all else equal, higher rates raise the cost of financing a home purchase, which puts downward pressure on housing demand and residential investment. Also, builders' capacity for funding new construction falls, albeit sometimes with a delay, when interest rates rise. Indeed, residential investment, which grew 15.5 percent during the four quarters of 2012, slowed to a 6.7 percent rate of growth during 2013. The slowdown is accounted for by diminishing increases in starts as well as a drop in commissions in the fourth quarter of 2013 due to a decline in sales of existing homes. But for the year as a whole, new home sales increased 17 percent in 2013, while housing starts rose by a comparable amount.

Another indication that housing market activity is holding steady: households remain optimistic about home prices, according to the Reuters/Michigan Survey of Consumers. Housing affordability remains high and 77

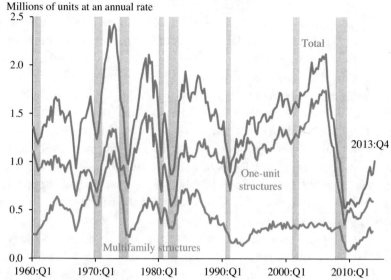

Figure 2-15
Housing Starts, 1960–2013

Millions of units at an annual rate

Total

2013:Q4

One-unit
structures

Multifamily structures

Note: Shading denotes recession.
Source: Census Bureau, New Residential Construction.

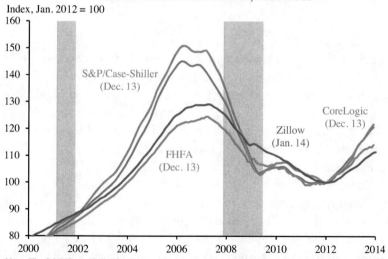

Figure 2-16
National House Price Indexes, 2000–2013

Index, Jan. 2012 = 100

S&P/Case-Shiller
(Dec. 13)

CoreLogic
(Dec. 13)

Zillow
(Jan. 14)

FHFA
(Dec. 13)

Note: The S&P/Case-Shiller, FHFA, and CoreLogic indexes all adjust for the quality of homes sold but
only cover homes that are bought or sold, whereas Zillow reflects prices for all homes on the market.
Shading denotes recession.
Source: Zillow; CoreLogic; FHFA; S&P/Case-Shiller.

percent of households report that it is a "good time to buy a house" (Reuters/Michigan Survey of Consumers).

At a more fundamental level, pent-up demand for housing due to suppressed levels of household formation since 2009 is likely to boost housing demand and to help absorb the large supply of vacant homes and homes still in the foreclosure process. During the Great Recession, the number of new households forming each year dropped to below 1 million a year and has remained low ever since. As Figure 2-17 shows, during the housing bubble of the mid-2000s more homes were built than were consistent with the underlying rate of household formation based on demographic trends that would call for about 1.6 million new housing units a year. This oversupply peaked in 2007 and—because of low levels of home construction—this oversupply began to fall. And by 2011, the oversupply turned into an undersupply. The increase in the stock of homes now lags behind the usual rates of household formation.

As employment prospects improve, household formation is likely to pick up. However, the extent to which the increase in the number of households translates into stronger housing demand depends critically on the easing of credit standards (that might have been over-tightened following the financial crisis), particularly for first-time homebuyers. In 2013, lending standards eased somewhat for prime residential mortgages, according to the Federal Reserve's Senior Loan Officer Opinion Survey, and this easing helped support a rise in mortgage purchase originations from the low levels seen in recent years.

Energy

In 2013, the United States continued to benefit from developments in the oil and gas sectors, as well as from growth in energy efficiency and the production and integration of renewable energy. As shown in Figure 2-18, net petroleum imports have fallen from more than 12 million barrels a day in 2005 to approximately 6.2 million barrels a day in 2013. Moreover, as shown in Figure 2-19, beginning in October 2013, domestic crude oil production exceeded crude oil imports for the first time since 1995.

Crude and refined oil products constitute the vast majority of the country's energy imports. This reduction in energy imports has multiple benefits: it has been a major driver of the improvement in the U.S. balance of trade, it reduces the vulnerability of the U.S. economy to foreign oil supply disruptions, and it supports American jobs both in energy production and in manufacturing. The dramatic increase in domestic oil and natural gas production added about 0.2 percentage point to U.S. GDP growth in both 2012 and 2013.

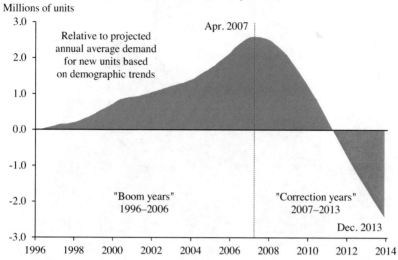

Figure 2-17
**Cumulative Over- and Under-Building of Residential
and Manufactured Homes, 1996–2013**

Source: Census Bureau, New Residential Construction (completions) and Manufactured
Homes Survey (placements); CEA (1998); CEA calculations.

The ongoing trend toward reduced energy imports is driven both by roughly stable energy demand and increases in domestic energy supply. Overall, economy-wide energy use has declined 0.8 percent at an annual rate since 2007. The increase in domestic energy supply reflects major gains in unconventional oil and natural gas production. The sharp increase in unconventional domestic gas production has led to a 73 percent drop in the wholesale (Henry Hub) price of natural gas from a high of $13.42 in October 2005 to $3.68 in October 2013. The United States is now the largest producer of natural gas in the world, and the 2013 International Energy Outlook projects that the United States will remain the largest producer through 2030 (U.S. Energy Information Administration 2013). Since 2007, over 50,000 jobs have been created in oil and natural gas extraction alone, with more than 160,000 jobs being created along the oil and natural gas supply chain. Low natural gas prices also help manufacturing as discussed below, and have been an important driver in the reduction of U.S. carbon dioxide emissions as electricity production has shifted from coal to cleaner-burning natural gas. Indeed, between 2010 and 2013, the total U.S. carbon dioxide emissions from energy consumption decreased by 4.3 percent. In addition to providing cost savings to consumers today, this reduction in greenhouse gas emissions will benefit future generations.

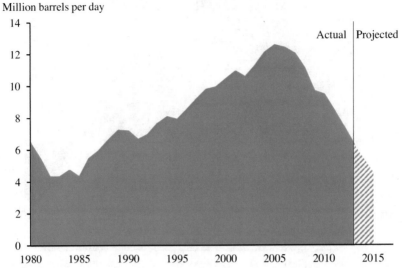

Figure 2-18
Petroleum Net Imports, 1980–2015

Million barrels per day

Source: Energy Information Admnistration, Monthly Energy Review, Short-Term Energy
Outlook.

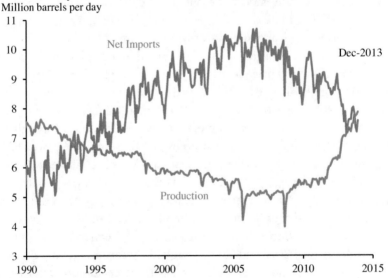

Figure 2-19
Monthly Crude Oil Production and Net Imports, 1990–2013

Million barrels per day

Note: This data is not seasonally adjusted.
Source: Energy Information Administration, Petroleum Supply Monthly.

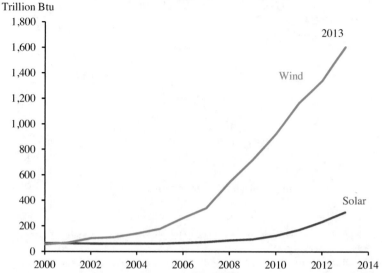

Figure 2-20
Wind and Solar Energy Production, 2000–2013

Trillion Btu

Note: Data for 2013 are projections.
Source: Energy Information Adminstration, Monthly Energy Review, Short-Term Energy Outlook.

The other part of the energy supply story, shown in Figure 2-20, is the dramatic growth in wind and solar electricity production, which have each more than doubled since President Obama took office. In 2012, a record 13 gigawatts of new wind power capacity was installed, roughly double the amount of newly installed capacity in 2011. More than 5 gigawatts were installed in December 2012 alone as firms scrambled to take advantage of the expiring 2.3 cent per kilowatt-hour production tax credit (Congress later extended the tax credit for 2013). These 13 gigawatts of new wind capacity represented the largest share of additions to total U.S. electric generation capacity in 2012.

In addition to increased domestic supply, energy imports have declined because of reduced energy demand across all the main energy sectors. As shown in Figure 2-21, gasoline demand per capita rose through the early 2000s and plateaued in the mid-2000s before dropping substantially during the recession. As the economy has recovered, however, gasoline demand per capita has continued to fall. Some of this continued decline in gasoline demand stems from the relatively high real gasoline prices shown in Figure 2-21, but that is only a partial explanation. Increasing fuel efficiency brought about by Federal fuel efficiency standards also played a role; and, in 2012, the Administration finalized fuel economy standards that, together with the Administration's first round of standards, will nearly double the

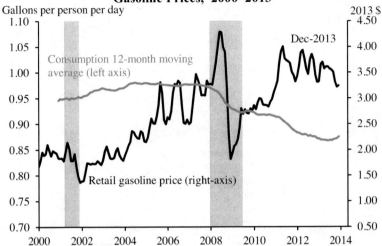

Figure 2-21
**U.S. Per Capita Consumption of Gasoline and Real
Gasoline Prices, 2000–2013**

Note: Retail gasoline prices deflated using PCE chain price index. Consumption includes
residential, commercial, industrial and transporation sectors.
Source: Energy Information Administration, Monthly Energy Review; Census Bureau; CEA
calculations.

fuel economy of light- duty vehicles to the equivalent of 54.5 miles per gal-
lon by the 2025 model year from 2010 levels. Further, beginning in model
year 2014, medium- and heavy-duty trucks must meet new energy efficiency
standards as well, which will increase their fuel efficiency by 10 to 20 percent
by 2018.

Despite these significant improvements in energy efficiency and
reductions in energy-related carbon dioxide emissions, continued work is
needed to reduce greenhouse gas emissions. In June 2013, the President laid
out his Climate Action Plan (summarized in Box 2-3), which aims to reduce
both greenhouse gas emissions and the impact of climate change on future
generations.

Labor Markets

The major U.S. labor market indicators continued to recover during
2013 even as the unemployment rate remained unacceptably high. As shown
in Figure 2-22, the unemployment rate dropped 1.2 percentage points during the 12 months of 2013, somewhat faster than the average 0.9 percentage
point annual drop during the three preceding years. Similarly, as shown in
Figure 2-23, establishment employment finished its third year of growth at

Box 2-3: The Climate Action Plan

In 2009, the President committed the United States to cut greenhouse gas emissions by approximately 17 percent below 2005 levels by 2020. The President's June 25, 2013 Climate Speech noted that, "Climate change represents one of our greatest challenges of our time, but it is a challenge uniquely suited to America's strengths." Following that speech, the President laid out a three-pronged approach to addressing the challenges of climate change: 1) reduce carbon emissions in the United States; 2) prepare America for the impacts of climate change; and 3) lead international efforts to fight climate change and adapt to its impacts.

The United States has already made substantial progress toward the 2020 emissions reduction goal. In 2012, U.S. carbon emissions declined to their lowest levels in nearly 20 years while the economy continued to grow. The Administration has continued to build on this progress by proposing tough new rules to cut carbon pollution from new fossil-fuel-fired power plants and by developing new rules to reduce carbon pollution from existing power plants, as well as by proposing new energy efficiency standards for appliances, announcing new funding for advanced fossil-energy projects, and other important actions. These steps will help to protect the welfare of future generations and will put America in a position to achieve sustainable economic growth by relying on the Nation's clean energy sources.

The Climate Action Plan also lays out steps to ensure that the country is ready to manage the inevitable and already realized impacts of climate change. For example, the Administration will lead an effort to assist State and local governments to make our infrastructure, communities, and natural resources more resilient, including through strengthening our roads, bridges, and shorelines to better protect people's homes, businesses and everyday lives from severe weather worsened by climate change.

Climate change is a global challenge that cannot be solved by any single country; therefore, it is imperative for the United States to couple action at home with leadership internationally. America must help forge a truly global solution to this global challenge by galvanizing international action to significantly reduce emissions (particularly among the major emitting countries), preparing for climate impacts, and driving progress through international negotiations.

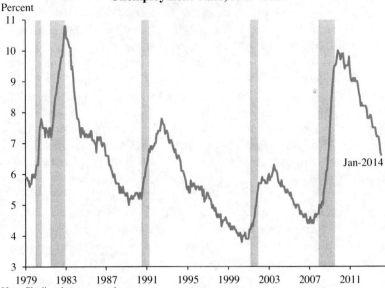

Figure 2-22
Unemployment Rate, 1979–2014

Percent

Jan-2014

Note: Shading denotes recession.
Source: Bureau of Labor Statistics, Current Population Survey.

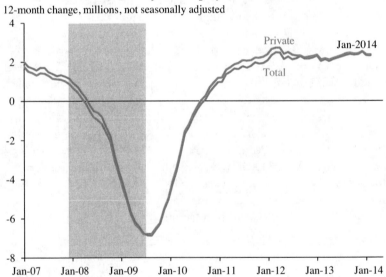

Figure 2-23
Nonfarm Payroll Employment, 2007–2014

12-month change, millions, not seasonally adjusted

Private   Jan-2014

Total

Note: Total excludes temporary decennial Census workers. Shading denotes recession.
Source: Bureau of Labor Statistics, Current Employment Statistics.

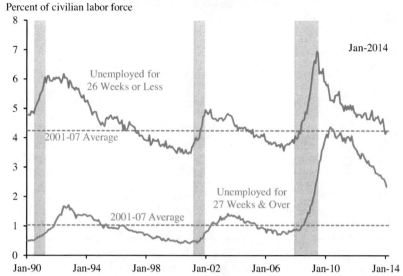

Figure 2-24
Unemployment Rate by Duration, 1990–2014

Percent of civilian labor force

Note: Shading denotes recession.
Source: Bureau of Labor Statistics, Current Population Survey.

roughly 2.3 million a year (or about 190,000 a month)[2]. The strength of the labor market was not matched by the growth of output, with some puzzling developments in the relation between the unemployment rate and GDP, and also the relationship between employee-hours and output (productivity).

The current elevation of the unemployment rate is entirely due to long-term unemployment. In December 2013, the unemployment rate for workers unemployed 26 weeks or less fell to lower than its average in the 2001-07 period, while the unemployment rate for workers unemployed 27 weeks or more remained higher than at any time prior to the Great Recession. But the long-term unemployment rate has declined by 1.1 percentage points in the last two years, a steeper decline than the 0.5 percentage point drop in the short-term unemployment rate over that period (Figure 2-24).

---

[2] The Department of Labor conducts several labor market surveys. The household survey—conducted in cooperation with the Bureau of Census—queries 60,000 households every month with a variety of questions including whether members of that household were working or looking for a job, and this survey is the source of the unemployment rate, among other important statistics. The Establishment (or Payroll) survey queries employers about how many workers they employed, how many hours did they work, and what they were paid. The Establishment survey is the source of the most quoted figures for job growth. The Job Openings and Labor Turnover Survey (JOLTS) (a relatively new survey, begun in 2000) also queries employers about their job openings (vacancies) as well as their hiring, quits, and layoffs.

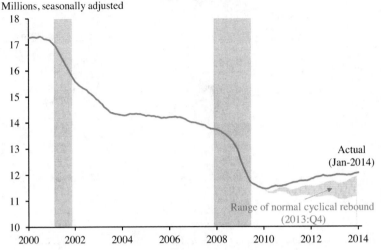

Figure 2-25
**Predicted vs. Actual Manufacturing
Payroll Employment, 2000–2014**

Millions, seasonally adjusted

Note: Gray shading denotes recession. Blue shading denotes the 95% confidence interval of the normal cyclical rebound.
Source: Bureau of Labor Statistics, Current Employment Statistics; CEA calculations.

Of the 2.3 million increase in payroll employment during the 12 months of 2013, about 4 percent was in manufacturing, 7 percent was in construction, and 90 percent was in the private service-providing industries. Within the service-providing industries, the sectors showing the strongest job growth were professional and business services (29 percent of total employment growth), retail trade (15 percent) and health care (9 percent of the total).

Over the course of the recovery, manufacturing has added 622,000 jobs since its trough. Some have pointed to this growth, following a decade of job losses, as indicating a resurgence in manufacturing, while others have suggested that this rebound simply reflects the normal cyclical pattern given the depth of the recession. The Council of Economic Advisers (CEA) analysis suggests that while the overall recovery did in fact contribute to the stabilization of manufacturing job losses, the job gains are about 500,000 above and beyond what would be associated with the historical cyclical pattern (Figure 2-25).

Further evidence of the healing of the job market comes from the number of job vacancies, which increased 6 percent during the 12 months through November (the latest available at press time). There are now 2.6 unemployed workers for each job vacancy, less than half of the number following the business-cycle trough in 2009, but still in excess of the average two-to-one ratio from 2001 to 2007.

Wage Growth and Price Inflation

Hourly compensation (including non-wage benefits) increased 2.0 percent during the 12 months of 2013, the fourth consecutive year of growth at around a 2-percent rate, according the Employment Cost Index. Prices in the nonfarm business sector increased at a 1.6 percent annual rate during these four years; so from the viewpoint of a typical employer, the real product hourly compensation increased 0.4 percent at an annual rate. These four-year growth rates for real hourly compensation were less than the 1.2 percent increase in labor productivity, and as a result, the labor share of nonfarm business output (and of gross domestic income) declined.

Growth in real wages (that is, take-home wages not including benefits) of production workers picked up to 0.7 percent in 2013 from a 0.1 percent decline a year earlier. Nominal wages increased 2.2 percent in 2013 (up from a year earlier) while prices for wage earners rose 1.5 percent (down from a year earlier).

Consumer prices excluding food and energy (the core CPI) rose 1.7 percent during the 12 months of 2013, down from 1.9 percent during 2012. Overall, consumer prices rose just 1.5 percent during the year as food prices increased only 1.1 percent and energy prices inched up 0.5 percent.

Although inflation edged lower in 2013, the relative stability of inflation during the recession and slow recovery presents a puzzle. During this period, the unemployment rate has been much higher than its long-term average, and higher than the rate that is generally considered consistent with stable inflation. Under these circumstances, conventional economic theory and historical experience would have expected declining inflation and perhaps even negative inflation. In contrast, inflation has remained fairly stable since the business-cycle peak with the 12-month change in core CPI inflation never falling below 0.6 percent, raising a puzzle of missing disinflation. Standard explanations of the missing disinflation focus on anchored expectations arising from increased Federal Reserve credibility associated with targeting an inflation rate of approximately 2 percent (for example, Fuhrer and Olivei 2010, Stock and Watson 2010, Ball and Mazumder 2011).

In addition to anchored expectations, a second factor behind the lack of disinflation appears to be the unusually high fraction of the long-term unemployed in this recovery. Those unemployed for only short durations search more intensely for a new job (Krueger and Mueller 2011) and are also potentially more likely to match with a good job, which suggests that the short-term unemployed put more downward pressure on wages than those

Box 2-4: Unemployment Duration and Inflation

A standard wage-price Phillips curve relates wage inflation, minus expected price inflation, to the unemployment rate. A benchmark specification uses previous-year price inflation as a proxy for expected price inflation (for example, Gordon 1990). In this specification, 2009-13 represents a cluster of outliers in which wages fell less than would have been expected based on historical relationships and the very-elevated unemployment rate. But some research, both older and recent, suggests that the composition of unemployment by duration can be important, in particular that the short-term unemployment rate might be a better measure of wage pressure than the total unemployment rate, perhaps because employers prefer to hire those who have spent less time since their last job or because job-search intensity declines with the duration of unemployment (Layard, Nickell, and Jackman 1991, Blanchard and Diamond 1994, Krueger and Mueller 2011, Stock 2011, Gordon 2013). In fact, as is shown in the Figure below, if this wage-price Phillips relation is expressed in terms of the short-term unemployment rate rather than the overall unemployment rate, the recovery is no longer an outlier.

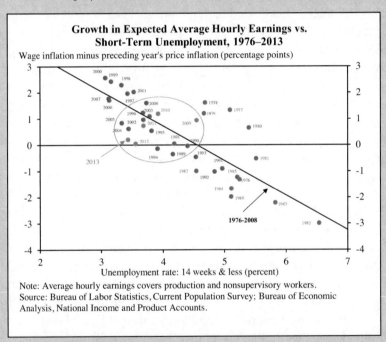

Growth in Expected Average Hourly Earnings vs. Short-Term Unemployment, 1976–2013

Wage inflation minus preceding year's price inflation (percentage points)

Unemployment rate: 14 weeks & less (percent)

Note: Average hourly earnings covers production and nonsupervisory workers.
Source: Bureau of Labor Statistics, Current Population Survey; Bureau of Economic Analysis, National Income and Product Accounts.

A second way to illustrate the lack of disinflation is to consider dynamic forecasts produced by a standard backwards-looking Phillips curve, in which the change in core price inflation depends on past core price inflation and a measure of economic slack. Estimating this model through 2007, then simulating it using the actual unemployment rate post-2007, but not using prices during that period (a method referred to as a dynamic simulation), permits judging whether the actual inflation path accords with what would have been predicted based on historical experience. As the Figure below shows, when the dynamic simulation is conducted using the total unemployment rate, the historical relationship would have predicted substantially more disinflation than actually occurred. In contrast, there is no missing disinflation when the measure of economic slack is the short-term unemployment rate. The wage-price Phillips curve in the figure above, and the dynamic price Phillips curve forecasts in the figure below, suggest that the short-term unemployment rate might be a better measure of effective economic slack than the long-term unemployment rate.

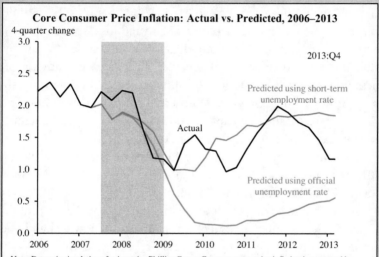

Core Consumer Price Inflation: Actual vs. Predicted, 2006–2013

Note: Dynamic simulation of price-price Phillips Curve. Core consumer price inflation is measured by the price index for consumer spending excluding food and energy in the National Income Accounts. Shading denotes recession.
Source: Bureau of Labor Statistics, Current Population Survey; Bureau of Economic Analysis, National Income and Product Accounts; CEA calculations.

who have been unemployed for more than six months. While the relationship between the overall unemployment rate and inflation in recent years is puzzling, the relationship between short-term unemployment and inflation is less so, as discussed in Box 2-4.

The 11-Year Forecast

Although real GDP has grown at a roughly 2 percent rate for each of the past three years, a foundation is in place for faster growth during 2014, as most components of demand point to faster growth while the supply side does not appear constraining. Although fiscal policy has generally increased the level of output, it has been a drag on GDP growth in the last several years and especially in 2013. The rate of decline in the deficit-to-GDP ratio will likely moderate in 2014 under the President's Budget policy as well as under current law, as noted earlier in this chapter. Consumer spending likely has adjusted by now to the expiration of the payroll tax cut, but it probably has not adjusted to the gains in housing and stock market wealth. End-of-2013 indicators suggest that growth among our European trading partners is looking up, suggesting stronger exports in 2014 than in 2013. While not much growth can be expected from real State and local spending, the latest quarterly data suggest that it will no longer be a substantial drag on overall growth. As discussed earlier in the chapter, firms appear ready to step up business investment if consumer spending picks up. Business investment will grow if everything else does. With the unemployment rate in January 2014 at 6.6 percent and the capacity utilization rate in manufacturing at about 77 percent, the economy has room to grow.

The Administration's economic forecast, as finalized on November 21, 2013 is presented in Table 2.1, and is the forecast that underpins the President's FY 2015 Budget. The Administration expects real GDP to accelerate from a 2.3 rate during the four quarters of 2013 to 3.3 percent during 2014. (Data released after the forecast was finalized show a slightly faster-than expected growth rate during 2013, 2.5 percent rather than 2.3 percent.) These projections, as is standard for the Administration's budget forecast, assume enactment of the President's Budget—including the Opportunity, Growth and Security initiative.

The forecast assumed that the unemployment rate would fall 0.5 percentage point in the four quarters of 2014. Since the forecast was finalized in November the unemployment rate has fallen from 7.3 percent (as first published for October) to 6.6 percent in January 2014, considerably faster than the pace forecasted by the Administration or by the consensus of private sector forecasters. As a result, the Administration's budget forecast of an unemployment rate averaging 6.9 percent in 2014 does not reflect the latest information and an updated projection would forecast a continued decline in the unemployment rate over the course of the year. A revised

Table 2–1
Administration Economic Forecast

	Nominal GDP	Real GDP (chain-type)	GDP price index (chain-type)	Consumer price index (CPI-U)	Unemploy-ment rate (percent)	Interest rate, 91-day Treasury bills (percent)	Interest rate, 10-year Treasury notes (percent)
	Percent change, Q4-to-Q4				Level, calendar year		
2012 (actual)	3.8	2.0	1.8	1.9	8.1	0.1	1.8
2013	3.6	2.3	1.3	1.1	7.5	0.1	2.3
2014	5.0	3.3	1.6	1.9	6.9	0.1	3.0
2015	5.2	3.4	1.8	2.1	6.4	0.3	3.5
2016	5.3	3.3	2.0	2.2	6.0	1.2	4.0
2017	5.3	3.2	2.0	2.3	5.6	2.3	4.3
2018	4.7	2.6	2.0	2.3	5.4	3.2	4.6
2019	4.6	2.5	2.0	2.3	5.4	3.6	4.7
2020	4.5	2.4	2.0	2.3	5.4	3.7	4.9
2021	4.4	2.3	2.0	2.3	5.4	3.7	5.0
2022	4.4	2.3	2.0	2.3	5.4	3.7	5.1
2023	4.4	2.3	2.0	2.3	5.4	3.7	5.1
2024	4.4	2.3	2.0	2.3	5.4	3.7	5.1

Note: These forecasts were based on data available as of November 21, 2013, and were used for the FY 2015 Budget. The interest rate on 91-day T-bills is measured on a secondary-market discount basis.

Source: The forecast was done jointly with the Council of Economic Advisers, the Department of Commerce, (the Bureau of Economic Analysis) and the Department the Treasury, and the Office of Management and Budget.

Administration forecast will be released in the Mid-Session Review of the Budget over the summer.

Real GDP is projected to grow in the 3.2-to-3.4 percent range during the four years through 2017, as the economy gradually uses up the slack suggested by the current elevated level of the unemployment rate. By the fourth quarter of 2017, the unemployment rate is expected to fall to 5.5 percent.

Nominal interest rates are currently low due to the fact that the economy has not fully healed together with monetary policy that has kept rates low across a wide range of Treasury securities. Consistent with the forward policy guidance at the time that the forecast was made, interest rates are projected to increase for maturities that extend through periods covering dates when the unemployment rate is expected to fall below 6.5 percent. Interest rates are expected to continue to climb as the economy approaches full employment. After that point, projected real interest rates (that is, nominal rates less the projected rate of inflation) will be close to their historical average. These interest-rate paths are close to those projected by the consensus of professional economists.

Growth in GDP over the Long Term

As discussed earlier, the growth rate of the economy over the long run is determined by the growth of its supply-side components, demographics, and technological change. The growth rate that characterizes the long-run trend in real U.S. GDP—or potential GDP—plays an important role in guiding the Administration's long-run forecast. Through 2020, potential real GDP is projected to grow at a 2.4 percent annual rate, before slowing to 2.3 percent during the three-year period 2021–24. These growth rates are slower than in the past because of the movement of the baby-boom generation into the retirement years. These growth rates for potential real GDP are based on the assumption of no change to immigration law. If, however, immigration law were to be revised along the lines of the Border Security, Economic Opportunity, and Immigration Modernization Act (S.744) that the Senate approved in June, the growth rate of potential real GDP would be higher, because of faster growth of the working-age population and increased total factor productivity growth (Box 2-5). The Budget totals reflect the effects of immigration reform by incorporating the CBO score directly into the Budget. This CBO score incorporates both direct policy effects and the broader economic impact. In order to avoid double counting with this estimate, the economic forecast does not reflect the effects of immigration reform.

Table 2-2 shows the Administration's forecast for the contribution of each supply-side factor to the growth in potential real GDP: the working-age population, the rate of labor force participation, the employed share of the labor force, the ratio of nonfarm business employment to household employment, the length of the workweek, labor productivity, and the ratio of real GDP to nonfarm output. Each column in Table 2-2 shows the average annual growth rate for each factor over a specific period of time. The first column shows the long-run average growth rates between the business-cycle peak of 1953 and the business-cycle peak of 2007, with business-cycle peaks chosen as end points to remove the substantial fluctuations within cycles. The second column shows average growth rates between the fourth quarter of 2007 and the third quarter of 2013, a period that includes the 2007–09 recession and the recovery so far. The third column shows the Administration's projection for the entire 11-year forecast period, from the third quarter of 2013 to the fourth quarter of 2024. And the fourth column shows average projected growth rates between the fourth quarter of 2020 and the fourth quarter of 2024; that is, the last four years of the forecast interval when the economy is assumed to settle into steady-state growth.

Table 2–2
Supply-Side Components of Actual and Potential Real GDP Growth, 1952–2024

Component	Growth rate[a]			
	History, peak-to-peak	Recent history, since peak	Forecast	Out-year forecast
	1953:Q2 to 2007:Q4[b]	2007:Q4 to 2013:Q3	2013:Q3 to 2024:Q4	2020:Q4 to 2024:Q4
1. Civilian noninstitutional population aged 16+	1.4	1.1	1.0	0.9
2. Labor force participation rate	0.2	–0.7	–0.2	–0.3
3. Employed share of the labor force	0.0	–0.5	0.2	0.0
4. Ratio of nonfarm business employment to household employment	0.0	–0.5	0.0	–0.4
5. Average weekly hours (nonfarm business)	–0.3	0.0	0.0	0.0
6. Output per hour (productivity, nonfarm business)[c]	2.2	1.7	2.1	2.2
7. Ratio of real GDP to nonfarm business output[c]	–0.2	–0.1	–0.3	–0.1
8. Sum: Actual real GDP[c]	3.3	1.1	2.7	2.3
9. Memo: Potential real GDP	3.3	2.0	2.3	2.3

a. All contributions are in percentage points at an annual rate, forecast finalized in November 2013. Total may not add up due to rounding.

b. 1953:Q2 and 2007:Q4 are business-cycle peaks.

c. Real GDP and real nonfarm business output are measured as the average of income- and product-side measures.

Note: Population, labor force, and household employment have been adjusted for discontinuities in the population series. Nonfarm business employment, and the workweek, come from the Labor Productivity and Costs database maintained by the Bureau of Labor Statistics.

Source: Bureau of Labor Statistics, Current Population Survey, Labor Productivity and Costs; Bureau of Economic Analysis, National Income and Product Accounts; Department of the Treasury; Office of Management and Budget; CEA calculations.

The population is projected to grow 1.0 percent a year, on average, over the projection period (line 1, column 3), following the projection published by the Social Security Administration. Over this same period, the labor force participation rate is projected to decline 0.2 percent a year (line 2, column 3). This projected moderate decline in the labor force participation rate reflects a balance of opposing influences: a negative demographic trend partially offset by increasing demand. The entry of the baby-boom generation into its retirement years is expected to reduce the participation rate trend by about 0.4 percent a year through 2020 and by about 0.3 percent during the 2020-24 period (as can be seen in column 4). During the next several years, however, rising labor demand due to the continuing business-cycle recovery is expected to offset some of this downward trend. Young adults, in particular, have been preparing themselves for labor-force entry through additional education. The share of young adults aged 16 to 24 enrolled in school between January 2008 and December 2012 rose well above its trend, enough to account for the entire decline in the labor force participation rate for this age group over this period. As these young adults

Box 2-5: Immigration Reform and Potential GDP Growth

Immigration reform would boost real GDP growth during the 10-year budget window and for the 10 years through 2034 too. Immigration reform would directly raise the growth of the working-age population. As a result, the labor force would grow faster as well. According to the Congressional Budget Office (CBO), the labor force would grow 0.35 percentage point a year faster through 2033 than without the legislation. The faster growth of the labor force would be the prime reason supporting an additional 0.3 percent a year of real GDP growth.

In addition, CBO also assumes that immigration reform would add to real GDP growth by boosting investment and raising the productivity of labor and capital (known as total factor productivity). Although immigrants constituted just 12 percent of the population in 2000, they accounted for 26 percent of the U.S.-based Nobel Prize winners between 1990 and 2000. Immigrants also comprised 25 percent of the founders of public-venture–backed companies started between 1990 and 2005, and they received patents at twice the rate of the native-born population.

complete their education, most are expected to enter or reenter the labor force.

The employed share of the labor force—which is equal to one minus the unemployment rate—is expected to increase at an average 0.2 percent a year over the next 11 years. It is expected to be unchanged after 2018 when the unemployment rate converges to the rate consistent with stable inflation. The workweek is projected to be roughly flat during the forecast period, somewhat less of a decline than its long-term historical trend of -0.3 percent. The workweek is expected to stabilize because some of the demographic forces pushing it down are largely spent, and because a longer workweek is projected to compensate for the anticipated decline in the labor force participation rate.

Labor productivity is projected to increase 2.1 percent a year over the forecast interval and 2.2 percent in the long run (line 6, columns 3 and 4), roughly the same as the average growth rate from 1953 to 2007 (line 6, column 1). The elevated rate of long-term unemployment poses some risk to the projection insofar as the human capital of workers may deteriorate with prolonged unemployment. That said, higher rates of school enrollment among young adults in recent years, as noted, should contribute to productivity growth in the coming years.

The ratio of real GDP to nonfarm business output is expected to subtract from GDP growth over the projection period (line 7, column 3), consistent with its long-run trend. The nonfarm business sector generally grows faster than government, households, and nonprofit institutions, where an accounting convention holds productivity growth to zero.

Summing the growth rates of all of its components, real GDP is projected to rise at an average 2.7 percent a year over the projection period (line 8, column 3), somewhat faster than the 2.3 percent annual growth rate for potential real GDP (line 9, column 3). Actual GDP is expected to grow faster than potential GDP primarily because of the projected rise in the employment rate (line 3, column 3) as millions of currently unemployed workers find jobs.

Real potential GDP (line 9, column 4) is projected to grow more slowly than the long-term historical growth rate of 3.3 percent a year (line 9, column 1). As discussed earlier, the projected slowdown in real potential GDP growth primarily reflects the lower projected growth rate of the working-age population and the retirement of the baby-boom cohort. If the effects of immigration reform were incorporated into this forecast, however, then it would show a higher real potential GDP growth rate.

CONCLUSION

As of December 2013, private payroll employment had increased for 46 months, and more gains are expected during the coming year. The economy is well situated for a pickup in growth, with households having made progress in deleveraging and building wealth, with housing demand gathering momentum, with inflation that is low and stable, and especially with the four-year period of fiscal consolidation now largely behind us. This past year's budget brinksmanship has receded into legislation that will provide some stability during the coming year. If international economies and markets are stable or improving, that would support exports. The energy sector has also supported sustainable growth with substantial increases in domestic energy supply, declines in energy imports, and progress toward reducing carbon dioxide emissions. With these foundations, the Administration forecast projects an increase in growth during the next few years. The growth rate over the budget window will be limited, however, by demographic forces that lower the participation rate, although immigration reform would both raise the participation rate and raise the growth rate of the working-age population.

Even with this growth, however, the economy would remain below its full potential and the unemployment rate would remain unacceptably high. Additional sound policies would speed the return of the economy to its full potential, including policies like investments in infrastructure and increasing certainty through business tax reform. Conversely, adverse policy developments in the United States or adverse shocks in the United States or abroad could impede this favorable scenario.

CHAPTER 3

THE ECONOMIC IMPACT OF THE AMERICAN RECOVERY AND REINVESTMENT ACT FIVE YEARS LATER

On February 17, 2009, President Obama signed into law the American Recovery and Reinvestment Act of 2009, also known as the Recovery Act, or "ARRA." At the time, the country was going through the worst economic and financial crisis since the Great Depression. In the year leading up to the passage of the Act, private employers shed 4.6 million jobs and another 698,000 were lost that February alone. Trillions of dollars of household wealth had been wiped out, and the economy's total output, as measured by real gross domestic product (GDP), was in the midst of its most severe downturn since World War II.

The purpose of the Recovery Act was to provide countercyclical fiscal support for the economy as part of a suite of monetary and fiscal policies aimed at containing the already-severe recession that, had it spiraled further, could have resulted in a second Great Depression. The Act was also intended to lay the foundation for a stronger and more resilient economy in the future.

In the four years following the Recovery Act, the President built on this initial step, signing into law over a dozen fiscal measures aiming to speed job creation. These measures, which extended key elements of the Recovery Act and provided new sources of support, were motivated by a deepening understanding of the severity of the initial shocks to the economy, as well as by new challenges that subsequently arose. These additional measures nearly doubled the size and impact of the Recovery Act's fiscal support to the economy through the end of 2012.

Nearly half of the jobs measures in the Recovery Act and subsequent legislation, or $689 billion, were tax cuts—with most of them directed at families. The other half was for investments in critical areas such as rebuilding bridges and roads, supporting teacher jobs, or providing temporary help for those who found themselves unemployed because of the impact of the Great Recession.

The economic picture today is much brighter. GDP per capita started expanding in the third quarter of 2009 and reached its pre-crisis level in about four years, considerably faster than the historical record suggests is the typical pace of recovery following a systemic financial crisis.[1] Since 2010, the U.S. economy has also consistently added over 2 million private-sector jobs a year, bringing the overall unemployment rate down to its lowest level since October 2008. Job growth has been broad-based across sectors and has withstood significant headwinds, including more recent fiscal contraction at all levels of government, and concerns stemming from the European sovereign debt crisis.

As part of the unprecedented accountability and transparency provisions included in the Recovery Act, the Council of Economic Advisers (CEA) was charged with providing to Congress quarterly reports on the effects of the Recovery Act on overall economic activity, and on employment in particular. In this chapter, CEA provides an assessment of the effects of the Act through the third quarter of 2013, and of subsequent jobs measures through 2012.

This chapter assesses the role of the Recovery Act and the subsequent jobs measures in helping to facilitate the economic turnaround since 2009. It updates previous estimates from the Council of Economic Advisers and other sources on the Act's contribution to employment and output growth, and expands the estimates to reflect the impact of the full set of fiscal measures undertaken. The chapter also considers how many investments contained in the Recovery Act have laid the groundwork for a more productive economy in the years ahead and will support growth long after the spending authorized by the Act has fully phased out.

Consistent with the preponderance of evidence from numerous private-sector, academic, and government analyses, this chapter finds that the Recovery Act substantially boosted employment and output. CEA estimates that, by itself, the Recovery Act saved or created an average of 1.6 million jobs a year for four years through the end of 2012 (cumulatively, equivalent to about 6 million job-years, where a job-year is defined as one full-time job for one year). In addition, the Recovery Act alone raised the level of GDP by between 2 and 2.5 percent from late 2009 through mid-2011. The Recovery Act also helped individuals, businesses, and State and local governments directly affected by the downturn, and put the economy on a

---

[1] See Reinhart and Rogoff (forthcoming).

better trajectory for long-run growth by undertaking targeted investments in education, energy, and health care, among other areas.

Combining effects of the Recovery Act and additional countercyclical fiscal legislation that followed, CEA estimates that the cumulative gain in employment was about 9 million job-years through the end of 2012. The cumulative boost to GDP from 2009 through 2012 is equivalent to 9.5 percent of fourth quarter 2008 GDP.

While these estimates are substantial, they still understate the full impact of the Administration's economic policies in tackling the Great Recession due to being based only on the effect of fiscal measures. CEA estimates do not account for the broader set of responses that included policies to stabilize the financial system, rescue the auto industry, and provide support for the housing sector—in addition to the independent actions undertaken by the Federal Reserve.

THE 2007-09 RECESSION AND THE EARLY POLICY RESPONSES

In the run-up to the 2007-09 recession, the country experienced a dramatic escalation in home prices starting in the mid-1990s, fueled by lax mortgage underwriting standards and an abundance of global capital in search of a safe, dollar-denominated return. This escalation came to an abrupt halt in 2006. Home prices stopped rising and then started falling, eventually dropping by 30 percent nationwide and even more in some areas. Millions of homeowners found themselves "under water"—that is, their mortgage loan balances exceeded the value of their homes—and many were unable to make scheduled mortgage payments.

Fallout from the housing crisis quickly spread to the broader economy through a complex web of opaque financial instruments and questionable business practices, including excessive leverage and an overreliance on short-term debt (Financial Crisis Inquiry Report 2011). Investors pulled back from risky assets and, during one fateful week in September 2008, the investment bank Lehman Brothers went out of business, a prominent money market fund "broke the buck" (meaning that depositors could no longer count on getting their money back in its entirety, an almost unprecedented event), and the large insurance firm American International Group (AIG) teetered on the edge of bankruptcy until the U.S. government provided $85 billion in financial support.

This financial turmoil led to sharp declines in real economic activity. From the third quarter of 2007 through the first quarter of 2009, the economy lost more than $13 trillion in wealth, nearly one-fifth of the total, because of rapidly declining stock and house prices. This was much larger than the initial decline in wealth at the outset of the Great Depression.[2] Falling asset prices reduced the value of collateral and further restricted the availability of credit and, as credit dried up, many small businesses and even some large, well-known corporations reported trouble meeting basic expenses such as payroll. Faced with extraordinary uncertainty about the economic future, businesses stopped hiring, laid off workers, and shelved investment plans. As housing and financial wealth plummeted and concerns over job security mounted, consumers cut back on spending. The effect was immediate and drastic: in the fourth quarter of 2008, personal consumption expenditures fell by nearly 5 percent and private investment shrunk 31 percent at an annual rate.

Most economic forecasters underestimated the magnitude of the toll these shocks would take on the economy, in large part because the United States had not gone through a systemic financial crisis since the Great Depression. Forecasts made at the time were also subject to considerable uncertainty about the spillovers to the rest of the world, and about how the economy would respond to other macroeconomic policy interventions after the federal funds rate had already hit zero. As shown in Table 3-1, in December 2008, for example, the Blue Chip panel of economic forecasters projected that real GDP would fall at a 1.4 percent annual rate in the first half of 2009, less than half the 2.9 percent annualized rate of decline that actually occurred. Moreover, the Blue Chip panel of forecasters estimated that the unemployment rate would rise to 7.7 percent in the second quarter of 2009, well below the actual rate of 9.3 percent. Other indicators showed similarly large deteriorations relative to forecasts.

Initial Policy Responses

As the economy slid into recession, Congress and the Bush Administration enacted the Economic Stimulus Act of 2008 in February. They designed the Act to counteract a short recession by providing temporary support to consumer spending, but it was not sufficient to reverse the emerging distress and, by design, did not have long-lasting effects. In fall 2008, as the initially mild recession turned into a full-blown financial crisis, the U.S. government mounted a coordinated emergency response to prevent a meltdown of the financial system.[3] The Federal Reserve, which had progressively cut its federal funds target rate several times over the previous

---

[2] See Romer (2011).
[3] A comprehensive timeline of the policy actions taken by the U.S. government can be found on the Federal Reserve Bank of St. Louis website http://timeline.stlouisfed.org/

Table 3–1
Forecasted and Actual Real GDP Growth and Unemployment Rate

	Real GDP Growth[a]			Unemployment Rate		
	Blue Chip[b]	Survey of Professional Forecasters[c]	Actual	Blue Chip	Survey of Professional Forecasters	Actual
2008:Q4	−4.1	−2.9	−8.3	6.7	6.6	6.9
2009:Q1	−2.4	−1.1	−5.4	7.3	7.0	8.3
2009:Q2	−0.4	0.8	−0.4	7.7	7.4	9.3

Note: a. Percent change from prior quarter at an annualized rate.
b. Blue Chip forecasts for both GDP and Unemployment were reported on December 10, 2008.
c. Survey of Professional Forecasters forecasts for both GDP and Unemployment were reported on November 17, 2008.

Source: Blue Chip Economic Indicators; Survey of Professional Forecasters; Bureau of Labor Statistics, Current Population Survey; Bureau of Economic Analysis, National Income and Product Accounts.

year, lowered the rate still further in December 2008 to near zero, where it remains to this day.

To prevent runs on banks and other financial institutions, the Treasury Department established a temporary guarantee program for money market mutual funds and the Federal Deposit Insurance Corporation expanded its guarantee on bank deposits and debt. The Bush Administration proposed and Congress approved the Troubled Asset Relief Program (TARP), providing up to $700 billion to stabilize troubled banks, automakers, insurance companies, secondary markets for consumer and small business loans, and the housing sector.[4]

These early policy responses proved fundamental to rescuing the global financial system. They helped repair the balance sheets of both financial and non-financial institutions, restored investor confidence, and restored the flow of credit to struggling businesses and families. Nevertheless, the economy continued to deteriorate, and aggregate demand remained depressed. With the traditional tool of monetary policy, the federal funds rate, reaching its lower bound of zero, conventional countercyclical monetary policy could go no further, and the Federal Reserve ultimately opted for additional, non-standard measures.

AN OVERVIEW OF THE RECOVERY ACT AND SUBSEQUENT JOBS MEASURES

Amid very real concerns about a substantial and protracted fall in GDP accompanied by persistent elevated unemployment, the incoming

---

[4] The Dodd-Frank Wall Street Reform and Consumer Protection Act (Dodd-Frank Act) later reduced that amount to $475 billion. A detailed description of the TARP can be found on the Treasury website http://www.treasury.gov/initiatives/financial-stability/Pages/default.aspx

Obama Administration and the 111th U.S. Congress took immediate action. In December 2008, the President-Elect and the transition team proposed the overall scope and elements of what they called the American Recovery and Reinvestment Act. Just days after the President's inauguration, on January 26, 2009, House Appropriations Committee Chair David Obey introduced H.R. 1 with the same name on the floor of the U.S. House of Representatives. The legislation passed the House and Senate soon afterwards. By February 13, both houses of Congress agreed to a compromise measure, which the President signed into law on February 17, 2009.

The Recovery Act

In early 2008, before the Nation realized the full extent of the economic challenge, fiscal expansion policy was guided by the "3T's" advocated by Summers (2007), Sperling (2007), and Elmendorf and Furman (2008): timely, targeted, and temporary. By the end of 2008, however, it was clear that the recession had turned into a major financial crisis and that a new approach was needed, what Former Treasury Secretary Lawrence Summers called "speedy, substantial, and sustained."[5]

Several principles guided the new Administration's policymaking. First, the fiscal effort was to be implemented speedily, unlike previous incoming presidents' economic programs, which were generally not passed until they were six months or more into office. Second, it should be substantial, given the very large scope of the economic problem. Finally, it should be a sustained effort that would not only have significant spend-out over the first two years, but would continue some temporary support thereafter. The new approach would require a mix of instruments, with some being faster to spend-out, such as tax cuts and other temporary assistance that put cash in the hands of households who immediately needed it. Other components would be more lagged but have larger cumulative countercyclical impacts and greater longer-run benefits, such as investments in infrastructure and innovation. In all cases, however, the measures would end and would not have long-term impacts on the Federal Government's primary budget deficit.[6]

Goals of the Recovery Act. Overall, this approach was embodied in the stated goals of the Recovery Act, as written into the legislation:

(1) To preserve and create jobs and promote economic recovery;

(2) To assist those most impacted by the recession;

(3) To provide investments needed to increase economic efficiency by spurring technological advances in science and health;

---

[5] Speech at the Wall Street Journal CEO Council conference in Washington, DC, Nov 19, 2008.
[6] The primary deficit excludes interest payments on the national debt.

(4) To invest in transportation, environmental protection, and other infrastructure that will provide long-term economic benefits;

(5) To stabilize State and local government budgets, in order to minimize and avoid reductions in essential services and counterproductive State and local tax increases.

Scale of the Recovery Act. At passage, CBO estimated that the Recovery Act would cost $787 billion, although this estimate would increase as the full magnitude of the recession became apparent. The most recent CBO estimates show that the fiscal support from the Recovery Act will total $832 billion through 2019.[7] Of this total, $69 billion was allocated to a routine set of patches for the Alternative Minimum Tax (AMT). This part of the Act, a continuation of a long-standing practice, is best thought of as ongoing fiscal policy, not as a temporary fiscal impulse designed specifically to counter the effects of an economic recession. Excluding the AMT patch, the Recovery Act provided a total fiscal impulse of $763 billion.

Composition of the Recovery Act. The initial cost projections of the Recovery Act showed the law would be fairly evenly distributed across tax cuts ($212 billion), expansions to mandatory programs such as Medicaid and unemployment benefits ($296 billion), and discretionary spending ($279 billion) in areas ranging from direct assistance to individuals to investments in infrastructure, education, job training, energy, and health information technology. More specifically, Figure 3-1 shows how Recovery Act policies excluding the AMT patch can be divided into five functional categories: individual tax cuts, business tax incentives, State fiscal relief, aid to directly impacted individuals, and public investments.[8]

Timing of the Recovery Act Spend-Out. The Nation felt the early effects of the Recovery Act almost immediately, as enhanced Medicaid payments started to flow to states on March 13, 2009 and individual income tax withholdings were reduced by April 1, 2009. As of the third quarter of 2009, roughly one-quarter of all spending and tax cuts had occurred, with another half spread across the four quarters after that, roughly consistent with CBO projections as of 2009. By September 30, 2013, the Federal Government had disbursed $805 billion on Recovery Act programs, as shown in Table 3-2.

As shown in Table 3-3, individual tax cuts, aid to States, and aid to individuals directly affected by the recession were among the first Recovery

---

[7] CBO's original estimate of the cost of the Recovery Act, $787 billion (CBO 2009b), was revised to $862 billion (CBO 2010a), then to $814 billion (CBO, 2010b), $821 billion (CBO 2011a), $831 billion (CBO 2012a), $830 billion (CBO 2013a), and most recently to $832 billion (CBO 2014). The estimates evolved because economic conditions deteriorated more than had been assumed in earlier projections, resulting in higher-than-expected use of certain assistance programs.

[8] Additional detail on these components of the Recovery Act can be found in Appendix 1.

Figure 3-1
Recovery Act Programs by Functional Categories

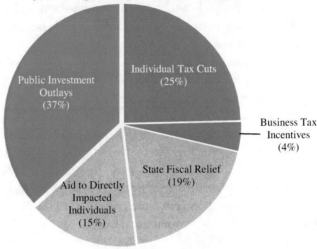

Note: Percentages may not add to 100 due to rounding. Data does not include AMT Relief.
Source: Office of Management and Budget, Agency Financial and Activity Reports; Department of the
Treasury, Office of Tax Analysis, based on the FY2013 Mid-Session Review.

Act programs to take effect, providing the largest initial boost to spending in fiscal year 2009. Each of these categories tapered after 2010, with only a small amount of outlays in 2012 and 2013, while public investment outlays now constitute the bulk of continuing Recovery Act expenditures.

Accountability, Transparency, and Oversight. In keeping with the Administration's commitment to the highest standards of accountability, transparency, and oversight, the Recovery Act took unprecedented steps to track and report the use of Federal funds and to prevent waste, fraud, and abuse. The Act established a Recovery Accountability Transparency Board comprised of an independent director and 12 agency inspectors general, as well as a Recovery Implementation Office that reported directly to the Vice President. Recipients (including vendors, nonprofit organizations, and State and local governments) were required to report regularly to the Board on their use of funds and the number of jobs created or saved.[9]

All of the information received from agencies and recipients has been posted on a website (www.recovery.gov). Users can sort and display data on funding in different ways (by category of funding, by agency, by state), making it easy to obtain and analyze information. The website also offers the opportunity for the public to report fraud or waste. Reported instances

---

[9] Title XV, Section 1512

Table 3–2
An Overview of Recovery Act Fiscal Impact

	Billions of Dollars, Fiscal Years					
	2009	2010	2011	2012	2013	Total Through 2013
Outlays	110.7	197.1	112.7	56.8	35.0	512.4
Obligations	256.3	196.1	41.2	21.8	18.5	533.8
Tax Reductions	69.8	188.7	37.2	−5.4	1.9	292.2
Sum of Outlays and Tax Reductions	180.5	385.8	149.9	51.4	37.0	804.6

Note: Items may not add to total due to rounding.
Source: Office of Management and Budget, Agency Financial and Activity Reports; Department of the Treasury, Office of Tax Analysis based on the FY2013 Mid-Session Review.

Table 3–3
Recovery Act Programs by Functional Categories

	Billions of Dollars, Fiscal Years					
	2009	2010	2011	2012	2013	Total Through 2013
Individual Tax Cuts	42.9	91.3	46.6	0.4	0.4	181.7
AMT Relief	13.8	69.6	−14.4	0.0	0.0	69.0
Business Tax Incentives	23.1	18.2	−5.9	−3.7	−2.9	28.8
State Fiscal Relief	43.8	63.3	26.0	6.0	4.0	143.0
Aid to Directly Impacted Individuals	31.8	49.5	15.5	8.8	5.9	111.5
Public Investment Outlays	25.1	94.0	82.0	39.9	29.6	270.5
Total	180.5	385.8	149.9	51.4	37.0	804.6

Note: Items may not add to total due to rounding.
Source: Office of Management and Budget, Agency Financial and Activity Reports; Department of the Treasury, Office of Tax Analysis based on the FY2013 Mid-Session Review.

of waste, fraud, and abuse remain low—at less than 1 percent of all grant awards.

Subsequent Jobs Measures

While the Recovery Act was the first and largest fiscal action undertaken after the financial crisis to create jobs and strengthen the economy, many subsequent actions extended, expanded, and built on the Recovery Act. Parts of the Recovery Act were extended to address the continuing needs of the economy, including Emergency Unemployment Compensation, accelerated depreciation of business investment for tax purposes (that is, "bonus depreciation"), measures for teacher jobs, and aid to states for Medicaid. In other cases, new measures expanded on elements of the Recovery Act, such as the temporary payroll tax cut in 2011 and 2012, which was nearly 50 percent larger than the Making Work Pay credit it replaced, and an even greater allowance for businesses to write off the cost of investments when computing their tax liability (that is, "expensing"). The following measures built on the goals of the Recovery Act and are counted as part of the fiscal impulse in the analysis that follows: the cash-for-clunkers program enacted in summer 2009, an expanded homebuyer tax credit and business tax incentives in fall 2009, the HIRE Act tax credit and additional infrastructure investment incentives in March 2010, a small business tax cut and credit bill in fall 2010, veterans hiring incentives in fall 2011, plus the additional payroll tax cut extensions and unemployment insurance extensions passed in 2011 and 2012. All told, these subsequent jobs measures, listed in Table 3-4, provided an additional $674 billion in countercyclical fiscal support through the end of 2012. This total excludes routine or expected policies such as continuing the 2001 and 2003 tax cuts, passing so-called "tax extenders" to address regularly expiring tax provisions, and fixing Medicare's Sustainable Growth Rate formula.[10]

Of the $674 billion in fiscal support following the Recovery Act, 31 percent was accounted for by the payroll tax cut from 2011 to 2012, 24 percent was accounted for by extended unemployment insurance, and the remainder included a variety of actions such as relief for States and tax incentives for businesses. Figure 3-2 shows a breakout of the policies of the Recovery Act and the subsequent jobs legislation.

In addition, the President proposed further measures for the economy that were not passed by Congress, most notably the American Jobs Act, which was proposed in September 2011 and would have provided additional investments—totaling $447 billion—in everything from infrastructure to teacher jobs to a robust tax credit for small business hiring.[11]

Automatic Countercylical Measures

In addition to Obama Administration policies, previously enacted laws have built-in provisions that allow for automatic support when economic conditions worsen. For example, personal income tax payments decline when income declines, and spending on unemployment insurance picks up as more individuals struggle to find work. These automatic

---

[10] This category includes items like the Research and Experimentation tax credit, the tax deduction for State and local sales taxes for States without income taxes, and numerous other tax provisions that have been routinely extended as a group in the past. Going forward, the President's budget is proposing that all tax extenders are either made permanent and paid for or allowed to expire.

[11] See http://www.whitehouse.gov/the-press-office/2011/09/08/fact-sheet-american-jobs-act

Table 3–4
Fiscal Support for the Economy Enacted After the Recovery Act

	Billions of Dollars	
	2009–12	2009–19
Enacted 2009		
Worker, Homeownership, and Business Assistance Act (HR 3548)	35	24
Supplemental Appropriations Act of 2009 (HR 2346) (Cash for Clunkers)	3	3
Defense Appropriations Act of 2010 (HR 3326) (Unemployment Insurance and COBRA)	18	18
Enacted 2010		
Temporary Extension Act of 2010 (HR 4691)	9	9
Hiring Incentives to Restore Employment Act (HR 2847)	13	15
Continuing Extension Act of 2010 (HR 4851)	16	16
Unemployment Compensation Act of 2010 (HR 4213)	33	34
FAA Safety Improvement Act (HR 1586) (Education Jobs/ FMAP Extension)	26	12
Small Business Jobs Act (HR 5297)	68	10
Tax Relief, Unemployment Insurance Reauthorization, and Job Creation Act (HR 4853)	309	237
Enacted 2011		
Temporary Payroll Tax Cut Continuation Act (HR 3765)	28	29
VOW to Hire Heroes Act (HR 674)	0	–0
Enacted 2012		
Middle Class Tax Relief and Job Creation Act of 2012 (HR 3630)	98	123
American Taxpayer Relief Act of 2012 (HR 8)	17	178
Total	674	709

Note: All measures use prospective CBO cost estimates for 2009–19. Routine tax extenders have been removed from the cost estimates. Column 1 contains data through the end of calendar year 2012, while Column 2 contains data through the end of fiscal year 2019.
Source: Congressional Budget Office; Joint Committee on Taxation.

responses—known as "automatic stabilizers"—can help moderate business cycles (as shown for instance by Auerbach and Feenberg (2000) and Follette and Lutz (2010)) in addition to alleviating the human costs of economic downturns.

As has been the case over the last several decades, automatic stabilizers also played a significant role during the most recent recession and recovery. Although CBO (2014) estimated that most fiscal expansion came from enacted legislation or discretionary fiscal policy, automatic stabilizers accounted for about one-quarter of the countercyclical fiscal expansion that occurred in FY 2009, and a much larger fraction thereafter as shown in Figure 3-3.

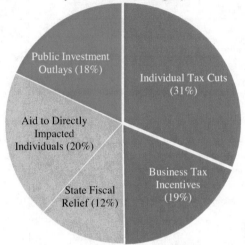

Figure 3-2
**Recovery Act and Subsequent Fiscal Measures
by Functional Category**

Public Investment
Outlays (18%)

Individual Tax Cuts
(31%)

Aid to Directly
Impacted
Individuals (20%)

State Fiscal
Relief (12%)

Business Tax
Incentives
(19%)

Note: Percentages may not add to 100 due to rounding. Data does not include AMT Relief.
Source: Office of Management and Budget, Agency Financial and Activity Reports; Department of
the Treasury, Office of Tax Analysis, based on the FY2013 Mid-Session Review; Congressional
Budget Office.

Figure 3-3
Automatic Stabilizers and the Budget Balance, 2009–2013

Federal Budget Deficit as a Percent of GDP

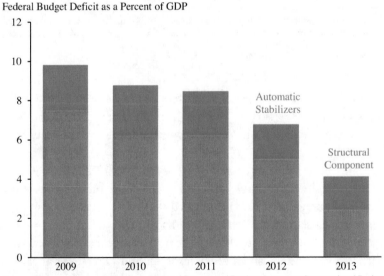

Source: Bureau of Economic Analysis, National Income and Product Accounts; Congressional Budget
Office, The Budget and Economic Outlook: 2014 to 2024.

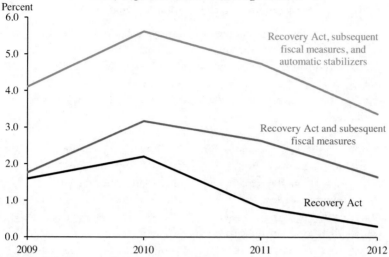

Figure 3-4
Fiscal Expansion as a Percentage of GDP

Percent

Recovery Act, subsequent fiscal measures, and automatic stabilizers

Recovery Act and subesquent fiscal measures

Recovery Act

Note: Data is displayed in calendar year terms for all series.
Source: Congressional Budget Office, The Budget and Economic Outlook: 2014 to 2024; Office of Management and Budget; Bureau of Economic Analysis, National Income and Product Accounts.

Total Fiscal Response

All told, the Great Recession triggered a substantial fiscal response. Figure 3-4 illustrates the scale of the Recovery Act and of the other major fiscal measures implemented by the Administration. As noted earlier, fiscal policy represented only one part of the Administration's broader economic strategy to foster recovery and protect households, as described more fully in Box 3-1.

NEAR-TERM MACROECONOMIC EFFECTS OF THE RECOVERY ACT AND SUBSEQUENT FISCAL LEGISLATION

This chapter reviews the range of evidence on the effect of the Recovery Act. In particular, it shows that a wide range of approaches— including model-based estimates by CEA, CBO and private forecasters, cross-state evidence and international evidence—all find that the Recovery Act had a large positive impact on employment and output.

Overall, CEA estimates that the Recovery Act saved or created about 6 million job-years (where a job-year is the equivalent of one full time job for one year) through 2012 and raised GDP by between 2 and 2.5 percent in FY 2010 and part of FY 2011. These estimates are consistent with estimates

Box 3-1: Other Administration Policy Responses to the Economic Crisis

The Recovery Act was part a comprehensive policy response to the economic crisis, one that included stabilizing the financial system, helping responsible homeowners avoid foreclosure, and aiding small businesses. Highlighted here are some of the other key non-fiscal programs (not counting the important steps taken independently by the Federal Reserve).

Housing. The Administration took several steps to strengthen the housing market. The most important initiative, the Making Home Affordable Program (MHA), provided several ways to help struggling homeowners avoid foreclosure. A detailed description is available at www.makinghomeaffordable.gov. The Home Affordable Modification Program was the cornerstone of the initiative, allowing eligible homeowners to reduce their monthly mortgage payments through loan modifications. Among the many other MHA programs, the Home Affordable Refinancing Program helped homeowners who, because of plummeting home prices, were "underwater" on their mortgages or in danger of becoming so, allowing them to refinance at a lower interest rate. The MHA also committed funds to help struggling homeowners in hard-hit areas (under the Hardest Hit Fund).

In addition, the Administration created the Consumer Financial Protection Bureau to establish safe mortgage standards to protect homebuyers and homeowners, among other purposes. The Administration also helped negotiate the National Mortgage Servicing Settlement with the largest mortgage servicers. While the housing market continues to heal, housing is in much better shape overall than it was just a few years ago. Home prices are about 15 percent higher than they were at the end of 2011, and sales of new and existing homes are higher than at the end of 2011 while the number of seriously delinquent mortgages is now at its lowest level since 2008.

Auto Industry. Recognizing that a collapse of the auto industry would have resulted in huge job losses and the devastation of many communities, the Administration, under the Troubled Asset Relief Program (TARP), provided financial support to auto companies to keep them afloat. The Administration committed additional assistance to Chrysler and General Motors, while at the same time working on a comprehensive restructuring of these companies. Since then, these auto companies have become profitable again, and auto sales have been trending up since 2009. The auto industry has added more than 420,000 jobs since June 2009. In December 2013, the Treasury sold its remaining shares of General Motors.

Financial Industry. TARP and other programs implemented during the height of the financial crisis helped prevent a meltdown of the global financial system, but did not solve many longer-running, more structural problems. The Administration pushed for an overhaul of the financial regulatory system, and its proposals eventually led to the Dodd-Frank Wall Street Reform and Consumer Protection Act of 2010. Among its many provisions, the Dodd-Frank Act required stress tests to assess the health of financial institutions, provided tools for orderly liquidations of large financial firms, and increased the transparency of derivatives markets. As a result of these actions, large banks are now much better capitalized and credit flows have resumed. While some of the Dodd-Frank Act's provisions are still being implemented and much work remains to be done, the financial system has become less vulnerable and families are better protected when making important financial decisions.

Small Businesses. Small business struggled under the weight of weak consumer demand and tight credit in the recession, and the Administration provided support in several ways. Specifically, the Administration extended the guarantees and the availability of Small Business Administration loans and created new programs such as the Small Business Lending Funds and the State Small Business Credit Initiative. It also helped small businesses indirectly by providing TARP funds to small and large banks across the country. Bank credit to small businesses, which had contracted sharply during the recession, has been expanding since 2011.

made by CBO (2013a) and by independent academic studies, which use a variety of methodologies and data sources. Adding the estimated effect of subsequent fiscal policy measures, CEA model finds that the combined effect of these actions increased GDP above what it otherwise would have been by more than 2 percent a year for three years, and created or saved about 9 million job-years through 2012. Moreover, research on economic growth generally finds that these types of benefits have a long-lasting impact on the economy even after the initial policy impetus has expired. This is even more true when the policy itself included significant measures for long-term growth, as described later in this chapter.

Model-Based Estimates of the Macroeconomic Effects of the Recovery Act and Subsequent Fiscal Legislation

Evaluating effects of fiscal policy in general, and the Recovery Act in particular, is challenging for several reasons. Appendix 2 describes these challenges, and how economists have addressed them, in greater detail. A key issue is that estimating effects entails comparing what actually happened with what might have happened (what economists call the "counterfactual"). However, because counterfactual outcomes are not actually observed, other methods are needed.

Estimating the Short-run Macroeconomic Effect of Fiscal Policy. A key concept for estimating the macroeconomic effects of fiscal policy is what economists call the fiscal multiplier. The fiscal expenditure multiplier is the change in GDP resulting from a $1 increase in government expenditures, and the tax multiplier is the change in GDP resulting from a $1 decrease in taxes. Because a $1 increase in spending or decrease in taxes has ripple effects in subsequent transactions as it passes through the broader economy, theory suggests that the fiscal multiplier may be greater than one—a $1 increase in spending or reduction in taxes may support an increase in output of more than $1.

The standard theory of fiscal policy in a recession holds that when government demand goes up, firms hire workers and raise production, which boosts employment, income, and GDP. The initial effect is amplified as workers spend additional income, and businesses purchase more raw materials and make investments to meet increased demand. In its most basic form, the government spending multiplier is the sum of the first-round direct effect of spending on GDP, the second-round effect with consumption by those paid for providing goods and services, and the subsequent-round effects. In this model, the multiplier effect depends on the marginal propensity to consume (MPC)—the fraction of an additional dollar of income that is spent rather than saved.[12] Because the MPC is thought to be large, especially in a recession when individuals face problems borrowing, models can generate multipliers much higher than one. Tax cuts also increase individual income, but the multiplier effect on overall output is generally thought to be slightly less than it is for government expenditures. Because the individual receiving the tax cut saves part of it, the first-round effect on overall spending is smaller, making the subsequent ripple effects smaller as well. Thus, the basic multiplier for a tax cut is less than the government spending multiplier; specifically, the tax multiplier is the spending multiplier times the MPC.

The model is a useful conceptual starting point, but it makes many simplifications. Appendix 2 to this chapter reviews recent theoretical research on the effects of fiscal policy, especially in a deep recession. This research suggests that, in normal times, fiscal multipliers can be small both because consumers save a substantial fraction of a temporary fiscal measure and because monetary policy tends to counteract the fiscal measure in an

---

[12] This basic multiplier thus equals $1 + MPC + MPC^2 + \ldots = 1/(1 - MPC)$.

attempt to maintain stable inflation. In a severe recession, however, especially when monetary policy is constrained by the fact that interest rates cannot drop below zero (the zero lower bound), fiscal multipliers can be much larger. Taking further into account the fact that long-term unemployment can lead to transitions out of the labor force, with a resulting long-term effect of depressing output and employment (an effect referred to as "hysteresis"), multipliers can be larger yet for fiscal policies that support aggregate demand and reduce the average duration of unemployment.

Numerical estimates of fiscal multipliers are typically computed using historical data on fiscal interventions and macroeconomic outcomes, and Appendix 2 also discusses the recent empirical research on this topic. This empirical work provides estimates of multipliers for different types of fiscal interventions (government spending and individual income tax cuts). Once estimated, the resulting multipliers can be used to estimate the macroeconomic effect of the Recovery Act; that is, to compare what happened under the Recovery Act with what likely would have happened in its absence.

CEA's and CBO's Estimates of the Recovery Act. To estimate the effect of the Recovery Act on GDP, CEA applied a different fiscal multiplier to each component, and then aggregated the effects of each component to arrive at the overall GDP effect. For government spending (corresponding to public investment outlays and income and support payments) and for tax cuts, CEA used multipliers derived from the empirical estimates of the spending and tax multipliers discussed in Appendix 2. For other components of the Act, such as State and local fiscal relief, CEA used a multiplier equal to a weighted average of one or both of the tax and spending multipliers.[13]

The CBO used a similar approach in its quarterly reports on the effects of the Recovery Act (although their estimates include the impact of AMT relief and so are not completely comparable to CEA estimates).[14] Because of the range of estimates of multipliers in the economic literature, CBO provided an upper and a lower bound for the fiscal multipliers on the various components of the Act. As shown in Table 3-5, CEA multipliers are within the range suggested by CBO (2013a).

The multipliers presented here indicate that the Recovery Act had a large effect on output. As shown in Figure 3-5, the Recovery Act quickly raised the level of GDP in the first half of 2009, jump-starting the

---

[13] For State and local fiscal relief, CEA assumed that 60 percent of the transfer is used to avoid spending reductions, and 30 percent is used to avoid tax increases. One-time tax rebates and one-time payments to seniors, veterans, and disabled are assumed to have half of the effects of conventional tax cuts. The effect of business tax incentives is very uncertain. Conservatively, the multiplier to this component is set equal to 1/12 of the spending multiplier. See CEA (2009a).

[14] CBO's methodology is described in Reichling and Whalen (2012).

Table 3–5

Table 3–5
Estimated Output Multipliers for Different Types of Fiscal Support

	CEA	CBO Low	CBO High
Public Investment Outlays[a]	1.5	0.5	2.5
State and Local Fiscal Relief	1.1	0.4	1.8
Income and Support Payments[b]	1.5	0.4	2.1
One-time Payments to Retirees	0.4	0.2	1.0
Tax Cuts to Individuals	0.8	0.3	1.5
Business Tax Incentives	0.1	0.0	0.4

Note: The CEA multipliers show the impact of a permanent change in the component of 1% of GDP after 6 quarters, or, equivalently, the cumulative impact of a one-time change of 1% of GDP over 6 quarters. The CBO multiplers show the cumulative impact of a one-time change of 1% of GDP over several quarters.

a. Includes transfer payments to state and local government for infrastructure and tax incentives to businesses directly tied to certain types of spending.

b. Includes such programs as unemployment compensation, COBRA, and SNAP

Source: Congressional Budget Office, Estimated Impact of the American Recovery and Reinvestment Act on Employment and Economic Output from October 2012 Through December 2012; CEA Calculations.

recovery. According to these estimates, the Act raised GDP by 2 to 2.5 percent between the fourth quarter of 2009 and the second quarter of 2011, and it continued to exert a positive effect even as it was winding down in 2012. These numbers are almost entirely within the range of those implied by the CBO analysis, with the exception being a few quarters in late 2012 and early 2013, when CEA estimate is slightly higher.

Using the historical relation between increases in GDP and employment, CEA and CBO also estimated the number of jobs generated by the Recovery Act. According to CEA model, the Recovery Act increased employment by more than 2.3 million in 2010 alone, and continued to have substantial effects into 2012, as demonstrated in Figure 3-6. Cumulating these gains through the end of FY 2013, the Recovery Act is estimated to have generated about 6.4 million job-years. These estimates are also within the range of CBO's upper- and lower-range estimates of 1.6 to 8.3 million job-years.

CEA Estimates of the Recovery Act and Subsequent Fiscal Measures Combined. The combined effect of the Recovery Act and the subsequent countercyclical fiscal legislation is substantially larger and longer lasting than the effect of the Recovery Act alone.[15] The Recovery Act represents only about half of total fiscal support for the economy from the beginning of 2009 through the fourth quarter of 2012. Moreover, as shown in Figures 3-7 and 3-8, the bulk of the effects of the other fiscal measures occurred as

---

[15] CEA's estimates of the effects of the subsequent fiscal measures are based on CBO's initial cost estimates, not actual spending. CEA assigned each of the subsequent fiscal measures to the same functional categories that were used to analyze the Recovery Act, and then applied the corresponding multipliers as discussed above. Quarterly costs were interpolated when only annual cost estimates were available.

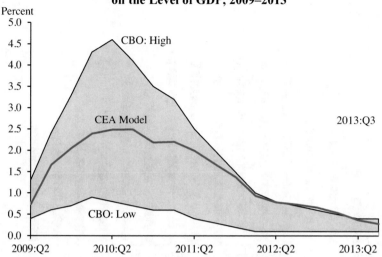

Figure 3-5
**Estimates of the Effects of the Recovery Act
on the Level of GDP, 2009–2013**

Source: Congressional Budget Office, Estimated Impact of the American Recovery and Reinvestment
Act on Employment and Economic Output in 2013; CEA calculations.

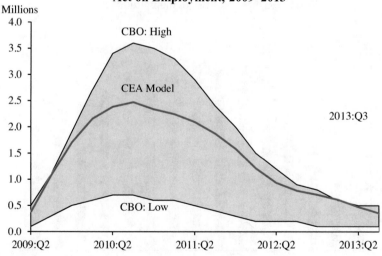

Figure 3-6
**Estimates of the Effects of the Recovery
Act on Employment, 2009–2013**

Source: Congressional Budget Office, Estimated Impact of the American Recovery and Reinvestment
Act on Employment and Economic Output in 2013; CEA calculations.

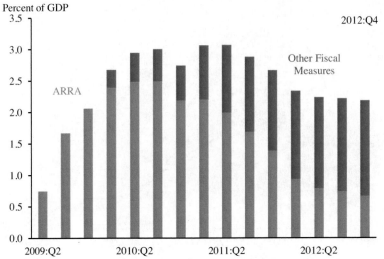

Figure 3-7
**Quarterly Effect of the Recovery Act and Subsequent
Fiscal Measures on GDP, 2009–2012**

Source: Bureau of Economic Analysis, National Income and Product Accounts; Congressional Budget
Office; CEA calculations.

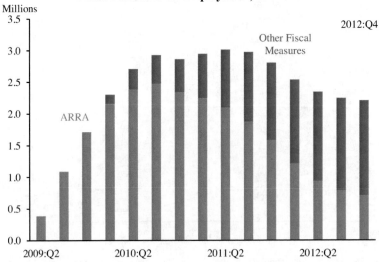

Figure 3-8
**Quarterly Effect of the Recovery Act and Subsequent
Fiscal Measures on Employment, 2009–2012**

Source: Bureau of Economic Analysis, National Income and Product Accounts; Congressional Budget
Office; CEA calculations.

the Recovery Act was phasing down. These other measures thus served to sustain the recovery as effects of the Recovery Act waned. CEA multiplier model indicates that by themselves these additional measures increased the level of GDP by between 1.0 and 1.5 percent each quarter from mid-2011 through the end of calendar year 2012. Altogether, summing up the effects for all quarters through the end of calendar year 2012, the Recovery Act and subsequent fiscal measures raised GDP by an average of more than 2.4 percent of GDP annually—totaling a cumulative amount equal to about 9.5 percent of fourth quarter 2008 GDP.

The contribution of all fiscal measures to employment is equally substantial. Other fiscal measures beyond the Recovery Act are estimated to have raised employment by 2.8 million job-years, cumulatively, through the end of calendar year 2012. Adding these jobs to those created or saved by the Recovery Act, the combined countercyclical fiscal measures created or saved more than 2.3 million jobs a year through the end of 2012—or 8.8 million job-years in total over the entire period.

Estimates from Private Forecasters. Private forecasters and domestic and international institutions have used large-scale macroeconomic models, mostly to estimate the effects of either the Recovery Act by itself or other policies in isolation. The models used by these individuals and organizations generally employ a similar multiplier-type analysis as is found in CEA and CBO work, although they vary considerably in their structure and underlying assumptions. Although no outside estimates of the total impact of *all* the fiscal measures are available, Table 3-6 displays the estimates of the impact of the Recovery Act offered by several leading private-sector forecasters before the Act was fully implemented. Despite the differences in the models, these private-sector forecasters all estimated that the Recovery Act would raise GDP substantially from 2009 to 2011, including a boost to GDP of between 2.0 and 3.4 percent in 2010.

Taking a broader view that incorporates fiscal measures in addition to the Recovery Act, Blinder and Zandi (2010) estimate the effect of the fiscal policies enacted through 2009 (the Economic Stimulus Act, the Recovery Act, cash for clunkers, the unemployment insurance benefits extensions of 2009). They find that these policies raised the level of GDP in 2009 by 3.4 percent in the third quarter and by 4.3 percent in the fourth quarter.

Cross-State Evidence

A different approach to estimating the effect of fiscal policy is to use variation in spending across states. As noted earlier, estimates of the effects of macroeconomic policy are inherently difficult because the counterfactual outcome is not observed. One way economists have attempted to address

Table 3–6
Estimates of the Effects of the Recovery Act on the Level of GDP

	Percent				
	2009	2010	2011	2012	2013
CEA: Model Approach	+1.1	+2.4	+1.8	+0.8	+0.3
CBO: Low	+0.4	+0.7	+0.4	+0.1	+0.1
CBO: High	+1.7	+4.1	+2.3	+0.8	+0.3
Goldman Sachs	+0.9	+2.3	+1.3	—	—
HIS Global Insight	+0.8	+2.2	+1.6	+0.6	—
James Glassman, JP Morgan Chase	+1.4	+3.4	+1.7	0.0	—
Macroeconomic Advisers	+0.7	+2.0	+2.1	+1.1	—
Mark Zandi, Moody's Economy.com	+1.1	+2.6	+1.7	+0.4	—

Note: Firm estimates were obtained from and confirmed by each firm or forecaster, and collected in CEA's Ninth Quarterly Report.

Sources: Congressional Budget Office, Estimated Impact of the American Recovery and Reinvestment Act on Employment and Economic Output from October 2012 Through December 2012; CEA Ninth Quarterly Report; CEA Calculations.

this difficulty is to isolate a component of the Act that was implemented in a random or quasi-random manner across different states, mimicking a randomized controlled trial used for research in other disciplines like medicine. If some states received more Recovery Act funds than others for reasons unrelated to their economic needs, then this portion of the funds can allow for an independent, unbiased evaluation of the effects, much like two groups of individuals participating in a drug trial that receive different dosages of the same medicine.

A notable drawback of using State-level data, however, is that this approach estimates local, not economy-wide, multipliers. These local multipliers do not incorporate out-of-state spending effects, nor do they incorporate the general equilibrium and monetary policy feedback effects that are the focus of much of the theoretical work discussed above and in the Appendix. [16]

One portion of the Act that was distributed independently of states' immediate economic needs was the additional grants to states for Medicaid. Under the Act, states received a 6.2 percentage point increase in their expected Federal reimbursement rate (the Federal Medical Assistance Percentage).[17] This increase was worth more to states that spent more per capita on Medicaid before the recession (in FY 2007). To the extent that

[16] See Nakamura and Steinsson (forthcoming) and Farhi and Werning (2012) for formal discussion of the relationship between local multipliers and the economy-wide multiplier.

[17] In addition, states were "held harmless" from planned reductions in FMAP rates due to personal income growth prior to the recession and they received an additional increment in the FMAP linked to local unemployment. The analysis presented here relies only on the 6.2 percent (non-cyclical) increase.

Figure 3-9
Change in Nonfarm Employment

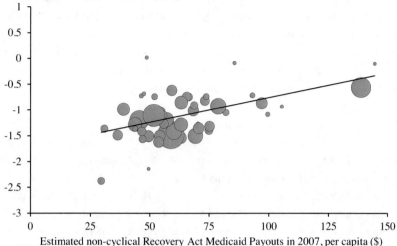

Percent of State Population, January-July 2009

Estimated non-cyclical Recovery Act Medicaid Payouts in 2007, per capita ($)

Note: Size of circle is proportional to 2008 state population.
Source: Centers for Medicare and Medicaid Services, Data Compendium; Bureau of Labor Statistics, Current Employment Statistics; CEA Calculations.

the relative severity of the recession at the state level was unrelated to its previous level of per-capita Medicaid spending, this portion of funds might be thought of "as if" randomly assigned. In other words, the spending was effectively independent of the strength or weakness of the state-level economy once the recession hit. As Figure 3-9 shows, states that received more funds stemming from this non-cyclical part of the formula tended to exhibit greater employment gains through the first half of 2009 compared with states receiving less funds.

Refining this approach, Chodorow-Reich et al. (2012) found that each additional $100,000 of formula-based Medicaid grants generated an additional 3.8 job-years, which translates into a $26,000 cost per job. Other academic papers following a similar approach, but assessing broader measures of Recovery Act spending, reached similar conclusions. For example, Wilson (2012) estimates a cost per job of about $125,000 for all Recovery Act spending programs other than those implemented by the Department of Labor (mostly unemployment insurance). Feyrer and Sacerdote (2011) and Conley and Dupor (2013) also find positive effects of the Act on employment, although the ranges of effects estimated in both papers include magnitudes similar to those discussed above as well as somewhat smaller effects.

International Comparison

The 2008 crisis reverberated worldwide. In addition to seeing sharp reductions in output and employment, many countries also experienced large government budget deficits because of countercyclical fiscal policies and a fall in tax revenues caused by the recession. These changes in budget deficits across countries can be used to derive an international estimate of the impact of fiscal policy. The International Monetary Fund's (IMF) early estimates using pre-crisis cross-country data suggested expenditure multipliers averaging 0.5, although with substantial variation across countries.[18] However, subsequent research by IMF (2012) and Blanchard and Leigh (2013) reassessed this earlier work and estimated multipliers substantially above 1.0 during the crisis, consistent with the discussion earlier in this chapter about recent fiscal multipliers in the United States.

This international evidence also suggests that the structural reductions in government budget deficits (or "fiscal consolidation") implemented by many countries has had a large negative impact on economic activity in the short run, at least when interest rates are low or at the zero lower bound and when there is already substantial economic slack. Previous research, summarized in Alesina and Ardagna (2010), hypothesized that fiscal consolidation can sometimes boost GDP because it increases investors' confidence and lowers interest rates. But Blanchard and Leigh's (2013) results, as well as findings by Perotti (2011) and Guajardo, Leigh, and Pescatori (forthcoming), point instead to significant short-run costs of deficit reductions and suggest a more gradual strategy of fiscal consolidation, as explained for instance in Blanchard, Dell'Ariccia, and Mauro (2010).

It is notable that the United States is one of only two of the 12 countries that experienced systemic financial crises in 2007 and 2008 but have seen real GDP per working-age person return to pre-crisis levels (see Box 3-2). Although this does not provide any specific evidence on the effect of U.S. fiscal measures, it is consistent with the proposition that the full set of U.S. policy interventions made a sizable difference in reversing the downward spiral of falling employment and output.

Benchmarking the Economy's Performance Since 2009

While the bulk of the available evidence indicates that the Recovery Act and subsequent fiscal legislation helped avert what might have become a second Great Depression and paved the way for stronger economic growth, many households continue to struggle with the after-effects of the recession. In addition, from a macroeconomic perspective, the average rate of

---

[18] See for example Ilzetzki, Mendoza, and Vegh (2011).

real GDP growth in this recovery (2.4 percent a year) has been slower than many would have liked. Some critics have argued that this slower growth is evidence that economic policymaking has gone awry, and that the interventions undertaken since 2008 have had unintended detrimental consequences on growth. Taylor (forthcoming) argues that fiscal policy not only failed to help but actually hurt the economy.

As discussed earlier, it is impossible to infer the causal impact of a set of policies from the observed outcomes because these observed outcomes do not reveal what would have happened absent the policy interventions. The research that attempts to answer that counterfactual conclusion using a variety of different methods has generally come to the conclusion that the Recovery Act and subsequent measures had a large positive impact on growth and employment.

In particular, claims based on the recovery are often based in part on a misleading apples-to-oranges comparison to past growth and also fail to take into account the key features of the recession and recovery. First, the economy's *potential* growth rate is slower now than it has been in previous post-World War II recoveries for long-standing reasons unrelated to the Great Recession or the policies that followed in its wake. This lower rate of potential growth reflects several key factors: slowing growth in the working-age population as baby boomers move into retirement, a plateauing of female labor force participation following several decades of transformative increases, and a slowdown in productivity growth. CBO (2012a) estimates that slower growth of potential GDP accounts for about two-thirds of the difference between observed real GDP growth in the current recovery and growth on average in the preceding postwar recoveries, an estimate that is in line with other recent studies (see the 2013 *Economic Report of the President* for further discussion).

Second, the economy has encountered a long list of additional headwinds in recent years. This list includes international events like the European sovereign debt crisis, the tsunami and nuclear accident in Japan, and the disruption of Libya's oil supply. It includes extreme weather like Hurricane Sandy and the 2012 drought that was described by the U.S. Department of Agriculture as the "most severe and extensive drought in at least 25 years."[19] It includes fiscal austerity at the state and local level that intensified as the Recovery Act began to phase out and has cost hundreds of thousands of additional job losses even during the expansion period. And it includes measures like the sequester which CBO estimated took 0.6 percentage point off growth in 2013, the 16-day government shutdown

---

[19] http://www.ers.usda.gov/topics/in-the-news/us-drought-2012-farm-and-food-impacts.aspx#.UulMXfldV5A

Box 3-2: The U.S. Recovery in Comparative International and Historical Context

The 2007-09 recession was the most severe recession experienced by the United States since World War II. The so-called Great Recession lasted 18 months from the business-cycle peak in December 2007 to the trough in June 2009, nearly twice the 10-month average length of the previous post-war recessions. The 2007-09 recession was also the sharpest, with a 4.5 percent peak-to-trough drop in real GDP, compared to an average decline of 2 percent in previous post-war recessions.

Most importantly, the 2007-09 recession was the only post-war U.S. recession associated with a systemic financial crisis. Severe financial crises tend to have long-lasting effects that can stymie an economic rebound in several ways. First, households burdened by high debt and losses on their assets can be reluctant to increase spending for an extended period of time, instead choosing to pay down debt and repair their finances. Business and residential investment can also be slow to resume, because over-leveraged banks and other financial institutions reduce the supply of credit as they reestablish the health of their balance sheets. When both credit supply and demand are suppressed, low interest rates induced by conventional monetary policy have a more limited impact than they otherwise would.

The U.S. economy has performed better over the past five years than would be suggested by the historical record of financial crises. Although the financial shocks that the United States suffered in 2007 and 2008 were similar to, if not larger than, the shocks that set off the Great Depression, the outcome was strikingly different. In the recent crisis, GDP per working-age person returned to its pre-crisis level in about four years, while it took 11 years in the United States during the Great Depression and, on average, 10 years in the 13 other countries affected

that the Bureau of Economic Analysis (BEA) estimated *directly* subtracted 0.3 percentage point from growth in the fourth quarter, and dangerous brinksmanship around the debt limit in 2011 and 2013.

In addition, the unique after-effects of financial crises discussed in Box 3-2 have also created substantial challenges for faster growth. The Great Recession was the first downturn brought about by a systemic financial crisis in nearly 80 years. Macroeconomic data from the Great Depression is limited, and models based on more readily available post-World War II data do not contain any comparable benchmark for the shock that hit the economy in 2008. Many of these models are still being refined to include more extensive and detailed linkages between the macroeconomy and the financial sector, based on lessons learned as a result of the crisis.

by systemic crises during the 1930s identified by Reinhart and Rogoff (2009).

The Figure below compares the performance of the U.S. economy with that of the other economies hit by the recent financial crisis. Of the 12 countries that suffered systemic financial crises in 2007 and 2008, real GDP per working-age adult has recovered to its pre-crisis levels in only the United States and Germany.[1]

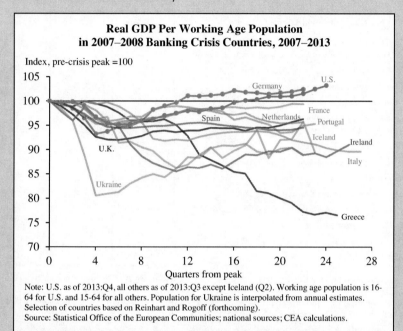

Real GDP Per Working Age Population in 2007–2008 Banking Crisis Countries, 2007–2013

Index, pre-crisis peak =100

Quarters from peak

Note: U.S. as of 2013:Q4, all others as of 2013:Q3 except Iceland (Q2). Working age population is 16-64 for U.S. and 15-64 for all others. Population for Ukraine is interpolated from annual estimates. Selection of countries based on Reinhart and Rogoff (forthcoming).
Source: Statistical Office of the European Communities; national sources; CEA calculations.

---

[1] For a historical account of financial crises in the United States and abroad, see Reinhart and Rogoff (2009) and Laeven and Valencia (2012).

All these factors must be taken into account in assessing the economy's performance in recent years—and understanding what would have happened without the significant policy actions that are described in this chapter.

Effects of the Recovery Act in Providing Relief for Individuals

As noted at the outset of this chapter, the Recovery Act had goals beyond preserving and creating jobs and promoting economic recovery. This section evaluates the impact of the Recovery Act in helping those most affected by the recession weather an extraordinarily trying period.

Table 3–7
Tax Relief and Income Support in the Recovery Act and Subsequent Measures, 2009-2012

	Billions of Dollars		
	Recovery Act	Subsequent Legislation	Total
Making Work Pay	112.2	—	112.2
Payroll Tax Cut	—	206.8	206.8
Other tax relief for individuals and families			
EITC third child and marriage penalty	6.0	4.3	10.3
Child tax credit refundability	18.7	12.3	31.0
American Opportunity tax credit	17.8	11.3	29.1
Partial exemption of tax on unemployment benefits	6.5	—	6.5
Sales tax deduction for vehicle purchase	1.3	—	1.3
First-time homebuyer tax credit	4.6	12.0	16.6
Unemployment Insurance			
Emergency Unemployment Compensation and Extended Benefits	43.2	160.6	203.8
Additional $25 payment	14.1	—	14.1
Unemployment Insurance Modernization	3.5	—	3.5
COBRA	9.2	9.8	19.1
Supplemental Nutrition Assistance Program	37.6	0.4	38.0
$250 Payment to Seniors, Veterans, and the Disabled	13.8	—	13.8
Wounded Warrior Tax Credit	—	0.3	0.3
TANF emergency fund	4.7	—	4.7
Total	293.3	417.8	711.1

Note: Data consist of cumulative outlays through the end of calendar year 2012. Items may not add to total due to rounding.

Source: Department of the Treasury, Office of Tax Analysis; Office of Management and Budget, Agency Financial and Activity Reports; Congressional Budget Office.

The Recovery Act included substantial assistance for middle-class families, unemployed workers struggling to find a job, and households in poverty or in danger of slipping into poverty. Many of these measures were extended or retooled in subsequent legislation. This assistance was partly to help families maintain their consumption even when income fell and credit dried up, a phenomenon economists refer to as "consumption smoothing." But the support was also motivated by the fact that people would quickly spend a large fraction of this assistance boosting aggregate demand and, in turn, job creation. Table 3-7 shows the programs that provided direct assistance to individuals.

Tax Cuts for Families

The Recovery Act's income support and individual tax cut provisions allowed households to maintain their purchasing power through one of the

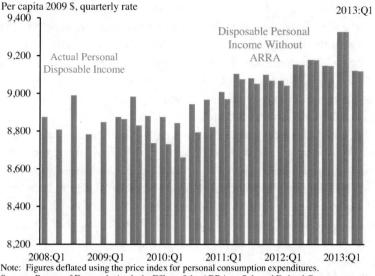

Figure 3-10
Disposable Personal Income With and Without ARRA

Per capita 2009 $, quarterly rate

Note: Figures deflated using the price index for personal consumption expenditures.
Sources: Bureau of Economic Analysis, Effect of the ARRA on Selected Federal Government
Sector Transactions, National Income and Product Accounts.

worst recessions of the century. The Making Work Pay tax credit in effect in 2009 and 2010 provided 95 percent of workers with a tax cut worth $400 for a typical single worker and $800 for a typical married couple. Without these provisions, aggregate real disposable personal income would have been $354 billion lower than what it actually was in 2009. As shown in Figure 3-10, despite $300 billion in lost private wages and salaries, real disposable incomes actually grew throughout calendar year 2009 (CEA 2010b), primarily due to tax cuts for families, the largest of which was the Making Work Pay tax credit in the Recovery Act. The Making Work Pay credit was replaced by the even-larger payroll tax cut in 2011 and 2012 that provided a tax cut for all 160 million workers, with $1,000 for the typical worker making $50,000 per year.

Unemployment Insurance

Regular state-based unemployment insurance (UI) programs typically provide benefits for 26 weeks, but as the average duration of unemployment rose to record highs in the 2007-09 recession and its wake, additional steps were needed. The Recovery Act expanded unemployment insurance in several ways. First, the Act provided for a 100 percent Federal contribution to the Extended Benefits program, which has been in place since 1970 to assist states that experience especially sharp increases in unemployment but has traditionally been jointly financed by Federal and State governments. The Recovery Act also extended the Emergency Unemployment Compensation (EUC) program enacted in 2008, which extended the duration of benefits available under Extended Benefits. It also provided an additional $25 a week in benefits through the end of 2009 and offered incentive funds for States that chose to modernize their unemployment insurance systems. Subsequent to the Recovery Act, Congress passed several more extensions and expansions of unemployment insurance, and another round of reforms aimed at assisting people searching for work.

Effects of Unemployment Insurance on Workers. In total, 24 million U.S. workers have received extended unemployment insurance benefits. Counting workers' families, over 70 million people have been supported by extended UI benefits, including more than 17 million children. Benefits have helped a broad swath of individuals, including 4.8 million with a bachelor's degree or higher. The impact was profound: the Census Bureau estimates that from 2008 to 2012, unemployment insurance kept over 11 million people out of poverty.

Beyond providing income support and keeping families out of poverty, unemployment benefits also affect labor markets. As discussed in the Executive Office of the President report on unemployment insurance (Council of Economic Advisers and Department of Labor, 2014), elevated unemployment rates in recent years were driven by declines in the demand for labor, with only slight reductions in labor supply stemming from unemployment insurance extensions. Moreover, as shown by Chetty (2008), unemployment benefits can also have a positive effect on labor productivity, because they give people time to search for a job better suited to their skills.

In addition to supporting incomes, unemployment benefits deter the long-term unemployed from dropping out of the labor force. After the extension of the unemployment benefits program in 2008, the long-term unemployed dropped out of the labor force at a considerably reduced rate, and Rothstein (2011) suggests that most of the small increase in unemployment rates due to extended benefits can be attributed to this phenomenon. While job-finding rates for the long-term unemployed remain low, keeping people in the labor market increases the chance that they will eventually resume working, which supports the economy's long-run potential.

Unemployment Insurance Reforms. The Recovery Act also included the most significant reforms to unemployment insurance in decades through a $7 billion fund to incentivize states to modernize their UI systems and to update eligibility rules to reflect the changing labor market. States received an incentive payment if they implemented some suggested improvements to their eligibility rules. These suggested improvements included allowing a worker to become eligible based on his or her most recent earnings (rather than earnings in the previous calendar year) or when quitting a job because of certain circumstances (compelling family responsibilities, a relocating spouse, domestic violence, or sexual assault). Proposed reforms also included offering benefits to individuals seeking only part-time work and providing for a dependent allowance.

Overall, states invested $3.5 billion of Recovery Act funds toward these modernization efforts. The law prompted 41 states to make nearly 100 reforms to their unemployment insurance programs. Numerous states expanded eligibility to workers whose job loss was due to compelling family circumstances, with 13 states adding coverage for domestic violence, 14 states adding coverage to care for a sick family member, and 16 states extending coverage to a relocating spouse.

In February 2012, the President signed into law more reforms to unemployment insurance—many of which were originally proposed in the American Jobs Act—including measures to help the long-term unemployed get back to work. Specifically, the new law created opportunities for states to test new strategies to help the long-term unemployed find new work. The Administration also expanded "work-sharing" programs across the country, which will help prevent layoffs by encouraging struggling employers to reduce hours for workers rather than cut headcount. Additionally, for the first time, the reforms allowed the long-term unemployed who were receiving federal benefits to start their own businesses, while also providing support to states to expand entrepreneurship programs.

Protecting the Most Vulnerable. The Recovery Act and subsequent legislation also included a range of proposals focused on protecting the most vulnerable. These measures included expanding the Earned Income Tax Credit (EITC) and the refundable portion of the child tax credit, both of which provide an additional reward to work for low-income families. The Administration also sought to ensure that the Making Work Pay credit was refundable, so that it benefited not just middle-class families but moderate-income working families as well. The Recovery Act expanded the Supplemental Nutrition Assistance Program (SNAP) to help families through tough times while also providing emergency benefits through Temporary Assistance to Needy Families (TANF), including subsidies to encourage hiring of low-income parents. The Recovery Act also ended or prevented homelessness for over 1.3 million families through the Homelessness Prevention and Rapid Rehousing Program.

All told, the pre-existing social insurance system combined with the expansions in the Recovery Act and subsequent extensions were very effective in preventing a large rise in the poverty rate, despite a substantial downturn in the economy. Even though the economy was dealt its most severe blow since the Great Depression, Wimer et al. (2013) find that from 2007 to 2010, the poverty rate measured to include the effects of antipoverty policy measures rose just half a percentage point. Excluding these measures, the poverty rate would have risen 4.5 percentage points—nine times greater than the actual increase. Chapter 6 further discusses the effects of the Administration's policies on reducing poverty.

THE EFFECT OF THE RECOVERY ACT
ON LONG-TERM GROWTH

The Recovery Act and subsequent jobs measures also contained a large number of provisions that were aimed at strengthening long-term growth. In designing the Act, the Administration believed that it was not just the quantity of the fiscal support that mattered, but the quality of it as well. In this sense, the Administration took to heart a lesson that has been pointed out by many but can be traced back as early as the 19th century to a French writer and politician named Frederic Bastiat. Bastiat (1848) wrote of a shopkeeper's careless son who broke a window in the storefront. When a crowd of onlookers gathered to inspect the damage, Bastiat took objection to the discussion that ensued: "But if, on the other hand, you come to the conclusion, as is too often the case, that it is a good thing to break windows, that it causes money to circulate, and that the encouragement of industry in general will be the result of it, you will oblige me to call out, 'Stop there!'"

For this reason, the Recovery Act was designed not just to provide an immediate, short-term boost to the economy, but also to make investments that would enhance the economy's productivity and overall capacity even after the direct spending authorized by the Act had phased out. The Act's investments in expanding broadband infrastructure and laying the ground-work for high-speed rail, to take two examples, are a far cry from the broken window in Bastiat's parable because they do so much more than simply restore things to how they once were. Rather, these types of investments will raise the economy's potential output for years to come, from a rural school that can now offer its students and teachers high-speed Internet access, to a business that has a new option to transport its goods more quickly.

As shown in Table 3-8, the Recovery Act included $300 billion of these types of investments in areas such as clean energy, health information technology, roads, and worker skills and training. Figure 3-11 suggests that the timing of these investments was relatively more spread out than some of the Act's other measures, consistent with the longer-term focus of these projects.

Table 3–8
Recovery Act Long Term Growth Investment by Category

	Billions of Dollars
	Estimated Cost (2009–2019)[a]
Capital	
Construction of Transportation Infrastructure	30.0
Environmental Cleanup and Preservation	28.0
Construction of Buildings	23.9
Public Safety and Defense	8.9
Economic Development	14.6
Memo: Business Tax Incentives	*11.7*
Labor	
Pell Grants	17.3
Special Education	12.2
Help for Disadvantaged Children	13.0
Other Human Capital	10.3
Technology	
Scientific Research	18.3
Clean Energy	78.5
Health and Health IT	32.0
Broadband	6.9
Other	6.7
Total Public Investment[b]	300.6

Note: a. Estimated cost includes appropriations and tax provisions through 2019:Q3.
b. Items may not add to total due to rounding. Total excludes Business Tax Incentives.
Source: Office of Management and Budget; Department of the Treasury, Office of Tax Analysis based on the FY2011 budget; CEA calculations.

Protecting and Expanding Investments in Physical Capital

The Recovery Act and subsequent jobs measures were designed to expand both private capital and public capital.

Business Tax Incentives for Private Capital. The theory behind incentivizing private capital holds that, at a time of systemic financial crisis, firms might not have access to sufficient capital through financial markets to invest or might be overly deterred from investing due to uncertainty, as explained in a report by the Treasury's Office of Tax Policy (2010a). To overcome these impediments to private investment, the Recovery Act and subsequent measures included business tax cuts designed to increase cash flows—like extended periods for net operating loss carrybacks and bonus depreciation—that, in effect, constituted an interest-free loan to businesses. Some economic research (House and Shapiro 2008) has shown that bonus depreciation policies can noticeably raise investment. At low interest rates, these measures had a small net present value cost to the Federal Government, but provided resources to credit-constrained firms to

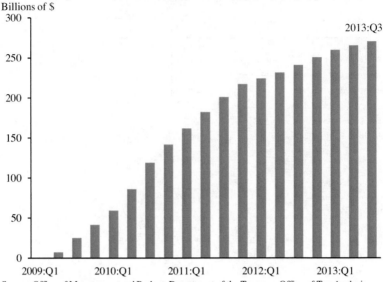

Figure 3-11
Recovery Act Cumulative Public Investment Outlays, 2009–2013

Billions of $

Source: Office of Management and Budget; Department of the Treasury, Office of Tax Analysis,
based on the FY2013 Mid-Session Review.

support investment. Building on this approach, in fall 2010 the President proposed 100 percent expensing for business investment, which, as passed by Congress in December 2010, became the largest temporary business investment tax incentive in history.

Transportation and Other Investments in Public Capital. A modern and effective transportation infrastructure network is both necessary for the economy to function and a prerequisite for future growth. Numerous studies have found evidence of large private-sector productivity gains from public infrastructure investments, as highlighted in a report by the Department of Treasury and CEA (2012).[20] The early stage of the recovery has been a particularly opportune time to undertake such investments because of the high level of underutilized resources in the economy and low construction costs. The Treasury report also points out that transportation investments can create middle-class jobs and lower transportation costs, which would otherwise weigh on household budgets.

The Recovery Act allocated $48 billion to programs administered by the Department of Transportation, with almost 60 percent for highways and 37 percent for public transportation and intercity passenger rail. The magnitude of this aid was substantial. While it is difficult to estimate what transportation expenditures would have been without the Recovery Act,

---

[20] Many of these studies are summarized in Munnell (1992) and Fernald (1999).

total highway spending in 2010 was about $27 billion (or 24 percent) higher than in 2007. This increase occurred in a period when user revenues (such as fuel taxes and other fees), the usual source of funding for states for transportation projects, were declining. Moreover, an equal dollar amount of expenditures was more effective during the recession, because construction costs for highways (as measured by the National Highway Construction Cost Index) declined about 20 percent between mid-2008 and mid-2009, and remained relatively flat through 2011.[21]

In addition to these direct programs, the Recovery Act also provided indirect support for transportation projects through Build America Bonds. The Federal Highway Administration estimated that 26 percent of the total funds raised by Build America Bonds (or $48 billion) were used by states for transportation projects. Further, a Recovery Act provision that temporarily exempted Private Activity Bonds (PABs) from the Alternative Minimum Tax (AMT) enabled airports across the country to access credit at affordable rates. The Federal Aviation Administration estimated that 24 U.S. airports issued $12.7 billion in bonds under the Recovery Act AMT exemption, realizing $1.06 billion of present value savings ($1.8 billion in gross savings) through early November 2010.

With these funds, shovels went in on more than 15,000 transportation projects across the Nation. The Department of Transportation estimates that these projects will improve nearly 42,000 miles of road, mend or replace over 2,700 bridges, and provide funds for over 12,220 transit vehicles. The Recovery Act also made the largest-ever investments in American high-speed rail, constructing or improving approximately 6,000 miles of high-performance passenger rail corridors and procurement of 120 next-generation rail cars or locomotives.

Finally, the Recovery Act initiated the Transportation Investment Generating Economic Recovery (TIGER) grant program, which allowed the Department of Transportation to invest in critical projects that were difficult to fund through traditional means. The TIGER program included a competitive process that encouraged innovation and regional collaboration. The program made extensive use of benefit-cost analysis to evaluate project applications, and required grant recipients to track the performance of their projects once launched to ensure that they achieve the promised benefits. The program also allowed many cities, counties, and other government entities to access direct Federal funds for the first time. The initial $1.5 billion TIGER program was deemed so successful that it was extended five additional times and is currently in effect through September 2014.

---

[21] See Transportation Investments in Response to Economic Downturns, Special Report 312, Transportation Research Board of the National Academies.

The Recovery Act also invested in restoring or otherwise improving infrastructure to allow Americans to safely and easily access public lands and waters. Investments included about $1 billion to the National Park Service, Fish and Wildlife Service, and Forest Service for deferred maintenance of facilities and trails and for other critical repair and rehabilitation projects. These projects help support the infrastructure needed to sustain the outdoor recreation economy and contribute to the enjoyment of public lands.

The Recovery Act included funding for programs administered by the Environmental Protection Agency (EPA) to protect and promote both a healthier environment and jobs. These investments have generated substantial environmental benefits, such as cleaning up contaminated land and putting that land back to economic use, reducing air pollution from diesel engines, and reducing contaminants in both surface water and drinking water. EPA's Brownfields program used $100 million in Recovery Act funds to leverage additional funds and cleaned up 1,566 acres of properties that are now ready for reuse, far exceeding the original target of 500 acres. The Act's funding led to 30,900 old diesel engines being retrofitted, replaced, or retired, which has reduced lifetime emissions of carbon dioxide by 840,300 tons and particulate matter by 3,900 tons.[22] More than 3,000 water quality infrastructure projects and Clean Water projects are improving or maintaining sewage treatment infrastructure for over 78 million people nationwide, as another Act investment. The Recovery Act funds have also enabled 693 drinking water systems, serving over 48 million Americans, to return to compliance with Safe Drinking Water Act standards.[23]

Protecting and Expanding Investments in Human Capital

The Recovery Act was also aimed at protecting and expanding human capital. Saving and creating jobs helps protect human capital, in part, by preventing the loss of skills—including job search skills—that can come from prolonged periods of unemployment. The evidence shows that protracted unemployment in Europe in the 1980s and 1990s resulted in sustained loss of human capital (Blanchard and Summers 1986, Ljungqvist and Sargent 1998). Helping workers better connect with jobs, whether through unemployment insurance reforms or job subsidies in the TANF emergency fund, has helped protect human capital.

Significant investments and reforms in education were critical to actually expanding human capital. State and local governments typically provide more than 90 percent of the funding for elementary and secondary education and about 40 percent of the funding for public institutions of

---

[22] See Environmental Protection Agency (2013).

[23] See http://www.epa.gov/recovery/accomplishments.html

higher education in the United States. As the economy slowed in 2008, State revenues declined, putting pressure on education budgets.

The Recovery Act dramatically increased funding for education through Title I grants to local education agencies (LEAs), School Improvement Grants, and grants for special education. In addition, the Act increased student aid and support for post-secondary institutions to invest in new buildings and research in innovative health and energy technologies. In response to these grants, recipients reported that more than 800,000 education job-years were saved or created, keeping teachers, principals, librarians, and counselors as well as university faculty and staff on the job.

States also reported that they used State Fiscal Stabilization Funds from the Recovery Act to restore sizable shares of K-12 education funding. For example, the Recovery Act restored 9 percent of K-12 education funding in California, Indiana, Alabama and Oregon; 12 percent of such funding in Florida, Wisconsin and South Carolina; and 23 percent of K-12 education funding in Illinois in fiscal year 2009. In at least 31 states, Recovery Act funds prevented or lessened tuition increases at public universities, including universities in Massachusetts, Minnesota, and Virginia. Without this influx of State Fiscal Stabilization Funds, these states would have endured drastic cuts in education funding.

The Recovery Act launched the innovative Race to the Top Program with $4.35 billion. Race to the Top is a competitive grant program designed to encourage and reward States to implement critical reforms designed to help close the achievement gap and improve student outcomes, including better student assessments; better data systems to provide teachers and parents with information about student progress; new steps to develop and support effective teachers; and efforts to turn around low-achieving schools. Encouraged by the incentives included in Race to the Top, states across the country chose to adopt more rigorous academic standards aligned to higher expectations for college and career readiness. To date, 19 states, representing 45 percent of all K-12 students, have received Race to the Top funds; and to compete for funds, 34 states modified state education laws and policies in ways known to improve education.

The Recovery Act also expanded the Pell Grant program, raising the maximum grant from $4,731 to $5,550, and it created the American Opportunity Tax Credit to modify and replace the Hope higher education credit (this policy was later extended by the Tax Relief, Unemployment Insurance Reauthorization and Job Creation Act of 2010 and the American Taxpayer Relief Act of 2012). The passage of the Health Care and Education Reconciliation Act of 2010 enabled further expansion of the Pell Grant award. Together, these efforts to expand higher education opportunity helped individuals who chose to return to school or remain in school to bolster their skills in a demanding job market. As a result, the Pell Grant program offered $36.5 billion in aid to more than 8.8 million undergraduate students in FY 2010, compared to roughly half as much aid, $18.3 billion, for 6.2 million students in FY 2008 (U.S. Department of Education, 2011). The largest growth in Pell Grant applications came from students in the lowest-income categories. For tax year 2009, 8.3 million tax returns claimed $14.4 billion in American Opportunity Tax Credits. This level of education credits (including the lifetime learning credit) was a nearly $10 billion increase from the prior year (U.S. Department of the Treasury, 2010b).

Investments in Technology and Innovation

Some of the highest returns to investment are in the area of innovation. Often, innovation produces large returns for the economy as a whole, but since businesses do not capture all these society-wide returns, they tend to underinvest in innovation. For example, firms may not undertake research and development even though it would benefit the rest of their industry, other industries, and their regional economies. In general, looking across a range of industries, economists have estimated that the divergence between private and social returns to investment may be as great as two-to-one (for instance, Hall et al. 2009). This is especially true when investments can result in externalities that are not captured by the entity making the investment. For instance, in the energy sector, there are substantial climate and national security benefits to cleaner energy that are not fully internalized in the form of financial rewards for individual firms. The Recovery Act made a significant impact on innovation—complementing the other measures this Administration has taken to encourage innovation.

Scientific Research. The Recovery Act provided a one-time supplemental appropriation of over $3 billion for the National Science Foundation and $1 billion for the National Aeronautics and Space Administration. It also increased support for the National Institute of Standards and Technology and provided the Advanced Research Projects Agency-Energy (ARPA-E) with funding of $400 million. The ARPA-E is charged with researching transformative energy technologies. So far it has pioneered research into so-called second-generation biofuels, which utilize agricultural and municipal waste, as well as more efficient batteries, superconducting wires, and vehicles powered by natural gas.

Clean energy. Clean energy was the focus of more than $90 billion in government investment and tax incentives in the Recovery Act. The purpose of these investments was to help create new jobs, reduce dependence on foreign oil, enhance national security, and improve the environment

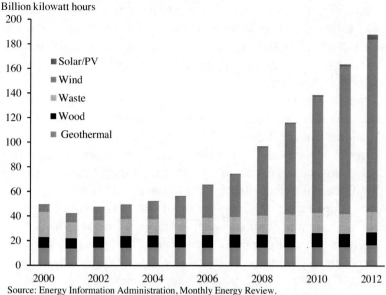

Figure 3-12
Advanced Renewable Electric Power Net Generation, 2000–2012

Billion kilowatt hours

Source: Energy Information Administration, Monthly Energy Review.

by countering climate change. Key targets included energy efficiency (with programs such as the weatherization assistance program), renewable generation (with investments in wind turbines, solar panels, and other renewable energy sources), and grid modernization. Many of these clean energy programs were administered though the $38 billion Recovery Act portfolio of the Department of Energy.

Using the multiplier model described earlier in the chapter, CEA estimated that clean energy investment created or saved about 650,000 job-years, directly or indirectly, through 2012.[24] These investments have started to drive changes in energy production, as highlighted, for instance, by Aldy (2013). Owing in large part to these clean energy incentives and investments, renewable wind, solar, and geothermal energy have increased their contributions to U.S. energy supply each year since 2008. For instance, as shown in Figure 3-12, wind electricity net generation nationwide grew by 145 percent from 2008 to 2012. Solar thermal and photovoltaic electricity net generation more than quadrupled during the same period. Meanwhile, carbon dioxide emissions from the electric power sector fell approximately 14 percent over

---

[24] See CEA's (2010a) second report on the Recovery Act of 2009 for a detailed discussion on the macroeconomic effects of clean energy investment. The latest estimates are presented in CEA's (2010c) fourth quarterly report.

the period, even though total power generation declined by only about 2 percent.

Many of the clean energy provisions of the Recovery Act were designed to bring in private funds through co-investment. For example, through Energy Cash Assistance, individuals and businesses that installed certain types of renewable energy generation received a grant equal to 30 percent of the project's cost.

Of course, not every investment in clean energy will ultimately result in a transformative technology. Because funding is often directed to projects based on ideas that are at the frontier of scientific research, there is a certain degree of risk involved. But given the grave economic, environmental, and national security consequences of climate change, these types of investments must continue. An independent review released in 2012 found that, on the whole, the Department of Energy loan guarantee programs are expected to perform well and hold even less risk than initially envisioned by Congress.

Health Care Information Systems. The Health Information Technology for Economic and Clinical Health (HITECH) Act, enacted as a part of the Recovery Act, encouraged adoption and use of health information technology. The core of the HITECH Act is a set of financial incentives to health care providers to adopt and make "meaningful use" of electronic health records. The HITECH Act also provided $2 billion to the Department of Health and Human Services to fund activities to encourage the diffusion of health information technology, such as investing in infrastructure and disseminating best practices. The Act also made a variety of other changes, including provisions to facilitate data sharing across health care providers to support coordinated care and protect patient privacy.

Fully integrated electronic health record systems allow immediate and complete access to all relevant patient information. These innovations have the potential to greatly improve coordination of care—for example, by limiting the unnecessary duplication of tests and procedures—and also to reduce medical errors, thereby lowering health care costs. Chapter 5 further explains the benefits of fully integrated electronic health record (EHR)systems and discusses the dramatic increase in the share of medical providers using electronic health records in recent years.

Broadband. The Recovery Act helped increase access to broadband and drive its adoption across the country, both directly through grants, and indirectly through tax incentives such as increased expensing of investment costs.[25] It provided $4.4 billion through the Department of Commerce's National Telecommunications and Information Administration to deploy

---

[25] See the Office of Science and Technology Policy and the National Economic Council report *Four years of broadband growth* (2013).

broadband infrastructure (for instance, laying new fiber-optic cables or upgrading wireless towers, and connecting key institutions such as schools, libraries, hospitals, and public safety facilities) and support public computer centers (establishing new public computer facilities to provide broadband access to the general public or specific vulnerable and underserved populations). The funding also encouraged sustainable adoption of broadband (for instance, through digital literacy training and outreach campaigns), led to the publication of the National Broadband Map (www.broadbandmap.gov), and supported state broadband leadership and capacity building activities (through, for example, local broadband planning teams and information technology assistance provided to small businesses, schools, libraries, and local governments). The Recovery Act also provided $2.5 billion through the Department of Agriculture Rural Utilities Service to expand broadband access in rural areas.

Because of these grants, over 110,000 miles of broadband infrastructure have been added or improved, and high-speed connection has been made available to about 20,000 community institutions. These projects have also delivered about 16 million hours of technology training to more than 4 million users.

In part as a result of the Recovery Act and related policies, broadband access has risen substantially in recent years. Chapter 5 discusses broadband development in more depth.

Fiscal Sustainability and the Recovery Act

The Recovery Act and subsequent fiscal measures were part of an overall fiscally responsible economic strategy that cut the deficit in the medium and long run. Moreover, given the economic context in which the jobs measures were passed, these measures alone had little if any impact on long-run fiscal sustainability.

The Recovery Act is entirely temporary—it cost $763 billion over the first decade (not counting the extension of the AMT patch) and it has no long-term impact on non-interest outlays or revenues. Overall, assuming the CBO score, the Act at most added less than 0.1 percentage point to the 75-year fiscal gap.

These estimates are small but may nevertheless overstate the true cost of the Recovery Act. To the degree that the Act successfully expanded output and boosted employment, those gains would result in additional revenue and less spending on countercyclical programs than would otherwise have occurred. Taking the estimates presented in this chapter for the increase in GDP over the 2009-12 period—and assuming these increases led to additional tax revenue at 18 percent of GDP, roughly the recent historical average—then the resulting increase in revenue would alone be enough to offset roughly one-quarter of the Act's cost.

Moreover, to the degree that effects on output are persistent—a factor that is not captured in the estimates in this chapter but is assumed by the IMF (2009) and Reifschneider, Wascher, and Wilcox (2013), then the positive fiscal feedback effects could be even larger. DeLong and Summers (2012) have shown, for example, that with plausible multipliers and persistence in output effects, it is possible that the additional output associated with the Recovery Act, and associated additions to revenue and reductions to debt, could result in a *reduced* debt-to-GDP ratio by the end of the decade.

These estimates do not reflect the potential benefits for long-term growth of the productivity-enhancing investments in the Recovery Act. For example, if an infrastructure project has a total rate of return of 10 percent, and if overall revenues are about 18 percent of GDP, then it would have a rate of return to the Federal taxpayer of about 2 percent. Given the Federal borrowing costs at the time of the Recovery Act, the investment would conceivably pay for itself over time and reduce Federal debt as a share of GDP as the investment produces returns.

None of these estimates should be taken as conclusive or as a suggestion that official budget scoring should take these feedback effects into account. When the economy is operating at full employment, and monetary policy is not constrained by the zero lower bound, many of these macroeconomic feedback effects would be less relevant or not even operative at all. Moreover, if fiscal policy actions raised the specter of substantially larger and less sustainable future deficits and debt, that could reduce confidence and raise interest rates, undermining any beneficial economic feedback. But in this case, these measures were passed at the same time that the Administration was also laying out steps for longer-term deficit reduction and reducing the fiscal gap by passing major deficit-reduction measures, including the Affordable Care Act and the Budget Control Act.

As a result, given the overall context of highly insufficient aggregate demand, monetary policy operating at the zero lower bound, and other measures for medium- and long-term deficit reduction, fiscal measures to support jobs have the potential for even larger impacts on output and thus greater associated revenue feedbacks and a much lower long-run fiscal cost, if they have any long-run fiscal cost at all.

CONCLUSION

The Recovery Act and subsequent jobs measures were designed to help propel the economy out of the worst contraction since the Great Depression and to set the stage for stronger future growth. Considerable evidence suggests the Federal Government's efforts to jump-start the economy were successful. CEA estimates that the Recovery Act provided an important and timely boost to GDP in 2009 and 2010, and led to the creation of about 6.4 million additional job-years through 2013—estimates that are in line with those of CBO and of other forecasting groups. Other fiscal efforts enacted subsequent to the Recovery Act brought the total to 8.8 million job-years.

The Administration's actions have been guided by the notion that fiscal support measures would only be needed for a temporary period, and this view is being borne out. Most temporary measures to support the economy expired in 2013, most notably the payroll tax cut. Businesses and households are now in far better shape as a result of several years of deleveraging, and private-sector growth has led the way since 2010. Although many challenges linger, and supportive measures like emergency unemployment insurance remain necessary given the unacceptably high rate of long-term unemployment, the economy has the potential for even stronger growth in 2014.

Public policy, in particular public investment in areas like research, infrastructure, and innovation, will continue to play an important role in the economy. The President is proposing additional investments and reforms in all of these areas. But, in these cases, investments are part of a longer-term, sustained commitment to expanding the productive capacity of the economy without the same need for immediate countercyclical support.

Overall, the Recovery Act and subsequent measures are one of the main reasons why the U.S. economy was able to return to record levels of per working-age population GDP within just over four years of the onset of the recession and to bring the unemployment rate down by 0.8 percentage point per year—when many other countries with systemic financial crises have not seen their GDP per working-age population fully recover or their unemployment rates start a sustained fall. In the longer run, the benefits of all of these efforts will be more difficult to isolate from other simultaneous changes, but they will be no less profound in terms of their cumulative impact on the economic well-being of the Nation.

Appendix 1: Components of the Recovery Act and Subsequent Fiscal Measures

Table 3-9 reports the actual budgetary impact of the Recovery Act from its inception through the latest data available (the end of fiscal year 2013).

Table 3-10 reports the budgetary impact classified into the six broad functional categories shown also in Figure 3-1: individual tax cuts,

Alternative Minimum Tax relief, business tax incentives, State fiscal relief, aid to directly impacted individuals, and public investments. The following sections of this appendix will discuss each of these categories in more detail.

Tax Relief

Within the first three categories of tax cuts, major programs included the Making Work Pay tax credit, which provided a 6.2 percent credit on earnings up to a maximum value of $400 for individuals and $800 for couples, phasing out starting at income above $75,000 and $150,000, respectively (estimated to cost about $116 billion between 2009 and 2011). The credit was administered through reducing tax withholdings and the Internal Revenue Service required that companies reduce withholding by April 1, 2009. In addition, the legislation made $250 one-time payments to seniors, veterans, and people with disabilities. The Recovery Act included the Making Work Pay tax credit for 2009 and 2010. In December of 2011 Congress enacted a 2-percentage point reduction of the Social Security payroll tax for 2011 that was extended through 2012 and expired at the start of 2013.

Additionally, the Recovery Act provided tax credits for families, such as an expansion of the child tax credit, including making it refundable for more low-income families (at a total estimated cost of $15 billion), expansions of the earned income tax credit for married couples and families with more than three children ($5 billion), and the American Opportunity Tax Credit to help make college more affordable. All of these measures have since been extended through 2017, and the President's Budget for 2014 proposes to make them permanent—rendering them among the only items from the Recovery Act intended to be permanent.

The Recovery Act also raised the exemption amount for the AMT to $46,700 for individual taxpayers and $70,950 for joint filers, at an estimated cost of $70 billion. Because this was a widely expected continuation of previous AMT patches, this component of the Recovery Act did not represent a net new fiscal impetus for the economy and is not included in CEA's macroeconomic estimates.

For businesses, the legislation provided cost-effective incentives to expand investment by allowing businesses to immediately deduct half of the cost of their investments (bonus depreciation) and also to extend the period over which small firms (except those receiving TARP funds) could claim losses and expense capital purchases. Businesses buying back or exchanging their own debt at a discount were also allowed to defer any resulting income. All of these measures were designed to improve the cash flow for firms that might be facing credit constraints and to increase incentives to invest. Long-run costs to the Federal Government were limited because the measures

Table 3–9
Recovery Act Outlays, Obligations, and Tax Reductions

Through the end of[a]	Outlays	Obligations	Tax Reductions	Sum of Outlays and Tax Reductions[b]
2009:Q1	8.6	30.5	2.4	11.0
2009:Q2	47.7	127.3	35.6	83.3
2009:Q3	54.4	98.5	31.8	86.2
2009:Q4	53.5	57.6	30.2	83.7
2010:Q1	46.7	48.2	64.9	111.6
2010:Q2	46.4	41.7	77.3	123.6
2010:Q3	50.6	48.6	16.4	66.9
2010:Q4	40.7	20.8	8.4	49.1
2011:Q1	25.0	6.2	31.9	56.9
2011:Q2	25.1	5.0	−5.1	20.0
2011:Q3	21.9	9.2	2.1	23.9
2011:Q4	17.7	5.7	2.0	19.6
2012:Q1	14.3	5.2	−4.0	10.4
2012:Q2	12.8	6.5	−3.0	9.8
2012:Q3	12.0	4.4	−0.5	11.6
2012:Q4	11.2	5.8	0.5	11.7
2013:Q1	11.0	6.2	0.7	11.7
2013:Q2	7.2	4.0	0.4	7.7
2013:Q3	5.6	2.5	0.4	5.9
Total Through 2013:Q3[b]	512.4	533.8	292.2	804.6

Notes: a. Data on outlays and obligations are for the last day of each calendar quarter.
b. Items may not add to total due to rounding.
Source: Office of Management and Budget, Agency Financial and Activity Reports; Department of the Treasury, Office of Tax Analysis based on the FY2013 Mid-Session Review.

largely advanced tax benefits that companies would receive anyway. The 50 percent bonus depreciation was subsequently extended and expanded to 100 percent expensing, and the net operating loss carryback was extended to larger firms. In addition, the Recovery Act included incentives for investments in renewables and advanced energy manufacturing, and in areas undergoing significant distress through State and local government-issued Recovery Zone Bonds. The Recovery Act also increased funding for the New Markets Tax Credit and provided incentives to hire unemployed veterans and disconnected youth.

Table 3–10
Recovery Act Fiscal Stimulus by Functional Category

Through the end of[a]	Individual Tax Cuts	AMT Relief	Business Tax Incentives	State Fiscal Relief	Aid to Directly Impacted Individuals	Public Investment Outlays	Total[b]
2009:Q1	2.3	0.0	0.1	8.5	0.0	0.0	11.0
2009:Q2	26.3	7.8	12.5	19.6	9.6	7.4	83.3
2009:Q3	14.3	6.0	10.5	15.6	22.2	17.6	86.2
2009:Q4	15.8	3.5	9.0	15.5	23.4	16.5	83.7
2010:Q1	43.3	11.4	6.9	16.2	16.1	17.7	111.6
2010:Q2	22.4	47.5	4.9	16.6	5.2	27.0	123.6
2010:Q3	9.8	7.2	−2.6	15.0	4.7	32.8	66.9
2010:Q4	8.6	0.0	−1.5	14.6	4.7	22.6	49.1
2011:Q1	25.5	4.6	−1.5	4.4	3.5	20.4	56.9
2011:Q2	12.2	−19.0	−1.5	4.7	3.3	20.3	20.0
2011:Q3	0.3	0.0	−1.5	2.3	4.1	18.7	23.9
2011:Q4	0.1	0.0	−0.9	1.9	2.4	16.2	19.6
2012:Q1	0.3	0.0	−0.9	1.7	2.2	7.1	10.4
2012:Q2	0.0	0.0	−0.9	1.2	2.2	7.3	9.8
2012:Q3	−0.0	0.0	−0.9	1.2	2.0	9.3	11.6
2012:Q4	0.1	0.0	−0.7	0.9	1.6	9.9	11.7
2013:Q1	0.3	0.0	−0.7	1.3	1.6	9.2	11.7
2013:Q2	0.0	0.0	−0.7	1.2	1.6	5.5	7.7
2013:Q3	−0.0	0.0	−0.7	0.6	1.1	5.0	5.9
Total Through 2013:Q3[b]	181.7	69.0	28.8	143.0	111.5	270.5	804.6

Notes: a. Data on outlays and obligations are for the last day of each calendar quarter.
b. Items may not add to total due to rounding.
Source: Office of Management and Budget, Agency Financial and Activity Reports; Department of the Treasury, Office of Tax Analysis based on the FY2013 Mid-Session Review.

Aid to Affected Individuals

An expansion in unemployment benefits offered significant aid to individuals.[26] Typically, American workers who have lost their jobs are entitled to 26 weeks of benefits under the unemployment insurance (UI) program, which tends to replace about half of lost earnings and is paid for entirely by the states through payroll taxes levied on employers. In June 2008, Congress created the Emergency Unemployment Compensation (EUC) program, which provided an additional 13 weeks of federally financed compensation in all states to eligible individuals who had exhausted their UI benefits. The

---

[26] For a comprehensive discussion of the various employment benefits programs implemented in recent years, see the Council of Economic Advisers and the Department of Labor report *The economic benefits of extending unemployment insurance* (2014).

Recovery Act extended and expanded the EUC program to reflect that fact that with jobs increasingly scarce the optimal balance of unemployment insurance shifted towards covering people for a longer period of time. It also provided 100 percent Federal funding of the pre-existing Extended Benefit (EB) program, which provides an additional 13 or 26 weeks of benefits in states where unemployment is exceptionally high and rising. (EB costs are usually borne half by the Federal Government and half by the States.)

The Recovery Act also added $25 a week to benefits and exempted the first $2,400 in yearly unemployment benefits from taxes. The CBO (2009a) estimated the total costs of these changes to the unemployment compensation system at $39 billion. In addition, the Federal government offered states incentives to modernize their UI programs, picking up the cost of new provisions allowing workers to become eligible based on recent earnings (rather than those from the previous calendar year) and extending benefits to part-time job seekers.

The Recovery Act provided a 13 percent increase in SNAP payments and lifted several restrictions governing the length of time that individuals could collect food stamps, at an estimated cost of $20 billion. For the first time, the Federal Government agreed to temporarily pay 65 percent of health insurance premiums for laid off workers who wanted to continue with their employer-sponsored health insurance. Other aid to individuals included funds for job training and improving skills of the hard to employ and young workers.

The Recovery Act devoted substantially more resources compared with previous antirecessionary policies to investments in education and research and development. The legislation increased the Pell Grant maximum by $500 to $5,550, at an estimated cost of $17 billion over ten years. The Recovery Act also boosted Title I aid and other programs for disadvantaged children ($13 billion) and funds for special education ($12 billion).

State Fiscal Relief

The Recovery Act provided unprecedented support for State and local governments, which often face budget challenges in a recession because their revenues rise and fall with the economy, while pressures on spending, especially on programs targeted to the disadvantaged, tend to move in the opposite direction. The result can be budget shortfalls, or gaps between expected revenues and expenditures. These gaps pose problems for state residents already affected by the downturn, and for the larger economy because most State and local governments are generally bound by constitutional or statutory requirements to balance their operating budgets each year. As shown by Poterba (1994), states and localities have to raise taxes or cut spending, precisely when doing so can most harm recovery.

To dampen such counterproductive tax increases or budget cuts, the Recovery Act boosted Federal Medicaid payments by $87 billion, including a 6.2 percent across-the-board increase in the Federal matching rate, plus delays of a planned reimbursement cut for some states (based on income growth before the recession) and an increment of aid linked to local unemployment conditions. It also established a $53.6 billion State Fiscal Stabilization Fund to be administered by the Department of Education, but with some funds available for other "high priority needs" such as public safety. Unlike most previous increases in Federal grants to States and localities during a recession, these transfers were available for general fiscal relief or left to local discretion to use, as long as recipients met basic maintenance of effort or minimal spending requirements.

Beyond direct spending, the Recovery Act made new types of borrowing available for State and local governments. Build America Bonds (BABs) allowed State and local governments to access non-traditional markets, including pension funds and international investors who would not normally purchase U.S. municipal bonds because they do not owe U.S. income taxes and therefore do not benefit from these bonds' tax-exempt status. Under BABs, State and local issuers could offer higher taxable interest rates on bonds and choose to make a Federal income tax credit available to buyers or to take a direct subsidy offsetting 35 percent of their borrowing costs. State and local governments issued $181 billion of Build America Bonds before the program expired at the end of 2010. The Treasury Department has estimated that this action saved issuers $20 billion in present value of borrowing costs as well as alleviating supply pressures in the tax-exempt market (Department of the Treasury 2011).

Investments

The Recovery Act made numerous investments in human capital, clean energy, health information technology, roads, and the skills of U.S. workers.[27] For example, the Recovery Act provided an additional $27.5 billion for highway construction, $18 billion for public transit and inter-

---

[27] CEA counts as public investment any Recovery Act expenditure or tax program that directly results in activity that increases the capital stock of the Federal government, State and local governments, or private firms. We also count provisions that affect the Nation's human capital and knowledge capital, areas not measured in the national income accounts but which economists have identified as crucial to generating long-run economic growth. Note that tax programs are included if they function similarly to direct spending. In other words, entities can claim tax benefits only when associated spending occurs (e.g., the Advanced Energy Manufacturing Tax Credit).

city passenger rail, $10 billion for water infrastructure, and $18 billion for government facilities. It also made available $57 billion for investment in smarter grid technology, renewable energy, and energy efficiency improvements through a combination of grants, loans, and pilot programs, including $5 billion to help low-income households weatherize their homes. Scientific projects from the National Science Foundation, National Institutes of Health, NASA, the Department of Energy, and others received over $15 billion for scientific facilities, research, and instrumentation. Additionally, the Recovery Act provided $7 billion to expand broadband Internet access in underserved areas of the country. The Recovery Act also provided several investments in health care and health information technology, including an $18 billion measure to encourage hospitals and physicians to computerize medical records, $2 billion for Community Health Centers, $1 billion for fighting preventable chronic diseases, and $1 billion for researching the effectiveness of various medical treatments. In total, more than $100 billion of the investments—including some tax incentives—were explicitly targeted at innovation.[28]

Subsequent Fiscal Measures

Table 3-11 shows the total fiscal support provided by the Administration, by fiscal year, with a brief description of the main programs for each measure. (These data were summarized in Table 3-4.) All measures use prospective CBO cost estimates. These totals only include measures explicitly designed to address job creation and provide relief and do not include routine extensions, like so-called "tax extenders" or the fix to Medicare's Sustainable Growth Rate formula.

APPENDIX 2: FISCAL MULTIPLIERS: THEORY AND EMPIRICAL EVIDENCE

Although the multiplier described in the text is simple and intuitive, it relies on several unrealistic assumptions, and much research in macroeconomic theory over the past four decades has focused on overcoming those conceptual problems. For example, because deficit spending in a recession could be offset by higher taxes in a boom, Barro (1974) argued that forward-looking individuals might save much or all of a tax cut in anticipation of higher taxes later. Although the extreme version of this argument requires consumers who are unrealistically liquid and prescient, in general

---

[28] Executive Office of the President and Office of the Vice President, *The Recovery Act: Transforming the American Economy through Innovation,* August 2010.

Table 3-11

Fiscal Support for the Economy Enacted After the Recovery Act

	2009	2010	2011	2012	2013	2014	2015	2016	2017	2018	2019	2009–12	2009–19	Description
Worker, Homeownership, and Business Assistance Act (HR 3548)	0	46	−3	−6	−4	−3	−2	−1	−1	−1	−0	35	24	Expanded weeks in UI (by 20 weeks) • Extended first time homebuyers tax credit
Supplemental Appropriations Act of 2009 (HR 2346)	1	2	0	0	0	0	0	0	0	0	0	3	3	Cash for Clunkers
Defense Appropriations Act of 2010 (HR 3326)	0	16	2	0	−0	−0	−0	−0	−0	0	0	18	18	Extended UI/COBRA 2 months
Temporary Extension Act of 2010 (HR 4691)	0	7	1	0	0	0	0	0	0	0	0	9	9	Extended UI/COBRA 1 month
Hiring Incentives to Restore Employment Act (HR 2847)	0	4	6	3	1	1	0	0	0	−0	0	13	15	Hiring tax credit • Subsidized bonds for school construction and renewable energy
Continuing Extension Act of 2010 (HR 4851)	0	13	2	0	0	0	0	0	−0	0	0	16	16	Extended UI/COBRA 2 months
Unemployment Compensation Act of 2010 (HR 4213)	0	9	25	2	0	0	0	0	0	0	0	33	34	Extended UI 6 months • Extended first time homebuyers tax credit
FAA Safety Improvement Act (HR 1586)	0	0	23	2	0	−3	−5	−3	−2	−1	−0	26	12	Education Jobs Fund • Extension of FMAP relief
Small Business Jobs Act (HR 5297)	0	0	80	−9	−12	−10	−22	−12	−4	−2	−1	68	10	Small business lending fund • Small business tax cut and bonus depreciation for all businesses
Tax Relief, Unemployment Insurance Reauthorization, and Job Creation Act (HR 4853)	0	0	158	145	22	−27	−21	−16	−12	−7	−5	309	237	Payroll tax cut for 2011 • Extended UI through 2011 • Extension of expanded AOTC, EITC, and CTC
Temporary Payroll Tax Cut Continuation Act (HR 3765)	0	0	0	27	2	0	0	0	0	0	0	28	29	Payroll tax and UI through February 2012
VOW to Hire Heroes Act (HR 674)	0	0	0	−0	1	−0	−0	−1	−0	−0	−0	0	−0	Returning Heroes and Wounded Warrior tax credits
Middle Class Tax Relief and Job Creation Act of 2012 (HR 3630)	0	0	0	90	33	−0	−0	−0	0	0	0	98	123	Payroll tax and UI through end of 2012
American Taxpayer Relief Act of 2012 (HR 8)	0	0	0	0	68	55	9	15	18	17	−4	17	178	Extended UI through 2013 • Extension of expanded AOTC, EITC, and CTC • Extension of small business tax cut and bonus depreciation
Total	1	98	294	253	113	13	−40	−18	−0	6	−11	674	709	

Note: All measures use prospective CBO cost estimates for 2009–19. Routine tax extenders have been removed from the cost estimates. Columns for individual years contain data in fiscal year terms. The column for 2009–2012 total contains data through the end of calendar year 2012, while the column for 2009–2019 contains data through the end of fiscal year 2019.

Source: Congressional Budget Office; Joint Committee on Taxation.

introducing forward-looking behavior by consumers and firms planning for the future changes the dynamics and magnitude of Keynesian multipliers.

Forward-Looking Models with Rigidities

Many modern macroeconomic models combine forward-looking behavior with some form of slow-moving prices or wages, sometimes called "New Keynesian" models. In normal times, when monetary policy is unconstrained and interest rates can vary, these models tend to imply fiscal expenditure multipliers that are positive but smaller than one, as shown for instance by Cogan et al. (2010) and Coenen et al. (2012), in part because of increases in the interest rate from monetary policy which partially offsets the fiscal expansion.

The onset of low interest rates has spurred considerable interest in how these models perform when monetary policy is constrained by the zero lower bound, that is, when the nominal federal funds rate falls to zero, as in the recent recession. For instance, Eggertson (2001), Christiano, Eichenbaum, and Rebelo (2011) and Woodford (2011) have shown that when nominal interest rates are near zero, government spending can be particularly effective and generate spending multipliers that are greater than one; at the zero lower bound, expansionary fiscal policies can increase inflation expectations and thereby reduce real interest rates, which spurs investment and consumption, and monetary policy does not counteract fiscal policy. Coenen et al. (2012) simulate the effect of the Recovery Act spending in some forward-looking models with rigidities, both conventional models (such as Smets and Wouters (2007)) and models augmented by the zero lower-bound effects. Their results show that the standard models imply a notable increase in output for several years, but with multipliers smaller than one, while the models augmented by zero-lower-bound effects imply multipliers that are much larger than one over the first few years.

The 2007-09 recession was unusual both because the Federal Reserve was at the zero lower bound and because of its severity. This severity raises the specter of high unemployment and—because the path to recovery from a deep shock is long—unusually long spells of unemployment. Long-term unemployment can lead to deterioration of skills and to stigmatization, which makes finding employment even more difficult. For these and other reasons, the longer the spell of unemployment, the less likely is an individual to find a job in any given month, and the more likely he or she is to remain unemployed or stop looking for a job altogether. This can lead to a vicious circle: persistent slack demand means many people out of work and long spells of unemployment, which in turn reduces the chances of the unemployed finding a job, which perpetuates slack and further lengthens spells. Because the resulting unemployment dynamics depend on the path of unemployment, not just on its current level, this phenomenon is often referred to as "hysteresis" in the rate of unemployment.

The potential for hysteresis in unemployment—the economy getting stuck at high rates of unemployment for an extended period—provides a further argument for activist fiscal policy, and models that build in hysteresis effects can have large and sustained multipliers (see for example Phelps 1972, Blanchard and Summers 1986, Ball 2009, and DeLong and Summers 2012). Reifschneider, Wascher, and Wilcox (2013) stress the relevance of these channels to the current recovery. Their research shows that the financial crisis damaged the productive capacity of the economy, by causing a steep decline in capital accumulation, lower productivity growth, and structural damages to the labor market, and a large portion of this damage to the productive capacity stemmed from weak demand. These results suggest that under such conditions fiscal policy can continue to have a meaningful effect on output with a substantial lag.

This recent work has moved far beyond the basic multiplier. It shows that fiscal and monetary policy can influence each other in substantial ways. While fiscal multipliers might be less than the basic model suggests in mild recessions and when monetary policy is unconstrained, they can be large when monetary policy is at the zero lower bound. In addition, fiscal expansion in a deep recession can have additional long-term benefits, and therefore high multipliers, by shortening spells of unemployment, minimizing the erosion of human capital, and increasing future productivity.

Time Series Evidence

Evaluations of fiscal effects using the structural models described above reflect the economic theory used to construct the models. The reliability of the resulting estimates therefore depends on the reliability of the underlying macroeconomic theory. A complementary approach to evaluating the effects of fiscal policy is instead to use models that rely less on economic theory and more on historical empirical evidence.

The main challenge to credibly implementing this data-driven approach is using just enough theory, or finding enough independent variation in the data, to estimate the causal effect of fiscal policy on the economy: simply noting that two variables move together does not establish causality. For example, if Congress passed countercyclical fiscal policy whenever a recession loomed, a figure plotting the countercyclical policy variable and GDP growth would show that countercyclical policy occurred at the beginning of recessions. An analyst might conclude, incorrectly, that this policy caused the recession, when in fact the policy was itself caused by the recognized onset of the recession. Analysis based on this hypothetical figure suffers from two central problems in the estimation of causal effects from observational (as opposed to experimental) data: simultaneous causality (the looming recession spurred Congressional action and the fiscal policy potentially affected the course of the economy) and the presence of other omitted, confounding factors (perhaps the Federal Reserve moved countercyclically and it was those actions, not Congress's, that muted the recession). The latter problem of omitted variables can be partially addressed using multiple regression methods, but the problem of simultaneous causality requires other approaches, and relying on simple plots or multiple regression can lead to misleading results.[29] Because such plots or regressions are uninformative, a vast literature developed over the past four decades uses more sophisticated methods to estimate causal effects in general and the effect of fiscal policy in particular.[30]

Evaluation of the effects of fiscal policy in general, and the Recovery Act in particular, faces several additional challenges. First, the effect of activist fiscal policy must be disentangled from the automatic stabilizers built into the tax and safety net system. Second, the effect of fiscal policy unfolds over time, so there is not a single causal effect but rather a sequence of dynamic causal effects, including long-lasting effects of investment on productivity that could last for many years. Third, different fiscal policy instruments (expenditures, taxes, transfers) will in general have different effects. Fourth, as discussed above, theory suggests that the effect of fiscal policy could depend on the economic environment, and in particular could depend both on the severity of the recession and on the reaction of monetary policy.

A vast body of empirical literature now employs time-series data to estimate the macroeconomic effect of fiscal policy. Broadly speaking, this

---

[29] The multiple regression analysis in Taylor (2011), which estimates the effect of fiscal policy in the 2000s, addresses in part the problem of omitted variables but not the problem of simultaneous causality. Taylor measures the direct impact of fiscal policy on income by the component of disposable income due to countercyclical fiscal policy from 2009-based on the 2001, 2008, and Recovery Act fiscal programs. The level of quarterly consumption is then regressed on contemporaneous values of on personal income, the fiscal policy measure, wealth, and oil prices. Thus this regression controls for the separate effects of oil price movements, in case they co-move with fiscal policy. As observed in the text, however, the sign and magnitude of the coefficient on fiscal policy is ambiguous *a-priori* because of simultaneous causality: it could be positive, zero, or negative. As it turns out, the coefficient is positive but small, a finding that is consistent with fiscal policy having a large positive effect which, in the regression, is offset by the fact that Congress passed it in a recession, or with fiscal policy having little effect. Because of simultaneous causality, this regression analysis, like its graphical equivalent, sheds little light on the question of the effect of fiscal policy.

[30] The field of the econometric estimation of causal effects has seen tremendous advances in both methods and applications; for a review see Angrist and Pischke (2010), Sims (2010), and Stock (2010). For additional methodological discussion of simultaneous causality, see Stock and Watson (2010, Chapters 9 and 12).

literature uses two different approaches to isolate (to "identify") the effect of fiscal policy. The first is to impose a minimal amount of structure on an otherwise unrestricted time series model, typically a so-called structural vector autoregression. In an influential contribution, Blanchard and Perotti (2002) assume that, because of implementation lags and limitations on the information considered by policymakers, fiscal policy does not respond immediately to other economic shocks. Under this assumption, any unpredicted movements in the fiscal variable (that is, movements that differ from what standard fiscal policy would have suggested) are unrelated to contemporaneous economic shocks, so the effect of fiscal policy can be estimated by tracing out the effect of those unpredicted movements on output and employment. Using this approach, Blanchard and Perotti (2002) estimate the government spending multiplier on GDP to be in the range 0.9 to 1.2. Ramey (2011b) reviews the large body of research that uses structural vector autoregressions to build on this approach to identifying the effects of fiscal shocks. The common theme of this work is using a component of fiscal policy—in Blanchard-Perotti (2002), the unpredictable component—which is "as-if random" in the sense that it is unrelated to other economic shocks.

A second approach to identifying the effect of fiscal policy is to exploit external information, such as institutional or historical knowledge, to find changes in fiscal policy that are in effect random (that is, independent of macroeconomic conditions), which can in turn be used to trace out the fiscal effect. Because this information falls outside the time series model being estimated, this approach is called the method of external instruments. In this vein, Ramey and Shapiro (1998) and Ramey (2011a) use expenditures on wars and military buildups, arguing that they are determined by international and political, not economic, considerations. These authors estimate GDP multipliers in the range of 0.6 and 1.2. Romer and Romer (2010), instead, use narrative evidence from Presidential and Congressional records and similar documents to identify tax changes that were not implemented in response to current or forecasted economic conditions. They find that the identified tax cuts have a sustained and large effect on output, with multipliers as high as 3. Mertens and Ravn (2012) use Romer and Romer's (2010) narrative to distinguish between the effects of anticipated and unanticipated tax changes and, surprisingly and in contrast to Ramey (2011a), find little difference in the two effects. Additional recent contributions include Favero and Giavazzi (2012) and Mertens and Ravn (2013). Estimates of fiscal policy effects obtained using this so-called method of external instruments are reviewed in Ramey (2011b) and Stock and Watson (2012).

The foregoing time series estimates are predicated upon fiscal multipliers having the same size in booms and in recessions. Recent work by

Auerbach and Gorodnichenko (2012) suggests that while the spending multiplier can be relatively small during expansions, it can be much greater than one during recessions. These results are consistent with conventional models in recessions, but with neoclassical ones in booms, and suggest that multipliers obtained also using fiscal policy changes that happen in booms (such as the military buildup used by Ramey and Shapiro (1998) and Ramey (2011a) to identify fiscal shocks) could underestimate the effect of the policies in recessions.

Finally, a different approach is to use consumer-level microeconomic data on specific policy events, as highlighted by Parker (2011). For instance, looking at the 2001 and 2008 tax rebates, which reached recipients in different months, Johnson, Parker, and Souleles (2006) and Parker, Souleles, Johnson, and McClelland (2011) show that a sizable fraction of the rebate was spent, especially by lower income or liquidity constrained households. Their results indicate that income transfers can be an effective way to raise consumption in the short run. This approach has the advantage of directly estimating consumption effects, although it does not capture the full dynamic, indirect response of the economy to the fiscal shock.

Cross-Sectional Multipliers

In addition to the works on the Recovery Act cited in the cross-state evidence section, recent work has also exploited other sources of cross-sectional variation in government spending to estimate the size of the fiscal multiplier. For instance, looking at the effects of windfall returns on pension funds, Shoag (2013) estimated a local output multiplier of 2.1. Suarez, Serrato, and Wingender (2011) reached a similar conclusion using on changes in Federal transfers due to the decennial census. Nakamura and Steinsson (2011) detected a 1.5 local multiplier based on regional differences in Federal defense spending.

Table 3-12 summarizes the fiscal multipliers implied by the economic literature on state-level effects of fiscal policies.

Table 3–12
Summary of Cross-Sectional Fiscal Multiplier Estimates

Study	Source of Variation	Regional Multiplier	Cost per Job
Chodorow-Reich et al. (2011)	Formulaic spending in American Recovery and Reinvestment Act of 2009	2.1	$26,000
Wilson (2011)	Formulaic spending in American Recovery and Reinvestment Act of 2009	—	$125,000
Suarez Serrato and Wingender (2011)	Impact of decennial census on Federal transfers	1.9	$30,000
Shoag (2010)	Windfall returns on pension investments	2.1	$35,000
Nakamura and Steinsson (2011)	Regional distribution of changes in defense spending	1.5	—

Source: Romer (2012).

CHAPTER 4

RECENT TRENDS IN HEALTH CARE COSTS, THEIR IMPACT ON THE ECONOMY, AND THE ROLE OF THE AFFORDABLE CARE ACT

Dramatic progress is being made in addressing one of the enduring problems of the U.S. health care system: the fact that millions of Americans lack access to quality, affordable health insurance. Since January 1, the Affordable Care Act (ACA) has extended coverage to millions of Americans, and the Congressional Budget Office (CBO) estimates that, by 2016, the ACA will reduce the number of people without health insurance by 25 million (CBO 2014). If all states elect to take up the ACA's Medicaid expansion, the ACA will reduce the number of people without health insurance even further.

But the U.S. health care system also faces another enduring challenge: decades of rapid growth in health care spending. While much of this historical increase reflects the development of new treatments that have greatly improved health and well-being (Cutler 2004), most agree that the system suffers from serious inefficiencies that hike costs and reduce the quality of care that patients receive. Another key goal of the ACA was to begin wringing these inefficiencies out of the health care system, simultaneously reducing the growth of health care spending—and its burden on families, employers, and State and Federal budgets—and increasing the quality of the care delivered.

This chapter analyzes recent trends in U.S. health care costs and documents a dramatic slowdown in recent years. According to the final data on national health expenditures, real per-capita health spending grew at an average annual rate of just 1.1 percent from 2010 to 2012. Preliminary data as well as projections by the Office of the Actuary at the Centers for Medicare and Medicaid Services (CMS) imply this slow growth continued in 2013, and the CMS projections show real per-capita health spending growth averaging just 1.2 percent over the three years since 2010. These spending growth rates are the lowest rates on record for any two- and three-year periods, and less than one-third the long-term historical average of 4.6 percent that stretches back to 1960. Moreover, they have occurred at a time when the aging of the population would have been expected to modestly increase the growth rate of health care spending.

The historically slow growth in health costs has appeared not only in health care spending, but also in the prices paid for health care goods and services. Measured using personal consumption expenditure price indices, health care inflation is currently running at around 1 percent on a year-over-year basis, a level not seen since 1963. Health care inflation measured using the consumer price index (CPI) for medical care is at levels not seen since 1972. Health care inflation measured relative to general price inflation is also unusually low in historical terms.

An important question is what has caused these trends and whether they are likely to persist in the years ahead. Although the slowdown is not yet fully understood, the evidence available to date supports several conclusions about its causes and the role of the Affordable Care Act.

The 2007-09 recession and its aftermath have likely played some role in the recent slowdown in health costs, and this portion of the slowdown is likely to fade as the economic recovery continues. However, several pieces of evidence imply that the slowdown in health care cost growth is more than just an artifact of the 2007-09 recession: something has changed. The fact that the health cost slowdown has persisted even as the economy is recovering; the fact that it is reflected in health care prices, not just utilization; and, the fact that it has also shown up in Medicare, which is more insulated from economic trends, all imply that the current slowdown is the result of more than just the recession and its aftermath. Rather, much of the slowdown appears to reflect "structural" changes in the U.S. health care system, suggesting that at least part of this trend—although it is uncertain how much—is likely to persist. This conclusion is consistent with a substantial body of recent research that seeks to quantify the recession's contribution to the slowdown and has found that the recession alone cannot explain recent trends.

While various non-recession factors unrelated to the ACA appear to be contributing to the recent slow growth in spending—including a long-term decline in the development of new prescription drugs and a long-term increase in cost-sharing in employer sponsored plans—the ACA is also playing a meaningful role. For example, by curtailing excessive Medicare payments to private insurers and medical providers, the law has contributed to the recent slow growth in health care prices and spending, reducing health care price inflation by an estimated 0.2 percentage points each year since 2010.

The ACA's measures to reduce costs and improve quality by improving the payment incentives faced by medical providers also appear to be beginning to bear fruit. For example, hospital readmission rates have turned sharply lower since the ACA began penalizing hospitals that readmit a larger number of patients soon after discharge. Similarly, the ACA has substantially increased health care provider participation in payment models designed to promote high-quality, integrated care. These are hopeful signs and provide reason to believe that, as the ACA's payment reforms continue to take effect over the coming years, they will make an important contribution to extending the recent slowdown.

An emerging literature also suggests that the ACA's payment reforms, which operate primarily through Medicare (and, to a lesser extent, through Medicaid), may generate "spillover" benefits throughout the health system. This literature finds that when Medicare reduces payments to medical providers, private payers tend to follow suit, and also finds that the same is true for changes to the *structure* of how Medicare pays providers. Some recent evidence also suggests that changes in payment structures by one insurer may benefit patients covered by other insurers, even if those other insurers do not adopt the new payment structures. One possibility is that changes by one insurer induce changes in providers' "practice styles" that affect all patients that providers see. This evidence suggests that the ACA's reforms to the Medicare payment system may be, in economic terms, "public goods."

The presence of spillover benefits would imply that the contribution of the ACA to the recent slowdown in health costs growth is considerably larger than previously understood. As noted above, ACA provisions that curb excessive Medicare payments to private insurers and medical providers have directly reduced health care price inflation by an estimated 0.2 percent a year since 2010. A calculation accounting for spillovers raises this estimate to 0.5 percent a year—a substantial share of the recent slowdown in health care price inflation.

This chapter concludes with a consideration of the economic benefits of a sustained slowdown in health care costs. Over the long run, slower growth in health care spending that is achieved without compromising the quality of care will raise living standards. These gains may be substantial. If even just one-third of the recent slowdown in spending can be sustained, health care spending a decade from now will be about $1,200 per person lower than if growth returned to its 2000-07 trend, the lion's share of which will accrue to workers as higher wages and to Federal and State governments as lower costs.

Recent Congressional Budget Office estimates offer a concrete illustration of the potential for improvements in the Federal fiscal outlook. Since August 2010, CBO has reduced its projections of combined Medicare and Medicaid spending in 2020 by $168 billion and 0.5 percent of gross domestic product (GDP). The $168 billion reduction represents a 13 percent reduction in previously projected spending on these programs and primarily reflects the recent slow growth in health care spending. These revisions are, however, distinct from the deficit reduction directly attributable to the ACA, which CBO estimates will be substantial. Due in large part to the ACA's role in slowing the growth of health care spending, CBO estimates that the provisions of the ACA will directly reduce deficits by about $100 billion over the coming decade and by an average of 0.5 percent of GDP a year over the following decade.

Slower growth in long-term health spending also reduces employers' compensation costs in the short run, increasing firms' incentives to hire additional workers. This chapter surveys the available evidence on the likely effects on employment to conclude that short-run employment gains could be substantial, although the magnitude of these gains is quite uncertain.

This chapter proceeds as follows. The first section quantifies the recent slowdown in health care costs. The second section discusses possible factors behind the slowdown in costs, and also discusses the effects of the ACA on quality of care so far and in the future. The final section discusses the slowdown's potential economic benefits.

RECENT TRENDS IN HEALTH CARE COSTS

To document the historically slow growth in health care costs seen in recent years, this section uses the National Health Expenditure (NHE) Accounts, which were recently updated by the Office of the Actuary at the Centers for Medicare and Medicaid Services (CMS) to incorporate data through 2012 (Martin et al. 2014). These data permit a detailed and comprehensive look at recent trends in the Nation's health care spending.

The analysis is extended through 2013 using the most recent NHE projections, which were published by CMS in September 2013 (Cuckler et al. 2013) and reflect Medicare and Medicaid spending data and macroeconomic data available through June 2013 (CMS Office of the Actuary 2013).[1]

---

[1] The final health spending growth rate for 2012, as reported by CMS in January 2014, came in approximately 0.2 percentage points below what CMS had projected in September 2013. To account for this lower base in 2012, this analysis uses CMS' projections of the 2013 growth rate of health spending, not the level of health spending.

Table 4–1

Category	Average annual growth from 2010 through...		Historical average annual growth		
	2012	2013	1960–2010	2000–2007	2007–2010
Total national health expenditures	1.1	1.2	4.6	4.0	1.9
Major payers (per enrollee)					
Private insurance	0.9	1.2	N/A	5.2	4.1
Medicare	−0.3	−0.4	N/A	5.5	2.4
Medicaid	−1.6	−0.1	N/A	0.4	0.3
Major categories of spending					
Hospital care	1.6	1.6	4.5	4.0	3.2
Physician and clinical services	1.7	1.6	4.6	3.2	1.7
Prescription drugs	−1.1	−1.3	4.6	6.3	0.5
Home health and skilled nursing care	0.9	1.2	6.6	3.0	2.9

Note: Inflation adjustments were made using the GDP deflator. Per-enrollee growth figures are not available for the 1960-2010 period because Medicare and Medicaid did not exist in 1960 and because CMS does not provide enrollment by insurance type for years before 1987.

Source: Centers for Medicare and Medicaid Services, National Health Expenditure Accounts and National Health Expenditure Projections; Bureau of Economic Analysis, National Income and Product Accounts; CEA calculations..

NHE "tracking" estimates constructed by the Altarum Institute using data on health spending from the Bureau of Economic Analysis imply that final estimates of NHE for 2013 will come in very close to the CMS projection (Altarum 2014).

Table 4-1 summarizes recent trends in spending growth, and Figure 4-1 depicts these trends graphically. From 2010 through 2012, the last year for which final data are available, real per capita national health expenditures grew at an annual rate of just 1.1 percent. The CMS projections show slow growth continuing through 2013, with the annual average real per-capita growth averaging just 1.2 percent. These slow growth rates since 2010 are less than one-third of the long-term historical average growth rate of 4.6 percent and substantially below the average growth rates recorded from 2000-07 and over the three years immediately prior to 2010.[2] These growth rates since 2010 are, in fact, the lowest on record; from 1960, the first year the NHE data are available, through the present, no other two- and three-year periods saw lower growth rates.

The slow growth is reflected in all three payer categories depicted in Figure 4-3, which appears on page 157. Real per enrollee spending growth

---

[2] The periods 2000-07 and 2007-10 were chosen as comparison periods in order to facilitate the discussion in the next section of the role of the 2007-09 recession in driving recent trends.

Box 4-1: Two Measures of Growth in Health Care Costs: Spending and Prices

This report examines two different measures of growth in health care costs: growth in the prices of health care goods and services and growth in total spending on health care goods and services. These two types of data are useful for answering different questions.

The growth in health care prices tells us how the amount of money needed to purchase a given amount of health care—a bypass surgery, a doctor's visit, or a tablet of aspirin—is changing over time. By contrast, the growth in health care spending captures not only changes in the prices of health care good or services (like the price of a doctor's visit), but also changes in the quantity of health care goods and services consumed (like the number of doctor's visits made).

In theory, increases in health care prices (above general price growth) are unambiguously bad for consumers since they reduce the amount of health care a consumer can buy with a given number of (real) dollars. By contrast, increases in health care spending can be good or bad. If spending rises because consumers are receiving more care and that care improves health, then spending increases are a good thing. If, on the other hand, spending rises because the price of care is rising or because consumers are receiving additional care that does not improve health, then higher spending is a bad thing. Concern about the long-term growth in health care spending reflects a belief that much of that growth reflects higher prices or increased use of low-value care.

In practice, measuring changes in health care prices is more challenging than in the idealized discussion presented above. In light of the rapid technological change that has been seen in the health care sector, comparing goods and services over time can be difficult. For example, an appendectomy done in 1990 and an appendectomy done in 2010 might be treated as the "same item" in a health care price index, but it is likely that the 2010 version of the procedure reflects substantial improvements in surgical technique relative to its 1990 counterpart, improvements in quality that may be important for health outcomes and of great value to patients. As a result, simply knowing that the price of an appendectomy has risen from 1990 to 2010 is not enough to determine whether someone in need of an appendectomy was better off in 1990 or in 2010; one must somehow account for the fact that the 2010 patient is effectively purchasing a greater quantity of "improved health" than the 1990 patient.

Cutler et al. (1998) document that these measurement challenges are a substantial problem in practice. Focusing on care for heart attack patients, the authors show that mortality outcomes for these patients have improved dramatically in ways not accounted for in major price indices. As a result, these indices dramatically overstate the extent to which rising medical prices are making people worse off over time.

As a final note, to the degree that statistical agencies have gotten better at measuring quality improvements over time, long-term comparisons of health care price inflation can be misleading. Indeed, it is possible that some of the long-term decline in health care price inflation depicted in Figure 4-2 results from methodological improvements of this kind. However, methodological improvements of this kind are unlikely to play a substantial role over short time periods, and they likely play little or no role in explaining the sharp declines in health care price inflation over the last few years.

in private insurance over the 2010-13 period is less than one-quarter its level from 2000-07 and less than one-third its level from 2007-10. The change in Medicare spending growth has been similarly dramatic, with real growth in per beneficiary Medicare costs essentially ceasing over this period. In Medicaid, the already slow growth in real per beneficiary costs seen in recent years has continued and turned slightly negative from 2010 to 2013.

The slowdown is similarly broad-based when looking across spending categories. Real per capita growth in spending on hospital care—the largest single category of spending, accounting for almost one-third of total spending—is growing at less than half the long-term historical average rate and more than 1 percentage point slower than the most recent historical period. Prescription drugs have seen particularly sharp reductions in growth, with spending actually shrinking in real per capita terms at a 1.3 percent annual rate over the last three years. Physician and clinical services and home health and skilled nursing care show similarly slow growth rates in a historical context.

Panel A of Table 4-2 documents a similar slowdown in the growth of prices paid for health care goods and services, which is also depicted in Figure 4-2. Health care inflation, whether measured using the personal consumption expenditure (PCE) price indices or the CPI for medical care, is running at half or less the rate seen historically, and below the rates seen over the last decade. Indeed, year-over-year inflation as measured using PCE data is currently running at around 1 percent, a level last seen in 1963. The recent behavior of the CPI for medical care is similar, with recent months' year-over-year inflation rates reaching low levels not seen since 1972.

It is important to note that this slow growth in prices for health care goods and services is not simply a reflection of the fact that the prices of all goods and services have grown slowly in recent years. Panel B demonstrates

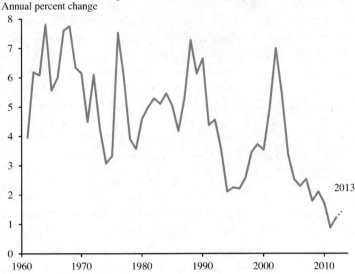

Figure 4-1
Growth in Real Per Capita National Health Expenditures, 1961–2013

Annual percent change

2013

Note: Data for 2013 is a projection.
Source: Centers for Medicare and Medicaid Services, National Health Expenditure Accounts;
Bureau of Economic Analysis, National Income and Product Accounts; CEA calculations.

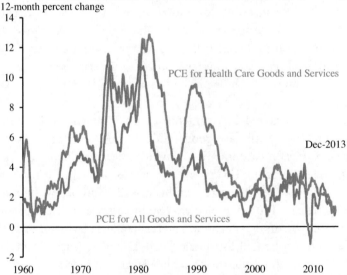

Figure 4-2
General and Health Care Price Inflation, 1960–2013

12-month percent change

PCE for Health Care Goods and Services

Dec-2013

PCE for All Goods and Services

Source: Bureau of Economic Analysis, National Income and Product Accounts; CEA
calculations.

Category	Fre-quency	Available through	Annual growth, ACA–present	Historical average annual growth		
				1960–ACA	2000–2007	2007–ACA
Panel A: Health care inflation						
PCE prices for health care goods & services	Monthly	Dec–13	1.7	5.4	3.3	2.8
CPI for medical care	Monthly	Dec–13	2.9	5.9	4.3	3.5
Panel B: Health care inflation relative to general price inflation						
PCE prices for health care goods & services	Monthly	Dec–13	0.1	1.7	1.0	1.2
CPI for medical care	Monthly	Dec–13	0.8	1.7	1.6	1.8
Panel C: Employer premiums for family coverage (adjusted for inflation)						
KFF/HRET survey	Annual	2013	4.1	N/A	6.8	3.0
MEPS–IC	Annual	2012	3.7	N/A	6.4	3.4
Panel D: PCE spending on health care goods & services (adjusted for inflation and population)						
PCE spending for health care goods & services	Monthly	Dec–13	2.2	4.7	3.9	1.4

Note: For monthly data, end points for periods starting or ending in a listed year are treated as occurring in July of that year. Time periods listed as starting or ending with the ACA start with March 2010 for monthly series and 2010 for annual series. PCE stands for personal consumption expenditures. PCE for health care goods and services includes the following categories of spending: health care, pharmaceutical and other medical products, therapeutic appliances and equipment, and net health insurance. Price indices for these categories are combined to construct a Fisher index for the aggregate, and it is growth in this index that is reported in Panel A and Panel B. In Panel D, the PCE spending data are adjusted for inflation using the general PCE deflator and BEA's population series. CPI stands for consumer price index. Employer premium growth is adjusted for inflation using the GDP deflator. Because MEPS-IC data are not available for 2007, the figures shown for that series reflect average growth rates for the period 2000-2006 and 2006-2010.

Source: Bureau of Economic Analysis, National Income and Product Accounts; Bureau of Labor Statistics, Consumer Price Index; Kaiser Family Foundation, Employer Health Benefits Survey; Agency for Healthcare Research and Quality, Medical Expenditure Panel Survey, Insurance Component; CEA calculations.

that health care inflation *relative* to general price inflation has also been unusually low over the last few years.

Panel C of Table 4-2 examines trends in employer premiums, as documented in two major surveys of employers. In both surveys, premium growth rates are more than 2.5 percentage points below the 2000-07 trend. Panel D tracks real per capita consumption spending for health care goods and services, based on data from the Bureau of Economic Analysis. By this measure, spending growth is running at about half the rate seen in the first portion of the last decade, and even farther below its longer-term historical average. While these series do suggest that growth may have increased slightly since 2010, they are consistent with the other available data in showing that current growth rates are very low, whether measured against short-term or long-term historical experience. In addition, premium growth in particular may not exactly track underlying cost trends on a year-to-year basis because premiums must be set before actual costs for the year are known. Over the long-run, however, slower growth in health costs will likely be fully reflected in the premiums individuals and employers pay.

WHAT IS HAPPENING NOW, AND WHAT WILL HAPPEN NEXT?

A natural—and important—question becomes: What is driving the recent slow growth in health care costs? The answer to this question can shed light on whether the current slow growth will last, and what policies could help make that occur. Indeed, slowdowns can be temporary; the early- and mid-1990s also saw several years of slow growth in health care costs, but costs accelerated once again in the late 1990s and early 2000s.

While final conclusions about the causes of the recent slow growth and its persistence await additional data and analysis, some conclusions are possible with the data currently available. Most importantly, the recent slow growth does not appear to be the result of idiosyncratic factors affecting a single category of spending or a particular payer. As documented in Table 4-1, the slowdown has affected all major payers and each of the major categories of spending. The search for explanations must, therefore, look for factors affecting behavior system-wide. The first part of this section examines the role of the 2007-09 recession, the second part discusses potential non-ACA, non-recession explanations for the recent slow growth, and the third part considers the role of the Affordable Care Act, both to date and in the future.

The Role of the 2007-09 Recession

Some have identified the 2007-09 recession and its aftermath as a potential driver of system-wide changes. For example, job losses may have caused reductions in insurance coverage that curtailed access to health care, or the accompanying falls in families' disposable incomes could have forced households to prioritize other needs over medical care. Alternatively, disruptions in financial markets could have depleted providers' cash reserves or reduced their ability to borrow in order to invest in new equipment or facilities, leading to lower utilization in subsequent years.[3] If the recession

---

[3] The NHE data do show a very sharp reduction in investment in equipment and structures in the health care sector over 2009 and 2010 of about 12 percent in real per capita terms. It is worth noting, however, that this contraction followed two years of very strong investment growth. Moreover, even as financial conditions have normalized, investment has remained subdued, suggesting that providers do not view themselves as having incurred a substantial investment deficit, nor suggesting an imminent investment-driven rebound in health care cost growth.

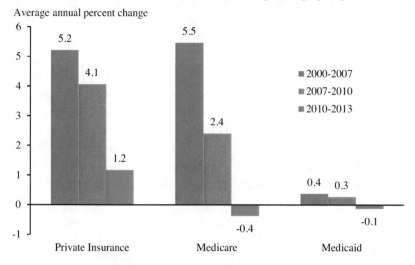

Figure 4-3
Growth in Real Per Enrollee Health Spending by Payer

Average annual percent change

- 2000-2007
- 2007-2010
- 2010-2013

Notes: Figures for 2013 are projections.
Source: Centers for Medicare and Medicaid Services; Bureau of Economic Analysis, National Income and Product Accounts; CEA calculations.

were the primary driver of the current slow growth in health spending, then growth would likely return to its earlier rapid rate as the economic recovery continues.

Three features of the recent slow growth in health care costs are inconsistent with the theory that this slow growth results only from the recession, suggesting that a substantial portion of the recent slowdown is "structural" and likely to persist. First, and most simply, the slowdown has now persisted well beyond the end of the recession. The Great Recession began in December 2007 and concluded by June 2009. Since that time, the economy has recorded four years of steady growth. Yet, as shown in Table 4-1 and Figure 4-3, health spending growth has remained subdued relative to the years during and immediately following the recession. While the economy may affect health spending with a lag, if the recession were the primary force driving the slowdown, more substantial acceleration would likely be visible by now.

Second, as documented in Table 4-1 and Figure 4-3, the slowdown has affected Medicare in addition to the private sector, a fact highlighted in a recent analysis by CBO economists (Levine and Buntin 2013). Because seniors are generally more insulated from a weak labor market, this fact undermines the notion that the slowdown results primarily from economic disruptions attributable to the recession. In addition, Levine and Buntin find that even those seniors who did experience relatively larger economic disruptions during the recession did not spend less on health care. Levine and Buntin also document, using State-level data, that Medicare spending growth has historically risen when unemployment rises—the opposite of the pattern required for the economic downturn to explain the slowdown in cost growth.[4]

Third, the recent behavior of health care inflation is difficult to square with the theory that the slowdown is primarily a result of the recession. As documented in Table 4-2 and Figure 4-2, health care inflation has decelerated sharply of late, even when measured *relative* to inflation in the broader economy. While there are a variety of plausible mechanisms by which the recession could reduce the quantity of health care services people demand, and thus reduce total spending, it is difficult to explain why a recession should cause a reduction in the growth rate of health care prices *relative to* price growth in other sectors of the economy.

Many recent studies have also attempted to directly quantify the role of the recession in driving recent slow growth in health care spending. These analyses, which use a variety of methods, have generally concluded that, while the recession likely has depressed health care spending growth in recent years, health spending is low in historical terms even after accounting for the recession, and a substantial fraction of the slowdown likely reflects structural changes that are likely to persist. The remainder of this section provides a review of this growing literature.

Chandra, Holmes, and Skinner (2013) provide one approach to evaluating the role of the recession. They survey the available micro-econometric estimates of the effect of income on the demand for health care. Virtually all such estimates in the existing literature are small, with the largest credible estimates of the income elasticity being the 0.7 estimate provided by Acemoglu et al. (2013). Applying this upper-bound estimate to the observed slowdown in GDP growth, they show that the slow economic growth in recent years explains less than half of the recent slow growth in health spending. Although they express some uncertainty about the future outlook for health spending, they nevertheless project that a substantial fraction of the slowdown will persist, due in part to the potential of payment reforms included in the Affordable Care Act.

Ryu et al. (2013) take another approach. They examine the role of two specific mechanisms by which the recession could have affected health

[4] The 2013 *Economic Report of the President* undertakes a related analysis (CEA, 2013). The report analyzes changes in state-level unemployment from 2007-09 to state-level health spending growth over that period. While that analysis finds that unemployment is associated with lower health spending growth, the effect is small and cannot explain a substantial fraction of the recent downturn in health spending.

care cost growth: by reducing insurance coverage via job loss and by causing firms to offer their employees leaner health plans that require greater cost-sharing. Focusing on the period 2009-11, they find that recent reductions in spending growth are, if anything, larger among employed individuals, and that increases in cost-sharing can account for only one-fifth of the slowdown. On the basis of their results, they advise a "cautious optimism that the slowdown in health spending may persist."

Another set of studies evaluates the effect of the recession by estimating the historical relationship between economic growth and health spending growth and using this estimated relationship to simulate how health spending would have evolved had the recession not occurred. Econometric time series analyses like these have the important advantage that, by virtue of their nationwide, aggregate approach, they can capture the effects of a wide variety of potential mechanisms connecting economic growth to health spending growth. But the nationwide, aggregate nature of these analyses is also a weakness; it can be difficult to plausibly control for important confounding factors, and the paucity of data (only about 50 years of data, or about 50 total data points, are available) can make these analyses sensitive to seemingly innocuous changes in methodology, as demonstrated by Chandra, Holmes, and Skinner. The current literature does not, unfortunately, provide persuasive evidence on which econometric specifications are likely to provide the most reliable results.

Cutler and Sahni (2013) estimate a model relating current health spending growth to a five-year average of economic growth. Based on their results, they estimate that spending growth in 2011 and 2012 would have been on the low end of the historical range even accounting for the recession, and that more than half of the slowdown over the longer period 2003-12 is due to factors other than the recession. They conclude that "fundamental changes" are underway in the health sector, changes that are not attributable to the recession alone.

A contrary perspective comes from an analysis from the Kaiser Family Foundation and the Altarum Institute (KFF and Altarum 2013). They estimate a model relating current health spending growth to economic growth the current year and each of the prior five years and general price inflation in the current year and each of the prior two years. On the basis of their estimated model, the authors conclude that most of the slowdown in health care spending from the 2001-03 period to the 2008-12 period is attributable to the macroeconomic factors, although they still attribute 23 percent of the slowdown to non-macroeconomic factors.

It is important to note, however, that the authors' calculation applies to the slowdown in nominal health spending growth over this period, while the slowdown in real (that is, inflation-adjusted) health spending growth is of greater economic interest. Because inflation was, on average, lower during the 2008-12 period than during the 2001-03 period, the authors' approach overstates the role of macroeconomic factors in explaining the slowdown in real spending growth. In addition, the authors' model, by virtue of its relative complexity, is particularly subject to the shortcomings of the time series approach described above. Indeed, the model estimated by KFF and Altarum has one particularly unusual feature: the effect of reduced economic growth on health spending actually peaks four years later. While not impossible, such lags seem implausibly long.

Non-ACA Factors Affecting Health Spending Growth

As discussed above, the recession does not provide a full, or even necessarily a major, explanation for the recent slow growth in health spending. While additional factors may be identified in the future, two non-ACA factors have received substantial attention to date—although it is important to note that at least one non-ACA factor is modestly increasing health spending growth.

The long-term trend toward increased patient cost-sharing is one factor that can plausibly explain why slow growth has affected many different categories of spending at the same time (Cutler and Sahni 2013; Ryu et al. 2013; Chandra, Holmes, and Skinner 2013). The Kaiser Family Foundation/ Health Research and Educational Trust Employer Health Benefits Survey indicates that recent increases in cost-sharing in employer plans have been substantial; the typical deductible in an employer plan has increased from $584 in 2006 to $1135 in 2013, a 70 percent increase after adjusting for inflation (Kaiser Family Foundation 2013a).

Some research suggests that the observed increase in cost-sharing is having an effect. As noted above, Ryu et al. (2013) examine the importance of increased cost-sharing in the employer context and conclude that it can account for 20 percent of the reduction in growth over the 2009-11 period. Chandra, Holmes, and Skinner (2013) evaluate the role of increased cost-sharing using estimates from the literature of how utilization responds to cost-sharing. They conclude that cost-sharing may have played a larger role, although the precision of their estimates is limited by the poor quality of the available data on recent changes in cost-sharing and the current incomplete understanding of how cost-sharing affects utilization.

While it seems possible and perhaps likely that increased cost-sharing is playing a role, it cannot be the whole story. As discussed in detail above, the slowdown in Medicare fee-for-service spending has been even more dramatic than the slowdown in the private sector, and there have been no substantial changes to the core Medicare benefit design in recent years that parallel the changes seen in the private sector.

The striking slowdown in prescription drug spending, documented in Table 4-1, also factors into the slow growth trend. Various sources attribute this sharp drop in prescription drug spending to the expiration of patent protection for many important drugs. Due to a slowdown in the invention of new drugs that stretches back more than a decade, the drugs that have come off patent in recent years are not being replaced by more-recently patented drugs. As a result, the share of prescriptions accounted for by generic drugs—which typically cost much less—has increased sharply, substantially reducing costs (Aitken, Berdnt, and Cutler 2009; Cutler and Sahni 2013; IMS 2013). However, these changes in the prescription drug market are probably only making a modest contribution to aggregate trends in health spending since prescription drugs account for less than 10 percent of total health spending.

There is, however, at least one easily identified factor working against the recent slowdown: the aging of the U.S. population. In recent decades, population aging has made a small positive contribution to the growth of U.S. health spending; White (2007) estimates that over the period 1970-2002, population aging added about 0.3 percentage points to annual growth. The contribution of population aging to health care spending growth appears to have increased by a small amount in recent years. Using data on the age distribution from the U.S. Census Bureau, data on spending by age reported by Yamamato (2013), and a methodology similar to that used by Yamamato, the CEA estimates that population aging added about 0.5 percent to annual growth in health care spending over the 2000-07 and 2007-10 periods and added about 0.8 percent to growth over the 2010-13 period.[5] These demographic headwinds mean that the slowdown in the growth of

---

[5] As Yamamato notes, this methodology assumes that spending does not change discontinuously at age 65 when individuals transition to Medicare. It also does not account for differences in coverage mix by age in the under-65 population. It does not appear that accounting for these factors would meaningfully alter the results, but further research in this area would be worthwhile.

health care costs for an individual of any particular age is actually slightly larger than shown in Table 4-1.[6]

The Role of the Affordable Care Act

The evidence discussed above shows that the recession is not the sole cause of the recent slow growth in health spending, and that the other factors identified to date cannot explain the magnitude or broad scope of the slowdown. What, then, is the Affordable Care Act's role in driving changes in the Nation's health care system? To be sure, the ACA is not the sole cause of the slowdown. Health care spending growth had slowed somewhat even before the ACA was passed (as shown in Table 4-1), the recession and other changes in the health system have certainly made contributions (as discussed above), and many of the ACA's reforms have yet to take full effect.

Nevertheless, the ACA's reforms aimed at driving out waste and improving quality are contributing in a meaningful way to recent slow growth in health costs—including by building on pre-existing trends in delivery system reform and initiating new ones—and are likely to make larger contributions in the future. Recent economic research also provides support for the premise that implementing reforms in Medicare can reduce the cost and improve the quality of care system-wide. This research supports the idea that the ACA will play an important role in slowing health care

---

[6] The effect of changing demographics on per beneficiary spending by particular payers may differ from the effect on the overall population. The average age of Medicare beneficiaries is currently falling as the youngest baby boomers reach age 65. Consistent with that, Levine and Buntin (2013) estimate that changes in the age mix of Medicare beneficiaries had no effect on per beneficiary growth in Medicare spending over the 2000-07 period, but subtracted 0.2 percentage points over the 2007-10 period. Calculations like those in the main text suggest that these changes in age mix *subtracted* somewhat more from growth, on the order of 0.4 percentage points, over the 2010-13 period. This represents a modest, but not trivial, share of the overall slowdown in Medicare spending growth.

In addition, changes in beneficiary mix (that are not primarily attributable to the aging of the population) appear to have had a larger effect on recent trends in per beneficiary Medicaid spending. Over the period 2000-10, Medicaid enrollment among children, parents, and pregnant women increased substantially more rapidly than did enrollment among elderly and disabled individuals (Kaiser Family Foundation, 2013b). The resulting change in enrollment mix lowered per beneficiary costs since non-elderly, non-disabled beneficiaries generally use less health care. Holahan and McMorrow (2012) estimate that this change in enrollment mix subtracted 1.5 percentage points from the annual growth of Medicaid spending per beneficiary spending over the 2000-10 period. However, enrollment data reported by the Kaiser Family Foundation suggest that, if anything, changes in enrollment mix have actually increased per beneficiary costs since 2010. Thus, adjusting for enrollment mix would make the slowdown in per beneficiary Medicaid costs over the 2010-13 period more dramatic than shown in Table 4-1.

**Box 4-2: How Will the ACA's Coverage Expansion
Affect Total Spending Growth?**

As the Affordable Care Act's coverage expansion takes effect, total national health care spending will likely grow at an elevated rate for a few years, reflecting the cost of covering an additional 25 million people (Cuckler et al. 2013; CBO 2014). This one-time increase in costs is more than justified by the benefits of bringing quality, affordable health insurance coverage to millions of Americans who lack this protection today. So the additional cost is neither a surprise, nor a cause for concern.

These increases in total national health expenditures are also not directly relevant for most individuals and employers, for whom what matters is how much they are paying in premiums or other costs. When a previously uninsured person purchases coverage through the Marketplace or receives it through Medicaid, that does increase total national health expenditures, but it has no direct effect on costs for someone who previously had coverage through their employer or the individual market.

Moreover, one-time changes of this kind will tell us nothing about the underlying trend in health spending, and it is this underlying trend that, as discussed in Section 3, will shape Americans' living standards over the long run. In addition, the ACA's Medicare reforms are slated to continue to phase in over years beyond 2014, and the ACA's mechanisms for generating new innovative reforms aimed at reducing costs and improving quality are just beginning to generate results. As a result, the savings from these and other aspects of the ACA are likely to grow substantially in the years ahead. This is an important reason why the Congressional Budget Office estimates that the extent to which the ACA will reduce the deficit grows dramatically over time (CBO 2012b).

It is also worth noting that the projected increase in growth over the next few years is not particularly large. Even after accounting for transient effects attributable to the ACA's coverage expansion, CMS projects that annual real per capita growth in national health expenditures will never exceed 3.4 percent over the next decade. As shown in Table 4-1, these rates are below the average growth rate recorded over the 2000-07 period and far below the longer-term historical average.

cost growth over the long term, but also suggests that its provider payment reforms may be having a larger-than-anticipated impact today.

Reductions in excessive Medicare payments to providers and health plans. The ACA has already had one easily quantifiable effect on the nation's health care spending: reducing excessive payments previously identified by independent experts (for example, MedPAC (2009)). The original CBO cost estimate for the ACA found that its reforms to Medicare would save $17 billion in fiscal year 2013, attributable primarily to reductions in payments to private insurers that provide coverage through Medicare Advantage and adjustments in annual updates to Medicare provider payment rates (CBO 2010a).[7] Estimated savings of $17 billion constitute about 0.6 percent of national health expenditures in 2013. Spread out over the three years from 2010 to 2013, this implies that the ACA alone accounts for a 0.2 percentage point reduction in the growth of national health expenditures over this period, making a meaningful contribution to explaining the slow growth in health spending observed over these three years. The analysis by Cutler and Sahni (2013) reaches similar conclusions. These reductions will continue to phase in over the years ahead and continue to reduce the growth of Medicare spending.

Deployment of new payment models. The ACA also includes many reforms intended to identify and promote payment models that encourage efficient care delivery, reduce care fragmentation, and reward physicians, hospitals, and others that invest in providing high-quality care rather than just a high quantity of care.

The ACA made direct changes in Medicare payment systems aimed at achieving these goals, including creating the readmissions reduction and shared savings programs discussed in detail below and various "value-based" purchasing initiatives that tie provider reimbursement to measures of the quality of the care received by patients. The ACA also provided additional financial assistance to states through Medicaid to establish health homes to improve care management for patients with chronic conditions.

In addition, the ACA created the Center for Medicare and Medicaid Innovation (the "Innovation Center") to experiment with diverse new payment approaches, including bundled payments, various accountable care models, and multi-payer initiatives, each of which will be touched on later in this section. To date, more than 50,000 health care providers from across every state are participating in an Innovation Center initiative. The Secretary of Health and Human Services has the authority to take successful pilots to scale.

Finally, through the Patient-Centered Outcomes Research Institute, the ACA is funding efforts to identify which treatments work—and for which patients—and to identify strategies for translating that evidence into practice. By giving providers the information they need to provide efficient,

---

[7] This chapter also cites a CBO estimate of the budgetary effect of repealing the ACA from July 2012, which suggests that repeal would increase Medicare spending in FY 2013 by $4 billion, a much smaller sum than the $17 billion cited here. However, as discussed in the CBO letter, because it would have been too late to unwind some ACA provisions for FY 2013 and due to other effects, this estimate does not reflect the full effect of the ACA in that year.

high-quality care, this research initiative directly complements the ACA's efforts to change provider incentives.

The full benefits of the initiatives described above will only be realized in the years to come. However, the next two subsections discuss a pair of payment reforms—the ACA's incentives to reduce hospital readmissions and its deployment of accountable care payment models—that are already beginning to show results.

Incentives to reduce hospital readmissions. The ACA made important changes in how Medicare's hospital payment system treats hospital readmissions—cases in which a patient returns to the hospital soon after being discharged. Historically, nearly one-in-five Medicare patients were readmitted within 30 days of discharge, and it is commonly believed that many of these readmissions result from low-quality care during the initial admission or poor planning for how the patient will obtain care after discharge. Prior to the ACA reform, hospitals faced no financial incentive to invest in activities aimed at reducing readmissions, and could actually be made financially worse off by doing so since they lose payment for the avoided readmissions. This misalignment of incentives likely both increased costs and reduced quality.

The ACA aims to correct these incentives by penalizing hospitals with high readmission rates for patients with a specified set of diagnoses. Many of the rules governing these penalties were finalized in August 2011. The penalties took effect at the start of FY 2013 (October 2012), but because penalties for a given fiscal year are based on hospitals' readmission rates in prior years, hospitals' incentives to begin reducing readmissions began as soon as the rules were finalized (or earlier, to the extent that hospitals anticipated the structure of the payment rules).[8] The number of conditions included in the program and the maximum penalty amount will grow over time.

Figure 4-4 provides evidence that this readmission policy has begun changing patterns of care. After having been flat for several years, overall 30-day hospital readmission rates for Medicare patients turned sharply lower soon after the program rules were finalized, and, as of July 2013, were more than one percentage points below their average level from 2007-11. From January 2012 through August 2013, this reduction corresponded to 130,000 avoided readmissions (CMS, 2013a). The sharp change in trend—and its timing—implies that the readmissions program played an important role in causing these changes, although other efforts to reduce readmissions were underway during this period as well. Among those other activities were efforts by the Department of Health and Human Services efforts to actively

---

[8] Under current program rules, a hospital's penalties in a given fiscal year are based on its readmission rate during the three-year period that ended five quarters earlier.

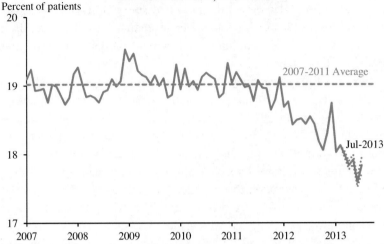

Figure 4-4
**Medicare 30-Day, All-Condition Hospital
Readmission Rate, 2007–2013**

Percent of patients

2007-2011 Average

Jul-2013

Notes: Recent months are based on preliminary data. The dotted blue lines depict the range in which
the final estimates are likely to fall.
Source: Centers for Medicare and Medicaid Services, Office of Information Products and Data
Analytics.

engage hospitals and community-based organizations in improving discharge processes through the Partnership for Patients and the Community-
Based Care Transitions Program (Gerhardt et al. 2013).

Accountable care payment models. Another important ongoing
ACA reform is the creation of "accountable care" payment models through
the Medicare Shared Savings Program and the Innovation Center. These
programs seek to realign provider incentives to encourage provision of
efficient, high-quality care. Under fee-for-service payment systems, providers delivering more efficient care often end up financially worse off because
lower service volume translates into lower payments from Medicare. In
addition, since provider payments were based on service volume, the pre-
ACA payment system gave providers no direct financial incentive to deliver
high-quality care. Prevailing fee-for-service payment systems also pay each
provider separately without regard to how services furnished by that provider fit into the patient's broader plan of care, and thus create no incentive
for efficient coordination of care across providers.

Under these accountable care programs, a provider or group of providers can seek designation as an Accountable Care Organization (ACO).
ACOs are eligible to share in the savings created when they reduce the cost
of caring for patients assigned to them, which encourages providers to be
efficient in the use of additional services. In addition, because the ACOs earn

shared savings based on the total costs of a patient's care across all providers and not merely the costs for any particular visit or procedure, ACOs have incentives to invest in care coordination and avoid duplication. Perhaps most important, ACOs must achieve designated benchmarks for the quality of care received by their patients in order to be eligible for shared savings, which provides strong incentives to ensure that patients receive high-quality care.

Today, more than 360 organizations serving 5.3 million Medicare beneficiaries have adopted the ACO model, and the number of beneficiaries covered will likely grow in the years ahead. A preliminary evaluation of the Pioneer ACO program (the Innovation Center ACO program for large and advanced systems) found that costs for beneficiaries aligned with Pioneer ACOs grew more slowly from 2011 to 2012 than costs for similar beneficiaries not aligned with ACOs (L&M Policy Research, 2013). The annual cost savings for each enrollee aligned with a Pioneer ACO in 2012, the first year of the program, were estimated to be at least $150, more than 1 percent of average Medicare spending per beneficiary in that year. In addition, overall, the ACOs performed better than fee-for-service benchmarks on all quality measures for which comparable data are available (CMS 2013b). Academic research on similar private models also suggests that these payment models can achieve their intended purpose of reducing costs while improving quality (Song et al. 2012).

The Innovation Center is experimenting with related payment models through its Bundled Payment for Care Improvement Initiative, which got underway in 2013.[9] Under these models, Medicare will make a single "bundled" payment for all services provided during an "episode" of care connected to a hospital stay, rather than paying separately for each service provided during that episode. In the model using the most comprehensive bundle definition, this payment will cover the hospital stay, physician services provided during the stay, and post-hospital care. The Innovation Center is also testing models with narrower bundles covering only services provided during the hospital stay or only services provided after the hospital stay. Although the details vary across payment models, the bundled payment will then be allocated across the participating providers according to

---

[9] These models build on several earlier Medicare demonstration projects, with the most similar being the Acute Care Episode (ACE) demonstration, a much smaller demonstration that concluded in 2013.

agreements among the providers themselves.[10] The models are being tested for a set of common types of hospital care episodes that account for a significant fraction of all hospital stays.

Much like the accountable care payment models, these bundled payment models encourage providers to be more efficient because providers receive no additional payment for providing additional services (if the service is included in the bundle). Similarly, because all providers involved in an episode of hospital care are jointly accountable for the total cost of the care episode, the bundled payment structure gives providers strong incentives to coordinate their activities, with attendant benefits for efficiency and quality of care. Because of this scope for increased efficiency, Medicare can (and does under the models being tested) set the bundled payment amount below the total amount it would pay under the existing fee-for-service payment systems. The efficiency gains from these sources could be substantial. CBO recently estimated that if a bundled payment model that covered services provided during and after the hospital stay and used a 5 percent savings target were phased in nationwide starting in 2017, the savings to Medicare would total $47 billion over 10 years (CBO 2013c).

Recent research on cross-payer "spillovers." In evaluating the direct effects of the ACA's Medicare and Medicaid reforms so far and considering their likely effects going forward, an important question is how these reforms will influence the rest of the health care system. Recent empirical work in economics and health policy strengthens the premise that reforms to public-sector health programs that reduce waste and improve quality will have spillover benefits for the private sector.[11]

---

[10] The bundled payment is administered in different ways under the different models. In the model covering only services during the hospital stay, the bundled payment is paid "prospectively" to a single entity (e.g. the hospital), which is then responsible for paying the other providers involved in episode. In the other models, Medicare continues to pay providers according to the existing fee-for-service rules. If total fee-for-service payments are below the bundled payment amount, Medicare pays the excess to a designated provider, which distributes that excess among the other involved providers. If total fee-for-service payments are above the bundled payment amount, the reverse occurs. In principle, the two structures change provider incentives in similar ways.

[11] This growing literature is contrary to the traditional view in some health policy circles, which held that efforts to achieve savings in Medicare (or Medicaid) cause medical care providers to increase the prices they charge to private insurers in order to recover the lost revenue, and, thus, reforms in Medicare simply "shift" costs to the private sector rather than reducing them. The empirical support for this view was always inconsistent, and, as argued by Dranove (1988) and Morrissey (1994), this view has important conceptual shortcomings. In particular, for hospitals to be able to increase the prices charged to private payers after a reduction in Medicare payment rates, they must have been willingly charging a price below what the market would bear prior to the reduction in Medicare rates. For a comprehensive overview of this literature, particularly the older literature, see Frakt (2011; 2013).

In particular, various recent studies suggest that efforts by Medicare to reduce excessive payments for particular services are likely to generate corresponding savings for private insurers and their enrollees. Clemens and Gottlieb (2013) study how the prices that private insurers pay to physicians change when Medicare changes its prices, exploiting a natural experiment created by regional differences in the effect of earlier reforms to the way Medicare pays physicians. They find that when Medicare reduces the price it pays for services, private insurers are able to reduce the amount they pay for care by similar amounts.

White (2013) and White and Wu (2013) undertake a similar analysis focused on Medicare payment to hospitals that exploits natural experiments created by cross-hospital differences in the effect of earlier Medicare payment changes. White (2013) finds that when Medicare reduces its payment rates, private payers reduce their payment rates by approximately 77 percent of that amount. White and Wu (2013) find that for each dollar of Medicare savings, private insurers realize additional savings of 55 cents.

The implications of these estimates are striking. For example, the $17 billion in Medicare savings estimated to have been achieved in FY 2013 as a result of reducing excessive Medicare payments. Using the same logic applied previously, these estimated savings correspond to a 0.2 percentage point reduction in the average growth of health care prices over the period 2010-13. If just half of these price reductions spilled over to the rest of the health care system to the extent estimated by White (2013), then the implied reduction in health care inflation economy-wide due to these Medicare changes would be about 0.5 percent.[12] In this scenario, the ACA would be playing a significant role in driving the observed slow growth in health care prices—representing about half of the recent slowdown in health care inflation relative to general price inflation.[13]

Potentially even more important, the work by Clemens and Gottlieb provides evidence that the benefits of the ACA's improvements to the *structure* of public-sector payment systems may be realized system-wide, not just among enrollees of those programs. Again focusing on Medicare

[12] The reductions in excessive payments to Medicare Advantage plans are less likely to "spill over" to general private-sector payment rates (although to the extent they lead MA-participating insurers to negotiate lower provider payment rates, such spillovers could occur under certain models of spillovers). Since the Medicare Advantage reductions account for about half of the estimated $17 billion in payment reductions in 2013, the calculation in the text assumes that only half of this reduction would spill over.

[13] Of course, effect on total spending may be smaller or larger to the extent that these price changes induce changes in volume. Indeed, the estimates of White and Wu, referenced above, as well as estimates reported by He and Mellor (2012) suggest that volume changes will generally work to offset these price spillovers. However, even under the estimates of White and Wu (2013), the savings to private insurers as a result of Medicare changes would be substantial.

payment for physician services, they show that Medicare payment changes that increase payment for some services and reduce payment for others tend to be matched by private insurers. Clemens and Gottlieb's results provide empirical support for the widely believed notion that Medicare's payment structure serves as the "starting point" in negotiations between providers and private insurers in many circumstances, in which case changes in Medicare will reasonably quickly get picked up in the private sector as well. This evidence is consistent with historical experience. Medicare introduced "prospective" payment for inpatient services in the 1980s, under which all care during an inpatient admission was covered via a single payment determined based on the patient's diagnosis; virtually all private insurers pay hospitals using this type of system today.

Some recent evidence suggests that spillover benefits from the ACA's public-sector payment reforms may occur even if private payers do not directly adopt these payment models. McWilliams et al. (2013) study the Alternative Quality Contract (AQC)—a contract similar to accountable care payment structures currently being deployed by CMS–that Blue Cross Blue Shield of Massachusetts has been experimenting with since 2009. Research cited above (Song et al. 2012) finds that the AQC reduces costs and improves quality for patients whose care is directly subject to the contract. The research by McWilliams et al. finds, however, that patients associated with AQC-participating providers whose care was *not* subject to the contract (in this case, Medicare patients) also experienced improvements. In this case, the cost savings amounted to 3.4 percent, on average, and was accompanied by improvement on some quality measures. The results may arise because providers adopt a single "practice style" for all their patients, so that when incentives from one induce a provider to change its approach in ways that improve efficiency or quality, all patients seen by that provider benefit.

Taken together, the evidence of cross-payer spillovers reviewed above suggests that not only are reforms to the structure of the public-sector payment systems helpful in reducing costs and improving quality system-wide, but that the public sector may be essential to fully realizing the potential for improvement. In economic terms, the presence of spillovers means that payment system reforms are "public goods"—investments that generate benefits for many people other than the purchaser and for which the purchaser cannot capture all the resulting benefits (Clemens and Gottlieb 2013). Because no individual investor captures the full benefits of investment in public goods, the private market generates too few of them. As with other public goods, one solution to the underinvestment is for the government to invest directly, in this case by implementing reforms through Medicare and Medicaid.

Recognizing the importance of other payers' decisions in determining providers' response to new payment arrangements, CMS has launched demonstration projects that actively engage multiple payers. Incorporating multiple payers into reform efforts at the outset may increase the possibility that the payment models that emerge can easily cross payer boundaries, once proven. These initiatives also recognize that engaging private payers in reform efforts is important for Medicare and Medicaid beneficiaries themselves, in light of the evidence described above that spillovers can run in both directions: from Medicare and Medicaid to the private sector, and vice versa.

Two multi-payer initiatives merit special mention. Through the Comprehensive Primary Care Initiative, CMS has enlisted public and private payers in eight states to join with Medicare to invest in primary care practices, with the potential for shared savings after two years. Another promising effort is the State Innovation Models Initiative, which provides grants to states that wish to make statewide, multi-payer changes to provider payment systems. With support from this program, Oregon has embarked upon an effort to move its Medicaid beneficiaries, State employees, and individuals who have purchased coverage through the state's ACA-created health insurance marketplace into ACO-like payment models. Arkansas has undertaken an initiative involving public and private payers aimed at ensuring that half of Arkansans have access to a patient-centered medical home by 2016, and expanding its existing system of episode-based payment.

ECONOMIC BENEFITS OF SLOW HEALTH SPENDING GROWTH

Slower growth in health care costs has the potential to bring three important economic benefits: higher living standards; lower deficits, potentially generating faster economic growth; and, at least in the short run, higher employment. This section of the report considers the implications of slower growth in health care costs across these variables.

Higher Living Standards

All else equal, when the health sector consumes less of the Nation's output, more resources are available for meeting other needs. As a result, reductions in health care spending that stem from improving efficiency or eliminating low-value care have the potential to improve living standards. Because of the large share of the Nation's resources devoted to health care, even relatively modest reductions can have very large effects on economic well-being.

Box 4-3: The Cost Slowdown and ACA Reforms are Reducing Medicare Beneficiaries' Out-of-Pocket Costs

As discussed in the text, reductions in Medicare spending growth have substantial benefits for the Federal budget. Lower growth also has substantial benefits for Medicare beneficiaries, both because it reduces their cost-sharing obligations and because many pay a premium to enroll in Medicare Parts B and D, and premiums are set to cover a specified fraction of the government's cost of providing that coverage. Due in large part to the broader trends discussed in this chapter, the base Medicare Part D premium is down 5 percent in inflation-adjusted terms relative to 2010 (Figure 4-5). Similarly, the standard Medicare Part B premium for 2014 is essentially unchanged in inflation-adjusted terms relative to 2009. (The standard Medicare Part B premium is down 11 percent in inflation-adjusted terms relative to 2010. However, it is more meaningful to compare to 2009; for technical reasons, many beneficiaries paid the 2009 premium in 2010 and 2011, and, for these same reasons, the standard Part B premium is anomalously high in those years (SSA 2013).)

At the same time as Medicare premiums have remained flat, features of the ACA are directly reducing out-of-pocket costs for Medicare enrollees. Under the ACA, Medicare beneficiaries receive a wide range of preventive services without cost-sharing requirements. CMS estimates that 34 million Medicare beneficiaries received at least one such service during 2012 (CMS 2013c). Through a combination of discounts on brand-name drugs and additional coverage, the ACA is also closing the "donut hole" in Medicare Part D—a range of drug spending over which beneficiaries enrolled in the "standard" Medicare Part D plans were previously required to cover the full cost of their medications. CMS estimates that 3.5 million Medicare beneficiaries who reached the coverage gap realized average savings of $706 on brand-name drugs in 2012, while 2.8 million Medicare beneficiaries realized savings of nearly $40 per person on generic drugs (CMS 2013c).

These benefits accrue to families through two primary channels. First, standard economics implies that, in the long run, reductions in the cost of providing benefits such as health insurance are passed through to workers in the form of higher wages since employers must compete for workers (Summers 1989). This theoretical prediction has received empirical support (Gruber and Krueger 1991; Gruber 1994; Baicker and Chandra 2006). Second, as discussed in detail below, lower health care costs have significant benefits for the Federal budget, which ultimately permit lower taxes or increased investment in other valued public services.

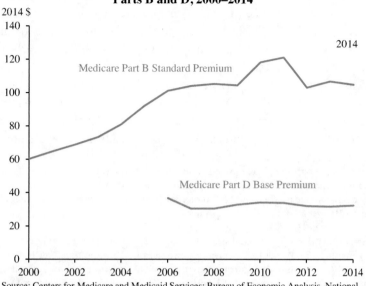

Figure 4-5
**Inflation-Adjusted Premiums for Medicare
Parts B and D, 2000–2014**

2014 $

Medicare Part B Standard Premium

2014

Medicare Part D Base Premium

2000   2002   2004   2006   2008   2010   2012   2014

Source: Centers for Medicare and Medicaid Services; Bureau of Economic Analysis, National
Income and Product Accounts; CEA calculations.

One straightforward way of illustrating the magnitude of the potential impacts is to consider the effect of continuing the slow growth of the last few years. To that end, recall from Table 4-1 that national health expenditures have grown at a 1.2 percent real per capita annual rate from 2010-13, whereas health spending grew at a 4.0 percent rate from 2000-07. Suppose that even just one-third of that slowdown continued, so that instead of returning to the recent historical rate of 4.0 percent, real per capita health care costs instead grew at a 3.1 percent rate, similar to the rate projected in the recent work by Chandra, Holmes and Skinner (2013). Under this illustrative scenario, the savings after a decade would amount to about $1,200 per person. As discussed above, these savings would materialize primarily in the form of higher wages and lower State and Federal costs.

Lower Deficits

In 2013, the Federal Government devoted 22 percent of the U.S. budget, or 4.6 percent of GDP, to Medicare and Medicaid. For this reason, the future path of health care costs has major implications for the long-term budget outlook.

Over the last three years, CBO has made a series of downward revisions to its forecast of future spending on Medicare and Medicaid (CBO

2010a; 2011; 2012c; 2013a; 2014), which are depicted in Figure 4-6. From the projections CBO published in August 2010 to its most recent set of projections in February 2014, CBO has reduced its estimate of Medicare and Medicaid spending in 2020 (the latest year covered by all of the projections examined here) by $168 billion and 0.5 percent of GDP.[14] This $168 billion represents a 13 percent reduction in spending relative to CBO's earlier projection of spending on these programs.

These reductions primarily reflect lower projections of future growth in health care costs.[15] To that point, in a recent presentation, CBO Director Douglas Elmendorf commented: "The slowdown in health care cost growth has been sufficiently broad and persistent to persuade us to make significant

---

[14] In July 2013, the Bureau of Economic Analysis (BEA) released comprehensive revisions to the National Income and Product Accounts that increased BEA's estimate of GDP in recent years by more than 3 percent. CBO projections of GDP released before and after these revisions are, therefore, not directly comparable.

The figures reported in the text and displayed in Figure 4-6 account for this issue in the following manner. For May 2013, CBO released two sets of GDP projections, one before and one after the BEA revisions; the figures shown use the GDP projections released after the BEA revisions. For earlier CBO baselines, CEA adjusted CBO's projections of GDP upward by the ratio of CBO's post- and pre-revision May 2013 GDP projections. Without these adjustments, the reduction in projected Medicare and Medicaid spending as a share of GDP in 2020 from CBO's August 2010 baseline to its February 2014 baseline would be 0.6 percent, rather than the 0.5 percent reported in the text, and the decline in Medicare and Medicaid spending shown in Figure 4-6 would be larger.

[15] Several factors other than recent slow growth in health care costs have affected CBO's projections of Medicare and Medicaid spending over this period. These factors work in different directions. First, CBO has revised its general economic projections in ways that, on net, increase projected future Medicare and Medicaid spending by around $25 billion. Second, CBO estimates issued after June 2012 incorporate the Supreme Court decision in NFIB v. Sebelius. CBO materials indicate that this ruling reduced projected Medicaid spending in 2020 by roughly $30 billion as of July 2012, although this figure has likely fluctuated as CBO has changed its assumptions about how many states will adopt the Medicaid expansion. For more detailed information, see CBO's analysis of the budgetary effects of the Supreme Court decision (CBO 2012c) and CBO's March 2012 baseline (CBO 2012a). Third, projections issued in August 2011 and later incorporate the effects of sequestration under the Budget Control Act, which CBO estimated in May 2013 would reduce Medicare spending by $11 billion in 2020 (CBO 2013a).

CBO itself has cited somewhat larger figures when discussing the extent to which it has revised down its projections in response to slower health care cost growth. For example, CBO recently reported that slower growth in health costs has led it to revise down its estimate of Medicare spending in 2020 by $109 billion since March 2010 (CBO 2014), whereas the comparable figure based on the approach in the text is $87 billion. CBO's figure is larger because it excludes the changes due to updated economic projections discussed above, because it considers a slightly different time period, and because its figure appears to apply to gross, rather than net, Medicare spending. On the other hand, CBO's figure excludes the effect of sequestration, which partially offsets these differences. The estimates presented in the text were chosen over the estimates presented by CBO to simplify exposition and presentation.

**Box 4-4: Premiums on the ACA Marketplaces
are Lower than Projected**

The Congressional Budget Office recently reported that actual 2014 premiums on the ACA Marketplaces are about 15 percent below its earlier estimates (CBO 2014). This has two important benefits. First, lower premiums will mean lower costs for many families, including those with incomes too high to qualify for premium tax credits and those that wish to purchase more comprehensive coverage than that offered by the second-lowest cost silver plan. Second, lower premiums will result in lower Federal costs for premium tax credits and cost-sharing assistance. While CBO states that it has not yet decided whether to mark down its premium estimates for years beyond 2014, estimates by Spiro and Gruber (2013) suggest that such a revision would result in Federal savings of more than $100 billion over ten years.

While it is not yet fully understood why premiums on the ACA Marketplaces are lower than expected, this may be another benefit of the recent slow growth in health care spending. The Marketplaces may also have proved better than expected at encouraging insurers to compete on price (Spiro and Gruber 2013). A related possibility is that the Marketplaces attracted greater-than-expected participation by insurers; premiums appear to be substantially lower in areas with more participating insurers (ASPE 2013).

downward revisions to our projections of Federal health care spending" (Elmendorf 2013).

For comparison, in CBO's most recent long-term budget outlook, CBO projected that the current law 25-year fiscal gap—a measure of the annual fiscal adjustment required to stabilize the debt as a share of the economy over the next 25 years—is just 0.9 percent of GDP (CBO 2013b). Without these recent improvements in the outlook for Federal health spending, the Nation's medium-run fiscal problem would therefore be about half again as large.

It is important to note that the reductions in projected Medicare and Medicaid spending described above are separate from the deficit reduction that CBO estimates will occur as a direct result of the ACA. The most recent CBO estimates indicate that the ACA will reduce the deficit by about $100 billion over the decade 2013-22, and that it will reduce the deficit, on average, by about 0.5 percent of GDP in the subsequent decade (CBO 2012b). CBO notes that these deficit-reducing effects are likely to continue to grow in following decades.

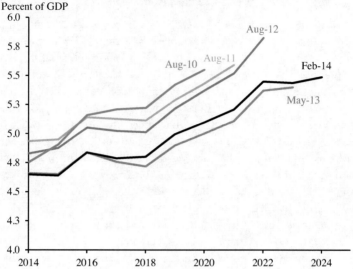

Figure 4-6
Recent CBO Projections of Medicare and Medicaid Outlays

Percent of GDP

Notes: Medicare outlays reflect spending net of offsetting receipts. Medicaid spending reflects Federal spending only.
Sources: Congressional Budget Office, Budget and Economic Outlook; CEA calculations.

Higher Employment and Economic Growth

Slower growth in health care costs reduces the growth of the health insurance premiums paid by employers. As discussed above, in the long run, because employers must compete for workers, reductions in the cost of health care are likely to be passed through to workers in the form of higher wages. Thus, over the long run, changes in the growth rate of health care costs are unlikely to substantially affect employer's hiring costs and decisions.[16]

In the short run, however, the picture may differ. Wage setting is subject to various "rigidities" that mean that lower health insurance costs may not be fully passed through in the short and medium run, potentially reducing employer costs and spurring hiring (Sommers 2005). Rigidities of this kind may be particularly important in the aftermath of the 2007-09 recession, as abnormally low inflation has increased the importance of constraints on the adjustment of nominal wages (Daly et al. 2012).

---

[16] Faster growth in health insurance costs could reduce employment through another mechanism. In particular, if workers do not value the additional health spending, then the combination of more expensive health insurance and lower wages could make employment less attractive over time, inducing them to reduce their labor supply. Because evidence suggests that workers' labor supply is only modestly responsive to the returns to work, these effects are likely to be modest in size.

There is relatively little empirical literature on the effect of slower growth in employer health insurance premiums on employment, and there is no consensus among economists about the likely size of these effects. There are, however, at least two empirical studies suggesting that these effects could be substantial.

Baicker and Chandra (2006) use variation in employer health insurance costs resulting from within-state changes in medical malpractice costs over time to estimate the effect of higher health insurance premiums on employment. They find that a 10 percent reduction in insurance premiums increases the share of working-age individuals who are employed by 1.2 percentage points. This estimate suggests that the recent slowdown in the growth of health insurance premiums could have had a substantial positive effect on employment.

Sood, Ghosh, and Escarce (2009) take an alternative approach to quantifying the effect of faster premium growth on employment. Specifically, they examine whether industries that provide insurance to a large share of their employees experience relatively lower employment growth during periods when health costs are growing particularly rapidly. They find that, for an industry that provides health insurance to all of its workers, increasing health insurance premiums by 1 percent reduces the industry's employment by 1.6 percent relative to an industry that insures none of its workers.

Translating the Sood, Ghosh, and Escarce estimates into effects on aggregate employment is difficult because their results could arise either because higher health insurance costs reduce employment overall or because they cause a reallocation of employment from high-coverage industries to low-coverage industries. Cutler and Sood (2010) make one set of plausible assumptions about the importance of these two types of employment changes, and given their estimates of the effect of the ACA on the path of health care costs, find that the ACA will increase job growth by 250,000 to 400,000 a year by the second half of this decade.

In the longer run, lower deficits due to the ACA and the slowdown in health costs also have the potential to improve economic growth. Reductions in long-term deficits increase national saving, which increases capital accumulation and reduces foreign borrowing, and thereby increase national income and living standards over time. As discussed in detail in a 2009 CEA report on the potential benefits of health care reform for the economy, this means that even modest sustained reductions in health care cost growth can generate substantial economic benefits (CEA 2009).

CONCLUSION

The evidence is clear that recent trends in health care spending and price growth reflect, at least in part, ongoing structural changes in the health care sector. The slowdown may be raising employment today and, if continued, will substantially raise living standards in the years ahead. The evidence also suggests that the Affordable Care Act is already contributing to lower spending and price growth, and that these effects will grow in the years ahead, bringing lower-cost, higher-quality care to Medicare and Medicaid beneficiaries and to the health system as a whole. But realizing these benefits will require additional action, including continuing aggressive implementation of the ACA's reforms, taking full advantage of the ACA's mechanisms for developing and deploying innovative new payment models, and pressing forward with new efforts that build on the ACA's approach to reducing health spending system-wide, such as the reform proposals in the President's recent budgets.

CHAPTER 5

FOSTERING PRODUCTIVITY GROWTH

In 1870, a family farmer planting corn in Iowa would have expected to grow 35 bushels an acre. Today, that settler's descendant can grow nearly 180 bushels an acre and uses sophisticated equipment to work many times the acreage of his or her forbearer. Because of higher yields and the use of time-saving machinery, the quantity of corn produced by an hour of farm labor has risen from an estimated 0.64 bushel in 1870 to more than 60 bushels in 2013. This 90-fold increase in labor productivity—that is, bushels of corn (real output) an hour—corresponds to an annual rate of increase of 3.2 percent compounded over 143 years. In 1870, a bushel of corn sold for approximately $0.80, about two days of earnings for a typical manufacturing worker; today, that bushel sells for approximately $4.30, or 12 minutes worth of average earnings.[1]

This extraordinary increase in corn output, fall in the real price of corn, and the resulting improvement in physical well-being, did not come about because we are stronger, harder-working, or tougher today than the early settlers who first plowed the prairies. Rather, through a combination of invention, more advanced equipment, and better education, the Iowa farmer today uses more productive strains of corn and sophisticated farming methods to get more output an acre. Today's farmer harnesses more capital equipment, such as advanced planters and combines, to plant more acres, and has the know-how to operate this sophisticated equipment.

Technological advances such as corn hybridization, fertilizer technology, disease resistance, and mechanical planting and harvesting have resulted from decades of research and development. While the government has supported some of this research and its dissemination—for example, through basic biological research and land-grant universities—much of this research occurred in the private sector. However, the government has

---

[1] Sources: Parker and Klein (1966), 1870 *Census of Manufacturers*, Iowa State University Extension Service (2013), Bureau of Labor Statistics, USDA *Economic Research Service*.

facilitated this private-sector technological innovation by providing the infrastructure to transport and sell increasing quantities of the products and a regulatory and legal environment, such as the U.S. patent system, which clarifies and enforces rights to inventions (more generally, to intellectual property) so that the private sector can reap the rewards of research. These property rights create incentives for innovators, while also allowing others to build on their inventions. The improvements in productivity made possible by technological progress have appeared not just in agriculture, but also throughout the U.S. economy.

The framework of government support for technological innovation is facing new challenges that stem from an ever-changing scientific and legal landscape. Many of these challenges center on the best way to support and encourage development of intellectual property which now encompasses improvements, not just to tractor design, but also technological changes to the software that optimizes its performance. Farmers can now use the Internet to do market research, purchase inputs, make direct sales, and participate in online crop and livestock auctions. Other challenges involve issues surrounding the allocation of the electromagnetic spectrum in a way that supports the efficient development of new wireless and communications technologies that will improve productivity and connectivity—for the farmer in the combine's cab as well as for millions of other consumers and businesses—while weighing national security and other concerns. These challenges also include striking the appropriate balance between the need for the government to support fundamental research, which can have large positive externalities that will not be realized by any individual private actor, and the importance of private-sector innovation in driving technology forward.

Another set of challenges relates to how the gains from innovation are shared. In the decades following World War II, productivity improvements translated relatively automatically into compensation increases for families across the income spectrum. But starting in the 1970s, inequality began its relentless rise and productivity growth became increasingly disconnected from compensation growth for typical families. The trends in inequality are related to the trends in productivity, as well as to other broad economic trends. Some of the technological changes over the past three decades, especially those related to information technology, have raised the relative reward to skills obtained through advanced academic study. Thus, the slowing growth of educational attainment both potentially slows innovation and increases inequality by raising the returns to the most highly educated workers. Although expanding the size of markets through globalization can help increase the productivity of the economy, it can also create challenges for inequality.

This chapter begins with a review of the history of productivity growth since World War II, emerging inequality trends, and the government's role in fostering productivity growth. It then focuses on two important current issues in more detail: wired and wireless broadband infrastructure and the efficient allocation of the electromagnetic spectrum; and, new challenges to the U.S. patent system posed by standard-essential patents and patent-assertion entities.

TRENDS IN TOTAL FACTOR PRODUCTIVITY

The most commonly used measure of productivity is *labor productivity*—that is, real output per hour worked. Over the long run, improvements in labor productivity translate into growth of output, wages, and income. Labor productivity can grow for multiple reasons: more capital per worker (increased capital intensity), increased labor skills (a more experienced workforce, more and better education and training), and technological advances that improve the quality and productivity for a given level of capital and labor skills (inventions, technological progress, process improvements, and other factors).

Because of the importance of technological progress in enhancing long-run growth, economists also use another measure of productivity called *total factor productivity*, or TFP, which proxies for the effect of technological progress. From 1948 to 2012, labor productivity growth in the private nonfarm business sector has averaged 2.2 percent per year, and total factor productivity growth, as measured by the series on multifactor productivity produced by the Bureau of Labor Statistics (BLS), has averaged 1.1 percent per year. This growth of productivity has not been constant, however, and can usefully be thought of as occurring in three episodes: a period of fast productivity growth through the early 1970s, a period of slow productivity growth through the mid-1990s, and a period of somewhat faster productivity growth since then, but still not as fast as in the 1950s and 1960s.

Labor Productivity, Total Factor Productivity, and Multifactor Productivity

The growth rate of labor productivity equals the growth rate of output, minus the growth rate of labor input (worker hours), thus yielding the growth rate of output per worker hour. In contrast, the growth rate of TFP is the growth rate of output, minus the growth rate of output that would be expected solely from the growth rate of the inputs to production. The resulting gap between the actual growth rate of output and the growth rate arising solely because of the growth of inputs is also known as the Solow residual, and is a measure of how well those inputs are combined. Thus, the growth rate of TFP tracks a broadly defined concept of technological change that encompasses scientific innovation and invention, managerial innovations, effects of reorganization of the production process, and other efficiency improvements that do not accrue uniquely to a single measured input.

The concept of total factor productivity is appealing because it estimates the contribution of technological developments to economic growth, and because it can be applied at the level of an industry as well as to the overall economy. In practice, measuring TFP poses several challenges. First, TFP is not observed directly and instead must be estimated using measured inputs and estimates of how the inputs contribute to output. Second, the inputs discussed so far have been capital and labor, but other inputs to production also include, in particular, energy, materials, and business services. Third, for a given level of other inputs, output can increase by hiring better-trained or higher-skilled workers; so for the purpose of measuring TFP, the desired concept of labor input captures changes in both the quantity and quality of labor input. Because labor quality is not observed, proxies such as age and education must be used. Both academics and the U.S. Government have tackled these and other measurement challenges, and have developed estimates of the growth of TFP. This chapter uses an estimate of TFP produced by the Bureau of Labor Statistics called *multifactor productivity*, or MFP, which is described in Box 5-1.[2]

Postwar U.S. Productivity Growth

According to the BLS measure of labor productivity shown in Table 5-1, an American worker could produce more than four times as much output per hour in 2012 as in 1948.[3] Because MFP takes into account the

---

[2] One of the many other challenges in estimating total factor productivity is that the intensity of utilization of inputs varies over the business cycle. For example, because hiring and training workers is expensive, firms might retain some workers in a mild downturn, so that fluctuations in output are greater than fluctuations in employment (a relationship which, when recast in terms of the unemployment rate, is known as Okun's Law). The BLS MFP series does not adjust for changes in factor utilization, which can produce cyclical fluctuations in MFP. Basu, Fernald, and Kimball (2006) provide an approach to adjusting for such cyclical variation, and a quarterly TFP series produced using their method is currently maintained by the Federal Reserve Bank of San Francisco (Fernald 2012).

[3] This discussion of postwar productivity performance cites statistics for nonfarm private businesses. Recall the earlier discussion about how productivity growth in farming allowed fewer resources to be devoted to it. By 1947, farming accounted for less than a nine percent share of GDP. Today that share is about one percent.

Box 5-1: Measuring Multifactor Productivity

The Bureau of Labor Statistics (BLS) publishes annual data on multifactor productivity, covering the private business sector, the private nonfarm business sector, the manufacturing sector, and 18 industries within the manufacturing sector.

Private business-sector output is a chain-type, annual-weighted (Fisher-Ideal) index constructed after excluding general government, nonprofit institutions, private households (including owner-occupied housing), and government enterprises from gross domestic product (GDP). The input measure is an aggregation of two inputs, labor and capital. Labor input is obtained by chained Tornqvist aggregation of the hours worked in private business by all persons, classified by age, education, and gender with weights determined by each group's share of total labor compensation. Capital inputs are measured based on the flow of services derived from physical assets. For each of 60 industries in the private-business sector, quantities of each capital asset are aggregated into a Tornqvist index, using estimated rental prices. Current-dollar capital costs are found by multiplying the rental price for each asset by the asset's constant-dollar stock, adjusting for capital composition effects. Finally, the combined input (labor and capital) measure is constructed via another Tornqvist index, taking as weights each inputs' share of total costs derived from the National Income and Product Accounts.

Manufacturing is treated somewhat differently. The output measure, known as sectoral output, is the value of production shipped to purchasers outside the domestic industry, either to satisfy final demand or to use as an input in other industries. Because additional inputs to manufacturing can be tracked, the input measures available include not just capital and labor, but also energy, non-energy materials, and purchased business services input. Intra-industry purchases are removed to avoid double counting. The resulting aggregate input is referred to by the acronym KLEMS—capital (K), labor (L), energy (E), materials (M) and services (S). Given these inputs and outputs, multifactor productivity is computed for 18 3-digit and 86 4-digit North American Industry Classification System (NAICS) manufacturing industries and for the manufacturing sector as a whole using the Tornqvist aggregation methods described above for the private business-sector manufacturing.

growth of capital and other factors, labor productivity growth generally exceeds MFP growth. For example, even absent technological change, labor can be more productive simply by using more capital; that is, by increasing the capital-labor ratio or so-called capital deepening. Mathematically, the growth rate of labor productivity is the sum of the MFP growth rate, the

Table 5–1
Sources of Productivity Improvement, Nonfarm Private Business, 1948–2012

Source	Improvement (multiple)	Contribution to Labor Productivity Growth (percent)
Composition of Labor	1.15	10
Capital	1.74	38
MFP	2.10	52
Labor Productivity	4.21	100

Source: Bureau of Labor Statistics, Productivity and Costs, Multifactor Productivity.

contribution of changes in labor quality (as measured by changes in the composition of the workforce), and the contribution of the growth in the amount of capital per worker.[4] The final column of Table 5-1 gives this decomposition, showing that 10 percent of the growth in labor productivity is due to improvements in the composition of labor (primarily greater educational attainment), 38 percent is due to increases in the amount of capital the worker has at his or her disposal, and 52 percent is due to increases in broad technological progress as measured by MFP.

The growth rates of the BLS measures of labor productivity and multifactor productivity have varied over time and are shown in Figure 5-1. Over the past 60 years, labor productivity has on average grown just over 1 percentage point faster than MFP: from 1953-2012, labor productivity grew at an annual rate of 2.2 percent per year, and MFP grew at an annual average rate of 1.1 percent per year.

As can be seen in Figure 5-1, both labor productivity and MFP are quite volatile from year to year. One reason for this volatility is measurement error in the estimation of both series; indeed, proper measurement of the inputs and outputs is a daunting task and for this reason alone not too much should be read into the growth of productivity in any one year. Another reason is that these series, and the gap between them, varies cyclically. For example, MFP growth fell—in fact, took on negative values—during the recessions that started in 1969, 1980-81, 1990, and 2007. These negative values do not mean that, during recessions, firms make negative technological

---

[4] Suppose aggregate production can be represented by the Cobb-Douglas production function, $Y = AL^{\alpha}K^{1-\alpha}$, where Y is real output, L is labor input measured in labor-quality units, K is capital, and A summarizes the contribution of technology to production, that is, A is TFP, and α is a constant. Then output per worker-hour (H) is $Y/H = A(L/H)^{\alpha}(K/H)^{1-\alpha}$. Thus the annual growth of output per worker, that is, the growth of labor productivity, is the sum of the growth of A, that is, the growth of TFP, plus α times the growth of L/H, that is, the growth of labor quality per worker-hour, plus $1-\alpha$ times the growth of K/H, that is, the growth of the capital-labor ratio. By using Tornqvist aggregation, the BLS MFP measure allows shares (α) to change over time and does not require an aggregate Cobb-Douglas production function.

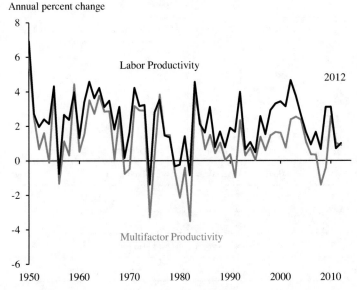

Figure 5-1
Nonfarm Private Business Productivity Growth, 1949 –2012

Annual percent change

Source: Bureau of Labor Statistics, Productivity and Costs, Multifactor Productivity.

progress or collectively forget about the innovations they have produced over the preceding years. Rather, such declines in MFP could come about from changes in relative prices, so that existing methods of production are no longer the optimal way to combine inputs to produce output. Negative MFP growth can also arise from variation in the utilization rates of capital and labor over the business cycle.

From the perspective of policies to foster long-term economic growth, these annual and cyclical fluctuations are less relevant than long-term trends in the growth rates of productivity. Figure 5-2 shows a centered 15-year moving average of the growth rates of labor productivity and MFP; and, Table 5-2 summarizes the compound annual growth rates of these series over 10- and 20-year periods ending in 2012, as well as the 60-year period from 1953-2012.

Table 5-2 and Figure 5-2 tell a similar story, which has two parts. First, over the long run the gap between labor productivity growth and MFP growth has fluctuated in a small range, with a difference of between 1.0 and 1.3 percentage points in decadal averages. Moreover, there is no noticeable trend in this gap: the mean difference in the growth rates of these two productivity measures over 2003-12 is within 0.2 percentage point of the mean difference over 1953-62. The stability of the difference between these

Table 5–2
Nonfarm Private Business Productivity Growth

10-year Average annual rates of change			
Period	Multifactor Productivity	Labor Productivity	Difference
1953–1962	1.5	2.6	1.1
1963–1972	1.9	2.8	1.0
1973–1982	−0.1	1.1	1.2
1983–1992	1.1	2.2	1.1
1993–2002	1.1	2.4	1.3
2003–2012	0.9	1.9	1.0

20-year Average annual rates of change			
Period	Multifactor Productivity	Labor Productivity	Difference
1953–1972	1.7	2.7	1.0
1973–1992	0.5	1.6	1.1
1993–2012	1.0	2.1	1.1

60-year Average annual rates of change			
1953–2012	1.1	2.2	1.1

Source: Bureau of Labor Statistics, Productivity and Costs, Multifactor Productivity.

measures underscores the role of broad technological change—as measured by MFP—as a key driver of long-term growth of output per worker.

Second, over the past 60 years the long-term mean growth rates of labor productivity and MFP have varied substantially, in what appear to be three episodes. The first episode, the 1950s through early 1970s, experienced high growth of MFP (and of labor productivity), with MFP growth averaging 1.7 percent per year from 1953 through 1972. The second episode, the late 1970s through early 1990s, experienced much lower MFP growth, averaging 0.5 percent per year. The third episode, from the mid-1990s through the present, experienced an intermediate level of MFP growth of 1.0 percent per year.

Because productivity is the key to raising output per person, a great deal of academic research has focused on understanding why productivity growth varies over time. Research points to several factors that contributed to the productivity slowdown of the 1970s. A major culprit seems to be the sharp rise in energy prices during the 1970s that made less energy-intensive technologies more attractive, thus changing the optimal way to combine inputs and reducing MFP growth (Jorgenson 1988, Nordhaus 2004). One lesson learned from this period is how important energy cost fluctuations are in determining the growth of potential output.

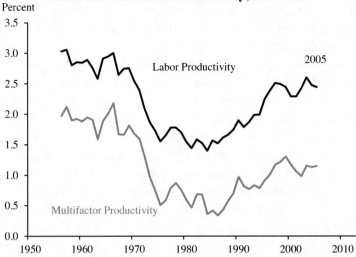

Figure 5-2
15-Year Centered Moving Average of Annual Growth Rates for Labor and Multifactor Productivity, 1956–2005

Percent

Source: Bureau of Labor Statistics, Productivity and Costs, Multifactor Productivity; CEA Calculations.

Another explanation is due to rapid changes in the labor force in the 1970s, primarily shifting the workforce to newer, less-experienced workers. The Baby Boom generation (the cohort born between 1946 and 1964) came of age in the 1970s and 1980s, lowering the overall work experience of the economy. This was a period of rapid entry of women into the workforce for the first time, a shift that also temporarily reduced the overall level of workforce experience in the economy (Feyrer 2007, 2011). Moreover, the rapid entry of these new workers into the workforce outpaced investment, slowing the growth of the capital-labor ratio.

Another possible part of the story is that productivity growth in the 1950s and 1960s was temporarily spurred by large public investments such as the interstate highway system and the commercialization of military innovations from World War II like the jet engine and synthetic rubber.

The productivity rebound of the 1990s and 2000s is widely attributable to the information technology (IT) revolution. For the nine years from 1996 to 2005, MFP grew at 1.6 percent per year, a rate not seen in a nine-year period since the mid-1960s. Although many of the basic technologies that facilitated this growth, like the personal computer and the software to run it, were invented in the 1970s and 1980s; improvements in speed, breadth of applications, and the ability of firms to exploit this technology stretched through the ensuing decades. The BLS MFP measure suggests that much of the productivity improvement resulted from technological and process improvements, a position supported, for example, by Basu, Fernald, Oulton, and Srinivasan (2004). Alternatively, Jorgenson (2001) and Jorgenson and Ho (2012) emphasize the importance of the accumulation of physical IT capital. Oliner, Sichel, and Stiroh (2007) provide a detailed review of the literature on the 1990s productivity boom.

A key current question is what the rate of productivity growth will be going forward—will the U.S. economy maintain the pace of recent decades, will new innovations accelerate the pace of productivity growth, or will productivity growth revert to the slower rates before the recent boom? MFP growth fell sharply in the recession, grew sharply in the early stages of the recovery, and has averaged 1 percent for 2011 and 2012. These large cyclical swings make it difficult to assess whether there has been a recent change in the rate of technological progress, relative to the late 1990s and early 2000s. The academic literature reaches mixed findings concerning whether the IT productivity boom was temporary.[5] This literature also requires qualification because it predates the substantial data revisions to historical GDP and productivity that were released in the summer of 2013, which substantially revised upwards estimated productivity growth in some years in the 2000s.

Some contributions to this debate look further into the future. While some economists predict labor productivity growth could decline in coming decades because the scope for future transformative general-purpose inventions is limited (Gordon 2012), others argue that IT is in fact a general-purpose invention and, at least in the medium run, presents an ongoing stream of opportunities for workplace reorganization and efficiency gains, as well as spin-off technologies and improvements.[6] Bernanke (2012) argued that making these improvements often requires more than just purchasing hardware and software, and realizing potential productivity gains can require changes within and between organizations and thus take a considerable time to be fully realized.[7]

Ultimately, it is very hard to predict future growth rates in innovation, and there is no economic reason that these growth rates should be constant over time. Moreover, the past four decades have seen substantial changes in

---

[5] The findings in the literature on recent productivity growth trends tend to depend on the statistical approaches used to discern different productivity regimes. Authors that adopt discrete breaks or regime shifts, including Kahn and Rich (2011) and Fernald (2012), tend to conclude that the productivity growth boom has passed, whereas Oliner, Sichel, and Stiroh (2007), who use methods in which productivity growth evolves more slowly, find less of a slowdown.

[6] An example of such now-possible workplace reorganization is telecommuting; see, for example, Bloom, Liang, Roberts and Ying (2013); Noonan and Glass (2012), Bailey and Kurland (2002); and Busch, Nash, and Bell (2011).

[7] These issues are argued in the February 2013 TED debate between Gordon and Brynjolfsson.

the extent to which productivity gains translate into higher incomes across the board, the topic of the next section.

Productivity Growth and Inequality Growth

Productivity improvements provide more output that has the potential to benefit society broadly. Through the early 1970s, productivity gains led to increases in labor compensation. Since then, however, productivity growth has not translated into commensurate growth in labor compensation, and income inequality has increased markedly.

Trends in Inequality, Productivity Growth, and Compensation

Real output per hour was 99 percent higher by the end of 1972 than in 1947, while real average hourly earnings (GDP deflator) grew by 73 percent. Figure 5-3 shows that since the early 1970s, the paths of labor productivity and average hourly earnings diverged more widely. As a result, by the end of September 2013 real output per hour was 107 percent higher than at the end of 1972, but average hourly earnings had only grown 31 percent.[8]

Table 5-3 examines the real output per hour and average hourly earnings for private production and nonsupervisory workers by decade. From 1953 to 1962, productivity growth exceeded the average annual rate of change in hourly earnings by only 0.4 percentage point. In the next decade, the difference in growth had ticked up to 0.6 percentage point. However, from 1973 through 2012 labor productivity grew 1.4 percentage points faster than earnings.

Since the 1970s, these trends generally have been worse for lower-income households than for higher-income households (DiNardo, Fortin, Lemieux 1996; Piketty and Saez 2003; Lemieux 2008; CEA 2012; Haskel, Lawrence, Leamer, and Slaughter 2012).[9] In particular, the income growth in the top percentile of the income distribution has been much stronger than other percentiles. For example, the Congressional Budget Office (CBO 2011) reports that from 1979 to 2007, real before-tax income at the median of the household income distribution increased by about 19 percent, while

---

[8] An alternative series from BLS measures real total hourly compensation (CPI deflator) for all nonfarm workers. This measure includes benefits as well as earnings. Since 1972, total hourly compensation has increased more than hourly earnings, but still only by 46 percent. BLS decompositions of compensation into real wage and benefit shares have been available since 1991. Since then, real wages grew 7 percent and benefits grew 22 percent, with the strongest benefit growth in the magnitude of employer contribution to health insurance.

[9] Figure 6-2 of this report suggests that the relative slow growth in income of the lower quintiles may have subsided some recently, particularly during the Great Recession and its near-term recovery. It is too soon to tell whether this has any implication for longer-term trends.

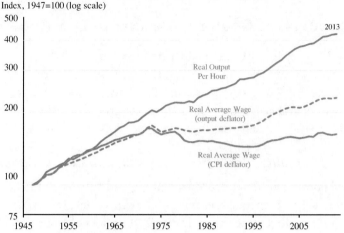

Figure 5-3
Growth in Productivity and Average Wage, 1947–2013

Index, 1947=100 (log scale)

Real Output
Per Hour

Real Average Wage
(output deflator)

Real Average Wage
(CPI deflator)

2013

Note: Real output per hour is for all workers in the nonfarm business sector. Average wage is for private production and nonsupervisory workers. Output deflator is the price index for nonfarm business output. CPI deflator is the CPI-W. Data on wages before 1964 reflects SIC-based industry classifications.
Source: Bureau of Labor Statistics, Productivity and Costs, Current Employment Statistics; CEA calculations.

incomes for the top 1 percent of households have increased by around 200 percent.[10]

Technological Change and Inequality

The lesson from Figure 5-3 is that productivity growth is important for wage growth, but that does not mean that it automatically leads to wage growth. One possibility is that the sources of labor productivity and MFP growth since the early 1970s are qualitatively different than earlier, and that these different sources of growth drove the trends in inequality over the last 40 years. In the early 1990s, a broad consensus emerged among economists that an increase in the demand for skill relative to the supply of educated labor was the primary driver of the sharp rise in inequality in the 1980s (Bound and Johnson 1995; Katz and Murphy 1992; and Juhn, Murphy, and Pierce 1993). It soon became accepted that "skill-biased technological change" (SBTC) was the most important cause of increased inequality (Berman, Bound, and Griliches 1994; Krueger 1993). The crux of the argument is that, as computer technology became increasingly less expensive, relative demand increased for workers with complementary skills. This explanation has remained popular among economists with few modifications to the basic argument until recently (for example, Acemoglu 2002).

---

[10] The CBO notes that it chose 1979 and 2007 as points of comparison because there are cyclical fluctuations in inequality measures and both years are business cycle peaks.

Table 5–3
Average Annual Rates of Change in the Nonfarm Business Sector

Period	Real Output per Hour of all Workers	Average Hourly Earnings for Private Production and Nonsupervisory Workers	Difference (p.p.)
1953–1962	2.5	2.1	0.4
1963–1972	2.7	2.1	0.6
1973–1982	1.1	–0.4	1.4
1983–1992	2.2	0.4	1.8
1993–2002	2.3	1.8	0.5
2003–2012	2.1	1	1.1

Note: Both series are deflated by the price index for output in the nonfarm business sector. Data on earnings before 1964 reflect SIC–based industry classifications.
Sources: Bureau of Labor Statistics, Productivity and Costs, Current Employment Statistics; CEA Calculations.

While this hypothesis has remained influential, there are reasons to question the primary role of technology in causing the inequality changes that emerged in the 1980s. For example, many other industrialized nations, such as Germany and Japan, experienced similar technology shocks in the 1980s, but saw little or no increase in wage inequality. This led some economists to expand the framework for explaining inequality to acknowledge the importance of wage-setting institutions in mediating technology shocks (Freeman and Katz 1995). This critique gained more force with other researchers finding that changes in institutions—especially the decline in the real value of the minimum wage and labor unions—could account for much of the rise in inequality in the 1980s, at least in the bottom of the distribution (Lee 1999 and DiNardo, Fortin, and Lemieux 1996). An additional challenge to the skill-biased technological change hypothesis is that the timing of changes in inequality do not line up well with the nature of technological change across decades. Inequality in the bottom of the distribution rose in the 1980s, but has been flat or declining since then. However, much of the widespread business adoption of IT, including the Internet, occurred in the 1990s, and those innovations were at least as significant as the changes in the 1980s (Card and DiNardo 2002). In fact, inequality in the top of the distribution did continue to rise, but after rising sharply in the 1980s, inequality at the bottom of the distribution has been flat or declining since.

Goldin and Katz (2008) focus on changes in the growth of the supply of skills rather than on episodic increases in technological change. Using the ratio of college to non-college workers as a measure of the relative supply of skills, they show this relative skill supply grew by 3.9 percent from 1960 to 1980. But in 1980, as confirmed by Heckman and LaFontaine (2010) and others, this increase slowed as high school graduation rates stopped improving and college completion rates slowed. Goldin and Katz (2008) show that a constant increase in the demand for relative skill, combined with the post-1980 slowdown in the supply of relative skill, explains the time path of the logarithm of the college wage premium, which is one measured aspect of wage inequality.[11] The nature of rising wage inequality started to change around the early 1990s, becoming increasingly concentrated in the top end of the wage distribution. The ratio of the 90th to the 50th percentile of the wage distribution continued to grow at roughly the same rate it had since the early 1980s, whereas inequality at the bottom (the 50-10 ratio) declined somewhat after the late 1980s. Piketty and Saez (2006) find that income gains have increasingly concentrated in the top 10 percent and top 1 percent since the 1980s. The result has been a "polarization" or a "hollowing out" of the wage distribution, with relative wage growth in the bottom and especially the top of the wage distribution relative to the middle (Goos and Manning 2007; Autor 2010; Acemoglu and Autor 2011; Lemieux 2006).

Autor and coauthors refine the earlier skill-biased technological change literature and argue that the changes in inequality are driven by technological change that substitutes for some tasks but not others (Autor, Levy, and Murnane 2003; Autor, Katz, and Kearney 2006; Acemoglu and Autor 2011). In particular, this new research argues that computer technologies complement non-routine cognitive tasks, which tend to be highly paid; substitute for routine tasks, which tend to be in occupations with wages in the middle of the distribution; and have little effect on manual tasks that tend to be associated with lower wages. This technological explanation for polarization has been controversial, however, and Mishel, Shierholz, and Schmitt (2013) suggest that the theory does not explain the timing of changes in polarization, and more generally that occupational employment and wage trends do not explain a large part of the trends in wages or inequality over time. Moreover, one of the most striking changes in inequality over the past three decades—the sharp growth of incomes at the very top of the distribution—is unlikely to be related to technological changes or to a relative demand for skill (Alvaredo, Atkinson, Piketty, and Saez 2013).

This discussion has focused on whether increases in productivity translate into increases in earnings or lead to increasing inequality. A related, less-understood question is whether increasing inequality might

---

[11] This theory is based on evidence from before 2008. The U.S. economy has long had some skills shortage, which tended to turn up in the form of wage differentials rather than unemployment. It does not account for the large shock in aggregate demand that characterized the Great Recession, or the shock-driven unemployment rates from which the economy is still recovering.

directly dampen productivity growth, and this question is addressed further in Box 5-2.

POLICIES TO FOSTER PRODUCTIVITY GROWTH AND TO HELP ENSURE THAT EVERYONE BENEFITS FROM IT

The benefits of technological progress do not accrue only to those who develop new processes and inventions; they also spill over to the population at large. For this reason, the U.S. Government has a role in supporting and enabling technological development. This government role includes: directly funding or providing incentives for research and development (R&D); providing an institutional, legal, and regulatory environment that protects competition, defines and supports intellectual property rights, and thereby encourages private innovation; and developing human capital through education, especially in scientific and technological fields. In addition, the government has a role in ensuring that everyone benefits from those technological advances.

Investments in R&D often have "spillover" effects; that is, a part of the returns to the investment accrue to parties other than the investor. As a result, investments that are worth making for society at large might not be profitable for any one firm, leaving aggregate R&D investment below the socially optimal level (for example, Nelson 1959). This tendency toward underinvestment creates a role for research that is performed or funded by the government as well as by nonprofit organizations such as universities.

These positive spillovers can be particularly large for basic scientific research. Discoveries made through basic research are often of great social value because of their broad applicability, but are of little value to any individual private firm, which would likely have few, if any, profitable applications for them. The empirical analyses of Jones and Williams (1998) and Bloom et al. (2012) suggest that the optimal level of R&D investment is two to four times the actual level. Akcigit et al. (2013) also find underinvestment in basic research (although, contrary to the bulk of the literature, they find overinvestment in applied research), and suggest policies that are specifically targeted at basic research.

Consistent with the presence of large spillover benefits, most basic research in the United States is funded by the government and other nonprofit entities. As Figure 5-4 shows, over half comes from government sources, and less than one-quarter comes from private industry. However, expenditures on basic research are only a fraction of total R&D expenditures, as seen in Figure 5-5, and the private-sector share of funding for applied research and development is much higher than it is for basic research.

Box 5-2: Does Inequality Affect Productivity?

Although conventional economic models do not include the equality of the income distribution as a determinant of economic output, some recent research has focused on whether increasing income inequality might reduce the growth rate of productivity. There are at least three channels that could produce this link and, in each, an underlying source of income inequality potentially leads to slower productivity. The first channel is through disparities in access to, and the quality of, publicly funded secondary education: inequality in educational quality leads to disparities in skills, so an increase in labor hours might not increase labor quality, slowing labor productivity growth. For example, Goldin and Katz (2008) argue that in the 19th and early 20th centuries, greater access to education in the United States than in Europe resulted in the United States having higher rates of labor productivity growth. In the United States today, the relevant channel is not likely related to access to public schools, but more likely geographic disparity in resources available to students at those schools.

A second channel is that greater income inequality creates disparities in the ability to pay for privately funded education, especially pre-kindergarten and college.[1] This channel too is relevant because of the increasing expense of post-secondary education.

A third channel, discussed by Acemoglu and Robinson (2011), is that sufficiently powerful and entrenched elites have an incentive to use resources to protect their interest rather than encourage growth. The relevance of Acemoglu and Robinson's examples of extractive societies drawn from world history—ancient Rome, the Mayans, slave-dependent economies in the early Americas, and so forth—to the United States today is less clear than that of the other channels.

There have been some attempts to use cross-country differences as sources of variation for econometric studies of the link from inequality to productivity growth. Those attempts, however, confront a variety of data availability and measurement issues, including comparable measures of inequality (Fields 2001) and insufficient variables to avoid spurious effects being loaded onto the inequality measure (Banerjee and Duflo 2003). In any event, the question of whether the increases in U.S. inequality over the past two decades have dampened, or could dampen, productivity growth remains an important source of concern.

---

[1] Except for programs like Head Start, pre-kindergarten education is privately financed. Heckman, Pinto and Savelyev (2012) contribute and list literature demonstrating the importance of early childhood intervention to subsequent schooling and other life outcomes. At the college level, nearly all students pay at least some of their educational expenses.

Figure 5-4
**Basic Research Expenditures in the U.S.
by Source Funding, 2010**

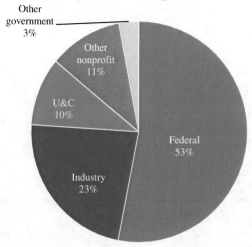

Source: National Science Foundation, National Patterns of R&D Resources: 2010-11 update.

In addition to direct funding of R&D, the government also provides financial incentives for private R&D investment through tax policy.
Government can also facilitate private R&D investment and technological
progress by providing an institutional, legal, and regulatory framework that
clarifies and enforces intellectual property rights and thereby ensures that
innovators reap enough financial rewards from their innovations to provide
sufficient incentive to engage in a closer-to-optimal level of R&D.[12]

One important type of intellectual property right is patents. A patent grants the inventor a temporary exclusive right over the invention.
Exercising that right results in high prices and profits for investments that
are successfully commercialized, and those profits provide an incentive to
invent. However, the exercise of the exclusive right will also raise prices on
inventions that would have been created even with weaker patent protection
or with none at all, and these higher prices harm consumers. Moreover,
because patented inventions are sometimes used as inputs in creating
additional innovations, the higher prices created by patents (as well as the
associated legal and administrative burdens, such as negotiating licenses)
could slow down subsequent innovation. As discussed further below, a
central economic challenge of patent policy is to strike the right balance

---

[12] Research in development economics suggests that a key factor in the economic performance
of a country is its "institutions," such as rule of law and clear property rights (Hall and Jones
1999, Rodrik et al., 2004).

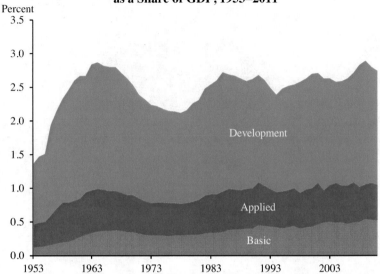

Figure 5-5
**Composition of Total R&D Spending
as a Share of GDP, 1953–2011**

Source: National Science Foundation, National Patterns of R&D Resources: 2010-11 update.

between providing an economic incentive to invent and the potential harm from the exercise of patent rights. At a minimum, it is important to ensure that patents are not wrongly issued, but rather are only issued for inventions that are non-obvious, useful, and inventive.

The government can also lay the groundwork for greater creativity and invention by supporting the development of human capital. Investments and improvements in education and training, particularly in the Science, Technology, Engineering, and Mathematics (STEM) fields, foster the innovation workforce of the future.[13] The productivity of these workers can be enhanced by investment in "innovation clusters," which are dense concentrations of firms and of highly skilled personnel, usually close to a major research university, whose mutual proximity can further promote innovation (see Greenstone, Hornbeck, and Moretti 2008).

Immigration reform is another human capital policy that has the potential to increase the pace of innovation. Studies have found that foreign-nationals living in the United States authored or co-authored over 25 percent of U.S. patent applications in 2006, and that over 75 percent of patents awarded to the top 10 patent-producing American universities in 2011 had at

---

[13] As discussed in Delgado et al. (2012), one determinant of a country's economic performance is its science and innovation infrastructure. The authors include in this category a number of elements that can be influenced by supportive government policy, such as the quality of scientific research institutions and the quality of math and science education.

least one foreign-born inventor. Moreover, the innovation benefits of immigration are not confined to the immigration of innovators. Immigration of low-skilled workers, as well as immigration of high-skilled workers who are not innovators, can spur innovation indirectly by increasing specialization. When more non-innovators are present to specialize more completely in their occupations, they enable innovators to specialize more completely in theirs. The Congressional Budget Office (2013) projects that the additional immigration resulting from the Border Security, Economic Opportunity, and Immigration Modernization Act, as passed by the Senate, would raise total factor productivity by roughly 0.7 percent in 2023 and by roughly 1.0 percent in 2033 as a result of increased innovation and task specialization.

Finally, the government has an important role in ensuring that access to the technologies that catalyze productivity growth, and to the technologies and products that are the fruits of that productivity growth, are broadly available throughout American society. Sharing these benefits increases welfare directly, and also ensures that the broad population maintains the technological skills needed in the workplace and for the education of current and future generations.

This chapter now turns from a general discussion of the role of government policy in achieving technological progress to a focus on two key current areas that are important for productivity growth and that are also a focus of the Administration's policies: telecommunications and patent reform.

TELECOMMUNICATIONS AND PRODUCTIVITY GROWTH

The telecommunications industry is an important one for fostering productivity growth. Improved telecommunications infrastructure, particularly fast and widely accessible wired and wireless broadband networks, is a critical factor in enabling important technological advances in business, health care, education, public safety, entertainment, and more. Government policies have an important role to play in facilitating and catalyzing these improvements, as discussed below. In this chapter, telecommunications policy is discussed in particular detail, in part due to its importance, and in part because it serves as a good illustration of more general economic and policy principles.

Innovation and Investment

The telecommunications sector is a major success story in the U.S. economy. A recent White House (2013) report, *Four Years of Broadband Growth*, documents many of the striking facts, including:

- Just two of the largest U.S. telecommunications companies account for greater combined stateside investment than the top five oil/gas companies, and nearly four times more than the big three auto companies combined, as seen in Figure 5-6.

- Between 2009 and 2012, annual investment in U.S. wireless networks grew more than 40 percent, from $21 billion to $30 billion. During that period, investment in European wireless networks remained flat, and wireless investment in Asia (including China) rose only 4 percent. The report projected that U.S. wireless network investment would increase further in 2013, to $35 billion.

- The United States leads the world in the availability of advanced 4G wireless broadband Internet services such as LTE; nearly half of the global subscriber base for 4G LTE is in the United States.

- The United States ranks among the top countries in the world in the amount of currently licensed spectrum available for mobile broadband.

This infrastructure is at the center of a vibrant ecosystem that includes smartphone design, mobile applications development, and the use of these technologies to effect broader changes in the economy and society—all of it centered in the United States. The mobile applications industry is forecast to generate more than $25 billion in revenue in 2013, rising to $74 billion in 2017, with nearly 2 million applications available for download at the two largest mobile app stores. Improved telecommunications has also contributed to changes in the way that business is organized, and in ways that may lead to further improvements in productivity. An example of this is discussed in Box 5-3.

Four Key Areas for Telecommunications Policy

The U.S. Government can support innovation and investment in telecommunications through the same general policies discussed above: direct government investment in research and development; catalyzing private innovation through policies such as reforming and extending the Research and Experimentation Tax Credit; catalyzing technological infrastructure investment in areas like broadband; and ensuring that everyone benefits from broadband technologies.

Government Investments in Research and Development. As discussed above, spillover benefits to research and development, especially for basic science and technology, creates a role for direct government investment. Perhaps the most famous government investment in telecommunications technology was the Defense Advanced Research Projects Agency (DARPA) development of the Internet. But DARPA has provided other important defense-based public research contributions as well. These contributions

Figure 5-6
Relative Investment of the Telecommunications Sector, 2011

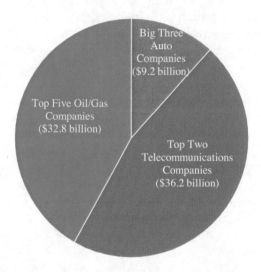

Big Three
Auto
Companies
($9.2 billion)

Top Five Oil/Gas
Companies
($32.8 billion)

Top Two
Telecommunications
Companies
($36.2 billion)

Source: Progressive Policy Institute.

include the radio and, more recently, Global Positioning Systems, which today are central to a huge number of consumer applications.

Today, the Department of Defense (DOD) continues to play an important role in telecommunications research, particularly in helping to develop ideas and technologies for sharing of electromagnetic spectrum frequency bands between different users, including between government and private users. This, as discussed further below, has been identified as important for efficient spectrum management in the future (PCAST 2012). For example, DOD has solicited innovative research proposals aimed at efficient and reliable sharing of spectrum between radar and communications systems. All told, $100 million in Federal investments are being targeted toward spectrum sharing and advanced communications through the National Science Foundation (NSF), DARPA, and the Commerce Department.

Catalyzing Private Investment. Reforming, expanding, and making permanent the Research and Experimentation Tax Credit would increase investment in telecommunications technology, accelerating innovation. Immigration reform would accelerate innovation as well. Reforming the patent system is also important in this industry, especially for technology deployed in smartphones, which are complex devices that embody thousands of patents. The increasing frequency of patent disputes in this area suggests that there may be increasing costs to navigating the appropriate

Box 5-3: Just-in-Time Manufacturing

The just-in-time (JIT) approach to manufacturing aims to maximize profits by dramatically reducing inventories and their costs. By minimizing the time that inventory is held, the system allows a fixed amount of inventory space to be used more productively; that is, by processing more goods through the fixed spaced during a fixed amount of time. Agrawal (2010) delineates channels through which the JIT approach can reduce costs, improve quality and customer service, maintain flexibility, and promote logistical efficiency. Many of these channels now rely on improved information and telecommunications technology. Since JIT requires precise coordination between demand and supply, the contemporaneous tracking of each is essential. On the supply side, Zhang et al. (2012) argue that radio frequency identification technology can provide firms with precise, accurate, real-time information on materials as they pass through the manufacturing process. But technology that makes JIT feasible is only one requirement. Other studies (Hur, Jeong and Suh 2009, Tayal 2012, Fairris and Brenner 2001, Agrawal 2010, Sim and Koh 2003) show that organizational experimentation, innovation, and learning in using the technology can also be necessary to realizing productivity gains.

licenses. If these costs are high enough to adversely affect the introduction of new products, then patent reform is particularly important for the telecommunications industry.

Catalyzing Technological Infrastructure Investment. The Federal Government funded the country's first investment in telecommunications infrastructure, a telegraph line from Washington D.C. to Baltimore built in the 1840s. But since then, appropriately, the vast majority of technological infrastructure investment has been private. Over the course of decades, an extraordinary expansion of telecommunications infrastructure made basic telephone service available to nearly every resident of the country, far sooner than in most other countries, which is a remarkable achievement given the large size and relatively low population density of the United States.

Public policy encouraged these investments. Many private carriers, as regulated monopolies, were permitted to charge high rates for long-distance calls, business service, and the telephones themselves. A portion of the resulting funds were required to be used to subsidize basic local phone service, particularly in rural and other areas that are costly to serve due to low population density and geographic factors. The Telecommunications Act of 1996 sought to reform and improve upon telecommunications regulation by enabling greater competition, particularly in local and long-distance telephone service, and by rationalizing, and making explicit, the subsidy system supporting service in high-cost areas. Substantial additional private investment followed.

In recent years, the U.S. Government has further facilitated private telecommunications investment through favorable tax policy. In 2010, the President proposed and signed into law the largest temporary investment incentive in history—100-percent expensing—that, together with the bonus depreciation that preceded and followed it, played a critical role in increasing and accelerating investment, including the substantial increases in both wired and wireless investment in the telecommunications sector. For example, two major companies in a joint statement said that, "despite the downturn in the economy, the cable communications sector has been able to continue steady investment and to retain jobs as a result of policies like 100-percent expensing."

Catalyzing investment in mobile broadband infrastructure is especially important given the rapidly growing usage and the scarcity of electromagnetic spectrum for carrying wireless broadband traffic. In 2010, Federal Communication Commission experts predicted that the needs for broadband capacity will overwhelm available spectrum (the "spectrum crunch"). If allowed to happen, this would result in higher prices for mobile broadband services, as well as reduced growth in broadband-based innovation, services, and employment. The scarcity of broadband capacity can be alleviated through increased investment (denser transmission infrastructure means more traffic on a given spectrum frequency), fuller deployment of spectrum already licensed to wireless carriers, spectrum license consolidation, technological advancement, and improvements in spectrum policy.

One important initiative is to seek to reallocate public spectrum when it has a more valuable private use. The Federal Government is a major user of spectrum, as Figure 5-7 shows. Most of this usage involves national security and law enforcement functions, as shown in Figure 5-8. Federal use of spectrum is valuable, but it is not costless. As an economic matter, if a particular spectrum band would produce a larger net social surplus in private hands than in public hands, then it should be reallocated, and vice-versa. That is, the Federal Government can alleviate spectrum scarcity by having government agencies vacate certain spectrum bands entirely, or share them with private users, when this can be achieved without compromising the agencies' vital missions (which in many cases involve safety-of-life and national security) and when the associated costs of relocating government operations out of those bands are justified by the social value that will be unlocked as a result of the reallocation to the private sector. The vacated

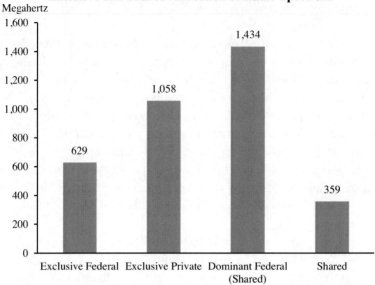

Figure 5-7
Exclusive and Shared Allocation of Radio Spectrum

Source: National Telecommunications and Information Administration (2009).

spectrum could then be auctioned off to commercial users or, if appropriate, made widely available on an unlicensed basis (more on this below). The Federal user would be relocated to alternative spectrum that could be used more intensively and economically, particularly if additional resources were made available for investment in newer equipment.

In addition to economizing on its aggregate spectrum usage, the government can further alleviate spectrum scarcity by rationalizing spectrum allocation. There are some spectrum bands that, above and beyond the properties that make them valuable in general (for example, strong propagation through buildings and in rural areas), are particularly valuable for commercial applications, such as if they are complementary to other commercial spectrum bands. In those cases, value can be unlocked by having the government relocate from those bands to other bands that do not have that property—again, under the condition that this can be done without compromising vital missions and that the relocation costs are not prohibitively high.

Box 5-4 describes several spectrum investment policies that have been undertaken or proposed by the Administration.

There is also substantial scope to reallocate some spectrum currently licensed to private entities to a more valuable use in wireless broadband. Some incumbent firms, such as over-the-air broadcast television stations, hold rights to spectrum that are much more valuable as wireless broadband

Figure 5-8
Federal Agencies with Most Spectrum Assignments

Note: "Other Federal Agencies" includes Interior, Agriculture, Energy, Commerce, and the other remaining 48 agencies and departments with spectrum frequency assignments.
Source: National Telecommunications and Information Adminstration, Government Master file (2010); Government Accountability Office Analysis.

spectrum. The 2010 National Broadband Plan introduced the idea of "incentive auctions" as a tool to help meet the nation's spectrum needs by giving those rights-holders a share of the auction proceeds if they relinquish their rights. In the Spectrum Act of 2012, Congress authorized the Federal Communications Commission to conduct incentive auctions and directed that the FCC use this innovative tool for an incentive auction of broadcast television spectrum. In September 2012, the FCC adopted a Notice of Proposed Rulemaking in order to develop a rulemaking record that will enable the Commission to meet the challenges presented by the Spectrum Act's unique grant of authority. The magnitude of potential gains to social surplus are enormous when broadcasters with access to new, more-efficient transmission technologies that use less spectrum, or with a small and shrinking base of over-the-air viewers and annual revenue in the low millions of dollars, will have an incentive to relinquish spectrum that, when reconfigured for commercial broadband use, will be sold for hundreds of millions of dollars to companies that will use it to improve services for a vastly greater number of broadband customers.

Some spectrum can be used effectively without being licensed at all, but rather made available for anyone to use on an unlicensed basis. Just as some roads seldom experience traffic jams, in some instances certain spectrum bands do not become highly congested even when access is free.

Box 5-4: Spectrum Investment Policies

In 2010, the President issued a Presidential Memorandum called "Unleashing the Wireless Broadband Revolution," which directed the Secretary of Commerce, working through the National Telecommunications and Information Administration (NTIA), to collaborate with the Federal Communications Commission (FCC) to make available a total of 500 megahertz (MHz) of Federal and nonfederal spectrum over the next 10 years, suitable for both mobile and fixed wireless broadband use, nearly doubling the amount of spectrum available for such purposes. The Secretary of Commerce has been facilitating discussions between agencies and nonfederal entities that have produced an unprecedented level of information-sharing and collaboration to identify opportunities for agencies to relinquish or share spectrum, currently focusing on the 1695-1710 MHz band, the 1755-1850 MHz band, the 3550-3650 MHz band, and the 5350-5470 and 5850-5925 MHz bands.

The President's fiscal year 2015 budget would invest $7.5 million to monitor spectrum use by Federal agencies in high-priority markets to identify opportunities for repurposing spectrum through auctions, while protecting Federal missions. This budget proposal builds on the Middle Class Tax Relief and Job Creation Act of 2012 by proposing to authorize use of a spectrum license user fee for licenses not currently awarded via auctions (for example, international satellite licenses), to promote efficient utilization of spectrum. This fee would raise nearly $5 billion over the next 10 years, and would continue to encourage more efficient allocation and use of spectrum.

Unlicensed spectrum plays an important role in the broadband ecosystem, enabling Wi-Fi, Bluetooth, "smart homes," and more, which operate on unlicensed spectrum using devices whose power is low enough that interference among numerous devices sharing the spectrum is not a major concern. It also helps to alleviate scarcity in licensed spectrum bands. This is because a great deal of mobile usage is not the "on-the-go/in transit" mobile usage that must be transmitted on a carrier's licensed mobile network, but rather is so-called "nomadic" usage (for example, at home, office, or other fixed location), that is amenable to carriage mostly by a wired broadband connection and then wirelessly completed using a nearby unlicensed Wi-Fi router. For this reason, the licensed carriers are investing heavily in the deployment and use of Wi-Fi networks. The value of this unlicensed spectrum has been estimated at $16 billion to $37 billion per year.

In February, the FCC proposed to make available up to 195 megahertz of additional spectrum in the 5-gigahertz band for unlicensed wireless devices, a 35 percent increase. This band was selected for unlicensed use in part because the presence of incumbent users of this band, including automobile makers that have been developing short-range communications capabilities that could greatly improve traffic safety and efficiency, make it a poor candidate for being vacated and auctioned off for licensed use. To unlock the value of the band for unlicensed use, the FCC has also proposed to create a more flexible regulatory environment, and to streamline existing rules and equipment authorization procedures for devices throughout this band. Currently ongoing is the process of identifying regulatory changes that strike the best balance between unlocking the value of this spectrum for unlicensed use on the one hand, and avoiding harmful interference with incumbent users on the other.

Clearing Federal Government spectrum for exclusive licensed use, and making it available for shared unlicensed use, remain viable solutions in the near term. However, given the dramatic spectrum challenge and the fact that much of the lowest-hanging fruit for reallocation has already been picked, it is also important to focus on newer and more innovative ideas. These ideas include new advances in the sharing of spectrum between different users, particularly between government and private users. Innovation in spectrum sharing is both promising and necessary, as there are some spectrum bands that the government cannot vacate entirely, but that nevertheless have unused capacity, and that with appropriate processes and procedures in place could be shared, accommodating some valuable private usage without compromising mission-critical functions.

The President's Council of Advisors on Science and Technology (PCAST) released a report estimating that "in the best circumstances, the amount of effective capacity that can be obtained from a given band of spectrum can be increased thousands of times over current usage through dynamic sharing techniques that make optimal use of frequency, geography, time and certain other physical properties of the specific new radio systems (PCAST 2012)."

The 2010 Presidential Memorandum that set the Administration's spectrum goal contemplated the sharing of Federal Government spectrum as one means of achieving that goal. More recently, in June 2013, another Presidential Memorandum established a Spectrum Policy Team in the Executive Office of the President, which was charged with the mandate to "monitor and support advances in spectrum sharing policies and technologies." That Memorandum also contains measures to facilitate research, development, testing, and evaluation of technologies to enhance spectrum sharing and other spectrum-related efficiencies.

To stimulate investment in more advanced forms of spectrum sharing, the Defense Advanced Research Projects Agency (DARPA) is soliciting innovative research proposals aimed at efficient and reliable sharing of spectrum between radar and communications systems. Consistent with its history of promoting groundbreaking technological breakthroughs for both military and commercial use, DARPA is seeking "innovative approaches that enable revolutionary advances" in spectrum sharing, specifically in the spectrum bands that are most amenable to broadband and communications services. The program may fund multi-year projects designed either to significantly modify existing radar and communications systems or to unveil new system architectures redesigned from the ground up.

By itself, making additional Federal spectrum available for commercial use, whether on an exclusive or a shared basis, is unlikely to be sufficient to keep up with the exploding demand for bandwidth. The ambitious goal of freeing up 500 MHz of spectrum would nearly double the amount of wireless spectrum available for mobile broadband over the course of a decade, but even that may not be enough to keep up with spectrum usage growth. Therefore, it is important to do everything from increasing investments in wired broadband networks that can offload some of the demand (often making the last connection wireless, but through Wi-Fi rather than cellular), to increasing the density of wireless cells, to encouraging technological innovations for using spectrum more efficiently.

The Administration is trying to help with these efforts in a variety of other ways, including the June 2012 Executive Order issued by the President specifying a number of steps that will ease and facilitate carriers' access to Federal land and buildings for purposes of deploying broadband infrastructure, including cell towers.

Ensuring Everyone Benefits. It is important to ensure broad participation in the benefits of broadband telecommunications technologies, because broad participation allows more people to use those benefits to develop their talents, which lead to higher economic growth and higher living standards in the future. One element of broad participation is ensuring that technology and its products are affordable. To that end, vigorous antitrust enforcement is critical to ensure that that prices are not inflated and choices not limited by lack of competition. This has been a focus of the law enforcement agencies, and is also important as a policy consideration going forward.

The Obama Administration has made critical investments in expanding broadband to underserved communities. The American Recovery and Reinvestment Act of 2009 included $6.9 billion in funding to upgrade the nation's broadband infrastructure, with $4.4 billion administered by the Department of Commerce's National Telecommunications and Information

Administration, and $2.5 billion by the Department of Agriculture's Rural Utilities Service. Of these funds, a total of $4.4 billion (as of the end of May 2013) went to fund more than more than 325 broadband projects through the Broadband Technology Opportunities Program and the Broadband Initiatives Program. The Federal Communications Commission has also played an important role in expanding broadband deployment in unserved and underserved areas through Universal Service Reform and the establishment of a $4.5 billion annual Connect America Fund, which reallocates funds previously used to support voice service.

Education researchers have long believed that technology holds the potential to profoundly impact the classroom experience, from allowing students to interact with course content in new and personalized ways to helping teachers understand what lessons and techniques are most effective. By making the ever-expanding collection of educational resources available on the Internet accessible to teachers and students in classrooms, technologically equipped schools enhance learning by gaining access to those resources, rather than being limited to resources that are physically at hand.

Although more high quality research on the effectiveness of online educational tools is still needed, these tools do show promise. A meta-analysis of experimental or quasi-experimental studies of the effects of online education conducted by the Department of Education in 2010 found that students who receive instruction that combines online and face-to-face elements performed better than students who received either exclusively online, or exclusively face-to-face, instruction. Other factors such as instruction time or curriculum may contribute to this positive effect, but the meta-analysis suggests that further research on designing, implementing, and evaluating these blended approaches may be worthwhile.

Instruction methods that incorporate computers have also shown promise in mathematics education. Barrow, Markman, and Rouse (2009) found that students who were randomly assigned to participate in and complete computerized math lessons at their own pace scored 0.17 to 0.25 standard deviations higher on mathematics achievement tests than students who received traditional instruction. Computer-aided mathematics instruction has been shown to have similar effects in other contexts. In an experimental study, Banerjee et al. (2007) find that playing educational math games on computers for two hours a week improved the math scores of impoverished elementary school students in India by 0.47 standard deviations. In another experiment, Carillo, Onofa, and Ponce (2010) find poor Ecuadoran elementary school students who used adaptive math and language software for three hours a week improved their math scores by 0.30 standard deviations.

Because current uses of technology can enhance learning and the potential of future developments is untold, it is critically important that all students have access to 21st century classrooms. The ConnectED program, announced by President Obama in June 2013, takes important steps to ensure that the benefits of improvements in educational technology will be made widely available. While initiatives like the FCC's E-Rate program, established under the Telecommunications Act of 1996, have helped bring Internet access to almost every school in the nation, many schools do not have access to the fast broadband speeds enjoyed by most businesses and households. Further, the E-Rate program was designed primarily to bring Internet access to the school, with less priority on ensuring that access was available throughout the school, such as via Wi-Fi technology. As a result, 62 percent of school districts say their bandwidth needs will outstrip their connections within the next 12 months, and 99 percent say that this will happen within three years.

ConnectED will bring high-speed broadband and wireless Internet access to 99 percent of America's students in their school classrooms and libraries within five years. To make the most of this enhanced connectivity, ConnectED will refocus existing professional development funds to train teachers to take full advantage of these resources in order to improve student learning. Finally, by equipping schools with the broadband Internet access necessary to make use of high-tech educational devices, ConnectED will deepen the market for such devices, as well as the digital educational content with which they interact, spurring private-sector innovation in this area.

The President has called on the FCC to modernize the E-Rate program, and has also called on the expertise of the NTIA, in order to deliver this connectivity and meet the goal of connecting 99 percent of America's students to the digital age within five years through next-generation broadband and high-speed wireless in their schools and libraries. Answering that call, the FCC announced in February 2014 that it would invest $2 billion to connect 20 million students over the next two years, representing a crucial down-payment on reaching the President's goal. The initiative, however, is not just about infrastructure. The President announced in February over $750 million in private sector commitments to help fill out this vision of a connected classroom through the digital devices, content and learning software, home wireless access, and teacher training necessary to make the best possible use of this infrastructure. By leveraging all these resources, we are making substantial progress toward a world-class education for every student that does not depend on their family's income or on the zip code in which they were born.

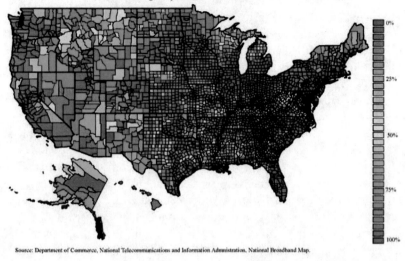

Figure 5-9
**Percentage of Households with Access to Download Speeds
of 6 Megabit per Second or Greater**

Source: Department of Commerce, National Telecommunications and Information Administration, National Broadband Map.

Finally, it is crucial that the benefits of broadband technology growth be consistent with privacy and security. Also, the free expression of ideas must be protected, so technological development must proceed in a way that is consistent with an open Internet.

Challenges to Broad Adoption of Telecommunications Technology

Broad adoption of telecommunications technologies faces several challenges. For example, these technologies are unevenly adopted across different education and income levels. Home broadband adoption is more than twice as high for college graduates as for high school dropouts. Overall, 30 percent of Americans do not use broadband at home, and many of these non-users are in lower-income households. Rural areas also lag in adoption. As illustrated in Figure 5-9, nearly all urban residents have access to 6 megabits per second downloads, but only 82 percent of residents in rural communities can access those speeds, and the disparity becomes even larger at faster speeds.

One reason some households do not adopt broadband is cost: unlike the sharp price declines seen for technological hardware, such as computers, the prices consumers pay for Internet access have remained steady or risen. But while broadband prices have not fallen sharply, the speeds that are available at a given price today are often considerably faster than the available speeds at the same price several years ago, which means that value for money

Box 5-5: Electronic Health Records

Technological advances in Health Information Technology, especially Electronic Health Records (EHR), hold the promise of improving patient care and lowering health care costs. Patients are often treated by multiple providers for the same condition or for related conditions. Because the correct treatment by one provider often depends upon what other providers are doing, effective coordination of care between providers can improve health outcomes. Effective coordination also helps to control costs, as it avoids both the costs of treating follow-on problems resulting from uncoordinated care and the unnecessary duplication of tests and procedures.

Some ways of improving care coordination among health care providers involves changing the way they are paid for their services. The Affordable Care Act of 2010 (ACA) included a variety of such reforms that are currently in various stages of implementation, many of which are discussed in Chapter 4. But other ways involve the application of better technology, notably EHR systems. As the name would suggest, these systems enable the creation of a permanent, sharable record of every aspect of a patient's care, including test results, past treatments, and providers' notes. In a fully integrated EHR system, each provider has immediate and complete access to all relevant patient information, which has the potential to greatly improve coordination of care and also to reduce medical errors.

EHR systems have additional functionality as well, such as providing automatic alerts when treatments are inconsistent with each other or when a scheduled test has been missed. The systems can also be used to improve quality more broadly by allowing hospitals and other providers to keep better track of outcomes and to identify problem areas.

EHR adoption has been promoted by Administration policy. The Health Information Technology for Economic and Clinical Health (HITECH) Act, enacted as part of the American Recovery and Reinvestment Act of 2009, encouraged adoption and use of health information technology, including EHR systems.

Key programs established by the HITECH Act were the Medicare and Medicaid EHR programs. These programs provide financial incentives to hospitals and health care professionals to adopt EHR systems, and require that they demonstrate "meaningful use" of the systems. The meaningful use criteria, which become increasingly rigorous over time, require providers to demonstrate that they are using EHR systems to capture patient health information, assist in clinical decision making, track quality of care, and securely exchange patient information across health care settings to facilitate coordinated care.

Providers who adopt and demonstrate meaningful use of EHR systems by 2014 (for Medicare) and by 2016 (for Medicaid) are eligible for bonus payments from those programs. The Medicare program, but not the Medicaid program, also includes a payment reduction to providers that do not adopt and demonstrate meaningful use of EHR systems. Medicare providers who have not demonstrated meaningful use by 2015 are subject to penalties that grow over time; for example, for physicians, penalties start at 1 percent in 2015 and grow to 3 percent or more in subsequent years. The Congressional Budget Office estimated that the Medicaid EHR program would award bonuses of $12.7 billion through 2019, while the Medicare EHR program would make bonus payments net of penalties of $20 billion over that period (CBO 2009).

The HITECH Act also provided $2 billion to the Department of Health and Human Services to fund activities to encourage the diffusion of health information technology, such as investing in infrastructure and disseminating best practices. The Act also made a variety of other changes, including provisions to facilitate data sharing across health care providers to support coordinated care and protect patient privacy.

The share of medical providers using EHRs has risen dramatically in recent years. Data from the National Ambulatory Medical Care Survey show that the share of office-based physicians using an advanced EHR system (which are generally more sophisticated than those required meet the early-stage "meaningful use" criteria) rose from 17 percent in 2008 to 40 percent in 2012 (Hsiao and Hing 2014), and data from the American Hospital Association's annual survey of hospitals show that the share of hospitals that had adopted such a system rose from 9 percent to 44 percent over the same period (Charles et al., 2013). Consistent with this rapid progress for advanced systems, the Department of Health and Human Services has estimated that, as of the end of April 2013, over half of eligible physicians and more than 80 percent of eligible hospitals have adopted an EHR system and met the criteria for meaningful use (HHS 2013).

has improved. Further, while international comparisons are difficult (due to variations in factors like taxes, government subsidies, geography, population density, and product bundles), the United States compares favorably in a number of respects, including entry-level pricing for slower but still useful broadband speeds.

A surprisingly large number of households cite a different factor for their decision not to subscribe to home Internet service: a perceived lack of relevance to their day-to-day lives. Private- and public-sector broadband adoption programs address this by focusing on educating non-subscribers about the array of services and support mechanisms that are available online, like job listings and training, educational tools, health care services, and government resources.

While this chapter has focused heavily on telecommunications technology, there are many other areas where technological advances promise large social and economic benefits, and where public policy can play an important role. One important example, discussed in Box 5-5, is Electronic Health Records and related technologies.

PATENTS

The rights that prospective innovators have to the economic returns on their innovations are known as intellectual property (IP) rights, of which one major category is patents, which apply to inventions. Patents are granted on inventions in many different areas of technology, as shown in Figure 5-10. The basic economic logic behind patent protection is simple: successful inventions are valuable to society, as they lead to new and better products. But attempting to invent is costly and risky. If successful inventions could be easily imitated by competitors, then prospective inventors may be in a position where they lose if their invention fails, but gain little or nothing if it succeeds. This diminishes the incentive to expend resources and effort on inventing, and the reduced rate of invention is harmful to society. To prevent this problem, patent protection allows inventors to enjoy a temporary exclusive right to their invention. The super-competitive pricing that results from this exclusivity provides an incentive to invest. Another benefit of patent protection is that patents are published, so they can be licensed and put to other socially valuable purposes other than those of the inventor. But patent protection can also harm consumers: for inventions that would have been created with weaker patent protection or even with no protection at all, patents simply lead to higher prices for the same inventions, not to additional inventions. The economically optimal strength of patent protection (for example, how many years a patent should run) is the one that best balances the benefit from accelerated invention with the harm from higher prices.

There are some additional effects of patent protection that also deserve mention. One effect is that some inventions are complementary to each other, meaning that the availability of one makes it easier to develop others. In those cases, the higher prices resulting from patent protection, as well as the related legal and administrative burdens (such as negotiating licenses), raise the cost of, and hence reduce the rate of, subsequent innovation. This effect is relevant for determining the economically optimal patent

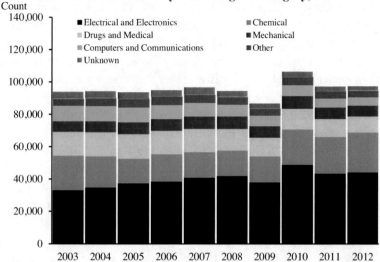

Figure 5-10

Patents Issued in the U.S. by Technological Category, 2003–2012

Count

- Electrical and Electronics
- Drugs and Medical
- Computers and Communications
- Unknown
- Chemical
- Mechanical
- Other

Note: "Unknown" indicates that a patent could not be assigned to a single technological category with a high enough probability.
Source: United States Patent and Trademark Office.

strength. Another effect is that, in some cases, patent rights can be used to harm rival firms or to extract license fees that do not correspond to the value of the patent. As discussed below, it is important to curb such behaviors by developing sound policies related to patent examination and enforcement. It is also important to ensure that patents are not wrongly issued, but rather are only issued for inventions that are non-obvious, useful, and inventive.

The chapter now turns to two specific patent issues that have been the subject of recent policy scrutiny: how to support standard setting by appropriate use of standard-essential patents, and the activities of Patent Assertion Entities and the effects of those activities.

Standard-Essential Patents

We take for granted that we can drive our car up to a gas pump and have the hose fit the car's nozzle. Similarly, that smartphones created by different manufacturers will communicate with each other. These are examples of *interoperability* that result from the standardization of certain product features. An interesting problem arises when an industry seeks to adopt an interoperability standard and the available choices for the standard may include patented inventions.

The nature of the economic problem is to develop a mechanism that determines when standardization would make market participants better off and, in such cases, provides parties with incentives to invent and propose the invention as a standard, while ensuring that all parties will later find it in their interest to implement the standard. The central premise of the economic theory of patents is that granting limited exclusive rights through the issuing of patents provides an incentive for private investment in invention; absent such rights, the entity making the investment may not receive sufficient returns to make the investment worthwhile. These exclusive rights are not meant to preclude similar technologies from being developed and marketed. In principle, some degree of competition in consumer markets bounds the power conferred by these exclusive rights. But that bound is removed if a patented technology becomes the standard and is used in all products sold in the market. As a result, the patent holder may seek to charge higher prices than originally agreed on during the standard-setting process and to use the patent to inefficiently restrict access to the technology. Such behavior may delay implementation of the technology, as others who may adapt the technology exit the market or seek other ways around it. The sought-after standard then fails to become standard (for example, Gilbert 2011).

Because industry actors are most likely to understand the substantial complexities of new technologies and the potential products and markets for their dissemination, there is value in having the standards set voluntarily by industry-based standards-developing organizations (DOJ 2013). These organizations provide a place for industry actors to propose their patented technologies as part of a standard, and to reach consensus on the technologies incorporated into the standard (or to decide on no standard). After a decision is taken, a chosen patent becomes known as standard essential. Actual implementation of the agreed-on standard as an observed standard follows when all implementers and potential implementers pay an agreed justified price (reasonable, or both fair and reasonable) for the technology, and their access to the patented technology cannot be improperly restricted (there is not discrimination). By proposing a patent for use in the standard, the patent owner is giving up the power to charge higher per-unit prices for use of the technology, but enjoys returns from the diffusion of the technology more widely across more units.

Because the notion behind standard-developing organizations is voluntary collaboration, there is no guarantee that a standard will be produced. A standard-essential patent holder can refrain from committing to licensing on reasonable and non-discriminatory (RAND) terms.[14] In such cases, the declared standard is less likely to be the implemented standard and

---

[14] Sometimes the licensing commitment is to fair, reasonable and non-discriminatory terms.

market forces may be suggesting that a standard is not needed or may be best determined over time and in the marketplace directly (Farrell et al. 2007).

When voluntary agreement does produce a standard, there are instances when parties to the agreement do not feel that others are living up to the agreement. In such instances, when patent holders have committed to license on RAND terms, judicial and enforcement procedures should aim to reproduce the intent of the agreement; that is, to ensure that the patent holder receives a RAND royalty. Otherwise, judicial and enforcement procedures can tip the balance of power in favor of one party or the other, leading either to excessive market power in the hands of the patent holder or to non-payment of reasonable royalties by implementers, and to greater incentives against establishing a standard in the first place (Lemley and Shapiro 2005).

Patent Assertion Entities

In recent years, organizations known as Patent Assertion Entities (PAEs) have become common. PAEs brought 24 percent of all patent lawsuits in 2011, and over the 2007-11 period they brought approximately one-fifth of all patent lawsuits, covering about one-third of all defendants (GAO 2013). These PAEs purchase rights to patents belonging to other firms, and then assert them against firms or individuals who are using the patented technology. Some of this activity is valuable: incentives to invent are stronger if inventors know they can later sell their patent to, or merely engage the services of, a PAE that can assert it more effectively than they could do themselves. Also, in some cases, it may be efficient for PAEs to act as intermediaries by obtaining the rights to patents held by disparate inventors in order to decrease the transaction cost of negotiating licenses. However, many industry observers believe that PAEs often do not assert patents in good faith, but rather assert them simply in order to extract nuisance payments from firms looking to avoid costly and risky litigation. In some cases, these patents are valid but of low value, meaning that absent the high cost of litigation they would only command very low licensing fees. In other cases, the patents are invalid (or not infringed), and absent the high litigation costs they would not command any license fees at all (Scott Morton & Shapiro 2013).

This issue is particularly pronounced in smartphones and other consumer electronics devices (Chien 2012). Many of these products contain technology based on thousands of patents, and as shown in Figure 5-10 above, the number of patents issued in the "Electrical and Electronics" category has been increasing over the past decade. The large number of patents embodied in these products, and their complexity, often makes manufacturers subject to patent-infringement claims, with the associated threat of costly and risky litigation, from owners of low-value valid patents or even from

Box 5-6: The Leahy-Smith America Invents Act

The Leahy-Smith America Invents Act of 2011 took some important steps to update the U.S. patent system. The Act changed the system to give priority to the first inventor to file for a patent on a given invention, moving away from the "first-to-invent" priority system and bringing the United States in line with every other industrialized nation. This change eliminated the need for long, expensive administrative proceedings to resolve disputes among inventors who filed for patents on the same invention over who invented it first.

The Act also helps ensure that inventors have the opportunity to share their work early on by maintaining a form of the one-year "prior art" grace period that had been a feature of the previous system. The grace period excludes from the previous state of knowledge, against which the originality of a patent application is judged, any disclosures of details of the invention made within the year preceding the application date by the inventor, or by third parties who learned them from the inventor. The grace period allows inventors to publish their work, prepare application materials, or seek to raise funds to support their application without fear that those activities will later be a detriment to that application.

The Act also increases protections from patent infringement lawsuits for innovators who develop and deploy new products or methods but choose not to patent them, a common practice in the high-tech industry, by expanding the "prior user rights" infringement defense. Formerly applicable only to business practices patents, this defense— which exempts from liability users who can demonstrate that they independently developed and used the patented product or method that they are accused of infringing upon, and did so more than a year prior to the date the patent was filed—is now applicable to all types of patents.

owners of invalid patents. It is therefore an important public policy goal to find ways to reduce the cost of defending patent lawsuits, and also to reduce the number of invalid patents, either by reducing the number of invalid patents that are granted, or by making it easier for them to be challenged.

One important step toward resolving these patent-related problems, which disrupt the appropriate economic incentives to invent, has been taken in the form of the Leahy-Smith America Invents Act of 2011, discussed further in Box 5-6. The key provisions of the AIA, which went into full effect in 2012, are helping to improve the patent system for innovators by offering a fast-track option for patent processing, taking important steps to reduce the current patent backlog, and increasing the ability of Americans to protect their intellectual property abroad.

Several provisions of the America Invents Act may help address some of the problematic behavior of PAEs by developing at the Patent and Trademark Office new programs to create alternatives to litigation over patent validity, new methods for post-grant review of issued patents, and major steps to increase patent quality through clarifying and tightening standards. Yet challenges remain, notably the asymmetry between the cost to a PAE of bringing a patent lawsuit and the cost to a target firm of defending one, which enables PAEs to bring weak cases in the hopes of extracting a settlement.

In June 2013, the President issued a set of five executive actions and seven legislative recommendations to address these challenges. These included measures to make it more difficult for overly broad claims to receive patents in the first place, as well as to make it easier to challenge weak patents once they have been granted. The President's priorities also include measures to require greater clarity in patent applications regarding the precise nature of the claimed invention, as well as the identity of the patent holder. Other measures include ways to make it more difficult for patent holders to sue end-users (as opposed to manufacturers) of products that contain patented technology, and to provide judges with more discretion to award attorney fees and other costs to the prevailing party in patent lawsuits.

Congress has taken up these issues. In December 2013, the House of Representatives passed a bipartisan bill containing many of the Administration's priority items. A related bill is currently under consideration in the Senate Judiciary Committee.

Another important policy issue related to patents is the phenomenon of "pay-for-delay" settlements of patent lawsuits in the pharmaceutical industry. This is discussed in Box 5-7 below.

CONCLUSION

Productivity growth allows a given set of scarce resources to yield more output and a higher aggregate standard of living. When private actors face incentives that lead them to optimal investments in growth-enhancing technologies, government policy should be to not interfere. But at other times, a light touch from government is needed to align incentives or to act in place of incentives that are missing: in the form of conducting of its own research; or of subsidization of private research; or through appropriate intellectual property rights laws, regulation, and enforcement. Government also has a role to play in ensuring that all citizens benefit from productivity advances that can increase living standards—a step that can form a virtuous cycle that also increases productivity growth itself by tapping more of the potential of our citizens.

Box 5-7: Pay-For-Delay Settlements in Pharmaceutical Patent Cases

Out-of-court settlements of lawsuits are usually socially beneficial, as they allow disputes to be resolved without a costly trial. There are circumstances, however, where settlement of a patent lawsuit can be used as a means of extending market power, rather than as a means of efficiently resolving the dispute. In recent years, this has been a significant issue for certain cases involving pharmaceutical patents. In these cases, an incumbent seller of a branded drug files a patent infringement suit against one or more companies seeking Food and Drug Administration approval to sell a generic version of that drug. The patent at issue is often not the one covering the drug's active ingredient (for which assessing infringement is usually less complicated), but is instead a secondary patent, such as one covering a particular formulation of the drug (Hemphill and Sampat 2011). The generic entrant will deny the infringement, claiming that the patent is invalid, that its product does not infringe, or both. A patent lawsuit results, and is settled through an agreement specifying a date on which the generic entrant may begin selling its product, which is some time after the date of the settlement and before the patent expires. The settlement will also specify a payment from the branded incumbent to the generic entrant. Absent the settlement, the case would have gone to trial; had the incumbent won, the generic entrant would have been barred from entry until the end of the incumbent's patent term, and had the entrant won, it could have entered immediately and sold its product, assuming it had received FDA approval.

The willingness of the incumbent to agree to such a settlement may seem puzzling, as the payment appears to go the "wrong" way, from the alleged infringer to the infringed. But the ability to enter into such settlements can benefit the incumbent by enabling it to "purchase" later generic entry than would otherwise occur. In other words, settlements of patent disputes can be used as a vehicle for extending market power.

What drives these settlements is the fundamental economic principle that the profits of a single seller of a product are greater than the combined profits of two or more sellers, because a single seller has greater market power and so can extract a higher price from consumers. A settlement that delays generic entry of a drug therefore increases the aggregate profits on that drug. These extra profits create an incentive for a deal in which entry is delayed; both parties will accept such a deal as long as the extra profits are divided in such a way that each party is better off than it would be absent the deal (i.e., better off than by letting the patent lawsuit proceed to trial). For this reason, these settlements are often called "pay-for-delay" settlements.

Pay-for-delay settlements undermine existing laws (most notably the Hatch-Waxman Act) that encourage the development of generic drugs. When generic drugs enter a market, they are offered at a much lower price than is the branded drug, and they typically capture a large market share. For these reasons, generic entry results in considerable savings to consumers and to the health care system. The delay of generic entry due to pay-for-delay settlements greatly reduces those savings.

The ability of incumbent patent holders to enter into pay-for-delay settlements, and to thereby maintain their patent protection for a longer period, might be viewed as increasing the value of pharmaceutical patents, and hence increasing the incentive to invest in discovering new drugs. However, the value of any increased innovation arising from these settlements may be relatively small. The most socially valuable drug patents are often those covering new molecular entities. These patents are relatively unlikely to be successfully challenged, which means the generic entrant has little prospect of victory at trial or of a lucrative pay-for-delay settlement. As a result, banning such settlements may not significantly affect the incentive to invest in inventing new molecular entities. Instead, pay-for-delay settlements often involve patents on incremental improvements to existing drugs, often ones that make the drug just different enough that a prescription for the new version cannot be filled with an existing generic equivalent of the old version. The ability to enter into pay-for-delay settlements does encourage this type of innovation, but the social benefits are likely to be comparatively small in many cases.

Pay-for-delay settlements have been the subject of a considerable amount of litigation, culminating in a 2013 Supreme Court decision in FTC v. Actavis, involving a drug called AndroGel. The Court ruled that "pay for delay" settlements are not presumptively unlawful, but are also not immune from antitrust scrutiny, partially resolving earlier conflicting rulings by lower courts (see FTC v. Actavis 2013). The Court did not establish a concrete rule regarding how such settlements should be treated, however, so substantial uncertainty remains about how these lawsuits will be adjudicated in practice.

The Administration has proposed legislation that gives the Federal Trade Commission explicit authority to stop companies from entering into pay-for-delay agreements. For the reasons described above, such authority would likely generate billions of dollars in savings for consumers, and also for the Federal Government through lower pharmaceutical prices paid by Medicare, Medicaid, the Department of Defense, and the Veterans Administration (see CBO 2011 and FTC 2010).

CHAPTER 6

THE WAR ON POVERTY 50 YEARS LATER: A PROGRESS REPORT

President Lyndon B. Johnson declared an "unconditional war on poverty in America" on January 8, 1964, and within a few years oversaw the creation of an array of programs "aimed not only to relieve the symptom of poverty, but to cure it and, above all, to prevent it." In the 1964 Economic Report of the President, President Johnson's Council of Economic Advisers outlined the many key points of attack: "maintaining high employment, accelerating economic growth, fighting discrimination, improving regional economies, rehabilitating urban and rural communities, improving labor markets, expanding educational opportunities, enlarging job opportunities for youth, improving the Nation's health, promoting adult education and training, and assisting the aged and disabled." The report ended with the declaration that, "It is time to renew our faith in the worth and capacity of all human beings; to recognize that, whatever their past history or present condition, all kinds of Americans can contribute to their country; and to allow Government to assume its responsibility for action and leadership in promoting the general welfare."

The War on Poverty ushered in a new era of Federal Government leadership in providing income and nutrition support, access to education, skills training, health insurance and a myriad of other services to low-income Americans. During President Johnson's term, Congress passed more than a dozen major pieces of legislation that provided such foundational elements of our current social welfare system as the Civil Rights Act, the Economic Opportunity Act, the Food Stamp Act, Elementary and Secondary Education Act, the Manpower Act, Medicare, Medicaid, the Higher Education Act and the Child Nutrition Act. Since then, many of these programs have been reformed and updated, ensuring that the modern safety net assists families when they need it most, while also keeping them connected to the labor force.

Optimism was high at the outset of the War on Poverty. One of its architects predicted poverty would be eradicated within a generation and saw "on the horizon a society of abundance, free of much of the misery and degradation that have been the age-old fate of man (Council of Economic Advisers 1964)." The 50th anniversary of President Johnson's bold declaration provides an opportunity to assess our achievements in reducing poverty and to evaluate the record of the poverty-fighting programs created or enhanced in the wake of his declaration. There is no question that the material conditions of those in poverty have improved: the percentage of the poor with indoor plumbing has risen from 58 percent in 1960 to 99 percent in 2011;[1] infant mortality in counties with the highest levels of deprivation has fallen from 23.2 per 1,000 in 1969 to 9.1 per 1,000 in 2000;[2] and today all American children in poverty have access to affordable health insurance, as do poor adults in states that have taken up the Affordable Care Act's Medicaid expansion. But to what extent have we reduced the proportion of Americans living in poverty? Indeed, the poverty rate has declined considerably since the beginning of the War on Poverty, but how much of this improvement is due to the efforts of government? And what are the lessons this contains for future policy?

This chapter answers these questions by first confronting the challenges in measuring poverty, and highlighting the limitations of the official poverty measure for tracking progress in the War on Poverty. Using new historical estimates of poverty based on modern measurement methods, this chapter presents a more accurate picture of the changes in poverty over the past five decades, and estimates the contribution of the safety net to these changes. While the Council of Economic Advisers (CEA) reviewed research on the effects of antipoverty programs on work and earnings, health, food security, educational attainment, and other valued outcomes, this chapter focuses primarily on their impacts on poverty and economic mobility.[3] Finally, it discusses the role that President Obama has played in reducing material hardship among low-income Americans by expanding access to affordable health insurance and tax credits for working families, and by his proposals to help ensure that no parent who works full time will have to raise his or her children in poverty.

---

[1] CEA calculations using 1960 Census and 2011 American Community Survey data.
[2] These figures come from Singh and Kogan (2007). The analysis compares birth outcomes in counties in the top and bottom quintiles of a socioeconomic deprivation index based on Census information on education, occupation, wealth, income distribution, unemployment, poverty, and housing quality. The data are broken out into 5-year periods—the statistics cited compare 1969-74 to 1995-2000.
[3] See Bailey and Danziger (2013) for an authoritative assessment of the various components of the War on Poverty from economists' perspectives.

Measuring Poverty: Who is Poor in America?

Michael Harrington's influential 1962 book The Other America depicted the poor as inhabiting an "invisible land," a world described in the 1964 Economic Report of the President as "scarcely recognizable, and rarely recognized, by the majority of their fellow Americans." One early achievement of Johnson's War on Poverty was to cast light on the problem of poverty by developing an official poverty measure that has been released by the government in each year since August 1969.[4] While reasonable at the time, this measure has turned out to be ill-suited to capturing the progress subsequently made in the War. As a result, modern poverty measures tell a different story of who is poor, and especially how this has changed over time.

Measuring Poverty

Measuring poverty is not a simple task; even defining it is controversial. Just starting with a commonsense definition of the poor—"those whose basic needs exceed their means to satisfy them"—requires difficult conceptual choices regarding what constitutes basic needs and what resources should be counted in figuring a family's means. There are no generally accepted standards of minimum needs for most necessary consumption items such as housing, clothing, and transportation. Moreover, our ideas about minimum needs may change over time. For example, even some middle-income households did not have hot and cold running water indoors in 1963. Today, over 99 percent of all households have complete indoor plumbing.

The Official Poverty Measure

Mollie Orshansky, an economist in the Social Security Administration, developed the official poverty thresholds between 1963 and 1964 (Fisher 1992). At the time, the U.S. Department of Agriculture had a set of food plans derived using data from the 1955 Household Food Consumption Survey, the lowest cost of which was deemed adequate for "temporary or emergency use when funds are low." Because families in this survey spent about one-third of their incomes, on average, on food, Orshansky set the poverty threshold at three times the dollar cost of this "economy food plan," with adjustments for family size, composition, and whether the family lived on a farm.

These income thresholds that were first used as the poverty thresholds for the 1963 calendar year have served as the basis for the official poverty

---

[4] A similar poverty measure was adopted internally by the Office of Economic Opportunity in 1965.

Box 6-1: Flaws In The Official Poverty Measure

The official poverty measure (OPM) has several flaws that distort our understanding of both the level of poverty and how it has changed over time. Perhaps the most significant problem with the OPM is its measure of family resources, based on pre-tax income plus cash transfers (like cash welfare, social security, or unemployment insurance payments), but not taxes, tax credits, or non-cash transfers. As such it inhabits a measurement limbo between "market poverty" (based on pre-tax, pre-transfer resources) and "post-tax, post-transfer poverty" reflecting well-being after taking into account the impact of policies directed at the poor.

Several other shortcomings are more technical. First, the dollar value defining the cost of basic needs, or the poverty threshold, was set in the 1960s and has been updated each year since using an index of food prices at first, but then the Consumer Price Index (CPI) after 1969. The use of the CPI is one source of the problems with the official measure that limits its usefulness for historical comparison. Methodological advances in measuring prices (for example, rental equivalence treatment of housing costs, quality adjustments for some large purchases, and geometric averaging for similar goods) have shown that the CPI overstated inflation substantially prior to the early 1980s, leading to an inflated estimate of the cost of basic needs and thus higher measured poverty over time. Revising the OPM measure using the CPI-U-RS (a historical series estimated consistently using modern methods) results in a fall in poverty from 1966 to 2012 that is 3 percentage points greater than that depicted by the official measure. Another flaw with the OPM thresholds is that they do not accurately reflect geographic variation in costs of living or economies associated with family size and structure.

All current income-based poverty measures, including both the OPM and the Supplemental Poverty Measure (SPM), suffer from large underreporting of both incomes and benefits. For example, Meyer, Mok, and Sullivan (2009) show that in 1984, March CPS respondents reported only 75 percent of Aid to Families with Dependent Children/Temporary Assistance for Needy Families (AFDC/TANF) dollars, and this fell to 49 percent in 2004. For SNAP benefits, which are accounted for in the SPM but not the OPM, 71 percent of the value was reported in 1984 compared to 57 percent in 2004. Underreporting will tend to increase measured poverty, so increases in underreporting over time understate the decline in the poverty rate during this period. The underreporting also means that the estimated effects of government programs on poverty, as described below, are likely to be conservative lower-bound estimates of the true effects.

thresholds ever since. These dollar amounts have been adjusted for inflation to hold the real value of the income needed to be above poverty the same over time. There have been minor tweaks to the methodology involving which price index is used to adjust for inflation, and how adjustments are made for family structure and farm status.

In defining the family resources to be compared to the poverty line, Orshansky created the thresholds to be applied to after-tax money income—the income concept used in the 1955 Household Food Consumption Survey. However, she was forced to use pre-tax money income (including cash transfer payments) due to limitations in the Current Population Survey (CPS) data, the only source of nationally representative information on income. At the time, this was an adequate approximation of disposable income, as few low-income families had any federal income tax liability or credits owed, and in-kind transfers were not a quantitatively important feature of the safety net.

The Supplemental Poverty Measure

While Orshansky's measure provided a reasonable depiction of poverty in the 1960s, it has not aged well.[5] Today, for example, the value of the two largest non-health programs directing aid to the poor—the Earned Income Tax Credit (EITC) and Supplemental Nutrition Assistance Program (SNAP)—are entirely ignored by the official measure, making it impossible to assess the success of these tools in fighting poverty. Over the past five decades, researchers have pointed to many flaws in the official measure (Box 6-1), leading to the development of alternative measures of poverty with more comprehensive measures of both family needs and resources. The Census Bureau created a Supplemental Poverty Measure (SPM), which departs dramatically from the official measure in its methodology for calculating both the poverty thresholds and family resources.[6] This measure, first published in 2011, calculates poverty thresholds using recent expenditures by families at the 33rd percentile of the expenditure distribution on an array

---

[5] It should be noted that Orshansky herself noted many flaws with her measure, and believed it understated poverty. She argued it measured income inadequacy rather than adequacy, stating "if it is not possible to state unequivocally 'how much is enough,' it should be possible to assert with confidence how much, on an average, is too little" (Orshansky 1965).

[6] While the term "family" is used here, the SPM differs in its definition of a "family unit" when assuming the unit of individuals over which resources are shared. Most importantly, the SPM includes all related individuals living at the same address, but also cohabiting individuals and co-residing children in their care.

Box 6-2: A Consumption Poverty Measure

Consumption-based poverty measures the amount households spend relative to a threshold on goods and services, and estimates "service flows" from large, infrequent purchases like housing and automobiles. Meyer and Sullivan argue in a series of papers (2003, 2012a, 2012b, 2013) that consumption provides a better measure of resources for low-income households since it reflects accumulated assets, expected future income, access to credit, assistance from family and friends, non-market income, and the insurance value of government programs. They also argue that consumption data are more accurately reported relative to some safety net benefits included in the SPM, especially for households in or near poverty.

The figure below shows the trend in Meyer and Sullivan's (2013) measure of consumption poverty, updated through 2012 and normalized to have the same level as the SPM measure in 2012. Although the underlying methodologies differ, the trends in consumption poverty and SPM income poverty have been remarkably similar over time. For example, the declines in poverty between 1972 and 2012 shown by each measure are nearly identical.

It is difficult to identify the effects of particular government programs on consumption poverty because it is harder to identify and remove the consumption derived from particular government programs than it is with income under the SPM. However, the fact that the two measures are similar suggests that underreporting of benefits has little impact at the margin of determining whether someone is poor. Additionally, the similarities in the measure suggest that spending through savings, or borrowing from friends and family, is rarely able to keep someone out of poverty.

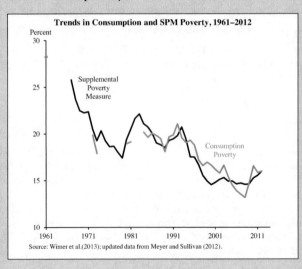

Trends in Consumption and SPM Poverty, 1961–2012

Source: Wimer et al.(2013); updated data from Meyer and Sullivan (2012).

of necessary items, including food, shelter, clothing, and utilities.[7] The dollar amount is calculated separately for families depending on whether they own or rent their home and whether they have a mortgage, and then increased by 20 percent to allow for other necessary expenses. Further adjustments are made based on differences in family size and structure, and, unlike in the official measure, the threshold is adjusted for geographic variation in living costs (Short 2013).

The Supplemental Poverty Measure also uses a more accurate measure of disposable income that accounts for both a greater number of income sources and a wider array of necessary expenditures. Unlike the official measure, the SPM uses a post-tax, post-transfer concept of resources that adds to family earnings all cash transfers and the cash-equivalent of in-kind transfers such as food assistance (for example, SNAP or free lunch) minus net tax liabilities, which can be negative for families receiving refundable tax credits like the EITC or CTC. Necessary expenditures on work and childcare are then subtracted from resources.

The Supplemental Poverty Measure also subtracts medical-out-of-pocket expenses from families' resources since those funds are not available to meet other needs. The SPM can thus be thought of as a measure of deprivation with respect to non-health care goods and services.[8] However, it does not provide an accurate picture of the benefits of health care. Instead, the SPM values health insurance only insofar as it reduces households' out-of-pocket medical costs and thus frees up resources for other uses. It misses benefits that may arise because insurance improves access to health care and may therefore improve health outcomes, or reduces stress caused by exposure to financial risk. As a result, the measured trend in SPM poverty may understate progress in decreasing economic hardship since the War on Poverty began by ignoring these benefits of increased access to insurance.

One important feature of the Supplemental Poverty Measure design is that the definition of minimum needs is adjusted each year based on recent data on family expenditures on necessities rather than adjusting a fixed bundle only for inflation. By considering families' expenditures on an array of necessary items, including food, shelter, clothing, and utilities—and

---

[7] More accurately, the thresholds are based on average expenditures on food, clothing, shelter, and utilities between the 30th and 36th percentiles of that distribution, multiplied by 1.2 to account for other necessary expenses and adjusted for geographic differences in cost of living and family size and structure.

[8] Korenman and Remler (2013) argue that the SPM's treatment of medical-out-of-pocket expenses actually does a poor job of capturing even deprivation of non-health care goods and services. They argue that households that are able to spend a large amount on health care are frequently those with substantial savings or other resources to draw on, and they present evidence that households with high out-of-pocket expenses frequently score lower on "direct" measures of hardship, like food insecurity.

then setting poverty rates based on how much families at the 33rd percentile spend—the SPM adjusts poverty thresholds as societies' spending patterns on these necessities shifts.[9] This type of threshold is "quasi-relative," in the sense that thresholds will tend to rise with income, but are not directly tied to income as in a purely relative definition of poverty, such as setting a threshold at half the median household income.

Alternatively, it is possible to create an "anchored" version of the Supplemental Poverty Measure, which is the focus in this chapter. The anchored version, like the official measure, fixes poverty thresholds based on expenditures on necessary items in a given year and then adjusts only for inflation in each year. This version allows for the use of the more comprehensive definition of resources in measuring poverty over time, while setting a fixed assessment of what constitutes basic needs spending on food, shelter, clothing, and utilities. The anchored measure is also more consistent with the vision of the War on Poverty architects, who believed that poverty can be eradicated. Eliminating poverty defined with a relative measure may be nearly impossible, as the threshold rises apace with incomes.[10]

Who is Poor?

In an attempt to "provide some understanding of the enemy" for Johnson's War, the 1964 Economic Report of the President presented tables depicting the "topography of poverty." As Table 1 shows, some of the landmarks have changed since 1960 while many remain the same. For 2012, the Table presents the poverty rates measured with both the official poverty measure and the Supplemental Poverty Measure.[11] The official measure is displayed for comparing the relative poverty of various groups in the two time periods, but should not be used for comparing changes in the levels of poverty between the two time periods due to the flaws in the official measure discussed above. The next section will provide trend data using a consistent

---

[9] So, for example, if families across the income spectrum spend more on, say, housing because preferences for or the ability to pay for space or bathrooms change then what is considered necessary for minimum housing will change.

[10] The SPM is a hybrid, "quasi-relative" measure such that when spending on necessities increases, the threshold defining who is poor also increases. It is unlikely to rise at the same rate as income, as with relative poverty measures, but will adjust more slowly since spending on necessities grows more slowly than income. Eliminating poverty under this quasi-relative definition is possible, depending on how a country's spending on necessities evolves as its income increases.

[11] This Table uses the official Supplemental Poverty Measure statistics published by the Census Bureau (Short 2013), whereas for historical comparisons below we rely on historical estimates produced by Wimer et al. (2013), described below. The series from Wimer et al. anchors its poverty measure at the 2012 SPM thresholds, so their estimated poverty rates for 2012 are very similar to those in Table 1.

Table 6-1
Poverty Rates by Selected Characteristics, 1959 and 2012

	1959	2012	
	Official Poverty Measure	Official Poverty Measure	Supplemental Poverty Measure
All People	24.3	15.1	16.0
Household Characteristics			
Head worked last year	17.8	10.0	10.5
Head did not work last year	55.7	27.4	29.2
Head married	18.9	7.9	10.2
Head single female	47.4	29.1	28.9
Individual Characteristics			
Less than high school (age 25-64)	25.3	33.9	35.8
High school (age 25-64)	10.2	15.6	17.5
College (adults 25-64)	6.7	4.5	5.9
Younger than 18	26.8	22.3	18.0
65 years and older	39.9	9.1	14.8
Female	24.9	16.4	16.7
African American	57.8	27.3	25.8
Hispanic	40.5	25.8	27.8
Asian	N/A	11.8	16.7
Native Alaskans/American Indians	N/A	34.2	30.3
White	19.5	9.8	10.7
Immigrant	23.0	19.3	25.4
Disabled (age 18-64)	N/A	28.4	26.5
Lives outside a metropolitan area	32.7	17.9	13.9

Note: Calculations based on characteristics of household heads exclude people living in group quarters.
Source: Census Bureau; CEA calculations.

measure. Since historical estimates of the SPM are available only starting in 1967, Table 1 shows only official poverty rates for 1959 using the 1960 Census.

Employment

Unsurprisingly, unemployment is one of the strongest predictors of poverty. In 1959, 55.7 percent of individuals in households where the head was out of work for a full year were poor—three times the rate of individuals in households where the head worked at least one week during the year. While this rate has declined to 29.2 percent, individuals in households where the head was out of work for a full-year were still three times as likely to be poor as those in households where the head worked.

However, even full-time employment is not enough to keep all families out of poverty today. A person working full-time, full-year in 2013 being paid the minimum wage earns $14,500 for the year. These earnings alone leave such workers below the poverty threshold if they have even one child. While the EITC, SNAP, and other benefits will help pull a family of two above the poverty line, for a larger family—such as one with three children—full-time, full-year minimum wage work combined with government assistance is unlikely to be enough to lift that family out of poverty.

Education Level

Education's role in poverty prevention has become more important over time: in 1959, high-school dropouts were 3.8 times more likely to be poor than college graduates; but in 2012, they were 6.1 times more likely to be poor (based on the SPM measure). The growth in the poverty gap by education is driven by growth in earnings inequality, which has led to much greater earnings for college graduates than for those with less education.

Children

As in 1959, the child poverty rate today is higher than the poverty rate of the overall population, although the SPM shows that children are disproportionately helped by our poverty-fighting programs. Once taxes and in-kind transfers are taken into account, the gap between child and non-child poverty falls. According to the official measure, the child poverty rate in 2012 was 22.3 percent—nearly 48 percent higher than the overall rate. But the official rate ignores the contributions of the most important antipoverty programs for children: the EITC and other refundable tax credits and SNAP. Including the value of these resources, the SPM estimates that 18 percent of children are poor—a rate that is 12.5 percent (2 percentage points) higher than the overall poverty rate.

The Elderly

One of the most heralded successes of the War on Poverty is the large reduction in elderly poverty rates. In 1959, poverty rates were highest among the elderly with 39.9 percent of people 65 and older living in poverty (based on OPM). Today, poverty rates of those 65 and older are below the national average. Using the SPM measure shows elderly poverty at 14.8 percent, which is more than 50 percent higher than when taken with the OPM measure. The reason for this difference is that the SPM subtracts

Box 6-3: Women and Poverty

While women continue to have a higher poverty rate than men, the gap has decreased over time as poverty has fallen more for women than for men. The following chart shows that the gap between working-age women and men has decreased from 4.7 percent to 1.7 percent from 1967 to 2012.

The decline in the poverty rate among women has been tempered by an increase in the number of single mothers, who have higher rates of poverty. The share of working-age women who are single mothers rose from 11.6 to 16.1 percent between 1967 and 2012. Had the poverty rates of demographic groups (based on marriage and motherhood only) remained as they were in 1967, this change would have increased poverty rates for working-age women by 2.1 percentage points. In fact, poverty rates of women in all marriage and motherhood groups fell due to increased work, rising education, and smaller families (Cancian and Reed 2009), as well as to the increased impact of the safety net described in this chapter.

The effect of government transfer and social insurance programs on poverty is slightly larger for women than for men. These programs reduced the 2012 poverty rate by 8.1 percentage points for working-age women compared to 6.4 percentage points for working-age men. This gender difference has been fairly stable over time, indicating that growth in these programs does not explain the narrowing poverty gap shown above. Rather, the closing of the gender poverty gap appears to be due to increases in women's education and employment rates relative to men.

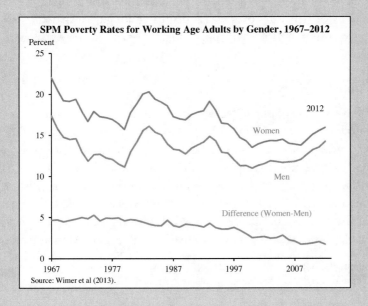

SPM Poverty Rates for Working Age Adults by Gender, 1967–2012

Source: Wimer et al (2013).

expenditures on medical expenses from a family's resources, and the elderly tend to have much higher medical expenses. Indeed, if the out-of-pocket medical costs were not subtracted, the measured elderly poverty rate would be only 8.4 percent—lower than their official poverty rate of 9.1 percent.[12] In the absence of Medicare and Medicaid, out-of-pocket medical expenses of the elderly would almost certainly cause their poverty to be much higher than the SPM poverty rate of 14.8 percent.

Women

Women are more likely than men to be in poverty, with a 2012 poverty rate of 16.7 percent compared to 15.3 percent among men. This gap largely reflects higher poverty among single women, both those age 18-64 (22.9 percent compared to 20.2 percent among single men) and those age 65 or older (21.2 percent compared to 16.1 percent among single men).

Childcare responsibilities help explain the poverty gap for single working-age women. Almost one-third (31.0 percent) of single women age 18-64 lived with their children in 2012, among whom the poverty rate was 27.5 percent. Just over one-third (35.2 percent) of single mothers age 18-64 were employed full-time, full-year in 2012, compared to 44.6 percent of single working-age males and 43.3 percent of single working-age women without children at home. Increased support for childcare for young children has been shown to positively affect mothers' employment hours and earnings (Connelly and Kimmel 2003; Misra, Budig, and Boeckmann 2011). The high poverty rate among older single women relative to men reflects a combination of lower Social Security benefits due to lower lifetime earnings; lower rates of pension coverage; and greater longevity that increases the chances of outliving their private savings (Anzick and Weaver 2001, SSA 2012).

Race and Ethnicity

Poverty rates have fallen for all racial and ethnic groups over time and gaps by race have shrunk slightly. However, troubling gaps still remain. In 1959, nearly three-fifths of African Americans were in poverty, which was nearly three times the poverty rate of Whites. The fraction of African Americans in poverty has fallen by more than half since then; yet at 25.8 percent, the SPM poverty rate for African Americans is still more than double the rate of 10.7 percent for Whites. Today, the SPM poverty rate among Hispanics is 27.8 percent, similar to that among African Americans.

---

[12] Accounting for out-of-pocket medical expenses raises measured poverty for nonelderly adults and children by 2.9 and 3.1 percentage points, respectively.

However, this reflects smaller declines in poverty among Hispanics over the past 50 years. Among both African Americans and Hispanics, the official and supplemental poverty rates tell similar stories. However, the SPM reveals that Asian Americans have a slightly higher poverty rate than the national average—at 16.7 percent—while their OPM poverty rate is lower than the national average. The higher SPM rate for Asian Americans reflects, in part, the fact that they tend to live in high-cost metropolitan areas (for example, Los Angeles and New York City) and the SPM poverty thresholds are higher in such places due to its geographic adjustments for cost of living. Finally, while measures of poverty among American Indians and Alaska Natives are not available in the earlier period, currently they have the highest rates of poverty of any race and ethnicity group at 30.3 percent in 2012.

People with Disabilities

Over one-fourth of working-age people with disabilities are estimated to live in poverty, using both the OPM (28.4 percent) and SPM (26.5 percent) measures. This largely reflects their low employment rates. The effective poverty rate of people with disabilities may be understated due to the extra costs that often accompany disability, such as for home and vehicle renovations, assistive equipment, personal assistance, and other items and services that may not be covered by insurance or government programs (Sen 2009: 258, She and Livermore 2007, Fremstad 2009, Schur, Kruse, and Blanck 2013: 32-33).

Rural and Urban Communities

The official poverty measure overestimates rural poverty since rural communities tend to have lower costs of living than urban areas and the official measure does not take geographic cost-of-living differences into account. However, the OPM has revealed that significant poverty persists in rural communities throughout the country today. The Economic Research Service of the U.S. Department of Agriculture estimates that 85 percent of persistent poverty counties—counties that have been in high poverty (over 20 percent based on the OPM) for at least 30 years—are in rural areas.[13] The gap between poverty rates outside and within metropolitan areas, though, has narrowed since 1959 when poverty rates outside metropolitan areas were more than double the rates within these areas. In fact, the adjustments

---

[13] See http://www.ers.usda.gov/topics/rural-economy-population/rural-poverty-well-being/geography-of-poverty.aspx#.UurSXhBdXA0

for different housing costs across geographic areas in the SPM show that poverty rates are higher in metropolitan areas than in rural areas today.[14]

Assessing the War on Poverty

This section presents new historical estimates of the poverty rate from 1967 to 2012 based on the Supplemental Poverty Measure and shows that substantial progress has been made in reducing poverty since President Johnson began major policy initiatives as part of his fight against poverty. In the past 45 years, the poverty rate fell from 25.8 to 16.0 percent—a reduction of over one-third. CEA documents that much of this decline was due to the increased poverty-reducing effects of the safety net expansion set in motion during the Johnson Administration. Based on a measure of pre-tax, pre-transfer income, the poverty rate would be about as high today as in 1967: over 28 percent. These analyses show that safety net programs lifted 45 million people from poverty in 2012 and, between 1968 and 2012, prevented 1.2 billion "person years" from living below the poverty line. This section first reviews changes in the economy that provide context for understanding the lack of growth in market incomes in the bottom part of the distribution over this time period. The section then presents estimates of poverty trends since 1967, measured using modern methods.

Context

The architects of the War on Poverty were confident they would live to see poverty eradicated. Looking at the data at their disposal at the time, it is easy to see how an analyst might have believed the end of poverty was on the horizon. Figure 6-1 shows the trend in the official poverty measure—the only consistently available measure tracking poverty until recently—from 1959 through 2012. Based on the trend in poverty observed between 1959 and 1968, one would have indeed forecast—extrapolating linearly—that poverty would be eradicated by 1980. Poverty fell by a remarkably consistent rate of about 1.15 percentage points a year over that 10-year period, but the official poverty measure stopped declining afterwards, reaching its lowest point in 1973.

As previously noted, the OPM is a measure of cash income that does not include non-cash benefits or tax credits. While it does not accurately capture the trend in poverty over time, it is nonetheless worth considering why the improvement in this measure of cash income slowed so abruptly in

---

[14] This comparison may be affected by significant differences among geographic areas in costs other than housing, such as transportation. In addition, there may be differences in housing quality that are not captured by the differences in housing costs.

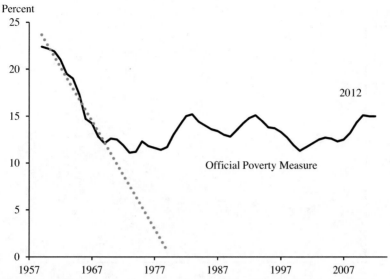

Figure 6-1
Trends in the Official Poverty Measure, 1959–2012

Percent

Source: Bureau of Labor Statistics, Current Population Survey, Annual Social and Economic Supplement;
CEA calculations.

the early 1970s. The first, and clearest, answer is that Social Security expansions during the 1960s brought the rate of poverty among the elderly down rapidly before leveling in the 1970s (Engelhardt and Gruber 2006). In 1959, 39.9 percent of those 65 and older were in poverty, but by 1974 that fraction had fallen to 14.6 percent (based on the OPM). Over the next 38 years, the elderly poverty rate fell further to 9.1 percent in 2012. The deceleration in poverty reduction is less pronounced for nonelderly adults and children. In fact, using the SPM measure that accounts for expansions of the EITC and non-cash transfers, children's poverty had greater declines in the 1990s than in the 1960s or 1970s.

Growth in inequality has also helped put the brakes on improvements in cash income for most households. Economic growth is an important determinant of poverty (Blank 2000) as long as the gains are shared with those in the bottom of the income distribution. When growth fails to benefit the bottom, it cannot play a role in eradicating poverty. As such, the distribution of income can have a profound impact on the level of poverty. While the real economy grew at an annual rate of about 2.1 percent during the 1970s and 1980s, since 1980 economic growth has not produced the "rising tide" heralded by President Kennedy, as rising inequality left incomes at the bottom relatively unchanged (DiNardo, Fortin, Lemieux 1996, Piketty and Saez 2003, Lemieux 2008). As shown in Figure 6-2, incomes in the top

Figure 6-2
Average Real Household Income by Quintile, 1967–2012

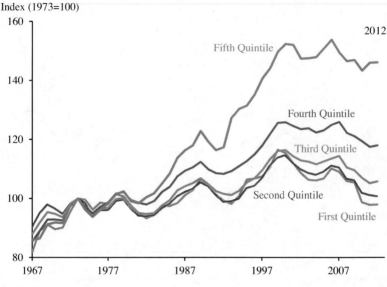

Source: Census Bureau.

20 percent of the income distribution rose dramatically until the 2000s and are about 50 percent higher today than in 1973. By contrast, real household incomes in the bottom 60 percent of the income distribution stagnated until the mid-1990s expansion, and today are little changed from the business cycle peak in 1973.

A large group of poverty scholars have pointed to this rise in inequality as a leading explanation for the lack of progress in reducing poverty since 1980 (for example, Blank 1993; Gottschalk and Danziger 1995, 2003; Hoynes, Page, and Stevens 2006).

The failure of the minimum wage to keep up with inflation is an important reason why inequality increased in the 1980s (DiNardo, Fortin, and Lemieux 1996, Lee 1999), and progress in the fight against poverty has slowed. President Johnson extended both the level and scope of the minimum wage, with its peak reached in real terms in 1968. Since then, the minimum wage has risen and fallen, but today its level of $7.25 an hour is the same in real terms as in 1950. At this level, even factoring in the subsidy provided by the EITC, a single parent of two kids working full time would still have income near the poverty line.

Several studies have documented a tight link between the value of the minimum wage and measures of wage inequality in the bottom part of the income distribution (Lee 1999, DiNardo, Fortin, and Lemieux 1996). For

Box 6-4: Social Programs Serve All Americans

While the safety net provides crucial support for families in poverty, far more Americans benefit from the safety net than are poor in any given year. Of course, all Americans benefit from Social Security and Medicare support for the aged, shielding both them and their families from low income in retirement and the costs of adverse health shocks. And many people benefit from social insurance programs that are not means-tested. For example, nearly half of all Americans will benefit from unemployment insurance at some point over a 20-year period.

But even programs targeting primarily low-income families serve a very high fraction of Americans at some point in their lives. A recent study using administrative tax records from 1989 to 2006 found that over 50 percent of tax-filers with children benefited from the EITC at some point over the 19-year period (Dowd and Horowitz 2011). Moreover, CEA analysis of the National Longitudinal Study of Youth 1979 finds that of all individuals aged 14 to 22 in 1979, over the 32-year period from 1978 to 2010:

- 29.6 percent benefitted from SNAP;
- 34.2 percent received support from SNAP, AFDC/TANF, or SSI; and
- 69.2 percent received income from SNAP, AFDC/TANF, SSI, or UI.

Looking at a broader array of programs, a large fraction of the population benefits in any given year as well. According to the 2013 Annual Demographic and Economic Supplement of the Current Population Survey, nearly half (47.5 percent) of all households received support from either refundable tax credits, SNAP, Unemployment Insurance, SSI, housing assistance, school lunch, TANF, Women, Infants, and Children (WIC), Medicaid or Disability Insurance.

An important feature of the safety net that is often overlooked: for most programs the majority of beneficiaries receive assistance for only a short period when their earnings drop for some reason, and then they bounce out again. Research has shown, for example, that 61 percent of all EITC recipients claimed the credit for two years or less (Dowd and Horowitz 2011); and, half of all new SNAP participants in the mid-2000s left the program within 10 months.[1]

---

[1] See: http://www.fns.usda.gov/sites/default/files/BuildingHealthyAmerica.pdf

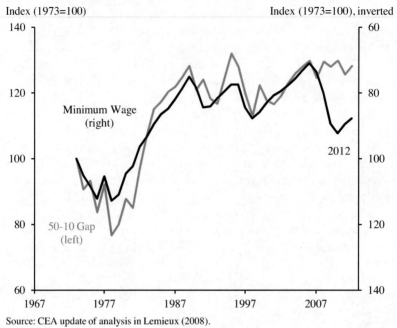

Figure 6-3
Women's 50-10 Wage Gap vs Real Minimum Wage, 1973–2012

Index (1973=100)   Index (1973=100), inverted

Minimum Wage
(right)

2012

50-10 Gap
(left)

Source: CEA update of analysis in Lemieux (2008).

example, as shown in Figure 6-3, changes in the ratio of the median wage to the 10th percentile of the wage distribution (the "50-10 wage gap")—a measure of inequality in the bottom of the wage distribution—for women correlate very closely with changes in the real value of the minimum wage.[15] The best research suggests that increases in the minimum wage do not result in job losses large enough to undermine the goal of raising incomes for the poor (Dube, Lester, Reich 2010). Moreover, a recent meta-analysis by Doucouliagos and Stanley (2009) covering over 1,000 estimates of minimum wage effects finds "no evidence of a meaningful adverse employment effect." Finally, a recent analysis and review of the literature by Dube (2013) finds consistent evidence across studies that a 10 percent increase in the minimum wage decreases the poverty rate by about 2.4 percent.

Another important factor in rising inequality and slow wage growth among low- and middle-income workers has been the decline in unionization. The percent of U.S. workers represented by unions has nearly halved from 23.3 percent in 1983 to 12.4 percent in 2013.[16] This decline has contributed to inequality because unions reduce inequality by raising the wages

---

[15] The figure updates an analysis in Lemieux (2008), who graciously shared data.
[16] Retrieved from http://www.bls.gov/cps/cpslutabs.htm, January 30, 2014.

of low- and middle-income workers and compressing the returns to skill (DiNardo, Fortin, and Lemieux 1996; DiNardo and Lemieux 1997).

Many observers have implicated various demographic changes—most prominently, increased immigration and a decline in two-parent families—as additional factors behind the lack of progress in market incomes in the lower part of the distribution. The recent literature on immigration rejects the claim that competition from immigrants has had a meaningfully adverse effect on the wages or poverty rates of native workers (Peri 2013). Because the country-of-origin composition of immigrants has increasingly shifted toward poorer countries, however, immigration has had a mechanical effect on poverty rates. Card and Raphael (2013) estimate that changes in the population shares and the country of origin of the foreign born increased overall poverty rates (based on OPM) by 3.7 percentage points between 1970 and 2009. While some immigrant households that may have seen their incomes rise as a result of coming to the United States, many still fall below the poverty line here. But other analysts focusing on different time periods generally find much smaller compositional effects. For example, Hoynes, Page, and Stevens (2006) find that increased immigration accounts for only a 0.1 percentage point increase in poverty between 1979 and 1999.

Another dramatic change since the 1960s is a large increase in the number of people living in single-female headed households. As shown in Table 1, individuals in such households typically have double the poverty rates of the national average, so this change also tends to increase the poverty rate. Using decomposition techniques, Hoynes, Page, and Stevens (2006) show that changes in family structure alone accounted for a 3.7 percentage point increase in the (OPM) poverty rate between 1967 and 2003.[17] In fact, women's poverty rates declined over this time period due to their educational attainment, labor force participation, higher earnings, and they had fewer children (Reed and Cancian 2001). Moreover, changes in family structure can both cause and be caused by changes in economic circumstances.

The last three decades have also seen a historic rise in incarceration, which has led to greater poverty. The fraction of the population in prison rose from 221 per 100,000 in 1980 to 762 per 100,000 in 2008 (Western and Pettit 2010).[18] In the short term, imprisonment removes wage earners from the family, which reduces their family's income and increases the probability of their children growing up in poverty. For example, Johnson (2008) finds

---

[17] Like all decompositions, the reference period matters. If the decomposition is performed using 2009 poverty rates rather than those in 1970, the predicted increase is 2.8 percentage points.

[18] Research suggests the increase is driven primarily by increased sentencing severity rather than increases in criminal activity (Caplow and Simon 1999, Nicholson-Crotty and Meier 2003).

that child poverty increases by 8.5 percentage points and family income falls by an average of $8,700 while a father is in prison.

There are also long-term negative impacts on earnings from incarceration that lead to higher rates of poverty among those with a criminal record. Offenders' wages are lower by between 3 and 16 percent after incarceration (Raphael 2007; Western 2002) and employment and labor force participation are also negatively affected. Research shows that each additional percentage point of imprisonment of African American men is associated with a reduction in employment or labor force participation of young African American men of approximately 1.0 to 1.5 percentage points. This relationship implies that the increases in incarceration over the last three decades have reduced employment and labor force participation among young African American males by 3 to 5 percentage points (Holzer 2007). Holzer also notes that, while the magnitude of the effect of incarceration on White and Latino offenders is less clear, most studies find that their experience with employment and labor force participation after incarceration is similar to that of African American men.

Together, the factors described above created headwinds in the fight on poverty. Evaluating the precise impact of these factors is beyond the scope of this report, but it is likely that their combined influence was to exert modest upward pressure on poverty rates. As shown below, the fact that "market poverty" stayed relatively constant over this time period suggests that improvements in education or other factors may have offset the adverse effects of these demographic and other changes. Previous studies based on the OPM support this notion. For example, Mishel et al. (2013) suggest that the impact of increases in education in reducing poverty were slightly greater than the adverse impact of changing demographics.

Correcting the Historical Account of Poverty Since the 1960s

The official poverty measure introduced by President Johnson's administration ignores, by design, the most important antipoverty programs introduced during and after the War on Poverty. In particular, resources from nutrition assistance, tax credits for working families, and access to health insurance are not considered when computing whether a family is poor by the traditional metric.

The Census Bureau has published the Supplemental Poverty Measure only as far back as 2009. But recent research by poverty scholars on alternate measures of poverty all find that the official poverty rate displayed in Figure 6-1 dramatically understates the decline in poverty since the 1960s (Fox et al. 2013, U.S. Census Bureau 2013, Meyer and Sullivan 2013, Sherman 2013). Work by Wimer, Fox, Garfinkel, Kaushal, and Waldfogel (2013) is particularly valuable since they estimate poverty rates from 1967 to 2012 following the SPM methodology for computing family resources. They also measure poverty using an "anchored" measure that uses a fixed poverty threshold based on expenditures on necessary items in 2012, adjusted only for inflation in each year (with inflation measured using a historically consistent series, the CPI-U-RS).[19]

Figure 6-4 shows a striking fact: poverty has declined by 38 percent since 1967, according to the anchored SPM measure. And, unlike the OPM, it continued to fall after the early 1970s. The figure shows the evolution of the poverty rate using the anchored SPM measure of poverty from 1967 to 2012, compared with the official poverty rate reproduced from Figure 6-1. Using the more accurate SPM measure of family resources changes the historical account of poverty in the United States significantly: between 1967 and 2012, poverty rates fell by 9.8 percentage points—from 25.8 to 16.0 percent. The trend in the SPM depicted in Figure 6-4 is very similar to that of an alternative measure of poverty based on consumption data, which Meyer and Sullivan (2013) argue is a better measure of material hardship (Box 6-2).

Figure 6-4 shows that the fraction of Americans in poverty fell smoothly between 1967 and 1979 to a low of 17.4 percent, a period where the discrepancy with the trend shown by the official measure is driven primarily by more accurate accounting for inflation in the 1970s. After rising steeply during the double-dip recession of the early 1980s, poverty rates fell slightly until rising again with the early 1990s recession.

In contrast to the depiction of the OPM, the steepest declines in the fraction of people in poverty occurred during the economic expansion of the 1990s. During that period, poverty fell from 20.7 percent in 1993 to 14.6 percent in 2000, the lowest poverty rate observed since 1967. As shown in Figure 6-2, economic growth in the 1990s provided a strong boost to low-income households as earnings grew even in the bottom one-fifth of incomes, in contrast to the experience of any other decade since the 1960s. Dramatic increases in the value of the EITC leveraged this upswing in the

---

[19] The "anchored poverty" measure allows progress to be measured against a constant definition of living standards. Using the SPM methodology of updating poverty thresholds each year to reflect rising expenditures on food, clothing, shelter, and utilities shows less of a decline in poverty since the real value of the poverty thresholds rise over time (Fox et al. 2013). Data constraints prevent Wimer et al. (2013) from following the SPM methodology exactly. The most important discrepancy from the Census procedure is that Wimer et al. do not adjust the poverty thresholds for geographic differences in living costs. It is worth noting that an alternative measure anchors poverty thresholds based on necessary expenditures in 1967, and adjusts for inflation each year afterwards. Both measures show similar declines in poverty, but using expenditures in 2012 gives a higher level of poverty in every period since increased real spending on necessities over time has led to a higher SPM poverty threshold.

labor market to further encourage work and channel even more resources to low-income working families.

One last, and remarkable, fact shown in Figure 6-4 is that the poverty rate ticked up only slightly during the Great Recession after remaining steady for most of the 2000s. Despite the largest rise in unemployment since the Great Depression, the poverty rate rose by only 0.5 percentage points overall between 2007 and 2010. As discussed below, this shows how effective the safety net and its expansion through the 2009 American Recovery and Reinvestment Act (the Recovery Act) have been. Since much of the credit for this is due to expansions in SNAP and tax credits, the official poverty rate fails to capture this crucial success.

The poverty rates for children and for working-age adults follow a similar pattern to the overall trend shown in Figure 6-4. The fraction of children living in poverty declined from 29.4 percent in 1967 to 18.7 percent in 2012; for working-age adults, the poverty rate fell from 19.8 to 15.1 percent over the same period. For the elderly, the trend in poverty is one of near continuous decline. Poverty fell quite rapidly up until the early 1980s, driven by large growth in per capita Social Security payments, from 46.5 percent in 1967 to 20.7 percent in 1984. Elderly poverty fell further during the 1990s expansion to a low of 16.5 percent in 1999, and then ticked up slightly in the 2000s. Driven in part by the Recovery Act stimulus payments, elderly poverty declined from 17.6 percent to 15.2 percent between 2007 and 2009, and it remained at that level in 2012.

Measuring the Direct Impact of Antipoverty Efforts

The fact that poverty rates have fallen overall, even as household incomes in the bottom of the distribution have stagnated since the 1980s, suggests a substantial direct role that policies have played in improving the well-being of the poor. Wimer et al. (2013) estimate the magnitude of this impact by constructing "counterfactual" poverty measures that simulate the fraction of the population that would have been poor in the absence of all government transfers, including the overall tax system.[20] In other words, they estimate the fraction of families that would have incomes below the poverty line if the value of all cash, in-kind, and tax transfers they received (or paid if the family owed taxes on net) were not counted. Comparing the difference between this measure of "market poverty" and the SPM poverty

---

[20] While this is a "static" exercise in that it assumes that individual earnings themselves are not affected by the existence of safety net programs, this chapter later reviews research on the effects of programs on employment and earnings and finds that such effects are generally small where they exist, and not large enough to meaningfully alter the conclusions from this simplification (Ben-Shalom, Moffitt, and Scholz 2010).

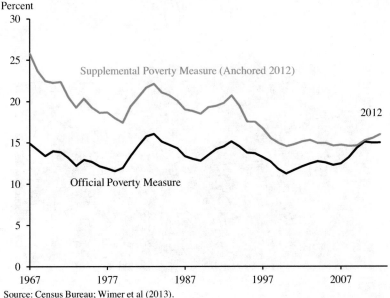

Figure 6-4
Official vs Anchored Supplemental Poverty Rates, 1967–2012

Source: Census Bureau; Wimer et al (2013).

rate provides a measure of the reduction in poverty accounted for by government transfers. Figure 6-5 shows the results of this analysis. The height of the overall shaded region indicates the poverty rate counting only market income, while the height of the region shaded in black is the SPM poverty rate shown in Figure 6-4. The difference, shaded in green, represents the percentage of the population lifted from poverty by the safety net and the net effect of the tax system.[21]

In part because of the rising inequality in earnings described above, market poverty increased over the past 45 years by 1.7 percentage points from 27.0 percent in 1967 to 28.7 percent in 2012. In contrast, poverty rates that are measured including taxes and transfers—these taxes and transfers are the green-shaded region in Figure 6-5—fell through most of this period. Government transfers reduced poverty by 1.2 percentage points in 1967. This impact grew to about 7.4 percentage points by 1975 due to the

---

[21] There are two counterfactuals estimated by Wimer et al. that are used in this report to discuss the impact of the safety net. For most estimates of the impact of the safety net we use a counterfactual poverty rate that strips away ("zeroes out") all cash and in-kind transfers, as well as refundable tax credits but continues to subtract any "normal" tax liability from family resources. In this section, we define "market poverty" similarly, only this measure additionally zeroes out all tax liabilities. Since poor families near the poverty line tend to have positive tax liabilities, market poverty rates are slightly—about 1.8 percentage points in 2012—lower (since we assume families can keep the taxes they in fact must pay).

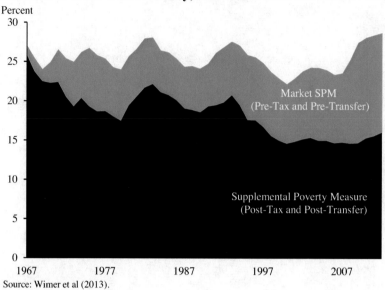

Figure 6-5
Trends in Market and Post-Tax, Post-Transfer Poverty, 1967–2012

Percent

Market SPM
(Pre-Tax and Pre-Transfer)

Supplemental Poverty Measure
(Post-Tax and Post-Transfer)

Source: Wimer et al (2013).

expansion of the safety net spurred by the War on Poverty, and hovered around that level until the Great Recession when it increased to 12.7 percentage points in 2012.

Despite an increase in "market poverty" of 4.5 percentage points between 2007 and 2010, the actual SPM poverty rate rose only 0.5 percentage points due to the safety net. In fact, the 2009 Recovery Act reduced poverty by 1.7 percentage points in 2010 through its extensions to the safety net as discussed below. Overall, for the entire 45-year period, the poverty decline of 9.8 percentage points is almost entirely accounted for by the increased effectiveness of the safety net. [22]

Figure 6-6 shows a similar analysis of the effect of the safety net on trends in deep poverty and highlights two important features of the safety net often overlooked. First, the safety net improves the well-being of many more individuals than is reflected in the standard accounting of how many individuals are lifted from poverty: in 2012, about one in twenty (5.3 percent) Americans lived in deep poverty, yet without government transfers the number would be closer to one in five (18.8 percent).

Second, the safety net almost entirely eliminates cyclical swings in the prevalence of deep poverty. Figure 6-6 shows that despite large increases in

---

[22] As described earlier, the underreporting of government income and benefits means that this is likely to be a conservative lower-bound estimate of the effect of the safety net.

deep market poverty driven by the business cycle, there is little if any rise in actual deep poverty due to the supports provided by the safety net.

Again, this phenomenon is especially visible during the Great Recession, when the prevalence of deep poverty ticked upward by only 0.2 percentage points despite an increase in market deep poverty of 3.3 percentage points. This corresponds to more than 9.5 million men, women, and children prevented from living below half the poverty line during the Great Recession. Over the 45 years shown in Figure 6-6, deep "market poverty" actually rises from 14.9 to 18.8 percent. Despite that increase, the fraction of those in deep poverty fell from 8.2 to 5.3 percent.

THE ROLE OF ANTIPOVERTY PROGRAMS: A CLOSER LOOK

This section presents further detail on antipoverty effects of specific components of the safety net. In particular, it highlights the impact that different groups of programs—cash transfers, in-kind transfers, and tax credits—have on the poverty rates of different age groups. It also shows how the relative importance of programs for nonelderly adults and children has changed since the start of the War on Poverty.

The section then refutes the concern critics have raised that the existence of safety net programs may undermine growth in market incomes as well as our efforts to fight poverty. The social safety net has increasingly been designed to reward and facilitate work increasing participation rates—in many cases, requiring work. Even where programs are not explicitly designed to require work, the highest-quality studies suggest that adverse earnings effects of safety net programs are nonexistent or very small, in part due to reforms over the past two decades that, for example, have phased out benefits gradually with increases in earnings to minimize disincentives to work.

Finally, this section presents findings on the level of economic mobility of individuals born into poverty in the United States, and the results of recent research showing the potentially large returns to social spending in terms of long-term outcomes of children in families receiving support.

Antipoverty Effects of Specific Programs

This section illustrates the role that various antipoverty programs have had in improving the well-being of different populations, and how the relative impacts of these programs have evolved since the War on Poverty began. It is based on an effectively "static" analysis that zeroes out income derived from various public programs to ask what effect this would have on

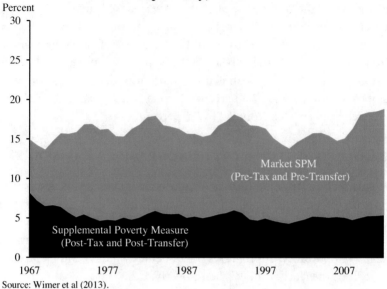

Figure 6-6
**Trends in Market and Post-Tax, Post-Transfer
Deep Poverty, 1967–2012**

Percent

Market SPM
(Pre-Tax and Pre-Transfer)

Supplemental Poverty Measure
(Post-Tax and Post-Transfer)

1967   1977   1987   1997   2007

Source: Wimer et al (2013).

poverty. The next subsection considers some of the broader impacts that these programs have on employment and earnings.

Table 2 shows the impact of various safety net programs on overall poverty, and for three separate age groups: children, adults age 19 to 64, and elderly adults age 65 and over. The safety net program with the single greatest impact is Social Security, which provides income to the elderly, people with disabilities, and surviving spouses and children, reducing the overall poverty rate by 8.6 percentage points in 2012. The program's impacts on elderly poverty are profound: without Social Security income, the poverty rate of the elderly would be 54.7 percent, rather than its rate of 14.8 percent in 2012. On the other end of the age spectrum, refundable tax credits like the EITC and the Child Tax Credit (CTC) have large impacts on child poverty—reducing the fraction of children in poverty by 6.7 percentage points.

Tax credits also reduce the poverty rates of nonelderly adults by 2.3 percentage points. The Supplemental Nutrition Assistance Program also has a dramatic effect on poverty, reducing child poverty by 3.0 percentage points and overall poverty rates by 1.6 percentage points.

Finally, unemployment insurance (UI) reduced poverty by 0.8 percent overall in 2012. This effect, as with the effects for other programs, was less than at the height of the Great Recession when more people were without work: in 2010, for example, unemployment insurance reduced poverty by 1.5 percentage points overall (Short 2012).

As noted, all of these estimates ignore the incentives to alter work behavior created by government programs and are not definitive causal estimates of the impact of the different programs on poverty. For example, Social Security may affect market incomes by changing retirement and savings incentives. Similarly, the estimates do not take into account the role that UI plays in keeping people attached to the labor force, or that the EITC plays in incentivizing additional hours of work and participation in the labor force. The importance of these considerations is discussed below.

Even programs with a small impact on overall poverty rates may be very effective in reducing poverty for certain populations or in alleviating hardship without lifting individuals out of poverty. For example, SSI reduces poverty rates by 1.1 percentage point overall, but this represents a large poverty reduction concentrated among a relatively small number of low-income recipients who are elderly or have a disability. TANF and General Assistance (state programs which typically provide limited aid to very poor individuals not qualifying for other aid) have only a small impact on the overall poverty rate at 0.2 percentage points, as TANF benefits are generally insufficient to bring people above the poverty level. However, by raising the incomes of those in poverty these programs have a much greater impact on reducing deep poverty.

Based on their historical estimates of SPM poverty rates, Wimer et al. (2013) conduct similar analyses to those in Table 2 for each year since 1967 for different groups of safety net programs. Their results shed light on how the safety net has changed over the past 50 years.

In aggregate, the antipoverty effects of three types of federal aid programs—support through cash programs like Social Security, SSI, and TANF; in-kind support like SNAP and housing assistance; and tax credits like the EITC and CTC—all increase over time, driving down overall poverty rates. The steady increase in the effect of each type of program masks some differences across the populations served by each program. For the elderly, for example, the trend is dominated by the growing real value of Social Security payments steadily driving down the elderly poverty rate.

For children, however, there is a shift in importance of the safety net's different components. Figure 6-7 shows the effect of eliminating various components of the safety net resources on the SPM poverty rate in three years corresponding to recession-driven peaks of the poverty rate. In the early 1970s recession, AFDC, and food stamps (now known as Supplemental Nutrition Assistance Program or SNAP) to a lesser extent, played the most important role in alleviating childhood poverty; and the EITC had not yet

Table 6–2
Poverty Rate Reduction from Government Programs, 2012

	All People	Children	Nonelderly Adults	65 Years and Older
Social Security	8.56	1.97	4.08	39.86
Refundable Tax Credits	3.02	6.66	2.25	0.20
SNAP	1.62	3.01	1.27	0.76
Unemployment Insurance	0.79	0.82	0.88	0.31
SSI	1.07	0.84	1.12	1.21
Housing subsidies	0.91	1.39	0.66	1.12
School lunch	0.38	0.91	0.25	0.03
TANF/General Assistance	0.21	0.46	0.14	0.05
WIC	0.13	0.29	0.09	0.00
Population (Thousands)	*311,116*	*74,046*	*193,514*	*43,245*

Note: Data are presented as percentage points.
Source: Census Bureau.

been introduced. Both in-kind transfers and the EITC had a small impact on child poverty in the early 1990s recession, but cash transfer programs still outweighed the poverty-reducing impact of both programs put together. During the Great Recession, however, we see that in-kind aid, cash-assistance, and tax credits all played similarly important roles in reducing poverty for families with children. This shift reflects both the large structural change away from cash welfare assistance during the 1990s, and expansion of both SNAP and tax credits through the Recovery Act.

Figure 6-8 is similar to Figure 6-7, only showing the impact of various transfer programs on deep poverty, or the fraction of individuals with incomes below 50 percent of the poverty threshold. This figure shows that for deep poverty, in-kind transfers have become the most important safety net program over time, and tax credits are less effective due to the paucity of work among families with very low resources.

The Effects of Antipoverty Programs on Work and Earnings

In his remarks before signing the cornerstone legislation of the War on Poverty, the Economic Opportunity Act, President Johnson declared: "Our American answer to poverty is not to make the poor more secure in their poverty but to reach down and to help them lift themselves out of the ruts of poverty and move with the large majority along the high road of hope and prosperity. The days of the dole in our country are numbered." He went on to describe the need to provide the poor with the means to lift themselves out of poverty through job training and employment services, among other strategies. In the past 20 years, this emphasis on promoting work through antipoverty programs intensified and we made dramatic changes to cash welfare and other programs that shifted the focus toward requiring or rewarding work.

The most important shift began with the introduction of the EITC in 1975. The EITC was expanded multiple times in the 1980s, 1990s, and 2000s as the safety net shifted increasingly toward work-based support. The EITC was expanded most recently in the 2009 Recovery Act, with those improvements extended in 2010 and 2013. Since 1996, the EITC has accounted for more support for low-income households than traditional cash welfare. In 2012, the EITC and the partially refundable CTC totaled $90 billion annually, more than four times the expenditures on the Temporary Assistance for Needy Families program.

Because the EITC is a supplement to labor market earnings, the credit provides strong incentives for those with otherwise low labor force attachment to increase their hours of work. However, because the credit is reduced as earnings continue to rise, it may also provide those with earnings above the phase-out threshold—above $22,870 for a married couple with three children—an incentive to reduce their earnings. Several studies have addressed these incentive effects, and reach similar conclusions: the EITC is associated with increased labor force participation, especially among single mothers, but it does not appear to substantially alter the hours or earnings of those already working (Eissa and Liebman 1996, Liebman 1998, Meyer and Rosenbaum 2001, Hotz and Scholz 2003, and Eissa and Hoynes 2005).[23] Taken together, these results suggest EITC expansions played an important role in increasing labor force participation among single mothers, without adversely affecting hours worked by those already working.

Meanwhile, the 1996 welfare reform law replaced AFDC with TANF and significantly strengthened work requirements in the cash assistance program. The Personal Responsibility and Work Opportunity Reconciliation Act of 1996 ended the entitlement to cash assistance and beneficiaries were generally required to work or participate in "work activities" to receive assistance. Moreover, the implicit tax rate on benefits in response to increased earnings—the benefit reduction rate—was reduced dramatically in many states. Matsudaira and Blank (2013) show that these changes increased the return to work, with potential income gains of over $1,842 (in 2000 dollars) for welfare recipients working 30 hours a week. At the same time, it should

---

[23] For example, Meyer and Rosenbaum (2001) suggest that EITC expansion accounts for about 60 percent of the roughly 10 percentage point rise in single mothers' employment rates relative to single mothers without children between 1984 and 1996.

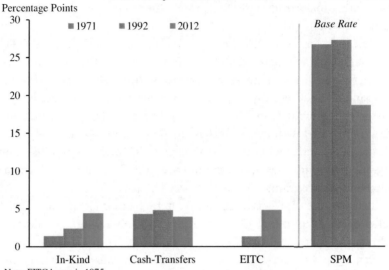

Figure 6-7
**Percentage Point Impact on SPM Child
Poverty for Selected Years**

Note: EITC began in 1975.
Source: Wimer et al (2013).

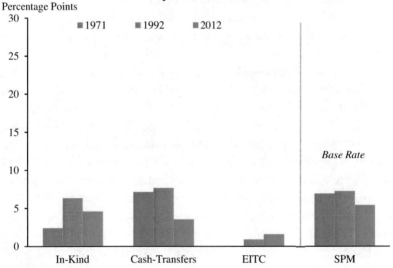

Figure 6-8
**Percentage Point Impact on Deep SPM Child
Poverty for Selected Years**

Note: EITC began in 1975.
Source: Wimer et al (2013).

be noted that researchers have found these reforms may have increased hardship among groups with high barriers to employment, highlighting the continued importance of programs that serve the most disadvantaged (Blank 2007; Danziger, Turner, and Seefeldt 2006).

While today's safety net has been reformed to promote work, it is important to note that careful research has shown that most assistance programs have only small, if any, disincentive effects on work. This suggests that the "static" estimates of the antipoverty effects of the programs shown above largely capture the actual full impact of these programs including any employment disincentives they may have—and may understate the poverty-reducing impacts of programs that effectively reward and facilitate work and thus increase market earnings. For example, examining labor supply behavior of individuals in the Oregon Health Insurance Experiment, Baicker et al. (2013) find that Medicaid recipients are not less likely to be employed nor do they earn less than they otherwise would have. Similarly, Hoynes and Schanzenbach (2012) study the initial rollout of SNAP (then food stamps) and find only small effects on labor supply. While there are no studies of the employment effects of the TANF program with its work requirements, prior studies of AFDC and the Negative Income Tax experiments of the 1970's suggest only modest disincentive effects of a program without an emphasis on work. Burtless (1986) found that a dollar of benefits reduces work earnings by 20 cents (total income is increased by 80 cents), but other evidence suggests the disincentive effects may have been even smaller (SRI International 1983).

Evaluating the weight of the evidence for all programs, Ben-Shalom, Moffitt, and Sholz (2011) conclude that the work disincentive effects of antipoverty programs have "basically, zero" effect on overall poverty rates. Going program by program, they conclude the behavioral effects of TANF are likely zero, and that the work disincentives induced by disability insurance, Medicare, and Unemployment Insurance might reduce the estimated "static" antipoverty effects of those programs by one-eighth or less. Although housing assistance provides significant benefits to some of the poorest households including the homeless, its effects on labor supply among those of working-age and free of disabilities are relatively modest. Shroder (2010) reports that the net negative impact of rental assistance on labor supply appears to vary among subgroups, may change over time, and seems rather small relative to the amounts paid out in subsidy. Jacob and Ludwig (2012) find that receipt of housing vouchers in Chicago during the welfare reform era reduced employment by 3.6 percentage points among able-bodied working-age individuals and reduced earnings an average 19 cents for each dollar of subsidies. Carlson et al. (2011) find employment effects in the same range for Wisconsin voucher recipients. Ben-Shalom, Moffitt, and Scholz estimate that the poverty rate among housing assistance recipients is 66.0 percent, and use the Jacob and Ludwig data to estimate that housing assistance lowers the poverty rate among recipients by 8.2 percentage points rather than the static estimate of 14.9 points. Finally, a recent study by Chetty, Friedman, and Saez (2012) of the EITC on the earnings distribution also finds that "the impacts of the EITC ... come primarily through its mechanical effects." They do find, however, that behavioral responses reinforce the effects of the safety net on deep poverty, so that the overall impact of the EITC might be somewhat greater than implied by the "static" estimates because of the increased work induced by the program.[24]

Economic Mobility

When economic mobility is high, individuals and families can lift themselves out of poverty by taking advantage of opportunities to improve their economic well-being. When economic mobility is low, it is difficult to change one's economic status and people may become stuck in poverty. Mobility can be measured either as relative mobility—the likelihood of moving up or down the income distribution—or absolute mobility, which is the likelihood of improving economic well-being in general without necessarily moving up in the income distribution (reflected in the saying, "a rising tide lifts all boats"). When there is low relative mobility, there are few opportunities for poor people to improve their standing in society by moving up the economic spectrum, and children from poor families are likely to continue to have low economic and social status as they become adults, even if their material well-being improves. When there is low absolute mobility, poor people and their children find it hard to escape the economic and material hardships of poverty.

While economic mobility in the United States allows some people to escape poverty, many do not. About half of the poorest individuals remain in the lowest one-fifth of the income distribution after 10 and 20 years, and no more than one-fourth make it to one of the top three income quintiles (Acs and Zimmerman 2008; Auten, Gee, and Turner 2013). Those who were in poor families as children are estimated to have 20 to 40 percent lower earnings as adults compared to those who did not grow up in poverty (Mayer 1997; Corcoran and Adams 1997; Corcoran 2001; Duncan et al.

---

[24] Unlike the earlier literature, they also find evidence of a slight downward adjustment of earnings for workers near 200 percent of the poverty line. This is consistent with the predictions of static labor supply theory since that level of earnings is in the phase-out region of the credit. This negative impact is small, however, and Chetty, Friedman, and Saez emphasize it is dominated by the (also small) positive impacts at low earnings levels.

2012). Among the children of low-earning fathers, about two-fifths of sons and one-fourth of daughters remained in the lowest earnings quintile when they became their father's age (Jäntti et al. 2006). Consistent with this, more than one-third of children who grew up in the lowest family income quintile were in the lowest quintile when they became adults (Isaacs 2008). Among children born in 1971 with parents in the lowest income quintile, 8.4 percent made it to the top quintile by age 26, compared to 9.0 percent of those born in 1986, indicating that the chance of moving up the income distribution has remained low and fairly stable over the past few decades (Chetty, Hendren, Kline, Saez, and Turner 2014).[25] More generally, studies find that about one-third to slightly less than one-half of parents' incomes are reflected in their children's incomes later in life (Chetty, Hendren, Kline, and Saez 2014, Black and Devereux 2011, Lee and Solon 2009), indicating that parents heavily influence children's economic fortunes.

The results of these studies imply strong lingering effects from growing up in poverty. The influence of poverty on future economic prospects stem not just from one's own family status, but from growing up in high-poverty neighborhoods that often have lower-quality schools, lower-paying jobs, higher crime rates, and other conditions that can create disadvantages (Sharkey 2009). Among children whose families were in the top three quintiles of family income, growing up in a high-poverty neighborhood raises the likelihood of downward mobility (falling at least one quintile) by 52 percent (Sharkey 2009). A comparison across geographic regions in the United States indicates that economic mobility is higher in areas with a larger middle class, less residential segregation between low-income and middle-income individuals, higher social capital, and lower rates of teen birth, crime, divorce, and children raised by single parents (Chetty, Hendren, Kline, and Saez 2014).

The above results mostly reflect relative mobility (moving up or down the economic spectrum). While absolute mobility (improving economic well-being without moving up the economic spectrum) has generally risen in the United States, the pace has slowed in recent decades. Comparing cohorts of men in their 30's, median personal income went up 5 percent from 1964 to 1994, but down 12 percent from 1974 to 2004 (Sawhill and Morton 2007). Counting all family income, income went up 32 percent between 1964 and 1994, and only 9 percent between 1974 and 2004. So the

---

[25] The stability of intergenerational mobility is also shown by comparing the correlation of parent and child income ranks over this period (Chetty, Hendren, Kline, Saez, and Turner 2014).

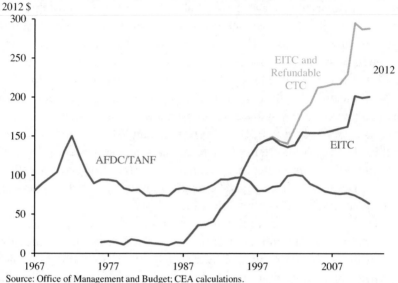

Figure 6-9
Real Per Capita Expenditures on Select Programs, 1967–2012

2012 $

EITC and
Refundable
CTC

2012

AFDC/TANF

EITC

Source: Office of Management and Budget; CEA calculations.

recent improvement in family income, which reflects the rising employment of women, was only one-third as large as in the earlier period.[26]

Despite the popular view that the United States is the land of opportunity, this Nation appears to have lower economic mobility than many other developed countries. Measuring mobility by the strength of the dependence of children's incomes on parents' incomes, the United States has similar mobility as the United Kingdom and Italy, but lower mobility than other European countries as well as Japan, Australia, and Canada (Solon 2002; Jäntti et al. 2006; Corak 2006, 2011).

Can anything be done to increase mobility? A study of data on families over time (including comparisons of twins and other siblings) found that genetics and shared upbringing play a statistically significant, but quantitatively minor role, in explaining adult earnings differences, indicating that environmental factors other than upbringing are largely responsible (Björklund, Jäntti, and Solon 2005). The large variation in mobility across countries and across regions (Chetty, Hendren, Kline, and Saez 2014) is further evidence for the fact that institutions and other potentially changeable factors can have a large impact on mobility.

---

[26] Using a different method to assess absolute mobility, about half of individuals moved out of the bottom income quintile in the 1984-94 and 1994-2004 periods when the quintile thresholds were fixed at the beginning of the period (Acs and Zimmerman, 2008).

Education appears to be one of the key factors that drive economic mobility. As shown in Figure 6-10, among families in the bottom fifth of the income distribution, almost half (45 percent) of the children who did not obtain college degrees remained in the poorest fifth as adults, while only one-sixth (16 percent) of the children who obtained college degrees remained in the poorest fifth (Isaacs, Sawhill, and Haskins 2008: 95).

The importance of education is also shown by the findings that economic mobility is higher in countries that have a greater public expenditure on education (Ichino, Karabarbounis, and Moretti 2009) and areas of the United States that have a higher-quality K-12 education system (Chetty, Hendren, Kline, and Saez 2014), and is improved for children in the poorest one-third of families when states increase spending on elementary and secondary education (Mayer and Lopoo 2008).

Intergenerational Returns

While much of the literature on mobility presented above is correlational, a handful of well-crafted studies that track the long-run outcomes of children exposed to safety net programs highlight the potential for investments in these programs to generate large returns.

Early childhood education has been found by many researchers to have dramatic, super-normal returns in terms of more favorable adult outcomes. The Head Start program created early in the War on Poverty has been heavily researched and the combined results show that it can "rightfully be considered a success for much of the past fifty years" (Gibbs, Ludwig, and Miller 2013: 61). Studies following children over time, and accounting for the influence of family background by comparing siblings, found that Head Start participants were more likely to complete high school and attend college (Garces, Thomas, and Currie 2002), and scored higher on a summary index of young adult outcomes that also included crime, teen parenthood, health status, and idleness (Deming 2009). The latter study found that Head Start closed one-third of the gap in the summary outcome index between children in families at the median and bottom quartiles of family income. Using a regression discontinuity research design that compared access to Head Start across counties, Ludwig and Miller (2007) found positive impacts of Head Start on schooling attainment, the likelihood of attending college, and mortality rates from causes that could be affected by Head Start. Gibbs, Ludwig, and Miller (2013) suggest the combination of the benefits due to Head Start might produce a benefit-cost ratio in excess of seven.

Randomized experiments studying the Perry Preschool Project, Abecedarian Project, Chicago Child-Parent Centers, Early Training Project, and Project CARE programs largely confirm these findings. A variety of

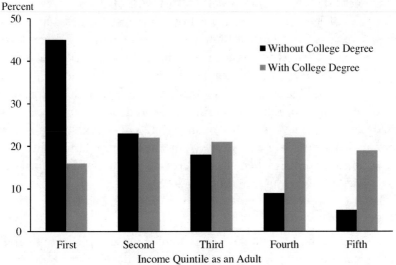

Figure 6-10
Economic Mobility for Children from First Income Quintile

Percent

■ Without College Degree
■ With College Degree

Income Quintile as an Adult

Note: Childhood income is the average family income from 1967-71. Adult Income is the average
from 1995, 1996, 1998, 2000, and 2002.
Source: Isaacs, Sawhill, and Haskins (2008).

well-done analyses find that the adult benefits for children—especially girls—
who participated included higher educational attainment, employment, and
earnings along with other benefits (Schweinhart et al. 2005; Anderson 2008;
Campbell et al. 2008; Heckman and Masterov 2007; Heckman et al. 2010;
Heckman et al. 2011). Heckman et al. (2009) find that the returns to one
preschool program (Perry) exceed the returns to equities.

In the past decade, researchers have identified long-run linkages
between early childhood (including exposure in-utero) health interventions
and long-term outcomes. For example, Almond, Chay, and Greenstone
(2006) document that the Johnson Administration used the threat of with-
held Federal funds for the newly introduced Medicare program to force
hospitals to comply with the Civil Rights Act mandate to desegregate,
resulting in dramatic improvements in infant health and large declines in
the black-white gap in infant mortality in the 1960s. Chay, Guryan, and
Mazumder (2009) show these improvements in access to health care and
health soon after birth had echoes in the form of large student achievement
gains for black teenagers in the 1980's, contributing to the decline in the
black-white test score gap. Their results suggest that improved health care
access and better early childhood health improve test scores by between 0.7
and 1 standard deviations—a very large impact that implies large increases
in lifetime earnings. For example, studying a different intervention, Chetty,

Friedman, and Rockoff (2011) find the financial value (the net present value at age 12 of the discounted increase in lifetime earnings) of a standard deviation increase in test scores to be $46,190 per grade.

While it may not be surprising that human capital interventions have long-run returns, recent studies have also found intergenerational effects on child outcomes from tax or near-cash transfers to their parents. That is, recent evidence suggests that government transfers that ameliorate child poverty by increasing family income have lasting, long-run benefits in terms of better child outcomes. For example, Hoynes, Schanzenbach, and Almond (2013) study the initial rollout of the Food Stamp (now SNAP) program between its initial pilot in 1961 and 1975. While Food Stamps are distributed as vouchers for food purchases, since their amount is generally less than households spend on food, the vouchers likely affect family behavior in the same manner as increased cash income (Hoynes and Schanzenbach 2009). Hoynes, Schanzenbach, and Almond find that exposure to Food Stamps led to improvements in adult health (reductions in the incidence of high blood pressure and obesity) and, for women, increased economic self-sufficiency. Similarly, Dahl and Lochner (2012) and Chetty, Friedman, and Rockoff (2011) find that family receipt of additional income from refundable tax credits improves the achievement test scores of children in the family. Chetty, Friedman, and Rockoff estimate that the implied increase in adult earnings due to improved achievement as a child is on the same order of magnitude, and probably greater, than the value of the tax expenditures.

The results discussed above highlight the crucial fact that government expenditures on the safety net have a strong economic justification. Not only do they help to propel struggling adults back onto their feet and protect them and their families from hardship, they improve opportunity and the adult outcomes of their children. As such, the poverty-reducing impact of these programs constitutes an important investment opportunity. To give a sense of the magnitude of this opportunity, Holzer et al. (2008) estimate the cost of childhood poverty at about $500 billion (in 2007 dollars) or about 4 percent of gross domestic product (GDP) annually in terms of foregone earnings, increased costs of crime, and higher health expenditures and lower health.

While the Holzer et al. study is correlational (though it attempts to correct for hereditary components of the intergenerational income correlation), the concern over bias in this estimate is overwhelmed by its magnitude. Based on Census Bureau estimates, the total poverty gap—the shortfall between family resources and the SPM poverty thresholds—among all families with children is about $59.8 billion in 2012, or 0.37 percent of GDP. Even if the Holzer et al. estimate was double the "true" causal effect of eliminating child poverty, the benefit would exceed the added costs five-fold. These numbers create a powerful case for renewed efforts to fight poverty.

THE OBAMA ADMINISTRATION'S RECORD AND AGENDA TO STRENGTHEN ECONOMIC SECURITY AND INCREASE OPPORTUNITY

The programs created during the War on Poverty and refined since have provided crucial support to Americans in need. But challenges clearly remain. In 2012, 49.7 million Americans, including 13.4 million children, lived below the poverty line—an unacceptable number in the richest nation in the world. There is clear evidence that antipoverty programs work, and we must redouble our efforts to enhance and strengthen our safety net.

At the same time, we must realize that while antipoverty programs are doing heroic work to lift struggling families from poverty, there is broad consensus among economists that a strong national recovery in the short run, and stronger economic growth in the long run, are necessary to sustain progress in the fight against poverty. Indeed, as our social safety net reinforces the economic benefits of work by supplementing wages for low earners, a strong labor market with jobs available for all is an essential partner in the fight against poverty. Given the growing economic inequality in the past few decades, we must strive for balanced growth that benefits all Americans. To do so, we must ensure that an economic expansion encompasses everyone, and commit to giving all Americans opportunities for lifelong learning and skills development to ensure a broad base of human capital that will be rewarded by good wages.

This section documents the Obama Administration's record in continuing the fight to expand opportunity and reduce poverty, and discusses the Administration's proposals to strengthen the safety net and to improve human capital and increase labor market earnings. These comprise a key part of the broader economic strategy to further the recovery and increase growth—all of which combat poverty.

Taking Immediate Action During the Economic Crisis

As the economy was sliding into the Great Recession, the Administration took action to strengthen the safety net and prevent millions of Americans from falling into poverty. The Recovery Act instituted a number of temporary antipoverty measures, including the creation of the Making Work Pay tax credit worth up to $800 for a married couple, a $250 Economic Recovery Payment for Social Security and SSI recipients; unemployment changes including an additional $25 a week (for up to 26 weeks) to regular UI beneficiaries, increased federal funding for the Extended Benefits program, incentives for states to modernize their UI system to reach part-time workers and recent workforce entrants, and reauthorized Emergency Unemployment Compensation; an increase in SNAP benefits; and an expansion of the Community Services Block Grant (CSBG). The Recovery Act also delivered nearly $100 billion to States, school districts, postsecondary institutions, and students to help address budget shortfalls and meet the educational needs of all. This total included $10 billion for the Title I Grants to Local Educational Agencies program, a flagship program of the War on Poverty's Elementary and Secondary Education Act of 1965, which currently serves more than 23 million students in high-poverty schools, helping ensure access to a high-quality public education.

In addition, the Recovery Act included expansions in tax credits that the Administration intends to make permanent. The EITC expansion increased the credit for families with three or more children, reflecting the fact that they have greater needs and higher poverty rates than families with two children. It also reduced the penalty that some low-income families faced when getting married. Together, these two provisions benefit about 6 million households a year by an average of $500. Further, the partial refundability of the CTC for working families was expanded, benefiting 12 million families by an average of $800 each. These changes were subsequently extended through 2017 and the President is proposing to make them permanent.

The impact of these emergency measures on poverty was dramatic. The Recovery Act played a large role in keeping Americans out of poverty during the recession, as shown in Figure 11.[27] In total, between 4.0 and 5.5 million people a year were kept out of poverty by these programs from 2009 to 2012. Without the Recovery Act, the Supplemental Poverty Rate would have been 1.8 percentage points higher in 2009 and 1.7 percentage points higher in 2010. Over the four years between 2009 and 2012, CEA estimates that 19.2 million person years were kept from poverty as a result of the expansions created by the Recovery Act alone (Figure 6-11). This calculation is conservative, in that it does not account for the impact of those expansions on employment through increased aggregate demand, and does not attempt to measure the impact of other components of the Recovery Act such as increased funding for Pell Grants and paying for COBRA for the unemployed.

---

[27] Estimates of the effects of the Recovery Act on poverty have been updated relative to our January 2014 report to reflect minor methodological improvements.

Expanding Health Care Security

The Affordable Care Act (ACA) ensures that all Americans have access to quality, affordable health insurance and provides financial incentives to states to expand their Medicaid programs to adults who are in or near poverty. As of January 2014, 26 states have adopted the Medicaid expansion. For moderate-income Americans, the ACA provides tax credits for the purchase of insurance through marketplaces and cost-sharing reductions. The Congressional Budget Office (CBO) estimates that, by 2016, these measures will increase the number of Americans with health insurance by 25 million (CBO 2013).

Americans of all income levels are already benefiting from insurance market reforms that ensure access to preventive services and no lifetime coverage limits. Further, Americans buying insurance are no longer forced to pay a higher premium because of their gender or health status, and can be confident that their insurance provides adequate financial protection. The ACA has also begun reforming the way the United States pays for health care to promote more efficiency and quality in the health system, the early results of which are discussed in a recent CEA report (CEA 2013) and in Chapter 4 of this report.

Nutrition programs like SNAP are vital to the economic livelihood of many families and communities, especially in a recessionary period. Every time a family uses SNAP benefits to put healthy food on the table, the benefits extend widely beyond those individuals. In fact, the U.S. Department of Agriculture's Economic Research Service estimates that an additional $1 billion in SNAP benefits supports an additional 8,900 to 17,900 full-time-equivalent jobs (Hanson 2010).

Rewarding Work

Work that pays enough to support a family is the most central anti-poverty measure. In 2013, the Obama Administration finalized rules to extend minimum wage and overtime protections to nearly 2 million direct-care workers who provide care assistance to elderly people and people with illnesses, injuries, or disabilities. This will ensure our nation's health aides, personal care aides, and certified nursing assistants receive the same basic protections already provided to most U.S. workers, while improving the quality and stability of care for those who rely on them.

Minimum wage and overtime protections have been a bulwark of protection against poverty, but the minimum wage has not kept pace with inflation. Today, a worker trying to support a family on the minimum wage is still living in poverty. That is why the President signed an Executive Order

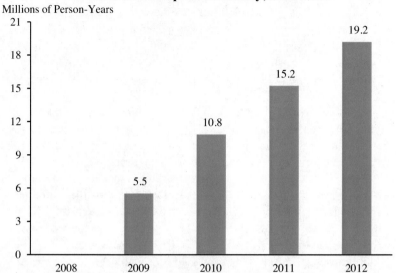

Figure 6-11
**Recovery Act and Subsequent Extensions: Cumulative
Person-Years Kept from Poverty, 2008–2012**

Millions of Person-Years

Source: Bureau of Labor Statistics, Current Population Survey, Annual Social and Economic
Supplement; CEA Calculations.

in 2014 to raise the minimum wage for workers on new and replacement Federal service and construction contracts to $10.10 an hour. This step will to ensure that no worker who provides services to the Federal government will raise their families in poverty, and will make Federal procurement more economical and efficient. An extensive body of research suggests that giving a raise to lower-income workers reduces turnover and raises morale, and can thus lower costs and improve productivity. To help insure that work is rewarded for millions more Americans, the President supports the Harkin-Miller bill to increase the minimum wage to $10.10 by 2016 (Box 6-5).

To further enhance economic security and incentivize work, the President has proposed to double the childless EITC to be worth up to $1,000 and lower the age threshold from 25 to 21 to help more lower-income young people, while continuing protections to ensure that it does not benefit, for example, typical full-time students. A small EITC for childless households was established in 1993, but its maximum value is expected to be only $503 in 2015 and is fully phased out for individuals making over $14,790 ($20,290 for married couples). This leaves a childless adult with wages equal to the poverty line with a federal tax burden (including income and payroll taxes) of $1,966 after receiving an EITC of $173, driving them deeper into poverty and making childless workers the sole demographic

Box 6-5: Raising the Minimum Wage

In 2013, the federal minimum wage was at the same inflation-adjusted level as it was in 1950. A full-time worker earning $7.25 per hour would not be able to keep a family of four out of poverty, even with the help of the EITC and CTC. Instead of allowing the value of the minimum wage to continue to erode while incomes at the top of the distribution soar, it is time to make the minimum wage a wage people can live on.

Raising the minimum wage to $10.10 per hour would help a large, diverse group of workers, and indexing it to inflation would ensure that its real value does not deteriorate over time, as it has after past increases. Over 28 million people earning wages near the minimum wage would be affected by such an increase, 46 percent of whom have household incomes below $35,000. Full-time workers earning exactly the minimum wage would see their earnings increase by $5,700, enough to move a family of four from 17 percent below the poverty line to 5 percent above it, once tax credit assistance is included. CEA estimates that raising the minimum wage to $10.10 by 2016 would lift roughly 2 million workers whose wages are currently near the minimum wage, and members of their families, out of poverty, while alleviating poverty for about 10 million more.

Opponents of increasing the minimum wage argue that the beneficiaries are largely middle-class teenagers, and those most in need of assistance are kept out of jobs by high wages. The available evidence does not support those claims. Among those workers who would be affected by increasing the minimum wage to $10.10, 92 percent are more than 18 years old. A large literature has considered the effects of minimum wages on employment, and the best evidence suggests there is little to no effect (Doucouliagos and Stanley 2009). While a higher minimum wage could increase compensation costs for employers, they could also reap benefits, including lower employee turnover rates and, by extension, lower costs of hiring and training new workers, as well as increased demand for their goods and services among low-wage workers.

driven deeper into poverty by the federal tax system. Under the President's proposal, a household at the poverty line would see its EITC expand to $848, more than eliminating its income taxes—although it would still pay net taxes on earnings when including payroll taxes.

Empowering Every Child with a Quality Education

To prepare Americans for the jobs of the future, we have to strengthen our investments in the Nation's educational system. The Administration has invested in coordinated state systems of early learning and proposed new policies building on evidence of how to create a foundation for success in the formative early years of life. High-quality early learning and development programs can help level the playing field for children from lower-income families on vocabulary, social and emotional development, and academic skills while helping students to stay on track and stay engaged in the early elementary grades. These programs generate a significant return on investment for society through a reduced need for spending on other services, such as remedial education, grade repetition, and special education, as well as increased later productivity and earnings. The Administration's comprehensive early-learning agenda invests in early childhood education, care, and development for our nation's youngest learners. In partnership with the states, the Preschool for All initiative would provide high-quality preschool for four-year olds from low- and moderate-income families, while encouraging states to serve additional four-year olds from middle-income families. The Administration has also proposed investments in high-quality early learning for infants and toddlers through new Early Head Start-Child Care Partnerships, as well as an extension and expansion of evidence-based voluntary home visiting programs that allow nurses, social workers, educators, and other professionals to connect pregnant women and vulnerable families with young children to tools that positively impact the child's health, development, and ability to learn.

Over the past 50 years, improvements in education at all levels have produced large returns for many Americans and played a key role in the economic mobility of children born to poor families. Because economic progress and educational achievement are inextricably linked, educating every American student to graduate from high school prepared for college and for a career is a national imperative. The President has articulated a goal for America to once again lead the world in college completion by the year 2020, and the Administration's education efforts aim toward this overarching objective. To provide a high-quality education to all American children, the Administration, in partnership with states, has advanced reforms of the Nation's K-12 education system to support higher standards that will prepare students to succeed in college and the workplace; efforts to recruit, prepare, develop, and advance effective teachers and principals; efforts to eliminate discrimination on the basis of race, color, national origin, gender, and disability in public school; efforts to ensure the use of data in the classroom; and a national effort to turn around our chronically lowest-achieving schools. The School Improvement Grants (SIG) program has invested over $5 billion in 1500 of the nation's lowest performing schools. The Promise Neighborhood Program, established by this Administration in 2010, has funded 58 neighborhoods across the country to design comprehensive projects that include a continuum of services and designed to combat the effects of poverty and improve education and life outcomes, from birth through college to career. The Administration has also put forward proposals to redesign the Nation's high schools to better engage students and to connect 99 percent of students to high-speed broadband and digital learning tools within the next five years. Continued investments and reforms are needed to ensure that all students have access to a high-quality education that prepares them for college and a career, and for success in today's global economy.

With the average earnings of college graduates at a level twice as high as that of workers with only a high school diploma, higher education is now the clearest pathway into the middle class. Our Nation suffers from a college attainment gap, as high school graduates from the wealthiest families are almost certain to continue on to higher education, while just over half of high school graduates in the poorest one-quarter of families attend college. This gap has increased over the past several decades. And while more than half of college students graduate within six years, the completion rate for low-income students is around 25 percent. To achieve the President's goal for college completion, ensure that America's students and workers receive the education and training needed for the jobs of today and tomorrow, and provide greater security for the middle class, the Administration is working to make college more accessible, affordable, and attainable for all American families. Under President Obama, Pell Grant funding was increased to serve over 3 million additional low-income students and the average grant was increased by more than $900. The Administration also created the American Opportunity Tax Credit to ease college costs for over 9 million families, and championed comprehensive reform of student loans that will save taxpayers $68 billion over the next decade. Finally, the Administration has launched an array of policies to contain college costs, and make it easier for students to manage their student debt through income-based repayment reforms, which limit student loan payments to a percentage of their income so that young workers will not be swamped by debt payments as they are establishing their households and careers.

Given the critical importance of education in expanding skills and opportunities, the Administration implemented several policies designed to increase college access and affordability for low-income students. Recognizing that the opportunity to acquire the skills to get and keep a good job starts early and through education, the President is also proposing to modernize America's high schools for real-world learning. The goal is to provide challenging, relevant experiences, and reward schools that develop new partnerships with colleges and employers, and that create classes that focus on technology, science, engineering, and other skills today's employers are demanding to fill jobs now and in the future.

Creating Jobs and Growing Our Economy

Building on the evidence that well-designed training programs can improve employment and earnings (Andersson et al. 2013), this Administration has proposed investing in subsidized employment and training opportunities for adults who are low-income or long-term unemployed. In 2009 and 2010, 372,000 low-income youth were placed into summer and year-round employment, and supported job opportunities were created for about 260,000 low-income individuals. In addition, the President continues to build public-private partnerships to provide opportunities for low-income youth.

The Administration is using all available tools to help people who have lost their jobs to find new work or to train for new careers in growth fields that will provide better jobs and paths to viable careers. This includes supporting training opportunities that lead directly to a job, and making sure our unemployment system promotes re-employment through wide-ranging reforms to the unemployment insurance program, some of which were adopted in the Middle Class Tax Relief and Jobs Creation Act of 2012, and continued investment in reemployment services, which have proven effective in speeding the return to work.

The President has proposed to build on these successes by further investing in creating job and work-based training opportunities for the long-term unemployed and youth seeking skills and wanting to get into the workplace.

This Administration has already invested $1.5 billion in community college-business partnerships in all 50 states to build capacity and develop curricula to train workers for jobs in growing industries. President Obama has proposed to build on these successes with further investments that will transform community college education and support Americans in getting training to enter skilled jobs.

Investing in and Rebuilding Hard-Hit Communities

Living in a high-poverty area presents various challenges, including crime, limited access to quality education, and scarcity of good jobs. Since these issues often interact with each other and compound the problems they create individually, it is very difficult for people, particularly children, to overcome the disadvantages created by and associated with poverty.

A child's zip code should never determine his or her destiny. To help provide ladders of opportunity so that every child has a chance to succeed, the Administration is working with State and local governments to focus public and private resources on transforming areas of high need into communities of opportunity.

The Administration's Promise Zones initiative focuses existing government resources on competitively selected communities and leverages private investment to create jobs, improve public safety, increase educational opportunities, and provide affordable housing. The Administration will designate 20 communities over the next several years with this intense and layered approach to community revitalization.

That approach includes working with local leadership, and bringing to bear the resources of the President's signature revitalization initiatives from the Department of Education, the Department of Housing and Urban Development, the Department of Agriculture, and the Department of Justice, to ensure that federal programs and resources support the efforts to turn around 20 of the highest poverty urban, rural and tribal communities across the country.

The Promise Zones initiative will build on existing programs, including HUD's Choice Neighborhoods and the Department of Education's Promise Neighborhoods grant programs. The Administration has invested $244 million in Choice and $157 million in Promise since 2010. For every federal dollar spent, Choice Neighborhoods has attracted eight dollars of private and other investment and has developed nearly 100,000 units of mixed-income housing in 260 communities, ensuring that low-income residents can afford to continue living in their communities. Promise Neighborhoods grants are supporting approximately 50 communities representing more than 700 schools. To help leverage and sustain grant work, 1,000 national, state, and community organizations have signed-on to partner with a Promise Neighborhood site. By expanding these programs, the Administration continues to support local efforts to transform low-income urban, rural, and tribal communities across the country.

CONCLUSION

The War on Poverty represented a dramatic shift in the Federal Government's priorities for helping those who are left behind in a growing economy. It set in motion a series of changes that transformed our social safety net and improved the well-being and economic outcomes of countless low-income Americans and their children. The architects of the War on Poverty believed that the combined effect of government policies attacking poverty on many fronts—providing income when earnings are low, providing access to health insurance, insuring that people have shelter and a minimal food budget, and providing access to education at all ages—would dramatically raise employment and earnings and reduce material hardship. In the years since 1964, this optimism and belief in the capacity of government to improve the lives of less fortunate Americans has at times given way to the cynical belief that the safety net is ineffective, or even exacerbates the problems of the poor by reducing the incentives for those able to work to do so.

The most important lesson from the War on Poverty is that government programs and policies can lift people from poverty; indeed they have for the past 50 years. Poverty rates fell from 25.8 percent in 1967 to 16 percent in 2012—a decline of nearly 40 percent. In 2012 alone, the combined effect of all federal tax, cash and in-kind aid programs was to lift approximately 14.5 percent of the population—over 45 million people—out of poverty.

But another lesson is that we cannot afford to simply embrace any program that purports to achieve this goal or attempt to freeze them in time. Instead, our antipoverty efforts have benefited from enormous changes in public policy since the 1960s, informed by a wealth of research on both successful and failed programs that provide important insights into what does and does not work in fighting poverty. Our safety net has evolved to put more emphasis on rewarding and supporting work, such as by providing greater support to working families through the EITC and refundable CTC, while also making it easier for them to get help from programs like SNAP and Medicaid. In 1967, we spent $19 billion in today's dollars on what was then called AFDC and nothing on the EITC. Today the EITC and partially refundable CTC are 3.8 times the size of the TANF program.[28] Meanwhile, the Affordable Care Act advances the goal of providing quality affordable health care to all Americans, with financial incentives to states to expand their Medicaid programs to adults who are in or near poverty and generous tax credits for moderate-income households. Our safety net remains imperfect, but these reforms and improvements represent important progress—and they also help many families work and raise the rewards to that work.

Nearly 50 million Americans still live in poverty, however, including 13.4 million children, and so there remains a need to do more to help the poor. The 1964 Economic Report of the President estimated that the total shortfall in income necessary to bring all poor families up to the poverty

---

[28] Based on CEA calculations using data from http://www.whitehouse.gov/sites/default/files/omb/budget/fy2014/assets/hist.pdf.

level was $11 billion (about $71 billion in today's dollars), or about 1.6 percent of the country's annual GDP. Our nation has grown much richer since, and today the total shortfall below poverty is only 0.6 percent of GDP. Continuing to make progress in closing that shortfall will require not just defending the programs that have helped reduce poverty but also continuing the efforts to strengthen the economy, increase growth and ensure that growth is reflected in broad-based wage gains so that families can lift themselves out of poverty.

CHAPTER 7

EVALUATION AS A TOOL FOR IMPROVING FEDERAL PROGRAMS

Since taking office, President Obama has emphasized the need to determine what works and what does not in government, and to use those answers to inform Federal policy and budget decisions. The President's 21st Century Management Agenda, submitted to Congress with the fiscal year 2010 Budget, set bold goals for building a more efficient, more effective government that contributes to economic growth and strengthens the foundations for economic prosperity (OMB 2009a). Today, evaluating Federal programs and interventions to understand their impact, and developing the infrastructure within agencies to support a sustained level of high-quality evaluations, remains an Administration priority. By rigorously testing which programs and interventions are most effective at achieving important goals, the government can improve its programs, scaling up the approaches that work best and modifying or discontinuing those that are less effective.

This Administration has supported the use of rigorous, high-quality "impact" evaluations to measure changes in a variety of outcomes targeted by Federal programs, ranging from earnings to health to electricity usage. Many factors affect whether Federal programs achieve their goals, and identifying impacts specifically attributable to programs is challenging. An impact evaluation is a particular type of program evaluation, and aims to measure the causal effect of a program or intervention on important program outcomes. This chapter focuses on impact evaluations. "Process" evaluations (another type of program evaluation) and performance measurement also contribute to building evidence about how well programs are working, but differ in important ways from impact evaluations (Box 7-1).

Building on the efforts of previous administrations, the Obama Administration is working to reform the Federal Government's approach to improving program performance. In addition to emphasizing transparency and accountability in tracking progress toward agencies' priority goals, this new approach also aims to complement and to draw on the Administration's

Box 7-1: Impact Evaluations, Process Evaluations, and Performance Measurement

Program managers use many approaches to assess how programs operate and how well they work. Impact evaluations aim to identify the causal effects of a program or intervention on some outcome or outcomes of interest. Impact evaluations are distinct from other types of program evaluation and performance measurement. For example:

- **Process evaluations** analyze the effectiveness of how programs deliver services relative to program design, professional standards, or regulatory requirements. For instance, a process evaluation might focus on whether a program is reaching the target number of participants or whether caseworkers are consistently following a specified protocol for providing services. Process evaluations help ensure that programs are running as intended, but in general these evaluations do not directly examine whether programs are achieving their outcome goals (GAO 2011).

- **Performance measurement** is a broader category that encompasses "the ongoing monitoring and reporting of program accomplishments, particularly progress toward pre-established goals" (GAO 2011). Typically, performance measures provide a descriptive picture of how a program is functioning and how participants are faring on various "intermediate" outcomes, but do not attempt to rigorously identify the causal effects of the program. For instance, performance measures for a job training program might capture how many individuals are served, what fraction complete the training, and what fraction are employed a year later. But these measures will not answer the question of how much higher these individuals' employment rates are as a result of having completed the training. Nonetheless, performance measures serve as important indicators of program accomplishments and can help establish that a program is producing apparently promising (or troubling) outcomes.

While process evaluations and performance measurement are useful at all stages of a program's maturity, they can be particularly useful for providing evidence about how programs are working in the early years of a program's history when impacts on program outcomes may not be detectable and rigorous, high-quality impact evaluations are not possible. A logic model—a tool that depicts the intended links between program investments and outcomes and helps to ensure program activities will achieve desired outcomes—can facilitate agency efforts to develop high-quality "intermediate" indicators of impacts as well as an understanding of alternative causal channels that can affect important program outcomes.

program evaluation efforts. For example, the Administration this year is establishing strategic reviews within agencies to strengthen the use of evidence in strategic and budget decisions.

This chapter provides an overview of the implementation and use of impact evaluation in Federal programs, with a special focus on the lessons learned so far in this Administration. It begins with a discussion of some challenges inherent in conducting rigorous impact evaluations in government programs. The chapter then focuses on Administration efforts to build and to use evidence, including actions taken on lessons learned from completed evaluations, launching new evaluations in areas where not enough is known, and creating a culture of evidence-building in Federal programs, especially grant programs. The final section identifies opportunities for further progress: for example, through increasing legislative support and removing legislative barriers, embedding evaluation into routine program operations, and using existing program data to measure outcomes and impacts.

Conducting Rigorous Impact Evaluations in Federal Programs

Science, business, and government routinely confront the problem of ascertaining the effect of a program, policy, or initiative. Is a newly developed drug effective in treating the condition for which it was developed? Does a new marketing strategy boost sales? Does a preschool program improve participants' outcomes, such as success in elementary school? Despite the different settings, these questions all focus on measuring the effect of an intervention or program on one or more outcomes of interest.

One basic approach to answering questions like these is to look at outcomes before and after the "treatment"—for instance, before and after taking a drug, before and after a new marketing strategy is rolled out, or before and after participation in an education program. Another straightforward approach is to compare outcomes for program participants with outcomes for non-participants. In complex policy environments, however, these simple approaches will often give the wrong answers. Take, for example, a job training program designed to help unemployed workers get jobs. The data may show that program participants were much more likely to be employed a year after the training program than before they entered the program. But if the unemployment rate has fallen substantially over the course of the program, then the gains may be due to the improving economy, not to the training program. Similarly, a government program offering start-up assistance to new businesses may appear to boost success rates. But if capable entrepreneurs are more likely than less capable ones to participate in the program, then self-selection of program participants, not the program itself, may be driving those better outcomes.

A strong impact evaluation needs a strategy for constructing more valid comparisons—specifically, for identifying "treatment" and "control" groups for which differences in outcomes can reasonably be attributed to the program or intervention rather than to some other factor. Impact evaluations conducted using rigorous, high-quality methods provide the greatest confidence that observed changes in outcomes targeted by the program are indeed attributable to the program or intervention. It is well recognized within Congress and other branches of government (for example, GAO 2012, National Research Council 2009), in the private sector (Manzi 2012), in non-governmental research organizations (Coalition for Evidence-Based Policy 2012, Walker et al. 2006), and in academia (for example, Imbens 2010; Angrist and Krueger 1999; Burtless 1995) that evaluations measuring impacts on outcomes using random assignment provide the most definitive evidence of program effectiveness.

Although the classic impact evaluation design entails random assignment of recipients into treatment and control groups as part of the experiment, the goal of constructing valid comparisons sometimes can be achieved by taking advantage of natural variation that produces as-if randomness, an approach referred to as a quasi-experiment. Quasi-experiments can sometimes be much less expensive than traditional large-scale random assignment experiments, and are discussed further below.

Estimation of Causal Effects of a Program or Intervention

The starting point for estimating the causal effect of a program or intervention is being precise about what constitutes a causal effect. Consider a treatment delivered at the individual level: either the individual received the treatment, or did not. The difference between the potential outcome if the individual received the treatment and the potential outcome if the individual did not is the effect of the treatment on the individual.[1] The challenge of estimating this treatment effect stems from the fact that any given individual either receives the treatment or does not (for example, a child either does or does not attend preschool). Thus, for any given person only one of two potential outcomes can be observed. The fact that we cannot directly observe the counterfactual outcome (for example, the earnings a person who

---

[1] No two individuals are the same, so in general the effect of a program or intervention differs from one individual to the next. For example, the effect of the preschool program could depend on the child's learning opportunities at home. Impact evaluation typically focuses on estimating an average causal effect, which is the average of the individual-level causal effects.

went to preschool would have had if they had, in fact, not gone to preschool) implies that we cannot directly measure the causal effect. This problem of observing only one of the potential outcomes for any given individual is the fundamental problem of causal inference (Holland 1986).

Randomization provides a solution to the problem of not observing the counterfactual outcome. If individuals are randomly assigned to treatment and control groups, then on average the individuals in the two groups are likely to be the same in terms of other characteristics that might affect outcomes. As a result, one can safely assume that ex-post differences between the groups are the result of the treatment. To take the preschool example, simply comparing test scores of all U.S. elementary school children who had attended preschool to all U.S. elementary school children who had not would not provide confidence that higher test scores for the first group were an effect of preschool. The scores might reflect differences in family background, elementary school resources, or other important factors between the two groups. On the other hand, if a group of three-year olds are randomly assigned to attend or not attend preschool, and the preschool group has higher test scores in third grade, we can attribute the test score gains to attending preschool because the two groups would not be systematically different along other dimensions that might impact learning.

In most cases, simple comparisons of treated and untreated individuals without random assignment will not produce valid comparisons because treatment status will be correlated with other important factors. For example, if potential preschool enrollees were initially screened so that those with the least learning opportunities outside school were placed in the program, then we might find that the treatment group (enrollees) has worse outcomes than the control group. However, the reason for this finding is that enrollees are more disadvantaged than non-enrollees. The variation between treatment and control groups affects ultimate outcomes both through the treatment and the differences in learning opportunities outside school. Thus, any comparison of outcomes between treatment and control groups would measure the combined effects of both the treatment and those differences in learning opportunities.

Because randomized experiments can be expensive or infeasible, researchers have also developed methods to use as-if random variation in what is known as a quasi-experiment. The necessary condition for a high-quality quasi-experimental design is that people are assigned to a treatment or control group in a way that mimics randomness. This can be done by forming treatment and control groups whose individuals have similar observable characteristics, and exploiting some rule that governs assignment to the treatment and control groups in a way that is plausibly unrelated to the outcome of interest.

One example of a quasi-experimental design that lends itself to estimating impacts of programs or interventions is when eligibility is determined based on one or more variables in a way that individuals who (just) qualify for the program are very much like those who (just) do not. If so, and if both eligible and ineligible applicants are tracked, then a method called regression discontinuity design can be used to compare the outcomes for individuals on the two sides of the threshold, controlling for other observable differences between the two groups.

Another example of quasi-experimental design is when a program varies across units for reasons unrelated to the program outcomes. Rothstein (2011), for example, exploits the fact that, due to different business cycle patterns combined with policy variation created by expirations and renewals of the Emergency Unemployment Compensation (EUC) program during the Great Recession, the number of available weeks of benefits available to jobseekers varied dramatically from month to month in differing ways across states. After controlling for local economic conditions, the haphazard nature of the changes in EUC benefit levels across states enabled estimation of EUC benefits on job-finding rates.

Describing the whole range of quasi-experimental approaches is beyond the scope of this chapter.[2] Quasi-experiments require stronger assumptions than randomized experiments and the debate around those assumptions makes it harder for quasi-experiments to be convincing, especially to non-experts. However, if the quasi-experimental variation used is plausibly unrelated to the outcomes of interest except through the treatment, quasi-experimental evidence can be convincing, with some methods and applications being nearly as compelling as randomized trials and others leaving more room for doubt.

Other Criteria for High-Quality, Successful Impact Evaluations

A strong impact evaluation also needs to address questions that are actionable and relate to outcomes that matter. In some cases, the actionable information might identify if a program is or is not effective. In other cases, the actionable information might identify which interventions are best at achieving important program outcomes, so that programs can be improved

---

[2] For more extensive introductions to impact evaluation (both randomized experiments and quasi-experiments), see Angrist and Pischke (2008, ch. 1) and Stock and Watson (2010, ch. 13). Shadish, Cook, and Campbell (2002) and Berk and Rossi (1998) provide more advanced textbook treatments, and Imbens and Wooldridge (2009) provide a survey of recent methodological developments in the field.

by adopting successful interventions more broadly. However, if there are legal or other impediments to expanding an evaluated small-scale intervention, then learning that the intervention works does not directly lead to an action that can improve a program at a national level. In such cases, it may be better to allocate scarce evaluation resources to testing more modest interventions or ways to run the program more effectively.

For the second of these criteria—outcomes that matter—the long-term goals of a program must be considered. For a preschool program, the number of students enrolled is an easy-to-measure intermediate outcome. However, preschool enrollment may or may not be related to ultimate outcomes, such as high school graduation rates, employment rates, or income. It is also important to consider program size and stage of development, as programs or interventions must be sufficiently mature, and treatment and control groups sufficiently large, to obtain credible estimates of impact.

Other issues must also be addressed to conduct policy-relevant impact evaluations in government programs. At the most practical level, rigorous evaluation requires adequate funding, staff expertise, and often cooperation across different parts of an agency (or across multiple agencies). Rigorous evaluation also requires support from top agency management and program managers. Further, many Federal programs have multiple goals, which can make it hard to take action on evaluation findings when the results support some goals but not others.

An important part of evaluating a program is remaining open to the findings, regardless of the outcome, to inform the best course of action to improve outcomes going forward. Findings of positive impacts provide important feedback that may indicate whether additional investment is warranted. Findings of no impact, either for all participants and program goals or for important subsets of the participants and program goals, also send valuable signals that modifications—including reallocating program funding to other strategies that could better achieve outcomes—are needed.

Lower-Cost Ways for Impact Evaluations to Facilitate Real-Time Learning

Large-scale random-assignment studies of social programs have been very influential, but also can be quite expensive, and their expense has been a major impediment to wide-scale adoption of learning and program improvement through randomization. For this reason, researchers have focused on lower-cost methods for learning about program effectiveness.

One lower-cost method is to build randomization into the design of the program, so that data on program performance can be tracked and evaluated on an ongoing basis. This strategy has been pioneered as a management tool in the private sector for ongoing product and process improvement. Indeed, some companies run thousands of randomized studies annually: by 2000, Capital One was running 60,000 studies annually using randomization methods, as they experimented with different strategies to determine what works. Google has also run randomized experiments in the tens of thousands in some years (Manzi 2012).

In the public sector, Federal agencies are also finding ways to conduct high-quality evaluation strategies at lower cost, including ways that employ the lessons learned from behavioral economics (Box 7-2). The U. S. Department of Agriculture's Food and Nutrition Service is conducting a range of rigorous demonstration projects to further develop the evidence base of effective strategies for programs that address food insecurity and improve nutrition among children; one such project implements low-cost environmental changes in lunchrooms to encourage students to make healthier food choices. One demonstration found that merely placing fruit in a colorful bowl in a convenient part of the lunch line can lead to an increase in fruit sales of up to 102 percent (Wansink, Just, and Smith 2011). Funding research for these simple, evidence-based interventions allows for the development of effective strategies to strengthen the nutrition and hunger safety net for the more than 30 million children fed by the National School Lunch Program.

Utilizing existing data and independent programmatic changes to measure outcomes is another strategy that agencies are using to minimize evaluation costs. For example, the Department of Justice's National Institute of Justice conducts impact evaluations of interventions that can help inform the approximately 18,000 local law enforcement agencies that do not individually have the resources to test interventions on their own. Hawaii's Opportunity Probation with Enforcement (HOPE) program was established as a demonstration pilot for drug-involved probationers in Hawaii. The pilot tested the efficacy of "swift and certain" sanctions against probationers who fail to meet the conditions of their probation. The randomized controlled experiment found that after one year, probationers who received very frequent drug testing (every other day) and—if they failed the drug test—an immediate court date and a modest but certain sanction (a night in jail), were 72 percent less likely to use drugs, 61 percent less likely to skip meetings with their supervisory officers, 55 percent less likely to be arrested for a new crime, and 53 percent less likely to have their probation revoked. These reductions led to HOPE participants being sentenced to an average of 48 fewer days in prison than those in the control group who received the traditional delayed but more severe sentence (National Institute of Justice). Because of the high costs associated with servicing inmates in prison,

Box 7-2: Using Behavioral Economics to Inform Potential Program Improvements

Increasingly, agencies are using insights from behavioral science to implement low-cost evaluations that can be used to improve program design. Utilizing randomized experiments or other rigorous evaluation designs, these studies examine aspects of program operations that can be re-designed to help people take better advantage of available programs and services—such as by simplifying application processes or highlighting the availability of student financial aid. Recently, the White House Office of Science and Technology Policy assembled a cross-agency team of behavioral science and evaluation experts—the U.S. Social and Behavioral Sciences Team—to help agencies identify promising opportunities for embedding behavioral insights into program designs and to provide the necessary technical tools to rigorously evaluate impact. Such low-cost, real-time experiments can help Federal programs operate more effectively and efficiently.

any intervention that reduces prison time can generate large savings. By making use of available administrative data, evaluations employing quasi-experimental and randomized controlled trial designs were implemented at a cost of only $150,000 and $230,000, respectively.[3] A follow-up analysis is examining the long-term impacts of the intervention; this model is also being piloted in four other locations.

The often-lengthy time between implementation and results of a rigorous evaluation can also discourage its use, but agencies are looking for ways to speed up the evaluation process to gain actionable insights more quickly. For example, the Center for Medicare and Medicaid Innovation (the "Innovation Center"), which was created by the Affordable Care Act of 2010, is using an innovative "Rapid Cycle" approach and high-quality evaluation methods to develop and test innovative payment and service delivery models designed to reduce expenditures while preserving or enhancing quality of care for Medicare, Medicaid and Children's Health Insurance Program beneficiaries. By giving more rapid feedback to health providers, as Box 7-3 shows, the Rapid Cycle approach provides actionable information, allows for more frequent course corrections, and supports continuous quality improvement (Shrank 2013).

---

[3] Cost estimates supplied by the Department of Justice's National Institute of Justice.

From its first months, the Administration embedded a strong evaluation focus into many new initiatives to learn what strategies work best and to scale up approaches backed by strong evidence. During the formulation of the FY 2011 Budget in fall 2009, the Office of Management and Budget (OMB) invited agencies to submit new evaluation proposals for building rigorous evidence and also encouraged agencies to demonstrate that new program initiatives were based on credible evidence of success or to include plans to collect evidence where none exists. The Administration has maintained its emphasis on using and building evidence in every subsequent budget (OMB 2010, 2011, 2012, 2013a, 2013b).

Uses of Evaluation

Agencies have used impact evaluations to inform policy and program decisions in a wide variety of ways.

Making the Unemployment Insurance System More Effective. Unemployment insurance (UI) provides an important safety net for workers who become unemployed. Occasionally, concerns are raised that UI payments could reduce an unemployed worker's incentive to find employment. While the evidence suggests that any such effects are small (Council of Economic Advisers and the Department of Labor 2013), the Federal Reemployment and Eligibility Assessment (REA) initiative started providing funds in 2005 to states and sought to reduce UI duration by combining in-person UI eligibility reviews with (1) labor market information, (2) developing a reemployment plan, and (3) offering a referral to reemployment services. The Department of Labor funded research using a randomized design that showed the REA initiative was effective in reducing the duration of UI (Benus et al. 2008). However, these studies focused on measuring reduced duration on UI and associated costs and not on other outcomes, such as return to employment or increased wages. These studies were followed by another randomized controlled trial which showed that the REAs were also effective at reducing joblessness when eligibility assessments were personalized and more closely integrated with the delivery of reemployment services (Poe-Yamagata et al. 2011). Consequently, the Administration proposed in the American Jobs Act to create a requirement that all Emergency Unemployment Compensation claimants receive both an REA and reemployment services; this was enacted in the Middle Class Tax Relief and Job Creation Act of 2012.[4] Evidence from rigorous evaluations is playing a role in making the REA initiative more effective and getting

---

[4] Public Law 112-96.

**Box 7-3: "Rapid Cycle" Evaluations in the Center
for Medicare and Medicaid Innovation**

The Center for Medicare and Medicaid Innovation (the "Innovation Center") has invested in building information systems and institutional capacity that permit a "Rapid Cycle" approach to testing a variety of new models. For instance, evaluators can gather real-time information and provide performance data to providers who adopted the same model, allowing these providers to understand and track their own performance, and to compare their performance with that of other providers. In the early stages of model implementation, the Innovation Center is applying this Rapid Cycle approach primarily to process evaluations (see Box 7-1), turning later to assessing the models' overall impacts (including impacts on important subgroups, where feasible) once there is reasonable assurance that the model has been in operation sufficiently long to detect impacts. When experimental conditions cannot be met due to logistical or other constraints, quasi-experimental methods are used, with multiple comparison groups for each treatment group identified where possible to provide robustness checks of the findings (Shrank 2013).

unemployed Americans back to work faster, and the Administration has sought to expand it to cover more workers. A modest increase in funding for REAs was included in the recently enacted Consolidated Appropriations Act of 2014.

Simplifying Applications for Student Aid. In many cases, actionable evidence on what works comes from field-generated, grant-funded research rather than from Federal program evaluations. In 2008, with support from the Department of Education's Federal Student Aid Office, Institute of Education Sciences, and other funders, university-based researchers worked with H&R Block to set up an experiment providing randomly selected low-income tax filers in North Carolina and Ohio with pre-populated Free Application for Federal Student Aid (FAFSA) forms and FAFSA assistance for themselves or their children, as well as with information about student aid. This relatively low-cost intervention had a surprisingly large effect on college enrollment outcomes. For example, college enrollment rates for high school seniors and recent high school graduates who received this help rose by about 25 percent—from 34 to 42 percent. Moreover, these gains persisted over time: three years after the intervention, treatment group students were 8 percentage points more likely to have been enrolled in college for at least two consecutive years (Bettinger et al. 2012).

The study's findings helped spur many important policy changes. Most notably, students and their families now have the option to pre-populate the FAFSA with the income information they have already provided the Internal Revenue Service on their tax returns, similar to the arrangement the researchers tested with H&R Block. This simplifies FAFSA completion for students, lowers the risk of errors, and as such should increase access to college among socioeconomically disadvantaged students and should lead to gains in college enrollment. As a complement, the Department of Education has also simplified the FAFSA application to make it easier to complete for all applicants, but especially for low-income students. In 2012, the Department of Education awarded a second grant to the research team to test the effects of FAFSA simplification at scale. The evaluation will use an experimental design and involve 9,000 tax-filing sites across the United States.

Institutionalizing Evidence-Based Decision-making in Grant Programs. In many programs, funds are distributed to states and local entities through competitive and formula grants. Grants to State and local governments have constituted roughly one-third of total outlays over the last 20 years, so increasing the use of evidence in informing policy in grant-supported programs could improve outcomes for a significant portion of outlays (Figure 7-1). Many effective program structures treat evaluation as an essential element in the decision-making framework, while also building in opportunities to scale up approaches that work and scale back or eliminate approaches that do not. As stated by then-OMB Director Peter Orszag, new initiatives should ideally have "evaluation standards built into their DNA" (OMB 2009b). The Administration has experimented with several models that embed both evidence building and evidence-based decisionmaking into the "DNA" of grant programs.

During this Administration, several initiatives have adopted a "tiered evidence" approach that embeds evidence-based decision making into program structure. Tiered evidence programs tie grant funding to the evidence base behind proposed interventions. In these programs, interventions that provide better evidence of success move to higher tiers and become eligible to receive more funding for expanded implementation and evaluation. The built-in mechanism for scaling up interventions that work helps prevent the troubling problem of not investing in programs with proven high returns.

A successful example of a three-tier approach is the Investing in Innovation program at the Department of Education. This program provides seed development grants of up to $3 million for high-potential and relatively untested interventions, validation grants of up to $12 million for interventions based on only a moderate amount of evidence, and scale-up grants of up to $20 million for potentially high-impact, transformative education interventions. Evidence of effectiveness is an "entry requirement"

Figure 7-1
Outlays for Grants to State and Local Governments, 1992–2012

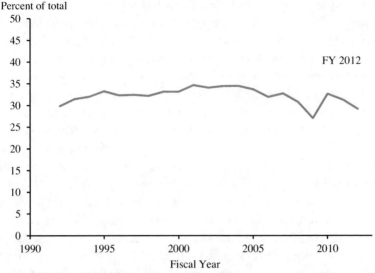

Percent of total

FY 2012

Fiscal Year

Note: Total excludes outlays for defense, interest and social security.
Source: Office of Management and Budget, FY 2014 Budget, Tables 3.1 and 12.2.

for validation and scale-up grants, and all grantees are expected to conduct an evaluation that will add to the evidence base on effectiveness. For the scale-up and validation grants, the grantee must make the data from their evaluations available to third-party researchers, consistent with applicable privacy requirements (Department of Education 2013a).

Similarly, the Maternal, Infant, and Early Childhood Home Visiting Program in the Department of Health and Human Services (HHS) was an early Administration initiative that uses a two-tiered evidence structure. Implemented in 2010 as part of the Affordable Care Act, this voluntary home visiting program uses trained professionals and paraprofessionals to provide support to vulnerable pregnant women and parents of young children to improve health, development, and well-being outcomes for at-risk children and their families. The Act required that at least 75 percent of the home visiting program funds be spent on proven, evidence-based approaches and allowed for the remainder to be spent on promising approaches as long as they are rigorously evaluated. Currently, 14 home visiting models meet the HHS criteria of "evidence-based approaches," and have been evaluated with a mix of randomized experiments and quasi-experiments using multiple measures of key outcomes (Paulsell et al. 2013). While the Act funded the home visiting program through 2014, the Administration has proposed to continue funding and expand the availability of voluntary evidence-based home visiting programs to reach additional families in need as part of a continuum of early childhood interventions.

In addition to tiered evidence structures, agencies have begun using other designs in competitive grant programs that encourage the use of evidence-based practices. One such design is the "Pay for Success" approach. In this performance-based model, philanthropic and private funding is leveraged and the government provides payment only after targeted outcomes are achieved. In 2012 and 2013, the Administration started supporting programs that use a Pay for Success model to fund preventive services, and which had outcomes that could be measured with credible evaluation methodologies. The first Pay for Success awards were for projects to prevent prison recidivism.[5] The Consolidated Appropriations Act of 2014 authorized up to $21.5 million for Pay for Success projects.

Even in more traditionally structured grant programs where funding is provided upfront, agencies are embedding more rigorous evaluation requirements into funding requirements. For example, upfront grants in the Department of Labor's Workforce Innovation Fund, first issued in 2011, fund promising but untested employment and training service and administrative strategies. These grants also fund well-tested ideas being adapted to new contexts as a way to significantly increase evidence about interventions that generate long-term improvements in public workforce system performance, such as reduced duration of unemployment. Grantees are required to conduct rigorous evaluations, and a national evaluation coordinator works with grantee evaluators to ensure consistent and high-quality evaluations (Department of Labor 2011).

Ending or Reducing Funding for Interventions or Programs. The Administration's commitment to evidence-based evaluation means terminating or reducing funding for a program when a body of evidence consistently shows that the program is not achieving its stated goals, helping to reduce the use of taxpayer dollars on ineffective programs. The FY 2012 Budget took this approach with the Mentoring Children of Prisoners (MCP) program run by the Department of Health and Human Services. Rigorous evaluations show that high-quality mentoring relationships lasting for at least 12 months can have positive impacts on youth, while relationships that do not last more than three months can actually have harmful effects on youth (Grossman and Rhodes 2002). According to the MCP program

---

[5] For example, the Department of Labor allocated nearly $24 million in Workforce Innovation Fund grants to pilot Pay for Success grants to increase employment and reduce recidivism among formerly incarcerated individuals (United States Interagency Council on Homelessness, 2013a). DOL required the grantees to employ rigorous evaluation methods in gauging impacts on outcomes, which was defined in the grant solicitation as an experimental or credible quasi-experimental evaluation design.

performance data, fewer than half of program participants each year were in matches that lasted at least 12 months and, in 2008 alone, as many as 27 percent of matches that ended prematurely ended within three months. An evaluation of one MCP-funded program suggested that premature terminations were the result of program performance and were independent of the demographics of the participants (Schlafer et al. 2009).

Interpreting the MCP performance data in light of the evidence from impact evaluations of other mentoring programs, the Administration concluded that the MCP was not as effective as it should be. As a result, the Administration proposed to reduce funding for the MCP, noting that other competitive grant programs could serve the youth targeted by the MCP, and that some of those programs, such as Promise Neighborhoods, utilize evidence-based practices. Congress ultimately eliminated funding for the program in the Continuing Appropriations Act of 2011.

Even Start, originally designed to improve family literacy in disadvantaged populations, was another program not meeting its stated goals that the Administration took steps to replace. While the literacy levels of Even Start children and parents improved, multiple national randomized experiments showed that parents and children in control groups who did not participate in Even Start (one-third of whom received other early childhood education or adult education services) had comparable improvements (see for example St. Pierre et al. 2003). The President's FY 2012 Budget proposed, and Congress approved, the elimination of separate funding for Even Start. The Administration has proposed incorporating it and other narrowly focused literacy programs into the newly created literacy component of the Effective Teaching and Learning program that would support competitive grants to states for high-quality, evidence-based literacy programs.

Building Evidence when Existing Evidence is Limited

In many of the examples highlighted above, evidence existed on what programs or interventions were most effective, and the key challenge facing policymakers was to act on that evidence. However, not enough is known about what works in many other important areas, and so the first step in evidence-based policymaking is to invest in developing evidence.

Reducing Electricity Use. Experts have long suggested time-varying pricing (more costly at times of peak demand) as a way of increasing the efficiency of electricity use, including reducing electricity demand. Such time-varying pricing could increase efficiency, defer investments in expensive new power plants, and reduce pollution. However, most electricity delivery systems have not invested in the in-home technologies necessary to allow residential consumers to respond to time-varying prices. In addition, regulators have been hesitant to approve varying rates, and private companies have been reluctant to invest in modernizing their systems without knowing whether time-varying pricing will significantly impact consumer behavior. In recent years, the Federal Government, in partnership with states and utilities, invested in evaluating the impact of time-varying pricing on consumer behavior so that this information would be available to utilities, regulators, and states. These consumer behavior studies were implemented with American Recovery and Reinvestment Act funds and use randomized controlled experimental methods. Deciding which type of pricing strategy to use falls within State jurisdiction, rather than Federal, so these studies will allow State and local public utilities to make more informed decisions on pricing models (Cappers et al 2013). While these studies are still ongoing, two utilities and their regulators have decided to implement time-varying rates across their service territories based on the results observed to date. Such efforts can serve as an impetus to get more public utilities to adopt time-varying pricing.

Improving Health Care Delivery. In another example, the Affordable Care Act made a number of major investments in understanding how to improve quality and reduce cost in health care delivery, in addition to expanding access to affordable health insurance coverage. As described earlier in this chapter, the Center for Medicare and Medicaid Innovation (the "Innovation Center"), created by the Act, is using high-quality evaluation approaches to test innovative payment and service delivery models designed to reduce expenditures while preserving or enhancing quality of care for Medicare, Medicaid and Children's Health Insurance Program beneficiaries. Several ongoing Innovation Center payment reform initiatives—and early results from those initiatives—are discussed in Chapter 4. The Innovation Center will use the results of such model evaluations and actuarial data to identify best practices and determine which successful models could be implemented more broadly.

Better Outcomes for Youth with Disabilities. The Administration is also testing many different approaches aimed at youth with disabilities. The Promoting Readiness of Minors in Supplemental Security Income (PROMISE) is a joint initiative of the departments of Education, Health and Human Services, Labor, and the Social Security Administration. PROMISE aims to improve the education and employment outcomes for youth with disabilities who receive Supplemental Security Income (SSI) and their families, by improving coordination of services such as those available through the Individuals with Disabilities Education Act, the Vocational Rehabilitation State Grants program, Medicaid health and home and community based services, Job Corps, Temporary Assistance for Needy Families, and Workforce

Investment Act programs. The PROMISE program allows grantees (states or consortia of states) to design their own intervention models to serve youth and their families for three years with a two-year extension option, provided they include a minimum set of services. Grantees may also apply for waivers of funding restrictions or rules in individual programs that they believe will constrain their ability to achieve outcomes. Grantees agree to enroll a large number of youth (around 2,000) who are eligible to be served by a PROMISE intervention, and to allow random assignment to be used to assign half of eligible youth to the treatment group and the remaining youth to a control group that receives the services that child SSI recipients normally receive. The first grants were awarded in September 2013. To evaluate whether PROMISE can help child SSI recipients achieve better outcomes, a national evaluation will be conducted of all grantees to analyze intervention impacts on educational attainment, employment credentials and outcomes, and whether the interventions reduce long-term reliance on public benefits, and SSI payments in particular (Social Security Administration 2013).

Improving Outcomes For At-Risk Youth. The Administration also is working to identify approaches that help at-risk youth. The National Guard Youth Challenge (ChalleNGe) program, which has been rigorously evaluated, is designed to provide opportunities for adolescents who have dropped out of school but demonstrate a willingness to turn their lives around. Using random assignment, Millensky et al. (2011) found significant benefits to program participation in addition to higher earnings, as ChalleNGe graduates were more likely than the control group to have obtained a high school diploma or GED, to have earned college credits, and to be working three years after completing the program. Participation was projected to increase discounted lifetime earnings by over $40,000 (in 2010 dollars) (Perez-Arce et al. 2012). After considering education costs to the student and other non-earnings benefits, the ChalleNGe program was estimated to generate $2.66 for every dollar of program cost (Perez-Arce et al. 2012). The Administration now plans to test the application of the ChalleNGe model to adjudicated youth, through the Department of Labor's Reintegration of Ex-Offenders program.

Reducing Homelessness. Sharply reducing homelessness is a key focus of the Administration.[6] Although once considered an intractable problem, a broad body of research (including rigorous evaluations) documented that

---

[6] Spurred in part by the Homeless Emergency Assistance and Rapid Transition to Housing Act of 2009, the Obama Administration released *Opening Doors: The Federal Strategic Plan to End Homelessness* in 2010. The plan establishes ambitious goals to end veterans' and chronic homelessness as well as homelessness among youth and families. The U.S. Interagency Council on Homelessness serves to coordinate action by 19 member agencies (United States Interagency Council on Homelessness, 2013b).

there are models that effectively serve individuals experiencing chronic homelessness. The Department of Housing and Urban Development (HUD) has invested heavily in promoting these evidence-based approaches, and has re-oriented the Homelessness Assistance Grant Program away from such traditional approaches as transitional housing and toward more-effective permanent supportive housing (Figure 7-2). Because research on interventions that are effective for homeless families does not yet exist at the same level of rigor as for homeless individuals (Culhane et al. 2007), HUD has undertaken an experimental study of family homelessness called the Family Options Study. This study will compare several combinations of housing assistance and services in a multi-site experiment to determine which interventions work best to promote housing stability, family preservation, child well-being, adult well-being, and self-sufficiency. In addition to usual care, defined as remaining in emergency shelter and accessing whatever resources that would normally be available to families in shelter, three interventions are being studied: 1) subsidy only (a voucher primarily), 2) transitional housing, 3) rapid re-housing.[7]

FURTHERING THE EVIDENCE AGENDA

Relative to when President Obama first took office in January 2009, agencies are doing more to build actionable evidence to answer important program and policy questions. These efforts span a wide range of agencies and programs. While largely focused on improving the performance of programs that provide direct services to individuals and account for roughly 65 percent of total Federal outlays (OMB 2014), many agencies, including the Department of Commerce, the Small Business Administration, the Department of Agriculture, and the Treasury Department are also pursuing ways to incorporate impact evaluations in programs that provide assistance to businesses.

Instilling a culture of evidence-based decision making within agencies, and building the foundations that enable rigorous evaluations to guide new investments and drive policy, is neither quick nor easy. Evaluations of particular interventions or entire programs should not be isolated exercises that occur on an ad hoc basis, but rather planned in advance. Challenges always accompany efforts to enact significant change, but addressing several key elements can greatly facilitate agency efforts to improve the collection and use of evidence. While not a comprehensive list, these issues represent

---

[7] A summary of the study, as well as the Interim Report (which documents the study design process of randomization, and characteristics of the study population) can be found here: http://www.huduser.org/portal/family_options_study.html

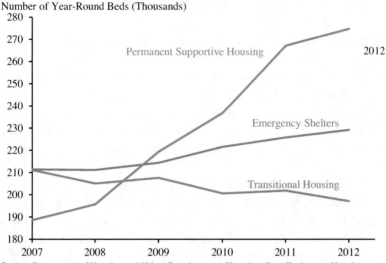

Figure 7-2
**Inventory of Beds for Homeless and Formerly
Homeless People, 2007–2012**

Number of Year-Round Beds (Thousands)

Permanent Supportive Housing

Emergency Shelters

Transitional Housing

2012

Source: Department of Housing and Urban Development, Homeless Data Exchange, Housing Inventory Count.

several major areas that provide either useful opportunities, or serve as barriers, in agency efforts to build and advance an evidence-based agenda.

Legislative Support for Evaluation

Authorizing legislation and appropriations bills can direct how agencies should use program funds for a wide variety of activities. Legislation can encourage stronger and more cost-effective evaluation in many ways. One is through language that recognizes the importance of conducting rigorous evaluations. Another is by making sure already-collected program data are made available for such statistical and analytical purposes.

Legislative Support for Rigorous Evaluations. Two ways that legislation can support rigorous evaluation is through set-asides and support for evaluation of demonstration programs. In recent years, with support of top management within agencies and the Administration, several agencies have had set-asides for evaluation specified in program legislation and appropriations. For example, the Consolidated Appropriations Act of 2012 first enabled the Secretary of Labor to reserve up to 0.5 percent of specific Department of Labor (DOL) appropriations for evaluations. Also, a set-aside of 5 percent of competitive grant funds in the Teacher Incentive Fund allows the Department of Education to conduct a rigorous national evaluation of the program and to share with grantees the results of current, rigorous research to help facilitate ongoing improvement. Additionally, authority to set-aside a percentage of program funds for evaluation is specified in some HHS and HUD programs, including several that received additional funding through the Affordable Care Act of 2010 and the American Recovery and Reinvestment Act of 2009.[8]

Many programs are funded through annual appropriations, which generally require obligation of those funds within a given fiscal year. However, the DOL set-aside for evaluation in the Consolidated Appropriations Act extends the deadline by which the DOL must obligate transferred evaluation funds to two years. Because designing rigorous evaluations takes time, a window beyond the standard one-year for obligating evaluation funds can in some cases enable agencies to plan and execute more thorough, higher-quality evaluations.

Legislation that specifies funding for demonstration pilots also provides important support for developing an evidence base. The legislatively authorized demonstrations being conducted by the Innovation Center are recent examples that illustrate the value of legislative support for evidence building.[9] As another example, the Department of Health and Human Services' child welfare waiver authority allows states to design and demonstrate a wide range of approaches for reforming child welfare and improving outcomes, including decreased first-time entries and re-entries into foster care, and improvements in various aspects of child developmental, behavioral, and social functioning. States are required to conduct rigorous impact evaluations as well as process evaluations as part of their waiver agreements.[10] In addition, the Administration is proposing to restore demonstration authority for the Disability Insurance program, while also providing new authority for the Social Security Administration and partner agencies to test early-intervention strategies that would help people with disabilities remain in the workforce.

Legislation can also encourage stronger evaluations through explicit language requiring grantees to participate in evaluations and by requiring use of proven interventions. The Healthy, Hunger-Free Kids Act, for

---

[8] While set-asides within programs are useful, some have noted that department-wide set-asides may have advantages over program-level set-asides by providing agencies with more flexibility over maximizing the return to evaluation investments. Also, set-asides will be used most effectively when agencies have a demonstrated capacity to manage evaluation funds.

[9] Prior to passage of the ACA, existing demonstration payment waiver authority allowed HHS to conduct Medicare demonstrations of the impacts of new service delivery methods and new payment approaches. However, due to statutory restrictions these demonstrations tended to be relatively small. The ACA provided the Secretary with more flexible authority for testing payment and delivery system innovations, and expanding them based on evidence. This work is conducted under the auspices of the CMMI.

[10] Child and Family Services Improvement and Innovation Act, Title II, Sec. 201, P.L. 112-34.

example, included a nondiscretionary provision that requires State and local grant recipients in a number of nutrition assistance programs, including the National School Lunch Program, the Special Supplemental Nutrition Program for Women, Infants and Children, and other programs authorized in the National School Lunch Act and the Child Nutrition Act to cooperate in evaluations conducted by or on behalf of the Department of Agriculture.[11] This Act also reformed the structure of the nutrition education provided through the Supplemental Nutrition Assistance Program, one of the Nation's main anchors of the social safety net that provides nutrition assistance to eligible low-income individuals and families. It established a new and improved Nutrition Education and Obesity Prevention Grant Program that requires a greater emphasis on evidence-based, outcome-driven interventions, with a focus on preventing obesity and coordinating with other programs for maximum impact and cost-effectiveness.

Legislative Support for Access to Data for Statistical Purposes, Including Evaluations. Existing laws can be explicit or implicit regarding whether information collected as part of administering programs can be used for statistical purposes integral to evaluation. Explicit and supportive laws can save significant time and effort in negotiating agreements to provide data for evaluations and can facilitate more and better analysis. For example, the Social Security Act explicitly states that one of the agency's datasets can be used for statistical and research activities conducted by Federal and State agencies.

Some legislation provides the agency head with broad authority to determine appropriate uses of program data. Given that the statistical uses of data in program evaluation often inform the context, policies, and operations of the same programs authorized by a given statute, agencies sometimes determine that their general statutory authority can grant sufficient authorization to provide administrative data to other Federal agencies for statistical purposes. For example, the Social Security Administration provides certain datasets for statistical and research purposes as described in its implementing regulations.

Multiple legitimate goals must be balanced when determining appropriate access to data, including reducing the burden of data collection on individuals and institutions and protecting personal privacy. Even so, careful crafting of legislative language can achieve those aims while still making data available for Federal researchers to rigorously evaluate and to improve

---

[11] U.S. Department of Agriculture, Food and Nutrition Service Final Rule, Cooperation in USDA Studies and Evaluations, and Full Use of Federal Funds in Nutrition Assistance Programs Nondiscretionary Provisions of the Healthy, Hunger-Free Kids Act of 2010, Public Law 111–296. Federal Register Vol 76, No. 125, June 29, 2011.

government programs. Key considerations include: avoiding vague or unclear authority to determine appropriate uses of program data; avoiding narrowly written statutory language that only allows access to data for narrowly defined programmatic reasons; or restricting a Federal agency's ability to collect data from grantees.

The information needs in programs managed at the State level could theoretically be addressed through non-Federal data systems, but this is not always possible. States or other grantees may not voluntarily develop comprehensive data systems in ways that are comparable across states, or have the capacity or incentive to make data available to researchers. When no feasible solutions exist to alleviate these issues, legislation may be warranted to authorize creation of Federal datasets accessible to researchers, or to establish requirements for State-held datasets that enable data exchange and comparability across states and to ensure access by researchers.

Building Evaluation into the Design of Programs

Many of the examples described earlier demonstrate the ways in which agencies are designing programs to facilitate evaluation. But agencies can still do more to embed rigorous evaluation designs into both new programs and existing programs.

New programs. The benefits of adopting evidence-based program designs, like the tiered evidence structure in the Investing in Innovation program and in HHS' home visiting program, include the ability to guide competitive grant funds to the strategies with a strong evidence base, while also requiring grantees to conduct evaluations where no evidence is yet available. Even without such a program structure, agencies implementing new programs over the past five years have increasingly required grantees to collect data and develop administrative data systems that can improve comparability and facilitate evaluation in addition to meeting program operating needs. For example, the Department of Education's Promise Neighborhoods initiative implemented in 2010 requires grantees to collect and track outcome data in an individual-level longitudinal data system to facilitate rigorous evaluation. This initiative aims to improve educational and developmental outcomes of children and youth in distressed communities.[12] To assist grantees in collecting high-quality and comparable data, the Education Department is providing grantees with extensive guidance on data collection and reporting (Comey et al. 2013).

---

[12] This program is based on the Harlem Children's Zone model, which was found to increase earnings for students, decrease the probability of committing crimes and decrease health disability probabilities—with the potential for providing large public benefits (Dobbie and Fryer 2011).

Other benefits of considering evaluation needs in the design of new programs include creating opportunities to save time and money by identifying evaluation data up front, minimizing burden on program respondents, and avoiding the loss of information all together that cannot be created too long after the fact. When not considered in the earliest stages of program design, a typical alternative to collecting the information needed for evaluation is to conduct surveys, which requires identifying expertise to design and test the surveys, gaining approval for their use, and then administering them to collect data, often long after the fact. Surveys add to the time and cost to build evidence, due to the time and skill involved in developing survey instruments that will yield high-quality data, the requirements for obtaining needed approvals, and the actual implementation of the survey.[13] Careful planning can help limit the need for evaluation-related surveys to data that cannot be obtained in any other way, such as information on post-program choices, earnings, or jobs necessary for identifying longer-term impacts of a program or intervention.

One of the most important ways the design of a program can facilitate evidence building is through careful consideration of how treatment and control groups can be established to facilitate impact evaluation. As discussed earlier, randomly assigning potential program participants to treatment and control groups enables the most credible impact evaluations. Several mechanisms exist for creating good comparison groups that allow for experimental or quasi-experimental techniques to be employed to produce high-quality estimates of program effectiveness.

Several options for enrolling potential participants in a program or intervention, presented in order of the rigor of evaluation they might support, are as follows:

1. Random assignment by lottery when capacity is limited. In many instances, due to limited funds or other constraints, a program or intervention cannot serve every person or entity that is eligible to apply. In such cases, rather than "first-come, first-serve" or other nonrandom devices, implementing a lottery to select which applicants may participate in a program or intervention generates a low-cost randomized experiment. This

---

[13] For example, the Paperwork Reduction Act (PRA), first enacted in 1980 and amended in 1995 (44 U.S.C., Chapter 35), requires Federal agencies to obtain OMB approval when an agency plans to collect information from ten or more persons using identical reporting, recordkeeping, or disclosure requirements. Among the PRA's goals are ensuring the greatest possible public benefit from and maximizing the utility of information created, collected, maintained, used, shared and disseminated by or for the Federal government and minimizing the burden for persons resulting from the collection of information by or for the Federal government. As a further example, some data collections are subject to review by Institutional Review Boards, in order to protect the rights of the human subjects of such research, a requirement under (42 USC 289) under 45 CFR 46.

strategy has been used recently to determine the impact of Medicaid access (Baicker et al. 2013), charter school attendance (Abdulkadiroglu et al. 2011), and small business entrepreneurship training (Benus et al. 2009). Note that the losers of the lottery need to be followed to track their outcome data.

2. Assignment based on a continuous "need score." A common objection to random assignment is that resources should be targeted to those with the greatest need, or those most likely to benefit. In this situation, program assignment might lend itself to a strong evaluation if it incorporates some sort of explicit, continuous, ranking of applicant need (or likely benefit), and bases program eligibility on some cutoff in need. For example, Ludwig and Miller (2007) study the effect of participating in Head Start on mortality rates for children by exploiting the fact that the Office of Economic Opportunity provided technical assistance to the 300 poorest counties in 1965. This created lasting differences in Head Start funding rates for counties with poverty levels just below and just above the poverty rate of the 300th poorest county. With this type of assignment rule, a regression discontinuity design can be used to study the impact of the program. The logic of the design is that individuals with "scores" just above and just below the threshold—in Ludwig and Miller, living in a county with a poverty rate just above or below the poverty rate of the 300th poorest county's rate—are likely to be similar to each other in ways that affect their outcomes, except that those just below receive the treatment (in this case, participation in Head Start). This design can deliver estimates of the effect of the program that are similar to randomized experiments.[14]

3. Staging the rollout of a large program. If a program will be introduced that will ultimately serve many participants spread across different geographic areas, or schools, or other natural groupings, staggering the rollout across time and space, with the rollout sequence chosen randomly, makes it much easier to evaluate. For example, suppose a mentoring program aimed at increasing college attendance will be introduced in a group of schools and the government hopes to learn about the effect of the program by estimating the change in college enrollment among students at the school before and after the program is introduced. If the program is introduced in only one school district, then any other changes that the school district introduced around the same time might affect the change in outcomes and bias the conclusion. Similarly, if the program is introduced in many different schools but all in the same year, then any other changes in policy, the economic climate, or other macro-economic conditions may be confounded

---

[14] On the other hand, the estimates from an RDD strictly pertain only to the types of participants "near" the cutoff. To the extent the impact varies across participants with different levels of need, this can be a limitation.

with the treatment effect and thus may "bias" the estimate of the treatment effect. Staggering the rollout of the program over time and space, using randomization and possibly further matching treatment and control units based on observable characteristics, helps to control for these potential biases, and thus allows for better estimates of a program's impact. This strategy has been used by Rothstein (2010) to study the effect of extended unemployment benefits.

The three strategies above create experiments or quasi-experiments that lend themselves to high-quality impact evaluations. In the absence of such devices, evaluators need to acknowledge the differences that do exist between program (or intervention) participants and non-participants and to use statistical techniques like multivariate regression and matching to control for these differences. Since these strategies all attempt to compare the outcomes of program participants and non-participants with similar characteristics, the success of the evaluation will be determined by the availability of good information on the characteristics of the population that are most predictive of the outcome under study, as well as the reasons why individuals choose to participate in a program. However, for these strategies to work, the variation between the treatment and control groups after using statistical or matching techniques to control for differences between these groups must be plausibly unrelated to the outcomes of interest, except through the effect of the treatment. There needs to be some part of that variation between the treatment and control groups that operates like randomization.

Existing Programs. Designing programs to facilitate evaluation may be relatively simpler in new programs than in existing programs, due to program manager reluctance in the latter to trying new strategies, concerns about equity among participants if the control group receives no services, and other reasons. But experiences at several agencies demonstrate these barriers can be overcome. Lotteries for oversubscribed programs are as applicable in longstanding programs as in new ones (see for example the Jacob and Ludwig (2012) study on impacts of housing vouchers). However, increasing opportunities for evidence-based decisionmaking in programs that allocate funds to states on the basis of formulas remain especially challenging, because evaluations and evidence-based funding allocations are not a requirement of States receiving the funds. Waiver authorities or other mechanisms to incentivize evaluations in these programs are only available in a few instances. A control that could prompt State and local grant recipients to do evaluations in these types of programs is a legislated requirement that a certain portion of funds be set aside for evidence-based grants or models of delivery. For example, in the Senate Appropriations Bill for FY 2014, the Substance Abuse and Mental Health Services Administration mental health block grant programs included language defining a 5 percent set-aside for evidence-based grants.[15]

There is still work to be done to embed evaluation and evidence-based decision making into more programs. Agencies can focus evaluation efforts in those programs that can help ensure that the agency's most critical program and policy questions are addressed.[16]

Developing the Capacity to Link to Other Administrative and Survey Data Sources

Increasingly, agencies are seeking opportunities to improve their evaluation approaches by supplementing their administrative program data with other available government data, where appropriate and while ensuring strong privacy protections. Using pre-existing data collected for other reasons, while maintaining strong privacy protections, provides a number of benefits. Several challenges arise when doing so, and the Administration is taking steps to address these challenges.

Benefits of using existing data resources. Using pre-existing administrative data collected for other reasons, while maintaining strong privacy protections, can help agencies answer important policy questions that could not otherwise easily be addressed with a single program database or survey. Administrative data provides the most complete and accurate source of information on program participation and can provide more accurate data on earnings, test scores, and other outcomes of interest. Indeed, the benefits of using pre-existing administrative data for evaluation and other statistical purposes have been widely acknowledged for some time. Data from multiple sources have been used in a number of impact evaluations, primarily to identify the characteristics of treatment and control groups, identify outcome variables which indicate the impacts of treatments, reduce study costs and reduce the burden on study participants by avoiding the need to collect the data via another survey (Coalition for Evidence-Based Policy 2012; Finkelstein et al. 2012; Bettinger et al. 2009; Jacob and Ludwig 2012). Linked datasets are also facilitating current evidence-building efforts in various agencies, such as in the Department of Health and Human Service's Office of Child Support Enforcement, which is currently implementing a child support-led employment services demonstration project with a random assignment impact evaluation (where treatment consists of extra services under the program, and the control group receives regular services that are available) and a cost-benefit analysis. The planned evaluation will draw on

---

[15] S. 1284, Report No. 113–71.
[16] Recognizing that agencies operate with scarce resources, OMB has encouraged agencies to adopt such a focus (OMB 2013b).

unemployment insurance wage and benefit records, as well as State administrative data on benefits in the Supplemental Nutrition Assistance Program and other public assistance programs, criminal justice system data and other data to more cost-effectively and accurately determine the effectiveness and the true costs and benefits of the program. As another example, HUD and HHS are pilot-testing links between HUD administrative data and HHS Medicare/Medicaid data, to build evidence on opportunities to improve the health of Medicare/Medicaid beneficiaries in HUD-assisted housing as well as the impact of housing assistance on health.

Challenges and Solutions. Nevertheless, accessing administrative data for these statistical uses is challenging. These data are collected to facilitate day-to-day program operations, including developing performance measures. Unless evaluation needs are considered in the database design stage, however, the meaningfulness of administrative data for conducting rigorous evaluation may be limited. Also, data definitions can vary dramatically across datasets; especially with State-level data, the definitions often vary across states and even counties. Aside from definitional differences, the quality of programmatic data—its completeness and accuracy—can vary dramatically across datasets. Significant data-quality gaps or errors can compromise analysis. It can also be costly to negotiate access to data on a state-by-state basis.

One key practical challenge is that agencies, in an attempt to be privacy sensitive, may not include in program databases unique identifiers for program applicants and participants. Such unique identifiers facilitate linking to data provided by subjects through other programs or even for the same program over time. Linking datasets through name and address matching or matching on other less unique variables can introduce bias and render the linked data unusable for rigorous analysis. While some agencies have an established history of allowing use of data (including identifying information) for statistical purposes, in many cases access to such data is not readily available due to real or perceived legal, policy, or operational barriers.[17] In some cases, extensive negotiations with the agency responsible for the data are needed to gain access to the data for use in evaluation studies; sometimes the efforts are not successful even after months or years of negotiations.

---

[17] One legal barrier is that when a program's authorizing statute is silent about whether access to data can be provided for statistical purposes (which includes evaluation), agencies need to make a determination about allowable uses. In such cases, agencies may conservatively interpret the lack of an express authority as a prohibition on providing data to another agency. However, as discussed in OMB memorandum M-14-06, agencies may be able to provide the data under their general statutory authority (OMB 2014).

To help address these barriers, the OMB recently issued guidance to assist both program and statistical agencies (and statistical components within agencies) in increasing the opportunities to use administrative data for statistical purposes, which includes evaluation.[18] In part, this guidance requires government departments to engage both program and statistical agencies in identifying administrative datasets of potential value for statistical purposes; communicating the importance to staff of promoting the use of administrative data for statistical purposes; and identifying several datasets with the most value for statistical purposes but which are not currently being provided, along with descriptions of critical barriers that appear to preclude providing access for statistical purposes. The guidance also offers tools to help agencies in these tasks, including guidance in understanding relevant legal requirements, a tool to facilitate more efficient interagency agreements, and a tool to assess administrative data quality developed under the auspices of the Federal Committee on Statistical Methodology. Departments must also report to the OMB on their efforts to foster collaboration and increase access to administrative data for statistical purposes.

Facilitating Researcher Access to Federal Data while Protecting Privacy

Some agencies have developed ways for researchers to access Federal data for statistical purposes in secure research environments that preserve the confidentiality of individual records. The Census Bureau and National Center for Health Statistics operate secure research data centers, in which qualified researchers with approved projects can use micro-data files for statistical research. The Retirement Research Consortium is a key tool that the Social Security Administration uses to facilitate policy-relevant research on retirement and Social Security. The consortium comprises three competitively selected research centers based at the University of Michigan, Boston College, and the National Bureau of Economic Research. The centers perform valuable research and evaluation of retirement policy, disseminate results, provide training and education awards, and facilitate the use of SSA's administrative data by outside researchers. Nonetheless, due to confidentiality restrictions, uneven interpretations of laws governing privacy of data provided to the government, and other reasons, many data sets remain

---

[18] Statistical purposes is defined in footnote 2 of the OMB memorandum M-14-06 (OMB 2014): [it] refers to "the description, estimation, or analysis of the characteristics of groups, without identifying the individuals or organizations that comprise such groups," (PL-107-347, Title V—Confidential Information Protection and Statistical Efficiency Act (CIPSEA), Section 502 (9)(A)). Statistical purposes exclude "any administrative, regulatory, law enforcement, adjudicatory, or other purpose that affects the rights, privileges, or benefits of a particular identifiable respondent" (PL-107-347, Title V—CIPSEA, Section 502 (5)(A)).

hard for researchers to access for statistical uses, and opportunities to link to researcher-collected data remain limited.

This Administration is committed to improving opportunities for researcher access in ways that fully maintain privacy protections of Federal program participants. HHS' Centers for Medicare and Medicaid Services' (CMS) Virtual Research Data Center is an innovative example of ways agencies are working to improve access to Federal agencies for their own use and for their grantees carrying out federally sponsored research activities. In late 2013, the Virtual Research Data Center began providing users with a dedicated workspace where they can upload external files and use them with CMS data to run analyses and download aggregate statistical files to their workstations. This model is a more-efficient, less-expensive, more-flexible and more-secure way for researchers to access a variety of Medicare and Medicaid program data, relative to the existing approach that entails cutting, encrypting, and shipping large quantities of information.

CONCLUSION

Whatever the findings, rigorous evaluations provide critical and credible feedback about whether the current design of a program is effective or whether program modifications are needed so that important program goals are met. Indeed, in some fields—including business and medicine—the vast majority of randomized controlled trials used to evaluate the efficacy of interventions and strategies find no positive effects of interventions (Coalition for Evidence-Based Policy 2013). Rigorous impact evaluations serve as important learning tools to guide management decisions about program investments. The Administration continues to support the use of these tools, broadly and often, to facilitate continuous improvement in government programs as well as to identify best practices and effective new approaches that can be shared with organizations delivering services funded with Federal dollars.

Over the last five years, Federal agencies have increasingly used rigorous impact evaluations to inform program decisions, including how to improve programs. Agencies are trying new approaches when the evidence indicates existing strategies are not yielding sufficiently positive impacts on important outcomes. They are restructuring programs to increase their effectiveness when evidence shows new strategies produce better results, and are developing evidence where an insufficient evidence base exists. And they are scaling up approaches that work, improving public policy and people's lives. As part of this effort, agencies are improving the collection and comparability of data to provide new opportunities for evaluation. They are also using cutting-edge technology to improve data access to other Federal agencies and to outside researchers while protecting privacy—strategies that can enable evaluations to be done more rapidly and at lower cost. The Administration continues to support these efforts to affect change. By using rigorous evaluation strategies to identify what works, and by taking steps to make needed modifications, agencies and taxpayers will have the greatest confidence that scarce resources are being used as efficiently as possible in meeting priority goals.

REFERENCES

CHAPTER 1

Almunia, Miguel, Agustin Benetrix, Barry Eichengreen, Kevin H. O'Rourke and Gisela Rua. 2010. "From Great Depression to Great Credit Crisis: similarities, differences and lessons." *Economic Policy* 25, no. 62: 219-265.

Bernanke, Ben S. 2012. "Monetary Policy since the Onset of the Crisis." Speech at the Federal Reserve Bank of Kansas City Economic Symposium. (http://www.federalreserve.gov/newsevents/speech/bernanke20120831a.htm).

____. 2014. "The Federal Reserve: Looking Back, Looking Forward." Speech at the Annual Meeting of the American Economic Association. (http://www.federalreserve.gov/newsevents/speech/bernanke20140103a.htm).

(CBO) Congressional Budget Office. 2013a. "Automatic Reductions in Government Spending—aka Sequestration." (http://www.cbo.gov/publication/43961).

____. 2013b. "The Economic Impact of S. 744, the Border Security, Economic Opportunity, and Immigration Modernization Act." (http://www.cbo.gov/publication/44346).

Greenspan, Alan. 2013. *The Map and the Territory: Risk, Human Nature, and the Future of Forecasting*. The Penguin Press.

Piketty, Thomas and Emmanuel Saez. 2003. "Income Inequality in the United States 1913–1998." *Quarterly Journal of Economics* 118, no. 1: 1–39.

_____. 2013. Data update to "Income Inequality in the United States 1913–1998." September (http://elsa.berkeley.edu/~saez/TabFig2012prel.xls).

Reinhart, Carmen M., and Kenneth S. Rogoff. Forthcoming. "Recovery from Financial Crises: Evidence from 100 Episodes." *American Economic Review.*

Romer, Christina D. 2009. "Back from the Brink." Speech at the Federal Reserve Bank of Chicago. (http://www.whitehouse.gov/assets/documents/Back_from_the_Brink2.pdf).

Wimer, Christopher, Liana Fox, Irwin Garfinkel, Neeraj Kaushal, and Jane Waldfogel. 2013.

"Trends in Poverty with an Anchored Supplemental Poverty Measure." Working Paper. New York: Columbia Population Research Center. (http://socialwork.columbia.edu/sites/default/files/file_manager/pdfs/News/Anchored%20SPM.December7.pdf).

CHAPTER 2

Ball, Laurence, and Sandeep Mazumder. 2011. "Inflation Dynamics and the Great Recession." *Brookings Papers on Economic Activity* 42, no. 1: 337-405.

Bank of Japan, Financial Markets Department. 2013. *Outline of Outright Purchases of Japanese Government Bonds.* Financial Market Department 1-3. April.

Blanchard, Oliver J., and Peter A. Diamond. 1994. "Ranking, Unemployment Duration, and Wages." *Review of Economic Studies* 61, no. 3: 417-34.

Board of Governors of the Federal Reserve System. 2009. "FRB/US Equation Documentation."

—— 2012. "Press Release: December 12, 2012." (http://www.federalreserve.gov/newsevents/press/monetary/20121212a.htm).

——. 2013a. "The October 2013 Senior Loan Officer Opinion Survey on Banking Lending Practices."

—— 2013b. "Press Release: June 19, 2013." (http://www.federalreserve.gov/newsevents/press/monetary/20130619a.htm).

—— 2013c. "Press Release: December 18, 2013." (http://www.federalreserve.gov/newsevents/press/monetary/20131218a.htm).

_____. 2014. "Press Release: January 29, 2014." (http://www.federalreserve.gov/newsevents/press/monetary/20140129a.htm).

(BEA) Bureau of Economic Analysis. 2013. "Comprehensive Revision: 1929 Through First Quarter 2013." U.S. Department of Commerce.

_____. 2014. "Technical Note: Gross Domestic Product Fourth Quarter of 2013 (Advance Estimate)." U.S. Department of Commerce. January.

(CBO) Congressional Budget Office. 2012. "Economic Effects of Policies Contributing to Fiscal Tightening in 2013." November.

—— 2013a. "Automatic Reductions in Government Spending aka Sequestration." February.

—— 2013b. "The Economic Impact of S. 744, the Border Security, Economic Opportunity, and Immigration Modernization Act." June.

(CEA) Council of Economic Advisers. 1997. *Economic Report of the President.* February.

—— 2013. "Comprehensive GDP Revision and Advance Estimate for the Second Quarter of 2013." July (http://www.whitehouse.gov/blog/2013/07/31/comprehensive-gdp-revision-and-advance-estimate-second-quarter-2013).

Database of State Incentives for Renewables and Efficiency. 2013. "Renewable Electricity Production Tax Credit (PTC)." October (http://dsireusa.org/incentives/incentive.cfm?Incentive_Code=US13F).

(DOT) Department of the Treasury. 2012. "Description of the Extraordinary Measures." December (http://web.archive.org/web/20131019163723/http:/www.treasury.gov/connect/blog/Documents/Sec%20Geithner%20LETTER%2012-26-2012%20Debt%20Limit.pdf).

(EIA) Energy Information Administration. 2013. "Industrial Sector Natural Gas Use Rising." June (http://www.eia.gov/todayinenergy/detail.cfm?id=11771).

—— 2013b. "International Energy Outlook." April (http://www.eia.gov/forecasts/ieo/pdf/ieorefngtab_1.pdf).

—— 2013c. "Oil and Gas Industry Employment Growing Much Faster than Total Private Sector Employment." August (http://www.eia.gov/todayinenergy/detail.cfm?id=12451).

(EPA) Environmental Protection Agency. 2011. "Paving the Way Toward Cleaner, More Efficient Trucks." August.

European Central Bank. 2012. "Press Release: Technical Features of Outright Monetary Transactions." September (http://www.ecb.europa.eu/press/pr/date/2012/html/pr120906_1.en.html).

—. 2013. "Monetary Policy." (http://www.ecb.europa.eu/mopo/html/index.en.html).

European Commission. 2013. "European Economic Forecast: Autumn 2013." November.

Executive Office of the President. 2013. "The President's Climate Action Plan." The White House. June.

Fuhrer, Jeffrey C., and Giovanni P. Olivei. 2010. "The Role of Expectations and Output in the Inflation Process: An Empirical Assessment." *Federal Reserve Bank of Boston Public Policy Brief,* no. 10-2: 1-39.

Gordon, Robert. 1990. "U.S. Inflation, Labor's Share, and the Natural Rate of Unemployment." Working Papers 2585. Cambridge, MA: National Bureau of Economic Research.

— 2013. "The Phillips Curve is Alive and Well: Inflation and the NAIRU During the Slow Recovery." Working Paper 19390. Cambridge, MA: National Bureau of Economic Research.

Layard, Richard, Stephen Nickells, and Richard Jackman. 1991. *Unemployment: Macroeconomic Performance and the Labor Market.* New York: Oxford University Press.

Krueger, Alan B., and Andreas I. Mueller. 2011. "Job Search and Job Finding in a Period of Mass Unemployment: Evidence from High-Frequency Longitudinal Data." Working Papers 1295. Princeton, NJ: Center for Economic Policy Studies.

Nalewaik, Jeremy J. 2010. "The Income- and Expenditure-Side Measures of U.S. Output Growth." *Brookings Papers on Economic Activity* 41, no. 1: 71-127.

(OMB) Office of Management and Budget. 2013. "Impacts and Costs of the Government Shutdown." (http://www.whitehouse.gov/blog/2013/11/07/impacts-and-costs-government-shutdown).

Office of the Press Secretary. 2012. "Obama Administration Finalizes Historic 54.5 MPG Fuel Efficiency Standards." The White House. (http://www.whitehouse.gov/the-press-office/2012/08/28/obama-administration-finalizes-historic-545-mpg-fuel-efficiency-standard).

(USTR) Office of the United States Trade Representative. 2013a. "Acting Deputy U.S. Trade Representative Endy Cutler Discussed Japan

and the TPP at the Peterson Institute for International Economics."
(http://www.ustr.gov/about-us/press-office/blog/2013/November/
Cutler-TPP-Japan-PIIE).

——2013b. "Ambassador Froman Discusses the Transatlantic Trade and
Investment Partnership at the Munich Security Conference."
(http://www.ustr.gov/about-us/press-office/blog/2013/November/
Froman-Munich-Security-Conference).

——2013c. "Statement of the Ministers and Heads of Delegation for the
Trans-Pacific Partnership Countries." (http://www.ustr.gov/tpp).

——2013d. "Weekly Trade Spotlight: The Benefits of the WTO Trade Facilitation Agreement to Small Business." (http://www.ustr.gov/about-us/
press-office/blog/2013/December/Benefits-of-WTO-Trade-Facili-
tation-Agreement-to-Small-Business).

——2013e. "White House Fact Sheet: Transatlantic Trade and Investment
Partnership (T-TIP)." (http://www.ustr.gov/about-us/press-office/
fact-sheets/2013/june/wh-ttip).

(OECD) Organization for Economic Cooperation and Development. 2013.
"General Assessment of the Macroeconomic Situation." *OECD
Economic Outlook*, no. 2: 9-66.

Polk. 2013. "Polk Finds Average Age of Light Vehicles Continues to Rise."
(https://www.polk.com/company/news/polk_finds_average_age_
of_light_vehicles_continues_to_rise).

Stock, James H. 2011. "Discussion of Ball and Mazumder, 'Inflation
Dynamics and the Great Recession." *Brookings Papers on Economic
Activity* 42, no. 1: 387-402.

Stock, James H., and Mark W. Watson. 2010. "Modeling Inflation After the
Crisis." Working Papers 16488. Cambridge, MA: National Bureau
of Economic Research.

Zindler, Ethan. 2013. "Burst of Construction in December Delivers Record
Year for US Wind." *Bloomberg New Energy Finance.* January 18.

CHAPTER 3

Aldy, Joseph E. 2013. "A Preliminary Assessment of the American Recovery
and Reinvestment Act's Clean Energy Package." *Review of Environmental Economics and Policy* 7(1): 136-155.

Alesina, Alberto,and Silvia Ardagna. 2010. "Large Changes in Fiscal Policy:
Taxes versus Spending." *Tax Policy and the Economy* 24: 35-68.

Angrist, Joshua D., and Jörn-Steffen Pischke. 2010. "The Credibility Revolution in Empirical Economics: How Better Research Design Is Taking the Con out of Econometrics." *Journal of Economic Perspectives* 24, no. 2: 3-30.

Auerbach, Alan J., and Daniel Feenberg. 2000. "The Significance of Federal Taxes as Automatic Stabilizers." *Journal of Economic Perspectives* 14(3): 37-56.

Auerbach, Alan, and Yuriy Gorodnichenko. 2012. "Measuring the Output Responses to Fiscal Policy." *American Economic Journal: Economic Policy* 4(2): 1-27.

Barro, Robert J. 1974. "Are Government Bonds Net Wealth?" *Journal of Political Economy* 82(6): 1095-1117.

Ball, Laurence M. 2009. "Hysteresis in Unemployment: Old and New Evidence." Working Paper 14818. Cambridge, MA: National Bureau of Economic Research.

Bastiat, Frédéric. 1848. "Selected Essays on Political Economy." Seymour Cain, trans. 1995. Library of Economics and Liberty. 3 February 2014.

Blanchard, Olivier, Giovanni Dell'Ariccia, and Paolo Mauro. 2010. "Rethinking Macroeconomic Policy." *IMF Staff Position Note*. Washington: International Monetary Fund.

Blanchard, Olivier, and Daniel Leigh. 2013. "Growth Forecast Errors and Fiscal Multipliers." *IMF Working Paper*.

Blanchard, Olivier, and Roberto, Perotti. 2002. "An Empirical Characterization of the Dynamic Effects of Changes in Government Spending and Taxes on Output." *Quarterly Journal of Economics*.

Blanchard, Olivier, and Lawrence H. Summers. 1986. "Hysteresis and the European Unemployment Problem." *NBER Macroeconomics Annual*, 1, 15-90. Cambridge, MA: National Bureau of Economic Research.

Blinder, Alan S., and Mark Zandi. 2010. "How the Great Recession was Brought to an End." Princeton University and Moody's Analytics.

Chetty, Raj. 2008. "Moral Hazard vs Liquidity and Optimal Unemployment Insurance." Working Paper 13967. Cambridge, MA: National Bureau of Economic Research.

Chodorow-Reich, Gabriel, Laura Feiveson, Zachary Liscow, and William Gui Woolston. 2012. "Does State Fiscal Relief During Recessions

Increase Employment? Evidence from the American Recovery and Reinvestment Act." *American Economic Journal: Economic Policy* 4, no. 3: 118-145.

Christiano, Lawrence, Martin Eichenbaum, and Sergio Rebelo. 2011. "When Is the Government Spending Multiplier Too Large?" *Journal of Political Economy* 119(1): 78-121.

Coenen, Gunter, et al. 2012. "Effects of Fiscal Stimulus in Structural Models." *American Economic Journal: Macroeconomics* 4(1): 22-68.

Cogan, John F., et al. 2010 "New Keynesian versus old Keynesian government spending multipliers." *Journal of Economic Dynamics and Control* 34(3): 281-295.

(CBO) Congressional Budget Office. 2009a. "Health Information Technology for Economic and Clinical Health Act."

____. 2009b. "Cost Estimate: H.R. 1, American Recovery and Reinvestment Act of 2009."

____. 2009c. "Cost Estimate: H.R. 3548, Worker, Homeownership, and Business Assistance Act of 2009."

____. 2010a. "The Budget and Economic Outlook: Fiscal Years 2010 to 2020."

____. 2010b. "The Budget and Economic Outlook: An Update."

____. 2010c. "Cost Estimate: H.R. 4691, the Temporary Extension Act of 2010, As Introduced on February 25, 2010."

____. 2010d. "Cost Estimate: Budgetary Effects of Hiring Incentives to Restore Employment Act, as Introduced by Senator Reid on February 11, 2010."

____. 2010e. "Cost Estimate: Amendment No. 3721 to H.R. 4851, the Continuing Extension Act, 2010, as Proposed by Senator Baucus."

____. 2010f. "Cost Estimate: Budgetary Effects of Senate Amendment 4425, the Unemployment Compensation Extension Act of 2010."

____. 2010g. "Cost Estimate: CBO Estimate of Changes in Revenues and Direct Spending for Senate Amendment 4594 in the Nature of a Substitute to H.R. 5297, the Small Business Jobs and Credit Act of 2010."

____. 2010h. "Cost Estimate: CBO Estimate of Changes in Revenues and Direct Spending for S.A. 4753, an amendment to H.R. 4852, the Tax Relief, Unemployment Insurance Reauthorization, and Job Creation Act of 2010."

____. 2010i. "Cost Estimate: Budgetary Effects of Senate Amendment 4575, containing proposals related to education, state fiscal relief, the Supplemental Nutrition Assistance Program, rescissions, and revenue offsets."

____. 2011a. "The Budget and Economic Outlook: Fiscal Years 2011 to 2021."

____. 2011b. "Cost Estimate: Budgetary Effects of Senate Amendment 927 to H.R. 674, as proposed by Senator Reid for Senator Tester."

____. 2011c. "Cost Estimate: H.R. 5297, the Small Business Jobs Act of 2010."

____. 2011d. "Cost Estimate: Budgetary Effects of the Temporary Payroll Tax Cut Continuation Act of 2011, as Posted on the Website of the House Committee on Rules on December 22, 2011."

____. 2012a. "The Budget and Economic Outlook: Fiscal Years 2012 to 2022."

____. 2012b. "Cost Estimate: Budgetary effects of the Conference Agreement for H.R. 3630, the Middle Class Tax Relief and Job Creation Act of 2012, as Posted on the Web Site of the House Committee on Rules on February 16, 2012."

____. 2012c. "Cost Estimate: Budgetary effects of the Conference Agreement for H.R. 3630, the Middle Class Tax Relief and Job Creation Act of 2012, as Posted on the Web Site of the House Committee on Rules on February 16, 2012."

____. 2013a. "Cost Estimate: Estimate of Budgetary Effects of H.R. 8, the American Taxpayer Relief Act of 2012, as passed by the Senate on January 1, 2013."

____. 2014a. "The Budget and Economic Outlook: 2014 to 2024."

____. 2014b. "Estimated Impact of the American Recovery and Reinvestment Act on Employment and Economic Output in 2013."

Conley, Timothy, and Bill Dupor. 2013. "The American Recovery and Reinvestment Act: Public Sector Jobs Saved, Private Sector Jobs Forestalled." *Journal of Monetary Economics.*

(CEA) Council of Economic Advisers. 2009a. "Estimates of Job Creation from the American Recovery and Reinvestment Act of 2009."

____. 2009b. "The Economic Impact of the American Recovery and Reinvestment Act of 2009." *First Quarterly* Report. September.

____. 2010a. "The Economic Impact of the American Recovery and Reinvestment Act of 2009." *Second Quarterly* Report. January.

____. 2010b. "The Economic Impact of the American Recovery and Reinvestment Act of 2009." *Third Quarterly* Report. April.

____. 2010c. "The Economic Impact of the American Recovery and Reinvestment Act of 2009." *Fourth Quarterly* Report. July.

____. 2011. "The Economic Impact of the American Recovery and Reinvestment Act of 2009." *Sixth Quarterly* Report. March.

____. 2013a. "The Economic Impact of the American Recovery and Reinvestment Act of 2009." *Ninth Quarterly* Report. February.

____. 2013b. "Economic Report of the President." March.

Council of Economic Advisers and the Department of Labor. 2014. "The Economic Benefits of Extending Unemployment Insurance." January.

Delong, J. Bradford, and Lawrence H. Summers. 2012. "Fiscal Policy in a Depressed Economy." *Brookings Papers on Economic Activity.* Spring.

Department of Education. 2011. "FY 2012 Department of Education Justifications of Appropriation Estimates to the Congress: Student Financial Assistance" in President's FY 2012 Budget Request for the U.S. Department of Education.

Department of the Treasury. 2010a. "The Case for Temporary 100 Percent Expensing: Encouraging Business to Expand now by Lowering the Cost of Investment."

____. 2010b. "The American Opportunity Tax Credit."

____. 2011. "Treasury Analysis of Build America Bonds Issuance and Savings."

Department of the Treasury and Council of Economic Advisers. 2012. "A New Economic Analysis of Infrastructure Investment." March.

Eggertson, Gauti B. 2001. "Real Government Spending in a Liquidity Trap." New York Federal Reserve.

Elmendorf, Douglas W., and Jason Furman. 2008. "If, When, How: A Primer on Fiscal Stimulus." Washington: Brookings Institution.

(EPA) Environmental Protection Agency. 2013. "American Recovery and Reinvestment Act Quarterly Performance Report – FY2013 Quarter 4 Cumulative Results as of September 30, 2013."

Executive Office of the President and Office of the Vice President. 2010. "The Recovery Act: Transforming the American Economy through Innovation".The White House.

Farhi, Emmanuel, and Ivan Werning. 2012. "Fiscal Multipliers: Liquidity Traps and Currency Unions." Working Paper 18321. Cambridge, MA: National Bureau of Economic Research.

Favero, Carlo, and Francesco Giavazzi. 2012. "Measuring Tax Multipliers: The Narrative Method in Fiscal VARs." *American Economic Journal: Economic Policy* 4(2): 69–94.

Fernald, John G. 1999. "Roads to Prosperity? Assessing the Link Between Public Capital and Productivity," *The American Economic Review,* Vol. 89, No. 3:619-638.

Feyrer, James, and Bruce Sacerdote. 2011. "Did the Stimulus Stimulate? Real Time Estimates of the Effects of the American Recovery and Reinvestment Act." Working Paper 16759. National Bureau of Economic Research.

Financial Crisis Inquiry Commission. 2011. *The Financial Crisis Inquiry Report.* New York: PublicAffairs.

Follette, Glenn, and Byron Lutz. 2010. "Fiscal Policy in the United States: Automatic Stabilizers, Discretionary Fiscal Policy Actions, and the Economy." *Finance and Economics Discussion Series.* Washington: Federal Reserve Board.

Guajardo, Jaime, Daniel Leigh, and Andrea Pescatori. Forthcoming. "Expansionary Austerity? New International Evidence." *Journal of the European Economic Association.*

Hall, Bronwyn H., Jacques Mairesse, Pierre Mohnen. 2009. "Measuring the Returns to R&D." Working Paper 15622. Cambridge, MA: National Bureau of Economic Research.

House, Christopher L., and Matthew D. Shapiro. 2008. "Temporary Investment Tax Incentives: Theory with Evidence from Bonus Depreciation." *American Economic Review* 98(3): 737-768.

Ilzetzki, Ethan, Enrique G. Mendoza, and Carlos A. Vegh. 2011. "How Big (Small?) are Fiscal Multipliers?" IMF Working Paper.

(IMF) International Monetary Fund. 2009 "What's the Damage? Medium Term Dynamics after Financial Crises." *World Economic Outlook October 2009: Sustaining the Recovery* Chapter 4, p. 121-151.

____. 2012. *World Economic Outlook April 2012: Growth Resuming, Dangers Remain."*

Johnson, David S., Jonathan A. Parker, and Nicholas S. Souleles. 2006. "Household Expenditure and the Income Tax Rebates of 2001." *American Economic Review* 96(5): 1589-1610.

Joint Committee on Taxation. 2009. "Estimated Budget Effects of the Revenue Provisions Contained in the Conference Agreement for H.R.1, The 'American Recovery and Reinvestment Tax Act of 2009.'"

____. 2010a. "Estimated Budget Effects of the Revenue Provisions Contained in Senate Amendment #4594 to H.R. 5297, The 'Small Business Jobs Act of 2010,' Scheduled for Consideration by the United States Senate on September 16, 2010."

____. 2010b. "Estimated Revenue Effects of the House Amendment to the Senate Amendment to H.R. 4853, The 'Middle Class Tax Relief Act of 2010,' Scheduled for Consideration by the House of Representatives on December 2, 2010."

____. 2012. "Estimated Revenue Effects of H.R. 8, The 'Job Protection and Recession Prevention Act of 2012.'"

Laeven, Luc, and Fabian Valencia. 2012. "Systemic Banking Crises Database: An Update."Working Paper WP/12/163. Washington: International Monetary Fund.

Ljungqvist, Lars, and Thomas J. Sargent. 1998. "The European Unemployment Dilemma." *Journal of Political Economy* 106(3): 514-550.

Mertens, Karel, and Morten O. Ravn. 2012. "Empirical Evidence on the Aggregate Effects of Anticipated and Unanticipated US Tax Policy Shocks." *American Economic Journal: Economic Policy* 4(2): 145–181.

Mertens, Karel, and Morten Ravn. 2013. "The Dynamic Effects of Personal and Corporate Income Tax Changes in the United States." *American Economic Review.* June.

Munnell, Alicia H, 1992. "Infrastructure Investment and Economic Growth," Journal of Economic Perspectives, vol. 6(4), pages 189-98, Fall. Pittsburg, PA: American Economic Association.

Nakamura, Emi, and Jón Steinsson. 2011. "Fiscal Stimulus in a Monetary Union: Evidence from U.S. Regions." Unpublished paper, New York: Columbia University.

Office of Science and Technology Policy, and The National Economic Council. 2013. "Four Years of Broadband Growth." The White House.

Parker, Jonathan A. 2011. "On Measuring the Effects of Fiscal Policy in Recessions." Working Paper 17240. Cambridge, MA: National Bureau of Economic Research.

Parker, Jonathan A., Nicholas S. Souleles, David S. Johnson, and Robert McClelland. 2011. "Consumer Spending and the Economic Stimulus Payments of 2008." Working Paper 16684. Cambridge, MA: National Bureau of Economic Research.

Perotti, Roberto. 2011. "The Austerity Myth: Gain Without Pain?" Working Paper 17571. Cambridge, MA: National Bureau of Economic Research.

Phelps, Edmund. 1972. "Inflation policy and unemployment theory." New York: WW Norton and Company.

Poterba, James M. 1994. "State Responses to Fiscal Crises: The Effects of Budgetary Institutions and Politics." *Journal of Political Economy* 102(4): 799-821.

Ramey, Valerie A. 2011a. "Identifying Government Spending Shocks: It's All in the Timing" *Quarterly Journal of Economics* 126, no. 1: 1-50.

____. 2011b. "Can Government Purchases Stimulate the Economy?" *Journal of Economic Literature* 49, no. 3: 673-85.

Ramey, Valerie A, and Matthew Shapiro. 1998. "Costly Capital Reallocation and the Effects of Government Spending." *Carnegie-Rochester Conference on Public Policy* 48: 145-94.

Reichling, Felix, and Charles Whalen. 2012. "Assessing the Short-Term Effects on Output Changes in Federal Fiscal Policies." Working Paper 2012-08. Congressional Budget Office.

Reinhart, Carmen M., and Kenneth S. Rogoff. 2009. *This time is different: Eight Centuries of Financial Folly.* Princeton, NJ: Princeton University Press.

____. Forthcoming. "Recovery from Financial Crises: Evidence from 100 Episodes." *American Economic Review.*

Reifschneider, Dave, William L. Wascher, and David Wilcox. 2013. "Aggregate Supply in the United States: Recent Developments and Implications for the Conduct of Monetary Policy." 14th *Jacques*

Polak Annual Research Conference. Washington: International Monetary Fund.

Romer, Christina D. 2011. "Back from the Brink." In *The International Financial Crisis: Have the Rules of Finance Changed?* Edited by Asli Demirgüç-Kunt, Douglas D. Evanoff, George G. Kaufman, pp. 15-31. World Scientific Publishing Company.

___. 2012. "Fiscal Policy In the Crisis: Lessons and Policy Implications." University of California-Berkeley, Department of Economics.

Romer, Christina D., and David H. Romer. 2010. "The Macroeconomic Effects of Tax Changes: Estimates Based on a New Measure of Fiscal Shocks." *American Economic Review* 100(3): 763-801.

Rothstein, Jesse. 2011. "Unemployment Insurance and Job Search in the Great Recession." *Brookings Papers on Economic Activity*, Fall.

Shoag, Daniel. 2013. "Using state pension shocks to estimate fiscal multipliers since the Great Recession." *The American Economic Review* 103(3): 121-124.

Sims, Christopher A. 2010. "But Economics Is Not an Experimental Science." *Journal of Economic Perspectives* 24, no. 2: 59-68.

Smets, Frank, and Rafael Wouters. 2007. "Shocks and Frictions in US Business Cycles: a Bayesian DSGE Approach." *American Economic Review* 97(3): 586-606.

Sperling, Gene. 2007. "Ways to Get Economic Stimulus Right This Time." Bloomberg.com. December 17.

Stock, James H. 2010. "The Other Transformation in Econometric Practice: Robust Tools for Inference." *Journal of Economic Perspectives* 24, no. 2: 83-94.

Stock, James H. and Mark W. Watson. 2012. "Disentangling the Channels of the 2007–09 Recession," *Brookings Papers on Economic Activity*. Spring.

Stock, James H., and Mark W. Watson. 2010. *Introduction to Econometrics*. 3rd ed. Boston, MA: Addison-Wesley.

Suarez Serrato, Juan Carlos, and Philippe Wingender. 2011. "Estimating the Incidence of Government Spending."

Summers, Lawrence H. 2007. "The State of the US Economy." Presentation at Brookings Institution Forum on December 19th, 2007.

____. 2008. Speech at the *Wall Street Journal*-CEO Council Conference. Washington, D.C., November 19.

Taylor, John B. 2011. "An Empirical analysis of the Revival of Fiscal Activism in the 2000s." *Journal of Economic Literature* 49(3): 686:702.

____. Forthcoming. "The Role of Policy in the Great Recession and the Weak Recovery." *American Economic Review, Papers and Proceedings*.

Transportation Research Board of the National Academies. 2013. "Transportation Investments in Response to Economic Downturns, Special Report 312."

Wilson, Daniel J. 2012. "Fiscal Spending Jobs Multipliers: Evidence from the 2009 American Recovery and Reinvestment Act." *American Economic Journal: Economic Policy*.

Wimer, Christopher, Liana Fox, Irwin Garfinkel, Neeraj Kaushal, and Jane Waldfogel. 2013. "Trends in Poverty with an Anchored Supplemental Poverty Measure." Working Paper 1- 25. New York: Columbia Population Research Center.

Woodford, Michael. 2011. "Simple Analytics of the Government Expenditure Multiplier." *American Economic Journal: Macroeconomics* (3), p. 1-35.

CHAPTER 4

Acemoglu, Daron, Amy Finkelstein, and Matthew J. Notowidigdo. 2013. "Income and Health Spending: Evidence from Oil Price Shocks." *Review of Economics and Statistics* 95, no. 4: 1079-1095.

Aitken, Murray, Ernst R. Berndt, and David M. Cutler. 2009. "Prescription Drug Spending Trends in the United States: Looking Beyond the Turning Point." *Health Affairs* 28, no. 1: 151-160.

Altarum Institute. 2014. "Insights from Monthly National Health Expenditures Estimates through November 2013." (http://altarum.org/ sites/default/files/uploaded-related-files/CSHS-Spending-Brief_ January%202014.pdf).

ASPE (Assistant Secretary for Planning and Evaluation, Office of). 2013. "Health Insurance Marketplace Premiums for 2014." Health and Human Services. (http://aspe.hhs.gov/health/reports/2013/Market-placePremiums/ib_marketplace_premiums.cfm).

Baicker, Katherine and Amitabh Chandra. 2006. "The Labor Market Effects of Rising Health Insurance Premiums." *Journal of Labor Economics* 24, no. 3: 609-634.

Chandra, Amitabh, Jonathan Holmes, and Jonathan Skinner. 2013. "Is This Time Different? The Slowdown in Healthcare Spending." Brookings Panel on Economic Activity. Washington: Brookings Institution. (http://www.brookings.edu/~/media/Projects/BPEA/Fall%202013/2013b%20chandra%20healthcare%20spending.pdf).

Centers for Medicare and Medicaid Services Office of the Actuary. 2013. "Projections of National Health Expenditures: Methodology and Model Specification."

(CMS) Centers for Medicare and Medicaid Services. 2013a. "New Data Shows Affordable Care Act Reforms Are Leading to Lower Hospital Readmission Rates for Medicare Beneficiaries." (http://blog.cms.gov/2013/12/06/new-data-shows-affordable-care-act-reforms-are-leading-to-lower-hospital-readmission-rates-for-medicare-beneficiaries/).

——.. 2013b. "Pioneer Accountable Care Organizations succeed in improving care, lowering costs." News Release. (http://www.cms.gov/Newsroom/MediaReleaseDatabase/Press-Releases/2013-Press-Releases-Items/2013-07-16.html).

——. 2013c. "The Affordable Care Act: A Stronger Medicare Program." (http://www.cms.gov/apps/files/Medicarereport2012.pdf).

Clemens, Jeffrey and Joshua D. Gottlieb. 2013. "Bargaining in the Shadow of a Giant: Medicare's Influence on Private Payment Systems." Working Paper 19503. Cambridge, MA: National Bureau of Economic Research.

(CBO) Congressional Budget Office. 2010a. "Cost Estimate of H.R. 4872, Reconciliation Act of 2010 (Final Health Care Legislation)." (http://www.cbo.gov/publication/21351).

——. 2010b. "The Budget and Economic Outlook: An Update." (http://www.cbo.gov/publication/21670).

——. 2011. "The Budget and Economic Outlook: An Update." (http://www.cbo.gov/publication/41586).

——. 2012a. "Updated Budget Projections: Fiscal Years 2012 to 2022." (http://www.cbo.gov/publication/43119).

_____. 2012b. "Letter to the Honorable John Boehner providing an estimate for H.R. 6079, the Repeal of Obamacare Act." (http://www.cbo.gov/publication/43471).

_____. 2012c. "Estimates for the Insurance Coverage Provisions of the Affordable Care Act Updated for the Recent Supreme Court Decision." (http://www.cbo.gov/sites/default/files/cbofiles/attachments/43472-07-24-2012-CoverageEstimates.pdf).

_____. 2012d. "An Update to the Budget and Economic Outlook: Fiscal Years 2012 to 2022." (http://www.cbo.gov/publication/43539).

_____. 2013a. "Updated Budget Projections: Fiscal Years 2013 to 2023." (http://www.cbo.gov/publication/44172).

_____. 2013b. "The 2013 Long-Term Budget Outlook." (http://www.cbo.gov/publication/44521).

_____. 2013c. "Health-Related Options for Reducing the Deficit: 2014 to 2023." (http://www.cbo.gov/sites/default/files/cbofiles/attachments/44906-HealthOptions.pdf).

_____. 2014. "The Budget and Economic Outlook: Fiscal Years 2014 to 2024." (http://www.cbo.gov/publication/45010).

(CEA) Council of Economic Advisers. 2009. "The Economic Case for Health Care Reform." (http://www.whitehouse.gov/assets/documents/CEA_Health_Care_Report.pdf).

_____. 2013. *Economic Report of the President.* (http://www.whitehouse.gov/administration/eop/cea/economic-report-of-the-President/2013).

Cuckler, Gigi A., et al. 2013. "National Health Expenditure Projections, 2012-22: Slow Growth Until Coverage Expands And Economy Improves." *Health Affairs* 32 (September): 1-12.

Cutler, David. 2004. *Your Money or Your Life: Strong Medicine for America's Health Care System.* New York: Oxford University.

Cutler, David and Neeraj Sood. 2010. "New Jobs Through Better Health Care: Health Care Reform Could Boost Employment by 250,000 to 400,000 a Year this Decade." Washington: Center for American Progress. (http://www.americanprogress.org/issues/2010/01/pdf/health_care_jobs.pdf).

Cutler, David and Nikhil R. Sahni. 2013. "If Slow Rate of Health Care Spending Growth Persists, Projections May Be Off by $770 Billion." *Health Affairs* 32 (September): 841-850.

Daly, Mary, Bart Hobijn, and Brian Lucking. 2012. "Why Has Wage Growth Stayed Strong?" Federal Reserve Board of San Francisco. (http://www.frbsf.org/economic-research/publications/economic-letter/2012/april/strong-wage-growth/).

Dranove, David. 1988. "Pricing by Non-Profit Institutions." *Journal of Health Economics* 7 (March): 47-57.

Elmendorf, Douglas. 2013. "The Slowdown in Health Care Spending." Presentation to the Brookings Panel on Economic Activity. Washington: Brookings Institution. September 19 (http://www.cbo.gov/publication/44596).

Frakt, Austin B. 2011. "How Much Do Hospitals Cost Shift? A Review of the Evidence." *The Milbank Quarterly* 89, no. 1: 90-130.

_____. 2013. "The End of Hospital Cost Shifting and the Quest for Hospital Productivity." *Health Services Research* 49 (September): 1-10.

Gerhardt, Geoffrey, et al. 2013. "Medicare Readmission Rates Showed Meaningful Decline in 2012." *Medicare & Medicaid Research Review* 3, no. 2: E1-E12.

Gruber, Jonathan and Alan B. Krueger. 1991. "The Incidence of Mandated Employer-Provided Insurance: Lessons From Workers' Compensation Insurance." In *Tax Policy and the Economy, Volume 5*, edited by David Bradford, pp. 111-144. Cambridge, MA: MIT Press.

Gruber, Jonathan. 1994. "The Incidence of Mandated Maternity Benefits." *American Economic Review* 84, no. 3: 622-641.

He, Daifeng and Jennifer M. Mellor. 2012. "Hospital volume responses to Medicare's Outpatient Prospective Payment System: Evidence from Florida." *Journal of Health Economics* 31: 730-743.

Holahan, John and Stacey McMorrow. 2012. "Medicare, Medicaid, and the Deficit Debate." Washington: Urban Institute. (http://www.urban.org/UploadedPDF/412544-Medicare-Medicaid-and-the-Deficit-Debate.pdf).

IMS Institute for Healthcare Informatics. 2013. "Declining Medicine Use and Costs: For Better or Worse?" (http://static.correofarmaceutico.com/docs/2013/05/20/usareport.pdf).

Kaiser Family Foundation. 2013a. "2013 Employer Health Benefits Survey." (http://kff.org/private-insurance/report/2013-employer-health-benefits).

_____. 2013b. "Medicaid Enrollment: June 2012 Data Snapshot." (http://kaiserfamilyfoundation.files.wordpress.com/2013/08/8050-06-medicaid-enrollment.pdf).

Kaiser Family Foundation and Altarum Institute. 2013. "Assessing the Effects of the Economy on the Recent Slowdown in Health Spending." (http://kff.org/health-costs/issue-brief/assessing-the-effects-of-the-economy-on-the-recent-slowdown-in-health-spending-2).

Levine, Michael and Melinda Buntin. 2013. "Why Has Growth in Spending for Fee-for-Service Medicare Slowed?" Working Paper 2013-06. Congressional Budget Office.

Martin, Anne B., et al. 2014. "National Health Spending in 2012: Rate of Health Spending Growth Remained Low for the Fourth Consecutive Year." _Health Affairs_ 33, no. 1: 1-11.

McClellan, Mark, et al. 1998. "Are Medical Prices Declining? Evidence from Heart Attack Treatments." _The Quarterly Journal of Economics_ 113, no. 4: 991-1024.

McWilliams, J. Michael, Bruce Landon, Michael E. Chernew. 2013. "Changes in Health Care Spending and Quality for Medicare Beneficiaries Associated With a Commercial ACO Contract." _Journal of the American Medical Association_ 310, no. 8: 829-836.

MedPAC (Medicare Payment Advisory Commission). 2009. "Improving Incentives in the Medicare Program." (http://www.medpac.gov/documents/jun09_entirereport.pdf).

Morrissey, Michael A. 1994. _Cost Shifting in Health Care: Separating Evidence from Rhetoric._ Washington: American Enterprise Institute.

Ryu, Alexander J., et al. 2013. "The Slowdown in Health Care Spending in 2009-11 Reflected Factors Other than the Weak Economy and Thus May Persist." _Health Affairs_ 32, no. 5: 835-840.

Sisko, Andrea, et al. 2009. "Health Spending Projections Through 2018: Recession Effects Add Uncertainty to the Outlook." _Health Affairs_ 28, no. 2: 346-357.

Sood, Neeraj, Arkadipta Ghosh and Jose J. Escarce. 2009. "Costs, Use and Outcomes: Employer-Sponsored Insurance, Health Care Cost Growth, and the Economic Performance of U.S. Industries." _Health Services Research_ 44, no. 5: 1449-1464.

Sommers, Benjamin D. 2005. "Who Really Pays for Health Insurance? The Incidence of Employer-Provided Health Insurance with Sticky

Nominal Wages," *International Journal of Health Care Finance and Economics* 5, no. 1: 89-118.

Song, Zirui, et al. 2012. "The 'Alternative Quality Contract,' Based on a Global Budget, Lowered Medical Spending and Improved Quality." *Health Affairs* 31, no.8: 1885-1894.

Spiro, Topher and Jonathan Gruber. 2013. "The Affordable Care Act's Lower-Than-Projected Premiums Will Save $190 billion." Washington: Center for American Progress. October 21 (http://www.americanprogress.org/issues/healthcare/report/2013/10/23/77537/the-affordable-care-acts-lower-than-projected-premiums-will-save-190-billion/).

(SSA) Social Security Administration. 2013. "Annual Statistical Supplement, 2013." (http://www.ssa.gov/policy/docs/statcomps/supplement/).

Summers, Lawrence H. 1989. "Some Simple Economics of Mandated Benefits." *The American Economic Review* 79, no. 2: 177-183.

White, Chapin. 2007. "Health Care Spending Growth: How Different is the United States from the Rest of the OECD." *Health Affairs,* 26 no. 1: 154-161.

_____. 2013. "Contrary To Cost-Shift Theory, Lower Medicare Hospital Payment rates For Inpatient Care Lead To Lower Private Payment Rates." *Health Affairs* 32, no. 5: 935-943.

White, Chapin and Vivian Yaling Wu. 2013. "How Do Hospitals Cope with Sustained Slow Growth in Medicare Prices?" *Health Services Research* 49: 1-21.

Yamamato, Dale H. 2013. "Health Care Costs From Birth to Death." Health Care Cost Institute Independent Report Series. (http://www.healthcostinstitute.org/files/Age-Curve-Study_0.pdf).

CHAPTER 5

Acemoglu, Daron. 2002. "Directed Technical Change." *The Review of Economic Studies* 69, no. 4: 781-809.

Acemoglu, Daron, and David Autor. 2011 "Skill, Tasks and Technologies: Implications for Employment Earnings." In *The Handbook of Labor Economics,* edited by Orley Ashenfelter and David Card, vol. 4b. Amsterdam: Elsevier.

Acemoglu, Daron and James Robinson. 2012. *Why Nations Fail: The Origins of Power, Prosperity and Poverty.* New York: Crown Publishers.

Acemoglu, Daron and David Autor. 2012. "What Does Human Capital Do? A Review of Goldin and Katz's Race between Education and Technology." *Journal of Economic Literature*, 50(2): 426–463.

Agrawal, N. 2010. "Review on just in time techniques in manufacturing systems." In *Advances in Production Engineering & Management 5*, no.2: 101-110

Akcigit, Ufuk, Douglas Hanley, and Nicolas Serrano-Velarde. 2013. "Back to Basics: Basic Research Spillovers, Innovation Policy and Growth." Working Paper 19473. Cambridge, MA.: National Bureau of Economic Research.

Alvaredo, Facundo, Anthony B. Atkinson, Thomas Piketty, and Emmanuel Saez. 2013. "The Top 1 Percent in International and Historical Perspective." *Journal of Economic Perspectives*, 27(3): 3-20.

Autor, David. 2010. "The Polarization of Job Opportunities in the U.S. Labor Market, Implications for Employment and Earnings." Washington: Center for American Progress and The Hamilton Project.

Autor, David, Lawrence F. Katz, and Melissa S. Kearney. 2006. "The Polarization of the U.S. Labor Market." Working Paper 11986. Cambridge, MA: National Bureau of Economic Research.

Autor, David, Frank Levy, and Richard J. Murnane. 2003. "The Skill Content of Recent Technological Change: an Empirical Exploration." *Quarterly Journal of Economics* 116 (4): 1279-1333.

Ayres, Ian, and Peter Cramton. 1996. "Deficit Reduction Through Diversity: How Affirmative Action at the FCC Increased Auction Competition," *Stanford Law Review* 48: 761-815.

Bailey, Diane E., and Nancy B. Kurland. 1999. "The Advantages and Challenges of Working Here, There, Anywhere, and Anytime." *Organizational Dynamics* (Autumn): 1-16.

Bailey, Diane E., and Nancy B. Kurland. 2002. "A Review of Telework Research: Findings, New Directions, and Lessons for the Study of Modern Work." *Journal of Organizational Behavior* 23, no. 4: 383-400.

Baily, Martin N., and Robert J. Gordon. 1988. "The Productivity Slowdown, Measurement Issues, and the Explosion of Computer Power," *Brookings Papers on Economic Activity*, vol. 19(2): 347-432.

Bakia, Marianne, Karla Jones, Barbara Means, Robert Murphy, and Yukie Toyama. 2010. "Evaluation of Evidence-Based Practices in Online

Learning: A Meta-Analysis and Review of Online Learning Studies." U.S. Department of Education Office of Planning, Evaluation, and Policy Development Policy and Program Studies Service.

Banerjee, Abhijit V., and Esther Duflo. 2003. "Inequality and Growth: What Can the Data Say?" *Journal of Economic Growth* 8, no. 3: 267-299.

Banerjee, Abhijit, Shawn Cole, Esther Duflo, and Leigh Linden. 2007. "Remedying Education: Evidence from Two Randomized Experiments in India." *The Quarterly Journal of Economics*, 1235-1264.

Barrow, Lisa, Lisa Markman, and Cecilia Rouse. 2009. "Technology's Edge: The Educational Benefits of Computer-Aided Instruction." *The American Economic Journal: Economic Policy*, (1), 52-74.

Basu, Fernald, Oulton, and Srinivasan. 2004. "The Case of the Missing Productivity Growth, or Does Information Technology Explain Why Productivity Accelerated in the United States but Not in the United Kingdom?" Working Paper 10010. Cambridge, MA: National Bureau of Economic Research.

Basu, Susanto, John Fernald, and Miles Kimball. 2006. "Are Technology Improvements Contractionary?" *American Economic Review.* 96(5), 1418-48.

Berman, Eli, John Bound, and Zvi Griliches. 1994. "Changes in the Demand for Skilled Labor within U.S. Manufacturing: Evidence from the Annual Survey of Manufactures." *The Quarterly Journal of Economics* 109(2), 367–397.

Bernanke, Ben. 2013. "Economic Progress for the Long Run." Speech at Bard College. May 18.

Bernstein, Jared. 2013. "The Impact of Inequality on Growth," Washington: Center for American Progress.

Bloom, Kretschmer, and Van Reenen. 2006. "Work-Life Balance, Management Practices and Productivity." *Centre for Economic Performance* (January): 1-45.

Bloom, Nicholas, Mark Schankerman, and John Van Reenen. 2012. "Identifying Technology Spillovers and Product Market Rivalry." *Centre for Economic Performance* (December): 1-81.

Bloom, Liang, Roberts, and Ying. 2013. "Does Working from Home Work? Evidence from a Chinese Experiment." Working Paper. London: Centre for Economic Performance.

BLS (Bureau of Labor Statistics). "Private Nonfarm Business Sector: Multi-factor Productivity"

_____. "Private Nonfarm Business Sector: Output per Hour of all Persons"

_____. "Private Nonfarm Business Sector: Sources of Productivity Growth."

_____. "Private Nonfarm Business Sector: Real Output Per Hour."

_____. "Private Nonfarm Business Sector: Real Compensation Per Hour."

Bound, John and George Johnson. 1995. "What are the Causes of Rising Wage Inequality in the United States?" *Economic Policy Review* 1, no. 1: 9-17.

Bureau of Labor Statistics, Office of Productivity and Technology. 2013. *Net Multifactor Productivity and Cost, 1948-2012.*

Busch, Emily, Jenna Nash, and Bradford S. Bell. 2011. "Remote Work: An Examination of Current Trends and Emerging Issues." *Center for Advanced Human Resource Studies, Cornell University* (Spring): 1-12.

Card, David, and John DiNardo. 2002. "Skill Biased Technological Change and Rising Wage Inequality: Some Problems and Puzzles." *Journal of Labor Economics* 20(4), 733–783.

Carew, Diana, G. and Michael Mandel. 2013. *Progressive Policy Institute.* "U.S. Investment heroes of 2013: The Companies Betting on America's Future".

Carillo, Ponce, Mercedes Onofa, and Juan Ponce. 2010. "Information Technology and Student Achievement: Evidence from a Randomized Experiment in Ecuador." Washington: Inter-American Development Bank.

CBO (Congressional Budget Office). 2011a. "Trends in the Distribution of Household Income between 1979 and 2007."

_____. 2011b. "S. 27, Preserve Access to Affordable Generics Act."

_____. 2013. *The Economic Impact of S. 744, the Border Security, Economic Opportunity, and Immigration Modernization Act.* Government Printing Office.

Charles, Dustin, et al. 2013. "Adoption of Electric Health Record Systems among U.S. Non-federal Acute Care hospitals: 2008-2012." ONC Data Brief no. 9. The Office of the National Coordinator for Health Information Technology, U.S. Department of Health and Human Resources.

Chien, Colleen V. 2012. "Reforming Software Patents." *Legal Studies Research Paper Series*. Santa Clara, CA: Santa Clara University School of Law.

Coase, Ronald H. 1959. "The Federal Communications Commission," *Journal of Law and Economics* 2: 1-40.

Council of Economic Advisers, the National Economic Council, and the Office of Science & Technology Policy. 2013. "Patent Assertion and U.S. Innovation." The White House.

CEA (Council of Economic Advisers). _____. 2010. "Work-Life Balance and the Economics of Workplace Flexibility."(March).

_____. 2012 "The Economic Benefits of New Spectrum for Wireless Broadband."

Cramton, Peter and Jesse A. Schwartz. 2000. "Collusive Bidding: Lessons from the FCC Spectrum Auctions," *Journal of Regulatory Economics* 17: 229-252.

_____. 2002. "Collusive Bidding in the FCC Spectrum Auctions," *Contributions to Economic Analysis & Policy* 1: 1-18.

Deardorff, Alan V. 1991. "Welfare Effects of Global Patent Protection." *Economica* 59 (May): 35-51.

Delgado, Mercedes, Christian Ketels, Michael E. Porter, and Scott Stern. 2012. "The Determinants of National Competiveness." Working Paper 18249. Cambridge, MA.: National Bureau of Economic Research (July).

Department of Justice and United States Patent and Trademark Office. 2013. *Policy Statement on Remedies for Standard-Essential Patents Subject to Voluntary FRAND Commitments*. Government Printing Office.

DiNardo, John, Nicole M Fortin, and Thomas Lemieux. 1996. "Labor Market Institutions and the Distribution of Wages, 1973-1992: A Semiparametric Approach." *Econometrica* 64(5), 1001–1044.

Evenson, Robert, and Sunil Kanwar. 2003. "Does intellectual property spur technological change?" *Oxford Economic Papers* 55: 235-264.

Fairris, David, and Mark Brenner. 2001. "Workplace Transformation and the Rise in Cumulative Trauma Disorders: Is There a Connection?" *Journal of Labor Research* XXII, no.1 (Winter): 15-28.

Falvey, Rod, Neil Foster, and David Greenaway. 2006. "Intellectual Property Rights and Economic Growth." *Review of Development Economics* 10(4): 700-719.

Farrell, Joseph, John Hayes, Carl Shapiro, and Theresa Sullivan. 2007. "Standard Setting, Patents, and Hold-Up." *Antitrust Law Journal* 74, no. 3: 603-670.

Federal Trade Commission v. Actavis, Inc. et al. 570 U.S. __ (2013).

FTC (Federal Trade Commission). 2010. "Pay-for-delay: How drug company pay-offs cost consumers billions: An FTC staff study.".

Fernald, John. 2012. "Productivity and potential output before, during, and after the Great Recession." Working Paper 2012-18. Federal Reserve Bank of San Francisco.

Feyrer, James. 2007. "Demographics and Productivity." *The Review of Economics and Statistics* 89, 100-109.

_____. 2011. "The U.S. Productivity Slowdown, the Baby Boom, and Management Quality." *Journal of Population Economics* 24, 267-284.

Fields, Gary. 2001. "Distribution and Development, A New Look at the Developing World." *Journal of Development Economics,* Vol. 70: 238-243.

Foellmi, R. and Zweimuller, J. 2006. "Income Distribution and Demand-Induced Innovations."

Review of Economic Studies 73(4): 941-960.

Freeman, Richard B., and Lawrence F. Katz, eds. 1995. *Differences and Changes in Wage Structures*. Chicago, IL: University of Chicago Press.

Furman, Jason. 2013. "Remarks at AEI's Center on Internet, Communications and Technology Policy." Washington, D.C., September 17.

Galor, Oded. 2011.*"Inequality, Human Capital Formation and the Process of Development,"* Working Paper 17058. Cambrige: MA: National Bureau of Economic Research.

Galor, Oded and Omer Moav. 2000. "Ability-Biased Technological Transition, Wage Inequality, and Economic Growth," *Quarterly Journal of Economics,* 115, 469-497.

_____. 2004. "From Physical to Human Capital Accumulation: Inequality and the Process of Development." *Review of Economic Studies,* 71, 1001-1026.

Galor, Oded and Daniel Tsiddon. 1997. "The Distribution of Human Capital, Technological Progress, and Economic Growth." *Journal of Economic Growth*, 2, 93-124

GAO (Government Accountability Office). 2001. *Spectrum Management: NTIA Planning and Processes Need Strengthening to Promote the Efficient Use of Spectrum by Federal Agencies.* GAO-11-352.

_____. 2012. *Electronic Health Records: Number and Characteristics of Providers Awarded Medicaid Incentive Payments for 2011.* Government Printing Office.

_____. 2013a. *Assessing Factors That Affect Patent Infringement Litigation Could Help Improve Patent Quality.* GAO 13-465. Government Printing Office.

_____. 2013b. *Electronic Health Records: Number and Characteristics of Providers Awarded Medicare Incentive Payments for 2011-2012.* Government Printing Office.

Gilbert, Richard J. 2010-2011. "Deal or No Deal? Licensing Negotiations in Standard-Setting Organizations." *HeinOnline* 77 855-888.

Goos, Martin and Alan M. Manning, 2007. "Lousy and Lovely Jobs: the rising polarization of work in Britain. *Review of Economics and Statistics.* 89(1): 118-133.

Goldin, Claudia, and Lawrence F. Katz. 2008. "The Race between Education and Technology." Cambridge, MA: The Belknap Press of Harvard University Press.

Gordon, Robert J. 2012. "Is U.S. Economic Growth Over? Faltering Innovation Confronts the Six Headwinds." Working Paper 18315. Cambridge, MA.: National Bureau of Economic Research.

Greenstone, M., R. Hornbeck, and E. Moretti. 2010. "Identifying Agglomeration Spillovers: Evidence from Winners and Losers of Large Plant Openings," *Journal of Political Economy,* 118, 536-598.

Hall, Robert E., and Charles I. Jones. 1999. "Why Do Some Countries Produce So Much More Output Per Worker Than Others?" *The Quarterly Journal of Economics*: 83-116.

Haskel, Jonathan, Robert Z. Lawrence, Edward E. Leamer, and Matthew J. Slaughter. 2012. "Globalization and U.S. Wages: Modifying Classic Theory to Explain Recent Facts." *Journal of Economic Perspectives* 26, no. 2: 119-40.

Heckman, James J. and Paul A. LaFontaine. 2010. "The American High School Graduation Rate: Trends and Levels." *The Review of Economics and Statistics* 92, no. 2: 244-262.

Heckman, James J., Rodrigo Pinto, and Peter A. Savelyev. 2012. "Understanding the Mechanisms Through Which an Influential Early Childhood Program Boosted Adult Outcomes." Working Paper 18581, Cambridge, MA.:National Bureau of Economic Research.

Hemphill, C. Scott, and Bhaven N. Sampat. 2011. "When Do Generics Challenge Drug Patents?." Journal of Empirical Legal Studies 8.4: 613-649.

HHS (Department of Health and Human Services). 2013. "Doctors and hospitals' use of health IT more than doubles since 2012." May 22.

Holl, Adelheid, Rafael Pardo, and Ruth Rama. 2010. "Inside and outside the factory: Just-in time manufacturing systems, subcontracting and geographic proximity." *Regional Studies* 44, no. 5: 519-533.

_____. 2011. "Spatial Patterns of Adoption of Just-in-Time Manufacturing." Working Paper, No. 1. Spanish National Research Council.

Hong, Jun, George Huang, Pingyu Jiang, Ting Qu, Yingfeng Zahang, and Guanghui Zhou. 2010. "RFID-enabled real-time manufacturing information tracking infrastructure for extended enterprises." *Journal of Intelligent Manufacturing* 23 (November): 2357-2366.

Hsiao, Chun-Ju and Esther Hing. 2014. "Use and Characteristics of Electric Health Record Systems Among Office-based Physician Practices: United States, 2001-2013." *NCHS Data Brief* No. 143. U.S. Department of Health and Human Services.

Hur, Seung Min, Suho Jeong, and Suk-Hwan Suh. 2009. "An experimental approach to RFID system performance prediction model." *International Journal of Computer Integrated Manufacturing* 22, no. 7 (July): 686-697.

Iowa State University Extension Service. 2013. Corn Production, Harvest and Yield.

JEC (U.S. Congress Joint Economic Committee). 2010a. *The Pivotal Role of Government Investment in Basic Research.* Government Printing Office.

_____. 2010b. *Challenges and Opportunities for Job Creation in the Aftermath of the Great Recession.* Cong. 2 sess. Government Printing Office.

Jones, Charles J., and John C. Williams. 1998. "Measuring the Social Return to R&D." The Quarterly Journal of Economics (November): 1119-1135.

Jorgenson, Dale. 2001. "Information Technology and the US Economy." *The American Economic Review.* Vol 91 (No. 1). 1-32. March.

Jorgenson, Dale, Mun Ho, and Jon Samuels. 2012. "Information Technology and U.S. Productivity Growth." *Industrial Productivity in Europe,* 35-64. Northampton MA: Edward Elgar.

Jorgenson, Dale W. 1988. "Productivity and Postwar U.S. Economic Growth." *Journal of Economic Perspectives.* 2(4): 23-41.

Juhn, Chinhui, Kevin M. Murphy, and Brooks Pierce. 1993. "Wage Inequality and the Rise in Returns to Skill." *Journal of Political Economy* 101(3), 410–442.

Kahn, James and Robert Rich. 2011. "The Productivity Slowdown Reaffirmed." Federal Reserve Bank of New York.

Katz, Lawrence F. and Kevin M. Murphy. 1992. "Changed in Relative Wages, 1963-1987: Supply and Demand Factors." *The Quarterly Journal of Economics* 107, no. 1: 35-78.

Klein, Judith L.V., and William N. Parker. 1966. "Productivity Growth in Grain Production in the United States, 1840-60 and 1900-10." Working Paper 523-582. Cambridge, MA: National Bureau of Economic Research.

Krueger, Alan B. 1993. "How Computers Have Changed the Wage Structure: Evidence from Microdata, 1984-1989." *The Quarterly Journal of Economics* 108, no. 1: 33-60.

Kwerel, Evan R. and Gregory L. Rosston. 2000. "An Insiders' View of FCC Spectrum Auctions," *Journal of Regulatory Economics* 17: 253-289.

Lee, David. 1999. "Wage Inequality in the United States during the 1980s: Rising Dispersion or Falling Minimum Wage?" *Quarterly Journal of Economics.* 114(3), 977–1023.

Lemieux, Thomas. 2008. "The Changing Nature of Wage Inequality." *Journal of Population Economics* 21, no. 1: 21-48.

_____. 2006. "Post-Secondary Education and Increasing Wage Inequality," *American Economic Review* 96(2), 195–99.

Lemley, Mark A., and Carl Shapiro. 2005. "Probabilistic Patents." *Journal of Economic Perspectives* 19, no.2 (Spring): 75-98.

Mateyka, Peter J., and Melanie A. Rapino. 2012. "Home-Based Workers in the United States: 2010." *Household Economic Studies, U.S. Census Bureau* (October): 1-32.

Mishel, Lawrence, Heidi Shierholz, and John Schmitt. 2013. "Don't Blame the Robots: Assessing the Job Polarization Explanation of Growing Wage Inequality." Washington: Economic Policy Institute.

National Science Foundation. 2013. *National Patterns of R&D Resources: 2010-11 Update.*

National Telecommunications and information Administration. 2013. *National Broadband Map.* "US Broadband Availability Data."

Nelson, Richard, R. 1959. "The Simple Economics of Basic Scientific Research." *Journal of Political Economy* 297. 727-736.

Noonan, Mary C. and Jennifer L. Glass. 2012. "The hard truth about telecommuting." *Monthly Labor Review, Statistics* (June): 38-45. U.S. Bureau of Labor Statistics.

Nordhaus, William. 2004. "Retrospective on the Postwar Productivity Slowdown." Cowles Foundation Discussion Paper No. 494. Cambridge, MA: National Bureau of Economic Research.

Office of Science and Technology Policy and the National Economic Council. 2013. "*Four Years of Broadband Growth.*" The White House. (June).

Oliner, Sichel. And Stiroh, 2007. "Explaining a Productive Decade," Finance and Economics Discussion Series 2007-63, Board of Governors of the Federal Reserve System.

Pham, Duc Truong, and Paulette Pham. 2009. "FIT Manufacturing: Linking manufacturing, marketing and product innovation strategies to achieve long term economic sustainability." Wales, UK: Cardiff University.

Piketty, Thomas and Emmanuel Saez. 2003. "Income Inequality in the United States, 1919 1998." *The Quarterly Journal of Economics*118, no. 1: 1-39.

_____. 2006. "The Evolution of Top Incomes: A Historical and International Perspective." Working Paper 11955. Cambridge, Mass: national Bureau of Economic Research (January).

Presidential Memorandum. 2010. "Unleashing the Broadband Wireless Revolution." June 10.

President's Council of Advisors on Science and Technology. 2012. *Report to the President: Realizing the Full Potential of Government-Held Spectrum to Spur Economic Growth.* The White House.

Rodrik, Dani, Arvind Subramanian, and Francesco Trebbi. 2004. "Institutions Rule: The Primacy of Institutions Over Geography and

Integration in Economic Development." *Journal of Economic Growth* 9: 131-165.

Scott Morton, Fiona, and Carl Shapiro. 2013. "Strategic Patent Acquisitions." Working Paper. University of California at Berkeley. (July).

Shackleton, Robert. 2013. "Total Factor Productivity Growth in Historical Perspective." Working Paper 2013-01. Congressional Budget Office

Sim, Khim Ling, and Hian Chye Koh. 2003. "An Empirical Examination of Management Control Systems in Just-In-Time Manufacturing." *The Review of Business Information Systems* 7, no.3: 71-82.

Stalk, George. 1989. "Time-the next source of competitive advantage." *The McKinsey Quarterly* (Spring): 28-50.

Tayal, S.P. 2012. "Just In Time Manufacturing." *International Journal of Applied Engineering Research* 7, no.11.

USDA. 2013. *Farm Computer Usage and Ownership.* Government Printing Office.

U.S. House of Representatives. Committee on the Judiciary. 2011. *America Invents Act.* Report 112-98. Part 1 Cong.1 sess. Government Printing Office.

U.S. Patent and Trademark Office. 2013. US Patents by Technological Category.

Zhang, Yingfeng, Pingyu Jiang, George Huang, Ting Qu, Guangui Zhou, Jun Hong. 2012. "RFID-enabled real-time manufacturing information tracking infrastructure for extended enterprises."

CHAPTER 6

Acs, Gregory and Seth Zimmerman. 2008. "U.S. Intragenerational Economic Mobility from 1984-2004: Trends and Implications." Washington: The Pew Charitable Trusts.

Almond, Douglas, Kenneth Y. Chay, and Michael Greenstone. 2006. "Civil Rights, the War on Poverty, and Black-White Convergence in Infant Mortality in the Rural South and Mississippi." MIT Department of Economics Working Paper 07-04.

Anderson, Michael L. 2008. "Multiple Inference and Gender Differences in the Effects of Early Intervention: A Reevaluation of the Abecedarian, Perry Preschool, and Early Training Projects." *Journal of the American Statistical Association* 103, no. 484: 1481-1495.

Andersson, Fredrik, Harry J. Holzer, Julia I. Lane, David Rosenblum and Jeffrey Smith. 2013. "Does Federally-Funded Job Training Work? Nonexperimental Estimates of WIA Training Impacts Using Longitudinal Data on Workers and Firms," Working Paper 19446. Cambridge, MA: National Bureau of Economic Research.

Anzick, Michael A. and David A. Weaver. 2001. "Reducing Poverty Among Elderly Women." Working Paper Series Number 87. Office of Research, Evaluation, and Statistics, Social Security Administration.

Auten, Gerald, Geoffrey Gee, and Nicholas Turner. 2013. "Income Inequality, Mobility, and Turnover at the Top in the US, 1987–2010." *American Economic Review 103 (May, Papers and Proceedings, 2012): 168–172.*

Baicker, Katherine, Sarah L. Taubman, Heidi L. Allen, Mira Bernstein, Jonathan H. Gruber, Joseph P. Newhouse, Eric C. Schneider, Bill J. Wright, Alan M. Zaslavsky, and Amy N. Finkelstein. 2013. "The Oregon Experiment—Effects of Medicaid on Clinical Outcomes." *The New England Journal of Medicine* 368: 1713-1722.

Bailey, Martha J. and Sheldon Danziger, eds. 2013. *Legacies of the War on Poverty.* New York: Russell Sage Foundation.

Ben-Shalom, Yonatan, Robert A. Moffitt, and John Karl Scholz. 2011. "An Assessment of Anti-Poverty Programs in the United States." Working Paper 17042. Cambridge, MA: National Bureau of Economic Research.

Björklund, Anders, Markus Jäntti, and Gary Solon. 2005. "Influences of Nature and Nurture on Earnings Variation: A Report on a Study of Various Sibling Types in Sweden." In *Unequal Chances: Family Background and Economic Success,* edited by Samuel Bowles, Herbert Gintis, and Melissa Osborne Groves, pp. 145-164. Princeton University Press.

Black, Sandra E. and Paul J. Devereux. 2011. "Recent Developments in Intergenerational Mobility." In *Handbook of Labor Economics*, Volume 4B, edited by Orley Ashenfelter and David Card, pp. 1487–1541. Amsterdam: North Holland Publishing Co.

Blank, Rebecca M. 1993. "Public Sector Growth and Labor Market Flexibility: The United States vs. the United Kingdom." Working Paper 4338. Cambridge, MA: National Bureau of Economic Research.

_____. 2000. "Fighting Poverty: Lessons from Recent U.S. History." *Journal of Economic Perspectives* 14, no. 2: 3-19.

_____. 2007. "Improving the Safety Net for Single Mothers Who Face Serious Barriers to Work." *Future of Children* 17, no. 2: 183-197.

Burtless, Gary. 1986. "Social Security, Unanticipated Benefit Increases, and the Timing of Retirement." *Review of Economic Studies* 53, no. 5: 781-805.

Campbell, Frances A., Barbara H. Wasik, Elizabeth Pungello, Margaret Burchinal, Oscar Barbarin, Kirsten Kainz, Joseph J. Sparling, and Craig T. Ramey. 2008. "Young Adult Outcomes of the Abecedarian and CARE Early Childhood Educational Interventions." *Early Childhood Research Quarterly* 23, no. 4: 452–466.

Cancian, Maria and Deborah Reed. 2009. "Family structure, childbearing, and parental employment: Implications for the level and trend in poverty." *Focus* 26, no.2: 21-26.

Caplow, Theodore and Jonathan Simon. 1999. "Understanding Prison Policy and Population Trends." *Crime and Justice* 26: 63-120.

Card, David E. and Steven Raphael. 2013. *Immigration, Poverty, and Socioeconomic Inequality.* New York: Russell Sage.

Carlson, Deven, Robert Haveman, Thomas Kaplan, and Barbara Wolfe. 2011. "The Benefits and Costs of the Section 8 Housing Subsidy Program: A Framework and Estimates of First-Year Effects." *Journal of Policy Analysis and Management* 30, 2: 233–255.

Census Bureau. 2013. "Poverty – Experimental Measures." http://www. census.gov/hhes/povmeas/data/nas/tables/index.html

Chay, Kenneth Y., Jonathan Guryan, and Bhashkar Mazumder. 2009. "Birth Cohort and the Black-White Achievement Gap: The Roles of Access and Health Soon After Birth." Working Paper No. 15078. Cambridge, MA, National Bureau of Economic Research.

Chetty, Raj. 2008. "Moral Hazard versus Liquidity and Optimal Unemployment Insurance." *Journal of Political Economy* 116, no. 2: 173-234.

Chetty, Raj, John N. Friedman, and Jonah E. Rockoff. 2011. "New Evidence on the Long-Term Impacts of Tax Credits." Statistics of Income Paper Series. Internal Revenue Service.

Chetty, Raj, John N. Friedman, and Emmanuel Saez. 2012. "Using Differences in Knowledge Across Neighborhoods to Uncover the Impacts of the EITC on Earnings." Working Paper 18232. Cambridge, MA: National Bureau of Economic Research.

Chetty, Raj, John N. Friedman, Soren Leth-Peterson, Torben Heien Nielson, and Tore Olsen. 2013. "Subsidies vs. Nudges: Which Policies Increase Saving the Most?" Issue Brief 13-3. Center for Retirement Research at Boston College.

Chetty, Raj, Nathaniel Hendren, Patrick Kline, and Emmanuel Saez. 2014. "Where is the Land of Opportunity? The Geography of Intergenerational Mobility in the United States." Working Paper 19843. Cambridge, MA: National Bureau of Economic Research.

Chetty, Raj, Nathaniel Hendren, Patrick Kline, and Emmanuel Saez, and Nick Turner. 2014. "Is the United States Still a Land of Opportunity? Recent Trends in Intergenerational Mobility." Working Paper 19844. Cambridge, MA: National Bureau of Economic Research.

(CBO) Congressional Budget Office. 2013. "Growth in Means-Tested Programs and Tax Credits for Low-Income Households." http://www.cbo.gov/sites/default/files/cbofiles/attachments/43934-Means-TestedPrograms.pdf.

Connelly, Rachel and Jean Kimmel. 2003. "The Effect of Child Care Costs on the Employment and Welfare Recipiency of Single Mothers." *Southern Economic Journal* 69, no. 3: 498-519.

Corak, Miles. 2006. "Do Poor Children Become Poor Adults? Lessons from a Cross Country Comparison of Generational Earnings Mobility." IZA Discussion Paper No. 1993.

_____. 2011. "Inequality from generation to generation: the United States in Comparison." Graduate School of Public and International Affairs, University of Ottawa.

Corcoran, Mary. 2001. "Mobility, Persistence, and the Consequences of Child Poverty for Children: Child and Adult Outcomes." In *Understanding Poverty*, edited by Sheldon H. Danziger and Robert H. Haveman, pp. 127-140. Cambridge, MA: Harvard University Press.

Corcoran, Mary and Terry Adams. 1997. "Race, Sex, and the Intergenerational Transmission of Poverty." In *Consequences of Growing Up Poor*, edited by Greg J. Duncan and Jeanne Brooks-Gunn, pp. 461-517. New York: Russell Sage Foundation.

(CEA) Council of Economic Advisers. 1964. *Economic Report of the President*.

_____. 2013. "Trends in Health Care and Cost Growth and the Role of the Affordable Care Act."

Dahl, Gordon B. and Lance Lochner. 2012. "The Impact of Family Income on Child Achievement: Evidence from the Earned Income Tax Credit." *American Economic Review* 102, no. 5: 1927-1956.

Danziger, Sheldon and Peter Gottschalk. 1995. *America Unequal.* Cambridge, MA: Harvard University Press.

Danziger, Sheldon H., Lesley J. Turner, and Kristin S. Seefeldt. 2006. "Failing the Transition from Welfare to Work: Women Chronically Disconnected from Employment and Cash Welfare." *Social Science Quarterly* 87, no. 2: 227-249.

Deming, David. 2009. "Early Childhood Intervention and Life-Cycle Skill Development: Evidence from Head Start." *American Economic Journal: Applied Economics* 1, no. 3: 111-134.

DiNardo, John, Nicole M. Fortin, and Thomas Lemieux. 1996. "Labor Market Institutions and the Distribution of Wages, 1973-1992: A Semiparametric Approach." *Econometrica* 64, no. 5: 1001-1044.

DiNardo, John, and Thomas Lemieux. 1997. "Diverging Male Wage Inequality in the United States and Canada, 1981-1988: Do Institutions Explain the Difference?" *Industrial and Labor Relations Review* 50, no. 4: 629-651.

Doucouliagos, Hirstos and T.D. Stanley. 2009. "Publication Selection Bias in Minimum-Wage Research? A Meta-Regression Analysis." *British Journal of Industrial Relations* 47, no. 2: 406-428.

Dowd, Tim and John B. Horowitz. 2011. "Income Mobility and the Earned Income Tax Credit: Short-Term Safety Net or Long-Term Income Support." *Public Finance Review* 39, no. 5: 619-652.

Dube, Arindrajit, T. William Lester, and Michael Reich. 2010. "Minimum Wage Effects Across State Borders: Estimates Using Contiguous Counties." *The Review of Economics and Statistics* 92, no. 4: 945-964.

Dube, Arindrajit. 2013. "Minimum Wages and the Distribution of Family Incomes." University of Massachusetts, Amherst Working Paper. https://dl.dropboxusercontent.com/u/15038936/Dube_Minimum-WagesFamilyIncomes.pdf.

Duncan, Greg J., Katherine Magnuson, Ariel Kalil, Kathleen Ziol-Guest. 2012. "The Importance of Early Childhood Poverty." *Social Indicators Research* 108, no. 1: pp 87-98.

Eissa, Nada and Hilary W. Hoynes. 2005. "Behavioral Responses to Taxes: Lessons from the EITC and Labor Supply." Working Paper 11729. Cambridge, MA: National Bureau of Economic Research.

Eissa, Nada and Jeffrey B. Liebman. 1996. "Labor Supply Response to the Earned Income Tax Credit." *The Quarterly Journal of Economics* 111, no. 2: 605-637.

Engelhardt, Gary V., and Jonathan Gruber. 2006. "Social Security and the Evolution of Elderly Poverty." In *Public Policy and the Income Distribution*, edited by Alan J. Auerbach, David E. Card, and John M. Quigley, pp. 259-287. New York: Russell Sage Foundation.

Fisher, Gordon M. 1992. "The Development and History of the Poverty Thresholds." *Social Security Bulletin* 55, no. 4: 3-14.

Fox, Liana, Irwin Garfinkel, Neeraj Kaushal, Jane Waldfogel, and Christopher Wimer. 2013. "Waging War on Poverty: Historical Trends in Poverty Using the Supplemental Poverty Measure." Working Paper 13-01. New York: Columbia Population Research Center.

Fremstad, Shawn. 2009. "Half in Ten: Why Taking Disability into Account is Essential to Reducing Income Poverty and Expanding Economic Inclusion." Reports and Issue Briefs 2009-30. Washington: Center for Economic and Policy Research.

Garces, Eliana, Duncan Thomas, and Janet Currie. 2002. "Longer-Term Effects of Head Start." *American Economic Review* 92, no. 4: 999–1012.

Gibbs, Chloe, Jens Ludwig, and Douglas L. Miller. 2013. "Head Start Origins and Impacts." In *Legacies of the War on Poverty*, edited by Martha Bailey and Sheldon Danziger, pp. 39-65. New York: Russell Sage Foundation Press.

Gottschalk, Peter and Sheldon Danziger. 2003. "Wage Inequality, Earnings Inequality and Poverty in the U.S. Over the Last Quarter of the Twentieth Century." Working Papers in Economics 560. Boston College Department of Economics.

Hanson, Kenneth. 2010. "The Food Assistance National Income-Output Multiplier (FANIOM) Model and Stimulus Effects of SNAP." Economic Research Report No. 103. U.S. Department of Agriculture Economic Research Service.

Harrington, Michael. 1962. *The Other America.* New York: Simon and Schuster.

Heckman, James J. and Dimitriy V. Masterov. 2007. "The Productivity Argument for Investing in Young Children." *Applied Economic Perspectives and Policy* 29, no. 3: 446-493.

Heckman, James J., Seong Hyeok Moon, Rodrigo Pinto, Peter A. Savelyev, and Adam Yavitz. 2009. "The Rate of Return to the High/Scope Perry Preschool Program." Working Paper No. 15471. Cambridge, MA: National Bureau of Economic Research.

_____. 2010. "A New Cost-Benefit and Rate of Return Analysis for the Perry Preschool Program: A Summary." Working Paper No. 16180. Cambridge, Mass.: National Bureau of Economic Research.

Heckman, James J., Rodrigo Pinto, Azeem M. Shaikh, and Adam Yavitz. 2011. "Inference with Imperfect Randomization: the Case of the Perry Preschool Program." Working Paper No. 16935. Cambridge, MA: National Bureau of Economic Research.

Holzer, Harry J. 2007. "Collateral Costs: The Effects of Incarceration on the Employment and Earnings of Young Workers." IZA Discussion Paper No. 3118.

Holzer, Harry J., Diane Whitmore Schanzenbach, Greg J. Duncan, and Jens Ludwig. 2008. "The Economic Costs of Childhood Poverty in the United States." *Journal of Children and Poverty* 14, no. 1: 41-61.

Hotz, V. Joseph and John Karl Scholz. 2003. "The Earned Income Tax Credit." In *Means-Tested Transfer Programs in the U.S.*, edited by Robert A. Moffitt, pp. 141-198. Chicago: University of Chicago Press.

Hoynes, Hilary W., Marianne E. Page, and Ann Huff Stevens. 2006. "Poverty in America: Trends and Explanations." *Journal of Economic Perspectives* 92, no. 3: 748-765.

Hoynes, Hilary W. and Diane W. Schanzenbach. 2009. "Consumption Reponses to In-Kind Transfers: Evidence from the Introduction of the Food Stamp Program." *American Economic Journal: Applied Economics* 1, no. 4: 109-139.

_____. 2012. "Work incentives and the Food Stamp Program." *Journal of Public Economics* 96, no. 1: 151-162.

Hoynes, Hilary W., Diane W. Schanzenbach, and Douglas Almond. 2013. "Long Run Impacts of Childhood Access to the Safety Net." Working Paper 18535. Cambridge, MA: National Bureau of Economic Research.

Ichino, Andrea, Loukas Karabarbounis, and Enrico Moretti. 2009. "The Political Economy of Intergenerational Income Mobility." IZA Discussion Paper No. 4767.

Isaacs, Julia B. 2008. "Economic Mobility of Families across Generations." In *Getting Ahead or Losing Ground: Economic Mobility in America*, edited by Julia Isaacs, Isabel Sawhill and Ron Haskins. Washington: The Pew Charitable Trusts.

Isaacs, Julia B., Isabel Sawhill, and Ron Haskins. 2008. *Getting Ahead or Losing Ground: Economic Mobility in America*. Washington: The Pew Charitable Trusts.

Jacob, Brian A. and Jens Ludwig. 2012. "The Effects of Housing Assistance on Labor Supply: Evidence from a Voucher Lottery." *American Economic Review* 102, no. 1: 272-304.

Jäntti, Markus, Bernt Bratsberg, Knut Røed, Oddbjørn Raaum, Robin Naylor, Eva Österbacka, Anders Björklund, and Tor Eriksson. 2006. "American Exceptionalism in a New Light: A Comparison of Inter-generational Earnings Mobility in the Nordic Countries, the United Kingdom and the United States." IZA Discussion Paper No. 1938.

Johnson, Rucker C. 2008. "Ever-increasing Levels of Parental Incarceration and the Consequences for Children." In *Do Prisons Make us Safer?*, edited by S. Raphael and M. Stoll, 177-206. New York: Russell Sage Foundation.

Korenman, Sanders and Dahlia Remler. 2013. "Rethinking Elderly Poverty: Time for a Health Inclusive Poverty Measure?" Working Paper 18900. Cambridge, MA: National Bureau of Economic Research.

Lee, Chul-In and Gary Solon, 2009. "Trends in Intergenerational Income Mobility," *The Review of Economics and Statistics*, 91, no. 4: 766-772

Lee, David S. 1999. "Wage Inequality in the United States During the 1980s: Rising Dispersion or Falling Minimum Wage?" *Quarterly Journal of Economics* 114, no. 3: 977-1023.

Lemieux, Thomas. 2008. "The Changing Nature of Wage Inequality." *Journal of Population Economics* 21, no. 1: 21-48.

Liebman, Jeffrey B. 1998. "The Impact of the Earned Income Tax Credit on Incentives and Income Distribution." In *Tax Policy and the Economy, Volume 12*, edited by James M. Poterba, pp. 83-120. Cambridge, MA: National Bureau of Economic Research.

Ludwig, Jens and Douglas Miller. 2007. "Does Head Start Improve Children's Life Chances? Evidence from a Regression Discontinuity Design." *Quarterly Journal of Economics* 122, no. 1: 159-208.

Matsudaira, Jordan D. and Rebecca M. Blank. 2013. "The Impact of Earnings Disregards on the Behavior of Low-Income Families." *Journal of Policy Analysis and Management* 33, no. 1: 7-35.

Mayer, Susan E. and Leonard M. Lopoo. 2008. "Government Spending and Intergenerational Mobility." *Journal of Public Economics* 92, no. 1-2: 139-158.

Mayer, Susan E. 1997. *What Money Can't Buy: Family Income and Children's Life Chances.* Cambridge, MA: Harvard University Press.

Meyer, Bruce D., Wallace K. C. Mok, and James X. Sullivan. 2009. "The Underreporting of Transfers in Household Surveys: Its Nature and Consequences." Working Paper 15181. Cambridge, MA: National Bureau of Economic Research.

Meyer, Bruce D. and Dan T. Rosenbaum. 2001. "Welfare, the Earned Income Tax Credit, and the Labor Supply of Single Mothers." *Quarterly Journal of Economics* 116, no. 3: 1063-1114.

Meyer, Bruce D. and James X. Sullivan. 2003. "Measuring the Well-Being of the Poor Using Income and Consumption." Journal of Human Resources 38, Supplement: 1180-1220.

_____. 2012a. "Winning the War: Poverty from the Great Society to the Great Recession." *Brookings Papers on Economic Activity* 45, no. 2: 133-200.

_____. 2012b. "Identifying the Disadvantaged: Official Poverty, Consumption Poverty, and the New Supplemental Poverty Measure." Journal of Economic Perspectives 26, no. 3: 111-136.

_____. 2013. "Winning the War: Poverty from the Great Society to the Great Recession." Working Paper 18718. Cambridge, MA: National Bureau of Economic Research.

Mishel, Lawrence, Josh Bivens, Elise Gould, and Heidi Shierholz. *The State of Working America, 12th Edition.* A forthcoming Economic Policy Institute book. Ithaca, NY: Cornell University Press.

Misra, Joya, Michelle Budig, and Irene Boeckmann. 2011. "Work-Family Policies and the Effects of Children on Women's Employment Hours and Wages." *Community, Work and Family* 14, no. 2: 139-157.

Nicholson-Crotty, Sean and Kenneth J. Meier. 2003. "Crime and Punishment: The Politics of Federal Criminal Justice Sanctions." *Political Research Quarterly* 56, no. 2: 119-126.

Orshansky, Mollie. 1965. "Counting the Poor: Another Look at the Poverty Profile." *Social Security Bulletin* 28, no. 1: 3-29.

Peri, Giovanni. 2013. "Immigrant Workers, Native Poverty and Labor Market Competition." *Policy Brief, Center for Poverty Research* 1, no. 3.

Peters, Alan H. and Peter S. Fisher. 2002. "State Enterprise Zones: Have They Worked?" Kalamazoo, MI: W.E. Upjohn Institute for Employment Research Press.

Piketty, Thomas and Emmanuel Saez. 2003. "Income Inequality in the United States, 1913-1998." *Quarterly Journal of Economics* 118, no. 1: 1-39.

Raphael, Steven. 2007. "Early Incarceration Spells and the Transition to Adulthood." In *The Price of Independence: The Economics of Early Adulthood*, edited by Sheldon Danziger and Cecilia Elena Rouse, pp. 278-306. New York: Russell Sage Foundation.

Reed, Deborah and Maria Cancian. 2001. "Sources of Inequality: Measuring the Contributions of Income Sources to Rising Family Income Inequality." *Review of Income and Wealth* 47, no. 3: 321-333.

Sawhill, Isabel V. and John E. Morton. 2007. "Economic Mobility: Is the American Dream Alive and Well?" Washington: Economic Mobility Project, Pew Charitable Trusts.

Schur, Lisa A., Douglas L. Kruse, and Peter Blanck. 2013. *People with Disabilities: Sidelined or Mainstreamed?* Cambridge, England: Cambridge University Press.

Schweinhart, Lawrence J., Jeanne Montie, Zongping Xiang, W. Steven Barnett, Clive R. Belfield, and Milagros Nores. 2005. *Lifetime Effects: The High/Scope Perry Preschool Study Through Age 40*. Monographs of the High/Scope Educational Research Foundation. Ypsilanti, MI: High/Scope Press.

Sen, Amartya. 2009. *The Idea of Justice*. London: Allen Lane.

Singh, Gopal K. and Michael D. Kogan. 2007. "Persistent Socioeconomic Disparities in Infant, Neonatal, and Postneonatal Mortality Rates in the United States, 1969-2001." *Pediatrics* 119, no. 4: 928-939.

Sharkey, Patrick. 2009. "Neighborhoods and the Black-White Mobility Gap." Washington: Economic Mobility Project, Pew Charitable Trusts.

She, Peiyun and Gina A. Livermore. 2007. "Material Hardship, Poverty, and Disability Among Working-Age Adults." *Social Science Quarterly* 88, no. 4: 970-989.

Sherman, Arloc. 2013. "Official Poverty Measure Masks Gains Made Over Last 50 Years." Washington: Center on Budget and Policy Priorities. http://www.cbpp.org/files/9-13-13pov.pdf.

Short, Kathleen. 2012. "The Research Supplemental Poverty Measure: 2011" Current Population Reports.

_____. 2013. "The Research Supplemental Poverty Measure: 2012" Current Population Reports.

Shroder, Mark. 2010. "Housing Subsidies and Work Incentives." MPRA Paper 26019, University Library of Munich, Germany.

Solon, Gary. 2002. "Cross-Country Differences in Intergenerational Earnings Mobility." *Journal of Economic Perspectives* 16, no. 3: 59– 66.

SRI International. 1983. "Final Report of the Seattle/Denver Income Maintenance Experiment. Vol 1: Design and Results." Menlo Park, CA.

(SSA) Social Security Administration. 2012. *Income of the Population 55 or Older, 2010.* SSA Publication No. 13-11871.

Western, Bruce. 2002. "The Impact of Incarceration on Wage Mobility and Inequality."

American Sociological Review 67: 526-46.

Western, Bruce and Becky Pettit. 2010. "Incarceration and Social Inequality." *Daedalus* 139: 8-19.

Wimer, Christopher, Liana Fox, Irwin Garfinkel, Neeraj Kaushal, and Jane Waldfogel. 2013. "Trends in Poverty with an Anchored Supplemental Poverty Measure." Working Paper 1-25. New York: Columbia Population Research Center.

CHAPTER 7

Abdulkadiroglu, Atila, Joshua D Angrist, Susan M Dynarski, Thomas J Kane, Parag A Pathak. 2011. "Accountability and Flexibility in Public Schools: Evidence from Boston's Charters and Pilots." *The Quarterly Journal of Economics* 126, no. 2: 699-748.

Angrist, Joshua D., and Jörn-Steffen Pischke. 2008. *Mostly Harmless Econometrics: An Empiricist's Companion*. Princeton, NJ: Princeton University Press.

Angrist, Joshua. D., and Alan B. Krueger. 1999. "Empirical strategies in labor economics." In *Handbook of Labor Economics*, edited by O. Ashenfelter and D. Card, pp.1277-1366. Vol 3, Elsevier.

Baicker, Katherine, Amy Finkelstein, Jae Song, and Sarah Taubman. 2013. "The Impact of Medicaid on Labor Force Activity and Program Participation: Evidence from the Oregon Health Insurance Experiment." Working Paper. Cambridge, MA: National Bureau of Economic Research (October).

Benus, J. T. Shen, S. Zhang, M. Chan and B. Hansen. 2009. "Growing America Through Entrepreneurship: Final Evaluation of Project GATE." Columbia, MD: IMPAQ International LLC.

Benus, J., Poe-Yamagata, E., Wang, Y., & Blass, E. 2008. "Reemployment and Eligibility Assessment (REA) Study FY 2005 Initiative." Columbia, MD: IMPAQ International LLC.

Berk, Richard A., and Peter H. Rossi. 1998. *Thinking about Program Evaluation 2*. 2nd ed. London: Sage Publications, Inc.

Bettinger, E.P., B.T. Long, P. Oreopoulos and L. Sanbonmatsu. 2009. "The Role Of Simplification and Information In College Decisions: Results From The H&R Block FAFSA Experiment." Working Paper 15361. Cambridge, MA: National Bureau of Economic Research (September).

Burtless, G. 1995. (The case for randomized field trials in economic and policy research.) *The Journal of Economic Perspectives* 9, no. 2 (Spring): 63-84.

Cappers, Peter, Charles Goldman, and Annika Todd. 2013. "Smart Grid Investment Grant Consumer Behavior Study Analysis: Summary of Utility Studies." Environmental Energy Technologies Division, Lawrence Berkeley National Laboratory.

Card, David, Carlos Dobkin, and Nicole Maestas. 2009. "Does Medicare Save Lives?" *The Quarterly Journal of Economics* 124, no. 2: 597-636.

Coalition for Evidence-Based Policy. 2012. "Rigorous Program Evaluations on a Budget: How Low-Cost Randomized Controlled Trials are Possible in Many Areas of Social Policy." Washington, DC (March).

_____. 2013. "Practical Evaluation Strategies for Building a Body of Proven-Effective Social Programs." Washington, DC (October).

Comey, Jennifer, Kaitlin Franks, Lesley Freiman, Christopher Hayes, Reed Jordan, Peter A. Tatian, and Mary K. Winkler. 2013. "Measuring Performance: A Guidance Document for Promise Neighborhoods on Collecting Data and Reporting Results." Washington, DC: The Urban Institute (February).

Council Of Economic Advisers And Department Of Labor. 2013. "The Economic Benefits of Extending Unemployment Insurance" (December).

Culhane, D. P., S. Metraux, J.M. Park, M.A. Schretzman, M. A., and J. Valente. 2007. "Testing a Typology of Family Homelessness Based on Patterns of Public Shelter Utilization in Four U.S. Jurisdictions: Implications for Policy and Program Planning." *Housing Policy Debate*, 18(1), 1-28.

Department of Education. 2012. *Education Improvement Programs: Fiscal Year 2012 Budget Request.* http://www2.ed.gov/about/overview/budget/budget12/justifications/d-eip.pdf

_____. 2013a. *Investing in Innovation Fund (i3) Program Guidance and Frequently Asked Questions (FAQs).* http://www2.ed.gov/programs/innovation/faq.html

_____. 2013b. *Promise Neighborhoods: Purpose.* http://www2.ed.gov/programs/promiseneighborhoods/index.html

_____. 2013c. *PROMISE: Promoting Readiness of Minors in Supplemental Security Income.* http://www2.ed.gov/about/inits/ed/promise/index.html#about

Department of Labor. 2011. *Employment and Training Administration Notice of Availability of Funds and Solicitation for Grant Applications for Workforce Innovation Fund Grants.* SGA/DFA PY-11-05 at http://www.doleta.gov/workforce_innovation/applicant_information.cfm

_____. 2013. *Congressional Budget Justification: Employment and Training Administration.* http://www.dol.gov/dol/budget/2013/PDF/CBJ-2013-V1-05.pdf

Departments of Labor, Health and Human Services, and Education, and Related Agencies Appropriations Act, 2006, Title V, Part D (P.L. 109-149). http://www2.ed.gov/programs/teacherincentive/legislation.html)

Dobbie, Will and Roland G. Fryer. 2011. "Are High Quality Schools Enough to Increase Achievement Among the Poor? Evidence from the Harlem Children's Zone." American Economic Journal: Applied Economics 3 (July):158-187.

Finkelstein, Amy, Sarah Taubman, Bill Wright, Mira Bernstein, Jonathan Gruber, Joseph P. Newhouse, Heidi Allen, Katherine Baicker, and the Oregon Health Study Group. 2012. "The Oregon Health Insurance Experiment: Evidence from the First Year." *Quarterly Journal of Economics* 127(3): 1057-1106 (August).

General Accounting Office. 2011. *Performance Measurement and Evaluation: Definitions and Relationships.* GAO-11-646SP, May.

_____. 2012. "Designing Evaluations: 2012 Revision." U.S. Government Accountability Office, GAO-12-208G, January.

Grossman, J.B., and J.E. Rhodes. 2002. "The test of time: Predictors and effects of duration in youth mentoring programs." *American Journal of Community Psychology* (30), 199-219.

Jacob, Brian A., Jens Ludwig. 2012. "The Effects of Housing Assistance On Labor Supply: Evidence From A Voucher Lottery." *American Economic Review* 102(1): 272–304.

Holland, Paul W. 1986. "Statistics and Causal Inference." *Journal of the American Statistical Association* 81, no. 396: 945-960.

Imbens, Guido W. and Jeffrey M. Woolridge. 2009. "Recent Developments in the Econometrics of Program Evaluation." *Journal of Economic Literature* 47, no. 1: 5-86.

Imbens, Guido W. 2010. "Better LATE Than Nothing: Some Comments on Deaton (2009) and Heckman and Urzua (2009)." *Journal of Economic Literature* 48 (June 2010): 399-423.

Ludwig, J. and D. L. Miller. 2007. "Does Head Start improve children's life chances? Evidence From a Regression Discontinuity Design." *Quarterly Journal of Economics* 122 no. 1: 159-208.

Manzi, Jim. 2012. *Uncontrolled: The Surprising Payoff of Trial-and-Error for Business, Politics, and Society.* New York: Basic Books.

Millensky, Megan, et al. 2011. "Staying on Course: Three-Year Results of the National Guard Youth ChalleNGe Evaluation. MDRC. http://www.mdrc.org/sites/default/files/full_510.pdf

National Institute of Justice. 2012. *"Swift and Certain" Sanctions in Probation Are Highly Effective: Evaluation of the Hope Program.* http://

www.nij.gov/topics/corrections/community/drug-offenders/
hawaii-hope.htm

National Research Council and Institute of Medicine. 2009. *Preventing Mental, Emotional, and Behavioral Disorders Among Young People: Progress and Possibilities.* Committee on Prevention of Mental Disorders and Substance Abuse Among Children, Youth and Young Adults: Research Advances and Promising Interventions. Mary Ellen O'Connell, Thomas Boat, and Kenneth E. Warner, Editors. Board on Children, Youth, and Families, Division of Behavioral and Social Sciences and Education. Washington, DC: The National Academies Press. Online at http://www.nap.edu/catalog.php?record_id=12480.

Office of Management and Budget. 2009a. *Analytical Perspectives: Budget of the U.S. Government,* February. At http://www.gpo.gov/fdsys/pkg/BUDGET-2010-PER/pdf/BUDGET-2010-PER.pdf

———. 2009b. *Building Rigorous Evidence to Drive Policy.* OMB Blogpost, http://www.whitehouse.gov/omb/blog/09/06/08/BuildingRigorousEvidencetoDrivePolicy

———. 2009c. *Increased Emphasis on Program Evaluations.* Memorandum M-10-01, October 7, 2009.

———. 2010. *Analytical Perspectives: Budget of the U.S. Government,* at http://www.gpo.gov/fdsys/pkg/BUDGET-2011-PER/pdf/BUDGET-2011-PER.pdf

———. 2011. *Analytical Perspectives: Budget of the U.S. Government,* February 14, 2011 at http://www.gpo.gov/fdsys/pkg/BUDGET-2012-PER/pdf/BUDGET-2012-PER.pdf

———. 2012. *Analytical Perspectives: Budget of the U.S. Government,* February 13, 2012 at http://www.gpo.gov/fdsys/pkg/BUDGET-2013-PER/pdf/BUDGET-2013-PER.pdf

———. 2013a. Creating a 21st Century Government, Budget of the United States Government, Fiscal Year 2014 http://www.whitehouse.gov/sites/default/files/omb/budget/fy2014/assets/21st_century.pdf

———. 2013b. *Next Steps in the Evidence and Innovation Agenda.* Memorandum M-13-17, July 26, 2013.

———. 2014. *Guidance for Providing and Using Administrative Data for Statistical Purposes.* Memorandum M-14-06, February 14, 2014.

Paulsell, Diane, S. Avellar, E. Sama Martin, P. Del Grosso. 2010. "Home visiting Evidence of Effectiveness Review: Executive Summary." Washington, DC:Mathematica Policy Research.

Perez-Arce, Francisco, et al. 2012. "A Cost-Benefit Analysis of the National Guard Youth ChalleNGe Program." RAND Corporation. http://www.rand.org/pubs/technical_reports/TR1193.html#key-findings

Poe-Yamagata, E., Benus, J., Bill, N., Carrington, H., Michaelides, M., & Shen, T. 2011. "Impact of the Reemployment and Eligibility Assessment (REA) Initiative." Columbia, MD: IMPAQ International LLC.

Rivkin, Steven G., Eric A. Hanushek and John F. Kain. 2005. "Teachers, Schools, and Academic Achievement." *Econometrica*, vol. 73 (2) (March): 417-458.

Rothstein, Jesse. 2011. "Unemployment Insurance and Job Search in the Great Recession." *Brookings Papers on Economic Activity* Fall 2011: 143-213.

Shadish, William R., Thomas D. Cook, and Donald Thomas Campbell. 2002. *Experimental and Quasi-Experimental Designs for Generalized Causal Inference.* Boston, MA: Houghton Mifflin.

Schlafer, Rebecca J., Poehlmann, Julie, Coffino, Brianna, Henneman, Ashley (2009). "Mentoring Children with Incarcerated Parents: Implications for Research, Practice, and Policy." *Family Relations* (58), 507-519.

Schochet, Peter Z., John Burghardt, and Sheena McConnell. 2008. "Does Job Corps Work? Impact Findings from the National Job Corps Study." *American Economic Review* 98:5, 1864-1886. http://www.jstor.org/stable/29730155?seq=2

Shadish, William R., Thomas D. Cook, and Donald Thomas Campbell. 2002. *Experimental and Quasi-Experimental Designs for Generalized Causal Inference.* Boston, MA: Houghton Mifflin.

Shrank, W. 2013. "The Center for Medicare and Medicaid Innovation's Blueprint for Rapid-Cycle Evaluation of New Care and Payment Models." *Health Affairs* 32(4):807-812.

Social Security Administration. 2013. *Solicitation: PROMISE Evaluation Statement of Work.* SSA-RFP-13-0018, July 16, 2013. https://www.fedconnect.net/FedConnect/PublicPages/PublicSearch/Public_Opportunities.aspx

Stock, James H., and Mark Watson. 2010. *Introduction to Econometrics.* 3rd ed. Boston, MA: Addison-Wesley.

St.Pierre, R., A. Ricciuti, F. Tao, C. Creps, J. Swartz, W. Lee, A. Parsad and T. Rimdzius. 2003. "Third National Even Start Evaluation: Program Impacts and Implications for Improvement." Abt Associates, Inc. and U.S. Department of Education.

United States Interagency Council on Homelessness. 2013a. "US Labor Department awards nearly $24 million in Pay for Success grants." September 26, 2013, available at http://usich.gov/media_center/news/us_labor_department_awards_nearly_24_million_in_pay_for_success_grants (accessed November 24, 2013).

United States Interagency Council on Homelessness, 2013b. "Opening Doors," available at http://usich.gov/opening_doors/ (accessed November 24, 2013).

Walker, Robert, Hoggart, Lesley, and Hamilton Gayle. 2006. "Making Random Assignment Happen: Evidence from the UK Employment Retention and Advancement (ERA) Demonstration." Policy Studies Institute (PSI), the Office for National Statistics (ONS), the Institute for Fiscal Studies (IFS) and MDRC for the UK Department for Work and Pensions.

Wansink, Brian, David Just, and Laura Smith. 2011. "Move the Fruit: Putting Fruit in New Bowls and New Places Doubles Lunchroom Sales." *Journal of Nutrition Education and Behavior* 43:4.

A P P E N D I X   A

REPORT TO THE PRESIDENT ON THE ACTIVITIES OF THE COUNCIL OF ECONOMIC ADVISERS DURING 2013

LETTER OF TRANSMITTAL

COUNCIL OF ECONOMIC ADVISERS
Washington, D.C., December 31, 2013

MR. PRESIDENT:

The Council of Economic Advisers submits this report on its activities during calendar year 2013 in accordance with the requirements of the Congress, as set forth in section 10(d) of the Employment Act of 1946 as amended by the Full Employment and Balanced Growth Act of 1978.

Sincerely yours,

Jason Furman, *Chairman*
Betsey Stevenson, *Member*
James H. Stock, *Member*

Council Members and Their Dates of Service

Name	Position	Oath of office date	Separation date
Edwin G. Nourse	Chairman	August 9, 1946	November 1, 1949
Leon H. Keyserling	Vice Chairman	August 9, 1946	
	Acting Chairman	November 2, 1949	
	Chairman	May 10, 1950	January 20, 1953
John D. Clark	Member	August 9, 1946	
	Vice Chairman	May 10, 1950	February 11, 1953
Roy Blough	Member	June 29, 1950	August 20, 1952
Robert C. Turner	Member	September 8, 1952	January 20, 1953
Arthur F. Burns	Chairman	March 19, 1953	December 1, 1956
Neil H. Jacoby	Member	September 15, 1953	February 9, 1955
Walter W. Stewart	Member	December 2, 1953	April 29, 1955
Raymond J. Saulnier	Member	April 4, 1955	
	Chairman	December 3, 1956	January 20, 1961
Joseph S. Davis	Member	May 2, 1955	October 31, 1958
Paul W. McCracken	Member	December 3, 1956	January 31, 1959
Karl Brandt	Member	November 1, 1958	January 20, 1961
Henry C. Wallich	Member	May 7, 1959	January 20, 1961
Walter W. Heller	Chairman	January 29, 1961	November 15, 1964
James Tobin	Member	January 29, 1961	July 31, 1962
Kermit Gordon	Member	January 29, 1961	December 27, 1962
Gardner Ackley	Member	August 3, 1962	
	Chairman	November 16, 1964	February 15, 1968
John P. Lewis	Member	May 17, 1963	August 31, 1964
Otto Eckstein	Member	September 2, 1964	February 1, 1966
Arthur M. Okun	Member	November 16, 1964	
	Chairman	February 15, 1968	January 20, 1969
James S. Duesenberry	Member	February 2, 1966	June 30, 1968
Merton J. Peck	Member	February 15, 1968	January 20, 1969
Warren L. Smith	Member	July 1, 1968	January 20, 1969
Paul W. McCracken	Chairman	February 4, 1969	December 31, 1971
Hendrik S. Houthakker	Member	February 4, 1969	July 15, 1971
Herbert Stein	Member	February 4, 1969	
	Chairman	January 1, 1972	August 31, 1974
Ezra Solomon	Member	September 9, 1971	March 26, 1973
Marina v.N. Whitman	Member	March 13, 1972	August 15, 1973
Gary L. Seevers	Member	July 23, 1973	April 15, 1975
William J. Fellner	Member	October 31, 1973	February 25, 1975
Alan Greenspan	Chairman	September 4, 1974	January 20, 1977
Paul W. MacAvoy	Member	June 13, 1975	November 15, 1976
Burton G. Malkiel	Member	July 22, 1975	January 20, 1977
Charles L. Schultze	Chairman	January 22, 1977	January 20, 1981
William D. Nordhaus	Member	March 18, 1977	February 4, 1979
Lyle E. Gramley	Member	March 18, 1977	May 27, 1980
George C. Eads	Member	June 6, 1979	January 20, 1981
Stephen M. Goldfeld	Member	August 20, 1980	January 20, 1981
Murray L. Weidenbaum	Chairman	February 27, 1981	August 25, 1982

COUNCIL MEMBERS AND THEIR DATES OF SERVICE

Name	Position	Oath of office date	Separation date
William A. Niskanen	Member	June 12, 1981	March 30, 1985
Jerry L. Jordan	Member	July 14, 1981	July 31, 1982
Martin Feldstein	Chairman	October 14, 1982	July 10, 1984
William Poole	Member	December 10, 1982	January 20, 1985
Beryl W. Sprinkel	Chairman	April 18, 1985	January 20, 1989
Thomas Gale Moore	Member	July 1, 1985	May 1, 1989
Michael L. Mussa	Member	August 18, 1986	September 19, 1988
Michael J. Boskin	Chairman	February 2, 1989	January 12, 1993
John B. Taylor	Member	June 9, 1989	August 2, 1991
Richard L. Schmalensee	Member	October 3, 1989	June 21, 1991
David F. Bradford	Member	November 13, 1991	January 20, 1993
Paul Wonnacott	Member	November 13, 1991	January 20, 1993
Laura D'Andrea Tyson	Chair	February 5, 1993	April 22, 1995
Alan S. Blinder	Member	July 27, 1993	June 26, 1994
Joseph E. Stiglitz	Member	July 27, 1993	
	Chairman	June 28, 1995	February 10, 1997
Martin N. Baily	Member	June 30, 1995	August 30, 1996
Alicia H. Munnell	Member	January 29, 1996	August 1, 1997
Janet L. Yellen	Chair	February 18, 1997	August 3, 1999
Jeffrey A. Frankel	Member	April 23, 1997	March 2, 1999
Rebecca M. Blank	Member	October 22, 1998	July 9, 1999
Martin N. Baily	Chairman	August 12, 1999	January 19, 2001
Robert Z. Lawrence	Member	August 12, 1999	January 12, 2001
Kathryn L. Shaw	Member	May 31, 2000	January 19, 2001
R. Glenn Hubbard	Chairman	May 11, 2001	February 28, 2003
Mark B. McClellan	Member	July 25, 2001	November 13, 2002
Randall S. Kroszner	Member	November 30, 2001	July 1, 2003
N. Gregory Mankiw	Chairman	May 29, 2003	February 18, 2005
Kristin J. Forbes	Member	November 21, 2003	June 3, 2005
Harvey S. Rosen	Member	November 21, 2003	
	Chairman	February 23, 2005	June 10, 2005
Ben S. Bernanke	Chairman	June 21, 2005	January 31, 2006
Katherine Baicker	Member	November 18, 2005	July 11, 2007
Matthew J. Slaughter	Member	November 18, 2005	March 1, 2007
Edward P. Lazear	Chairman	February 27, 2006	January 20, 2009
Donald B. Marron	Member	July 17, 2008	January 20, 2009
Christina D. Romer	Chair	January 29, 2009	September 3, 2010
Austan D. Goolsbee	Member	March 11, 2009	
	Chairman	September 10, 2010	August 5, 2011
Cecilia Elena Rouse	Member	March 11, 2009	February 28, 2011
Katharine G. Abraham	Member	April 19, 2011	April 19, 2013
Carl Shapiro	Member	April 19, 2011	May 4, 2012
Alan B. Krueger	Chairman	November 7, 2011	August 2, 2013
James H. Stock	Member	February 7, 2013	
Jason Furman	Chairman	August 4, 2013	
Betsey Stevenson	Member	August 6, 2013	

Report to the President on the Activities of the Council of Economic Advisers During 2013

The Council of Economic Advisers was established by the Employment Act of 1946 to provide the President with objective economic analysis and advice on the development and implementation of a wide range of domestic and international economic policy issues. The Council is governed by a Chairman and two Members. The Chairman is appointed by the President and confirmed by the United States Senate. The Members are appointed by the President.

The Chairman of the Council

Jason Furman was confirmed by the U.S. Senate on August 1, 2013. Prior to this role, Furman served as Assistant to the President for Economic Policy and the Principal Deputy Director of the National Economic Council.

From 2007 to 2008 Furman was a Senior Fellow in Economic Studies and Director of the Hamilton Project at the Brookings Institute. Previously, he served as a Staff Economist at the Council of Economic Advisers, a Special Assistant to the President for Economic Policy at the National Economic Council under President Clinton and Senior Adviser to the Chief Economist and Senior Vice President of the World Bank. Furman was the Economic Policy Director for Obama for America. Furman has also served as Visiting Scholar at NYU's Wagner Graduate School of Public Service, a visiting lecturer at Yale and Columbia Universities, and a Senior Fellow at the Center on Budget and Policy Priorities.

Alan B. Krueger resigned as Chairman on August 2, 2013 to return to Princeton University, where he is the Bendheim Professor of Economics and Public Affairs.

The Members of the Council

Betsey Stevenson was appointed by the President on August 6, 2013. She is on leave from the University of Michigan's Gerald R. Ford School of Public Policy and the Economics Department where she is an Associate Professor of Public Policy and Economics. She served as the Chief Economist of the US Department of Labor from 2010 to 2011.

James H. Stock was appointed by the President on February 7, 2013. He served as Chief Economist of the Council of Economic Advisers from September 12, 2012 until then. Dr. Stock is on leave from Harvard University, where he is the Harold Hitchings Burbank Professor of Political Economy. Dr. Stock served as the Chair of the Harvard University Department of Economics from 2006 to 2009.

Katharine G. Abraham resigned as Member of the Council on April 19, 2013 to return to the University of Maryland, where she is a professor in the Joint Program in Survey Methodology and faculty associate in the Maryland Population Research Center.

Areas of Activities

A central function of the Council is to advise the President on all economic issues and developments. In the past year, as in the four previous years, advising the President on policies to spur economic growth and job creation, and evaluating the effects of the policies on the economy, have been a priority.

The Council works closely with various government agencies, including the National Economic Council, the Office of Management and Budget, White House senior staff, and other officials and engages in discussions on numerous policy matters. In the area of international economic policy, the Council coordinates with other units of the White House, the Treasury Department, the State Department, the Commerce Department, and the Federal Reserve on matters related to the global financial system.

Among the specific economic policy areas that received attention in 2013 were: housing policies; health care cost growth and the Affordable Care Act; individual and corporate taxation; college affordability and ratings; regional development; the economic cost of carbon pollution; renewable fuel standards; energy policy; intellectual property and innovation; infrastructure investment; regulatory measures; trade policies; poverty and income inequality; unemployment insurance and the minimum wage; labor force participation; job training; and foreign direct investment. The Council also worked on several issues related to the quality of the data available for assessing economic conditions.

The Council prepares for the President, the Vice President, and the White House senior staff a daily economic briefing memo analyzing current economic developments and almost-daily memos on key economic data releases. Chairman Furman also presents a monthly briefing on the state of the economy and the Council's energy analysis to senior White House officials.

The Council, the Department of Treasury, and the Office of Management and Budget—the Administration's economic "troika"—are responsible for producing the economic forecasts that underlie the Administration's budget proposals. The Council initiates the forecasting process twice each year, consulting with a wide variety of outside sources, including leading private sector forecasters and other government agencies.

The Council was an active participant in the trade policy process, participating in the Trade Policy Staff Committee and the Trade Policy Review Group. The Council provided analysis and opinions on a range of trade-related issues involving the enforcement of existing trade agreements, reviews of current U.S. trade policies, and consideration of future policies. The Council also participated on the Trade Promotion Coordinating Committee, helping to examine the ways in which exports may support economic growth in the years to come. In the area of investment and security, the Council participated on the Committee on Foreign Investment in the United States (CFIUS), reviewing individual cases before the committee.

The Council is a leading participant in the Organisation for Economic Co-operation and Development (OECD), an important forum for economic cooperation among high-income industrial economies. The Council coordinated and oversaw the OECD's review of the U.S. economy. Chairman Furman is chairman of the OECD's Economic Policy Committee, and Council Members and staff participate actively in working-party meetings on macroeconomic policy and coordination and contribute to the OECD's research agenda.

The Council issued a wide range of reports in 2013 and early 2014. In June, the Council released a report assessing the economic benefits of reforming US's "broken immigration system." In October, the Council released a report analyzing the negative impact that the government shutdown and debt limit brinksmanship had on the economy. Also in October, the Council released a report describing why the US provides such an attractive investment climate for firms across the globe and how this is beneficial to the US. In November, the Council released a report analyzing the recent health care cost trends in addition to the contributions the Affordable Care

Act has had on reducing health care cost growth. In December, the Council worked with the Department of Labor to study the benefits of extending unemployment insurance. In January 2014, the Council released a progress report on the "War on Poverty" that Lyndon B. Johnson declared 50 years prior. In February 2014, the Council transmitted the final report on the fifth Anniversary of the Recovery Act to Congress. All of the aforementioned reports can be found on the Council's website, and some of them are incorporated into this annual report as well. (http://www.whitehouse.gov/administration/eop/cea/factsheets-reports.)

The Council continued its efforts to improve the public's understanding of economic developments and of the Administration's economic policies through briefings with the economic and financial press, speeches, discussions with outside economists, and regular updates on major data releases and postings of CEA's Reports on the White House and CEA blogs. The Chairman and Members also regularly met to exchange views on the economy with the Chairman and Members of the Board of Governors of the Federal Reserve System.

Public Information

The Council's annual *Economic Report of the President* is an important vehicle for presenting the Administration's domestic and international economic policies. It is available for purchase through the Government Printing Office, and is viewable on the Internet at www.gpo.gov/erp.

The Council frequently prepared reports and blog posts in 2013, and the Chairman and Members gave numerous public speeches. The reports, posts and texts of speeches are available at the Council's website, www.whitehouse.gov/cea. Finally, the Council published the monthly *Economic Indicators,* which is available online at www.gpo.gov/economicindicators.

The Staff of the Council of Economic Advisers

The staff of the Council consists of the senior staff, senior economists, economists, staff economists, research economists, a research assistant, and the administrative and support staff. The staff at the end of 2013 was:

Senior Staff

Jessica Schumer . . . . Chief of Staff

Steven N. Braun . . . . Director of Macroeconomic Forecasting

Alexander G. Krulic. . . . . General Counsel

Adrienne Pilot .... Director of Statistical Office

Archana Snyder .... Director of Finance and
Administration

Senior Economists

David J. Balan.................... Industrial Organization, Technology,
Health

Marco Cagetti.................... Macroeconomics

Jane K. Dokko.................... Housing

Matthew Fiedler.................. Health

Tracy M. Gordon .... Tax, Budget

Douglas Kruse.................... Labor, Disability

Jordan D. Matsudaira .... Labor, Education

Cynthia J. Nickerson .... Agriculture, Environment, Evaluation

Ronald J. Shadbegian.............. Energy, Environment

Kenneth A. Swinnerton............ International

Staff Economists

Zachary Y. Brown .... Labor, Health Housing

John Coglianese .... Labor, Public Finance,
Macroeconomics

Kevin Rinz....................... Labor, Education

Research Economists

Philip K. Lambrakos .... Macroeconomics

Cordaye T. Ogletree.............. Energy, Environment and
International

Krista Ruffini .... Health

Rudy Telles Jr. .... International, Technology

Research Assistants

Brendan Mochoruk................ Tax, Budget

Jenny Shen....................... Energy, Environment

David N. Wasser .... Labor, Immigration, Education

Statistical Office

The Statistical Office gathers, administers, and produces statistical information for the Council. Duties include preparing the statistical appendix to the *Economic Report of the President* and the monthly publication *Economic Indicators*. The staff also creates background materials for economic analysis and verifies statistical content in Presidential memoranda. The Office serves as the Council's liaison to the statistical community.

Brian A. Amorosi . . . . Statistical Analyst

Wenfan Chen . . . . Economic Statistician

Office of the Chairman and Members

Andrea Taverna . . . . Special Assistant to the Chairman

Natasha Lawrence . . . . Special Assistant to the Members

Matthew L. Aks . . . . Special Assistant to the Chairman and Research Economist

Administrative Office

The Administrative Office provides general support for the Council's activities. This includes financial management, human resource management, travel, operations of facilities, security, information technology, and telecommunications management support.

Doris T. Searles. . . . . Administrative and Information Management Specialist

Anna Y. Lee. Financial Systems Analyst

Interns

Student interns provide invaluable help with research projects, day-to-day operations, and fact-checking. Interns during the year were: Katherine Allsop, Brian Bendett, Rachel Burdick, Katherine Carpenter, Benjamin Clark, Brian Collopy, Christopher Gum, Thomas Hedin, Ashwin Kambhampati, Michael Kennedy, Samsun Knight, Katelyn Lamson, Catherine Mahoney, Brennan Mange, David McCarthy, Elliot Melaney, J Mintzmyer, Ivan Mogensen, Benjamin Murray, Andrew Olenski, Sarah Orzell, Patrick Rooney, Chase Ross, Michelle Saipe, Julian Sarafin, Leah Soffer, Courtney Spetko, Benjamin Sprung-Keyser, Mattie Toma, Kate Tomlinson, William Weber, Katherine Wen, Kayla Wilding, and Andrew Winslow.

Departures in 2013

In August, David P. Vandivier left his position as Chief of Staff.

The senior economists who resigned in 2013 (with the institutions to which they returned after leaving the Council in parentheses) were: Bevin Ashenmiller (Occidental University), Benjamin H. Harris (Brookings Institution), Susan Helper (Case Western University), Justin Joffrion (U.S. Air Force Academy), Chinhui Juhn (University of Houston), Paul Lengermann (Federal Reserve Board), Emily Y. Lin (U.S. Department of the Treasury), Rodney D. Ludema (Georgetown University), James M. Williamson (U.S. Department of Agriculture), and Wesley Yin (UCLA).

The economists who departed in 2013 were David Cho (Princeton University) and Judd N.L. Cramer (Princeton University). David served the CEA for more than two years and was a recipient of the Robert M. Solow Award for Distinguished Service.

The staff economists who departed in 2013 were Nicholas Li, Ben Meiselman, Nicholas Tilipman, Lee Tucker, and Jeffrey Y. Zhang.

The research economists who departed in 2013 were Carys Golesworthy, Dina Grossman, and Spencer Smith.

Petra S. Starke resigned from her position as General Counsel. Michael Bourgeois resigned from his position as Special Assistant to the Chairman. Emily C. Berret resigned from her position as Special Assistant to the Members. Sarah A. Murray resigned from her position as Economic Statistician. Thomas F. Hunt resigned from his position as Staff Assistant.

STATISTICAL TABLES RELATING TO INCOME, EMPLOYMENT, AND PRODUCTION

C O N T E N T S

INTEREST RATES, MONEY STOCK, AND GOVERNMENT FINANCE
—*Continued*

General Notes

Detail in these tables may not add to totals due to rounding.

Unless otherwise noted, all dollar figures are in current dollars.

Because of the formula used for calculating real gross domestic product (GDP), the chained (2009) dollar estimates for the detailed components do not add to the chained-dollar value of GDP or to any intermediate aggregate. The Department of Commerce (Bureau of Economic Analysis) no longer publishes chained-dollar estimates prior to 1999, except for selected series.

Symbols used:
    p Preliminary.
    ... Not available (also, not applicable).

Data in these tables reflect revisions made by source agencies through February 28, 2014. In particular, tables containing national income and product accounts (NIPA) estimates reflect revisions released by the Department of Commerce in July 2013 and tables containing estimates from the current employment statistics (CES) survey reflect revisions released by the Department of Labor in February 2014.

Excel versions of these tables are available at *www.gpo.gov/erp*.

Notes on Streamlining

With extensive economic data now available online, the 2014 statistical appendix has been streamlined. Tables that have been retained (some in modified form) are listed on the following page, matched to their 2013 table numbers.

Data presented in the past remain available to the public through their source agencies. For each table in last year's statistical appendix, the Sources section starting on page 397 lists source agency (or agencies), website, and data program for the data featured, along with selected contact information.

2013-TO-2014 TABLE NUMBER MATCH

2013	2014	Title
B-1	B-2	Gross domestic product
B-2	B-2	Real gross domestic product
B-3	B-3	Quantity and price indexes for gross domestic product
B-4	B-1	Percent changes in real gross domestic product
B-25	B-5	Real exports and imports of goods and services
B-33	B-9	Median money income and poverty status of families and people, by race
B-35	B-11	Civilian population and labor force
B-42	B-12	Civilian unemployment rate
B-44	B-13	Unemployment by duration and reason
B-46	B-14	Employees on nonagricultural payrolls by major industry
B-47	B-15	Hours and earnings in private nonagricultural industries
B-49	B-16	Productivity and related data, business and nonfarm business sectors
B-56	B-8	New private housing units started, authorized, and completed and houses sold
B-60	B-10	Consumer price indexes for major expenditure classes
B-63	B-10	Changes in special consumer price indexes
B-69	B-18	Money stock and debt measures
B-73	B-17	Bond yields and interest rates
B-78	B-19	Federal receipts, outlays, surplus or deficit, and debt
B-79	B-20	Federal receipts, outlays, surplus or deficit, and debt, as percent of GDP
B-80	B-21	Federal receipts and outlays, by major category, and surplus or deficit
B-81	B-22	Federal receipts, outlays, surplus or deficit, and debt
B-82	B-23	Federal and State and local government current receipts and expenditures
B-86	B-24	State and local government revenues and expenditures
B-87	B-25	U.S. Treasury securities outstanding by kind of obligation
B-89	B-26	Estimated ownership of U.S. Treasury securities
B-91	B-6	Corporate profits by industry
B-97	B-7	Real farm income
B-112	B-4	Growth rates in real gross domestic product, by area and country

Historical data may be subject to revision, so source agencies should be consulted for data no longer shown on these pages. Early data that remain static and are not available on a source agency website, however, may be found in previous issues of the *Economic Report of the President* at *www.gpo. gov/erp* and *fraser.stlouisfed.org.*

Statistical agencies and data aggregators also offer tools allowing users to download, graph, map, and program data themselves. The Federal Reserve Bank of St. Louis, a notable aggregator of economic data, features an online database at its Federal Reserve Economic Data (FRED) site comprising more than 154,000 economic time series from 59 national, international, public, and private data sources. In addition to mobile apps and other data tools, FRED provides application programming interfaces (APIs) to allow developers to create applications or programs that directly utilize its website content. For more information, see *www.research.stlouisfed.org/fred2.*

Table B–1. Percent changes in real gross domestic product, 1965–2013

[Percent change from preceding period; quarterly data at seasonally adjusted annual rates]

Year or quarter	Gross domestic product	Personal consumption expenditures			Gross private domestic investment								Change in private inventories
					Total	Fixed investment							
						Total	Nonresidential					Residential	
		Total	Goods	Services			Total	Structures	Equipment	Intellectual Property Products			
1965	6.5	6.3	7.1	5.5	13.8	10.4	16.7	15.9	18.2	12.7		-2.6	
1966	6.6	5.7	6.3	4.9	9.0	6.2	12.3	6.8	15.5	13.2		-8.4	
1967	2.7	3.0	2.0	4.1	-3.5	-.9	-.3	-2.5	-1.0	7.8		-2.6	
1968	4.9	5.7	6.2	5.3	6.0	7.0	4.8	1.4	6.1	7.5		13.5	
1969	3.1	3.7	3.1	4.4	5.6	5.9	7.0	5.4	8.3	5.4		3.1	
1970	.2	2.4	.8	3.9	-6.1	-2.1	-.9	.3	-1.8	-.1		-5.2	
1971	3.3	3.8	4.2	3.5	10.3	6.9	.0	-1.6	.8	.4		26.6	
1972	5.2	6.1	6.5	5.7	11.3	11.4	8.7	3.1	12.7	7.0		17.4	
1973	5.6	5.0	5.2	4.7	10.9	8.6	13.2	8.2	18.5	5.0		-.6	
1974	-.5	-.8	-3.6	1.9	-6.6	-5.6	.8	-2.2	2.1	2.9		-19.6	
1975	-.2	2.3	.7	3.8	-16.2	-9.8	-9.0	-10.5	-10.5	.9		-12.1	
1976	5.4	5.6	7.0	4.3	19.1	9.8	5.7	2.4	6.1	10.9		22.1	
1977	4.6	4.2	4.3	4.1	14.3	13.6	10.8	4.1	15.5	6.6		20.5	
1978	5.6	4.4	4.1	4.6	11.6	11.6	13.8	14.4	15.1	7.1		6.7	
1979	3.2	2.4	1.6	3.1	3.5	5.8	10.0	12.7	8.2	11.7		-3.7	
1980	-.2	-.3	-2.5	1.6	-10.1	-5.9	.0	5.9	-4.4	5.0		-20.9	
1981	2.6	1.5	1.2	1.7	8.8	2.7	6.1	8.0	3.7	10.9		-8.2	
1982	-1.9	1.4	.7	2.0	-13.0	-6.7	-3.6	-1.6	-7.6	6.2		-18.1	
1983	4.6	5.7	6.4	5.2	9.3	7.5	-.4	-10.8	4.6	7.9		42.0	
1984	7.3	5.3	7.2	3.9	27.3	16.2	16.7	13.9	19.4	13.7		14.8	
1985	4.2	5.3	5.3	5.3	-.1	5.5	6.6	7.1	5.5	9.0		2.3	
1986	3.5	4.2	5.6	3.2	.2	1.8	-1.7	-11.0	1.1	7.0		12.4	
1987	3.5	3.4	1.8	4.5	2.8	.6	.1	-2.9	.4	3.9		2.0	
1988	4.2	4.2	3.7	4.5	2.5	3.3	5.0	.7	6.6	7.1		-.9	
1989	3.7	2.9	2.5	3.2	4.0	3.2	5.7	2.0	5.3	11.7		-3.2	
1990	1.9	2.1	.6	3.0	-2.6	-1.4	1.1	1.5	-2.1	8.4		-8.5	
1991	-.1	.2	-2.0	1.6	-6.6	-5.1	-3.9	-11.1	-4.6	6.4		-8.9	
1992	3.6	3.7	3.2	4.0	7.3	5.5	2.9	-6.0	5.9	6.0		13.8	
1993	2.7	3.5	4.2	3.1	8.0	7.7	7.5	-.3	12.7	4.2		8.2	
1994	4.0	3.9	5.3	3.1	11.9	8.2	7.9	1.8	12.3	4.0		9.0	
1995	2.7	3.0	3.0	3.0	3.2	6.1	9.7	6.4	12.1	7.3		-3.4	
1996	3.8	3.5	4.5	2.9	8.8	8.9	9.1	5.7	9.5	11.3		8.2	
1997	4.5	3.8	4.8	3.2	11.4	8.6	10.8	7.3	11.1	13.0		2.4	
1998	4.4	5.3	6.7	4.6	9.5	10.2	10.8	5.1	13.1	10.8		8.6	
1999	4.8	5.5	7.9	4.1	8.4	8.8	9.7	.1	12.5	12.4		6.3	
2000	4.1	5.1	5.2	5.0	6.5	6.9	9.1	7.8	9.7	8.9		.7	
2001	1.0	2.5	3.0	2.2	-6.1	-1.6	-2.4	-1.5	-4.3	.5		.9	
2002	1.8	2.5	3.9	1.8	-.6	-3.5	-6.9	-17.7	-5.4	-.5		6.1	
2003	2.8	3.1	4.8	2.2	4.1	4.0	1.9	-3.9	3.2	3.8		9.1	
2004	3.8	3.8	5.1	3.2	8.8	6.7	5.2	-.4	7.7	5.1		10.0	
2005	3.4	3.5	4.1	3.2	6.4	6.8	7.0	1.7	9.6	6.5		6.6	
2006	2.7	3.0	3.6	2.7	2.1	2.0	7.1	7.2	8.6	4.5		-7.6	
2007	1.8	2.2	2.7	2.0	-3.1	-2.0	5.9	12.7	3.2	4.8		-18.8	
2008	-.3	-.4	-2.5	.8	-9.4	-6.8	-.7	6.1	-6.9	3.0		-24.0	
2009	-2.8	-1.6	-3.0	-.8	-21.6	-16.7	-15.6	-18.9	-22.9	-1.4		-21.2	
2010	2.5	2.0	3.4	1.2	12.9	1.5	2.5	-16.4	15.9	1.9		-2.5	
2011	1.8	2.5	3.4	2.1	4.9	6.2	7.6	2.1	12.7	4.4		.5	
2012	2.8	2.2	3.3	1.6	9.5	8.3	7.3	12.7	7.6	3.4		12.9	
2013 ᵖ	1.9	2.0	3.6	1.1	5.5	4.5	2.8	1.4	3.1	3.4		12.1	
2010: I	1.6	2.1	4.0	1.2	13.6	.8	4.2	-25.0	31.2	-1.6		-12.2	
II	3.9	3.3	5.2	2.4	22.3	13.6	11.4	11.8	23.3	-2.0		23.2	
III	2.8	2.8	3.8	2.2	13.7	-.4	8.3	-5.8	18.0	6.1		-30.7	
IV	2.8	4.3	7.6	2.6	-3.5	8.5	8.6	7.7	11.8	5.0		7.9	
2011: I	-1.3	2.1	2.7	1.8	-7.5	-.5	-.9	-29.8	12.0	3.7		1.7	
II	3.2	1.5	.2	2.1	14.2	8.6	9.9	33.7	4.3	4.9		2.7	
III	1.4	2.1	1.2	2.5	2.5	14.8	16.7	28.4	20.3	5.3		6.1	
IV	4.9	2.4	5.0	1.1	31.9	10.0	9.5	14.4	10.2	5.5		12.2	
2012: I	3.7	2.9	4.6	2.1	10.5	8.6	5.8	7.0	8.3	1.3		23.0	
II	1.2	1.9	2.2	1.7	-1.6	4.7	4.5	6.9	5.3	1.8		5.7	
III	2.8	1.7	3.7	.7	6.5	2.7	.3	5.9	-3.9	2.8		14.1	
IV	.1	1.7	3.7	.6	-2.4	11.6	9.8	17.6	8.9	5.7		19.8	
2013: I	1.1	2.3	3.7	1.5	4.7	-1.5	-4.6	-25.7	1.6	3.7		12.5	
II	2.5	1.8	3.1	1.2	9.2	6.5	4.7	17.6	3.3	-1.5		14.2	
III	4.1	2.0	4.5	.7	17.2	5.9	4.8	13.4	.2	5.8		10.3	
IV ᵖ	2.4	2.6	3.2	2.2	4.5	3.8	7.3	.2	10.6	8.0		-8.7	

See next page for continuation of table.

TABLE B–1. Percent changes in real gross domestic product, 1965–2013—*Continued*

[Percent change from preceding period; quarterly data at seasonally adjusted annual rates]

Year or quarter	Net exports of goods and services			Government consumption expenditures and gross investment					Final sales of domestic product	Gross domestic purchases[1]	Gross domestic income[2]	Gross national product[3]
	Net exports	Exports	Imports	Total	Federal			State and local				
					Total	National defense	Non-defense					
1965		2.8	10.6	3.2	0.8	-1.3	7.9	6.6	5.9	6.9	6.4	6.5
1966		6.9	14.9	8.7	10.7	12.9	3.6	6.2	6.1	6.9	6.0	6.5
1967		2.3	7.3	7.9	10.1	12.5	1.9	5.0	3.3	3.0	3.0	2.7
1968		7.8	14.9	3.4	1.5	1.6	1.3	6.0	5.1	5.2	5.0	4.9
1969		4.8	5.7	.2	-2.4	-4.1	3.9	3.5	3.2	3.2	3.3	3.1
1970		10.8	4.3	-2.0	-6.1	-8.2	1.0	2.9	.9	-.1	-.1	.2
1971		1.7	5.3	-1.8	-6.4	-10.2	5.6	3.1	2.7	3.5	3.0	3.3
1972		7.5	11.2	-.5	-3.1	-6.9	7.2	2.2	5.2	5.5	5.5	5.3
1973		18.9	4.6	-.3	-3.6	-5.1	.2	2.8	5.2	4.8	5.8	5.9
1974		7.9	-2.3	2.3	.7	-1.0	4.6	3.7	-.3	-1.2	-.6	-.4
1975		-.6	-11.1	2.2	.5	-1.0	3.9	3.6	1.0	-1.1	-.5	-.4
1976		4.4	19.6	.5	.2	-.5	1.6	.8	4.0	6.5	5.1	5.5
1977		2.4	10.9	1.2	2.2	1.0	4.7	.4	4.4	5.3	4.8	4.7
1978		10.5	8.7	2.9	2.5	.8	6.0	3.3	5.5	5.5	5.5	5.5
1979		9.9	1.7	1.9	2.3	2.7	1.7	1.5	3.6	2.5	2.4	3.5
1980		10.8	-6.6	1.9	4.4	3.9	5.4	-.2	.6	-1.9	-.1	-.3
1981		1.2	2.6	1.0	4.5	6.2	1.0	-2.0	1.5	2.7	3.0	2.4
1982		-7.6	-1.3	1.8	3.7	7.2	-3.6	.1	-.6	-1.3	-1.0	-1.8
1983		-2.6	12.6	3.8	6.5	7.3	4.7	1.3	4.3	5.9	3.3	4.6
1984		8.2	24.3	3.6	3.3	5.2	-1.4	3.8	5.4	8.7	7.8	7.1
1985		3.3	6.5	6.8	7.9	8.8	5.7	5.7	5.4	4.5	4.0	3.9
1986		7.7	8.5	5.4	5.9	6.9	3.1	5.0	3.8	3.7	3.0	3.3
1987		10.9	5.9	3.0	3.8	5.1	.2	2.2	3.1	3.2	4.3	3.4
1988		16.2	3.9	1.3	-1.3	-.2	-4.3	3.9	4.4	3.3	5.1	4.3
1989		11.6	4.4	2.9	1.7	-.2	7.2	4.0	3.5	3.1	2.5	3.7
1990		8.8	3.6	3.2	2.1	.3	7.3	4.1	2.1	1.5	1.5	2.0
1991		6.6	-.1	1.2	.0	-1.0	2.4	2.2	.2	-.7	.0	-.2
1992		6.9	7.0	.5	-1.5	-4.5	5.9	2.1	3.3	3.6	3.3	3.5
1993		3.3	8.6	-.8	-3.5	-5.1	.0	1.2	2.7	3.3	2.2	2.7
1994		8.8	11.9	.1	-3.5	-4.9	-.8	2.8	3.4	4.4	4.4	3.9
1995		10.3	8.0	.5	-2.6	-4.0	.0	2.7	3.2	2.6	3.4	2.8
1996		8.2	8.7	1.0	-1.2	-1.6	-.5	2.4	3.8	3.9	4.3	3.8
1997		11.9	13.5	1.9	-.8	-2.7	2.8	3.6	4.0	4.7	5.1	4.4
1998		2.3	11.7	2.1	-.9	-2.1	1.3	3.8	4.5	5.5	5.3	4.4
1999		4.6	11.4	3.4	2.0	1.5	2.7	4.2	4.9	5.7	4.5	4.9
2000		8.4	12.8	1.9	.3	-.9	2.3	2.8	4.2	4.8	4.7	4.2
2001		-5.7	-2.9	3.8	3.9	3.5	4.7	3.7	1.9	1.1	1.1	1.1
2002		-1.9	3.4	4.4	7.2	7.0	7.4	2.9	1.2	2.3	1.4	1.7
2003		1.6	4.3	2.2	6.8	8.5	4.1	-.4	2.8	3.1	2.2	2.9
2004		9.4	11.0	1.6	4.5	6.0	2.0	-.1	3.4	4.2	3.7	3.9
2005		6.0	6.1	.6	1.7	2.0	1.3	.0	3.4	3.5	3.6	3.3
2006		8.9	6.1	1.5	2.5	2.0	3.5	.9	2.6	2.6	4.0	2.4
2007		8.9	2.3	1.6	1.7	2.5	.3	1.5	2.0	1.1	.1	2.2
2008		5.7	-2.6	2.8	6.8	7.5	5.5	.3	.2	-1.3	-.8	.0
2009		-9.1	-13.7	3.2	5.7	5.4	6.2	1.6	-2.0	-3.8	-2.6	-3.0
2010		11.5	12.8	.1	4.4	3.2	6.4	-2.7	1.0	2.9	2.7	2.8
2011		7.1	4.9	-3.2	-2.6	-2.3	-3.0	-3.6	2.0	1.7	2.5	2.1
2012		3.5	2.2	-1.0	-1.4	-3.2	1.8	-.7	2.6	2.6	2.5	2.7
2013 p		2.7	1.4	-2.3	-5.2	-7.0	-1.9	-.2	1.7	1.7		
2010: I		6.4	11.9	-2.9	3.8	-1.8	14.8	-7.1	.0	2.5	.5	1.7
II		9.5	20.2	2.9	8.5	6.4	12.3	-.8	2.8	5.5	2.8	3.9
III		10.9	14.5	-.3	3.7	7.6	-2.8	-3.1	.9	3.5	5.2	2.6
IV		12.4	.9	-4.1	-2.7	-3.5	-1.2	-5.0	4.5	1.4	1.6	3.2
2011: I		3.8	2.8	-7.5	-10.5	-14.2	-3.5	-5.4	-.3	-1.3	2.0	-.5
II		4.9	.7	-1.3	1.8	6.8	-6.5	-3.4	2.4	2.6	2.3	3.1
III		7.0	4.9	-2.5	-3.4	2.4	-13.1	-1.9	3.0	1.2	2.2	1.9
IV		2.7	5.9	-1.5	-3.1	-10.2	11.3	-.4	2.1	5.3	2.6	4.8
2012: I		4.2	.7	-1.4	-2.5	-6.7	5.4	-.6	3.4	3.1	5.4	3.0
II		3.8	2.5	.3	-.2	-1.0	1.2	.6	2.2	1.1	-.6	1.4
III		.4	.5	3.5	8.9	12.5	2.8	-.2	2.2	2.7	.9	2.4
IV		1.1	-3.1	-6.5	-13.9	-21.6	1.0	-1.0	2.2	-.5	4.9	.3
2013: I		-1.3	.6	-4.2	-8.4	-11.2	-3.6	-1.3	.2	1.4	2.4	.6
II		8.0	6.9	-.4	-1.6	-.6	-3.1	.4	2.1	2.5	3.2	2.7
III		3.9	2.4	.4	-1.5	-.5	-3.1	1.7	2.5	3.9	1.8	4.4
IV p		9.4	1.5	-5.6	-12.8	-14.4	-10.1	-.5	2.3	1.4		

[1] Gross domestic product (GDP) less exports of goods and services plus imports of goods and services.
[2] Gross domestic income is deflated by the implicit price deflator for GDP.
[3] GDP plus net income receipts from rest of the world.

Note: Percent changes based on unrounded GDP quantity indexes.

Source: Department of Commerce (Bureau of Economic Analysis).

TABLE B–2. Gross domestic product, 1999–2013

[Quarterly data at seasonally adjusted annual rates]

Year or quarter	Gross domestic product	Personal consumption expenditures			Gross private domestic investment							
		Total	Goods	Services	Total	Fixed investment						Change in private inventories
						Total	Nonresidential				Residential	
							Total	Structures	Equipment	Intellectual Property Products		
					Billions of dollars							
1999	9,665.7	6,316.9	2,286.8	4,030.1	1,884.2	1,823.4	1,361.6	283.9	713.6	364.0	461.8	60.8
2000	10,289.7	6,801.6	2,452.9	4,348.8	2,033.8	1,979.2	1,493.8	318.1	766.1	409.5	485.4	54.5
2001	10,625.3	7,106.9	2,525.2	4,581.6	1,928.6	1,966.9	1,453.9	329.7	711.5	412.6	513.0	−38.3
2002	10,980.2	7,385.3	2,598.6	4,786.7	1,925.0	1,906.5	1,348.9	282.9	659.6	406.4	557.6	18.5
2003	11,512.2	7,764.4	2,721.6	5,042.8	2,027.9	2,008.7	1,371.7	281.8	669.0	420.9	636.9	19.3
2004	12,277.0	8,257.8	2,900.3	5,357.5	2,276.7	2,212.8	1,463.1	301.8	719.2	442.1	749.7	63.9
2005	13,095.4	8,790.3	3,080.3	5,710.1	2,527.1	2,467.5	1,611.5	345.6	790.7	475.1	856.1	59.6
2006	13,857.9	9,297.5	3,235.8	6,061.7	2,680.6	2,613.7	1,776.3	415.6	856.1	504.6	837.4	67.0
2007	14,480.3	9,744.4	3,361.6	6,382.9	2,643.7	2,609.3	1,920.6	496.9	885.8	537.9	688.7	34.5
2008	14,720.3	10,005.5	3,375.7	6,629.8	2,424.8	2,456.8	1,941.0	552.4	825.1	563.4	515.9	−32.0
2009	14,417.9	9,842.9	3,198.4	6,644.5	1,878.1	2,025.7	1,633.4	438.2	644.3	550.9	392.2	−147.6
2010	14,958.3	10,201.9	3,362.8	6,839.1	2,100.8	2,039.3	1,658.2	362.0	731.8	564.3	381.1	61.5
2011	15,533.8	10,711.8	3,602.7	7,109.1	2,232.1	2,195.6	1,809.9	380.6	832.7	596.6	385.8	36.4
2012	16,244.6	11,149.6	3,769.7	7,379.9	2,475.2	2,409.1	1,970.0	437.3	907.6	625.0	439.2	66.1
2013 ᵖ	16,797.5	11,496.2	3,886.6	7,609.6	2,673.7	2,565.7	2,049.0	457.1	939.4	652.5	516.8	107.9
2010: I	14,672.5	10,042.3	3,304.9	6,737.4	1,989.5	1,977.5	1,594.4	352.4	682.7	559.2	383.1	12.1
II	14,879.2	10,134.7	3,325.6	6,809.1	2,092.7	2,042.6	1,641.8	364.5	719.0	558.3	400.8	50.1
III	15,049.8	10,234.3	3,362.4	6,871.9	2,164.6	2,043.0	1,677.4	361.1	751.2	565.1	365.6	121.5
IV	15,231.7	10,396.3	3,458.4	6,937.9	2,156.5	2,094.1	1,719.3	370.1	774.4	574.8	374.7	62.4
2011: I	15,242.9	10,527.1	3,532.2	6,995.0	2,120.4	2,098.9	1,721.8	340.8	798.0	582.9	377.1	21.5
II	15,461.9	10,662.6	3,588.2	7,074.4	2,199.9	2,154.1	1,773.1	370.1	809.9	593.1	381.0	45.8
III	15,611.8	10,778.6	3,622.3	7,156.3	2,222.2	2,235.7	1,848.9	397.5	849.8	601.6	386.8	−13.5
IV	15,818.7	10,878.9	3,668.2	7,210.7	2,385.7	2,293.8	1,895.7	413.9	873.0	608.8	398.1	91.9
2012: I	16,041.6	11,019.1	3,729.3	7,289.7	2,453.6	2,350.7	1,932.3	422.0	895.4	614.9	418.4	102.9
II	16,160.4	11,100.2	3,738.4	7,361.8	2,454.0	2,387.1	1,961.4	431.3	907.9	622.2	425.7	66.8
III	16,356.0	11,193.6	3,784.9	7,408.7	2,493.3	2,411.7	1,968.0	438.3	902.2	627.5	443.7	81.6
IV	16,420.3	11,285.5	3,826.1	7,459.4	2,499.9	2,486.9	2,018.2	457.8	925.0	635.4	468.8	13.0
2013: I	16,535.3	11,379.2	3,851.8	7,527.4	2,555.1	2,491.7	2,001.4	429.1	928.0	644.3	490.3	63.4
II	16,661.0	11,427.1	3,848.5	7,578.6	2,621.0	2,543.8	2,030.6	452.6	934.6	643.5	513.2	77.2
III	16,912.9	11,537.7	3,912.8	7,624.8	2,738.0	2,593.2	2,060.5	470.7	935.8	654.1	532.6	144.8
IV ᵖ	17,080.7	11,640.7	3,933.2	7,707.6	2,780.5	2,634.2	2,103.3	475.9	959.1	668.2	531.0	146.3
					Billions of chained (2009) dollars							
1999	12,071.4	7,788.1	2,460.9	5,344.8	2,231.4	2,165.9	1,510.1	494.9	662.4	391.1	633.4	75.5
2000	12,565.2	8,182.1	2,588.3	5,611.6	2,375.5	2,316.2	1,647.7	533.5	726.9	426.1	637.9	66.2
2001	12,684.4	8,387.5	2,666.6	5,736.3	2,231.4	2,280.0	1,608.4	525.4	695.7	428.0	643.7	−46.2
2002	12,909.7	8,600.4	2,770.2	5,840.0	2,218.2	2,201.1	1,498.0	432.5	658.0	425.9	682.7	22.5
2003	13,270.0	8,866.2	2,904.5	5,965.6	2,308.7	2,289.5	1,526.1	415.8	679.0	442.2	744.5	22.6
2004	13,774.0	9,205.6	3,051.9	6,154.1	2,511.3	2,443.9	1,605.4	414.1	731.2	464.9	818.9	71.4
2005	14,235.6	9,527.8	3,177.2	6,349.4	2,672.6	2,611.0	1,717.4	421.2	801.6	495.0	872.6	64.3
2006	14,615.2	9,814.9	3,292.5	6,519.8	2,730.0	2,662.5	1,839.6	451.5	870.8	517.5	806.6	71.6
2007	14,876.8	10,035.5	3,381.8	6,650.4	2,644.1	2,609.6	1,948.4	509.0	898.3	542.4	654.8	35.5
2008	14,833.6	9,999.2	3,297.8	6,700.6	2,396.0	2,432.6	1,934.4	540.2	836.1	558.8	497.7	−33.7
2009	14,417.9	9,842.9	3,198.4	6,644.5	1,878.1	2,025.7	1,633.4	438.2	644.3	550.9	392.2	−147.6
2010	14,779.4	10,035.9	3,308.7	6,727.2	2,120.4	2,056.2	1,673.8	366.3	746.7	561.3	382.4	58.2
2011	15,052.4	10,291.3	3,419.9	6,871.1	2,224.6	2,184.6	1,800.5	374.1	841.7	586.1	384.3	33.6
2012	15,470.7	10,517.6	3,534.1	6,982.7	2,436.0	2,365.3	1,931.8	421.6	905.9	605.8	433.7	57.6
2013 ᵖ	15,759.0	10,723.0	3,660.1	7,062.3	2,569.6	2,472.5	1,986.3	427.4	934.2	626.3	486.4	83.0
2010: I	14,597.7	9,915.4	3,247.0	6,668.3	2,012.9	1,997.9	1,615.0	359.7	697.7	557.6	383.0	9.8
II	14,738.0	9,995.3	3,288.0	6,707.2	2,116.9	2,062.8	1,659.3	369.8	735.2	554.7	403.5	48.8
III	14,839.3	10,063.7	3,319.1	6,744.6	2,185.7	2,060.8	1,692.8	364.4	766.2	563.0	368.1	116.2
IV	14,942.4	10,169.0	3,380.5	6,788.5	2,166.1	2,103.1	1,728.1	371.2	787.8	570.0	375.1	58.1
2011: I	14,894.0	10,221.3	3,402.8	6,818.2	2,124.3	2,100.7	1,724.1	339.8	810.6	575.2	376.7	22.0
II	15,011.3	10,258.9	3,404.6	6,854.1	2,196.1	2,144.4	1,765.3	365.3	819.2	582.0	379.2	42.9
III	15,062.1	10,311.9	3,415.2	6,896.6	2,209.9	2,219.8	1,835.0	388.9	858.0	589.6	384.9	−11.0
IV	15,242.1	10,373.1	3,457.0	6,915.5	2,368.2	2,273.4	1,877.3	402.2	879.1	597.6	396.2	80.6
2012: I	15,381.6	10,447.8	3,495.8	6,951.2	2,427.8	2,320.8	1,903.8	409.0	896.9	599.6	417.2	89.2
II	15,427.7	10,496.8	3,514.7	6,981.4	2,418.0	2,347.9	1,925.0	416.0	908.5	602.3	423.0	56.8
III	15,534.0	10,541.0	3,546.7	6,993.4	2,456.5	2,363.5	1,926.4	422.0	899.5	606.4	437.3	77.2
IV	15,539.6	10,584.8	3,579.2	7,004.7	2,441.8	2,429.1	1,971.9	439.4	918.8	614.9	457.5	7.3
2013: I	15,583.9	10,644.0	3,611.9	7,031.1	2,470.1	2,420.0	1,949.0	407.9	922.5	620.6	471.2	42.2
II	15,679.7	10,691.9	3,639.6	7,051.5	2,524.9	2,458.4	1,971.3	424.8	929.9	618.3	487.1	56.6
III	15,839.3	10,744.2	3,680.0	7,063.6	2,627.2	2,494.0	1,994.7	438.4	930.4	627.0	499.2	115.7
IV ᵖ	15,932.9	10,812.1	3,708.8	7,102.8	2,656.2	2,517.5	2,030.1	438.6	954.0	639.2	487.9	117.4

See next page for continuation of table.

[Quarterly data at seasonally adjusted annual rates]

Year or quarter	Net exports of goods and services			Government consumption expenditures and gross investment					Final sales of domestic product	Gross domestic pur-chases [1]	Gross domestic income [2]	Gross national product [3]
	Net exports	Exports	Imports	Total	Federal			State and local				
					Total	National defense	Non-defense					
	Billions of dollars											
1999	−261.4	989.2	1,250.6	1,726.0	610.4	382.7	227.7	1,115.6	9,604.9	9,927.1	9,698.1	9,692.8
2000	−380.1	1,094.3	1,474.4	1,834.4	632.4	391.7	240.7	1,202.0	10,235.2	10,669.8	10,384.3	10,326.8
2001	−369.0	1,028.8	1,397.8	1,958.8	669.2	412.7	256.5	1,289.5	10,663.5	10,994.3	10,736.8	10,677.1
2002	−425.0	1,004.7	1,429.7	2,094.9	740.6	456.8	283.8	1,354.3	10,961.7	11,405.2	11,050.3	11,028.8
2003	−500.9	1,043.4	1,544.3	2,220.8	824.8	519.9	304.9	1,396.0	11,493.0	12,013.2	11,524.3	11,580.3
2004	−614.8	1,183.1	1,797.9	2,357.4	892.4	570.2	322.1	1,465.0	12,213.2	12,891.8	12,283.5	12,367.1
2005	−715.7	1,310.4	2,026.1	2,493.7	946.3	608.3	338.1	1,547.4	13,035.8	13,811.1	13,129.2	13,189.0
2006	−762.4	1,478.5	2,240.9	2,642.2	1,002.0	642.4	359.6	1,640.2	13,790.9	14,620.3	14,073.2	13,926.3
2007	−709.8	1,665.7	2,375.5	2,801.9	1,049.8	678.7	371.0	1,752.2	14,445.9	15,190.1	14,460.1	14,606.8
2008	−713.2	1,843.1	2,556.4	3,003.2	1,155.6	754.1	401.5	1,847.6	14,752.3	15,433.5	14,621.2	14,893.2
2009	−392.2	1,583.8	1,976.0	3,089.1	1,217.7	788.3	429.4	1,871.4	14,565.5	14,810.1	14,345.7	14,565.1
2010	−518.5	1,843.5	2,362.0	3,174.0	1,303.9	832.8	471.1	1,870.2	14,896.7	15,476.7	14,915.2	15,164.2
2011	−568.7	2,101.2	2,669.9	3,158.7	1,304.1	835.8	468.2	1,854.7	15,497.4	16,102.6	15,587.5	15,794.6
2012	−547.2	2,195.9	2,743.1	3,167.0	1,295.7	817.1	478.6	1,871.3	16,178.5	16,791.8	16,261.6	16,497.4
2013 *p*	−497.3	2,259.8	2,757.0	3,124.9	1,245.9	770.8	475.1	1,879.0	16,689.6	17,294.8	......	......
2010: I	−495.1	1,746.4	2,241.4	3,135.7	1,269.2	811.9	457.3	1,866.5	14,660.4	15,167.5	14,627.4	14,875.9
II	−529.7	1,807.0	2,336.7	3,181.5	1,304.6	829.3	475.2	1,876.9	14,829.0	15,408.9	14,793.7	15,084.3
III	−543.8	1,860.3	2,404.0	3,194.7	1,321.6	846.3	475.3	1,873.1	14,928.2	15,593.5	15,050.5	15,249.5
IV	−505.3	1,960.4	2,465.7	3,184.2	1,320.1	843.5	476.6	1,864.2	15,169.3	15,737.0	15,189.0	15,447.2
2011: I	−554.7	2,029.5	2,584.1	3,150.0	1,297.4	822.0	475.4	1,852.6	15,221.4	15,797.6	15,326.2	15,491.2
II	−572.2	2,095.5	2,667.7	3,171.7	1,315.4	844.2	471.2	1,856.3	15,416.2	16,034.1	15,513.6	15,712.1
III	−553.7	2,143.4	2,697.1	3,164.6	1,308.5	851.6	456.9	1,856.1	15,625.3	16,165.5	15,694.9	15,884.0
IV	−594.4	2,136.2	2,730.7	3,148.5	1,294.9	825.6	469.3	1,853.6	15,726.8	16,413.1	15,815.3	16,091.0
2012: I	−590.8	2,173.4	2,764.2	3,159.7	1,291.8	816.3	475.5	1,867.9	15,938.7	16,632.4	16,104.6	16,289.6
II	−557.9	2,197.4	2,755.3	3,164.1	1,293.8	816.7	477.1	1,870.3	16,093.6	16,718.3	16,150.3	16,419.2
III	−524.4	2,199.2	2,723.5	3,193.5	1,322.1	841.9	480.2	1,871.4	16,274.4	16,880.4	16,269.6	16,603.7
IV	−515.8	2,213.7	2,729.5	3,150.7	1,275.2	793.7	481.5	1,875.4	16,407.3	16,936.1	16,522.0	16,677.3
2013: I	−523.1	2,214.2	2,737.3	3,124.1	1,255.0	775.8	479.2	1,869.1	16,471.9	17,058.4	16,690.9	16,772.7
II	−509.0	2,238.9	2,747.9	3,121.9	1,252.6	776.3	476.3	1,869.3	16,583.8	17,170.0	16,847.8	16,907.9
III	−500.2	2,265.8	2,766.0	3,137.5	1,251.2	777.3	473.9	1,886.3	16,768.1	17,413.2	17,004.6	17,175.9
IV *p*	−456.8	2,320.1	2,776.9	3,116.2	1,224.8	753.7	471.1	1,891.4	16,934.4	17,537.5	......	......
	Billions of chained (2009) dollars											
1999	−382.3	1,174.1	1,556.4	2,451.7	815.3	516.9	298.5	1,643.6	12,000.3	12,474.6	12,111.9	12,108.9
2000	−482.7	1,272.4	1,755.1	2,498.2	817.7	512.3	305.4	1,689.1	12,500.4	13,069.5	12,680.6	12,614.3
2001	−504.2	1,200.5	1,704.7	2,592.4	849.8	530.0	319.7	1,751.5	12,731.7	13,213.5	12,817.6	12,750.2
2002	−584.9	1,178.1	1,763.0	2,705.8	910.8	567.3	343.3	1,802.4	12,889.9	13,520.1	12,992.1	12,970.8
2003	−641.6	1,197.2	1,838.8	2,764.3	973.0	615.4	357.5	1,795.3	13,247.9	13,937.1	13,283.9	13,352.2
2004	−731.9	1,309.3	2,041.2	2,808.2	1,017.1	652.7	364.5	1,792.8	13,702.7	14,529.1	13,781.3	13,879.0
2005	−777.1	1,388.4	2,165.5	2,826.2	1,034.8	665.5	369.4	1,792.3	14,170.1	15,036.2	14,272.3	14,340.8
2006	−786.2	1,512.4	2,298.6	2,869.3	1,060.9	678.8	382.1	1,808.8	14,543.6	15,424.8	14,842.3	14,690.9
2007	−703.6	1,647.3	2,350.9	2,914.4	1,078.7	695.6	383.1	1,836.1	14,839.2	15,600.8	14,856.1	15,009.7
2008	−546.9	1,741.8	2,288.7	2,994.8	1,152.3	748.1	404.2	1,842.4	14,868.9	15,392.0	14,733.8	15,009.0
2009	−392.2	1,583.8	1,976.0	3,089.1	1,217.7	788.3	429.4	1,871.4	14,565.5	14,810.1	14,345.7	14,565.1
2010	−462.6	1,765.6	2,228.1	3,091.4	1,270.7	813.5	457.1	1,820.8	14,717.7	15,244.5	14,736.7	14,966.5
2011	−445.9	1,890.5	2,336.4	2,992.3	1,237.9	794.6	443.3	1,754.5	15,014.4	15,501.1	15,104.3	15,286.7
2012	−430.8	1,957.4	2,388.2	2,963.1	1,220.3	769.1	451.2	1,742.8	15,403.2	15,902.3	15,487.0	15,693.1
2013 *p*	−412.3	2,010.0	2,422.3	2,896.3	1,157.4	715.0	442.4	1,738.6	15,665.8	16,170.4	......	......
2010: I	−413.6	1,700.4	2,113.9	3,084.3	1,247.8	798.6	449.2	1,836.5	14,584.3	15,011.5	14,552.8	14,782.7
II	−474.3	1,739.3	2,213.6	3,106.2	1,273.4	811.0	462.4	1,832.8	14,686.3	15,215.4	14,653.4	14,925.1
III	−504.9	1,784.9	2,289.8	3,103.5	1,285.0	825.9	459.1	1,818.5	14,718.3	15,348.5	14,840.1	15,020.5
IV	−457.5	1,837.7	2,295.2	3,071.5	1,276.4	818.6	457.7	1,795.2	14,881.8	15,402.5	14,900.5	15,137.8
2011: I	−456.5	1,854.7	2,311.3	3,012.0	1,241.6	787.8	453.7	1,770.5	14,871.9	15,354.0	14,975.4	15,119.2
II	−438.3	1,876.9	2,315.2	3,002.4	1,247.0	800.8	446.2	1,755.5	14,961.8	15,451.6	15,061.5	15,235.6
III	−433.9	1,908.9	2,342.8	2,983.2	1,236.4	805.6	430.8	1,746.9	15,072.7	15,498.4	15,142.2	15,306.4
IV	−454.7	1,921.7	2,376.4	2,971.7	1,226.7	784.2	442.5	1,745.0	15,151.3	15,700.5	15,238.8	15,485.7
2012: I	−439.2	1,941.4	2,380.6	2,961.3	1,219.1	770.7	448.3	1,742.2	15,278.9	15,822.4	15,441.9	15,600.2
II	−435.3	1,959.8	2,395.1	2,963.5	1,218.5	768.8	449.7	1,745.0	15,360.8	15,864.4	15,418.0	15,656.2
III	−436.5	1,961.6	2,398.0	2,988.8	1,244.6	791.8	452.8	1,744.3	15,444.9	15,971.4	15,451.9	15,751.1
IV	−412.1	1,967.0	2,379.1	2,938.8	1,198.9	745.0	453.9	1,739.8	15,528.3	15,950.8	15,636.0	15,764.8
2013: I	−422.3	1,960.5	2,382.7	2,907.4	1,172.8	723.1	449.8	1,734.3	15,536.4	16,005.8	15,730.6	15,789.7
II	−424.4	1,998.4	2,422.9	2,904.5	1,168.2	722.0	446.2	1,736.0	15,616.2	16,104.1	15,855.4	15,893.9
III	−419.8	2,017.6	2,437.3	2,907.4	1,163.9	721.2	442.7	1,743.2	15,711.1	16,258.5	15,925.2	16,067.4
IV *p*	−382.8	2,063.5	2,446.2	2,866.2	1,124.7	693.6	431.1	1,741.1	15,799.4	16,313.1	......	......

[1] Gross domestic product (GDP) less exports of goods and services plus imports of goods and services.
[2] For chained dollar measures, gross domestic income is deflated by the implicit price deflator for GDP.
[3] GDP plus net income receipts from rest of the world.

Source: Department of Commerce (Bureau of Economic Analysis).

GDP, Income, Prices, and Selected Indicators | 369

TABLE B-3. Quantity and price indexes for gross domestic product, and percent changes, 1965-2013

[Quarterly data are seasonally adjusted]

| | Index numbers, 2009=100 | | | | | | Percent change from preceding period [1] | | | | | |
| | Gross domestic product (GDP) | | | Personal consumption expenditures (PCE) | | Gross domestic purchases price index | Gross domestic product (GDP) | | | Personal consumption expenditures (PCE) | | Gross domestic purchases price index |
Year or quarter	Real GDP (chain-type quantity index)	GDP chain-type price index	GDP implicit price deflator	PCE chain-type price index	PCE less food and energy price index		Real GDP (chain-type quantity index)	GDP chain-type price index	GDP implicit price deflator	PCE chain-type price index	PCE less food and energy price index	
1965	27.555	18.744	18.720	18.680	19.325	18.321	6.5	1.8	1.8	1.4	1.3	1.7
1966	29.373	19.270	19.246	19.155	19.761	18.829	6.6	2.8	2.8	2.5	2.3	2.8
1967	30.179	19.830	19.805	19.637	20.367	19.346	2.7	2.9	2.9	2.5	3.1	2.7
1968	31.660	20.673	20.647	20.402	21.240	20.163	4.9	4.3	4.3	3.9	4.3	4.2
1969	32.653	21.692	21.663	21.326	22.237	21.149	3.1	4.9	4.9	4.5	4.7	4.9
1970	32.721	22.835	22.805	22.325	23.281	22.287	.2	5.3	5.3	4.7	4.7	5.4
1971	33.798	23.996	23.964	23.274	24.377	23.449	3.3	5.1	5.1	4.3	4.7	5.2
1972	35.572	25.038	25.005	24.070	25.164	24.498	5.2	4.3	4.3	3.4	3.2	4.5
1973	37.580	26.399	26.366	25.367	26.125	25.888	5.6	5.4	5.4	5.4	3.8	5.7
1974	37.385	28.763	28.734	28.008	28.196	28.510	-.5	9.0	9.0	10.4	7.9	10.1
1975	37.311	31.435	31.395	30.347	30.557	31.116	-.2	9.3	9.3	8.4	8.4	9.1
1976	39.321	33.161	33.119	32.012	32.414	32.821	5.4	5.5	5.5	5.5	6.1	5.5
1977	41.133	35.213	35.173	34.091	34.494	34.977	4.6	6.2	6.2	6.5	6.4	6.6
1978	43.421	37.685	37.643	36.479	36.801	37.459	5.6	7.0	7.0	7.0	6.7	7.1
1979	44.800	40.795	40.750	39.713	39.478	40.729	3.2	8.3	8.3	8.9	7.3	8.7
1980	44.690	44.485	44.425	43.977	43.092	44.962	-.2	9.0	9.0	10.7	9.2	10.4
1981	45.850	48.663	48.572	47.907	46.856	49.087	2.6	9.4	9.3	8.9	8.7	9.2
1982	44.974	51.630	51.586	50.552	49.880	51.875	-1.9	6.1	6.2	5.5	6.5	5.7
1983	47.057	53.664	53.623	52.728	52.465	53.696	4.6	3.9	3.9	4.3	5.2	3.5
1984	50.473	55.570	55.525	54.723	54.644	55.482	7.3	3.6	3.5	3.8	4.2	3.3
1985	52.613	57.347	57.302	56.660	56.897	57.150	4.2	3.2	3.2	3.5	4.1	3.0
1986	54.460	58.510	58.458	57.886	58.849	58.345	3.5	2.0	2.0	2.2	3.4	2.1
1987	56.346	59.941	59.949	59.649	60.717	59.985	3.5	2.4	2.6	3.0	3.2	2.8
1988	58.715	62.042	62.048	61.973	63.288	62.091	4.2	3.5	3.5	3.9	4.2	3.5
1989	60.875	64.455	64.460	64.640	65.868	64.515	3.7	3.9	3.9	4.3	4.1	3.9
1990	62.044	66.848	66.845	67.439	68.491	67.039	1.9	3.7	3.7	4.3	4.0	3.9
1991	61.998	69.063	69.069	69.651	70.885	69.111	-.1	3.3	3.3	3.3	3.5	3.1
1992	64.202	70.639	70.644	71.493	73.019	70.719	3.6	2.3	2.3	2.6	3.0	2.3
1993	65.965	72.322	72.325	73.277	75.006	72.323	2.7	2.4	2.4	2.5	2.7	2.3
1994	68.628	73.859	73.865	74.802	76.679	73.835	4.0	2.1	2.1	2.1	2.2	2.1
1995	70.493	75.402	75.406	76.354	78.323	75.420	2.7	2.1	2.1	2.1	2.1	2.1
1996	73.169	76.776	76.783	77.980	79.799	76.728	3.8	1.8	1.8	2.1	1.9	1.7
1997	76.453	78.097	78.096	79.326	81.194	77.851	4.5	1.7	1.7	1.7	1.7	1.5
1998	79.855	78.944	78.944	79.934	82.198	78.358	4.4	1.1	1.1	.8	1.2	.7
1999	83.725	80.071	80.071	81.109	83.290	79.578	4.8	1.4	1.4	1.5	1.3	1.6
2000	87.149	81.894	81.891	83.128	84.744	81.641	4.1	2.3	2.3	2.5	1.7	2.6
2001	87.977	83.767	83.766	84.731	86.277	83.206	1.0	2.3	2.3	1.9	1.8	1.9
2002	89.539	85.055	85.054	85.872	87.749	84.359	1.8	1.5	1.5	1.3	1.7	1.4
2003	92.038	86.754	86.754	87.573	89.048	86.196	2.8	2.0	2.0	2.0	1.5	2.2
2004	95.534	89.130	89.132	89.703	90.751	88.729	3.8	2.7	2.7	2.4	1.9	2.9
2005	98.735	91.989	91.991	92.260	92.710	91.850	3.4	3.2	3.2	2.9	2.2	3.5
2006	101.368	94.816	94.818	94.728	94.785	94.782	2.7	3.1	3.1	2.7	2.2	3.2
2007	103.182	97.338	97.335	97.099	96.829	97.370	1.8	2.7	2.7	2.5	2.2	2.7
2008	102.883	99.208	99.236	100.063	98.824	100.243	-.3	1.9	2.0	3.1	2.1	3.0
2009	100.000	100.000	100.000	100.000	100.000	100.000	-2.8	.8	.8	-.1	1.2	-.2
2010	102.507	101.215	101.211	101.654	101.287	101.528	2.5	1.2	1.2	1.7	1.3	1.5
2011	104.400	103.203	103.199	104.086	102.743	103.884	1.8	2.0	2.0	2.4	1.4	2.3
2012	107.302	105.008	105.002	106.009	104.632	105.599	2.8	1.7	1.7	1.8	1.8	1.7
2013 p	109.301	106.487	106.590	107.210	105.935	106.852	1.9	1.4	1.5	1.1	1.2	1.2
2010: I	101.247	100.509	100.513	101.282	100.911	101.036	1.6	1.3	1.4	1.4	1.0	1.8
II	102.220	100.972	100.958	101.398	101.179	101.285	3.9	1.9	1.8	.5	1.1	1.0
III	102.923	101.432	101.418	101.698	101.427	101.609	2.8	1.8	1.8	1.2	1.0	1.3
IV	103.638	101.948	101.936	102.239	101.632	102.183	2.8	2.1	2.1	2.1	.8	2.3
2011: I	103.302	102.354	102.342	102.996	101.959	102.900	-1.3	1.6	1.6	3.0	1.3	2.8
II	104.115	103.024	103.002	103.938	102.522	103.792	3.2	2.6	2.6	3.7	2.2	3.5
III	104.468	103.651	103.650	104.529	103.039	104.307	1.4	2.5	2.5	2.3	2.0	2.0
IV	105.716	103.782	103.783	104.880	103.452	104.538	4.9	.5	.5	1.3	1.6	.9
2012: I	106.683	104.296	104.291	105.471	104.010	105.124	3.7	2.0	2.0	2.3	2.2	2.3
II	107.003	104.751	104.750	105.750	104.482	105.383	1.2	1.8	1.8	1.1	1.8	1.0
III	107.741	105.345	105.292	106.193	104.849	105.742	2.8	2.3	2.1	1.7	1.4	1.4
IV	107.780	105.640	105.667	106.622	105.187	106.150	.1	1.1	1.4	1.6	1.3	1.6
2013: I	108.087	105.994	106.105	106.909	105.542	106.467	1.1	1.3	1.7	1.1	1.4	1.2
II	108.751	106.165	106.259	106.878	105.711	106.526	2.5	.6	.6	-.1	.6	.2
III	109.859	106.685	106.778	107.387	106.077	107.010	4.1	2.0	2.0	1.9	1.4	1.8
IV p	110.508	107.103	107.204	107.666	106.410	107.406	2.4	1.6	1.6	1.0	1.3	1.5

[1] Quarterly percent changes are at annual rates.

Source: Department of Commerce (Bureau of Economic Analysis).

TABLE B–4. Growth rates in real gross domestic product by area and country, 1995–2014

[Percent change]

Area and country	1995–2004 annual average	2005	2006	2007	2008	2009	2010	2011	2012	2013[1]	2014[1]
World	3.6	4.7	5.2	5.3	2.7	−.4	5.2	3.9	3.1	3.0	3.7
Advanced economies	2.8	2.8	3.0	2.7	.1	−3.4	3.0	1.7	1.4	1.3	2.2
Of which:											
United States	3.4	3.4	2.7	1.8	−.3	−2.8	2.5	1.8	2.8	1.9	2.8
Euro area[2]	2.2	1.7	3.2	3.0	.4	−4.4	2.0	1.5	−.7	−.4	1.0
Germany	1.3	.8	3.9	3.4	.8	−5.1	3.9	3.4	.9	.5	1.6
France	2.2	1.8	2.5	2.3	−.1	−3.1	1.7	2.0	.0	.2	.9
Italy	1.6	.9	2.2	1.7	−1.2	−5.5	1.7	.4	−2.5	−1.8	.6
Spain	3.7	3.6	4.1	3.5	.9	−3.8	−.2	.1	−1.6	−1.2	.6
Japan	1.1	1.3	1.7	2.2	−1.0	−5.5	4.7	−.6	1.4	1.7	1.7
United Kingdom	3.4	3.2	2.8	3.4	−.8	−5.2	1.7	1.1	.3	1.7	2.4
Canada	3.2	3.2	2.6	2.0	1.2	−2.7	3.4	2.5	1.7	1.7	2.2
Other advanced economies	4.0	4.2	4.8	5.0	1.7	−1.1	5.9	3.2	1.9	2.2	3.0
Emerging market and developing economies	4.9	7.3	8.3	8.7	5.8	3.1	7.5	6.2	4.9	4.7	5.1
Regional groups:											
Central and eastern Europe	4.0	5.9	6.4	5.4	3.2	−3.6	4.6	5.4	1.4	2.5	2.8
Commonwealth of Independent States[3]	2.9	6.7	8.8	8.9	5.3	−6.4	4.9	4.8	3.4	2.1	2.6
Russia	2.8	6.4	8.2	8.5	5.2	−7.8	4.5	4.3	3.4	1.5	2.0
Excluding Russia	3.2	7.7	10.6	9.9	5.6	−3.1	6.0	6.1	3.3	3.5	4.0
Developing Asia	7.1	9.5	10.3	11.5	7.3	7.7	9.8	7.8	6.4	6.5	6.7
China	9.2	11.3	12.7	14.2	9.6	9.2	10.4	9.3	7.7	7.7	7.5
India[4]	6.2	9.3	9.3	9.8	3.9	8.5	10.5	6.3	3.2	4.4	5.4
ASEAN-5[5]	4.0	5.4	5.5	6.2	4.7	1.8	7.0	4.5	6.2	5.0	5.1
Latin America and the Caribbean	2.5	4.7	5.6	5.7	4.2	−1.2	6.0	4.6	3.0	2.6	3.0
Brazil	2.5	3.2	4.0	6.1	5.2	−.3	7.5	2.7	1.0	2.3	2.3
Mexico	2.4	3.2	5.0	3.1	1.2	−4.5	5.1	4.0	3.7	1.2	3.0
Middle East, North Africa, Afghanistan, and Pakistan	4.6	6.0	6.7	5.9	5.0	2.8	5.2	3.9	4.1	2.4	3.3
Sub-Saharan Africa	4.5	6.3	6.4	7.1	5.7	2.6	5.6	5.5	4.8	5.1	6.1
South Africa	3.1	5.3	5.6	5.5	3.6	−1.5	3.1	3.5	2.5	1.8	2.8

[1] All figures are forecasts as published by the International Monetary Fund. For the United States, the second estimate by the Department of Commerce shows that real GDP rose 1.9 percent in 2013.

[2] In 2014, consists of: Austria, Belgium, Cyprus, Estonia, Finland, France, Germany, Greece, Ireland, Italy, Latvia, Luxembourg, Malta, Netherlands, Portugal, Slovak Republic, Slovenia, and Spain.

[3] Includes Georgia, which is not a member of the Commonwealth of Independent States but is included for reasons of geography and similarity in economic structure.

[4] Data and forecasts are presented on a fiscal year basis and output growth is based on GDP at market prices.

[5] Consists of Indonesia, Malaysia, Philippines, Thailand, and Vietnam.

Note: For details on data shown in this table, see *World Economic Outlook,* October 2013, and *World Economic Outlook Update,* January 2014, published by the International Monetary Fund.

Sources: Department of Commerce (Bureau of Economic Analysis) and International Monetary Fund.

TABLE B–5. Real exports and imports of goods and services, 1999–2013

[Billions of chained (2009) dollars; quarterly data at seasonally adjusted annual rates]

Year or quarter	Exports of goods and services					Imports of goods and services				
	Total	Goods [1]			Services [1]	Total	Goods [1]			Services [1]
		Total	Durable goods	Nondurable goods			Total	Durable goods	Nondurable goods	
1999	1,174.1	819.0	533.8	287.7	354.4	1,556.4	1,286.1	724.1	572.2	267.7
2000	1,272.4	902.0	599.3	301.9	368.2	1,755.1	1,454.4	833.9	623.9	297.2
2001	1,200.5	846.5	549.5	300.1	352.3	1,704.7	1,407.3	781.6	640.5	294.7
2002	1,178.1	817.1	518.7	305.1	360.5	1,763.0	1,459.9	814.7	658.7	300.0
2003	1,197.2	832.4	528.0	311.3	364.1	1,838.8	1,531.3	849.7	697.9	303.8
2004	1,309.3	902.8	586.0	321.6	406.3	2,041.2	1,701.4	968.1	744.0	335.7
2005	1,388.4	969.2	641.1	331.8	418.4	2,165.5	1,814.7	1,050.2	773.0	346.1
2006	1,512.4	1,060.5	710.1	353.6	450.8	2,298.6	1,922.2	1,143.8	785.9	371.6
2007	1,647.3	1,140.4	771.1	372.6	506.2	2,350.9	1,957.5	1,172.9	792.3	389.0
2008	1,741.8	1,210.4	810.4	402.9	530.5	2,288.7	1,885.1	1,128.2	764.2	401.1
2009	1,583.8	1,064.7	671.9	392.8	519.1	1,976.0	1,587.3	893.1	694.2	388.7
2010	1,765.6	1,217.2	784.6	433.1	548.1	2,228.1	1,828.0	1,096.6	735.7	399.4
2011	1,890.5	1,303.9	855.5	450.9	586.3	2,336.4	1,923.4	1,194.6	740.7	411.8
2012	1,957.4	1,353.2	896.4	460.9	603.7	2,388.2	1,964.3	1,280.6	710.3	422.8
2013 ᵖ	2,010.0	1,384.9	913.7	474.9	624.8	2,422.3	1,988.4	1,327.9	694.7	433.2
2010: I	1,700.4	1,170.6	743.5	427.1	529.6	2,113.9	1,722.9	1,008.5	715.6	390.7
II	1,739.3	1,203.3	781.5	422.7	535.6	2,213.6	1,818.4	1,084.4	737.4	394.4
III	1,784.9	1,228.4	794.9	434.2	556.3	2,289.8	1,881.4	1,134.6	751.8	407.5
IV	1,837.7	1,266.4	818.5	448.5	571.0	2,295.2	1,889.2	1,158.8	737.9	404.9
2011: I	1,854.7	1,280.0	832.0	449.1	574.3	2,311.3	1,909.8	1,172.1	745.9	399.8
II	1,876.9	1,291.6	851.3	443.5	585.0	2,315.2	1,906.5	1,170.2	744.8	407.4
III	1,908.9	1,309.8	864.9	448.3	599.2	2,342.8	1,923.1	1,202.9	734.2	419.0
IV	1,921.7	1,334.3	873.9	462.7	586.6	2,376.4	1,954.4	1,233.0	738.0	420.9
2012: I	1,941.4	1,340.2	897.5	448.4	600.7	2,380.6	1,958.6	1,268.1	715.2	420.8
II	1,959.8	1,357.3	898.3	462.9	601.9	2,395.1	1,970.7	1,284.6	712.8	423.2
III	1,961.6	1,362.8	897.8	468.3	598.0	2,398.0	1,972.7	1,282.1	716.3	424.2
IV	1,967.0	1,352.6	892.0	464.0	614.2	2,379.1	1,955.1	1,287.6	696.8	423.1
2013: I	1,960.5	1,342.8	890.5	456.7	617.5	2,382.7	1,954.0	1,284.6	698.1	428.3
II	1,998.4	1,373.4	921.2	458.4	624.9	2,422.9	1,989.6	1,324.2	698.5	432.6
III	2,017.6	1,392.2	916.6	479.0	625.1	2,437.3	2,001.4	1,342.1	695.0	435.2
IV ᵖ	2,063.5	1,431.3	926.7	505.4	631.8	2,446.2	2,008.9	1,360.7	687.3	436.7

[1] Certain goods, primarily military equipment purchased and sold by the Federal Government, are included in services. Repairs and alterations of equipment are also included in services.

Source: Department of Commerce (Bureau of Economic Analysis).

TABLE B–6. Corporate profits by industry, 1965–2013

[Billions of dollars; quarterly data at seasonally adjusted annual rates]

Year or quarter	Total	Corporate profits with inventory valuation adjustment and without capital consumption adjustment												Rest of the world
		Domestic industries												
		Total	Financial			Nonfinancial								
			Total	Federal Reserve banks	Other	Total	Manu-factur-ing	Trans-porta-tion [1]	Utilities	Whole-sale trade	Retail trade	Infor-mation	Other	
SIC: [2]														
1965	81.9	77.2	9.3	1.3	8.0	67.9	42.1	11.4	....	3.8	4.9	....	5.7	4.7
1966	88.3	83.7	10.7	1.7	9.1	73.0	45.3	12.6	....	4.0	4.9	....	6.3	4.5
1967	86.1	81.3	11.2	2.0	9.2	70.1	42.4	11.4	....	4.1	5.7	....	6.6	4.8
1968	94.3	88.6	12.9	2.5	10.4	75.7	45.8	11.4	....	4.7	6.4	....	7.4	5.6
1969	90.8	84.2	13.6	3.1	10.6	70.6	41.6	11.1	....	4.9	6.4	....	6.5	6.6
1970	79.7	72.6	15.5	3.5	12.0	57.1	32.0	8.8	....	4.6	6.1	....	5.8	7.1
1971	94.7	86.8	17.9	3.3	14.6	69.0	40.0	9.6	....	5.4	7.3	....	6.7	7.9
1972	109.3	99.7	19.5	3.3	16.1	80.3	47.6	10.4	....	7.2	7.5	....	7.6	9.5
1973	126.6	111.7	21.1	4.5	16.6	90.6	55.0	10.2	....	8.8	7.0	....	9.6	14.9
1974	123.3	105.8	20.8	5.7	15.1	85.1	51.0	9.1	....	12.2	2.8	....	10.0	17.5
1975	144.2	129.6	20.4	5.6	14.8	109.2	63.0	11.7	....	14.3	8.4	....	11.8	14.6
1976	182.1	165.6	25.6	5.9	19.7	140.0	82.5	17.5	....	13.7	10.9	....	15.3	16.5
1977	212.8	193.7	32.6	6.1	26.5	161.1	91.5	21.2	....	16.4	12.8	....	19.2	19.1
1978	246.7	223.8	40.8	7.6	33.1	183.1	105.8	25.5	....	16.7	13.1	....	22.0	22.9
1979	261.0	226.4	41.8	9.4	32.3	184.6	107.1	21.6	....	20.0	10.7	....	25.2	34.6
1980	240.6	205.2	35.2	11.8	23.5	169.9	97.6	22.2	....	18.5	7.0	....	24.6	35.5
1981	252.0	222.3	30.3	14.4	15.9	192.0	112.5	25.1	....	23.7	10.7	....	20.1	29.7
1982	224.8	192.2	27.2	15.2	12.0	165.0	89.6	28.1	....	20.7	14.3	....	12.3	32.6
1983	256.4	221.4	36.2	14.6	21.6	185.2	97.3	34.3	....	21.9	19.3	....	12.3	35.1
1984	294.3	257.7	34.7	16.4	18.3	223.0	114.2	44.7	....	30.4	21.5	....	12.1	36.6
1985	289.7	251.6	46.5	16.3	30.2	205.1	107.1	39.1	....	24.6	22.8	....	11.4	38.1
1986	273.3	233.8	56.4	15.5	40.8	177.4	75.6	39.3	....	24.4	23.4	....	14.7	39.5
1987	314.6	266.5	60.3	16.2	44.1	206.2	101.8	42.0	....	18.9	23.3	....	20.3	48.0
1988	366.2	309.2	66.9	18.1	48.8	242.3	132.8	46.8	....	20.4	19.8	....	22.5	57.0
1989	373.1	305.9	78.3	20.6	57.6	227.6	122.3	41.9	....	22.0	20.9	....	20.5	67.1
1990	391.2	315.1	89.6	21.8	67.8	225.5	120.9	43.5	....	19.4	20.3	....	21.3	76.1
1991	434.2	357.8	120.4	20.7	99.7	237.3	109.3	54.5	....	22.3	26.9	....	24.3	76.5
1992	459.7	386.6	132.4	18.3	114.1	254.2	109.8	57.7	....	25.3	28.1	....	33.4	73.1
1993	501.9	425.0	119.9	16.7	103.2	305.1	122.9	70.1	....	26.5	39.7	....	45.8	76.9
1994	589.3	511.3	125.9	18.5	107.4	385.4	162.6	83.9	....	31.4	46.3	....	61.2	78.0
1995	667.0	574.0	140.3	22.9	117.3	433.7	199.8	89.0	....	28.0	43.9	....	73.1	92.9
1996	741.8	639.8	147.9	22.5	125.3	492.0	220.4	91.2	....	39.9	52.0	....	88.5	102.0
1997	811.0	703.4	162.2	24.3	137.9	541.2	248.5	81.0	....	48.1	63.4	....	100.3	107.6
1998	743.8	641.1	138.9	25.6	113.3	502.1	220.4	72.6	....	50.6	72.3	....	86.3	102.8
1999	762.2	640.2	154.6	26.7	127.9	485.6	219.4	49.3	....	46.8	72.5	....	97.6	122.0
2000	730.3	584.1	149.7	31.2	118.5	434.4	205.9	33.8	....	50.4	68.9	....	75.4	146.2
NAICS: [2]														
1998	743.8	641.1	138.9	25.6	113.3	502.1	193.5	12.8	33.3	57.3	62.5	33.1	109.7	102.8
1999	762.2	640.2	154.6	26.7	127.9	485.6	184.5	7.2	34.4	55.6	59.5	20.8	123.5	122.0
2000	730.3	584.1	149.7	31.2	118.5	434.4	175.6	9.5	24.3	59.5	51.3	−11.9	126.1	146.2
2001	698.7	528.3	195.0	28.9	166.1	333.3	75.1	−.7	22.5	51.1	71.3	−26.4	140.2	170.4
2002	795.1	636.3	270.7	23.5	247.2	365.6	75.1	−6.0	11.1	55.8	83.7	−3.1	149.0	158.8
2003	959.9	793.3	306.5	20.1	286.5	486.7	125.3	4.8	13.5	59.3	90.5	16.3	177.1	166.6
2004	1,215.2	1,010.1	349.4	20.0	329.4	660.7	182.7	12.0	20.5	74.7	93.2	52.7	224.9	205.0
2005	1,621.2	1,382.1	409.7	26.6	383.1	972.4	277.7	27.7	30.8	96.2	121.7	91.3	327.2	239.1
2006	1,815.7	1,559.6	415.1	33.8	381.3	1,144.4	349.7	41.2	55.1	105.9	132.5	107.0	353.1	256.2
2007	1,708.9	1,355.5	301.5	36.0	265.5	1,054.0	321.9	23.9	49.5	103.2	119.0	108.4	328.2	353.4
2008	1,345.5	938.8	95.4	35.1	60.4	843.4	240.6	28.8	30.1	90.6	80.3	92.2	280.8	406.7
2009	1,474.8	1,122.0	362.9	47.3	315.5	759.2	171.4	22.4	23.8	89.3	108.7	81.2	262.3	352.8
2010	1,793.8	1,398.6	405.3	71.6	333.8	993.3	284.9	44.6	29.8	102.2	118.3	94.7	318.7	395.2
2011	1,791.3	1,354.8	384.1	75.9	308.1	970.7	303.9	32.1	11.1	96.3	116.1	87.4	323.7	436.6
2012	2,180.0	1,761.1	477.4	71.7	405.7	1,283.7	404.3	51.5	37.1	137.8	149.2	110.6	393.2	418.9
2011: I	1,672.2	1,244.3	377.8	72.4	305.4	866.5	278.1	29.8	3.9	74.4	112.2	85.3	283.0	427.8
II	1,782.3	1,354.9	364.6	80.0	284.6	990.3	291.5	33.3	29.7	94.7	109.1	92.4	339.5	427.3
III	1,805.4	1,354.6	348.8	76.6	272.2	1,005.8	314.5	30.3	3.2	110.3	114.9	86.7	346.0	450.8
IV	1,905.4	1,465.2	445.1	74.7	370.4	1,020.1	331.7	35.1	7.9	105.9	128.2	85.1	326.2	440.2
2012: I	2,142.5	1,726.7	462.5	73.4	389.1	1,264.2	408.7	53.4	34.5	128.8	149.9	110.3	378.6	415.9
II	2,169.8	1,740.5	447.7	72.6	375.1	1,292.8	410.5	53.5	39.4	146.5	145.3	116.6	381.0	429.3
III	2,186.6	1,774.0	507.2	67.5	439.8	1,266.8	387.8	52.2	40.8	131.6	142.5	112.9	399.0	412.5
IV	2,221.1	1,803.0	492.1	73.3	418.7	1,310.9	410.1	47.1	33.6	144.4	159.0	102.5	414.2	418.1
2013: I	2,180.0	1,781.5	486.9	70.0	416.9	1,294.6	389.7	54.5	38.3	150.2	148.9	124.2	388.9	398.5
II	2,248.6	1,845.5	511.9	82.1	429.8	1,333.6	381.8	57.6	47.2	151.1	169.9	131.8	394.2	403.1
III	2,288.2	1,868.4	521.6	90.4	431.2	1,346.8	392.4	61.3	50.2	154.7	166.0	118.3	403.9	419.8

[1] Data on Standard Industrial Classification (SIC) basis include transportation and public utilities. Those on North American Industry Classification System (NAICS) basis include transportation and warehousing. Utilities classified separately in NAICS (as shown beginning 1998).
[2] SIC-based industry data use the 1987 SIC for data beginning in 1987 and the 1972 SIC for prior data. NAICS-based data use 2002 NAICS.

Note: Industry data on SIC basis and NAICS basis are not necessarily the same and are not strictly comparable.

Source: Department of Commerce (Bureau of Economic Analysis).

Table B–7. Real farm income, 1950–2014

[Billions of chained (2009) dollars]

Year	Total [2]	Total	Crops [3,4]	Livestock [4]	Forestry and services	Direct Government payments	Production expenses	Net farm income
1950	240.8	238.8	96.0	132.0	10.8	2.1	141.5	99.3
1951	260.9	258.9	95.6	152.1	11.2	1.9	152.3	108.6
1952	251.7	249.9	102.2	135.7	12.0	1.8	152.0	99.8
1953	226.8	225.4	93.1	120.1	12.2	1.4	141.3	85.4
1954	222.7	221.1	94.0	115.3	11.8	1.7	142.1	80.6
1955	215.1	213.6	91.6	110.0	12.0	1.5	142.4	72.6
1956	210.9	207.5	89.7	106.2	11.6	3.4	141.0	69.9
1957	208.8	202.7	81.9	109.0	11.7	6.1	142.2	66.5
1958	228.5	222.1	88.0	121.9	12.2	6.4	151.3	77.2
1959	219.3	215.4	85.5	116.8	13.1	3.9	157.3	62.0
1960	220.3	216.3	89.5	113.5	13.4	4.0	156.3	64.0
1961	229.0	220.5	89.3	117.4	13.8	8.4	161.4	67.5
1962	236.2	226.5	92.9	119.5	14.0	9.7	168.9	67.3
1963	239.2	229.9	98.9	116.4	14.6	9.4	174.3	64.9
1964	229.8	218.0	91.7	111.2	15.1	11.8	172.8	57.0
1965	248.3	235.2	101.5	118.4	15.3	13.1	179.5	68.8
1966	261.9	244.9	95.0	134.2	15.6	17.0	189.5	72.4
1967	254.8	239.2	96.9	126.0	16.3	15.5	192.5	62.2
1968	250.8	234.0	91.5	126.3	16.2	16.7	191.2	59.6
1969	260.0	242.6	90.7	135.2	16.6	17.5	194.1	65.9
1970	257.6	241.3	89.9	134.7	16.7	16.3	194.7	62.9
1971	258.9	245.8	97.6	131.1	17.0	13.1	196.3	62.6
1972	284.1	268.3	103.6	147.4	17.3	15.8	206.4	77.7
1973	374.7	364.8	163.1	183.2	18.5	9.9	244.5	130.1
1974	341.6	339.7	170.9	148.9	20.0	1.8	246.8	94.8
1975	319.9	317.3	160.3	136.8	20.2	2.6	238.7	81.2
1976	310.4	308.1	145.8	140.6	21.7	2.2	249.5	60.8
1977	308.9	303.7	145.3	134.4	24.1	5.2	252.4	56.5
1978	340.8	332.8	150.2	156.2	26.4	8.0	274.0	66.9
1979	369.5	366.1	163.4	174.5	28.2	3.4	302.3	67.2
1980	335.6	332.7	144.7	158.1	29.9	2.9	299.3	36.3
1981	341.8	337.8	162.2	144.7	31.0	4.0	286.5	55.2
1982	317.9	311.2	139.1	136.5	35.5	6.8	271.8	46.2
1983	286.7	269.4	106.0	130.5	32.9	17.3	260.1	26.6
1984	302.3	287.1	139.9	129.6	17.6	15.2	255.5	46.7
1985	280.9	267.4	128.4	120.3	18.7	13.4	231.2	49.7
1986	266.8	246.6	108.2	120.9	17.5	20.2	213.7	53.2
1987	281.0	253.0	107.6	126.4	19.1	27.9	217.6	63.4
1988	286.8	263.4	111.6	126.7	25.0	23.3	222.9	63.9
1989	297.3	280.4	126.4	129.5	24.5	16.9	225.1	72.1
1990	295.9	282.0	124.5	134.7	22.8	13.9	226.7	69.2
1991	278.1	266.2	117.6	126.3	22.3	11.9	219.8	58.3
1992	283.9	270.9	126.1	123.4	21.5	13.0	212.9	71.0
1993	283.5	265.0	114.3	127.2	23.5	18.5	218.9	64.6
1994	292.6	281.9	136.0	121.5	24.4	10.7	221.4	71.2
1995	279.6	270.0	127.2	116.4	26.4	9.7	226.9	52.7
1996	307.1	297.6	150.7	119.9	27.0	9.6	230.4	76.8
1997	304.8	295.2	144.1	123.3	27.8	9.6	239.1	65.7
1998	294.6	278.9	129.3	119.3	30.3	15.7	234.9	59.7
1999	293.4	266.5	115.9	118.9	31.8	26.9	233.8	59.6
2000	295.1	266.7	116.0	121.0	29.8	28.4	233.2	61.9
2001	298.3	271.5	113.4	127.0	31.1	26.8	232.8	65.5
2002	271.1	256.5	115.1	109.9	31.5	14.6	225.1	46.0
2003	298.2	279.2	125.2	121.0	33.0	19.0	227.9	70.3
2004	330.8	316.3	140.4	139.4	36.5	14.6	232.8	98.1
2005	324.5	298.0	124.3	137.5	36.1	26.5	238.9	85.6
2006	306.0	289.4	125.2	125.8	38.3	16.7	245.5	60.6
2007	348.8	336.6	155.2	142.2	39.2	12.2	276.9	71.9
2008	380.7	368.3	184.5	141.5	42.3	12.3	296.3	84.3
2009	343.3	331.2	168.6	119.8	42.7	12.2	283.0	60.4
2010	361.1	348.9	170.7	139.1	39.0	12.2	284.0	77.1
2011	417.1	407.0	200.5	159.5	47.1	10.1	302.8	114.3
2012	433.2	423.1	206.6	162.3	54.2	10.1	324.8	108.4
2013 _p_	453.0	442.5	216.0	169.9	56.6	10.5	330.5	122.5
2014 _p_	408.1	402.4	178.9	169.6	53.9	5.6	320.0	88.0

[1] The GDP chain-type price index is used to convert the current-dollar statistics to 2009=100 equivalents.
[2] Value of production, Government payments, other farm-related cash income, and nonmoney income produced by farms including imputed rent of farm dwellings.
[3] Crop receipts include proceeds received from commodities placed under Commodity Credit Corporation loans.
[4] The value of production equates to the sum of cash receipts, home consumption, and the value of the change in inventories.

Note: Data for 2013 and 2014 are forecasts.

Source: Department of Agriculture (Economic Research Service).

TABLE B–8. New private housing units started, authorized, and completed and houses sold, 1970–2014

[Thousands; monthly data at seasonally adjusted annual rates]

Year or month	New housing units started				New housing units authorized[1]				New housing units completed	New houses sold
	Type of structure				Type of structure					
	Total	1 unit	2 to 4 units[2]	5 units or more	Total	1 unit	2 to 4 units	5 units or more		
1970	1,433.6	812.9	84.9	535.9	1,351.5	646.8	88.1	616.7	1,418.4	485
1971	2,052.2	1,151.0	120.5	780.9	1,924.6	906.1	132.9	885.7	1,706.1	656
1972	2,356.6	1,309.2	141.2	906.2	2,218.9	1,033.1	148.6	1,037.2	2,003.9	718
1973	2,045.3	1,132.0	118.2	795.0	1,819.5	882.1	117.0	820.5	2,100.5	634
1974	1,337.7	888.1	68.0	381.6	1,074.4	643.8	64.4	366.2	1,728.5	519
1975	1,160.4	892.2	64.0	204.3	939.2	675.5	63.8	199.8	1,317.2	549
1976	1,537.5	1,162.4	85.8	289.2	1,296.2	893.6	93.1	309.5	1,377.2	646
1977	1,987.1	1,450.9	121.7	414.4	1,690.0	1,126.1	121.3	442.7	1,657.1	819
1978	2,020.3	1,433.3	125.1	462.0	1,800.5	1,182.6	130.6	487.3	1,867.5	817
1979	1,745.1	1,194.1	122.0	429.0	1,551.8	981.5	125.4	444.8	1,870.8	709
1980	1,292.2	852.2	109.5	330.5	1,190.6	710.4	114.5	365.7	1,501.6	545
1981	1,084.2	705.4	91.2	287.7	985.5	564.3	101.8	319.4	1,265.7	436
1982	1,062.2	662.6	80.1	319.6	1,000.5	546.4	88.3	365.8	1,005.5	412
1983	1,703.0	1,067.6	113.5	522.0	1,605.2	901.5	133.7	570.1	1,390.3	623
1984	1,749.5	1,084.2	121.4	543.9	1,681.8	922.4	142.6	616.8	1,652.2	639
1985	1,741.8	1,072.4	93.5	576.0	1,733.3	956.6	120.1	656.6	1,703.3	688
1986	1,805.4	1,179.4	84.0	542.0	1,769.4	1,077.6	108.4	583.5	1,756.4	750
1987	1,620.5	1,146.4	65.1	408.7	1,534.8	1,024.4	89.3	421.1	1,668.8	671
1988	1,488.1	1,081.3	58.7	348.0	1,455.6	993.8	75.7	386.1	1,529.8	676
1989	1,376.1	1,003.3	55.3	317.6	1,338.4	931.7	66.9	339.8	1,422.8	650
1990	1,192.7	894.8	37.6	260.4	1,110.8	793.9	54.3	262.6	1,308.0	534
1991	1,013.9	840.4	35.6	137.9	948.8	753.5	43.1	152.1	1,090.8	509
1992	1,199.7	1,029.9	30.9	139.0	1,094.9	910.7	45.8	138.4	1,157.5	610
1993	1,287.6	1,125.7	29.4	132.6	1,199.1	986.5	52.4	160.2	1,192.7	666
1994	1,457.0	1,198.4	35.2	223.5	1,371.6	1,068.5	62.2	241.0	1,346.9	670
1995	1,354.1	1,076.2	33.8	244.1	1,332.5	997.3	63.8	271.5	1,312.6	667
1996	1,476.8	1,160.9	45.3	270.8	1,425.6	1,069.5	65.8	290.3	1,412.9	757
1997	1,474.0	1,133.7	44.5	295.8	1,441.1	1,062.4	68.4	310.3	1,400.5	804
1998	1,616.9	1,271.4	42.6	302.9	1,612.3	1,187.6	69.2	355.5	1,474.2	886
1999	1,640.9	1,302.4	31.9	306.6	1,663.5	1,246.7	65.8	351.1	1,604.9	880
2000	1,568.7	1,230.9	38.7	299.1	1,592.3	1,198.1	64.9	329.3	1,573.7	877
2001	1,602.7	1,273.3	36.6	292.8	1,636.7	1,235.6	66.0	335.2	1,570.8	908
2002	1,704.9	1,358.6	38.5	307.9	1,747.7	1,332.6	73.7	341.4	1,648.4	973
2003	1,847.7	1,499.0	33.5	315.2	1,889.2	1,460.9	82.5	345.8	1,678.7	1,086
2004	1,955.8	1,610.5	42.3	303.0	2,070.1	1,613.4	90.4	366.2	1,841.9	1,203
2005	2,068.3	1,715.8	41.1	311.4	2,155.3	1,682.0	84.0	389.3	1,931.4	1,283
2006	1,800.9	1,465.4	42.7	292.8	1,838.9	1,378.2	76.6	384.1	1,979.4	1,051
2007	1,355.0	1,046.0	31.7	277.3	1,398.4	979.9	59.6	359.0	1,502.8	776
2008	905.5	622.0	17.5	266.0	905.4	575.6	34.4	295.4	1,119.7	485
2009	554.0	445.1	11.6	97.3	583.0	441.1	20.7	121.1	794.4	375
2010	586.9	471.2	11.4	104.3	604.6	447.3	22.0	135.3	651.7	323
2011	608.8	430.6	10.9	167.3	624.1	418.5	21.6	184.0	584.9	306
2012	780.6	535.3	11.4	233.9	829.7	518.7	25.9	285.1	649.2	368
2013 p	926.7	618.3	13.8	294.6	976.4	617.5	26.6	332.3	765.1	428
2012: Jan	723	513	....	194	714	461	22	231	540	338
Feb	713	462	....	243	739	486	26	227	566	366
Mar	707	483	....	214	785	477	23	285	588	349
Apr	754	505	....	240	749	484	23	242	667	352
May	711	515	....	181	806	499	23	284	613	369
June	757	530	....	219	785	501	24	260	628	360
July	741	512	....	217	839	520	29	290	673	369
Aug	749	537	....	205	827	520	28	279	686	374
Sept	854	591	....	254	921	559	29	333	651	384
Oct	864	595	....	252	908	570	26	312	741	365
Nov	842	576	....	256	933	574	29	330	677	398
Dec	983	620	....	345	943	584	30	329	672	396
2013: Jan	898	614	....	273	915	588	26	301	720	458
Feb	969	652	....	307	952	600	31	321	727	445
Mar	1,005	623	....	356	890	599	25	266	810	443
Apr	852	593	....	244	1,005	614	25	366	698	446
May	919	597	....	311	985	620	27	338	711	429
June	835	605	....	219	918	625	26	267	759	450
July	891	587	....	285	954	609	27	318	783	373
Aug	883	620	....	251	926	627	23	276	765	388
Sept	873	580	....	283	974	615	28	331	762	403
Oct	899	600	....	289	1,039	621	27	391	814	452
Nov	1,101	713	....	379	1,017	641	24	352	826	444
Dec p	1,048	681	....	344	991	610	26	355	778	427
2014: Jan p	880	573	....	300	945	599	27	319	814	468

[1] Authorized by issuance of local building permits in permit-issuing places: 20,000 places beginning with 2004; 19,000 for 1994–2003; 17,000 for 1984–93; 16,000 for 1978–83; 14,000 for 1972–77; and 13,000 for 1970–71.
[2] Monthly data do not meet publication standards because tests for identifiable and stable seasonality do not meet reliability standards.

Note: One-unit estimates prior to 1999, for new housing units started and completed and for new houses sold, include an upward adjustment of 3.3 percent to account for structures in permit-issuing areas that did not have permit authorization.

Source: Department of Commerce (Bureau of the Census).

TABLE B–9. Median money income (in 2012 dollars) and poverty status of families and people, by race, 2003-2012

Race, Hispanic origin, and year	Families[1]		Below poverty level				People below poverty level		Median money income (in 2012 dollars) of people 15 years old and over with income[2]			
			Total		Female householder, no husband present				Males		Females	
	Number (millions)	Median money income (in 2012 dollars)[2]	Number (millions)	Percent	Number (millions)	Percent	Number (millions)	Percent	All people	Year-round full-time workers	All people	Year-round full-time workers
TOTAL (all races)[3]												
2003	76.2	$65,767	7.6	10.0	3.9	28.0	35.9	12.5	$37,367	$51,813	$21,547	$39,516
2004[4]	76.9	65,715	7.8	10.2	4.0	28.3	37.0	12.7	37,094	50,649	21,476	39,039
2005	77.4	66,092	7.7	9.9	4.0	28.7	37.0	12.6	36,784	49,619	21,848	39,114
2006	78.5	66,514	7.7	9.8	4.1	28.3	36.5	12.3	36,744	51,198	22,792	39,846
2007	77.9	67,944	7.6	9.8	4.1	28.3	37.3	12.5	36,761	51,188	23,169	40,051
2008	78.9	65,607	8.1	10.3	4.2	28.7	39.8	13.2	35,363	50,952	22,253	39,125
2009[5]	78.9	64,323	8.8	11.1	4.4	29.9	43.6	14.3	34,452	52,629	22,434	39,858
2010[6]	79.6	63,434	9.4	11.8	4.8	31.7	46.3	15.1	33,915	52,814	21,878	40,480
2011	80.5	62,248	9.5	11.8	4.9	31.2	46.2	15.0	33,675	51,367	21,543	39,493
2012	80.9	62,241	9.5	11.8	4.8	30.9	46.5	15.0	33,904	50,683	21,520	40,019
WHITE, non-Hispanic[7]												
2003	54.0	74,827	3.3	6.1	1.5	20.4	15.9	8.2	40,363	57,795	22,847	42,493
2004[4]	54.3	74,143	3.5	6.5	1.5	20.8	16.9	8.7	40,938	57,110	22,409	42,451
2005	54.3	74,280	3.3	6.1	1.5	21.5	16.2	8.3	41,571	56,595	22,877	42,102
2006	54.7	75,008	3.4	6.2	1.6	22.0	16.0	8.2	41,639	57,446	23,604	42,006
2007	53.9	77,447	3.2	5.9	1.5	20.7	16.0	8.2	41,386	56,992	24,016	42,832
2008	54.5	74,724	3.4	6.2	1.5	20.7	17.0	8.6	39,893	55,822	23,193	42,091
2009[5]	54.5	72,087	3.8	7.0	1.7	23.3	18.5	9.4	39,377	56,167	23,485	43,103
2010[6]	53.8	72,561	3.9	7.2	1.7	24.1	19.3	9.9	39,127	57,555	22,868	43,526
2011	54.2	71,288	4.0	7.3	1.8	23.4	19.2	9.8	38,945	56,928	22,690	42,237
2012	54.0	71,478	3.8	7.1	1.7	23.4	18.9	9.7	38,751	56,247	22,902	42,171
BLACK[7]												
2003	8.9	42,907	2.0	22.3	1.5	36.9	8.8	24.4	27,448	41,734	20,700	34,484
2004[4]	8.9	42,725	2.0	22.8	1.5	37.6	9.0	24.7	27,581	38,558	21,101	35,428
2005	9.1	41,711	2.0	22.1	1.5	36.1	9.2	24.9	26,643	40,263	20,737	35,711
2006	9.3	43,581	2.0	21.6	1.5	36.6	9.0	24.3	28,543	40,401	21,755	35,230
2007	9.3	44,454	2.0	22.1	1.5	37.3	9.2	24.5	28,595	40,681	21,873	34,984
2008	9.4	42,528	2.1	22.0	1.5	37.2	9.4	24.7	26,931	41,176	21,538	34,324
2009[5]	9.4	41,116	2.1	22.7	1.5	36.7	9.9	25.8	25,411	42,136	20,842	34,758
2010[6]	9.6	40,643	2.3	24.1	1.7	38.7	10.7	27.4	24,533	39,727	20,689	35,850
2011	9.7	41,341	2.3	24.2	1.7	39.0	10.9	27.6	23,965	41,114	20,168	35,880
2012	9.8	40,517	2.3	23.7	1.6	37.8	10.9	27.2	24,923	39,816	20,021	35,090
ASIAN[7]												
2003	3.1	78,964	0.3	10.2	0.1	23.8	1.4	11.8	40,313	57,702	22,071	43,176
2004[4]	3.1	79,523	0.2	7.4	.0	13.6	1.2	9.8	40,137	56,906	24,946	44,508
2005	3.2	81,103	0.3	9.0	0.1	19.7	1.4	11.1	40,242	58,487	25,453	43,297
2006	3.3	84,968	0.3	7.8	0.1	15.4	1.4	10.3	42,611	59,333	25,283	45,835
2007	3.3	85,416	0.3	7.9	0.1	16.1	1.3	10.2	41,187	56,713	26,970	45,752
2008	3.5	78,465	0.3	9.8	0.1	16.7	1.6	11.8	39,038	55,224	24,644	47,144
2009[5]	3.6	80,315	0.3	9.4	0.1	16.9	1.7	12.5	39,961	57,193	26,059	47,772
2010[6]	3.9	79,210	0.4	9.3	0.1	21.1	1.9	12.2	37,725	55,293	24,814	44,146
2011	4.2	74,521	0.4	9.7	0.1	19.1	2.0	12.3	37,093	57,459	22,499	42,276
2012	4.1	77,864	0.4	9.4	0.1	19.2	1.9	11.7	40,227	60,253	23,335	46,371
HISPANIC (any race)[7]												
2003	9.3	42,786	1.9	20.8	0.8	37.0	9.1	22.5	26,283	32,976	17,031	28,791
2004[4]	9.5	43,080	2.0	20.5	0.9	38.9	9.1	21.9	26,203	32,696	17,567	29,532
2005	9.9	44,537	1.9	19.7	0.9	38.9	9.4	21.8	25,980	31,716	17,684	29,429
2006	10.2	45,552	1.9	18.9	0.9	36.0	9.2	20.6	26,707	33,676	17,945	29,260
2007	10.4	44,922	2.0	19.7	1.0	38.4	9.9	21.5	27,077	33,724	18,547	30,070
2008	10.5	43,153	2.2	21.3	1.0	39.2	11.0	23.2	25,597	33,292	17,507	29,263
2009[5]	10.4	42,530	2.4	22.7	1.1	38.8	12.4	25.3	23,825	33,868	17,352	29,848
2010[6]	11.3	41,387	2.7	24.3	1.3	42.6	13.5	26.5	23,610	33,534	17,157	30,641
2011	11.6	40,898	2.7	22.9	1.3	41.2	13.2	25.3	24,227	32,758	17,181	30,731
2012	12.0	40,764	2.8	23.5	1.3	40.7	13.6	25.6	24,592	32,516	16,725	29,508

[1] The term "family" refers to a group of two or more persons related by birth, marriage, or adoption and residing together. Every family must include a reference person.
[2] Adjusted by consumer price index research series (CPI-U-RS).
[3] Data for American Indians and Alaska natives, native Hawaiians and other Pacific Islanders, and those reporting two or more races are included in the total but not shown separately.
[4] For 2004, figures are revised to reflect a correction to the weights in the 2005 Annual Social and Economic Supplement.
[5] Beginning with data for 2009, the upper income interval used to calculate median incomes was expanded to $250,000 or more.
[6] Reflects implementation of Census 2010-based population controls comparable to succeeding years.
[7] The Current Population Survey allows respondents to choose more than one race. Data shown are for "white alone, non-Hispanic," "black alone," and "Asian alone" race categories. ("Black" is also "black or African American.") Family race and Hispanic origin are based on the reference person.

Note: Poverty thresholds are updated each year to reflect changes in the consumer price index (CPI-U).
For details see publication Series P–60 on the Current Population Survey and Annual Social and Economic Supplements.

Source: Department of Commerce (Bureau of the Census).

TABLE B–10. Changes in consumer price indexes, 1945–2013

[For all urban consumers; percent change]

December to December	All items	All items less food and energy					Food			Energy[4]		C-CPI-U[5]
		Total[1]	Shelter[2]	Medical care[3]	Apparel	New vehicles	Total[1]	At home	Away from home	Total[1]	Gasoline	
1945	2.2			2.6	4.9		3.5				-1.4	
1946	18.1			8.3	18.1		31.3				7.8	
1947	8.8			6.9	8.2		11.3				16.4	
1948	3.0			5.8	5.1	11.5	-.8	-1.1			6.2	
1949	-2.1			1.4	-7.4	4.0	-3.9	-3.7			1.6	
1950	5.9			3.4	5.3	.2	9.8	9.5			1.6	
1951	6.0			5.8	5.7	9.7	7.1	7.6			2.1	
1952	.8			4.3	-2.9	4.4	-1.0	-1.3			.5	
1953	.7		3.2	3.5	.7	-1.7	-1.1	-1.6			10.1	
1954	-.7		1.8	2.3	-.7	1.3	-1.8	-2.3	0.9		-1.4	
1955	.4		.9	3.3	.5	-2.3	-.7	-1.0	1.4		4.2	
1956	3.0		2.6	3.2	2.5	7.8	2.9	2.7	2.7		3.1	
1957	2.9		3.4	4.7	.9	2.0	2.8	3.0	3.9		2.2	
1958	1.8	1.7	.8	4.5	.2	6.1	2.4	1.9	2.1	-0.9	-3.8	
1959	1.7	2.0	2.0	3.8	1.3	-.2	-1.0	-1.3	3.3	4.7	7.0	
1960	1.4	1.0	1.6	3.2	1.5	-3.0	3.1	3.2	2.4	1.3	1.2	
1961	.7	1.3	.8	3.1	.4	.2	-.7	-1.6	2.3	-1.3	-3.2	
1962	1.3	1.3	.8	2.2	.6	-1.0	1.3	1.3	3.0	2.2	3.8	
1963	1.6	1.6	1.9	2.5	1.7	-.4	2.0	1.6	1.8	-.9	-2.4	
1964	1.0	1.2	1.5	2.1	.4	-.6	1.3	1.5	1.4	.0	.0	
1965	1.9	1.5	2.2	2.8	1.3	-2.9	3.5	3.6	3.2	1.8	4.1	
1966	3.5	3.3	4.0	6.7	3.9	.0	4.0	3.2	5.5	1.7	3.2	
1967	3.0	3.8	2.8	6.3	4.2	2.8	1.2	.3	4.6	1.7	1.5	
1968	4.7	5.1	6.5	6.2	6.3	1.4	4.4	4.0	5.6	1.7	1.5	
1969	6.2	6.2	8.7	6.2	5.2	2.1	7.0	7.1	7.4	2.9	3.4	
1970	5.6	6.6	8.9	7.4	3.9	6.6	2.3	1.3	6.1	4.8	2.5	
1971	3.3	3.1	2.7	4.6	2.1	-3.2	4.3	4.3	4.4	3.1	-.4	
1972	3.4	3.0	4.0	3.3	2.6	.2	4.6	5.1	4.2	2.6	2.8	
1973	8.7	4.7	7.1	5.3	4.4	1.3	20.3	22.0	12.7	17.0	19.6	
1974	12.3	11.1	11.4	12.6	8.7	11.4	12.0	12.4	11.3	21.6	20.7	
1975	6.9	6.7	7.2	9.8	2.4	7.3	6.6	6.2	7.4	11.4	11.0	
1976	4.9	6.1	4.2	10.0	4.6	4.8	.5	-.8	6.0	7.1	2.8	
1977	6.7	6.5	8.8	8.9	4.3	7.2	8.1	7.9	7.9	7.2	4.8	
1978	9.0	8.5	11.4	8.8	3.1	6.2	11.8	12.5	10.4	7.9	8.6	
1979	13.3	11.3	17.5	10.1	5.5	7.4	10.2	9.7	11.4	37.5	52.1	
1980	12.5	12.2	15.0	9.9	6.8	7.4	10.2	10.5	9.6	18.0	18.9	
1981	8.9	9.5	9.9	12.5	3.5	6.8	4.3	2.9	7.1	11.9	9.4	
1982	3.8	4.5	2.4	11.0	1.6	1.4	3.1	2.3	5.1	1.3	-6.7	
1983	3.8	4.8	4.7	6.4	2.9	3.3	2.7	1.8	4.1	-.5	-1.6	
1984	3.9	4.7	5.2	6.1	2.0	2.5	3.8	3.6	4.2	.2	-2.5	
1985	3.8	4.3	6.0	6.8	2.8	3.6	2.6	2.0	3.8	1.8	3.0	
1986	1.1	3.8	4.6	7.7	.9	5.6	3.8	3.7	4.3	-19.7	-30.7	
1987	4.4	4.2	4.8	5.8	4.8	1.8	3.5	3.5	3.7	8.2	18.6	
1988	4.4	4.7	4.5	6.9	4.7	2.2	5.2	5.6	4.4	.5	-1.8	
1989	4.6	4.4	4.9	8.5	1.0	2.4	5.6	6.2	4.6	5.1	6.5	
1990	6.1	5.2	5.2	9.6	5.1	2.0	5.3	5.8	4.5	18.1	36.8	
1991	3.1	4.4	3.9	7.9	3.4	3.2	1.9	1.3	2.9	-7.4	-16.2	
1992	2.9	3.3	2.9	6.6	1.4	2.3	1.5	1.5	1.4	2.0	2.0	
1993	2.7	3.2	3.0	5.4	.9	3.3	2.9	3.5	1.9	-1.4	-5.9	
1994	2.7	2.6	3.0	4.9	-1.6	3.3	2.9	3.5	1.9	2.2	6.4	
1995	2.5	3.0	3.5	3.9	.1	1.9	2.1	2.0	2.2	-1.3	-4.2	
1996	3.3	2.6	2.9	3.0	-.2	1.8	4.3	4.9	3.1	8.6	12.4	
1997	1.7	2.2	3.4	2.8	1.0	-.9	1.5	1.0	2.6	-3.4	-6.1	
1998	1.6	2.4	3.3	3.4	-.7	.0	2.3	2.1	2.5	-8.8	-15.4	
1999	2.7	1.9	2.5	3.7	-.5	-.3	1.9	1.7	2.3	13.4	30.1	
2000	3.4	2.6	3.4	4.2	-1.8	-.2	2.8	2.9	2.4	14.2	13.9	2.6
2001	1.6	2.7	4.2	4.7	-3.2	-.1	2.8	2.6	3.0	-13.0	-24.9	1.3
2002	2.4	1.9	3.1	5.0	-1.8	-2.0	1.5	.8	2.3	10.7	24.8	2.0
2003	1.9	1.1	2.2	3.7	-2.1	-1.8	3.6	4.5	2.3	6.9	6.8	1.7
2004	3.3	2.2	2.7	4.2	-.2	.6	2.7	2.4	3.0	16.6	26.1	3.2
2005	3.4	2.2	2.6	4.3	-1.1	-.4	2.3	1.7	3.2	17.1	16.1	2.9
2006	2.5	2.6	4.2	3.6	.9	-.9	2.1	1.4	3.2	2.9	6.4	2.3
2007	4.1	2.4	3.1	5.2	-.3	-.3	4.9	5.6	4.0	17.4	29.6	3.7
2008	.1	1.8	1.9	2.6	-1.0	-3.2	5.9	6.6	5.0	-21.3	-43.1	.2
2009	2.7	1.8	.3	3.4	1.9	4.9	-.5	-2.4	1.9	18.2	53.5	2.5
2010	1.5	.8	.4	3.3	-1.1	-.2	1.5	1.7	1.3	7.7	13.8	1.3
2011	3.0	2.2	1.9	3.5	4.6	3.2	4.7	6.0	2.9	6.6	9.9	2.9
2012	1.7	1.9	2.2	3.2	1.8	1.6	1.8	1.3	2.5	.5	1.7	1.5
2013	1.5	1.7	2.5	2.0	.6	.4	1.1	.4	2.1	.5	-1.0	1.3

[1] Includes other items not shown separately.
[2] Data beginning with 1983 incorporate a rental equivalence measure for homeowners' costs.
[3] Commodities and services.
[4] Household energy--electricity, utility (piped) gas service, fuel oil, etc.--and motor fuel.
[5] Chained consumer price index (C-CPI-U) introduced in 2002. Reflects the effect of substitution that consumers make across item categories in response to changes in relative prices. Data for 2013 are subject to revision.

Note. Changes from December to December are based on unadjusted indexes.
Series reflect changes in composition and renaming beginning in 1998, and formula and methodology changes in 1999.

Source: Department of Labor (Bureau of Labor Statistics).

TABLE B–11. Civilian population and labor force, 1929–2014

[Monthly data seasonally adjusted, except as noted]

Year or month	Civilian noninstitu-tional population [1]	Civilian labor force					Not in labor force	Civilian labor force participa-tion rate [2]	Civilian employ-ment/population ratio [3]	Unemploy-ment rate, civilian workers [4]
		Total	Employment			Unemploy-ment				
			Total	Agricultural	Non-agricultural					
	Thousands of persons 14 years of age and over							Percent		
1929		49,180	47,630	10,450	37,180	1,550				3.2
1930		49,820	45,480	10,340	35,140	4,340				8.7
1931		50,420	42,400	10,290	32,110	8,020				15.9
1932		51,000	38,940	10,170	28,770	12,060				23.6
1933		51,590	38,760	10,090	28,670	12,830				24.9
1934		52,230	40,890	9,900	30,990	11,340				21.7
1935		52,870	42,260	10,110	32,150	10,610				20.1
1936		53,440	44,410	10,000	34,410	9,030				16.9
1937		54,000	46,300	9,820	36,480	7,700				14.3
1938		54,610	44,220	9,690	34,530	10,390				19.0
1939		55,230	45,750	9,610	36,140	9,480				17.2
1940	99,840	55,640	47,520	9,540	37,980	8,120	44,200	55.7	47.6	14.6
1941	99,900	55,910	50,350	9,100	41,250	5,560	43,990	56.0	50.4	9.9
1942	98,640	56,410	53,750	9,250	44,500	2,660	42,230	57.2	54.5	4.7
1943	94,640	55,540	54,470	9,080	45,390	1,070	39,100	58.7	57.6	1.9
1944	93,220	54,630	53,960	8,950	45,010	670	38,590	58.6	57.9	1.2
1945	94,090	53,860	52,820	8,580	44,240	1,040	40,230	57.2	56.1	1.9
1946	103,070	57,520	55,250	8,320	46,930	2,270	45,550	55.8	53.6	3.9
1947	106,018	60,168	57,812	8,256	49,557	2,356	45,850	56.8	54.5	3.9
	Thousands of persons 16 years of age and over									
1947	101,827	59,350	57,038	7,890	49,148	2,311	42,477	58.3	56.0	3.9
1948	103,068	60,621	58,343	7,629	50,714	2,276	42,447	58.8	56.6	3.8
1949	103,994	61,286	57,651	7,658	49,993	3,637	42,708	58.9	55.4	5.9
1950	104,995	62,208	58,918	7,160	51,758	3,288	42,787	59.2	56.1	5.3
1951	104,621	62,017	59,961	6,726	53,235	2,055	42,604	59.2	57.3	3.3
1952	105,231	62,138	60,250	6,500	53,749	1,883	43,093	59.0	57.3	3.0
1953	107,056	63,015	61,179	6,260	54,919	1,834	44,041	58.9	57.1	2.9
1954	108,321	63,643	60,109	6,205	53,904	3,532	44,678	58.8	55.5	5.5
1955	109,683	65,023	62,170	6,450	55,722	2,852	44,660	59.3	56.7	4.4
1956	110,954	66,552	63,799	6,283	57,514	2,750	44,402	60.0	57.5	4.1
1957	112,265	66,929	64,071	5,947	58,123	2,859	45,336	59.6	57.1	4.3
1958	113,727	67,639	63,036	5,586	57,450	4,602	46,088	59.5	55.4	6.8
1959	115,329	68,369	64,630	5,565	59,065	3,740	46,960	59.3	56.0	5.5
1960	117,245	69,628	65,778	5,458	60,318	3,852	47,617	59.4	56.1	5.5
1961	118,771	70,459	65,746	5,200	60,546	4,714	48,312	59.3	55.4	6.7
1962	120,153	70,614	66,702	4,944	61,759	3,911	49,539	58.8	55.5	5.5
1963	122,416	71,833	67,762	4,687	63,076	4,070	50,583	58.7	55.4	5.7
1964	124,485	73,091	69,305	4,523	64,782	3,786	51,394	58.7	55.7	5.2
1965	126,513	74,455	71,088	4,361	66,726	3,366	52,058	58.9	56.2	4.5
1966	128,058	75,770	72,895	3,979	68,915	2,875	52,288	59.2	56.9	3.8
1967	129,874	77,347	74,372	3,844	70,527	2,975	52,527	59.6	57.3	3.8
1968	132,028	78,737	75,920	3,817	72,103	2,817	53,291	59.6	57.5	3.6
1969	134,335	80,734	77,902	3,606	74,296	2,832	53,602	60.1	58.0	3.5
1970	137,085	82,771	78,678	3,463	75,215	4,093	54,315	60.4	57.4	4.9
1971	140,216	84,382	79,367	3,394	75,972	5,016	55,834	60.2	56.6	5.9
1972	144,126	87,034	82,153	3,484	78,669	4,882	57,091	60.4	57.0	5.6
1973	147,096	89,429	85,064	3,470	81,594	4,365	57,667	60.8	57.8	4.9
1974	150,120	91,949	86,794	3,515	83,279	5,156	58,171	61.3	57.8	5.6
1975	153,153	93,775	85,846	3,408	82,438	7,929	59,377	61.2	56.1	8.5
1976	156,150	96,158	88,752	3,331	85,421	7,406	59,991	61.6	56.8	7.7
1977	159,033	99,009	92,017	3,283	88,734	6,991	60,025	62.3	57.9	7.1
1978	161,910	102,251	96,048	3,387	92,661	6,202	59,659	63.2	59.3	6.1
1979	164,863	104,962	98,824	3,347	95,477	6,137	59,900	63.7	59.9	5.8
1980	167,745	106,940	99,303	3,364	95,938	7,637	60,806	63.8	59.2	7.1
1981	170,130	108,670	100,397	3,368	97,030	8,273	61,460	63.9	59.0	7.6
1982	172,271	110,204	99,526	3,401	96,125	10,678	62,067	64.0	57.8	9.7
1983	174,215	111,550	100,834	3,383	97,450	10,717	62,665	64.0	57.9	9.6
1984	176,383	113,544	105,005	3,321	101,685	8,539	62,839	64.4	59.5	7.5
1985	178,206	115,461	107,150	3,179	103,971	8,312	62,744	64.8	60.1	7.2
1986	180,587	117,834	109,597	3,163	106,434	8,237	62,752	65.3	60.7	7.0
1987	182,753	119,865	112,440	3,208	109,232	7,425	62,888	65.6	61.5	6.2
1988	184,613	121,669	114,968	3,169	111,800	6,701	62,944	65.9	62.3	5.5
1989	186,393	123,869	117,342	3,199	114,142	6,528	62,523	66.5	63.0	5.3

[1] Not seasonally adjusted.
[2] Civilian labor force as percent of civilian noninstitutional population.
[3] Civilian employment as percent of civilian noninstitutional population.
[4] Unemployed as percent of civilian labor force.

See next page for continuation of table.

[Monthly data seasonally adjusted, except as noted]

Year or month	Civilian noninstitutional population [1]	Civilian labor force					Not in labor force	Civilian labor force participation rate [2]	Civilian employment/ population ratio [3]	Unemployment rate, civilian workers [4]
		Total	Employment			Unemployment				
			Total	Agricultural	Non-agricultural					
	Thousands of persons 16 years of age and over							Percent		
1990	189,164	125,840	118,793	3,223	115,570	7,047	63,324	66.5	62.8	5.6
1991	190,925	126,346	117,718	3,269	114,449	8,628	64,578	66.2	61.7	6.8
1992	192,805	128,105	118,492	3,247	115,245	9,613	64,700	66.4	61.5	7.5
1993	194,838	129,200	120,259	3,115	117,144	8,940	65,638	66.3	61.7	6.9
1994	196,814	131,056	123,060	3,409	119,651	7,996	65,758	66.6	62.5	6.1
1995	198,584	132,304	124,900	3,440	121,460	7,404	66,280	66.6	62.9	5.6
1996	200,591	133,943	126,708	3,443	123,264	7,236	66,647	66.8	63.2	5.4
1997	203,133	136,297	129,558	3,399	126,159	6,739	66,837	67.1	63.8	4.9
1998	205,220	137,673	131,463	3,378	128,085	6,210	67,547	67.1	64.1	4.5
1999	207,753	139,368	133,488	3,281	130,207	5,880	68,385	67.1	64.3	4.2
2000 [5]	212,577	142,583	136,891	2,464	134,427	5,692	69,994	67.1	64.4	4.0
2001	215,092	143,734	136,933	2,299	134,635	6,801	71,359	66.8	63.7	4.7
2002	217,570	144,863	136,485	2,311	134,174	8,378	72,707	66.6	62.7	5.8
2003	221,168	146,510	137,736	2,275	135,461	8,774	74,658	66.2	62.3	6.0
2004	223,357	147,401	139,252	2,232	137,020	8,149	75,956	66.0	62.3	5.5
2005	226,082	149,320	141,730	2,197	139,532	7,591	76,762	66.0	62.7	5.1
2006	228,815	151,428	144,427	2,206	142,221	7,001	77,387	66.2	63.1	4.6
2007	231,867	153,124	146,047	2,095	143,952	7,078	78,743	66.0	63.0	4.6
2008	233,788	154,287	145,362	2,168	143,194	8,924	79,501	66.0	62.2	5.8
2009	235,801	154,142	139,878	2,103	137,774	14,265	81,659	65.4	59.3	9.3
2010	237,829	153,889	139,064	2,206	136,858	14,825	83,941	64.7	58.5	9.6
2011	239,618	153,617	139,869	2,254	137,615	13,747	86,001	64.1	58.4	9.0
2012	243,284	154,975	142,469	2,186	140,283	12,506	88,310	63.7	58.6	8.1
2013	245,679	155,389	143,929	2,130	141,799	11,460	90,290	63.2	58.6	7.4
2011: Jan	238,704	153,198	139,287	2,270	137,036	13,910	85,506	64.2	58.4	9.1
Feb	238,851	153,280	139,422	2,266	137,182	13,858	85,571	64.2	58.4	9.0
Mar	239,000	153,403	139,655	2,260	137,471	13,748	85,597	64.2	58.4	9.0
Apr	239,146	153,566	139,622	2,143	137,438	13,944	85,580	64.2	58.4	9.1
May	239,313	153,526	139,653	2,230	137,395	13,873	85,787	64.2	58.4	9.0
June	239,489	153,379	139,409	2,253	137,136	13,971	86,110	64.0	58.2	9.1
July	239,671	153,309	139,524	2,225	137,215	13,785	86,362	64.0	58.2	9.0
Aug	239,871	153,724	139,904	2,344	137,470	13,820	86,147	64.1	58.3	9.0
Sept	240,071	154,059	140,154	2,232	137,904	13,905	86,012	64.2	58.4	9.0
Oct	240,269	153,940	140,335	2,211	138,283	13,604	86,330	64.1	58.4	8.8
Nov	240,441	154,072	140,747	2,251	138,500	13,326	86,368	64.1	58.5	8.6
Dec	240,584	153,927	140,836	2,362	138,454	13,090	86,658	64.0	58.5	8.5
2012: Jan	242,269	154,328	141,677	2,211	139,437	12,650	87,942	63.7	58.5	8.2
Feb	242,435	154,826	141,943	2,193	139,782	12,883	87,610	63.9	58.5	8.3
Mar	242,604	154,811	142,079	2,246	139,888	12,732	87,793	63.8	58.6	8.2
Apr	242,784	154,565	141,963	2,203	139,712	12,603	88,218	63.7	58.5	8.2
May	242,966	154,946	142,257	2,278	139,980	12,689	88,019	63.8	58.6	8.2
June	243,155	155,134	142,432	2,221	140,246	12,702	88,022	63.8	58.6	8.2
July	243,354	154,970	142,272	2,212	140,020	12,698	88,384	63.7	58.5	8.2
Aug	243,566	154,669	142,204	2,106	140,017	12,464	88,897	63.5	58.4	8.1
Sept	243,772	155,018	142,947	2,178	140,773	12,070	88,754	63.6	58.6	7.8
Oct	243,983	155,507	143,369	2,176	141,379	12,138	88,476	63.7	58.8	7.8
Nov	244,174	155,279	143,233	2,126	141,110	12,045	88,895	63.6	58.7	7.8
Dec	244,350	155,485	143,212	2,066	141,121	12,273	88,865	63.6	58.6	7.9
2013: Jan	244,663	155,699	143,384	2,057	141,234	12,315	88,963	63.6	58.6	7.9
Feb	244,828	155,511	143,464	2,070	141,393	12,047	89,317	63.5	58.6	7.7
Mar	244,995	155,099	143,393	2,020	141,350	11,706	89,896	63.3	58.5	7.5
Apr	245,175	155,359	143,676	2,048	141,604	11,683	89,815	63.4	58.6	7.5
May	245,363	155,609	143,919	2,081	141,860	11,690	89,754	63.4	58.7	7.5
June	245,552	155,822	144,075	2,091	142,021	11,747	89,730	63.5	58.7	7.5
July	245,756	155,693	144,285	2,171	142,081	11,408	90,062	63.4	58.7	7.3
Aug	245,959	155,435	144,179	2,205	141,918	11,256	90,524	63.2	58.6	7.2
Sept	246,168	155,473	144,270	2,208	142,058	11,203	90,695	63.2	58.6	7.2
Oct	246,381	154,625	143,485	2,208	141,449	11,140	91,756	62.8	58.2	7.2
Nov	246,567	155,284	144,443	2,139	142,317	10,841	91,283	63.0	58.6	7.0
Dec	246,745	154,937	144,586	2,229	142,337	10,351	91,808	62.8	58.6	6.7
2014: Jan	246,915	155,460	145,224	2,183	142,970	10,236	91,455	63.0	58.8	6.6

[5] Beginning in 2000, data for agricultural employment are for agricultural and related industries; data for this series and for nonagricultural employment are not strictly comparable with data for earlier years. Because of independent seasonal adjustment for these two series, monthly data will not add to total civilian employment.

Note: Labor force data in Tables B–11 through B–13 are based on household interviews and usually relate to the calendar week that includes the 12th of the month. Historical comparability is affected by revisions to population controls, changes in occupational and industry classification, and other changes to the survey. In recent years, updated population controls have been introduced annually with the release of January data, so data are not strictly comparable with earlier periods. Particularly notable changes were introduced for data in the years 1953, 1960, 1962, 1972, 1973, 1978, 1980, 1990, 1994, 1997, 1998, 2000, 2003, 2008 and 2012. For definitions of terms, area samples used, historical comparability of the data, comparability with other series, etc., see *Employment and Earnings* or concepts and methodology of the CPS at http://www.bls.gov/cps/documentation.htm#concepts.

Source: Department of Labor (Bureau of Labor Statistics).

TABLE B–12. Civilian unemployment rate, 1970–2014

[Percent [1]; monthly data seasonally adjusted, except as noted]

Year or month	All civilian workers	Males Total	Males 16–19 years	Males 20 years and over	Females Total	Females 16–19 years	Females 20 years and over	Both sexes 16–19 years	White[2]	Black and other[2]	Black or African American[2]	Asian (NSA)[2,3]	Hispanic or Latino ethnicity[4]	Married men, spouse present	Women who maintain families (NSA)[3]
1970	4.9	4.4	15.0	3.5	5.9	15.6	4.8	15.3	4.5	8.2	....	....	....	2.6	5.4
1971	5.9	5.3	16.6	4.4	6.9	17.2	5.7	16.9	5.4	9.9	....	....	....	3.2	7.3
1972	5.6	5.0	15.9	4.0	6.6	16.7	5.4	16.2	5.1	10.0	10.4	....	....	2.8	7.2
1973	4.9	4.2	13.9	3.3	6.0	15.3	4.9	14.5	4.3	9.0	9.4	....	7.5	2.3	7.1
1974	5.6	4.9	15.6	3.8	6.7	16.6	5.5	16.0	5.0	9.9	10.5	....	8.1	2.7	7.0
1975	8.5	7.9	20.1	6.8	9.3	19.7	8.0	19.9	7.8	13.8	14.8	....	12.2	5.1	10.0
1976	7.7	7.1	19.2	5.9	8.6	18.7	7.4	19.0	7.0	13.1	14.0	....	11.5	4.2	10.1
1977	7.1	6.3	17.3	5.2	8.2	18.3	7.0	17.8	6.2	13.1	14.0	....	10.1	3.6	9.4
1978	6.1	5.3	15.8	4.3	7.2	17.1	6.0	16.4	5.2	11.9	12.8	....	9.1	2.8	8.5
1979	5.8	5.1	15.9	4.2	6.8	16.4	5.7	16.1	5.1	11.3	12.3	....	8.3	2.8	8.3
1980	7.1	6.9	18.3	5.9	7.4	17.2	6.4	17.8	6.3	13.1	14.3	....	10.1	4.2	9.2
1981	7.6	7.4	20.1	6.3	7.9	19.0	6.8	19.6	6.7	14.2	15.6	....	10.4	4.3	10.4
1982	9.7	9.9	24.4	8.8	9.4	21.9	8.3	23.2	8.6	17.3	18.9	....	13.8	6.5	11.7
1983	9.6	9.9	23.3	8.9	9.2	21.3	8.1	22.4	8.4	17.8	19.5	....	13.7	6.5	12.2
1984	7.5	7.4	19.6	6.6	7.6	18.0	6.8	18.9	6.5	14.4	15.9	....	10.7	4.6	10.3
1985	7.2	7.0	19.5	6.2	7.4	17.6	6.6	18.6	6.2	13.7	15.1	....	10.5	4.3	10.4
1986	7.0	6.9	19.0	6.1	7.1	17.6	6.2	18.3	6.0	13.1	14.5	....	10.6	4.4	9.8
1987	6.2	6.2	17.8	5.4	6.2	15.9	5.4	16.9	5.3	11.6	13.0	....	8.8	3.9	9.2
1988	5.5	5.5	16.0	4.8	5.6	14.4	4.9	15.3	4.7	10.4	11.7	....	8.2	3.3	8.1
1989	5.3	5.2	15.9	4.5	5.4	14.0	4.7	15.0	4.5	10.0	11.4	....	8.0	3.0	8.1
1990	5.6	5.7	16.3	5.0	5.5	14.7	4.9	15.5	4.8	10.1	11.4	....	8.2	3.4	8.3
1991	6.8	7.2	19.8	6.4	6.4	17.5	5.7	18.7	6.1	11.1	12.5	....	10.0	4.4	9.3
1992	7.5	7.9	21.5	7.1	7.0	18.6	6.3	20.1	6.6	12.7	14.2	....	11.6	5.1	10.0
1993	6.9	7.2	20.4	6.4	6.6	17.5	5.9	19.0	6.1	11.7	13.0	....	10.8	4.4	9.7
1994	6.1	6.2	19.0	5.4	6.0	16.2	5.4	17.6	5.3	10.5	11.5	....	9.9	3.7	8.9
1995	5.6	5.6	18.4	4.8	5.6	16.1	4.9	17.3	4.9	9.6	10.4	....	9.3	3.3	8.0
1996	5.4	5.4	18.1	4.6	5.4	15.2	4.8	16.7	4.7	9.3	10.5	....	8.9	3.0	8.2
1997	4.9	4.9	16.9	4.2	5.0	15.0	4.4	16.0	4.2	8.8	10.0	....	7.7	2.7	8.1
1998	4.5	4.4	16.2	3.7	4.6	12.9	4.1	14.6	3.9	7.8	8.9	....	7.2	2.4	7.2
1999	4.2	4.1	14.7	3.5	4.3	13.2	3.8	13.9	3.7	7.0	8.0	....	6.4	2.2	6.4
2000	4.0	3.9	14.0	3.3	4.1	12.1	3.6	13.1	3.5	....	7.6	3.6	5.7	2.0	5.9
2001	4.7	4.8	16.0	4.2	4.7	13.4	4.1	14.7	4.2	....	8.6	4.5	6.6	2.7	6.6
2002	5.8	5.9	18.1	5.3	5.6	14.9	5.1	16.5	5.1	....	10.2	5.9	7.5	3.6	8.0
2003	6.0	6.3	19.3	5.6	5.7	15.6	5.1	17.5	5.2	....	10.8	6.0	7.7	3.8	8.5
2004	5.5	5.6	18.4	5.0	5.4	15.5	4.9	17.0	4.8	....	10.4	4.4	7.0	3.1	8.0
2005	5.1	5.1	18.6	4.4	5.1	14.5	4.6	16.6	4.4	....	10.0	4.0	6.0	2.8	7.8
2006	4.6	4.6	16.9	4.0	4.6	13.8	4.1	15.4	4.0	....	8.9	3.0	5.2	2.4	7.1
2007	4.6	4.7	17.6	4.1	4.5	13.8	4.0	15.7	4.1	....	8.3	3.2	5.6	2.5	6.5
2008	5.8	6.1	21.2	5.4	5.4	16.2	4.9	18.7	5.2	....	10.1	4.0	7.6	3.4	8.0
2009	9.3	10.3	27.8	9.6	8.1	20.7	7.5	24.3	8.5	....	14.8	7.3	12.1	6.6	11.5
2010	9.6	10.5	28.8	9.8	8.6	22.8	8.0	25.9	8.7	....	16.0	7.5	12.5	6.8	12.3
2011	8.9	9.4	27.2	8.7	8.5	21.7	7.9	24.4	7.9	....	15.8	7.0	11.5	5.8	12.4
2012	8.1	8.2	26.8	7.5	7.9	21.1	7.3	24.0	7.2	....	13.8	5.9	10.3	4.9	11.4
2013	7.4	7.6	25.5	7.0	7.1	20.3	6.5	22.9	6.5	....	13.1	5.2	9.1	4.3	10.2
2012: Jan	8.2	8.2	25.7	7.6	8.2	21.3	7.6	23.5	7.4	....	13.6	6.7	10.5	5.1	12.0
Feb	8.3	8.5	27.0	7.8	8.1	20.6	7.6	23.8	7.4	....	14.0	6.3	10.6	5.1	11.7
Mar	8.2	8.4	26.9	7.7	8.0	22.7	7.4	24.8	7.3	....	14.1	6.2	10.4	5.2	10.8
Apr	8.2	8.3	26.9	7.6	8.0	22.1	7.4	24.6	7.4	....	13.2	5.2	10.4	5.1	10.2
May	8.2	8.4	26.7	7.7	7.9	21.6	7.4	24.2	7.4	....	13.6	5.2	11.1	5.2	10.9
June	8.2	8.4	26.4	7.7	7.9	21.0	7.4	23.7	7.3	....	14.1	6.3	11.0	5.0	11.8
July	8.2	8.3	26.1	7.7	8.0	21.2	7.5	23.7	7.4	....	14.2	6.2	10.2	5.0	11.7
Aug	8.1	8.3	28.5	7.5	7.8	20.2	7.3	24.4	7.2	....	13.9	5.9	10.1	4.9	12.3
Sept	7.8	8.0	27.0	7.3	7.6	20.5	7.0	23.8	7.0	....	13.5	4.8	9.9	4.6	11.3
Oct	7.8	7.9	26.8	7.2	7.7	20.7	7.1	23.8	6.9	....	14.2	4.9	10.0	4.6	11.5
Nov	7.8	7.9	26.8	7.2	7.6	21.0	7.0	23.9	6.8	....	13.3	6.4	9.9	4.6	10.7
Dec	7.9	7.9	26.7	7.2	7.9	21.3	7.3	24.0	6.9	....	14.0	6.6	9.5	4.6	11.3
2013: Jan	7.9	8.0	26.5	7.4	7.7	20.6	7.2	23.5	7.1	....	13.8	6.5	9.7	4.6	11.3
Feb	7.7	7.9	27.2	7.2	7.6	23.2	7.0	25.2	6.8	....	13.8	6.1	9.5	4.5	11.0
Mar	7.5	7.6	25.8	6.9	7.5	22.1	6.9	23.9	6.7	....	13.2	5.0	9.2	4.3	10.7
Apr	7.5	7.8	25.9	7.1	7.2	21.6	6.6	23.7	6.6	....	13.1	5.1	9.0	4.4	10.3
May	7.5	7.9	26.8	7.2	7.1	21.3	6.5	24.1	6.6	....	13.5	4.3	9.1	4.4	9.9
June	7.5	7.8	27.7	7.0	7.3	19.7	6.8	23.8	6.6	....	13.5	5.0	9.1	4.4	10.7
July	7.3	7.7	26.9	7.0	6.9	19.8	6.4	23.4	6.6	....	12.6	5.7	9.5	4.3	10.5
Aug	7.2	7.7	25.0	7.0	6.8	20.1	6.2	22.6	6.4	....	12.9	5.1	9.3	4.3	11.0
Sept	7.2	7.7	24.1	7.0	6.7	18.1	6.2	21.3	6.3	....	13.0	5.3	8.9	4.3	8.8
Oct	7.2	7.5	24.4	6.9	6.9	19.6	6.4	22.0	6.3	....	13.0	5.2	9.0	4.5	9.5
Nov	7.0	7.3	23.3	6.7	6.7	18.3	6.2	20.8	6.1	....	12.4	5.3	8.7	4.2	9.7
Dec	6.7	6.8	21.1	6.3	6.5	19.3	6.0	20.2	5.9	....	11.9	4.1	8.3	3.8	8.7
2014: Jan	6.6	6.8	22.6	6.2	6.4	18.7	5.9	20.7	5.7	....	12.1	4.8	8.4	3.8	9.1

[1] Unemployed as percent of civilian labor force in group specified.
[2] Beginning in 2003, persons who selected this race group only. Prior to 2003, persons who selected more than one race were included in the group they identified as the main race. Data for "black or African American" were for "black" prior to 2003. Data discontinued for "black and other" series. See *Employment and Earnings* or concepts and methodology of the CPS at http://www.bls.gov/cps/documentation.htm#concepts for details.
[3] Not seasonally adjusted (NSA).
[4] Persons whose ethnicity is identified as Hispanic or Latino may be of any race.

Note: Data relate to persons 16 years of age and over.
See Note, Table B–11.

Source: Department of Labor (Bureau of Labor Statistics).

TABLE B–13. Unemployment by duration and reason, 1970–2014

[Thousands of persons, except as noted; monthly data seasonally adjusted [1]]

Year or month	Un-employ-ment	Duration of unemployment						Reason for unemployment					
		Less than 5 weeks	5–14 weeks	15–26 weeks	27 weeks and over	Average (mean) duration (weeks)[2]	Median duration (weeks)	Job losers[3]			Job leavers	Re-entrants	New entrants
								Total	On layoff	Other			
1970	4,093	2,139	1,290	428	235	8.6	4.9	1,811	675	1,137	550	1,228	504
1971	5,016	2,245	1,585	668	519	11.3	6.3	2,323	735	1,588	590	1,472	630
1972	4,882	2,242	1,472	601	566	12.0	6.2	2,108	582	1,526	641	1,456	677
1973	4,365	2,224	1,314	483	343	10.0	5.2	1,694	472	1,221	683	1,340	649
1974	5,156	2,604	1,597	574	381	9.8	5.2	2,242	746	1,495	768	1,463	681
1975	7,929	2,940	2,484	1,303	1,203	14.2	8.4	4,386	1,671	2,714	827	1,892	823
1976	7,406	2,844	2,196	1,018	1,348	15.8	8.2	3,679	1,050	2,628	903	1,928	895
1977	6,991	2,919	2,132	913	1,028	14.3	7.0	3,166	865	2,300	909	1,963	953
1978	6,202	2,865	1,923	766	648	11.9	5.9	2,585	712	1,873	874	1,857	885
1979	6,137	2,950	1,946	706	535	10.8	5.4	2,635	851	1,784	880	1,806	817
1980	7,637	3,295	2,470	1,052	820	11.9	6.5	3,947	1,488	2,459	891	1,927	872
1981	8,273	3,449	2,539	1,122	1,162	13.7	6.9	4,267	1,430	2,837	923	2,102	981
1982	10,678	3,883	3,311	1,708	1,776	15.6	8.7	6,268	2,127	4,141	840	2,384	1,185
1983	10,717	3,570	2,937	1,652	2,559	20.0	10.1	6,258	1,780	4,478	830	2,412	1,216
1984	8,539	3,350	2,451	1,104	1,634	18.2	7.9	4,421	1,171	3,250	823	2,184	1,110
1985	8,312	3,498	2,509	1,025	1,280	15.6	6.8	4,139	1,157	2,982	877	2,256	1,039
1986	8,237	3,448	2,557	1,045	1,187	15.0	6.9	4,033	1,090	2,943	1,015	2,160	1,029
1987	7,425	3,246	2,196	943	1,040	14.5	6.5	3,566	943	2,623	965	1,974	920
1988	6,701	3,084	2,007	801	809	13.5	5.9	3,092	851	2,241	983	1,809	816
1989	6,528	3,174	1,978	730	646	11.9	4.8	2,983	850	2,133	1,024	1,843	677
1990	7,047	3,265	2,257	822	703	12.0	5.3	3,387	1,028	2,359	1,041	1,930	688
1991	8,628	3,480	2,791	1,246	1,111	13.7	6.8	4,694	1,292	3,402	1,004	2,139	792
1992	9,613	3,376	2,830	1,453	1,954	17.7	8.7	5,389	1,260	4,129	1,002	2,285	937
1993	8,940	3,262	2,584	1,297	1,798	18.0	8.3	4,848	1,115	3,733	976	2,198	919
1994	7,996	2,728	2,408	1,237	1,623	18.8	9.2	3,815	977	2,838	791	2,786	604
1995	7,404	2,700	2,342	1,085	1,278	16.6	8.3	3,476	1,030	2,446	824	2,525	579
1996	7,236	2,633	2,287	1,053	1,262	16.7	8.3	3,370	1,021	2,349	774	2,512	580
1997	6,739	2,538	2,138	995	1,067	15.8	8.0	3,037	931	2,106	795	2,338	569
1998	6,210	2,622	1,950	763	875	14.5	6.7	2,822	866	1,957	734	2,132	520
1999	5,880	2,568	1,832	755	725	13.4	6.4	2,622	848	1,774	783	2,005	469
2000	5,692	2,558	1,815	669	649	12.6	5.9	2,517	852	1,664	780	1,961	434
2001	6,801	2,853	2,196	951	801	13.1	6.8	3,476	1,067	2,409	835	2,031	459
2002	8,378	2,893	2,580	1,369	1,535	16.6	9.1	4,607	1,124	3,483	866	2,368	536
2003	8,774	2,785	2,612	1,442	1,936	19.2	10.1	4,838	1,121	3,717	818	2,477	641
2004	8,149	2,696	2,382	1,293	1,779	19.6	9.8	4,197	998	3,199	858	2,408	686
2005	7,591	2,667	2,304	1,130	1,490	18.4	8.9	3,667	933	2,734	872	2,386	666
2006	7,001	2,614	2,121	1,031	1,235	16.8	8.3	3,321	921	2,400	827	2,237	616
2007	7,078	2,542	2,232	1,061	1,243	16.8	8.5	3,515	976	2,539	793	2,142	627
2008	8,924	2,932	2,804	1,427	1,761	17.9	9.4	4,789	1,176	3,614	896	2,472	766
2009	14,265	3,165	3,828	2,775	4,496	24.4	15.1	9,160	1,630	7,530	882	3,187	1,035
2010	14,825	2,771	3,267	2,371	6,415	33.0	21.4	9,250	1,431	7,819	889	3,466	1,220
2011	13,747	2,677	2,993	2,061	6,016	39.3	21.4	8,106	1,230	6,876	956	3,401	1,284
2012	12,506	2,644	2,866	1,859	5,136	39.4	19.3	6,877	1,183	5,694	967	3,345	1,316
2013	11,460	2,584	2,759	1,807	4,310	36.5	17.0	6,073	1,136	4,937	932	3,207	1,247
2012: Jan	12,650	2,461	2,880	1,942	5,524	40.1	20.9	7,270	1,253	6,017	928	3,303	1,252
Feb	12,883	2,584	2,842	2,021	5,352	40.0	20.0	7,167	1,160	6,007	1,035	3,360	1,383
Mar	12,732	2,724	2,792	1,924	5,292	39.4	19.6	7,051	1,148	5,903	1,101	3,300	1,392
Apr	12,603	2,621	2,839	1,951	5,106	39.3	19.2	6,859	1,099	5,760	987	3,360	1,357
May	12,689	2,575	3,018	1,677	5,392	39.6	19.8	6,980	1,143	5,838	906	3,395	1,347
June	12,702	2,741	2,804	1,839	5,331	40.0	19.8	7,106	1,264	5,842	929	3,193	1,318
July	12,698	2,708	3,037	1,780	5,166	38.8	17.2	7,121	1,383	5,738	873	3,365	1,298
Aug	12,464	2,832	2,834	1,845	5,003	39.1	18.2	6,885	1,231	5,654	953	3,336	1,264
Sept	12,070	2,517	2,825	1,853	4,875	39.4	18.7	6,508	1,170	5,338	956	3,303	1,268
Oct	12,138	2,619	2,850	1,774	5,021	40.3	20.0	6,511	1,058	5,452	1,018	3,321	1,306
Nov	12,045	2,636	2,777	1,796	4,767	39.2	18.6	6,434	1,082	5,351	929	3,336	1,349
Dec	12,273	2,688	2,876	1,862	4,772	38.0	17.8	6,475	1,110	5,365	1,000	3,615	1,296
2013: Jan	12,315	2,753	3,077	1,867	4,707	35.4	16.0	6,675	1,164	5,511	984	3,520	1,274
Feb	12,047	2,677	2,788	1,735	4,750	36.9	17.7	6,495	1,091	5,404	952	3,330	1,276
Mar	11,706	2,497	2,843	1,779	4,576	37.0	18.1	6,321	1,118	5,204	978	3,182	1,304
Apr	11,683	2,491	2,844	1,969	4,360	36.6	17.3	6,367	1,179	5,188	857	3,131	1,268
May	11,690	2,704	2,642	1,934	4,353	36.9	16.9	6,094	980	5,114	944	3,326	1,257
June	11,747	2,665	2,848	1,892	4,325	35.7	16.2	6,089	1,195	4,894	1,034	3,240	1,250
July	11,408	2,548	2,826	1,786	4,246	36.7	15.8	5,894	1,197	4,697	970	3,234	1,246
Aug	11,256	2,527	2,738	1,704	4,269	37.0	16.5	5,887	1,059	4,828	890	3,116	1,295
Sept	11,203	2,571	2,685	1,802	4,125	36.8	16.4	5,803	1,091	4,712	984	3,165	1,211
Oct	11,140	2,794	2,636	1,777	4,047	36.0	16.5	6,162	1,507	4,655	842	3,104	1,217
Nov	10,841	2,439	2,585	1,742	4,044	37.1	17.0	5,731	1,128	4,603	890	3,065	1,169
Dec	10,351	2,255	2,506	1,651	3,878	37.1	17.1	5,366	997	4,369	862	3,036	1,201
2014: Jan	10,236	2,434	2,429	1,689	3,646	35.4	16.0	5,407	986	4,421	818	2,937	1,184

[1] Because of independent seasonal adjustment of the various series, detail will not sum to totals.
[2] Beginning with January 2011, includes unemployment durations of up to 5 years; prior data are for up to 2 years.
[3] Beginning with January 1994, job losers and persons who completed temporary jobs.

Note: Data relate to persons 16 years of age and over.
See Note, Table B–11.

Source: Department of Labor (Bureau of Labor Statistics).

TABLE B–14. Employees on nonagricultural payrolls, by major industry, 1970–2014

[Thousands of jobs; monthly data seasonally adjusted]

Year or month	Total non-agricultural employment	Private industries									
		Total private	Goods-producing industries						Private service-providing industries		
			Total	Mining and logging	Construction	Manufacturing			Total	Trade, transportation, and utilities [1]	
						Total	Durable goods	Non-durable goods		Total	Retail trade
1970	71,006	58,318	22,179	677	3,654	17,848	10,762	7,086	36,139	14,144	7,463
1971	71,335	58,323	21,602	658	3,770	17,174	10,229	6,944	36,721	14,318	7,657
1972	73,798	60,333	22,299	672	3,957	17,669	10,630	7,039	38,034	14,788	8,038
1973	76,912	63,050	23,450	693	4,167	18,589	11,414	7,176	39,600	15,349	8,371
1974	78,389	64,086	23,364	755	4,095	18,514	11,432	7,082	40,721	15,693	8,536
1975	77,069	62,250	21,318	802	3,608	16,909	10,266	6,643	40,932	15,606	8,600
1976	79,502	64,501	22,025	832	3,662	17,531	10,640	6,891	42,476	16,128	8,966
1977	82,593	67,334	22,972	865	3,940	18,167	11,132	7,035	44,362	16,765	9,359
1978	86,826	71,014	24,156	902	4,322	18,932	11,770	7,162	46,858	17,658	9,879
1979	89,933	73,865	24,997	1,008	4,562	19,426	12,220	7,206	48,869	18,303	10,180
1980	90,533	74,158	24,263	1,077	4,454	18,733	11,679	7,054	49,895	18,413	10,244
1981	91,297	75,117	24,118	1,180	4,304	18,634	11,611	7,023	50,999	18,604	10,364
1982	89,689	73,706	22,550	1,163	4,024	17,363	10,610	6,753	51,156	18,457	10,372
1983	90,295	74,284	22,110	997	4,065	17,048	10,326	6,722	52,174	18,668	10,635
1984	94,548	78,389	23,435	1,014	4,501	17,920	11,050	6,870	54,954	19,653	11,223
1985	97,532	81,000	23,585	974	4,793	17,819	11,034	6,784	57,415	20,379	11,733
1986	99,500	82,661	23,318	829	4,937	17,552	10,795	6,757	59,343	20,795	12,078
1987	102,116	84,960	23,470	771	5,090	17,609	10,767	6,842	61,490	21,302	12,419
1988	105,378	87,838	23,909	770	5,233	17,906	10,969	6,938	63,929	21,974	12,808
1989	108,051	90,124	24,045	750	5,309	17,985	11,004	6,981	66,079	22,510	13,108
1990	109,527	91,112	23,723	765	5,263	17,695	10,737	6,958	67,389	22,666	13,182
1991	108,427	89,881	22,588	739	4,780	17,068	10,220	6,848	67,293	22,281	12,896
1992	108,802	90,015	22,095	689	4,608	16,799	9,946	6,853	67,921	22,125	12,828
1993	110,935	91,946	22,219	666	4,779	16,774	9,901	6,872	69,727	22,378	13,021
1994	114,398	95,124	22,774	659	5,095	17,020	10,132	6,889	72,350	23,128	13,491
1995	117,407	97,975	23,156	641	5,274	17,241	10,373	6,868	74,819	23,834	13,897
1996	119,836	100,297	23,409	637	5,536	17,237	10,486	6,751	76,888	24,239	14,143
1997	122,951	103,287	23,886	654	5,813	17,419	10,705	6,714	79,401	24,700	14,389
1998	126,157	106,248	24,354	645	6,149	17,560	10,911	6,649	81,894	25,186	14,609
1999	129,240	108,933	24,465	598	6,545	17,322	10,831	6,491	84,468	25,771	14,970
2000	132,019	111,230	24,649	599	6,787	17,263	10,877	6,386	86,581	26,225	15,280
2001	132,074	110,956	23,873	606	6,826	16,441	10,336	6,105	87,083	25,983	15,239
2002	130,628	109,115	22,557	583	6,716	15,259	9,485	5,774	86,558	25,497	15,025
2003	130,318	108,735	21,816	572	6,735	14,509	8,964	5,546	86,918	25,287	14,917
2004	131,749	110,128	21,882	591	6,976	14,315	8,925	5,390	88,246	25,533	15,058
2005	134,005	112,201	22,190	628	7,336	14,227	8,956	5,271	90,010	25,959	15,280
2006	136,398	114,424	22,530	684	7,691	14,155	8,981	5,174	91,894	26,276	15,353
2007	137,936	115,718	22,233	724	7,630	13,879	8,808	5,071	93,485	26,630	15,520
2008	137,170	114,661	21,335	767	7,162	13,406	8,463	4,943	93,326	26,293	15,283
2009	131,233	108,678	18,558	694	6,016	11,847	7,284	4,564	90,121	24,906	14,522
2010	130,275	107,785	17,751	705	5,518	11,528	7,064	4,464	90,034	24,636	14,440
2011	131,842	109,756	18,047	788	5,533	11,726	7,273	4,453	91,708	25,065	14,668
2012	134,104	112,184	18,420	848	5,646	11,927	7,470	4,457	93,763	25,476	14,841
2013 ᴾ	136,368	114,503	18,700	868	5,827	12,005	7,543	4,463	95,804	25,871	15,077
2012: Jan	133,188	111,246	18,304	840	5,627	11,837	7,395	4,442	92,942	25,355	14,818
Feb	133,414	111,474	18,327	846	5,622	11,859	7,419	4,440	93,147	25,368	14,803
Mar	133,657	111,720	18,377	849	5,627	11,901	7,447	4,454	93,343	25,396	14,808
Apr	133,753	111,822	18,396	850	5,630	11,916	7,460	4,456	93,426	25,417	14,833
May	133,863	111,953	18,394	853	5,613	11,928	7,470	4,458	93,559	25,457	14,827
June	133,951	112,028	18,411	852	5,620	11,939	7,480	4,459	93,617	25,447	14,814
July	134,111	112,200	18,465	851	5,635	11,979	7,518	4,461	93,735	25,451	14,802
Aug	134,261	112,336	18,452	849	5,647	11,956	7,492	4,464	93,884	25,470	14,802
Sept	134,422	112,495	18,436	846	5,648	11,942	7,477	4,465	94,059	25,495	14,834
Oct	134,647	112,750	18,452	839	5,666	11,947	7,481	4,466	94,298	25,545	14,861
Nov	134,850	112,961	18,484	846	5,687	11,951	7,493	4,458	94,477	25,618	14,915
Dec	135,064	113,176	18,536	851	5,720	11,965	7,505	4,460	94,640	25,638	14,917
2013: Jan	135,261	113,395	18,579	854	5,743	11,982	7,514	4,468	94,816	25,691	14,944
Feb	135,541	113,658	18,651	858	5,789	12,004	7,527	4,477	95,007	25,691	14,953
Mar	135,682	113,822	18,680	860	5,813	12,007	7,533	4,474	95,142	25,683	14,944
Apr	135,885	114,010	18,669	857	5,811	12,001	7,533	4,468	95,341	25,718	14,967
May	136,084	114,232	18,671	861	5,816	11,994	7,531	4,463	95,561	25,760	15,002
June	136,285	114,433	18,684	864	5,829	11,991	7,532	4,459	95,749	25,811	15,040
July	136,434	114,603	18,679	867	5,830	11,982	7,526	4,456	95,924	25,862	15,089
Aug	136,636	114,783	18,696	870	5,836	11,990	7,540	4,450	96,087	25,911	15,118
Sept	136,800	114,936	18,718	876	5,849	11,993	7,549	4,444	96,218	25,973	15,146
Oct	137,037	115,183	18,756	881	5,864	12,011	7,562	4,449	96,427	26,017	15,187
Nov	137,311	115,455	18,824	882	5,896	12,046	7,581	4,465	96,631	26,090	15,210
Dec ᴾ	137,386	115,544	18,811	883	5,874	12,054	7,583	4,471	96,733	26,172	15,272
2014: Jan ᴾ	137,499	115,686	18,887	890	5,922	12,075	7,598	4,477	96,799	26,182	15,260

[1] Includes wholesale trade, transportation and warehousing, and utilities, not shown separately.

Note: Data in Tables B–14 and B–15 are based on reports from employing establishments and relate to full- and part-time wage and salary workers in nonagricultural establishments who received pay for any part of the pay period that includes the 12th of the month. Not comparable with labor force data (Tables B–11 through B–13), which include proprietors, self-employed persons, unpaid family workers, and private household workers; which count persons as

See next page for continuation of table.

TABLE B–14. Employees on nonagricultural payrolls, by major industry, 1970–2014—*Continued*

[Thousands of jobs; monthly data seasonally adjusted]

Year or month	Private industries—Continued						Government			
	Private service-providing industries—Continued									
	Information	Financial activities	Professional and business services	Education and health services	Leisure and hospitality	Other services	Total	Federal	State	Local
1970	2,041	3,532	5,267	4,577	4,789	1,789	12,687	2,865	2,664	7,158
1971	2,009	3,651	5,328	4,675	4,914	1,827	13,012	2,828	2,747	7,437
1972	2,056	3,784	5,523	4,863	5,121	1,900	13,465	2,815	2,859	7,790
1973	2,135	3,920	5,774	5,092	5,341	1,990	13,862	2,794	2,923	8,146
1974	2,160	4,023	5,974	5,322	5,471	2,078	14,303	2,858	3,039	8,407
1975	2,061	4,047	6,034	5,497	5,544	2,144	14,820	2,882	3,179	8,758
1976	2,111	4,155	6,287	5,756	5,794	2,244	15,001	2,863	3,273	8,865
1977	2,185	4,348	6,587	6,052	6,065	2,359	15,258	2,859	3,377	9,023
1978	2,287	4,599	6,972	6,427	6,411	2,505	15,812	2,893	3,474	9,446
1979	2,375	4,843	7,312	6,768	6,631	2,637	16,068	2,894	3,541	9,633
1980	2,361	5,025	7,544	7,077	6,721	2,755	16,375	3,000	3,610	9,765
1981	2,382	5,163	7,782	7,364	6,840	2,865	16,180	2,922	3,640	9,619
1982	2,317	5,209	7,848	7,526	6,874	2,924	15,982	2,884	3,640	9,458
1983	2,253	5,334	8,039	7,781	7,078	3,021	16,011	2,915	3,662	9,434
1984	2,398	5,553	8,464	8,211	7,489	3,186	16,159	2,943	3,734	9,482
1985	2,437	5,815	8,871	8,679	7,869	3,366	16,533	3,014	3,832	9,687
1986	2,445	6,128	9,211	9,086	8,156	3,523	16,838	3,044	3,893	9,901
1987	2,507	6,385	9,608	9,543	8,446	3,699	17,156	3,089	3,967	10,100
1988	2,585	6,500	10,090	10,096	8,778	3,907	17,540	3,124	4,076	10,339
1989	2,622	6,562	10,555	10,652	9,062	4,116	17,927	3,136	4,182	10,609
1990	2,688	6,614	10,848	11,024	9,288	4,261	18,415	3,196	4,305	10,914
1991	2,677	6,561	10,714	11,556	9,256	4,249	18,545	3,110	4,355	11,081
1992	2,641	6,559	10,970	11,948	9,437	4,240	18,787	3,111	4,408	11,267
1993	2,668	6,742	11,495	12,362	9,732	4,350	18,989	3,063	4,488	11,438
1994	2,738	6,910	12,174	12,872	10,100	4,428	19,275	3,018	4,576	11,682
1995	2,843	6,866	12,844	13,360	10,501	4,572	19,432	2,949	4,635	11,849
1996	2,940	7,018	13,462	13,761	10,777	4,690	19,539	2,877	4,606	12,056
1997	3,084	7,255	14,335	14,185	11,018	4,825	19,664	2,806	4,582	12,276
1998	3,218	7,565	15,147	14,570	11,232	4,976	19,909	2,772	4,612	12,525
1999	3,419	7,753	15,957	14,939	11,543	5,087	20,307	2,769	4,709	12,829
2000	3,630	7,783	16,666	15,247	11,862	5,168	20,790	2,865	4,786	13,139
2001	3,629	7,900	16,476	15,801	12,036	5,258	21,118	2,764	4,905	13,449
2002	3,395	7,956	15,976	16,377	11,986	5,372	21,513	2,766	5,029	13,718
2003	3,188	8,078	15,987	16,805	12,173	5,401	21,583	2,761	5,002	13,820
2004	3,118	8,105	16,394	17,192	12,493	5,409	21,621	2,730	4,982	13,909
2005	3,061	8,197	16,954	17,630	12,816	5,395	21,804	2,732	5,032	14,041
2006	3,038	8,367	17,566	18,099	13,110	5,438	21,974	2,732	5,075	14,167
2007	3,032	8,348	17,942	18,613	13,427	5,494	22,218	2,734	5,122	14,362
2008	2,984	8,206	17,735	19,156	13,436	5,515	22,509	2,762	5,177	14,571
2009	2,804	7,838	16,579	19,550	13,077	5,367	22,555	2,832	5,169	14,554
2010	2,707	7,695	16,728	19,889	13,049	5,331	22,490	2,977	5,137	14,376
2011	2,674	7,697	17,332	20,228	13,353	5,360	22,086	2,859	5,078	14,150
2012	2,676	7,784	17,932	20,698	13,768	5,430	21,920	2,820	5,055	14,045
2013 ᴾ	2,685	7,880	18,560	21,102	14,242	5,464	21,864	2,766	5,048	14,050
2012: Jan	2,673	7,733	17,694	20,479	13,594	5,414	21,942	2,833	5,048	14,061
Feb	2,673	7,741	17,752	20,563	13,638	5,412	21,940	2,827	5,049	14,064
Mar	2,675	7,765	17,790	20,593	13,703	5,421	21,937	2,826	5,053	14,058
Apr	2,677	7,766	17,835	20,613	13,700	5,418	21,931	2,826	5,058	14,047
May	2,680	7,778	17,864	20,656	13,705	5,419	21,910	2,825	5,049	14,036
June	2,675	7,781	17,912	20,666	13,711	5,425	21,923	2,824	5,056	14,043
July	2,679	7,781	17,964	20,689	13,739	5,432	21,911	2,814	5,053	14,044
Aug	2,680	7,789	17,998	20,706	13,810	5,431	21,925	2,819	5,058	14,048
Sept	2,673	7,803	18,014	20,765	13,868	5,441	21,927	2,819	5,074	14,034
Oct	2,672	7,812	18,078	20,858	13,889	5,444	21,897	2,821	5,052	14,024
Nov	2,681	7,816	18,132	20,862	13,921	5,447	21,889	2,816	5,052	14,021
Dec	2,674	7,827	18,165	20,904	13,981	5,451	21,888	2,814	5,050	14,024
2013: Jan	2,673	7,835	18,210	20,921	14,028	5,458	21,866	2,809	5,034	14,023
Feb	2,692	7,847	18,295	20,948	14,078	5,456	21,883	2,810	5,049	14,024
Mar	2,694	7,853	18,362	20,989	14,112	5,449	21,860	2,789	5,056	14,015
Apr	2,688	7,863	18,434	21,040	14,145	5,453	21,875	2,791	5,053	14,031
May	2,686	7,872	18,511	21,069	14,198	5,465	21,852	2,768	5,047	14,037
June	2,685	7,885	18,570	21,084	14,249	5,465	21,852	2,767	5,034	14,051
July	2,697	7,901	18,621	21,108	14,272	5,463	21,831	2,756	5,025	14,050
Aug	2,669	7,897	18,663	21,172	14,306	5,469	21,853	2,749	5,039	14,065
Sept	2,682	7,896	18,700	21,181	14,315	5,471	21,864	2,744	5,051	14,069
Oct	2,688	7,903	18,753	21,212	14,380	5,474	21,854	2,732	5,057	14,065
Nov	2,689	7,899	18,826	21,237	14,417	5,473	21,856	2,739	5,060	14,057
Dec ᴾ	2,679	7,902	18,830	21,233	14,437	5,480	21,842	2,736	5,059	14,047
2014: Jan ᴾ	2,679	7,900	18,866	21,227	14,461	5,484	21,813	2,724	5,053	14,036

Note (cont'd): employed when they are not at work because of industrial disputes, bad weather, etc., even if they are not paid for the time off; which are based on a sample of the working-age population; and which count persons only once—as employed, unemployed, or not in the labor force. In the data shown here, persons who work at more than one job are counted each time they appear on a payroll.

Establishment data for employment, hours, and earnings are classified based on the 2012 North American Industry Classification System (NAICS). For further description and details see *Employment and Earnings*.

Source: Department of Labor (Bureau of Labor Statistics).

[Monthly data seasonally adjusted]

Year or month	Average weekly hours			Average hourly earnings			Average weekly earnings, total private			
	Total private	Manufacturing		Total private		Manufacturing (current dollars)	Level		Percent change from year earlier	
		Total	Overtime	Current dollars	1982–84 dollars [2]		Current dollars	1982–84 dollars [2]	Current dollars	1982–84 dollars [2]
1970	37.0	39.8	2.9	$3.40	$8.72	$3.24	$125.79	$322.54	4.2	−1.4
1971	36.7	39.9	2.9	3.63	8.92	3.45	133.22	327.32	5.9	1.5
1972	36.9	40.6	3.4	3.90	9.26	3.70	143.87	341.73	8.0	4.4
1973	36.9	40.7	3.8	4.14	9.26	3.97	152.59	341.36	6.1	−.1
1974	36.4	40.0	3.2	4.43	8.93	4.31	161.61	325.83	5.9	−4.5
1975	36.0	39.5	2.6	4.73	8.74	4.71	170.29	314.77	5.4	−3.4
1976	36.1	40.1	3.1	5.06	8.85	5.10	182.65	319.32	7.3	1.4
1977	35.9	40.3	3.4	5.44	8.93	5.55	195.58	321.15	7.1	.6
1978	35.8	40.4	3.6	5.88	8.96	6.05	210.29	320.56	7.5	−.2
1979	35.6	40.2	3.3	6.34	8.67	6.57	225.69	308.74	7.3	−3.7
1980	35.2	39.6	2.8	6.85	8.26	7.15	241.07	290.80	6.8	−5.8
1981	35.2	39.8	2.8	7.44	8.14	7.87	261.53	286.14	8.5	−1.6
1982	34.7	38.9	2.3	7.87	8.12	8.36	273.10	281.84	4.4	−1.5
1983	34.9	40.1	2.9	8.20	8.22	8.70	286.43	287.00	4.9	1.8
1984	35.1	40.6	3.4	8.49	8.22	9.05	298.26	288.73	4.1	.6
1985	34.9	40.5	3.3	8.74	8.18	9.40	304.62	284.96	2.1	−1.3
1986	34.7	40.7	3.4	8.93	8.22	9.60	309.78	285.25	1.7	.1
1987	34.7	40.9	3.7	9.14	8.12	9.77	317.39	282.12	2.5	−1.1
1988	34.6	41.0	3.8	9.44	8.07	10.05	326.48	279.04	2.9	−1.1
1989	34.5	40.9	3.8	9.80	7.99	10.35	338.34	275.97	3.6	−1.1
1990	34.3	40.5	3.9	10.20	7.91	10.78	349.63	271.03	3.3	−1.8
1991	34.1	40.4	3.8	10.51	7.83	11.13	358.46	266.91	2.5	−1.5
1992	34.2	40.7	4.0	10.77	7.79	11.40	368.20	266.43	2.7	−.2
1993	34.3	41.1	4.4	11.05	7.78	11.70	378.89	266.64	2.9	.1
1994	34.5	41.7	5.0	11.34	7.79	12.04	391.17	268.66	3.2	.8
1995	34.3	41.3	4.7	11.65	7.78	12.34	400.04	267.05	2.3	−.6
1996	34.3	41.3	4.8	12.04	7.81	12.75	413.25	268.17	3.3	.4
1997	34.5	41.7	5.1	12.51	7.94	13.14	431.86	274.02	4.5	2.2
1998	34.5	41.4	4.9	13.01	8.15	13.45	448.59	280.90	3.9	2.5
1999	34.3	41.4	4.9	13.49	8.27	13.85	463.15	283.79	3.2	1.0
2000	34.3	41.3	4.7	14.02	8.30	14.32	480.99	284.78	3.9	.3
2001	34.0	40.3	4.0	14.54	8.38	14.76	493.74	284.58	2.7	−.1
2002	33.9	40.5	4.2	14.97	8.51	15.29	506.60	288.00	2.6	1.2
2003	33.7	40.4	4.2	15.37	8.55	15.74	517.82	288.00	2.2	.0
2004	33.7	40.8	4.6	15.69	8.50	16.14	528.89	286.66	2.1	−.5
2005	33.8	40.7	4.6	16.12	8.44	16.56	544.05	284.84	2.9	−.6
2006	33.9	41.1	4.4	16.75	8.50	16.81	567.39	287.87	4.3	1.1
2007	33.8	41.2	4.2	17.42	8.59	17.26	589.27	290.61	3.9	1.0
2008	33.6	40.8	3.7	18.07	8.56	17.75	607.53	287.86	3.1	−.9
2009	33.1	39.8	2.9	18.61	8.88	18.24	616.01	293.86	1.4	2.1
2010	33.4	41.1	3.8	19.05	8.90	18.61	636.25	297.36	3.3	1.2
2011	33.6	41.4	4.1	19.44	8.77	18.93	653.19	294.79	2.7	−.9
2012 ᵖ	33.7	41.7	4.2	19.74	8.73	19.08	665.82	294.31	1.9	−.2
2013 ᵖ	33.7	41.9	4.3	20.13	8.78	19.30	677.67	295.51	1.8	.4
2012: Jan	33.8	41.8	4.2	19.58	8.73	19.02	661.80	295.00	2.6	−.6
Feb	33.7	41.8	4.1	19.60	8.72	19.01	660.52	293.73	2.1	−1.0
Mar	33.7	41.6	4.2	19.65	8.71	19.02	662.21	293.64	2.0	−.7
Apr	33.7	41.6	4.2	19.70	8.72	19.09	663.89	293.85	2.1	−.3
May	33.6	41.5	4.1	19.69	8.73	19.02	661.58	293.40	1.4	−.3
June	33.7	41.6	4.2	19.72	8.75	19.08	664.56	294.99	1.8	.2
July	33.7	41.7	4.2	19.76	8.77	19.11	665.91	295.71	1.4	.1
Aug	33.6	41.5	4.1	19.75	8.72	19.06	663.60	292.90	1.3	−.3
Sept	33.6	41.5	4.2	19.78	8.68	19.07	664.61	291.66	1.4	−.6
Oct	33.6	41.5	4.2	19.80	8.67	19.10	665.28	291.21	1.0	−1.2
Nov	33.7	41.6	4.1	19.85	8.72	19.15	668.95	293.73	1.4	−.3
Dec	33.7	41.7	4.3	19.89	8.74	19.14	670.29	294.53	1.6	−.1
2013: Jan	33.6	41.6	4.3	19.95	8.76	19.15	670.32	294.38	1.3	−.2
Feb	33.8	41.9	4.3	20.00	8.73	19.22	676.00	294.96	2.3	.4
Mar	33.8	41.9	4.4	20.02	8.76	19.22	676.68	296.16	2.2	.9
Apr	33.7	41.8	4.3	20.04	8.79	19.21	675.35	296.26	1.7	.8
May	33.7	41.8	4.3	20.06	8.78	19.25	676.02	295.94	2.2	.9
June	33.7	41.9	4.3	20.12	8.78	19.28	678.04	295.75	2.0	.3
July	33.5	41.7	4.3	20.15	8.77	19.27	675.03	293.89	1.4	−.6
Aug	33.7	41.9	4.3	20.17	8.78	19.33	679.73	295.74	2.4	1.0
Sept	33.6	41.9	4.3	20.21	8.78	19.35	679.06	295.10	2.2	1.2
Oct	33.6	41.9	4.4	20.25	8.80	19.37	680.40	295.71	2.3	1.5
Nov	33.7	42.0	4.5	20.30	8.82	19.42	684.11	297.09	2.3	1.1
Dec ᵖ	33.5	41.9	4.5	20.33	8.80	19.46	681.06	294.93	1.6	.1
2014: Jan ᵖ	33.5	41.7	4.3	20.39	8.82	19.47	683.07	295.40	1.9	.3

[1] For production employees in goods-producing industries and for nonsupervisory employees in private, service-providing industries; total includes private industry groups shown in Table B–14.

[2] Current dollars divided by the consumer price index for urban wage earners and clerical workers on a 1982–84=100 base.

Note: See Note, Table B–14.

Source: Department of Labor (Bureau of Labor Statistics).

[Index numbers, 2009=100; quarterly data seasonally adjusted]

Year or quarter	Output per hour of all persons		Output [1]		Hours of all persons [2]		Compensation per hour [3]		Real compensation per hour [4]		Unit labor costs		Implicit price deflator [5]	
	Business sector	Nonfarm business sector	Business sector	Nonfarm business sector	Business sector	Nonfarm business sector	Business sector	Nonfarm business sector	Business sector	Nonfarm business sector	Business sector	Nonfarm business sector	Business sector	Nonfarm business sector
1965	39.4	41.4	25.0	25.0	63.5	60.4	9.2	9.4	57.1	58.7	23.4	22.8	21.9	21.4
1966	41.0	42.9	26.7	26.8	65.2	62.4	9.8	10.0	59.3	60.4	24.0	23.3	22.4	21.9
1967	41.9	43.7	27.3	27.3	65.0	62.4	10.4	10.6	60.8	62.0	24.7	24.2	23.0	22.6
1968	43.4	45.2	28.6	28.7	66.0	63.5	11.2	11.4	62.9	64.0	25.8	25.2	23.9	23.4
1969	43.6	45.3	29.5	29.6	67.7	65.4	12.0	12.2	63.8	64.8	27.4	26.8	25.0	24.5
1970	44.5	46.0	29.5	29.6	66.3	64.3	12.9	13.0	64.9	65.6	28.9	28.3	26.1	25.6
1971	46.3	47.8	30.6	30.7	66.2	64.2	13.6	13.8	65.9	66.7	29.5	28.9	27.2	26.7
1972	47.8	49.4	32.6	32.7	68.2	66.3	14.5	14.7	67.9	68.8	30.3	29.7	28.2	27.5
1973	49.2	50.9	34.9	35.1	70.8	69.0	15.6	15.8	68.9	69.7	31.8	31.1	29.6	28.5
1974	48.4	50.1	34.3	34.6	71.0	69.1	17.1	17.3	67.9	68.7	35.3	34.6	32.5	31.4
1975	50.1	51.4	34.0	34.0	67.9	66.1	18.9	19.1	68.9	69.6	37.8	37.2	35.7	34.8
1976	51.7	53.2	36.3	36.4	70.1	68.5	20.4	20.6	70.3	70.9	39.5	38.7	37.6	36.7
1977	52.7	54.1	38.4	38.5	72.8	71.2	22.1	22.3	71.3	72.0	41.9	41.2	39.8	39.0
1978	53.3	54.8	40.8	41.1	76.6	74.9	23.9	24.2	72.2	73.1	44.9	44.2	42.6	41.6
1979	53.3	54.7	42.2	42.4	79.1	77.6	26.3	26.5	72.3	73.1	49.3	48.5	46.2	45.1
1980	53.3	54.7	41.8	42.0	78.5	76.9	29.1	29.4	72.1	72.8	54.6	53.8	50.3	49.4
1981	54.5	55.5	43.0	43.0	79.0	77.5	31.8	32.2	72.0	72.9	58.4	58.0	54.9	54.1
1982	54.1	55.0	41.7	41.6	77.2	75.8	34.2	34.6	72.9	73.7	63.2	62.9	58.1	57.5
1983	56.0	57.4	44.0	44.3	78.6	77.3	35.7	36.1	73.1	74.0	63.7	62.9	60.1	59.3
1984	57.6	58.6	47.9	48.1	83.2	82.0	37.3	37.7	73.3	74.1	64.7	64.3	61.8	61.0
1985	58.9	59.6	50.1	50.1	85.1	84.1	39.2	39.5	74.5	75.1	66.5	66.3	63.6	63.0
1986	60.6	61.4	52.0	52.0	85.8	84.8	41.4	41.8	77.3	78.0	68.4	68.1	64.4	63.9
1987	60.9	61.7	53.8	53.9	88.3	87.3	43.0	43.4	77.6	78.4	70.6	70.3	65.7	65.2
1988	61.8	62.7	56.1	56.3	90.8	89.8	45.2	45.6	78.8	79.5	73.2	72.7	67.8	67.2
1989	62.5	63.3	58.2	58.4	93.1	92.3	46.6	46.9	77.9	78.4	74.5	74.2	70.3	69.6
1990	63.9	64.5	59.2	59.3	92.6	91.9	49.6	49.9	79.0	79.3	77.6	77.3	72.6	71.9
1991	65.1	65.7	58.9	59.0	90.4	89.7	52.1	52.3	79.9	80.4	80.0	79.7	74.6	74.2
1992	68.0	68.5	61.3	61.3	90.2	89.5	55.1	55.5	82.6	83.1	81.1	81.0	75.8	75.4
1993	68.1	68.6	63.1	63.2	92.7	92.2	56.0	56.2	81.8	82.1	82.2	81.9	77.6	77.1
1994	68.6	69.3	66.2	66.2	96.4	95.5	56.5	56.9	80.9	81.4	82.3	82.1	79.0	78.6
1995	68.9	69.8	68.2	68.5	99.1	98.2	57.6	58.0	80.5	81.1	83.6	83.1	80.4	79.9
1996	70.9	71.6	71.4	71.6	100.7	99.9	60.0	60.4	81.7	82.2	84.6	84.3	81.6	81.0
1997	72.3	72.8	75.2	75.3	104.0	103.4	62.2	62.5	82.9	83.3	86.0	85.8	82.8	82.4
1998	74.5	75.0	79.1	79.3	106.1	105.7	65.9	66.1	86.6	86.9	88.4	88.1	83.2	82.9
1999	77.3	77.6	83.6	83.9	108.2	108.0	68.8	68.9	88.5	88.7	89.0	88.7	83.7	83.6
2000	79.9	80.2	87.4	87.5	109.4	109.1	73.8	74.0	91.9	92.1	92.4	92.2	85.3	85.2
2001	82.1	82.4	87.9	88.1	107.1	107.0	77.2	77.2	93.5	93.5	94.0	93.7	86.8	86.6
2002	85.6	85.9	89.5	89.7	104.5	104.4	78.9	79.0	94.1	94.2	92.2	91.9	87.4	87.4
2003	88.9	89.1	92.3	92.5	103.9	103.8	81.9	81.9	95.5	95.6	92.1	92.0	88.6	88.5
2004	91.8	91.9	96.5	96.6	105.2	105.2	85.7	85.7	97.3	97.3	93.4	93.3	90.7	90.3
2005	93.7	93.8	100.2	100.3	106.9	106.9	88.8	88.8	97.6	97.6	94.8	94.7	93.5	93.4
2006	94.6	94.6	103.3	103.5	109.2	109.3	92.3	92.3	98.2	98.2	97.5	97.5	96.1	96.0
2007	96.0	96.2	105.5	105.8	109.9	110.0	96.4	96.3	99.7	99.6	100.4	100.1	98.2	97.9
2008	96.8	96.9	104.3	104.5	107.7	107.8	99.0	98.9	98.6	98.5	102.2	102.0	99.7	99.4
2009	100.0	100.0	100.0	100.0	100.0	100.0	100.0	100.0	100.0	100.0	100.0	100.0	100.0	100.0
2010	103.3	103.3	103.1	103.2	99.9	99.9	102.0	102.1	100.3	100.4	98.8	98.8	101.1	101.0
2011	103.6	103.8	105.6	105.7	101.9	101.9	104.4	104.6	99.6	99.7	100.8	100.8	103.3	102.7
2012	105.1	105.3	109.5	109.7	104.1	104.1	107.2	107.4	100.1	100.3	102.0	102.0	105.1	104.6
2013 p	106.2	105.9	112.2	112.1	105.7	105.9	109.1	109.1	100.4	100.5	102.7	103.0	106.7	105.9
2010: I	102.5	102.6	101.5	101.5	98.9	98.9	100.7	100.7	99.3	99.4	98.2	98.2	100.5	100.4
II	102.9	102.9	102.7	102.7	99.8	99.7	101.9	102.0	100.6	100.7	99.0	99.1	100.9	100.8
III	103.6	103.5	103.7	103.7	100.2	100.2	102.5	102.5	100.8	100.9	98.9	99.0	101.3	101.2
IV	104.0	104.1	104.7	104.8	100.7	100.7	102.9	103.1	100.5	100.6	99.0	99.0	101.9	101.6
2011: I	103.1	103.2	104.2	104.2	101.0	101.0	104.5	104.7	101.0	101.2	101.4	101.5	102.4	101.9
II	103.6	103.7	105.2	105.4	101.6	101.7	104.4	104.4	99.7	99.8	100.8	100.7	103.0	102.5
III	103.5	103.7	105.7	105.9	102.1	102.1	105.0	105.2	99.6	99.8	101.5	101.5	103.8	103.2
IV	104.4	104.5	107.3	107.4	102.9	102.8	103.8	104.0	98.1	98.3	99.5	99.6	103.9	103.4
2012: I	104.7	104.8	108.6	108.7	103.7	103.7	106.0	106.3	99.6	99.8	101.3	101.3	104.4	103.8
II	105.0	105.2	109.1	109.2	103.8	103.8	106.5	106.8	99.9	100.1	101.4	101.5	104.9	104.4
III	105.6	105.8	110.0	110.3	104.2	104.2	106.7	106.9	99.5	99.7	101.1	101.1	105.5	105.0
IV	105.1	105.4	110.1	110.5	104.7	104.8	109.4	109.5	101.4	101.5	104.0	103.9	105.8	105.2
2013: I	105.2	104.9	110.5	110.4	105.0	105.2	108.1	108.0	99.9	99.8	102.7	103.0	106.3	105.4
II	105.7	105.4	111.4	111.3	105.4	105.6	109.1	109.1	100.8	100.8	103.2	103.5	106.4	105.6
III	106.6	106.3	112.9	112.8	105.9	106.1	109.4	109.5	100.5	100.5	102.7	103.0	106.9	106.2
IV p	107.3	107.1	114.1	114.1	106.4	106.5	109.8	109.9	100.6	100.7	102.3	102.6	107.1	106.5

[1] Output refers to real gross domestic product in the sector.
[2] Hours at work of all persons engaged in sector, including hours of employees, proprietors, and unpaid family workers. Estimates based primarily on establishment data.
[3] Wages and salaries of employees plus employers' contributions for social insurance and private benefit plans. Also includes an estimate of wages, salaries, and supplemental payments for the self-employed.
[4] Hourly compensation divided by consumer price series. The consumer price series for 1978-2012 is based on the consumer price index research series (CPI-U-RS), and for recent quarters is based on the consumer price index for all urban consumers (CPI-U).
[5] Current dollar output divided by the output index.

Source: Department of Labor (Bureau of Labor Statistics).

TABLE B–17. Bond yields and interest rates, 1942–2014

[Percent per annum]

Year and month	U.S. Treasury securities Bills (at auction)[1] 3-month	6-month	Constant maturities[2] 3-year	10-year	30-year	Corporate bonds (Moody's) Aaa[3]	Baa	High-grade municipal bonds (Standard & Poor's)	New-home mortgage yields[4]	Prime rate charged by banks[5]	Discount window (Federal Reserve Bank of New York)[5,6] Primary credit	Adjustment credit	Federal funds rate[7]
1942	0.326	....	....	....	....	2.83	4.28	2.36	....	1.50	....	[8]1.00	....
1943	.373	....	....	....	....	2.73	3.91	2.06	....	1.50	....	[8]1.00	....
1944	.375	....	....	....	....	2.72	3.61	1.86	....	1.50	....	[8]1.00	....
1945	.375	....	....	....	....	2.62	3.29	1.67	....	1.50	....	[8]1.00	....
1946	.375	....	....	....	....	2.53	3.05	1.64	....	1.50	....	[8]1.00	....
1947	.594	....	....	....	....	2.61	3.24	2.01	....	1.50–1.75	....	1.00	....
1948	1.040	....	....	....	....	2.82	3.47	2.40	....	1.75–2.00	....	1.34	....
1949	1.102	....	....	....	....	2.66	3.42	2.21	....	2.00	....	1.50	....
1950	1.218	....	....	....	....	2.62	3.24	1.98	....	2.07	....	1.59	....
1951	1.552	....	....	....	....	2.86	3.41	2.00	....	2.56	....	1.75	....
1952	1.766	....	....	....	....	2.96	3.52	2.19	....	3.00	....	1.75	....
1953	1.931	....	2.47	2.85	....	3.20	3.74	2.72	....	3.17	....	1.99	....
1954	.953	....	1.63	2.40	....	2.90	3.51	2.37	....	3.05	....	1.60	....
1955	1.753	....	2.47	2.82	....	3.06	3.53	2.53	....	3.16	....	1.89	1.79
1956	2.658	....	3.19	3.18	....	3.36	3.88	2.93	....	3.77	....	2.77	2.73
1957	3.267	....	3.98	3.65	....	3.89	4.71	3.60	....	4.20	....	3.12	3.11
1958	1.839	....	2.84	3.32	....	3.79	4.73	3.56	....	3.83	....	2.15	1.57
1959	3.405	3.832	4.46	4.33	....	4.38	5.05	3.95	....	4.48	....	3.36	3.31
1960	2.93	3.25	3.98	4.12	....	4.41	5.19	3.73	....	4.82	....	3.53	3.21
1961	2.38	2.61	3.54	3.88	....	4.35	5.08	3.46	....	4.50	....	3.00	1.95
1962	2.78	2.91	3.47	3.95	....	4.33	5.02	3.18	....	4.50	....	3.00	2.71
1963	3.16	3.25	3.67	4.00	....	4.26	4.86	3.23	5.89	4.50	....	3.23	3.18
1964	3.56	3.69	4.03	4.19	....	4.40	4.83	3.22	5.83	4.50	....	3.55	3.50
1965	3.95	4.05	4.22	4.28	....	4.49	4.87	3.27	5.81	4.54	....	4.04	4.07
1966	4.88	5.08	5.23	4.93	....	5.13	5.67	3.82	6.25	5.63	....	4.50	5.11
1967	4.32	4.63	5.03	5.07	....	5.51	6.23	3.98	6.46	5.63	....	4.19	4.22
1968	5.34	5.47	5.68	5.64	....	6.18	6.94	4.51	6.97	6.31	....	5.17	5.66
1969	6.68	6.85	7.02	6.67	....	7.03	7.81	5.81	7.81	7.96	....	5.87	8.21
1970	6.43	6.53	7.29	7.35	....	8.04	9.11	6.51	8.45	7.91	....	5.95	7.17
1971	4.35	4.51	5.66	6.16	....	7.39	8.56	5.70	7.74	5.73	....	4.88	4.67
1972	4.07	4.47	5.72	6.21	....	7.21	8.16	5.27	7.60	5.25	....	4.50	4.44
1973	7.04	7.18	6.96	6.85	....	7.44	8.24	5.18	7.96	8.03	....	6.45	8.74
1974	7.89	7.93	7.84	7.56	....	8.57	9.50	6.09	8.92	10.81	....	7.83	10.51
1975	5.84	6.12	7.50	7.99	....	8.83	10.61	6.89	9.00	7.86	....	6.25	5.82
1976	4.99	5.27	6.77	7.61	....	8.43	9.75	6.49	9.00	6.84	....	5.50	5.05
1977	5.27	5.52	6.68	7.42	7.75	8.02	8.97	5.56	9.02	6.83	....	5.46	5.54
1978	7.22	7.58	8.29	8.41	8.49	8.73	9.49	5.90	9.56	9.06	....	7.46	7.94
1979	10.05	10.02	9.70	9.43	9.28	9.63	10.69	6.39	10.78	12.67	....	10.29	11.20
1980	11.51	11.37	11.51	11.43	11.27	11.94	13.67	8.51	12.66	15.26	....	11.77	13.35
1981	14.03	13.78	14.46	13.92	13.45	14.17	16.04	11.23	14.70	18.87	....	13.42	16.39
1982	10.69	11.08	12.93	13.01	12.76	13.79	16.11	11.57	15.14	14.85	....	11.01	12.24
1983	8.63	8.75	10.45	11.10	11.18	12.04	13.55	9.47	12.57	10.79	....	8.50	9.09
1984	9.53	9.77	11.92	12.46	12.41	12.71	14.19	10.15	12.38	12.04	....	8.80	10.23
1985	7.47	7.64	9.64	10.62	10.79	11.37	12.72	9.18	11.55	9.93	....	7.69	8.10
1986	5.98	6.03	7.06	7.67	7.78	9.02	10.39	7.38	10.17	8.33	....	6.32	6.80
1987	5.82	6.05	7.68	8.39	8.59	9.38	10.58	7.73	9.31	8.21	....	5.66	6.66
1988	6.69	6.92	8.26	8.85	8.96	9.71	10.83	7.76	9.19	9.32	....	6.20	7.57
1989	8.12	8.04	8.55	8.49	8.45	9.26	10.18	7.24	10.13	10.87	....	6.93	9.21
1990	7.51	7.47	8.26	8.55	8.61	9.32	10.36	7.25	10.05	10.01	....	6.98	8.10
1991	5.42	5.49	6.82	7.86	8.14	8.77	9.80	6.89	9.32	8.46	....	5.45	5.69
1992	3.45	3.57	5.30	7.01	7.67	8.14	8.98	6.41	8.24	6.25	....	3.25	3.52
1993	3.02	3.14	4.44	5.87	6.59	7.22	7.93	5.63	7.20	6.00	....	3.00	3.02
1994	4.29	4.66	6.27	7.09	7.37	7.96	8.62	6.19	7.49	7.15	....	3.60	4.21
1995	5.51	5.59	6.25	6.57	6.88	7.59	8.20	5.95	7.87	8.83	....	5.21	5.83
1996	5.02	5.09	5.99	6.44	6.71	7.37	8.05	5.75	7.80	8.27	....	5.02	5.30
1997	5.07	5.18	6.10	6.35	6.61	7.26	7.86	5.55	7.71	8.44	....	5.00	5.46
1998	4.81	4.85	5.14	5.26	5.58	6.53	7.22	5.12	7.07	8.35	....	4.92	5.35
1999	4.66	4.76	5.49	5.65	5.87	7.04	7.87	5.43	7.04	8.00	....	4.62	4.97
2000	5.85	5.92	6.22	6.03	5.94	7.62	8.36	5.77	7.52	9.23	....	5.73	6.24
2001	3.44	3.39	4.09	5.02	5.49	7.08	7.95	5.19	7.00	6.91	....	3.40	3.88
2002	1.62	1.69	3.10	4.61	5.43	6.49	7.80	5.05	6.43	4.67	....	1.17	1.67
2003	1.01	1.06	2.10	4.01	....	5.67	6.77	4.73	5.80	4.12	2.12	....	1.13
2004	1.38	1.57	2.78	4.27	....	5.63	6.39	4.63	5.77	4.34	2.34	....	1.35
2005	3.16	3.40	3.93	4.29	....	5.24	6.06	4.29	5.94	6.19	4.19	....	3.22
2006	4.73	4.80	4.77	4.80	4.91	5.59	6.48	4.42	6.63	7.96	5.96	....	4.97
2007	4.41	4.48	4.35	4.63	4.84	5.56	6.48	4.42	6.41	8.05	5.86	....	5.02
2008	1.48	1.71	2.24	3.66	4.28	5.63	7.45	4.80	6.05	5.09	2.39	....	1.92
2009	.16	.29	1.43	3.26	4.08	5.31	7.30	4.64	5.14	3.25	.50	....	.16
2010	.14	.20	1.11	3.22	4.25	4.94	6.04	4.16	4.80	3.25	.72	....	.18
2011	.06	.10	.75	2.78	3.91	4.64	5.66	4.29	4.56	3.25	.75	....	.10
2012	.09	.13	.38	1.80	2.92	3.67	4.94	3.14	3.69	3.25	.75	....	.14
2013	.06	.09	.54	2.35	3.45	4.24	5.10	3.96	4.00	3.25	.75	....	.11

[1] High bill rate at auction, issue date within period, bank-discount basis. On or after October 28, 1998, data are stop yields from uniform-price auctions. Before that date, they are weighted average yields from multiple-price auctions.

See next page for continuation of table.

[Percent per annum]

Year and month	U.S. Treasury securities					Corporate bonds (Moody's)		High-grade municipal bonds (Standard & Poor's)[3]	New-home mortgage yields[4]	Prime rate charged by banks[5]	Discount window (Federal Reserve Bank of New York)[5,6]		Federal funds rate[7]
	Bills (at auction)[1]		Constant maturities[2]										
	3-month	6-month	3-year	10-year	30-year	Aaa[3]	Baa			High-low	Primary credit High-low	Adjustment credit High-low	
2009: Jan	0.12	0.31	1.13	2.52	3.13	5.05	8.14	5.13	5.11	3.25–3.25	0.50–0.50		0.15
Feb	.31	.46	1.37	2.87	3.59	5.27	8.08	5.00	5.09	3.25–3.25	0.50–0.50		.22
Mar	.25	.43	1.31	2.82	3.64	5.50	8.42	5.15	5.10	3.25–3.25	0.50–0.50		.18
Apr	.17	.37	1.32	2.93	3.76	5.39	8.39	4.88	4.96	3.25–3.25	0.50–0.50		.15
May	.19	.31	1.39	3.29	4.23	5.54	8.06	4.60	4.92	3.25–3.25	0.50–0.50		.18
June	.17	.32	1.76	3.72	4.52	5.61	7.50	4.84	5.17	3.25–3.25	0.50–0.50		.21
July	.19	.29	1.55	3.56	4.41	5.41	7.09	4.69	5.40	3.25–3.25	0.50–0.50		.16
Aug	.18	.27	1.65	3.59	4.37	5.26	6.58	4.58	5.32	3.25–3.25	0.50–0.50		.16
Sept	.13	.22	1.48	3.40	4.19	5.13	6.31	4.13	5.26	3.25–3.25	0.50–0.50		.15
Oct	.08	.17	1.46	3.39	4.19	5.15	6.29	4.20	5.14	3.25–3.25	0.50–0.50		.12
Nov	.06	.16	1.32	3.40	4.31	5.19	6.32	4.35	5.08	3.25–3.25	0.50–0.50		.12
Dec	.07	.17	1.38	3.59	4.49	5.26	6.37	4.16	5.01	3.25–3.25	0.50–0.50		.12
2010: Jan	.06	.15	1.49	3.73	4.60	5.26	6.25	4.22	5.04	3.25–3.25	0.50–0.50		.11
Feb	.10	.18	1.40	3.69	4.62	5.35	6.34	4.23	5.08	3.25–3.25	0.75–0.75		.13
Mar	.15	.22	1.51	3.73	4.64	5.27	6.27	4.22	5.09	3.25–3.25	0.75–0.75		.16
Apr	.15	.24	1.64	3.85	4.69	5.29	6.25	4.24	5.21	3.25–3.25	0.75–0.75		.20
May	.16	.23	1.32	3.42	4.29	4.96	6.05	4.15	5.12	3.25–3.25	0.75–0.75		.20
June	.12	.19	1.17	3.20	4.13	4.88	6.23	4.18	5.00	3.25–3.25	0.75–0.75		.18
July	.16	.20	.98	3.01	3.99	4.72	6.01	4.11	4.87	3.25–3.25	0.75–0.75		.18
Aug	.15	.19	.78	2.70	3.80	4.49	5.66	3.91	4.67	3.25–3.25	0.75–0.75		.19
Sept	.15	.19	.74	2.65	3.77	4.53	5.66	3.76	4.52	3.25–3.25	0.75–0.75		.19
Oct	.13	.17	.57	2.54	3.87	4.68	5.72	3.83	4.40	3.25–3.25	0.75–0.75		.19
Nov	.13	.17	.67	2.76	4.19	4.87	5.92	4.30	4.26	3.25–3.25	0.75–0.75		.19
Dec	.15	.20	.99	3.29	4.42	5.02	6.10	4.72	4.44	3.25–3.25	0.75–0.75		.18
2011: Jan	.15	.18	1.03	3.39	4.52	5.04	6.09	5.02	4.75	3.25–3.25	0.75–0.75		.17
Feb	.14	.17	1.28	3.58	4.65	5.22	6.15	4.92	4.94	3.25–3.25	0.75–0.75		.16
Mar	.11	.16	1.17	3.41	4.51	5.13	6.03	4.70	4.98	3.25–3.25	0.75–0.75		.14
Apr	.06	.12	1.21	3.46	4.50	5.16	6.02	4.71	4.91	3.25–3.25	0.75–0.75		.10
May	.04	.08	.94	3.17	4.29	4.96	5.78	4.34	4.86	3.25–3.25	0.75–0.75		.09
June	.04	.10	.71	3.00	4.23	4.99	5.75	4.22	4.61	3.25–3.25	0.75–0.75		.09
July	.03	.08	.68	3.00	4.27	4.93	5.76	4.24	4.55	3.25–3.25	0.75–0.75		.07
Aug	.05	.09	.38	2.30	3.65	4.37	5.36	3.92	4.29	3.25–3.25	0.75–0.75		.10
Sept	.02	.05	.35	1.98	3.18	4.09	5.27	3.79	4.36	3.25–3.25	0.75–0.75		.08
Oct	.02	.06	.47	2.15	3.13	3.98	5.37	3.94	4.19	3.25–3.25	0.75–0.75		.07
Nov	.01	.05	.39	2.01	3.02	3.87	5.14	3.95	4.26	3.25–3.25	0.75–0.75		.08
Dec	.02	.05	.39	1.98	2.98	3.93	5.25	3.76	4.18	3.25–3.25	0.75–0.75		.07
2012: Jan	.02	.06	.36	1.97	3.03	3.85	5.23	3.43	4.09	3.25–3.25	0.75–0.75		.08
Feb	.08	.11	.38	1.97	3.11	3.85	5.14	3.25	4.01	3.25–3.25	0.75–0.75		.10
Mar	.09	.14	.51	2.17	3.28	3.99	5.23	3.51	3.72	3.25–3.25	0.75–0.75		.13
Apr	.08	.14	.43	2.05	3.18	3.96	5.19	3.47	3.93	3.25–3.25	0.75–0.75		.14
May	.09	.14	.39	1.80	2.93	3.80	5.07	3.21	3.88	3.25–3.25	0.75–0.75		.16
June	.09	.14	.39	1.62	2.70	3.64	5.02	3.30	3.80	3.25–3.25	0.75–0.75		.16
July	.10	.14	.33	1.53	2.59	3.40	4.87	3.14	3.76	3.25–3.25	0.75–0.75		.16
Aug	.11	.14	.37	1.68	2.77	3.48	4.91	3.07	3.67	3.25–3.25	0.75–0.75		.13
Sept	.10	.13	.34	1.72	2.88	3.49	4.84	3.02	3.62	3.25–3.25	0.75–0.75		.14
Oct	.10	.15	.37	1.75	2.90	3.47	4.58	2.89	3.58	3.25–3.25	0.75–0.75		.16
Nov	.11	.15	.36	1.65	2.80	3.50	4.51	2.68	3.46	3.25–3.25	0.75–0.75		.16
Dec	.08	.12	.35	1.72	2.88	3.65	4.63	2.73	3.40	3.25–3.25	0.75–0.75		.16
2013: Jan	.07	.11	.39	1.91	3.08	3.80	4.73	2.93	3.41	3.25–3.25	0.75–0.75		.14
Feb	.10	.12	.40	1.98	3.17	3.90	4.85	3.09	3.49	3.25–3.25	0.75–0.75		.15
Mar	.09	.11	.39	1.96	3.16	3.93	4.85	3.27	3.61	3.25–3.25	0.75–0.75		.14
Apr	.06	.09	.34	1.76	2.93	3.73	4.59	3.22	3.66	3.25–3.25	0.75–0.75		.15
May	.05	.08	.40	1.93	3.11	3.89	4.73	3.39	3.55	3.25–3.25	0.75–0.75		.11
June	.05	.09	.58	2.30	3.40	4.27	5.19	4.02	3.64	3.25–3.25	0.75–0.75		.09
July	.04	.08	.64	2.58	3.61	4.34	5.32	4.51	4.07	3.25–3.25	0.75–0.75		.09
Aug	.04	.07	.70	2.74	3.76	4.54	5.42	4.77	4.33	3.25–3.25	0.75–0.75		.08
Sept	.02	.04	.78	2.81	3.79	4.64	5.47	4.74	4.44	3.25–3.25	0.75–0.75		.08
Oct	.05	.08	.63	2.62	3.68	4.53	5.31	4.50	4.47	3.25–3.25	0.75–0.75		.09
Nov	.07	.10	.58	2.72	3.80	4.63	5.38	4.51	4.39	3.25–3.25	0.75–0.75		.08
Dec	.07	.09	.69	2.90	3.89	4.62	5.38	4.55	4.37	3.25–3.25	0.75–0.75		.09
2014: Jan	.05	.07	.78	2.86	3.77	4.49	5.19	4.38	4.45	3.25–3.25	0.75–0.75		.07

[2] Yields on the more actively traded issues adjusted to constant maturities by the Department of the Treasury. The 30-year Treasury constant maturity series was discontinued on February 18, 2002, and reintroduced on February 9, 2006.

[3] Beginning with December 7, 2001, data for corporate Aaa series are industrial bonds only.

[4] Effective rate (in the primary market) on conventional mortgages, reflecting fees and charges as well as contract rate and assuming, on the average, repayment at end of 10 years. Rates beginning with January 1973 not strictly comparable with prior rates.

[5] For monthly data, high and low for the period. Prime rate for 1947–1948 are ranges of the rate in effect during the period.

[6] Primary credit replaced adjustment credit as the Federal Reserve's principal discount window lending program effective January 9, 2003.

[7] Since July 19, 1975, the daily effective rate is an average of the rates on a given day weighted by the volume of transactions at these rates. Prior to that date, the daily effective rate was the rate considered most representative of the day's transactions, usually the one at which most transactions occurred.

[8] From October 30, 1942 to April 24, 1946, a preferential rate of 0.50 percent was in effect for advances secured by Government securities maturing in one year or less.

Sources: Department of the Treasury, Board of Governors of the Federal Reserve System, Federal Housing Finance Agency, Moody's Investors Service, and Standard & Poor's.

TABLE B–18. Money stock and debt measures, 1974–2014

[Averages of daily figures, except debt end-of-period basis; billions of dollars, seasonally adjusted]

Year and month	M1 — Sum of currency, demand deposits, travelers checks, and other checkable deposits (OCDs)	M2 — M1 plus retail MMMF balances, savings deposits (including MMDAs), and small time deposits [2]	Debt [1] — Debt of domestic nonfinancial sectors	Percent change — From year or 6 months earlier [3] M1	Percent change — From year or 6 months earlier [3] M2	Percent change — From previous period [4] Debt
December:						
1974	274.2	902.1	2,069.1	4.3	5.4	9.2
1975	287.1	1,016.2	2,259.8	4.7	12.6	9.3
1976	306.2	1,152.0	2,503.0	6.7	13.4	10.8
1977	330.9	1,270.3	2,824.0	8.1	10.3	12.8
1978	357.3	1,366.0	3,207.9	8.0	7.5	13.8
1979	381.8	1,473.7	3,596.3	6.9	7.9	12.1
1980	408.5	1,599.8	3,944.3	7.0	8.6	9.5
1981	436.7	1,755.5	4,351.9	6.9	9.7	10.3
1982	474.8	1,906.4	4,773.1	8.7	8.6	10.4
1983	521.4	2,123.8	5,348.6	9.8	11.4	12.0
1984	551.6	2,306.8	6,134.8	5.8	8.6	14.8
1985	619.8	2,492.6	7,110.6	12.4	8.1	15.6
1986	724.7	2,729.2	7,953.0	16.9	9.5	11.9
1987	750.2	2,828.8	8,656.1	3.5	3.6	9.1
1988	786.7	2,990.6	9,437.0	4.9	5.7	9.1
1989	792.9	3,154.4	10,139.3	.8	5.5	7.3
1990	824.7	3,272.7	10,825.1	4.0	3.8	6.5
1991	897.0	3,371.6	11,295.2	8.8	3.0	4.4
1992	1,024.9	3,423.1	11,812.7	14.3	1.5	4.6
1993	1,129.6	3,472.4	12,494.8	10.2	1.4	5.6
1994	1,150.6	3,485.0	13,140.9	1.9	.4	5.1
1995	1,127.5	3,626.7	13,810.3	–2.0	4.1	5.0
1996	1,081.3	3,804.9	14,516.4	–4.1	4.9	5.1
1997	1,072.4	4,017.3	15,309.0	–.8	5.6	5.5
1998	1,095.3	4,356.4	16,307.0	2.1	8.4	6.5
1999	1,122.8	4,616.8	17,353.2	2.5	6.0	6.2
2000	1,088.5	4,903.5	18,227.9	–3.1	6.2	5.0
2001	1,183.3	5,405.6	19,374.9	8.7	10.2	6.4
2002	1,220.2	5,740.8	20,804.5	3.1	6.2	7.4
2003	1,306.1	6,036.0	22,520.1	7.0	5.1	8.0
2004	1,376.0	6,388.6	25,349.1	5.4	5.8	9.3
2005	1,374.8	6,651.5	27,696.1	–.1	4.1	9.3
2006	1,367.5	7,040.6	30,174.2	–.5	5.8	8.7
2007	1,375.0	7,444.0	32,765.2	.5	5.7	8.6
2008	1,603.8	8,166.2	34,724.9	16.6	9.7	6.0
2009	1,694.2	8,463.8	35,667.3	5.6	3.6	3.1
2010	1,836.2	8,766.0	37,039.9	8.4	3.6	4.0
2011	2,159.9	9,620.2	38,421.4	17.6	9.7	3.7
2012	2,447.2	10,406.8	40,286.2	13.3	8.2	4.9
2013	2,648.3	10,958.8		8.2	5.3	
2012: Jan	2,199.6	9,707.5		19.3	9.2	
Feb	2,212.1	9,760.0		9.0	5.7	
Mar	2,228.5	9,802.1	38,871.1	9.5	6.3	4.7
Apr	2,250.4	9,856.7		10.3	6.8	
May	2,254.2	9,886.0		8.6	6.4	
June	2,269.6	9,948.7	39,380.4	10.2	6.8	5.3
July	2,322.1	10,022.1		11.1	6.5	
Aug	2,346.7	10,086.0		12.2	6.7	
Sept	2,383.5	10,157.7	39,671.9	13.9	7.3	3.0
Oct	2,415.4	10,214.1		14.7	7.3	
Nov	2,407.7	10,279.9		13.6	8.0	
Dec	2,447.2	10,406.8	40,286.2	15.7	9.2	6.2
2013: Jan	2,464.5	10,442.6		12.3	8.4	
Feb	2,473.5	10,454.7		10.8	7.3	
Mar	2,476.4	10,519.8	40,731.2	7.8	7.1	4.4
Apr	2,517.8	10,553.7		8.5	6.6	
May	2,525.8	10,590.8		9.8	6.0	
June	2,529.1	10,639.0	41,074.1	6.7	4.5	3.4
July	2,558.3	10,702.2		7.6	5.0	
Aug	2,560.3	10,756.2		7.0	5.8	
Sept	2,587.0	10,802.2	41,431.9	8.9	5.4	3.5
Oct	2,625.8	10,900.1		8.6	6.6	
Nov	2,612.3	10,908.9		6.8	6.0	
Dec	2,648.3	10,958.8		9.4	6.0	
2014: Jan	2,683.0	11,011.5		9.7	5.8	

[1] Consists of outstanding credit market debt of the U.S. Government, State and local governments, and private nonfinancial sectors.
[2] Money market mutual fund (MMMF). Money market deposit account (MMDA).
[3] Annual changes are from December to December; monthly changes are from six months earlier at a simple annual rate.
[4] Annual changes are from fourth quarter to fourth quarter. Quarterly changes are from previous quarter at annual rate.

Note: For further information on the composition of M1 and M2, see the H6 release of the Federal Reserve Board. The Federal Reserve no longer publishes the M3 monetary aggregate and most of its components. Institutional money market mutual funds is published as a memorandum item in the H.6 release, and the component on large-denomination time deposits is published in other Federal Reserve Board releases. For details, see H.6 release of March 23, 2006.

Source: Board of Governors of the Federal Reserve System.

TABLE B–19. Federal receipts, outlays, surplus or deficit, and debt, fiscal years, 1947–2015

[Billions of dollars; fiscal years]

Fiscal year or period	Total			On-budget			Off-budget			Federal debt (end of period)		Addendum: Gross domestic product
	Receipts	Outlays	Surplus or deficit (−)	Receipts	Outlays	Surplus or deficit (−)	Receipts	Outlays	Surplus or deficit (−)	Gross Federal	Held by the public	
1947	38.5	34.5	4.0	37.1	34.2	2.9	1.5	0.3	1.2	257.1	224.3	238.9
1948	41.6	29.8	11.8	39.9	29.4	10.5	1.6	.4	1.2	252.0	216.3	262.4
1949	39.4	38.8	.6	37.7	38.4	−.7	1.7	.4	1.3	252.6	214.3	276.8
1950	39.4	42.6	−3.1	37.3	42.0	−4.7	2.1	.5	1.6	256.9	219.0	279.0
1951	51.6	45.5	6.1	48.5	44.2	4.3	3.1	1.3	1.8	255.3	214.3	327.4
1952	66.2	67.7	−1.5	62.6	66.0	−3.4	3.6	1.7	1.9	259.1	214.8	357.5
1953	69.6	76.1	−6.5	65.5	73.8	−8.3	4.1	2.3	1.8	266.0	218.4	382.5
1954	69.7	70.9	−1.2	65.1	67.9	−2.8	4.6	2.9	1.7	270.8	224.5	387.7
1955	65.5	68.4	−3.0	60.4	64.5	−4.1	5.1	4.0	1.1	274.4	226.6	407.0
1956	74.6	70.6	3.9	68.2	65.7	2.5	6.4	5.0	1.5	272.7	222.2	439.0
1957	80.0	76.6	3.4	73.2	70.6	2.6	6.8	6.0	.8	272.3	219.3	464.2
1958	79.6	82.4	−2.8	71.6	74.9	−3.3	8.0	7.5	.5	279.7	226.3	474.3
1959	79.2	92.1	−12.8	71.0	83.1	−12.1	8.3	9.0	−.7	287.5	234.7	505.6
1960	92.5	92.2	.3	81.9	81.3	.5	10.6	10.9	−.2	290.5	236.8	535.1
1961	94.4	97.7	−3.3	82.3	86.0	−3.8	12.1	11.7	.4	292.6	238.4	547.6
1962	99.7	106.8	−7.1	87.4	93.3	−5.9	12.3	13.5	−1.3	302.9	248.0	586.9
1963	106.6	111.3	−4.8	92.4	96.4	−4.0	14.2	15.0	−.8	310.3	254.0	619.3
1964	112.6	118.5	−5.9	96.2	102.8	−6.5	16.4	15.7	.6	316.1	256.8	662.9
1965	116.8	118.2	−1.4	100.1	101.7	−1.6	16.7	16.5	.2	322.3	260.8	710.7
1966	130.8	134.5	−3.7	111.7	114.8	−3.1	19.1	19.7	−.6	328.5	263.7	781.9
1967	148.8	157.5	−8.6	124.4	137.0	−12.6	24.4	20.4	4.0	340.4	266.6	838.2
1968	153.0	178.1	−25.2	128.1	155.8	−27.7	24.9	22.3	2.6	368.7	289.5	899.3
1969	186.9	183.6	3.2	157.9	158.4	−.5	29.0	25.2	3.7	365.8	278.1	982.3
1970	192.8	195.6	−2.8	159.3	168.0	−8.7	33.5	27.6	5.9	380.9	283.2	1,049.1
1971	187.1	210.2	−23.0	151.3	177.3	−26.1	35.8	32.8	3.0	408.2	303.0	1,119.3
1972	207.3	230.7	−23.4	167.4	193.5	−26.1	39.9	37.2	2.7	435.9	322.4	1,219.5
1973	230.8	245.7	−14.9	184.7	200.0	−15.2	46.1	45.7	.3	466.3	340.9	1,356.0
1974	263.2	269.4	−6.1	209.3	216.5	−7.2	53.9	52.9	1.1	483.9	343.7	1,486.2
1975	279.1	332.3	−53.2	216.6	270.8	−54.1	62.5	61.6	.9	541.9	394.7	1,610.6
1976	298.1	371.8	−73.7	231.7	301.1	−69.4	66.4	70.7	−4.3	629.0	477.4	1,790.3
Transition quarter ..	81.2	96.0	−14.7	63.2	77.3	−14.1	18.0	18.7	−.7	643.6	495.5	472.6
1977	355.6	409.2	−53.7	278.7	328.7	−49.9	76.8	80.5	−3.7	706.4	549.1	2,028.4
1978	399.6	458.7	−59.2	314.2	369.6	−55.4	85.4	89.2	−3.8	776.6	607.1	2,278.2
1979	463.3	504.0	−40.7	365.3	404.9	−39.6	98.0	99.1	−1.1	829.5	640.3	2,570.0
1980	517.1	590.9	−73.8	403.9	477.0	−73.1	113.2	113.9	−.7	909.0	711.9	2,796.8
1981	599.3	678.2	−79.0	469.1	543.0	−73.9	130.2	135.3	−5.1	994.8	789.4	3,138.4
1982	617.8	745.7	−128.0	474.3	594.9	−120.6	143.5	150.9	−7.4	1,137.3	924.6	3,313.9
1983	600.6	808.4	−207.8	453.2	660.9	−207.7	147.3	147.4	−.1	1,371.7	1,137.3	3,541.1
1984	666.4	851.8	−185.4	500.4	685.6	−185.3	166.1	166.2	−.1	1,564.6	1,307.0	3,952.8
1985	734.0	946.3	−212.3	547.9	769.4	−221.5	186.2	176.9	9.2	1,817.4	1,507.3	4,270.4
1986	769.2	990.4	−221.2	568.9	806.8	−237.9	200.2	183.5	16.7	2,120.5	1,740.6	4,536.1
1987	854.3	1,004.0	−149.7	640.9	809.2	−168.4	213.4	194.8	18.6	2,346.0	1,889.8	4,781.9
1988	909.2	1,064.4	−155.2	667.7	860.0	−192.3	241.5	204.4	37.1	2,601.1	2,051.6	5,155.1
1989	991.1	1,143.7	−152.6	727.4	932.8	−205.4	263.7	210.9	52.8	2,867.8	2,190.7	5,570.0
1990	1,032.0	1,253.0	−221.0	750.3	1,027.9	−277.6	281.7	225.0	56.6	3,206.3	2,411.6	5,914.6
1991	1,055.0	1,324.2	−269.2	761.1	1,082.5	−321.4	293.9	241.7	52.2	3,598.2	2,689.0	6,110.0
1992	1,091.2	1,381.5	−290.3	788.8	1,129.2	−340.4	302.4	252.3	50.1	4,001.8	2,999.7	6,434.7
1993	1,154.3	1,409.4	−255.1	842.4	1,142.8	−300.4	311.9	266.6	45.3	4,351.0	3,248.4	6,794.9
1994	1,258.6	1,461.8	−203.2	923.5	1,182.4	−258.8	335.0	279.4	55.7	4,643.3	3,433.1	7,197.8
1995	1,351.8	1,515.7	−164.0	1,000.7	1,227.1	−226.4	351.1	288.7	62.4	4,920.6	3,604.4	7,583.3
1996	1,453.1	1,560.5	−107.4	1,085.6	1,259.6	−174.0	367.5	300.9	66.6	5,181.5	3,734.1	7,978.3
1997	1,579.2	1,601.1	−21.9	1,187.2	1,290.5	−103.2	392.0	310.6	81.4	5,369.2	3,772.3	8,483.2
1998	1,721.7	1,652.5	69.3	1,305.9	1,335.9	−29.9	415.8	316.6	99.2	5,478.2	3,721.1	8,954.8
1999	1,827.5	1,701.8	125.6	1,383.0	1,381.1	1.9	444.5	320.8	123.7	5,605.5	3,632.4	9,514.0
2000	2,025.2	1,789.0	236.2	1,544.6	1,458.2	86.4	480.6	330.8	149.8	5,628.7	3,409.8	10,154.0
2001	1,991.1	1,862.8	128.2	1,483.6	1,516.0	−32.4	507.5	346.8	160.7	5,769.9	3,319.6	10,568.4
2002	1,853.1	2,010.9	−157.8	1,337.8	1,655.2	−317.4	515.3	355.7	159.7	6,198.4	3,540.4	10,879.4
2003	1,782.3	2,159.9	−377.6	1,258.5	1,796.9	−538.4	523.8	363.0	160.8	6,760.0	3,913.4	11,334.0
2004	1,880.1	2,292.8	−412.7	1,345.4	1,913.3	−568.0	534.7	379.5	155.2	7,354.7	4,295.5	12,090.7
2005	2,153.6	2,472.0	−318.3	1,576.1	2,069.7	−493.6	577.5	402.2	175.3	7,905.3	4,592.2	12,890.5
2006	2,406.9	2,655.1	−248.2	1,798.5	2,233.0	−434.5	608.4	422.1	186.3	8,451.4	4,829.0	13,686.6
2007	2,568.0	2,728.7	−160.7	1,932.9	2,275.0	−342.2	635.1	453.6	181.5	8,950.7	5,035.1	14,324.9
2008	2,524.0	2,982.5	−458.6	1,865.9	2,507.8	−641.8	658.0	474.8	183.3	9,986.1	5,803.1	14,756.1
2009	2,105.0	3,517.7	−1,412.7	1,451.0	3,000.7	−1,549.7	654.0	517.0	137.0	11,875.9	7,544.7	14,413.6
2010	2,162.7	3,457.1	−1,294.6	1,531.0	2,902.4	−1,371.4	631.7	554.7	77.0	13,528.8	9,018.9	14,791.4
2011	2,303.5	3,603.1	−1,299.6	1,737.7	3,104.5	−1,366.8	565.8	498.6	67.2	14,764.2	10,128.2	15,387.1
2012	2,450.2	3,537.1	−1,087.0	1,880.7	3,029.5	−1,148.9	569.5	507.6	61.9	16,050.9	11,281.1	16,094.2
2013	2,775.1	3,454.6	−679.5	2,101.8	2,820.8	−719.0	673.3	633.8	39.5	16,719.4	11,982.6	16,618.6
2014 (estimates)	3,001.7	3,650.5	−648.8	2,269.4	2,939.3	−669.9	732.3	711.2	21.1	17,892.6	12,902.7	17,332.3
2015 (estimates)	3,337.4	3,901.0	−563.6	2,579.5	3,143.4	−563.8	757.9	757.6	.3	18,713.5	13,591.8	18,219.4

Note: Fiscal years through 1976 were on a July 1–June 30 basis; beginning with October 1976 (fiscal year 1977), the fiscal year is on an October 1–September 30 basis. The transition quarter is the three-month period from July 1, 1976 through September 30, 1976.

See Budget of the United States Government, Fiscal Year 2015, for additional information.

Sources: Department of Commerce (Bureau of Economic Analysis), Department of the Treasury, and Office of Management and Budget.

[Percent; fiscal years]

Fiscal year or period	Receipts	Outlays		Surplus or deficit (−)	Federal debt (end of period)	
		Total	National defense		Gross Federal	Held by public
1942	9.9	23.8	17.4	−13.9	53.6	45.9
1943	13.0	42.6	36.1	−29.6	77.3	69.2
1944	20.5	42.7	37.0	−22.2	95.5	86.4
1945	19.9	41.0	36.6	−21.0	114.9	103.9
1946	17.2	24.2	18.7	−7.0	118.9	106.1
1947	16.1	14.4	5.4	1.7	107.6	93.9
1948	15.8	11.3	3.5	4.5	96.0	82.4
1949	14.2	14.0	4.8	.2	91.3	77.4
1950	14.1	15.3	4.9	−1.1	92.1	78.5
1951	15.8	13.9	7.2	1.9	78.0	65.5
1952	18.5	18.9	12.9	−.4	72.5	60.1
1953	18.2	19.9	13.8	−1.7	69.5	57.1
1954	18.0	18.3	12.7	−.3	69.9	57.9
1955	16.1	16.8	10.5	−.7	67.4	55.7
1956	17.0	16.1	9.7	.9	62.1	50.6
1957	17.2	16.5	9.8	.7	58.6	47.2
1958	16.8	17.4	9.9	−.6	59.0	47.7
1959	15.7	18.2	9.7	−2.5	56.9	46.4
1960	17.3	17.2	9.0	.1	54.3	44.3
1961	17.2	17.8	9.1	−.6	53.4	43.5
1962	17.0	18.2	8.9	−1.2	51.6	42.3
1963	17.2	18.0	8.6	−.8	50.1	41.0
1964	17.0	17.9	8.3	−.9	47.7	38.7
1965	16.4	16.6	7.1	−.2	45.4	36.7
1966	16.7	17.2	7.4	−.5	42.0	33.7
1967	17.8	18.8	8.5	−1.0	40.6	31.8
1968	17.0	19.8	9.1	−2.8	41.0	32.2
1969	19.0	18.7	8.4	.3	37.2	28.3
1970	18.4	18.6	7.8	−.3	36.3	27.0
1971	16.7	18.8	7.0	−2.1	36.5	27.1
1972	17.0	18.9	6.5	−1.9	35.7	26.4
1973	17.0	18.1	5.7	−1.1	34.4	25.1
1974	17.7	18.1	5.3	−.4	32.6	23.1
1975	17.3	20.6	5.4	−3.3	33.6	24.5
1976	16.6	20.8	5.0	−4.1	35.1	26.7
Transition quarter	17.2	20.3	4.7	−3.1	34.0	26.2
1977	17.5	20.2	4.8	−2.6	34.8	27.1
1978	17.5	20.1	4.6	−2.6	34.1	26.6
1979	18.0	19.6	4.5	−1.6	32.3	24.9
1980	18.5	21.1	4.8	−2.6	32.5	25.5
1981	19.1	21.6	5.0	−2.5	31.7	25.2
1982	18.6	22.5	5.6	−3.9	34.3	27.9
1983	17.0	22.8	5.9	−5.9	38.7	32.1
1984	16.9	21.5	5.8	−4.7	39.6	33.1
1985	17.2	22.2	5.9	−5.0	42.6	35.3
1986	17.0	21.8	6.0	−4.9	46.7	38.4
1987	17.9	21.0	5.9	−3.1	49.1	39.5
1988	17.6	20.6	5.6	−3.0	50.5	39.8
1989	17.8	20.5	5.4	−2.7	51.5	39.3
1990	17.4	21.2	5.1	−3.7	54.2	40.8
1991	17.3	21.7	4.5	−4.4	58.9	44.0
1992	17.0	21.5	4.6	−4.5	62.2	46.6
1993	17.0	20.7	4.3	−3.8	64.0	47.8
1994	17.5	20.3	3.9	−2.8	64.5	47.7
1995	17.8	20.0	3.6	−2.2	64.9	47.5
1996	18.2	19.6	3.3	−1.3	64.9	46.8
1997	18.6	18.9	3.2	−.3	63.3	44.5
1998	19.2	18.5	3.0	.8	61.2	41.6
1999	19.2	17.9	2.9	1.3	58.9	38.2
2000	19.9	17.6	2.9	2.3	55.4	33.6
2001	18.8	17.6	2.9	1.2	54.6	31.4
2002	17.0	18.5	3.2	−1.5	57.0	32.5
2003	15.7	19.1	3.6	−3.3	59.6	34.5
2004	15.6	19.0	3.8	−3.4	60.8	35.5
2005	16.7	19.2	3.8	−2.5	61.3	35.6
2006	17.6	19.4	3.8	−1.8	61.7	35.3
2007	17.9	19.0	3.8	−1.1	62.5	35.1
2008	17.1	20.2	4.2	−3.1	67.7	39.3
2009	14.6	24.4	4.6	−9.8	82.4	52.3
2010	14.6	23.4	4.7	−8.8	91.5	61.0
2011	15.0	23.4	4.6	−8.4	96.0	65.8
2012	15.2	22.0	4.2	−6.8	99.7	70.1
2013	16.7	20.8	3.8	−4.1	100.6	72.1
2014 (estimates)	17.3	21.1	3.6	−3.7	103.2	74.4
2015 (estimates)	18.3	21.4	3.5	−3.1	102.7	74.6

Note: See Note, Table B–19.

Sources: Department of the Treasury and Office of Management and Budget.

[Billions of dollars; fiscal years]

Fiscal year or period	Receipts (on-budget and off-budget)					Outlays (on-budget and off-budget)										Surplus or deficit (–) (on-budget and off-budget)
	Total	Individual income taxes	Corporation income taxes	Social insurance and retirement receipts	Other	Total	National defense		International affairs	Health	Medicare	Income security	Social security	Net interest	Other	
							Total	Department of Defense, military								
1947	38.5	17.9	8.6	3.4	8.5	34.5	12.8		5.8	0.2		2.8	0.5	4.2	8.2	4.0
1948	41.6	19.3	9.7	3.8	8.8	29.8	9.1		4.6	.2		2.5	.6	4.3	8.5	11.8
1949	39.4	15.6	11.2	3.8	8.9	38.8	13.2		6.1	.2		3.2	.7	4.5	11.1	.6
1950	39.4	15.8	10.4	4.3	8.9	42.6	13.7		4.7	.3		4.1	.8	4.8	14.2	–3.1
1951	51.6	21.6	14.1	5.7	10.2	45.5	23.6		3.6	.3		3.4	1.6	4.7	8.4	6.1
1952	66.2	27.9	21.2	6.4	10.6	67.7	46.1		2.7	.3		3.7	2.1	4.7	8.1	–1.5
1953	69.6	29.8	21.2	6.8	11.7	76.1	52.8		2.1	.3		3.8	2.7	5.2	9.1	–6.5
1954	69.7	29.5	21.1	7.2	11.9	70.9	49.3		1.6	.3		4.4	3.4	4.9	7.1	–1.2
1955	65.5	28.7	17.9	7.9	11.0	68.4	42.7		2.2	.3		5.1	4.4	4.9	8.9	–3.0
1956	74.6	32.2	20.9	9.3	12.2	70.6	42.5		2.4	.4		4.7	5.5	5.1	10.1	3.9
1957	80.0	35.6	21.2	10.0	13.2	76.6	45.4		3.1	.5		5.4	6.7	5.4	10.1	3.4
1958	79.6	34.7	20.1	11.2	13.6	82.4	46.8		3.4	.5		7.5	8.2	5.6	10.3	–2.8
1959	79.2	36.7	17.3	11.7	13.5	92.1	49.0		3.1	.7		8.2	9.7	5.8	15.5	–12.8
1960	92.5	40.7	21.5	14.7	15.6	92.2	48.1		3.0	.8		7.4	11.6	6.9	14.4	.3
1961	94.4	41.3	21.0	16.4	15.7	97.7	49.6		3.2	.9		9.7	12.5	6.7	15.2	–3.3
1962	99.7	45.6	20.5	17.0	16.5	106.8	52.3	50.1	5.6	1.2		9.2	14.4	6.9	17.2	–7.1
1963	106.6	47.6	21.6	19.8	17.6	111.3	53.4	51.1	5.3	1.5		9.3	15.8	7.7	18.3	–4.8
1964	112.6	48.7	23.5	22.0	18.5	118.5	54.8	52.6	4.9	1.8		9.7	16.6	8.2	22.6	–5.9
1965	116.8	48.8	25.5	22.2	20.3	118.2	50.6	48.8	5.3	1.8		9.5	17.5	8.6	25.0	–1.4
1966	130.8	55.4	30.1	25.5	19.8	134.5	58.1	56.6	5.6	2.5	0.1	9.7	20.7	9.4	28.5	–3.7
1967	148.8	61.5	34.0	32.6	20.7	157.5	71.4	70.1	5.6	3.4	2.7	10.3	21.7	10.3	32.1	–8.6
1968	153.0	68.7	28.7	33.9	21.7	178.1	81.9	80.8	5.3	4.4	4.6	11.8	23.9	11.1	35.1	–25.2
1969	186.9	87.2	36.7	39.0	23.9	183.6	82.5	80.8	4.6	5.2	5.7	13.1	27.3	12.7	32.6	3.2
1970	192.8	90.4	32.8	44.4	25.2	195.6	81.7	80.1	4.3	5.9	6.2	15.7	30.3	14.4	37.2	–2.8
1971	187.1	86.2	26.8	47.3	26.8	210.2	78.9	77.5	4.2	6.8	6.6	22.9	35.9	14.8	40.0	–23.0
1972	207.3	94.7	32.2	52.6	27.8	230.7	79.2	77.6	4.8	8.7	7.5	27.7	40.2	15.5	47.3	–23.4
1973	230.8	103.2	36.2	63.1	28.3	245.7	76.7	75.0	4.1	9.4	8.1	28.3	49.1	17.3	52.8	–14.9
1974	263.2	119.0	38.6	75.1	30.6	269.4	79.3	77.9	5.7	10.7	9.6	33.7	55.9	21.4	52.9	–6.1
1975	279.1	122.4	40.6	84.5	31.5	332.3	86.5	84.9	7.1	12.9	12.9	50.2	64.7	23.2	74.8	–53.2
1976	298.1	131.6	41.4	90.8	34.3	371.8	89.6	87.9	6.4	15.7	15.8	60.8	73.9	26.7	82.7	–73.7
Transition quarter	81.2	38.8	8.5	25.2	8.8	96.0	22.3	21.8	2.5	3.9	4.3	15.0	19.8	6.9	21.4	–14.7
1977	355.6	157.6	54.9	106.5	36.6	409.2	97.2	95.1	6.4	17.3	19.3	61.1	85.1	29.9	93.0	–53.7
1978	399.6	181.0	60.0	121.0	37.7	458.7	104.5	102.3	7.5	18.5	22.8	61.5	93.9	35.5	114.7	–59.2
1979	463.3	217.8	65.7	138.9	40.8	504.0	116.3	113.6	7.5	20.5	26.5	66.4	104.1	42.6	120.2	–40.7
1980	517.1	244.1	64.6	157.8	50.6	590.9	134.0	130.9	12.7	23.2	32.1	86.6	118.5	52.5	131.3	–73.8
1981	599.3	285.9	61.1	182.7	69.5	678.2	157.5	153.9	13.1	26.9	39.1	100.3	139.6	68.8	133.0	–79.0
1982	617.8	297.7	49.2	201.5	69.3	745.7	185.3	180.7	12.3	27.4	46.6	108.2	156.0	85.0	125.0	–128.0
1983	600.6	288.9	37.0	209.0	65.6	808.4	209.9	204.4	11.8	28.6	52.6	123.0	170.7	89.8	121.8	–207.8
1984	666.4	298.4	56.9	239.4	71.8	851.8	227.4	220.9	15.9	30.4	57.5	113.4	178.2	111.1	117.9	–185.4
1985	734.0	334.5	61.3	265.2	73.0	946.3	252.7	245.1	16.2	33.5	65.8	129.0	188.6	129.5	131.0	–212.3
1986	769.2	349.0	63.1	283.9	73.2	990.4	273.4	265.4	14.1	35.9	70.2	120.6	198.8	136.0	141.4	–221.2
1987	854.3	392.6	83.9	303.3	74.5	1,004.0	282.0	273.9	11.6	40.0	75.1	124.1	207.4	138.6	125.2	–149.7
1988	909.2	401.2	94.5	334.3	79.2	1,064.4	290.4	281.9	10.5	44.5	78.9	130.4	219.3	151.8	138.7	–155.2
1989	991.1	445.7	103.3	359.4	82.7	1,143.7	303.6	294.8	9.6	48.4	85.0	137.4	232.5	169.0	158.3	–152.6
1990	1,032.0	466.9	93.5	380.0	91.5	1,253.0	299.3	289.7	13.8	57.7	98.1	148.7	248.6	184.3	202.5	–221.0
1991	1,055.0	467.8	98.1	396.0	93.1	1,324.2	273.3	262.3	15.8	71.2	104.5	172.5	269.0	194.4	223.5	–269.2
1992	1,091.2	476.0	100.3	413.7	101.3	1,381.5	298.3	286.8	16.1	89.5	119.0	199.6	287.6	199.3	172.1	–290.3
1993	1,154.3	509.7	117.5	428.3	98.8	1,409.4	291.1	278.5	17.2	99.4	130.6	210.0	304.6	198.7	157.9	–255.1
1994	1,258.6	543.1	140.4	461.5	113.7	1,461.8	281.6	268.6	17.1	107.1	144.7	217.2	319.6	202.9	171.5	–203.2
1995	1,351.8	590.2	157.0	484.5	120.1	1,515.7	272.1	259.4	16.4	115.4	159.9	223.8	335.8	232.1	160.2	–164.0
1996	1,453.1	656.4	171.8	509.4	115.4	1,560.5	265.7	253.1	13.5	119.4	174.2	229.7	349.7	241.1	167.2	–107.4
1997	1,579.2	737.5	182.3	539.4	120.1	1,601.1	270.5	258.3	15.2	123.8	190.0	235.0	365.3	244.0	157.3	–21.9
1998	1,721.7	828.6	188.7	571.8	132.6	1,652.5	268.2	255.8	13.1	131.4	192.8	237.8	379.2	241.1	188.9	69.3
1999	1,827.5	879.5	184.7	611.8	151.5	1,701.8	274.8	261.2	15.2	141.0	190.4	242.5	390.0	229.8	218.1	125.6
2000	2,025.2	1,004.5	207.3	652.9	160.6	1,789.0	294.4	281.0	17.2	154.5	197.1	253.7	409.4	222.9	239.7	236.2
2001	1,991.1	994.3	151.1	694.0	151.7	1,862.8	304.7	290.2	16.5	172.2	217.4	269.8	433.0	206.2	243.1	128.2
2002	1,853.1	858.3	148.0	700.8	146.0	2,010.9	348.5	331.8	22.3	196.5	230.9	312.7	456.0	170.9	273.1	–157.8
2003	1,782.3	793.7	131.8	713.0	143.9	2,159.9	404.7	387.1	21.2	219.5	249.4	334.6	474.7	153.1	302.6	–377.6
2004	1,880.1	809.0	189.4	733.4	148.4	2,292.8	455.8	436.4	26.9	240.1	269.4	333.1	495.5	160.2	311.8	–412.7
2005	2,153.6	927.2	278.3	794.1	154.0	2,472.0	495.3	474.1	34.6	250.5	298.6	345.8	523.3	184.0	339.8	–318.3
2006	2,406.9	1,043.9	353.9	837.8	171.2	2,655.1	521.8	499.3	29.5	252.7	329.9	352.5	548.5	226.6	393.5	–248.2
2007	2,568.0	1,163.5	370.2	869.6	164.7	2,728.7	551.3	528.5	28.5	266.4	375.4	366.0	586.2	237.1	317.9	–160.7
2008	2,524.0	1,145.7	304.3	900.2	173.7	2,982.5	616.1	594.6	28.9	280.6	390.8	431.3	617.0	252.8	365.2	–458.6
2009	2,105.0	915.3	138.2	890.9	160.5	3,517.7	661.0	636.7	37.5	334.3	430.1	533.2	683.0	186.9	651.6	–1,412.7
2010	2,162.7	898.5	191.4	864.8	207.9	3,457.1	693.5	666.7	45.2	369.1	451.6	622.2	706.7	196.2	372.6	–1,294.4
2011	2,303.5	1,091.5	181.1	818.8	212.1	3,603.1	705.6	678.1	45.7	372.5	485.7	597.4	730.8	230.0	435.5	–1,299.6
2012	2,450.2	1,132.2	242.3	845.3	230.4	3,537.1	677.9	650.9	47.2	346.7	471.8	541.3	773.3	220.4	458.5	–1,087.0
2013	2,775.1	1,316.4	273.5	947.8	237.4	3,454.6	633.4	607.8	46.4	358.3	497.8	536.5	813.6	220.9	347.7	–679.5
2014 (estimates)	3,001.7	1,386.1	332.7	1,021.1	261.8	3,650.5	620.6	593.3	48.5	450.8	519.0	542.2	857.3	223.5	388.7	–648.8
2015 (estimates)	3,337.4	1,533.9	449.0	1,055.7	298.7	3,901.0	631.3	584.3	50.1	512.2	532.3	536.0	903.2	251.9	484.1	–563.6

Note: See Note, Table B–19.

Sources: Department of the Treasury and Office of Management and Budget.

TABLE B–22. Federal receipts, outlays, surplus or deficit, and debt, fiscal years 2010–2015

[Millions of dollars; fiscal years]

Description	Actual				Estimates	
	2010	2011	2012	2013	2014	2015
RECEIPTS, OUTLAYS, AND SURPLUS OR DEFICIT						
Total:						
Receipts	2,162,706	2,303,466	2,450,164	2,775,103	3,001,721	3,337,425
Outlays	3,457,079	3,603,059	3,537,127	3,454,605	3,650,526	3,900,989
Surplus or deficit (–)	–1,294,373	–1,299,593	–1,086,963	–679,502	–648,805	–563,564
On-budget:						
Receipts	1,531,019	1,737,678	1,880,663	2,101,829	2,269,389	2,579,548
Outlays	2,902,397	3,104,453	3,029,539	2,820,794	2,939,299	3,143,368
Surplus or deficit (–)	–1,371,378	–1,366,775	–1,148,876	–718,965	–669,910	–563,820
Off-budget:						
Receipts	631,687	565,788	569,501	673,274	732,332	757,877
Outlays	554,682	498,606	507,588	633,811	711,227	757,621
Surplus or deficit (–)	77,005	67,182	61,913	39,463	21,105	256
OUTSTANDING DEBT, END OF PERIOD						
Gross Federal debt	13,528,807	14,764,222	16,050,921	16,719,434	17,892,637	18,713,486
Held by Federal Government accounts	4,509,926	4,636,035	4,769,790	4,736,856	4,989,977	5,121,683
Held by the public	9,018,882	10,128,187	11,281,131	11,982,577	12,902,660	13,591,802
Federal Reserve System	811,669	1,664,660	1,645,285	2,072,283	....	....
Other	8,207,213	8,463,527	9,635,846	9,910,294	....	....
RECEIPTS BY SOURCE						
Total: On-budget and off-budget	2,162,706	2,303,466	2,450,164	2,775,103	3,001,721	3,337,425
Individual income taxes	898,549	1,091,473	1,132,206	1,316,405	1,386,068	1,533,942
Corporation income taxes	191,437	181,085	242,289	273,506	332,740	449,020
Social insurance and retirement receipts	864,814	818,792	845,314	947,820	1,021,109	1,055,744
On-budget	233,127	253,004	275,813	274,546	288,777	297,867
Off-budget	631,687	565,788	569,501	673,274	732,332	757,877
Excise taxes	66,909	72,381	79,061	84,007	93,528	110,539
Estate and gift taxes	18,885	7,399	13,973	18,912	15,746	17,526
Customs duties and fees	25,298	29,519	30,307	31,815	34,966	36,965
Miscellaneous receipts	96,814	102,817	107,014	102,638	117,564	131,689
Deposits of earnings by Federal Reserve System	75,845	82,546	81,957	75,767	90,422	88,292
All other	20,969	20,271	25,057	26,871	27,142	43,397
Legislative proposals [1]	....	....	....	....	....	2,000
OUTLAYS BY FUNCTION						
Total: On-budget and off-budget	3,457,079	3,603,059	3,537,127	3,454,605	3,650,526	3,900,989
National defense	693,485	705,554	677,852	633,385	620,562	631,280
International affairs	45,195	45,685	47,189	46,418	48,472	50,086
General science, space, and technology	30,100	29,466	29,060	28,908	28,718	30,839
Energy	11,618	12,174	14,858	11,042	13,375	8,620
Natural resources and environment	43,667	45,473	41,631	38,145	39,102	41,349
Agriculture	21,356	20,662	17,791	29,492	22,659	16,953
Commerce and housing credit	–82,316	–12,573	40,823	–83,199	–82,283	–31,430
On-budget	–87,016	–13,381	38,153	–81,286	–78,331	–30,472
Off-budget	4,700	808	2,670	–1,913	–3,952	–958
Transportation	91,972	92,966	93,019	91,673	95,519	97,825
Community and regional development	23,894	23,883	25,132	32,336	33,305	28,865
Education, training, employment, and social services	128,598	101,233	90,823	72,808	100,460	117,350
Health	369,068	372,504	346,742	358,315	450,795	512,193
Medicare	451,636	485,653	471,793	497,826	519,027	532,324
Income security	622,210	597,352	541,344	536,511	542,237	535,963
Social security	706,737	730,811	773,290	813,551	857,319	903,196
On-budget	23,317	101,933	140,387	56,009	26,204	32,388
Off-budget	683,420	628,878	632,903	757,542	831,115	870,808
Veterans benefits and services	108,384	127,189	124,595	138,938	151,165	158,524
Administration of justice	54,383	56,056	56,277	52,601	53,102	55,843
General government	23,014	27,476	28,036	27,755	22,407	25,706
Net interest	196,194	229,962	220,408	220,885	223,450	251,871
On-budget	314,696	345,943	332,801	326,535	323,689	348,074
Off-budget	–118,502	–115,981	–112,393	–105,650	–100,239	–96,203
Allowances	....	....	....	....	1,875	29,285
Undistributed offsetting receipts	–82,116	–88,467	–103,536	–92,785	–90,740	–95,653
On-budget	–67,180	–73,368	–87,944	–76,617	–75,043	–79,627
Off-budget	–14,936	–15,099	–15,592	–16,168	–15,697	–16,026

[1] Includes Undistributed Allowance for Immigration Reform.

Note: See Note, Table B–19.

Sources: Department of the Treasury and Office of Management and Budget.

TABLE B–23. Federal and State and local government current receipts and expenditures, national income and product accounts (NIPA), 1965–2013

[Billions of dollars; quarterly data at seasonally adjusted annual rates]

Year or quarter	Total government Current receipts	Total government Current expenditures	Total government Net government saving (NIPA)	Federal Government Current receipts	Federal Government Current expenditures	Federal Government Net Federal Government saving (NIPA)	State and local government Current receipts	State and local government Current expenditures	State and local government Net State and local government saving (NIPA)	Addendum: Grants-in-aid to State and local governments
1965	179.7	181.0	−1.4	120.4	125.9	−5.5	65.8	61.7	4.1	6.6
1966	202.1	203.9	−1.8	137.4	144.3	−7.0	74.1	68.9	5.2	9.4
1967	216.9	231.7	−14.8	146.3	165.7	−19.5	81.6	76.9	4.7	10.9
1968	251.2	260.7	−9.5	170.6	184.3	−13.7	92.5	88.2	4.3	11.8
1969	282.5	283.5	−1.0	191.8	196.9	−5.1	104.3	100.2	4.1	13.7
1970	285.7	317.5	−31.8	185.1	219.9	−34.8	118.9	115.9	3.0	18.3
1971	302.1	352.4	−50.2	190.7	241.5	−50.8	133.6	133.0	0.6	22.1
1972	345.4	385.9	−40.5	219.0	267.9	−48.9	156.9	148.5	8.4	30.5
1973	388.5	416.6	−28.0	249.2	286.9	−37.7	172.8	163.1	9.6	33.5
1974	430.0	468.3	−38.3	278.5	319.1	−40.6	186.4	184.1	2.3	34.9
1975	440.9	543.5	−102.5	276.8	373.8	−97.0	207.7	213.3	−5.6	43.6
1976	505.0	582.1	−77.1	322.2	402.1	−79.9	231.9	229.1	2.8	49.1
1977	566.7	630.1	−63.5	363.5	435.4	−71.9	257.9	249.5	8.4	54.8
1978	645.4	691.8	−46.4	423.6	483.4	−59.8	285.3	271.9	13.4	63.5
1979	728.6	764.9	−36.3	486.8	531.3	−44.5	305.8	297.6	8.2	64.0
1980	798.7	879.5	−80.9	533.0	619.3	−86.3	335.3	329.9	5.4	69.7
1981	918.0	999.7	−81.7	620.4	706.3	−85.8	367.0	362.9	4.1	69.4
1982	939.9	1,109.6	−169.7	618.0	782.7	−164.6	388.1	393.2	−5.1	66.3
1983	1,001.1	1,204.9	−203.7	644.2	849.2	−205.0	424.8	423.6	1.3	67.9
1984	1,113.9	1,285.4	−171.4	710.7	903.0	−192.3	475.6	454.7	20.9	72.3
1985	1,216.0	1,391.4	−175.4	775.3	970.9	−195.6	516.9	496.7	20.3	76.2
1986	1,291.7	1,483.9	−192.2	817.3	1,030.0	−212.7	556.8	536.4	20.4	82.4
1987	1,405.5	1,556.6	−151.1	899.0	1,062.1	−163.2	585.0	572.9	12.1	78.4
1988	1,505.5	1,645.9	−140.4	961.4	1,118.8	−157.3	629.9	612.9	17.0	85.7
1989	1,629.8	1,779.0	−149.2	1,040.8	1,197.5	−156.6	680.8	673.4	7.4	91.8
1990	1,710.9	1,918.3	−207.4	1,085.7	1,286.6	−200.9	729.6	736.0	−6.5	104.4
1991	1,761.0	2,032.3	−271.3	1,105.6	1,351.8	−246.2	779.5	804.6	−25.1	124.0
1992	1,846.0	2,216.1	−370.2	1,152.1	1,484.7	−332.7	835.6	873.1	−37.5	141.7
1993	1,950.1	2,299.1	−349.0	1,228.8	1,540.6	−311.8	877.1	914.3	−37.2	155.7
1994	2,094.0	2,374.6	−280.7	1,326.7	1,580.4	−253.7	934.1	961.0	−27.0	166.8
1995	2,218.2	2,490.6	−272.4	1,412.9	1,653.7	−240.8	979.8	1,011.4	−31.5	174.5
1996	2,382.3	2,573.2	−191.0	1,531.2	1,709.7	−178.5	1,032.6	1,045.0	−12.5	181.5
1997	2,559.3	2,648.8	−89.5	1,661.6	1,752.8	−91.2	1,085.8	1,084.1	1.7	188.1
1998	2,731.7	2,713.6	18.1	1,783.8	1,781.0	2.7	1,148.7	1,133.3	15.4	200.8
1999	2,903.4	2,827.6	75.8	1,900.7	1,834.2	66.5	1,221.8	1,212.6	9.2	219.2
2000	3,133.1	2,967.3	165.8	2,063.2	1,907.3	155.9	1,303.1	1,293.2	9.9	233.1
2001	3,118.2	3,169.5	−51.3	2,026.8	2,012.8	14.0	1,352.6	1,417.9	−65.3	261.3
2002	2,967.0	3,358.9	−391.9	1,865.8	2,136.7	−270.9	1,388.4	1,509.4	−120.9	287.2
2003	3,042.8	3,567.8	−524.9	1,889.9	2,293.5	−403.5	1,474.6	1,596.0	−121.4	321.7
2004	3,265.1	3,773.2	−508.1	2,022.2	2,422.0	−399.8	1,575.1	1,683.4	−108.4	332.2
2005	3,663.5	4,035.6	−372.0	2,298.1	2,603.5	−305.4	1,708.8	1,775.4	−66.6	343.4
2006	4,001.8	4,269.3	−267.5	2,531.7	2,759.8	−228.1	1,810.9	1,850.3	−39.4	340.8
2007	4,202.4	4,541.8	−339.4	2,660.8	2,927.5	−266.7	1,900.6	1,973.3	−72.7	359.0
2008	4,043.8	4,844.0	−800.2	2,505.7	3,140.8	−635.1	1,909.1	2,074.1	−165.1	371.0
2009	3,691.2	5,213.0	−1,521.7	2,230.1	3,479.9	−1,249.8	1,919.2	2,191.2	−271.9	458.1
2010	3,885.0	5,451.8	−1,566.8	2,391.7	3,721.3	−1,329.5	1,998.5	2,235.8	−237.3	505.3
2011	4,074.1	5,535.4	−1,461.3	2,516.7	3,764.9	−1,248.3	2,029.9	2,243.0	−213.1	472.5
2012	4,259.2	5,621.6	−1,362.3	2,663.0	3,772.7	−1,109.7	2,039.4	2,292.1	−252.7	443.2
2013 ᵖ	....	5,669.3	....	....	3,792.8	....	....	2,320.4	....	444.0
2010: I	3,780.5	5,393.2	−1,612.6	2,309.0	3,661.3	−1,352.3	1,963.7	2,224.0	−260.3	492.2
II	3,836.2	5,439.2	−1,603.0	2,363.1	3,703.1	−1,340.0	1,965.4	2,228.4	−262.9	492.3
III	3,933.2	5,474.9	−1,541.7	2,429.9	3,750.0	−1,320.1	2,020.5	2,242.1	−221.6	517.2
IV	3,989.9	5,500.0	−1,510.1	2,465.0	3,770.6	−1,305.7	2,044.5	2,248.9	−204.4	519.5
2011: I	4,051.7	5,507.0	−1,455.3	2,506.3	3,751.3	−1,244.9	2,040.7	2,251.1	−210.3	495.4
II	4,081.6	5,583.6	−1,502.0	2,523.1	3,836.4	−1,313.4	2,059.0	2,247.6	−188.6	500.5
III	4,075.1	5,529.9	−1,454.8	2,515.7	3,747.4	−1,231.7	2,013.1	2,236.3	−223.1	453.8
IV	4,088.0	5,521.3	−1,433.3	2,521.6	3,724.6	−1,203.0	2,006.7	2,236.9	−230.3	440.3
2012: I	4,233.7	5,568.9	−1,335.1	2,645.4	3,739.4	−1,094.0	2,024.4	2,265.5	−241.1	436.1
II	4,234.4	5,636.5	−1,402.1	2,641.1	3,787.9	−1,146.9	2,034.1	2,289.3	−255.2	440.7
III	4,248.5	5,627.9	−1,379.4	2,656.6	3,775.8	−1,119.3	2,039.6	2,299.7	−260.1	447.7
IV	4,320.3	5,653.0	−1,332.7	2,709.0	3,787.5	−1,078.5	2,059.7	2,313.9	−254.2	448.4
2013: I	4,547.3	5,630.1	−1,082.9	2,900.1	3,753.2	−853.1	2,078.7	2,308.5	−229.8	431.5
II	4,832.0	5,682.7	−850.7	3,166.9	3,820.1	−653.1	2,110.8	2,308.4	−197.6	445.7
III	4,623.3	5,699.3	−1,075.9	2,975.8	3,825.7	−850.0	2,103.2	2,329.2	−226.0	455.7
IV ᵖ	....	5,665.0	....	....	3,772.4	....	....	2,335.6	....	442.9

Note: Federal grants-in-aid to State and local governments are reflected in Federal current expenditures and State and local current receipts. Total government current receipts and expenditures have been adjusted to eliminate this duplication.

Source: Department of Commerce (Bureau of Economic Analysis).

TABLE B–24. State and local government revenues and expenditures, selected fiscal years, 1954–2011

[Millions of dollars]

Fiscal year [1]	General revenues by source [2]							General expenditures by function [2]				
	Total	Property taxes	Sales and gross receipts taxes	Individual income taxes	Corporation net income taxes	Revenue from Federal Government	All other [3]	Total [4]	Education	Highways	Public welfare [4]	All other [4,5]
1954	29,012	9,967	7,276	1,127	778	2,966	6,898	30,701	10,557	5,527	3,060	11,557
1955	31,073	10,735	7,643	1,237	744	3,131	7,583	33,724	11,907	6,452	3,168	12,197
1956	34,670	11,749	8,691	1,538	890	3,335	8,467	36,715	13,224	6,953	3,139	13,399
1957	38,164	12,864	9,467	1,754	984	3,843	9,252	40,375	14,134	7,816	3,485	14,940
1958	41,219	14,047	9,829	1,759	1,018	4,865	9,701	44,851	15,919	8,567	3,818	16,547
1959	45,306	14,983	10,437	1,994	1,001	6,377	10,514	48,887	17,283	9,592	4,136	17,876
1960	50,505	16,405	11,849	2,463	1,180	6,974	11,634	51,876	18,719	9,428	4,404	19,325
1961	54,037	18,002	12,463	2,613	1,266	7,131	12,562	56,201	20,574	9,844	4,720	21,063
1962	58,252	19,054	13,494	3,037	1,308	7,871	13,488	60,206	22,216	10,357	5,084	22,549
1963	62,891	20,089	14,456	3,269	1,505	8,722	14,850	64,815	23,776	11,135	5,481	24,423
1963–64	68,443	21,241	15,762	3,791	1,695	10,002	15,952	69,302	26,286	11,664	5,766	25,586
1964–65	74,000	22,583	17,118	4,090	1,929	11,029	17,251	74,678	28,563	12,221	6,315	27,579
1965–66	83,036	24,670	19,085	4,760	2,038	13,214	19,269	82,843	33,287	12,770	6,757	30,029
1966–67	91,197	26,047	20,530	5,825	2,227	15,370	21,198	93,350	37,919	13,932	8,218	33,281
1967–68	101,264	27,747	22,911	7,308	2,518	17,181	23,599	102,411	41,158	14,481	9,857	36,915
1968–69	114,550	30,673	26,519	8,908	3,180	19,153	26,117	116,728	47,238	15,417	12,110	41,963
1969–70	130,756	34,054	30,322	10,812	3,738	21,857	29,973	131,332	52,718	16,427	14,679	47,508
1970–71	144,927	37,852	33,233	11,900	3,424	26,146	32,372	150,674	59,413	18,095	18,226	54,940
1971–72	167,535	42,877	37,518	15,227	4,416	31,342	36,156	168,549	65,813	19,021	21,117	62,598
1972–73	190,222	45,283	42,047	17,994	5,425	39,264	40,210	181,357	69,713	18,615	23,582	69,447
1973–74	207,670	47,705	46,098	19,491	6,015	41,820	46,542	199,222	75,833	19,946	25,085	78,358
1974–75	228,171	51,491	49,815	21,454	6,642	47,034	51,735	230,722	87,858	22,528	28,156	92,180
1975–76	256,176	57,001	54,547	24,575	7,273	55,589	57,191	256,731	97,216	23,907	32,604	103,004
1976–77	285,157	62,527	60,641	29,246	9,174	62,444	61,125	274,215	102,780	23,058	35,906	112,472
1977–78	315,960	66,422	67,596	33,176	10,738	69,592	68,435	296,984	110,758	24,609	39,140	122,478
1978–79	343,236	64,944	74,247	36,932	12,128	75,164	79,822	327,517	119,448	28,440	41,898	137,731
1979–80	382,322	68,499	79,927	42,080	13,321	83,029	95,467	369,086	133,211	33,311	47,288	155,276
1980–81	423,404	74,969	85,971	46,426	14,143	90,294	111,599	407,449	145,784	34,603	54,105	172,957
1981–82	457,654	82,067	93,613	50,738	15,028	87,282	128,925	436,733	154,282	34,520	57,996	189,935
1982–83	486,753	89,105	100,247	55,129	14,258	90,007	138,008	466,516	163,876	36,655	60,906	205,080
1983–84	542,730	96,457	114,097	64,871	16,798	96,935	153,571	505,008	176,108	39,419	66,414	223,068
1984–85	598,121	103,757	126,376	70,361	19,152	106,158	172,317	553,899	192,686	44,989	71,479	244,745
1985–86	641,486	111,709	135,005	74,365	19,994	113,099	187,314	605,623	210,819	49,368	75,868	269,568
1986–87	686,860	121,203	144,091	83,935	22,425	114,857	200,350	657,134	226,619	52,355	82,650	295,510
1987–88	726,762	132,212	156,452	88,350	23,663	117,602	208,482	704,921	242,683	55,621	89,090	317,527
1988–89	786,129	142,400	166,336	97,806	25,926	125,824	227,838	762,360	263,898	58,105	97,879	342,479
1989–90	849,502	155,613	177,885	105,640	23,566	136,802	249,996	834,818	288,148	61,057	110,518	375,094
1990–91	902,207	167,999	185,570	109,341	22,242	154,099	262,955	908,108	309,302	64,937	130,402	403,467
1991–92	979,137	180,337	197,731	115,638	23,880	179,174	282,376	981,253	324,652	67,351	158,723	430,526
1992–93	1,041,643	189,744	209,649	123,235	26,417	198,663	293,935	1,030,434	342,287	68,370	170,705	449,072
1993–94	1,100,490	197,141	223,628	128,810	28,320	215,421	307,099	1,077,665	353,287	72,067	183,394	468,916
1994–95	1,169,505	203,451	237,268	137,931	31,406	228,771	330,677	1,149,863	378,273	77,109	196,703	497,779
1995–96	1,222,821	209,440	248,993	146,844	32,009	234,891	350,645	1,193,276	398,859	79,092	197,354	517,971
1996–97	1,289,237	218,877	261,418	159,042	33,820	244,847	371,233	1,249,984	418,416	82,062	203,779	545,727
1997–98	1,365,762	230,150	274,883	175,630	34,412	255,048	395,639	1,318,042	450,365	87,214	208,120	572,343
1998–99	1,434,029	239,672	290,993	189,309	33,922	270,628	409,505	1,402,369	483,259	93,018	218,957	607,134
1999–2000	1,541,322	249,178	309,290	211,661	36,059	291,950	443,186	1,506,797	521,612	101,336	237,336	646,512
2000–01	1,647,161	263,689	320,217	226,334	35,296	324,033	477,592	1,626,063	563,572	107,235	261,622	693,634
2001–02	1,684,879	279,191	324,123	202,832	28,152	360,546	490,035	1,736,866	594,694	115,295	285,464	741,413
2002–03	1,763,212	296,683	337,787	199,407	31,369	389,264	508,702	1,821,917	621,335	117,696	310,783	772,102
2003–04	1,887,397	317,941	361,027	215,215	33,716	423,112	536,386	1,908,543	655,182	117,153	340,523	795,622
2004–05	2,026,034	335,779	384,266	242,273	43,256	438,558	581,902	2,012,110	688,314	126,350	365,295	832,151
2005–06	2,197,475	364,559	417,735	268,667	53,081	452,975	640,458	2,123,663	728,917	136,502	373,846	884,398
2006–07	2,329,356	388,701	440,331	290,278	60,626	464,585	684,834	2,259,899	773,676	144,714	388,277	953,232
2007–08	2,421,977	409,540	449,945	304,902	57,231	477,441	722,919	2,406,183	826,061	153,831	408,920	1,017,372
2008–09	2,424,861	430,935	433,252	270,862	46,281	536,823	706,713	2,499,881	851,149	154,047	436,640	1,058,044
2009–10	2,502,548	440,577	432,470	260,315	43,865	623,081	702,241	2,542,553	858,259	155,688	460,835	1,067,772
2010–11	2,612,777	443,259	460,824	284,938	48,547	645,962	729,247	2,587,397	861,131	153,005	496,044	1,077,217

[1] Fiscal years not the same for all governments. See Note.
[2] Excludes revenues or expenditures of publicly owned utilities and liquor stores and of insurance-trust activities. Intergovernmental receipts and payments between State and local governments are also excluded.
[3] Includes motor vehicle license taxes, other taxes, and charges and miscellaneous revenues.
[4] Includes intergovernmental payments to the Federal Government.
[5] Includes expenditures for libraries, hospitals, health, employment security administration, veterans' services, air transportation, sea and inland port facilities, parking facilities, police protection, fire protection, correction, protective inspection and regulation, sewerage, natural resources, parks and recreation, housing and community development, solid waste management, financial administration, judicial and legal, general public buildings, other government administration, interest on general debt, and other general expenditures, not elsewhere classified.

Note: Except for States listed, data for fiscal years listed from 1963–64 to 2010–11 are the aggregation of data for government fiscal years that ended in the 12-month period from July 1 to June 30 of those years; Texas used August and Alabama and Michigan used September as end dates. Data for 1963 and earlier years include data for government fiscal years ending during that particular calendar year.

Source: Department of Commerce (Bureau of the Census).

[Billions of dollars]

End of year or month	Total Treasury securities outstanding [1]	Marketable							Nonmarketable				
		Total [2]	Treasury bills	Treasury notes	Treasury bonds	Treasury inflation-protected securities			Total	U.S. savings securities [3]	Foreign series [4]	Government account series	Other [5]
						Total	Notes	Bonds					
Fiscal year:													
1976	609.2	392.6	161.2	191.8	39.6	....	....	....	216.7	69.7	21.5	120.6	4.9
1977	697.8	443.5	156.1	241.7	45.7	....	....	....	254.3	75.6	21.8	140.1	16.8
1978	767.2	485.2	160.9	267.9	56.4	....	....	....	282.0	79.9	21.7	153.3	27.1
1979	819.1	506.7	161.4	274.2	71.1	....	....	....	312.4	80.6	28.1	176.4	27.4
1980	906.8	594.5	199.8	310.9	83.8	....	....	....	312.3	73.0	25.2	189.8	24.2
1981	996.8	683.2	223.4	363.6	96.2	....	....	....	313.6	68.3	20.5	201.1	23.7
1982	1,141.2	824.4	277.9	442.9	103.6	....	....	....	316.8	67.6	14.6	210.5	24.1
1983	1,376.3	1,024.0	340.7	557.5	125.7	....	....	....	352.3	70.6	11.5	234.7	35.6
1984	1,560.4	1,176.6	356.8	661.7	158.1	....	....	....	383.8	73.7	8.8	259.5	41.8
1985	1,822.3	1,360.2	384.2	776.4	199.5	....	....	....	462.1	78.2	6.6	313.9	63.3
1986	2,124.9	1,564.3	410.7	896.9	241.7	....	....	....	560.5	87.8	4.1	365.9	102.8
1987	2,349.4	1,676.0	378.3	1,005.1	277.6	....	....	....	673.4	98.5	4.4	440.7	129.8
1988	2,601.4	1,802.9	398.5	1,089.6	299.9	....	....	....	798.5	107.8	6.3	536.5	148.0
1989	2,837.9	1,892.8	406.6	1,133.2	338.0	....	....	....	945.2	115.7	6.8	663.7	159.0
1990	3,212.7	2,092.8	482.5	1,218.1	377.2	....	....	....	1,119.9	123.9	36.0	779.4	180.6
1991	3,664.5	2,390.7	564.6	1,387.7	423.4	....	....	....	1,273.9	135.4	41.6	908.4	188.5
1992	4,063.8	2,677.5	634.3	1,566.3	461.8	....	....	....	1,386.3	150.3	37.0	1,011.0	188.0
1993	4,410.7	2,904.9	658.4	1,734.2	497.4	....	....	....	1,505.8	169.1	42.5	1,114.3	179.9
1994	4,691.7	3,091.6	697.3	1,867.5	511.8	....	....	....	1,600.1	178.6	42.0	1,211.7	167.8
1995	4,953.0	3,260.4	742.5	1,980.3	522.6	....	....	....	1,692.6	183.5	41.0	1,324.3	143.8
1996	5,220.8	3,418.4	761.2	2,098.7	543.5	....	....	....	1,802.4	184.1	37.5	1,454.7	126.1
1997	5,407.6	3,439.6	701.9	2,122.2	576.2	24.4	24.4	....	1,968.0	182.7	34.9	1,608.5	141.9
1998	5,518.7	3,331.0	637.6	2,009.1	610.4	58.8	41.9	17.0	2,187.6	180.8	35.1	1,777.3	194.4
1999	5,647.3	3,233.0	653.2	1,828.8	643.7	92.4	67.6	24.8	2,414.3	180.0	31.0	2,005.2	198.1
2000	5,622.1	2,992.8	616.2	1,611.3	635.3	115.0	81.6	33.4	2,629.4	177.7	25.4	2,242.9	183.3
2001 [1]	5,807.5	2,930.7	734.9	1,433.0	613.0	134.9	95.1	39.7	2,876.7	186.5	18.3	2,492.1	179.9
2002	6,228.2	3,136.7	868.3	1,521.6	593.0	138.9	93.7	45.1	3,091.5	193.3	12.5	2,707.3	178.4
2003	6,783.2	3,460.7	918.2	1,799.5	576.9	166.1	120.0	46.1	3,322.5	201.6	11.0	2,912.2	197.7
2004	7,379.1	3,846.1	961.5	2,109.6	552.0	223.0	164.5	58.5	3,533.0	204.2	5.9	3,130.0	192.9
2005	7,932.7	4,084.9	914.3	2,328.8	520.7	307.1	229.1	78.0	3,847.8	203.6	3.1	3,380.6	260.5
2006	8,507.0	4,303.0	911.5	2,447.2	534.7	395.6	293.9	101.7	4,203.9	203.7	3.0	3,722.7	274.5
2007	9,007.7	4,448.1	958.1	2,458.0	561.1	456.9	335.7	121.2	4,559.5	197.1	3.0	4,026.8	332.6
2008	10,024.7	5,236.0	1,489.8	2,624.8	582.9	524.5	380.2	144.3	4,788.7	194.3	3.0	4,297.7	293.8
2009	11,909.8	7,009.7	1,992.5	3,773.8	679.8	551.7	396.2	155.5	4,900.1	192.5	4.9	4,454.3	248.4
2010	13,561.6	8,498.3	1,788.5	5,255.9	849.9	593.8	421.1	172.7	5,063.3	188.7	4.2	4,645.3	225.1
2011	14,790.3	9,624.5	1,477.5	6,412.5	1,020.4	705.7	509.4	196.3	5,165.8	185.1	3.0	4,793.9	183.8
2012	16,066.2	10,749.7	1,616.0	7,120.7	1,198.2	807.7	584.7	223.0	5,316.5	183.8	3.0	4,939.3	190.4
2013	16,738.2	11,596.2	1,530.0	7,758.0	1,366.2	936.4	685.5	250.8	5,142.0	180.0	3.0	4,803.1	156.0
2012: Jan	15,356.1	10,068.9	1,525.4	6,711.3	1,078.0	745.7	541.6	204.0	5,287.2	185.2	3.8	4,922.0	176.3
Feb	15,488.9	10,222.3	1,610.4	6,754.4	1,096.0	753.0	540.4	212.7	5,266.6	185.0	3.8	4,902.1	175.7
Mar	15,582.3	10,338.5	1,674.4	6,776.5	1,109.9	769.3	555.7	213.6	5,243.8	184.8	3.6	4,870.8	184.6
Apr	15,692.7	10,400.1	1,613.4	6,883.3	1,125.3	769.6	555.1	214.5	5,292.6	185.2	3.4	4,912.5	191.6
May	15,771.0	10,486.2	1,605.4	6,941.5	1,142.3	788.5	572.4	216.1	5,284.8	184.9	3.2	4,901.7	195.0
June	15,855.5	10,520.8	1,596.4	6,962.9	1,156.2	798.2	574.3	223.9	5,334.7	184.7	3.0	4,953.1	193.9
July	15,933.5	10,607.3	1,581.0	7,067.2	1,169.2	782.9	559.2	223.7	5,326.1	184.4	3.0	4,952.9	185.9
Aug	16,016.0	10,757.0	1,663.0	7,105.8	1,185.2	795.9	572.6	223.4	5,259.0	184.0	3.0	4,885.5	186.5
Sept	16,066.2	10,749.7	1,616.0	7,120.7	1,198.2	807.7	584.7	223.0	5,316.5	183.8	3.0	4,939.3	190.4
Oct	16,261.7	10,887.5	1,622.0	7,228.2	1,211.2	819.0	587.7	231.3	5,374.2	183.6	3.0	4,992.1	195.4
Nov	16,369.7	11,032.8	1,695.0	7,267.7	1,227.2	835.8	603.4	232.4	5,336.9	183.3	3.0	4,959.9	190.7
Dec	16,432.7	11,053.2	1,629.0	7,327.1	1,240.2	849.8	617.5	232.3	5,379.5	182.5	3.0	4,999.6	194.4
2013: Jan	16,433.8	11,115.3	1,607.9	7,386.2	1,253.2	860.9	629.7	231.2	5,318.5	182.2	3.0	4,943.7	189.6
Feb	16,687.3	11,308.4	1,742.0	7,422.5	1,269.2	867.7	628.1	239.6	5,379.0	182.0	3.0	5,008.1	185.8
Mar	16,771.6	11,398.3	1,791.0	7,435.0	1,282.2	883.0	642.8	240.3	5,373.4	181.7	3.0	4,999.0	189.7
Apr	16,828.8	11,416.8	1,694.9	7,528.0	1,295.2	891.6	649.4	242.2	5,412.1	181.5	3.0	5,032.2	195.4
May	16,738.8	11,397.3	1,606.9	7,564.9	1,311.2	907.2	664.3	242.9	5,341.5	181.2	3.0	4,958.8	198.5
June	16,738.2	11,394.9	1,569.9	7,581.7	1,324.2	913.4	663.7	249.7	5,343.3	180.9	3.0	4,972.7	186.7
July	16,738.6	11,483.5	1,556.0	7,680.1	1,337.2	904.6	654.5	250.1	5,255.1	180.6	3.0	4,901.6	170.0
Aug	16,738.8	11,586.3	1,638.0	7,666.5	1,353.2	923.0	672.2	250.7	5,152.5	180.2	3.0	4,809.7	159.5
Sept	16,738.2	11,596.2	1,530.0	7,758.0	1,366.2	936.4	685.5	250.8	5,142.0	180.0	3.0	4,803.1	156.0
Oct	17,156.1	11,695.0	1,545.0	7,811.3	1,379.2	944.6	686.3	258.3	5,461.1	179.7	3.0	5,125.9	152.5
Nov	17,217.2	11,791.7	1,621.0	7,801.8	1,395.2	958.8	700.2	258.6	5,425.5	179.6	3.0	5,092.1	150.9
Dec	17,352.0	11,869.4	1,592.0	7,881.7	1,408.2	972.6	714.7	257.9	5,482.5	179.2	3.0	5,152.9	147.5
2014: Jan	17,293.0	11,825.3	1,486.0	7,929.1	1,421.2	959.1	701.7	257.4	5,467.7	178.8	3.0	5,143.6	142.3

[1] Data beginning with January 2001 are interest-bearing and non-interest-bearing securities; prior data are interest-bearing securities only.
[2] Data from 1986 to 2002 and 2005 to 2014 include Federal Financing Bank securities, not shown separately. Beginning with data for January 2014, includes Floating Rate Notes, not shown separately.
[3] Through 1996, series is U.S. savings bonds. Beginning 1997, includes U.S. retirement plan bonds, U.S. individual retirement bonds, and U.S. savings notes previously included in "other" nonmarketable securities.
[4] Nonmarketable certificates of indebtedness, notes, bonds, and bills in the Treasury foreign series of dollar-denominated and foreign-currency-denominated issues.
[5] Includes depository bonds; retirement plan bonds through 1996; Rural Electrification Administration bonds; State and local bonds; special issues held only by U.S. Government agencies and trust funds and the Federal home loan banks; for the period July 2003 through February 2004, depositary compensation securities; and beginning August 2008, Hope bonds for the HOPE For Homeowners Program.

Note: In fiscal year 1976, the fiscal year was on a July 1–June 30 basis; beginning with October 1976 (fiscal year 1977), the fiscal year is on an October 1–September 30 basis.

Source: Department of the Treasury.

Interest Rates, Money Stock, and Government Finance | 395

TABLE B–26. Estimated ownership of U.S. Treasury securities, 2000–2013

[Billions of dollars]

End of month	Total public debt[1]	Federal Reserve and Intra-governmental holdings[2]	Held by private investors									
			Total privately held	Depository institutions[3]	U.S. savings bonds[4]	Pension funds		Insurance companies	Mutual funds[6]	State and local governments	Foreign and international[7]	Other investors[8]
						Private[5]	State and local governments					
2000: Mar	5,773.4	2,590.6	3,182.8	237.7	178.6	150.2	196.9	120.0	222.3	306.3	1,085.0	685.7
June	5,685.9	2,698.6	2,987.3	222.2	177.7	149.0	194.9	116.5	205.4	309.3	1,060.7	551.7
Sept	5,674.2	2,737.9	2,936.3	220.5	177.7	147.9	185.5	113.7	207.8	307.9	1,038.8	536.5
Dec	5,662.2	2,781.8	2,880.4	201.5	176.9	145.0	179.1	110.2	225.7	310.0	1,015.2	516.9
2001: Mar	5,773.7	2,880.9	2,892.8	196.0	184.8	153.4	177.3	113.3	225.5	316.9	1,012.5	513.1
June	5,726.8	3,004.2	2,722.6	195.5	185.5	148.5	183.1	112.1	221.2	324.8	983.3	368.5
Sept	5,807.5	3,027.8	2,779.7	195.7	186.5	149.9	166.8	111.5	235.2	321.2	992.2	420.7
Dec	5,943.4	3,123.9	2,819.5	192.8	190.4	145.8	155.1	115.4	261.2	328.4	1,040.1	390.2
2002: Mar	6,006.0	3,156.8	2,849.2	201.7	192.0	152.7	163.3	125.6	261.0	327.6	1,057.2	368.3
June	6,126.5	3,276.7	2,849.8	217.4	192.8	152.1	153.9	136.0	245.8	333.6	1,123.1	295.0
Sept	6,228.2	3,303.5	2,924.7	219.6	193.3	154.5	156.3	149.4	248.3	338.6	1,188.6	276.1
Dec	6,405.7	3,387.2	3,018.5	231.8	194.9	154.0	158.9	161.3	272.1	354.7	1,235.6	255.3
2003: Mar	6,460.8	3,390.8	3,070.0	162.6	196.9	166.0	162.1	163.5	282.7	350.0	1,275.2	310.9
June	6,670.1	3,505.4	3,164.7	155.0	199.2	170.5	161.3	166.0	285.4	347.9	1,371.9	307.7
Sept	6,783.2	3,515.3	3,267.9	158.0	201.6	168.2	155.5	168.5	271.0	356.2	1,443.3	345.8
Dec	6,998.0	3,620.1	3,377.9	165.3	203.9	172.4	148.6	166.4	271.2	361.8	1,523.1	365.2
2004: Mar	7,131.1	3,628.3	3,502.8	172.7	204.5	169.8	143.6	172.4	275.2	372.8	1,670.0	321.8
June	7,274.3	3,742.8	3,531.5	167.8	204.6	173.1	134.9	174.6	252.3	390.1	1,735.4	298.7
Sept	7,379.1	3,772.0	3,607.1	146.3	204.2	173.7	140.1	182.9	249.4	393.0	1,794.5	322.9
Dec	7,596.1	3,905.6	3,690.5	133.4	204.5	173.3	149.4	188.5	256.1	404.9	1,849.3	331.3
2005: Mar	7,776.9	3,921.6	3,855.3	149.4	204.2	176.8	157.2	193.3	264.3	429.3	1,952.2	328.7
June	7,836.5	4,033.5	3,803.0	135.9	204.2	180.4	165.9	195.0	248.6	461.1	1,877.5	334.4
Sept	7,932.7	4,067.8	3,864.9	134.0	203.6	183.6	161.1	200.7	246.6	493.6	1,929.6	312.0
Dec	8,170.4	4,199.8	3,970.6	129.4	205.2	184.4	154.2	202.3	254.1	512.2	2,033.9	294.8
2006: Mar	8,371.2	4,257.2	4,114.0	113.0	206.0	186.2	152.9	200.3	254.2	515.7	2,082.1	403.6
June	8,420.0	4,389.2	4,030.8	119.5	205.2	191.6	149.6	196.1	243.4	531.6	1,977.8	416.1
Sept	8,507.0	4,432.8	4,074.2	113.6	203.7	201.7	149.3	196.8	234.2	542.3	2,025.3	407.3
Dec	8,680.2	4,558.1	4,122.1	114.8	202.4	216.1	153.4	197.9	248.2	570.5	2,103.1	315.6
2007: Mar	8,849.7	4,576.6	4,273.1	119.8	200.3	219.6	156.3	185.4	263.2	608.3	2,194.8	325.3
June	8,867.7	4,715.1	4,152.6	110.4	198.6	220.6	162.3	168.9	257.6	637.8	2,192.0	204.4
Sept	9,007.7	4,738.0	4,269.7	119.7	197.1	225.4	153.2	155.1	292.7	643.1	2,235.3	248.0
Dec	9,229.2	4,833.5	4,395.7	128.9	196.5	228.7	144.2	141.9	343.5	647.8	2,353.2	210.1
2008: Mar	9,437.6	4,694.7	4,742.9	125.0	195.4	240.1	135.4	152.1	466.7	646.4	2,506.3	275.6
June	9,492.0	4,685.8	4,806.2	112.7	195.0	243.8	135.5	159.4	440.3	635.1	2,587.4	297.1
Sept	10,024.7	4,692.7	5,332.0	130.0	194.3	252.7	136.7	163.4	631.4	614.0	2,802.4	407.2
Dec	10,699.8	4,806.4	5,893.4	105.0	194.1	259.7	129.9	171.4	758.2	601.4	3,077.2	596.5
2009: Mar	11,126.9	4,785.2	6,341.7	125.7	194.0	272.4	137.0	191.0	714.3	588.2	3,265.7	853.6
June	11,545.3	5,026.8	6,518.5	140.8	193.6	281.6	146.6	200.0	704.3	588.4	3,460.8	802.4
Sept	11,909.8	5,127.1	6,782.7	198.2	192.5	291.1	146.8	210.2	660.4	582.7	3,570.6	930.1
Dec	12,311.3	5,276.9	7,034.4	202.5	191.3	302.1	151.9	222.0	660.0	584.1	3,685.1	1,035.5
2010: Mar	12,773.1	5,259.8	7,513.3	269.3	190.2	311.0	153.3	225.7	668.8	582.8	3,877.9	1,234.4
June	13,201.8	5,345.1	7,856.7	266.1	189.6	323.1	149.0	231.8	666.4	583.2	4,070.0	1,377.4
Sept	13,561.6	5,350.5	8,211.1	322.8	188.7	334.4	150.2	240.6	659.6	583.9	4,324.2	1,406.6
Dec	14,025.2	5,656.2	8,368.9	319.3	187.9	345.4	160.0	248.4	708.8	590.9	4,435.6	1,372.7
2011: Mar	14,270.0	5,958.9	8,311.1	321.0	186.7	353.7	165.3	253.3	746.6	579.8	4,481.4	1,223.2
June	14,343.1	6,220.4	8,122.7	279.4	186.0	364.1	166.5	254.5	764.4	569.3	4,690.6	845.8
Sept	14,790.3	6,328.0	8,462.4	293.8	185.1	380.2	165.4	259.4	808.4	552.6	4,912.1	905.4
Dec	15,222.8	6,439.6	8,783.3	279.7	185.2	391.1	173.3	271.8	898.2	545.4	5,006.9	1,031.6
2012: Mar	15,582.3	6,397.2	9,185.1	320.2	184.8	411.0	189.4	271.5	974.1	541.0	5,145.1	1,148.1
June	15,855.5	6,475.8	9,379.7	304.2	184.7	422.5	195.7	268.6	971.0	550.5	5,310.9	1,171.6
Sept	16,066.2	6,446.8	9,619.4	339.3	183.8	436.9	203.8	269.5	986.5	543.2	5,476.1	1,180.2
Dec	16,432.7	6,523.7	9,909.1	348.5	182.5	451.1	214.5	269.8	1,035.6	536.2	5,573.8	1,297.1
2013: Mar	16,771.6	6,656.8	10,114.8	340.1	181.7	465.1	225.9	268.2	1,107.5	534.4	5,725.0	1,267.0
June	16,738.2	6,773.3	9,964.9	302.3	180.9	478.9	226.0	266.2	1,076.0	535.8	5,595.0	1,303.8
Sept	16,738.2	6,834.2	9,904.0	295.3	180.0	492.9	233.6	265.0	1,083.0	498.0	5,652.9	1,203.3
Dec	17,352.0	7,205.3	10,146.6	....	179.2	....	....	....	....	....	5,794.9	....

[1] Face value.
[2] Federal Reserve holdings exclude Treasury securities held under repurchase agreements.
[3] Includes U.S. chartered depository institutions, foreign banking offices in U.S., banks in U.S. affiliated areas, credit unions, and bank holding companies.
[4] Current accrual value.
[5] Includes Treasury securities held by the Federal Employees Retirement System Thrift Savings Plan "G Fund."
[6] Includes money market mutual funds, mutual funds, and closed-end investment companies.
[7] Includes nonmarketable foreign series, Treasury securities, and Treasury deposit funds. Excludes Treasury securities held under repurchase agreements in custody accounts at the Federal Reserve Bank of New York. Estimates reflect benchmarks to this series at differing intervals; for further detail, see *Treasury Bulletin* and http://www.treasury.gov/resource-center/data-chart-center/tic/pages/index.aspx.
[8] Includes individuals, Government-sponsored enterprises, brokers and dealers, bank personal trusts and estates, corporate and noncorporate businesses, and other investors.

Note: Data shown in this table are as of February 21, 2014.

Source: Department of the Treasury.

SOURCES

For each table, this section lists source agency (or agencies), website, and data program for data featured; links and contact information are also provided. Table numbers correspond to those used in the 2013 statistical appendix. The 2014 statistical appendix has been streamlined and tables re-sequenced (details on pages 363–365).

NATIONAL INCOME OR EXPENDITURE

B–1. Gross domestic product
Department of Commerce (Bureau of Economic Analysis), *www.bea.gov*
GDP and Personal Income, *www.bea.gov/itable*
customerservice@bea.gov, (202) 606-9900

B–2. Real gross domestic product
Department of Commerce (Bureau of Economic Analysis), *www.bea.gov*
GDP and Personal Income, *www.bea.gov/itable*
customerservice@bea.gov, (202) 606-9900

B–3. Quantity and price indexes for gross domestic product, and percent changes
Department of Commerce (Bureau of Economic Analysis), *www.bea.gov*
GDP and Personal Income, *www.bea.gov/itable*
customerservice@bea.gov, (202) 606-9900

B–4. Percent changes in real gross domestic product
Department of Commerce (Bureau of Economic Analysis), *www.bea.gov*
GDP and Personal Income, *www.bea.gov/itable*
customerservice@bea.gov, (202) 606-9900

B–5. Contributions to percent change in real gross domestic product
Department of Commerce (Bureau of Economic Analysis), *www.bea.gov*
GDP and Personal Income, *www.bea.gov/itable*
customerservice@bea.gov, (202) 606-9900

B–6. Chain-type quantity indexes for gross domestic product
Department of Commerce (Bureau of Economic Analysis), *www.bea.gov*
GDP and Personal Income, *www.bea.gov/itable*
customerservice@bea.gov, (202) 606-9900

B–7. Chain-type price indexes for gross domestic product
Department of Commerce (Bureau of Economic Analysis), *www.bea.gov*
  GDP and Personal Income, *www.bea.gov/itable*
    customerservice@bea.gov, (202) 606-9900

B–8. Gross domestic product by major type of product
Department of Commerce (Bureau of Economic Analysis), *www.bea.gov*
  GDP and Personal Income, *www.bea.gov/itable*
    customerservice@bea.gov, (202) 606-9900

B–9. Real gross domestic product by major type of product
Department of Commerce (Bureau of Economic Analysis), *www.bea.gov*
  GDP and Personal Income, *www.bea.gov/itable*
    customerservice@bea.gov, (202) 606-9900

B–10. Gross value added by sector
Department of Commerce (Bureau of Economic Analysis), *www.bea.gov*
  GDP and Personal Income, *www.bea.gov/itable*
    customerservice@bea.gov, (202) 606-9900

B–11. Real gross value added by sector
Department of Commerce (Bureau of Economic Analysis), *www.bea.gov*
  GDP and Personal Income, *www.bea.gov/itable*
    customerservice@bea.gov, (202) 606-9900

B–12. Gross domestic product by industry, value added, in current dollars and as a percentage of GDP
Department of Commerce (Bureau of Economic Analysis), *www.bea.gov*
  GDP-by-industry, *www.bea.gov/itable*
    customerservice@bea.gov, (202) 606-9900

B–13. Real gross domestic product by industry, value added, and percent changes
Department of Commerce (Bureau of Economic Analysis), *www.bea.gov*
  GDP-by-industry, *www.bea.gov/itable*
    customerservice@bea.gov, (202) 606-9900

B–14. Gross value added of nonfinancial corporate business
Department of Commerce (Bureau of Economic Analysis), *www.bea.gov*
  GDP and Personal Income, *www.bea.gov/itable*
    customerservice@bea.gov, (202) 606-9900

B–15. Gross value added and price, costs, and profits of nonfinancial corporate business
Department of Commerce (Bureau of Economic Analysis), *www.bea.gov*
  GDP and Personal Income, *www.bea.gov/itable*
    customerservice@bea.gov, (202) 606-9900

B–16. Personal consumption expenditures
Department of Commerce (Bureau of Economic Analysis), *www.bea.gov*
  GDP and Personal Income, *www.bea.gov/itable*
    customerservice@bea.gov, (202) 606-9900

B-17. Real personal consumption expenditures
Department of Commerce (Bureau of Economic Analysis), *www.bea.gov*
GDP and Personal Income, *www.bea.gov/itable*
customerservice@bea.gov, (202) 606-9900

B-18. Private fixed investment by type
Department of Commerce (Bureau of Economic Analysis), *www.bea.gov*
GDP and Personal Income, *www.bea.gov/itable*
customerservice@bea.gov, (202) 606-9900

B-19. Real private fixed investment by type
Department of Commerce (Bureau of Economic Analysis), *www.bea.gov*
GDP and Personal Income, *www.bea.gov/itable*
customerservice@bea.gov, (202) 606-9900

B-20. Government consumption expenditures and gross investment by type
Department of Commerce (Bureau of Economic Analysis), *www.bea.gov*
GDP and Personal Income, *www.bea.gov/itable*
customerservice@bea.gov, (202) 606-9900

B-21. Real government consumption expenditures and gross investment by type
Department of Commerce (Bureau of Economic Analysis), *www.bea.gov*
GDP and Personal Income, *www.bea.gov/itable*
customerservice@bea.gov, (202) 606-9900

B-22. Private inventories and domestic final sales by industry
Department of Commerce (Bureau of Economic Analysis), *www.bea.gov*
GDP and Personal Income, *www.bea.gov/itable*
customerservice@bea.gov, (202) 606-9900

B-23. Real private inventories and domestic final sales by industry
Department of Commerce (Bureau of Economic Analysis), *www.bea.gov*
GDP and Personal Income, *www.bea.gov/itable*
customerservice@bea.gov, (202) 606-9900

B-24. Foreign transactions in the national income and product accounts
Department of Commerce (Bureau of Economic Analysis), *www.bea.gov*
GDP and Personal Income, *www.bea.gov/itable*
customerservice@bea.gov, (202) 606-9900

B-25. Real exports and imports of goods and services
Department of Commerce (Bureau of Economic Analysis), *www.bea.gov*
GDP and Personal Income, *www.bea.gov/itable*
customerservice@bea.gov, (202) 606-9900

B-26. Relation of gross domestic product, gross national product, net national product, and national income
Department of Commerce (Bureau of Economic Analysis), *www.bea.gov*
GDP and Personal Income, *www.bea.gov/itable*
customerservice@bea.gov, (202) 606-9900

B-27. Relation of national income and personal income
Department of Commerce (Bureau of Economic Analysis), *www.bea.gov*
GDP and Personal Income, *www.bea.gov/itable*
customerservice@bea.gov, (202) 606-9900

B–28. National income by type of income
Department of Commerce (Bureau of Economic Analysis), *www.bea.gov*
GDP and Personal Income, *www.bea.gov/itable*
customerservice@bea.gov, (202) 606-9900

B–29. Sources of personal income
Department of Commerce (Bureau of Economic Analysis), *www.bea.gov*
GDP and Personal Income, *www.bea.gov/itable*
customerservice@bea.gov, (202) 606-9900

B–30. Disposition of personal income
Department of Commerce (Bureau of Economic Analysis), *www.bea.gov*
GDP and Personal Income, *www.bea.gov/itable*
customerservice@bea.gov, (202) 606-9900

B–31. Total and per capita disposable personal income and personal consumption expenditures, and per capita gross domestic product
Department of Commerce (Bureau of Economic Analysis), *www.bea.gov*
GDP and Personal Income, *www.bea.gov/itable*
customerservice@bea.gov, (202) 606-9900

B–32. Gross saving and investment
Department of Commerce (Bureau of Economic Analysis), *www.bea.gov*
GDP and Personal Income, *www.bea.gov/itable*
customerservice@bea.gov, (202) 606-9900

B–33. Median money income and poverty status of families and people, by race
Department of Commerce (Bureau of Census), *www.census.gov*
Income, *www.census.gov/hhes/www/income/data/historical*
Poverty, *www.census.gov/hhes/www/poverty/data/historical*
ask.census.gov/newrequest.php, (301) 763-3243 (income),
(301) 763-3213 (poverty)

POPULATION, EMPLOYEMENT, WAGES, AND PRODUCTIVITY

B–34. Population by age group
Department of Commerce (Bureau of Census), *www.census.gov*
Population Estimates, *www.census.gov/popest/data/index.html*
ask.census.gov/newrequest.php, (301) 763-2422

B–35. Civilian population and labor force
Department of Labor (Bureau of Labor Statistics), *www.bls.gov*
Labor Force Statistics from the Current Population Survey, *www.bls.gov/cps*
cpsinfo@bls.gov, (202) 691-6378

B–36. Civilian employment and unemployment by sex and age
Department of Labor (Bureau of Labor Statistics), *www.bls.gov*
Labor Force Statistics from the Current Population Survey, *www.bls.gov/cps*
cpsinfo@bls.gov, (202) 691-6378

B–37. Civilian employment by demographic characteristic
Department of Labor (Bureau of Labor Statistics), *www.bls.gov*
   Labor Force Statistics from the Current Population Survey, *www.bls.gov/cps*
      cpsinfo@bls.gov, (202) 691-6378

B–38. Unemployment by demographic characteristic
Department of Labor (Bureau of Labor Statistics), *www.bls.gov*
   Labor Force Statistics from the Current Population Survey, *www.bls.gov/cps*
      cpsinfo@bls.gov, (202) 691-6378

B–39. Civilian labor force participation rate and employment/population ratio
Department of Labor (Bureau of Labor Statistics), *www.bls.gov*
   Labor Force Statistics from the Current Population Survey, *www.bls.gov/cps*
      cpsinfo@bls.gov, (202) 691-6378

B–40. Civilian labor force participation rate by demographic characteristic
Department of Labor (Bureau of Labor Statistics), *www.bls.gov*
   Labor Force Statistics from the Current Population Survey, *www.bls.gov/cps*
      cpsinfo@bls.gov, (202) 691-6378

B–41. Civilian employment/population ratio by demographic characteristic
Department of Labor (Bureau of Labor Statistics), *www.bls.gov*
   Labor Force Statistics from the Current Population Survey, *www.bls.gov/cps*
      cpsinfo@bls.gov, (202) 691-6378

B–42. Civilian unemployment rate
Department of Labor (Bureau of Labor Statistics), *www.bls.gov*
   Labor Force Statistics from the Current Population Survey, *www.bls.gov/cps*
      cpsinfo@bls.gov, (202) 691-6378

B–43. Civilian unemployment rate by demographic characteristic
Department of Labor (Bureau of Labor Statistics), *www.bls.gov*
   Labor Force Statistics from the Current Population Survey, *www.bls.gov/cps*
      cpsinfo@bls.gov, (202) 691-6378

B–44. Unemployment by duration and reason
Department of Labor (Bureau of Labor Statistics), *www.bls.gov*
   Labor Force Statistics from the Current Population Survey, *www.bls.gov/cps*
      cpsinfo@bls.gov, (202) 691-6378

B–45. Unemployment insurance programs, selected data
Department of Labor (Employment and Training Administration), *www.doleta.gov*
   Weekly Claims and Program Statistics, *www.ows.doleta.gov/unemploy/*
      ui-reports@uis.doleta.gov, (202) 693-3029

B–46. Employees on nonagricultural payrolls, by major industry
Department of Labor (Bureau of Labor Statistics), *www.bls.gov*
   Current Employment Statistics (National), *www.bls.gov/ces*
      cesinfo@bls.gov, (202) 691-6555

B–47. Hours and earnings in private nonagricultural industries
Department of Labor (Bureau of Labor Statistics), *www.bls.gov*
   Current Employment Statistics (National), *www.bls.gov/ces*
      cesinfo@bls.gov, (202) 691-6555

B-48. Employment cost index, private industry
Department of Labor (Bureau of Labor Statistics), *www.bls.gov*
Employment Cost Index, *www.bls.gov/ect*
ncsinfo@bls.gov, (202) 691-6199

B-49. Productivity and related data, business and nonfarm business sectors
Department of Labor (Bureau of Labor Statistics), *www.bls.gov*
Labor Productivity and Costs, *www.bls.gov/lpc*
dprweb@bls.gov, (202) 691-5606

B-50. Changes in productivity and related data, business and nonfarm business sectors
Department of Labor (Bureau of Labor Statistics), *www.bls.gov*
Labor Productivity and Costs, *www.bls.gov/lpc*
dprweb@bls.gov, (202) 691-5606

PRODUCTION AND BUSINESS ACTIVITY

B-51. Industrial production indexes, major industry divisions
Board of Governors of the Federal Reserve System, *www.federalreserve.gov*
G.17 – Industrial Production and Capacity Utilization, *www.federalreserve.gov/releases/g17*
www.federalreserve.gov/apps/contactus/feedback.aspx, (202) 452-3204

B-52. Industrial production indexes, market groupings
Board of Governors of the Federal Reserve System, *www.federalreserve.gov*
G.17 – Industrial Production and Capacity Utilization, *www.federalreserve.gov/releases/g17*
www.federalreserve.gov/apps/contactus/feedback.aspx, (202) 452-3204

B-53. Industrial production indexes, selected manufacturing industries
Board of Governors of the Federal Reserve System, *www.federalreserve.gov*
G.17 – Industrial Production and Capacity Utilization, *www.federalreserve.gov/releases/g17*
www.federalreserve.gov/apps/contactus/feedback.aspx, (202) 452-3204

B-54. Capacity utilization rates
Board of Governors of the Federal Reserve System, *www.federalreserve.gov*
G.17 – Industrial Production and Capacity Utilization, *www.federalreserve.gov/releases/g17*
www.federalreserve.gov/apps/contactus/feedback.aspx, (202) 452-3204

B-55. New construction activity
Department of Commerce (Bureau of Census), *www.census.gov*
Construction Spending, *www.census.gov/constructionspending*
ask.census.gov/newrequest.php, (301) 763-1605

B-56. New private housing units started, authorized, and completed and houses sold
Department of Commerce (Bureau of Census), *www.census.gov*
New Residential Construction, *www.census.gov/construction/nrc*
New Residential Sales, *www.census.gov/construction/nrs*
mcd.rcb.customer.service@census.gov, (301) 763-5160

B–57. Manufacturing and trade sales and inventories
Department of Commerce (Bureau of Census), *www.census.gov*
Manufacturing and Trade Inventories and Sales, *www.census.gov/mtis*
retail.trade@census.gov, (301) 763-2713
Retail Indicators, *www.census.gov/retail*
retail.trade@census.gov (monthly), (301) 763-2713
sssd.annual.retail.survey@census.gov (annual)
Manufacturers' Shipments, Inventories, and Orders, *www.census.gov/
manufacturing/m3*
ask.census.gov/newrequest.php, (301) 763-4832
Annual and Monthly Wholesale, *www.census.gov/wholesale*
sssd.wholesale.trade@census.gov, (301) 763-2703

B–58. Manufacturers' shipments and inventories
Department of Commerce (Bureau of Census), *www.census.gov*
Manufacturers' Shipments, Inventories, and Orders, *www.census.gov/
manufacturing/m3*
ask.census.gov/newrequest.php, (301) 763-4832

B–59. Manufacturers' new and unfilled orders
Department of Commerce (Bureau of Census), *www.census.gov*
Manufacturers' Shipments, Inventories, and Orders, *www.census.gov/
manufacturing/m3*
ask.census.gov/newrequest.php, (301) 763-4832

PRICES

B–60. Consumer price indexes for major expenditure classes
Department of Labor (Bureau of Labor Statistics), *www.bls.gov*
Consumer Price Index, *www.bls.gov/cpi*
cpi_info@bls.gov, (202) 691-7000

B–61. Consumer price indexes for selected expenditure classes
Department of Labor (Bureau of Labor Statistics), *www.bls.gov*
Consumer Price Index, *www.bls.gov/cpi*
cpi_info@bls.gov, (202) 691-7000

B–62. Consumer price indexes for commodities, services, and special groups
Department of Labor (Bureau of Labor Statistics), *www.bls.gov*
Consumer Price Index, *www.bls.gov/cpi*
cpi_info@bls.gov, (202) 691-7000

B–63. Changes in special consumer price indexes
Department of Labor (Bureau of Labor Statistics), *www.bls.gov*
Consumer Price Index, *www.bls.gov/cpi*
cpi_info@bls.gov, (202) 691-7000

B–64. Changes in consumer price indexes for commodities and services
Department of Labor (Bureau of Labor Statistics), *www.bls.gov*
Consumer Price Index, *www.bls.gov/cpi*
cpi_info@bls.gov, (202) 691-7000

B-65. Producer price indexes by stage of processing
Department of Labor (Bureau of Labor Statistics), *www.bls.gov*
Producer Price Indexes, *www.bls.gov/ppi*
ppi-info@bls.gov, (202) 691-7705

B-66. Producer price indexes by stage of processing, special groups
Department of Labor (Bureau of Labor Statistics), *www.bls.gov*
Producer Price Indexes, *www.bls.gov/ppi*
ppi-info@bls.gov, (202) 691-7705

B-67. Producer price indexes for major commodity groups
Department of Labor (Bureau of Labor Statistics), *www.bls.gov*
Producer Price Indexes, *www.bls.gov/ppi*
ppi-info@bls.gov, (202) 691-7705

B-68. Changes in producer price indexes for finished goods
Department of Labor (Bureau of Labor Statistics), *www.bls.gov*
Producer Price Indexes, *www.bls.gov/ppi*
ppi-info@bls.gov, (202) 691-7705

MONEY STOCK, CREDIT, AND FINANCE

B-69. Money stock and debt measures
Board of Governors of the Federal Reserve System, *www.federalreserve.gov*
H.6 – Money Stock, *www.federalreserve.gov/releases/h6*
Z.1 – Financial Accounts of the U.S., *www.federalreserve.gov/releases/z1*
www.federalreserve.gov/apps/contactus/feedback.aspx, (202) 452-3204

B-70. Components of money stock measures
Board of Governors of the Federal Reserve System, *www.federalreserve.gov*
H.6 – Money Stock, *www.federalreserve.gov/releases/h6*
www.federalreserve.gov/apps/contactus/feedback.aspx, (202) 452-3204

B-71. Aggregate reserves of depository institutions and the monetary base
Board of Governors of the Federal Reserve System, *www.federalreserve.gov*
H.3 – Aggregate Reserves/Monetary Base, *www.federalreserve.gov/releases/h3*
www.federalreserve.gov/apps/contactus/feedback.aspx, (202) 452-3204

B-72. Bank credit at all commercial banks
Board of Governors of the Federal Reserve System, *www.federalreserve.gov*
H.8 – Assets and Liabilities, *www.federalreserve.gov/releases/h8*
www.federalreserve.gov/apps/contactus/feedback.aspx, (202) 452-3204

B-73. Bond yields and interest rates
Board of Governors of the Federal Reserve System, *www.federalreserve.gov*
H.15 – Selected Interest Rates, *www.federalreserve.gov/releases/h15*
www.federalreserve.gov/apps/contactus/feedback.aspx, (202) 452-3204

B-74. Credit market borrowing
Board of Governors of the Federal Reserve System, *www.federalreserve.gov*
  Z.1 – Financial Accounts of the U.S., *www.federalreserve.gov/releases/z1*
  www.federalreserve.gov/apps/contactus/feedback.aspx, (202) 452-3204

B-75. Mortgage debt outstanding by type of property and of financing
Board of Governors of the Federal Reserve System, *www.federalreserve.gov*
  Mortgage Debt Outstanding, *www.federalreserve.gov/econresdata/releases/*
  mortoutstand
  www.federalreserve.gov/apps/contactus/feedback.aspx, (202) 452-3204

B-76. Mortgage debt outstanding by holder
Board of Governors of the Federal Reserve System, *www.federalreserve.gov*
  Mortgage Debt Outstanding, *www.federalreserve.gov/econresdata/releases/*
  mortoutstand
  www.federalreserve.gov/apps/contactus/feedback.aspx, (202) 452-3204

B-77. Consumer credit outstanding
Board of Governors of the Federal Reserve System, *www.federalreserve.gov*
  G.19 – Consumer Credit, *www.federalreserve.gov/releases/g19*
  www.federalreserve.gov/apps/contactus/feedback.aspx, (202) 452-3204

GOVERNMENT FINANCE

B-78. Federal receipts, outlays, surplus or deficit, and debt
Office of Management and Budget, *www.whitehouse.gov/omb*
  The Budget, *www.whitehouse.gov/omb/budget/historicals*
  (202) 395-3080
Department of the Treasury, *www.treasury.gov*
  Monthly Treasury Statement, *www.fms.treas.gov/mts*
  budget.reports@fms.treas.gov, (202) 622-2970

B-79. Federal receipts, outlays, surplus or deficit, and debt, as percent of gross domestic product
Office of Management and Budget, *www.whitehouse.gov/omb*
  The Budget, *www.whitehouse.gov/omb/budget/historicals*
  (202) 395-3080
Department of the Treasury, *www.treasury.gov*
  Monthly Treasury Statement, *www.fms.treas.gov/mts*
  budget.reports@fms.treas.gov, (202) 622-2970

B-80. Federal receipts and outlays, by major category, and surplus or deficit
Office of Management and Budget, *www.whitehouse.gov/omb*
  The Budget, *www.whitehouse.gov/omb/budget/historicals*
  (202) 395-3080
Department of the Treasury, *www.treasury.gov*
  Monthly Treasury Statement, *www.fms.treas.gov/mts*
  budget.reports@fms.treas.gov, (202) 622-2970

B–81. Federal receipts, outlays, surplus or deficit, and debt
Office of Management and Budget, *www.whitehouse.gov/omb*
The Budget, *www.whitehouse.gov/omb/budget/historicals*
(202) 395-3080
Department of the Treasury, *www.treasury.gov*
Monthly Treasury Statement, *www.fms.treas.gov/mts*
budget.reports@fms.treas.gov, (202) 622-2970

B–82. Federal and State and local government current receipts and expenditures, national income and product accounts (NIPA)
Department of Commerce (Bureau of Economic Analysis), *www.bea.gov*
GDP and Personal Income, *www.bea.gov/itable*
customerservice@bea.gov, (202) 606-9900

B–83. Federal and State and local government current receipts and expenditures, NIPA, by major type
Department of Commerce (Bureau of Economic Analysis), *www.bea.gov*
GDP and Personal Income, *www.bea.gov/itable*
customerservice@bea.gov, (202) 606-9900

B–84. Federal Government current receipts and expenditures, NIPA
Department of Commerce (Bureau of Economic Analysis), *www.bea.gov*
GDP and Personal Income, *www.bea.gov/itable*
customerservice@bea.gov, (202) 606-9900

B–85. State and local government current receipts and expenditures, NIPA
Department of Commerce (Bureau of Economic Analysis), *www.bea.gov*
GDP and Personal Income, *www.bea.gov/itable*
customerservice@bea.gov, (202) 606-9900

B–86. State and local government revenues and expenditures
Department of Commerce (Bureau of Census), *www.census.gov*
State and Local Government Finances, *www.census.gov/govs/local*
govs.finstaff@census.gov, (301) 763-5153

B–87. U.S. Treasury securities outstanding by kind of obligation
Department of the Treasury, *www.treasury.gov*
Monthly Statement of Public Debt, *www.treasurydirect.gov/govt/reports/pd/
mspd/mspd.htm*
treasury.bulletin@fms.treas.gov, (202) 622-2000

B–88. Maturity distribution and average length of marketable interest-bearing public debt securities held by private investors
Department of the Treasury, *www.treasury.gov*
Treasury Bulletin, *www.fms.treas.gov/bulletin*
treasury.bulletin@fms.treas.gov, (202) 622-2000

B–89. Estimated ownership of U.S. Treasury securities
Department of the Treasury, *www.treasury.gov*
Treasury Bulletin, *www.fms.treas.gov/bulletin*
treasury.bulletin@fms.treas.gov, (202) 622-2000

Corporate Profits and Finance

B–90. Corporate profits with inventory valuation and capital consumption adjustments
Department of Commerce (Bureau of Economic Analysis), *www.bea.gov*
    GDP and Personal Income, *www.bea.gov/itable*
        customerservice@bea.gov, (202) 606-9900

B–91. Corporate profits by industry
Department of Commerce (Bureau of Economic Analysis), *www.bea.gov*
    GDP and Personal Income, *www.bea.gov/itable*
        customerservice@bea.gov, (202) 606-9900

B–92. Corporate profits of manufacturing industries
Department of Commerce (Bureau of Economic Analysis), *www.bea.gov*
    GDP and Personal Income, *www.bea.gov/itable*
        customerservice@bea.gov, (202) 606-9900

B–93. Sales, profits, and stockholders' equity, all manufacturing corporations
Department of Commerce (Bureau of Census), *www.census.gov*
    Quarterly Financial Report, *www.census.gov/econ/qfr*
        csd.qfr@census.gov, (301)763-3359

B–94. Relation of profits after taxes to stockholders' equity and to sales, all manufacturing corporations
Department of Commerce (Bureau of Census), *www.census.gov*
    Quarterly Financial Report, *www.census.gov/econ/qfr*
        csd.qfr@census.gov, (301)763-3359

B–95. Historical stock prices and yields
New York Stock Exchange, *www.nyse.com*
Dow Jones & Co., *www.dowjones.com*
Standard & Poor's Financial Services, *www.standardandpoors.com*
Nasdaq Stock Market, *www.nasdaq.com*

B–96. Common stock prices and yields
New York Stock Exchange, *www.nyse.com*
Dow Jones & Co., *www.dowjones.com*
Standard & Poor's Financial Services, *www.standardandpoors.com*
Nasdaq Stock Market, *www.nasdaq.com*

Agriculture

B–97. Real farm income
Department of Agriculture (Economic Research Service), *www.ers.usda.gov*
    Farm Income and Wealth, *www.ers.usda.gov/data-products/farm-income-and-wealth-statistics*
        webadmin@ers.usda.gov, (202) 694-5000

B–98. Farm business balance sheet
Department of Agriculture (Economic Research Service), *www.ers.usda.gov*
    Farm Income and Wealth, *www.ers.usda.gov/data-products/farm-income-and-wealth-statistics*
        webadmin@ers.usda.gov, (202) 694-5000

B–99. Farm output and productivity indexes
Department of Agriculture (Economic Research Service), *www.ers.usda.gov*
Agricultural Productivity, *www.ers.usda.gov/data-products/agricultural-productivity-in-the-us*
webadmin@ers.usda.gov, (202) 694-5000

B–100. Farm input use, selected inputs
Department of Agriculture (Economic Research Service), *www.ers.usda.gov*
Agricultural Productivity, *www.ers.usda.gov/data-products/agricultural-productivity-in-the-us.aspx*
Major Land Uses, *www.ers.usda.gov/data-products/major-land-uses*
webadmin@ers.usda.gov, (202) 694-5000

B–101. Agricultural price indexes and farm real estate value
Department of Agriculture (National Agricultural Statistics Service), *www.nass.usda.gov*
Agricultural Prices, *usda.mannlib.cornell.edu/MannUsda/viewDocumentInfo.do?documentID=1002*
nass@nass.usda.gov, (800) 727-9540

B–102. U.S. exports and imports of agricultural commodities
Department of Agriculture (Economic Research Service), *www.ers.usda.gov*
U.S. Agricultural Trade, *www.ers.usda.gov/topics/international-markets-trade/us-agricultural-trade*
webadmin@ers.usda.gov, (202) 694-5000

INTERNATIONAL STATISTICS

B–103. U.S. international transactions
Department of Commerce (Bureau of Economic Analysis), *www.bea.gov*
International Transactions, *www.bea.gov/itable*
customerservice@bea.gov, (202) 606-9900

B–104. U.S. international trade in goods by principal end-use category
Department of Commerce (Bureau of Economic Analysis), *www.bea.gov*
International Transactions, *www.bea.gov/itable*
customerservice@bea.gov, (202) 606-9900

B–105. U.S. international trade in goods by area
Department of Commerce (Bureau of Economic Analysis), *www.bea.gov*
International Transactions, *www.bea.gov/itable*
customerservice@bea.gov, (202) 606-9900

B–106. U.S. international trade in goods on balance of payments (BOP) and Census basis, and trade in services on BOP basis
Department of Commerce (Bureau of Economic Analysis and Bureau of Census), *www.bea.gov* and *www.census.gov*
Foreign Trade, *www.census.gov/ft900*
ftd.data.dissemination@census.gov, (301) 763-2311 (goods)
International Transactions, *www.bea.gov/itable*
customerservice@bea.gov, (202) 606-9900 (services)

B-107. International investment position of the United States at year-end
Department of Commerce (Bureau of Economic Analysis), *www.bea.gov*
   International Investment, *www.bea.gov/itable*
      customerservice@bea.gov, (202) 606-9900

B-108. Industrial production and consumer prices, major industrial countries
Board of Governors of the Federal Reserve System, *www.federalreserve.gov*
   Industrial Production (IP), *www.federalreserve.gov/releases/g17*
Department of Labor (Bureau of Labor Statistics), *www.bls.gov*
   Consumer Price Index (CPI), *www.bls.gov/cpi*
French National Institute of Statistics and Economic Studies, *www.insee.fr/en*
   IP, *www.insee.fr/en/themes/indicateur.asp?id=10*
   CPI, *www.insee.fr/en/themes/indicateur.asp?id=29*
      portail-statistique-publique-dg@insee.fr
German Federal Statistics Office, *www.destatis.de/EN*
   IP, *www.destatis.de/EN/FactsFigures/EconomicSectors/IndustryManufacturing/*
   IndustryManufacturing
   CPI, *www.destatis.de/EN/FactsFigures/NationalEconomyEnvironment/Prices/*
   ConsumerPriceIndices/ConsumerPriceIndices
      www.destatis.de/EN/Service/Contact/Contact
Italian National Institute of Statistics, *www.istat.it/en*
   www.istat.it/en/contact-us
Japanese Ministry of Economy, Trade, and Industry, *www.meti.go.jp/english*
   IP, *www.meti.go.jp/english/statistics/tyo/iip*
   CPI, *www.stat.go.jp/english/data/cpi*
      www.meti.go.jp/honsho/comment_form/comments_send.htm
Statistics Canada, *www.statcan.gc.ca*
   Economic and Financial Data, *www.statcan.gc.ca/tables-tableaux/sum-som/l01/*
   cst01/dsbbcan-eng.htm
   infostats@statcan.gc.ca
United Kingdom Office for National Statistics, *www.ons.gov.uk*
   Economy, *www.ons.gov.uk/ons/taxonomy/index.html?nscl=economy*
   info@ons.gsi.gov.uk

B-109. Civilian unemployment rate, and hourly compensation, major industrial countries
Department of Labor (Bureau of Labor Statistics), *www.bls.gov*
   Labor Force Statistics from the Current Population Survey, *www.bls.gov/cps*
   International Labor Comparisons, *www.bls.gov/fls/*
      pressoffice@bls.gov, (202) 691-5902
The Conference Board, *www.conference-board.org*
   International Labor Comparisons, *www.conference-board.org/ilcprogram*

B-110. Foreign exchange rates
Board of Governors of the Federal Reserve System, *www.federalreserve.gov*
   H.10 – Foreign Exchange Rates, *www.federalreserve.gov/releases/h10*
      www.federalreserve.gov/apps/contactus/feedback.aspx, (202) 452-3204

B-111. International reserves

International Monetary Fund, *www.imf.org*
> International Financial Statistics, *www.imf.org/external/data.htm*
> International Reserves and Foreign Currency Liquidity, *www.imf.org/*
> *external/np/sta/ir/irprocessweb/colist.aspx*
>> *statisticsquery@imf.org, (202) 623-7764*

B-112. Growth rates in real gross domestic product

International Monetary Fund, *www.imf.org*
> World Economic Outlook, *www.imf.org/external/ns/cs.aspx?id=29*
>> *statisticsquery@imf.org, (202) 623-7764*